2009

SCREENWRITER'S & PLAYWRIGHT'S MARKET®

Chuck Sambuchino, Editor
Robin Mizell, Senior Editor
Charles Galvin, Assistant Editor
Emily Hoferer, Assistant Editor

WRITER'S DIGEST BOOKS

Publisher & Editorial Director, Writer's Digest Books: Jane Friedman
Managing Editor, Writer's Digest Market Books: Alice Pope

Screenwriter's & Playwright's Market Web site: www.screenandplaymarket.com
Writer's Market Web site: www.writersmarket.com
Writer's Digest Web site: www.writersdigest.com
F + W Media Bookstore: http://fwbookstore.com

Distributed in Canada by Fraser Direct
100 Armstrong Ave.
Georgetown, ON, Canada L7G 5S4
Tel: (905) 877-4411

Distributed in the U.K. and Europe by David & Charles
Brunel House, Newton Abbot, Devon, TQ12 4PU, England
Tel: (+44) 1626 323200, Fax: (+44) 1626 323319
E-mail: postmaster@davidandcharles.co.uk

Distributed in Australia by Capricorn Link
P.O. Box 704, Windsor, NSW 2756, Australia
Tel: (02) 4577-3555

Distributed in New Zealand by David Bateman Ltd.
P.O. Box 100-242, N.S.M.C., Auckland 1330, New Zealand
Tel: (09) 415-7664, Fax: (09) 415-8892

Distributed in South Africa by Real Books
P.O. Box 1040, Auckland Park 2006, Johannesburg, South Africa
Tel: (011) 837-0643, Fax: (011) 837-0645
E-mail: realbook@global.co.za

ISSN: 1944-2823
ISBN-13: 978-1-58297-552-8
ISBN-10: 1-58297-552-3

Cover design by Claudean Wheeler
Interior design by Clare Finney
Production coordinated by Greg Nock
Illustrations ©Dominique Bruneton/PaintoAlto

Attention Booksellers: This is an annual directory of F + W Media, Inc. Return deadline for this edition is December 31, 2009.

Contents

SUBMITTING YOUR WORK

PERSPECTIVES

MARKETS

RESOURCES

INDEXES

From the Editor

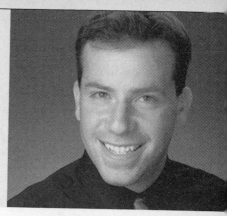

Fade in:

For years, there was talk within Writer's Digest Books about creating a new market resource for screenwriters and playwrights. After all, we've put together directories for magazine freelancers, poets, novelists, short story scribes and children's writers, so what about the ignored media of film and plays? Well the wait is no longer!

Thank you for picking up the first edition of *Screenwriter's & Playwright's Market*, a new annual resource. Our intent was simple: Create a single publication that has both instructional articles as well as a boatload of directory listings for writers of feature films, TV shows and stage plays. We've done our best to put together the ultimate resource for those that write for screen and stage—a book with more than 1,000 listings, but also more than 100 pages of informative articles.

Inside this book, you'll find articles on the craft—and even more so, the business—of writing. These articles, covering a whole host of topics, can help writers, new and experienced, navigate the road to Hollywood with success. If you're brand new to writing, why not start with Charles Galvin's article on formatting your screen and stage scripts (page 23). TV writers shouldn't miss advice on writing for existing shows, provided by writer and producer Ellen Sandler (page 40). If you've just polished the third draft of your screenplay and don't know what to do now, take a peek at the article on how to write film queries and synopses that agents want to see (page 51).

After the articles, dive into the listings! In this first edition of *SPM*, you can find the following: more than 150 contests for scriptwriters; hundreds of theaters and drama organizations open to reviewing new play scripts; contact information for managers and agents who represent screenwriters and playwrights; and conferences where you can mingle with peers and power players. There's much more, but you'd be better served to leaf through the pages than have me keep talking. I'm confident you'll be pleased. Lastly, I have to send out a special thank you to my great editorial team who worked on this book: managing editor Alice Pope, senior editor Robin Mizell, and assistant editors Charles Galvin and Emily Hoferer.

Please continue to stay in contact with me at www.screenandplaymarket.com, passing along success stories, improvement ideas, and news from the entertainment world.

Chuck Sambuchino
Editor
Screenwriter's & Playwright's Market
screenwriter@fwpubs.com

How to Use This Book

Seeing your screenplay or stage play come to life can be an overwhelming task, whether you're a brand new writer or have credits in another category on your résumé. More than likely, you're eager to start pursuing agents and anxious to hear your words spoken aloud by actors. But before you go directly to the listings in this book, take time to familiarize yourself with the worlds of writing for screen and stage. By doing so, you will be more prepared in your search and ultimately save yourself effort and unnecessary grief.

Read the articles

The book begins with feature articles that explain all about the craft and business of screenwriting, TV writing and playwriting. The articles are organized into four sections appropriate for each stage of the search process: **Getting Started**, **Sitting Down to Write**, **Submitting Your Work** and **Perspectives**. You may want to start by reading through each article, and then refer back to relevant articles during each stage of your search.

Decide what you're looking for

Listings in this book are markets for screenwriters, TV writers and playwrights. Make sure you know what you're writing and who you want to contact. If you're looking for representation, for instance, the **Managers and Agents** section lists each rep's contact information and explains what type of work the agency represents as well as how to submit your work for consideration.

If you want to test your writing's meddle against others, look through the **Contests** section and try and claim a top prize. The section will show you competitions of all shapes and sizes (not to mention possible entry fees), so check them all out before firing away material.

Utilize the extras

Aside from the articles and listings, the book offers a section of **Resources**. If you come across a term with which you aren't familiar, check out the Resources section for a quick explanation. Also, note the gray tabs along the edge of each page. The tabs block off each section so they are easier to flip to as you conduct your search.

Finally—and perhaps most importantly—are the **Indexes** in the back of the book. These can serve as an incredibly helpful way to start your search because they categorize the listings according to different criteria. For example, you can look for script agents by name or according to their specialties (romantic comedy, horror, etc.). Plus, there is a **General Index** that lists every agent, production company, contest and conference in the book.

Frequently Asked Questions

1 **Why do you include producers/agents who are not seeking new clients?** This book is designed to be a comprehensive resource, and we include some listings simply so writers know they exist and know not to contact them at this time. When we do not, writers will contact us and ask why a particular market/agency was not included in the book.

2 **Why do you exclude fee-charging agents and producers?** No WGA-endorsed managers or agents will charge an upfront fee to review work. They make money when you make money by taking a small percentage of what writers earn. Beware anything such as "marketing fees," "evaluation costs," "submission fees," or any other euphemism. If you pay a company money to review your work, you may very well get your stuff read, but they still have no legal binding to do anything besides say, "No thanks."

3 **Why are some contests and producers not listed in** *Screenwriter's & Playwright's Market*? For starters, we don't have infinite space to list everything, so we can only list as much as the page count will allow. Some markets may not have responded to our requests for information. And still others have contacted us personally requesting to not be listed.

4 **Can I submit my work simultaneously to different contests or different agents?** Typically, yes. Check the listings and individual websites to see if any individual or company requires an "exclusive submission," meaning they want to be the only person to be reviewing it for a period of time.

5 **If I have a literary agent, do I need another representative for my film work?** If you simply want to sell the movie rights to your book(s), then your literary agent will likely pair up with a co-agent in California to make that deal—meaning you don't have to do a thing. If you want to sell screenplays and stage plays but your agent has no expertise in those areas, you may indeed need another rep.

6 **Why didn't the contest or agent return my material?** There are a number of reasons why this occurred. Your submission could have been addressed wrong or gotten lost in the mail—never even reaching its destination. More than likely, though, the recipient (contest, producer, etc.) has a policy of not returning submissions. They are usually recycled to avoid time spent mailing materials back.

7 **Why don't you list more foreign listings and agents?** It's not that we don't want to—it's just that this is a new book and we've tried to compile as much useful information as we can. As the database grows, we will start to have more Canadian and other international listings. On this subject, keep in mind that when dealing with international listings, you must 1) include an international reply coupon instead of American stamps if you want something mailed back; and 2) be positive that the market in question accepts submissions from writers of all countries, and not just native scribes.

Listing Policy and Complaint Procedure

Listings in *Screenwriter's & Playwright's Market* are compiled from detailed questionnaires, phone interviews and information provided by the markets. The industry is volatile, and listings will change frequently—and sometimes, dramatically. Agents quit. Contests fold. Play competition deadlines get moved up one month. We rely on our readers for information on your dealings with the screenwriting and playwriting industries. If you find changes in information or evidence of any shady dealing, please contact the editor of this book at: Editor, Screenwriter's & Playwright's Market, 4700 E. Galbraith Road, Cincinnati, OH 45236, or e-mail us at screenwriter@fwpubs.com.

Listings are published free of charge and are not advertisements. Although the information is as accurate as possible, the listings are not endorsed or guaranteed by the editor or publisher of *SPM*. If you feel you have not been treated fairly by someone listed in this book, we advise you to take the following steps:

- First try to contact a listing representative. Sometimes one polite follow-up e-mail can clear up the matter. Politely relate your concern.

- Document all your correspondence with the listing. When you write to us with a complaint, provide the name of your manuscript, the date of your first contact with the listing, and the nature of your subsequent correspondence.

We will keep your letter on file and keep the concern in mind when attempting to contact them and verify their information. The number, frequency and severity of complaints will be considered when deciding whether or not to delete a market's listing from the next edition.

Screenwriter's & Playwright's Market reserves the right to exclude any listing for any reason.

Screenwriting Basics

The Scoop on Writing for a Visual Medium

by Chuck Sambuchino

Making a living as a screenwriter is a challenging endeavor to say the least. And if you're reading this, you've no doubt at least toyed with the idea of trying to tackle Hollywood and seek success in the realms of screenwriting and TV writing. This is an ambitious goal, so it's vital that you're well prepared for what lies ahead. And like in all things, it's important that you work smart—to make sure your time and effort is well spent.

So before you type the words "Fade In" on your computer (or at least go any further on the script), read on to learn the basics about writing for the screen.

IS IT A SCREENPLAY?

Here are some questions to ask yourself before you begin.

Can you create a compelling visual story?

Writing for movies and TV means writing with visuals in mind. It means telling your story through images just as much—if not more than—through words. Whether your tale is set on an exotic island or in a run-down apartment complex, you must help the reader imagine your scenes as you write them on the page.

Is the length right?

Feature-length screenplays run from 90-130 pages. If you feel yourself really struggling with length, you may have a good story that's just not a screenplay.

Are you making your story a screenplay just to make money?

Yes, there is money to be made in Hollywood—plenty of it, if you're good enough. But that's not a good enough reason to become a scriptwriter. As you develop your ideas, plot and character, pay attention to the medium where you most feel yourself drawn. Sometimes, a story is suited best as told through a novel, or as told through a series of TV episodes. Forcing a concept into the form of a screenplay for money's sake may produce an awkward finished product.

CHUCK SAMBUCHINO is the editor of *Screenwriter's & Playwright's Market*. He is also the editor of *Guide to Literary Agents* (www.guidetoliteraryagents.com/blog) and assists in editing *Writer's Market*.

Scripts to Read

Recently, the Writers Guild of America compiled their list of the top 101 screenplays of all time. Though we don't have enough space to list them all, here are the Top 20.

1. *Casablanca*
2. *The Godfather*
3. *Chinatown*
4. *Citizen Kane*
5. *All About Eve*
6. *Annie Hall*
7. *Sunset Boulevard*
8. *Network*
9. *Some Like It Hot*
10. *The Godfather: Part II*
11. *Butch Cassidy and the Sundance Kid*
12. *Dr. Strangelove*
13. *The Graduate*
14. *Lawrence of Arabia*
15. *The Apartment*
16. *Pulp Fiction*
17. *Tootsie*
18. *On the Waterfront*
19. *To Kill a Mockingbird*
20. *It's a Wonderful Life*

Also, know that each year, the Academy of Motion Picture Arts and Sciences nominates 10 screenplays for awards—five for the Best Original Screenplay Oscar, and five for the Best Screenplay Adapted from a Previously Published Work Oscar. Any nominated script is that year's crème de la crème in terms of screenwriting, and worth checking out.

Is your idea strong enough?

As you'll read in these pages, the idea for your movie must be strong or else you're already in a tough spot. If you consider yourself a writer who prides himself on things such as the quality of your prose, the complexity of your language and the mystique of your narrative, then you may want to stay away from screenwriting (at least for now). Scripts are processed quickly by readers and producers in Hollywood, so make sure that you're dealing with a concept that doesn't need a lot of preface before a reader can grasp what it's about. Are there exceptions to this? Of course. But you can never count on being that rarest-of-rare exception.

Are you OK with letting others change your ideas?

Perhaps in no other medium of writing is work changed so much—and so drastically—as in screenwriting. Scripts can be purchased for the concept alone; following the purchase, your work may be completely rewritten (a "page one rewrite") in accordance with a producer's vision of how to develop your idea in a different direction. Of course, this doesn't always happen—and the more success you have, the less it will—but you must prepare yourself.

Do you have a thick skin?

Here's an expression you'll hear more than once in this lifetime: "That's Hollywood!" The expression is used when someone gets ripped off, has their ideas stolen, has a deal fall through, or has a project stuck in Development Hell, etc. The stereotype that Hollywood is filled with sharks did not materialize for no reason. It's a slick business out west, and you'll meet plenty of people interested more in money than your creative artistry or livelihood. Enter the waters at your own risk.

And lastly: Do you love movies?

They say the best writers are great readers, and the same is true in this medium. To be a screenwriter, you must watch plenty of movies—and enjoy watching them. But if you're talking about making a living as a screenwriter, you're beyond simply "watching" films and TV shows. Now you must become a student of them. Break stories down; dissect them; reverse engineer a successful plot to figure out why things worked the way they did. Ask yourself: Do you have the patience to watch a good movie a second (and third and fourth . . .) time to deconstruct why it entertained you the first time through?

ADAPTING YOUR WORK AND OTHERS'

Adaptations are a tricky thing, and not to be rushed into. If you want to adapt an already-existing work, then you need to secure the rights to that story—a complicated process involving time and money. If you want to write about a true story and real people, that means securing life rights—another not-so-simple task.

Some writers compose scripts based on already-existing franchises or ideas, such as the next Batman movie or a script for *Ghostbusters III*. This is dangerous because the characters and concepts are not yours, and there is almost nothing you can do with the screenplay, even if it's good. There is only an infinitesimal chance it will sell, and managers may be unwilling to even look at it as a writing sample because they fear some legal repercussion when distributing the work around town.

Writing scripts for existing TV shows, on the other hand, is common and encouraged. It's a common way for TV writers to get their talent noticed and land a job.

Adapting your *own* work is a practical route for novelists and other writers. If your novel sells but Hollywood fails to snatch up the film rights and hire a screenwriter, you can always try writing the screenplay adaptation yourself. The odds are against success here, though, as novelists tend to get too close to their work and fail in adapting it to a vastly different

How I Broke In: 5 Tips for Writers

I was one of those writers who developed into a jack-of-all-trades: I was a studio development exec and a feature film producer; I consulted for production companies, movie stars and independent writers; I judged contests; and of course, I wrote (a few of my scripts were even optioned). There are many paths to getting paid in Hollywood, and mine took me in directions both surprising and strange (like the time I helped the stunt coordinator on a major feature rewrite a big chase sequence!). It wasn't easy, and it didn't happen overnight.

Here are five things I did along the way that can help you get on the road to success in Tinseltown:

1. **I picked up the phone.** If you can talk intelligently about your script and not waste anyone's time with stammering, high-maintenance demands or amateur theatrics, you can get your script read. Simply find out who is in the market for your kind of script, aim for the assistant to a junior executive, practice your 30-second pitch, pick up the phone and pretend to be a player, too. And by the way, the assistants will actually *read* your script because they are looking for the one that will catapult them into the office with a window.

2. **I treated assistants like my best friends.** Treat them well, and you may just slice and dice your way through the tangle of Hollywood without ever having to talk directly (or be avoided studiously) by an executive. And that's not a bad thing.

3. **I worked for free.** A lot. Once I'd had some on-the-job training with a studio production company, I was in a position to help others. I put as much energy into other people's projects as I did my own because that's how Hollywood works. You do favors, and then when it's your turn, people do favors for you. Plus it's a great education.

4. **I lived in LA.** You don't have to live in Hollywood to be a screenwriter, but it helps. You can absolutely sell your first screenplay living in Topeka, but if you want to be a contender for writing jobs or plan on pitching specs, think about moving. You can't take meetings at the drop of a hat if you're a plane ride away.

5. **I realized the importance of finding a niche.** Probably the most important advice I wish I'd gotten as a young writer: Pick a specialty and then hone it until I did it better than anyone. My early years as a writer involved a lot of experimenting; I had the voice, but I didn't have the theme. Over the years, I'd written a script in every major genre. This helped make me a great consultant, able to work with any kind of writer, but it didn't make me the most successful screenwriter. Don't get me wrong—I was happy with my successes—but if I had to do it over today, I would have focused on the one genre I most dearly wanted to write for the rest of my life and then I would have rode for broke.

Trai Cartwright (www.craftwrite.com) is a script consultant and contest judge who has had multiple scripts optioned. She now lives in Colorado.

medium. Peter Benchley's adaptation of his own novel, *Jaws,* for example, was a huge disappointment, and the script wasn't used. But then again, John Irving won an Academy Award for adapting his own book, *The Cider House Rules.*

Since you weren't commissioned to adapt your own work, you'll be writing it on spec, meaning that no money is promised or guaranteed. If done well, adapting your own published work into screenplay form can be a double boon for writers, as it may start the ball rolling on getting a film produced, and the adapted screenplay can serve as a writing sample to get you more assignments in Hollywood, if you ever considered making the jump.

LIVING IN HOLLYWOOD

One of the great things about being a freelance writer or novelist is that you can live anywhere. It's no coincidence that so many freelancers live in some nice area near Portland, or in Santa Fe, or on 25 acres in New Hampshire. But can you make a career out of screenwriting and live outside LA? It's possible, but not likely. Hollywood is a place of meetings and lunches, schmoozing and networking, discussions and assignments. You need to be close by, or at least be able to jump on a plane to California at a moment's notice.

It is definitely possible to begin your career in Hollywood and *then* move elsewhere, as you've already had face-to-face meetings with plenty of important contacts and they know your name.

PERSEVERANCE IS MANDATORY

A screenplay is no short story. It's a 110-page monster that will consume your life for quite a while—and that's just while writing it. After that, you'll be dealing with rewriting, queries, synopses, research, managers, pitching and everything else. Add it all up and you're looking at a lot of time dedicated to a single project. Make sure that you're ready to commit yourself to your writing or you could end up just another writer who has two-thirds of a finished screenplay sitting in a desk drawer somewhere, promising himself every Jan. 1 that *this* is the year it gets finished and makes the rounds.

While dedication and heart is mandatory with any medium of writing, you must also be brave and strong to wheel and deal in Hollywood, as you fight not only tough odds, but also a lot of people who will knock you down just to get ahead.

So—if you've read all this and still think that the medium of screenwriting is the best fit for your story—as well as a good fit for your career goals—then carry on, my wayward son. Let's get to work on advancing your writing career, and maybe you can be *commissioned* to write the next Batman movie.

Long Live the Idea

Finding a Great Concept

by Pamela Wallace

Creating a good movie is all about the idea. No matter how many hot stars you use or how much you spend on special effects or how over-the-top you make the marketing campaign, the secret to box-office success is an original, compelling story.

Before leaving Disney to co-found DreamWorks studios, Jeffrey Katzenberg drafted a memo that raised the bar for what movie executives call "high concept." The term referred to a fresh idea that could be summarized in a sentence or two: easy to understand, easy to sell to an audience. Katzenberg kicked high concept up a notch, insisting that only scripts with ingenious, powerful core ideas that could succeed without brilliant execution deserve the label.

Katzenberg wrote that stars, directors, writers, hardware and special effects can influence the success of a film. But these elements work only if they serve a good idea. In essence, he said, "The idea is king."

AIM FOR WIDE APPEAL

A great idea needs to translate into a compelling story. This happens when a central character goes through a transforming experience the audience can relate to. In *Raiders of the Lost Ark*, cocky Indiana Jones is humbled by the realization that there are forces even he shouldn't challenge. *Tootsie* is about a man who becomes a better man by pretending to be a woman. A successful story will stir emotions in its viewers, making them laugh or cry (both, in really good movies) or shriek in horror.

Deceptively simple, but universal ideas connect best with audiences: underdog triumphs (*The Karate Kid*), revenge (*Dirty Harry*), triumph of the human spirit (*The Color Purple*), coming-of-age (*Stand by Me*). "Connect with the viewer" is the mandate of every successful film.

Once executives and producers buy into a screenplay's central idea, their focus shifts to the next big issue: Is the story castable? In other words, are the leading roles appropriate for "bankable" stars? Or is the idea strong enough that you don't need stars (as in *Independence Day*)? Has this idea proved commercial in the past? Or, even better, is it a fresh take on a proven commodity?

The next deal-making issue is the audience. Who will want to see this movie? Will this idea appeal to a broad demographic? Production costs for a major summer release usually exceed $100 million, meaning a major film must be able to pull in at least two demographic segments of moviegoers to recoup expenses.

The Logline: Boiling It Down

A **logline** is a one-sentence description of what a story is about. Though "logline" is typically a Hollywood term, being able to concisely explain what your story is about is a universal concept—and that's why you need to know how to do it. Loglines are short, catchy, and mandatory.

Loglines are designed to be simple—that means one sentence, ideally. Two-sentence loglines are generally acceptable, but a reason should be clear why the story can't be summarized in one.

Examples

Two best friends who crash weddings as a way to pick up women find themselves breaking their own rules when they both fall head-over-heels for ladies at a high-profile reception.
 —Wedding Crashers

To track down a serial killer, an ambitious female FBI agent-in-training seeks help from an imprisoned psychiatrist, who is both a manipulative genius and a serial killer himself.
 —Silence of the Lambs

After he kills several assailants in an act of self-defense, a small-town restaurant owner suddenly finds himself being terrorized by the mob, who believe he is actually a former mafia killer who disappeared decades ago.
 —A History of Violence

A no-name boxer is plucked from obscurity (and the streets of Philadelphia, more literally) when he is given the opportunity to fight the World Heavyweight Champion.
 —Rocky

Thirty years after he failed to save President Kennedy, a veteran Secret Service agent must stop a psychopathic assassin from killing the current president.
 —In the Line of Fire

After being kicked out of their sport for fighting, two rival male figure skaters must join forces to compete in a pairs skating competition.
 —Blades of Glory

Why It's Important

OK, so you can craft witty dialogue and your characters are interesting in an existential sort of way. You're proud of your writing—but can you boil the tale down into one or two intriguing sentences? If you can't, you're in trouble. Every reader, manager and executive who sees your query or picks up your script will first peruse the logline, seeing if the story is interesting enough to warrant more attention.

Is it fair to judge a whole body of work on one sentence? Perhaps not, but it's somewhat understandable. Studios are in this business to make money, and they do so by people going to see their movies. But if they produce a film that's not easily summarized for viewers, then they can't get butts in the seats. No money. And *that's* why you need a solid logline.

Typically, studios target a primary audience, then go after a secondary and possibly tertiary group. *George of the Jungle* demonstrates this strategy. Ostensibly, George was a kid flick—after all, it was based on a cartoon character. But sexy Brendan Fraser—wearing nothing but a loincloth—combined with a witty script peppered with adult humor, turned a broad comedy into an entertaining movie for teens and enjoyable entertainment for adults (especially women).

The necessity of a great idea is borne out every year by the films that achieve the best profit vs. cost ratio. Small, relatively low-budget films often top the profit-making list above higher-profile movies. In 1997, a little British movie called *The Full Monty* cost a mere $3.5 million to produce but was the revenue ratio champ. In fact, that year's top five profitable films were each made for less than $6 million. What they lacked in bankable stars and special effects, they made up for with universally appealing concepts.

FINDING THE GREAT ONES

Where do winning concepts come from? I pull ideas from many sources—newspaper and magazine articles, my friends' lives, the lives of people in the news, my own life or unrealized fantasies. My concept for *Witness* came from reading news stories about an Amish baby, killed accidentally when non-Amish teenage boys threw rocks at the infant's carriage. As a mother myself, I ached for the parents. The idea for my CBS movie *Borrowed Hearts* reflected my childhood desire for the father I didn't have. On other occasions, I indulged my most romantic imaginings while writing three romance novels that were subsequently adapted into movies for the Showtime channel.

The common thread for all these projects was a subject or thought that touched my heart, that made me want to explore more deeply the feelings it evoked. I've tried to write stories that were market-driven, but they've never worked. I believe that's true for most writers. For an audience to love a movie, the writer has to love what he's written.

HIGH-VOLTAGE INSPIRATION

I know I'm on to a viable idea by the jolt of excitement I feel when it hits. It's heartfelt, it's deep, it's powerful. I'm compelled to grab the nearest pen and jot down as much as I can before it escapes.

Recognizing an idea with real film potential is part inspiration and part physical sensation, and it points to the essence of our creative energy. The best ideas are often the most intimate and personal. We resist examining these sensations because of the pain or fear they dredge up. This force is the core strength of the story that we want to communicate to the audience.

When *Borrowed Hearts* sold, the production company executive asked how I came up with the idea. I was reluctant to disclose that the story I wrote—a man "rents" a family for business purposes then falls in love with the single mother and her daughter—came from my therapist's suggestion that I get in touch with my inner child. When I couldn't "talk" to my imaginary younger self, I, instead, considered what that little girl would have wanted more than anything: a father. The plot evolved smoothly from there.

Borrowed Hearts was the No. 1-rated TV program of the week it aired, and the fourth-highest-rated TV movie of the season. All of that from a simple but profound childhood longing. When you're fighting through the difficulties of writing a screenplay, return to the initial idea. Why did it touch you? What do you want to express in the story? Never lose sight of that.

Your personal approach to an idea makes it uniquely yours. No other writer would explore that particular story exactly as you would. Your internal associations with an idea make it emotionally powerful. Ultimately, it's that power that makes your idea king.

Screenwriter FAQ

*The Pros Chime in on Some Common
(and Not So Common) Questions*

by Robin Mizell

What's the best way to break in to the screenwriting business?

You should never underestimate the importance of writing short films to get noticed. It goes against what you may have read in all the books, but you should really write scripts on spec and try to sell them. And Hollywood is the place to be in terms of getting meetings and meeting people who can give you a job. You don't necessarily have to move here with no prospects, but you can set up some meetings with some studios and maybe arrange a vacation around a visit. There's a lot of groundwork to cover, so have plenty of ideas ready to go when you get here and pound the pavement until you get your foot in the door.

—**Kevin Brodbin**'s *first script was* The Glimmer Man. *Later, writing with Frank Capello, he turned the Hellblazer comics into* Constantine.

What's your advice for writers starting out in the business?

Write, write, write! And then write some more! People seem to get hung up on finding an agent, as if that will suddenly make them writers. An agent won't make your dreams come true. Your talent and perseverance will. No one is born knowing how to write a screenplay. It takes practice and hard work. If your first script doesn't sell, write another one—and then another one. The cream really does rise to the top.

—**Andrea Berloff**'s *feature script* World Trade Center *was purchased and made into a film by director Oliver Stone.*

Are there jobs for freelance TV scriptwriters?

I gave out two assignments to assistants the first year. Frequently, the assistants on shows are writers who haven't gotten breaks yet. So if there's a script available to be written outside of a staff, the assistants are typically the first ones to get it. That's why people who are interested in writing for television take assistant jobs: 1) You learn how the process works, and 2) It puts you in a place where you can put a script on someone's desk and they can see your work. Then they may toss you a script when an opportunity comes up.

—**Allison M. Gibson** *has worked as writer on NBC's* Parenthood; *the creator, executive producer, and writer for WB's* Reba; *and a consultant on UPN's* Rock Me Baby.

ROBIN MIZELL is the senior editor of *Screenwriter's & Playwright's Market*. To learn more about her and her writing, visit www.robinmizell.com.

As someone who writes for plays, TV, and film, how do you feel that writing for each medium is different and unique?

The differences come down to what the audience can see. In plays, the audience gets the big picture. They can't see things close up. Words that the actors say are the most valuable commodity there. In TV, you've got a small screen, one step up from a play. Spoken words are important, but not as much as on the stage. The camera becomes transitional. It gives the writer more freedom to explore the relationship between a character and his/her various settings. In film, someone's quick glance can be the size of a building wall. You may not need as many words there because the minute features of the actors can tell the story and emotions without having to spend so much time explaining things to the audience.

—**Clay Stafford** *is a playwright, producer and screenwriter living in Nashville.*

Do networks or studios ever develop shows by newcomers?

It's rare, almost never, that a studio or network will even meet with a person with no TV experience, and even less likely they'd actually give money to a new writer to develop or produce their own series. Sometimes writers can cross over from feature film writing, but less so from theater. It happens, but you really have to earn your chops.

Staff writing is like an apprenticeship. If you're smart and attentive and lucky enough to work for people who allow you to be part of the process, you can learn everything you need to know. Once you have a sense of how a show operates, you can use that experience when you pitch to a studio or network, and they can trust you with the hundreds of thousands of dollars it costs to shoot a pilot.

—**Molly Newman** *is an Emmy Award-winning television writer and producer whose credits include* Frasier, Murphy Brown, *and* The Larry Sanders Show.

What are you looking for when a writer talks to you in person or contacts you via a query?

Personally, I look for some sense of concept and marketing—is the person hitting the commercial side of my brain? Or is the person boring me with unnecessary details about how the main character changes because of a tragedy? If the person's loglines seem to encapsulate a really good movie idea, I will usually ask to read a sample. A person's background can help, as well. I will lend weight to someone who claims to have a background in writing (journalism, advertising, etc.) or someone who has gone to film school.

Assuming the writer makes it past the query stage and I've read a good sample from the person, it's time to meet. When I sit down (or chat via phone) with a writer, I am essentially looking for someone that I am not afraid to put in a room with executives and producers. That person should be articulate and energetic. I've actually passed on representing people who come across as lethargic or argumentative. Life is too short.

—**Marc Manus** *is a script manager and the founder of Manus Entertainment in Hollywood.*

What makes a script salable in Hollywood?

For the vast majority of people, it's not just about selling a script, but actually making a career out of screenwriting—that's the end goal. Scripts that can't sell on the open market can open doors and get you writing assignments immediately and serve as a sample for your writing career. That's a lesson worth taking to heart. If you write a fantastic thriller or sword-and-sorcery epic, when they need a writer for one of those things, you're going to be the guy they call.

—**Zak Penn** *has written the screen adaptations of comic books for films such as* X2, Elektra, *and* X-Men: The Last Stand.

Advice from the Picket Lines

A year after receiving a bachelor's degree in film studies from the University of Colorado Denver, Liz Lorang decided to make the trip to Los Angeles to march on the picket lines with members of the Writers Guild of America, West, who were demanding a more favorable residuals agreement for their contributions to dramatic works distributed online. Lorang hoped to meet some of the writers who worked on her favorite television shows. If she talked to them while they were picketing, she thought, maybe they could offer her a little advice about launching her career as a scriptwriter.

Here is Lorang's account of what she learned by visiting the frontlines and marching in solidarity with other writers.

"The most important tip I received while speaking with writers is that while you're looking for work it's important to make sure you have amazing samples—both spec scripts and a script for an original TV series.

It's also all about who you know. If you don't have any connections, be adamant about making some. Most of the writers I spoke to were fortunate to know someone in the industry who helped them get started. Whether it was a showrunner, or simply a writer's assistant on a show, writers took full advantage of connections and worked their way up from the lowliest of assistants to full-fledged staff writers.

The great thing about L.A. is that it is obviously full of people in the film and television industry. When it comes to television writers, there is a definite community that supports and helps new and existing writers find work and keep working. Film screenwriters are more on their own in terms of having a screenplay produced. It could be said that a screenwriter is more of a lone wolf battling the Hollywood institution, while television writers have more of a network of people to rely on, partially due to the teamwork that goes into writing a show with a group of people. While on the picket line, I saw that the writers were interested in what others were working on and gave tips and advice to one another.

I love living in Denver and am not too excited about the thought of living in L.A and away from my immediate family. One writer informed me that it is simply necessary to live in L.A. during staffing season and pilot season, about four or five months out of the year—roughly between the months of March and July. After that, it's possible to write for a show by telecommuting.

Regardless of their backgrounds, the writers I met were all steadfast and dedicated to making it as writers in Hollywood. Even those who were out of work, not just because of the strike, were working on projects, keeping in touch with those they knew in the industry, and figuring out how to get work. Persistence is key, above anything else. Whether working or not, it's vital to keep writing, not only to polish your skills, but simply for the enjoyment of it."

Liz Lorang lives and works in Denver, and is writing a spec script she hopes will attract the attention of a Hollywood producer.

Is it challenging to write on a project where there are so many hands trying to stir the pot?

It's a whole different challenge, but yes, it is a challenge. Something like *Spider-Man*, there's a lot more people involved and, therefore, a lot more opinions and more possibilities for conflict. *Spider-Man* was a job I was up for and very, very much wanted. The studio was clear with everybody that nobody just gets this job handed to them, you have to come in and impress us. It was an audition. So I did as much prep work as I could, and I found all the relevant sections of the various comics that I was interested in, and put it all up on big posterboards, and went in there and pitched my little ass off. Happily, I got the job. Never underestimate the power of office products.

> —**David Koepp** *has worked on many franchise hits, series, sequels, and blockbusters, including* Jurassic Park, Mission Impossible, Spider-Man, *and* Indiana Jones and the Kingdom of the Crystal Skull.

What's more important—plot and storylines or character development?

It depends. If you're writing a pilot, it's all about the characters. How you sell it and whether or not people want to engage, they have to be invested in them. That being said, I think that it's much easier if you have strong stories to make sure the characters have something that they're fighting for. Character is always easier to expound upon if you've got a good story. It's all about finding a story that serves the characters well. On our show, the stories are dictated by the characters. If they're great stories, then the characters really pop.

> —**Marc Cherry** *is an executive producer and writer for* Desperate Housewives.

What's the most common thing you see new screenwriters doing wrong?

I think they overexplain. Unless your script is a parable or something that's not realistic, you shouldn't try to make it too profound or affecting or sentimental. A lot of new screenwriters don't write the way people talk. And often, what's not said is just as important as what is said.

> —**Diana Ossana** *collaborated with Larry McMurtry on the Oscar-winning adapted screenplay for* Brokeback Mountain.

What's a frequent obstacle for scriptwriters, and how should they deal with it?

In terms of the writing process, it's all about conquering procrastination. If you're serious about writing, you need to give yourself a block of time to write—before work, on vacation, or leave your job for a month. It's like going to the gym. Everybody says they want to go to the gym, but they never do unless there's a specific time or a reason or a friend picking them up. Don't get overwhelmed with screenwriting how-to books, because there's no real, one way to do it. Just write the script. Write it long and write it big, then trim it back and fix it. Just get something down on paper.

> —**Dan Fogelman** *created and co-produced the sitcom* Like Family, *wrote and produced* Lipshitz Saves the World *and* The 12th Man *for television, and created the film scripts for* Cars *and* Fred Claus.

What's your advice for dealing with rejection?

I've almost never had a script that wasn't turned down before it was bought. I've had scripts that were rejected for seven years that were bought and made into good movies. I don't take it to heart when material gets turned down, because it always happens the same way. Most of the producers and studio executives have all gone out and taken these writing courses to learn what to look for in a script and they're getting all the wrong criteria. Any time you write something really good, you're going to get turned down. If it's good, it's got to be original—and if it's original, it'll probably be turned down.

—**Larry Cohen** *recently had three thrillers*—Phone Booth, Cellular *and* Captivity—*produced on the big screen, while his TV writing career has ranged from* The Fugitive *to* NYPD Blue.

Playwriting Basics

Know the Dos and Don'ts Before Diving In

by Chuck Sambuchino

Stage plays are a medium all their own, no matter if you're writing a 10-minute script, a one-act, or a sprawling three-hour masterpiece. Plays are minimalist in nature, and rely heavily on excellent storytelling and compelling characters. The world of playwriting is typically one of little money and long hours—but a big payoff. In this medium, words reign—so a writer's snappy dialogue or in-depth character drama can come front and center, without worrying about how many producers want to change the script or add in a gratuitous sex scene to attract a new audience demographic.

Read on to discover the basics of plays and playwriting, and know whether that story you're concocting is best fit for the stage.

IS IT A PLAY?

Here are some questions to ask yourself before starting to create your story as a stage play.

Can the story move forward using a combination of dialogue and emotion?

Perhaps the greatest tool for any playwright is dialogue. That's most of what a play is: spoken words. A novel can have pages upon pages of description and characters' interior thoughts/monologue; meanwhile, films are a visual medium, where images are paramount. On stage, however, special effects are hard to come by, and you won't have a John Williams score in the background to help convey mood or tension—hence, the emphasis on dialogue and character.

Can you show exposition, backstory and setting through dialogue without making it sound like a paragraph in a book?

All you've got is a stage. Flashbacks are feasible, but complicated. Montages are not realistic. If one of your characters is supposed to enter a lush garden with plants and vines, you probably won't have a detailed set that reflects that. A playwright must describe the characters' surroundings through dialogue, but not overdo it. If you spend two minutes describing the view of the ocean, it can get boring for the audience.

CHUCK SAMBUCHINO is the editor of *Screenwriter's & Playwright's Market*. He is also the editor of *Guide to Literary Agents* (www.guidetoliteraryagents.com/blog) and assists in editing *Writer's Market*.

Are you prepared to be a marketer and advocate for your play, helping out wherever needed?

If you sell a screenplay, the work is now completely out of your hands. Try walking into a meeting of big-wig executives and suggesting a design for the movie poster—then you can enjoy being escorted from the building. Plays, on the other hand, often need all the help they can get. Plays that are produced by small- or medium-sized theaters need volunteers (read: you, the playwright) who will assist in publicity and marketing, from designing fliers to writing the press release.

Plays to Study

The best way to learn how to compose a great play is to read other great plays and analyze them. Your first step should be visiting the official Tony Awards Web site (www.tonyawards.com), which will reveal works nominated and awarded the honor of "Best Play" each year. Obviously, any of these works are of great caliber and worth a look. Outside of those with Tony nominations and anything by William Shakespeare, the following works should be sought out at the bookstore or online:

- *Angels in America*, by Tony Kushner
- *Arcadia*, by Tom Stoppard
- *Cat on a Hot Tin Roof*, by Tennessee Williams
- *Crimes of the Heart*, by Beth Henley
- *Dark of the Moon*, by Howard Richardson
- *A Doll's House*, by Henrik Ibsen
- *Fences*, by August Wilson
- *Glengarry Glen Ross*, by David Mamet
- *'night, Mother*, by Marsha Norman
- *Oedipus Rex (Oedipus the King)*, by Sophocles
- *Our Town*, by Thornton Wilder
- *Pygmalion*, by George Bernard Shaw
- *Six Degrees of Separation*, by John Guare
- *A Streetcar Named Desire*, by Tennessee Williams
- *The Cherry Orchard*, by Anton Chekhov
- *The Death of a Salesman*, by Arthur Miller
- *True West*, Sam Shepard
- *Waiting for Godot*, by Samuel Beckett.

Keep in mind that older plays are likely in the public domain, as their copyright has long since expired. For example, Shakespeare's works are free to read online, and it's easy to find works by Oscar Wilde, as well, among others. Here are a few starter Web sites to check out when searching for plays posted online:

- The Literature Page: www.literaturepage.com/category/plays.html
- Classic Reader: www.classicreader.com/
- The Virtual Library for Theatre and Drama: vl-theatre.com/list4.shtml
- Pro-play: www.singlelane.com/proplay/
- Chiff's Databases: www.chiff.com/art/theater/scripts.htm
- Simply Scripts: www.simplyscripts.com/

Can you engage an audience?

One of the most common mistakes of storytelling in any medium is releasing too much information too fast—commonly called an "information dump." Writers do not need to explain everything about the characters and the world they inhabit right at the beginning of the work. Audience members want to be more than spectators—they want to be *part* of the play and its happenings, as it helps them forget they're simply sitting down and watching actors.

Do not underestimate the value of having the audience ask questions. By not explaining things fully—meaning, you limit exposition and never hit the nail on the head—you connect with audience members and allow them to mentally engage the story, figuring things out for themselves. "When something is spelled out, or told directly to us, it simply becomes less fun because our participation is denied," says playwright Michael Wright, in his book, *Playwriting in Process*. "Imagine being told just before a game starts that 'your team will lose by one point on a missed shot with one second left in the game.'"

"THE PRACTICALITIES OF THE THEATER"
Cast size

Cast size should always be on your mind. Musicals, children's theater, and big-budget productions aside, theaters will usually look for plays will small cast sizes. A small cast requires less money for actors (especially when you're dealing with unions) and less hassle in getting people together for rehearsals. An old playwriting joke tells of a meeting between a writer and a producer. The producer asks, "How many actors will be needed for this play?" The writer responds, "That's the good news. Just one!" The producer pauses and says, "See if you cut that number down, then call me back."

Keep in mind that what's important here is a small *cast* size, not a small number of roles. David Lindsay-Abaire's play, *Wonder of the World*, for example, requires seven actors, but has many more characters than that. Six of the characters are major, and all the minor characters (such as a waitress, a helicopter pilot, a cop, etc.) are played by a seventh actor, who changes appearances.

Embracing simplicity

Plays are not superhero movies, and one of the biggest and most common amateur errors is to try to force a movie onto the stage. "When you have a scene, you have to write with the practicalities of the theater in mind," says Ted Swindley, creator of the musical *Always . . . Patsy Cline*. "Plays are not movies. You can't say, 'Scene 1: The Peer at Lake Michigan; Scene 2: A Skyscraper Penthouse; Scene 3: Central Park.' That is a nonrealistic play. Frankly, there are a lot of logistical things that producers will look at in a script. They may say, 'This is an interesting play, but it's got too many characters, it's too many costumes, it's got too many props.'"

When you're writing a play, keep basic things in mind. Is this set change possible? Do I really need to include these props in this scene? If a character is in a wedding dress in one scene, then the next scene requires them to be on their honeymoon, dressed casually, how will that transition work? Don't underestimate simplicity. "There are two reasons that certain plays are repeatedly produced," Swindley says. "One is that they make money and that they become popular—that's just economics . . . But there's also a practical reason why plays are done: They're really good plays that are really simple to produce. (Playwright) David Mamet's a prime example. Brilliant writer—simple to produce. It's all about his language."

Limiting stage directions and description

Looking back at Shakespeare's plays, it's astounding to see the lack of stage directions. Characters enter; they leave; many die—and that's about it. While playwrights today definitely have more leverage, stage plays are not a medium where you can describe action in depth. For example, if two characters fight, simply say, "They fight." Writing down a paragraph or two full of blow-by-blow action is the exact thing *not* to do.

Ideally, your play will be produced many times on many different stages—and the directors that tackle your work will not want to put on the exact same interpretation of another director; same goes for the actors. Directors will often black out some or all of a play's stage directions, so they can create their own vision of how to block the action. By the same token, if you feel you must preface every line of dialogue with an emotion, such as "nervous" or "holding back tears," you're limiting how actors can interpret your words.

8 Things That Can Ruin Your Play

Don't sabotage your work! Avoid these eight poisonous pitfalls that can get your work rejected:

1. Neglecting character arc and development. Not all characters can have a whole, dramatic arc throughout the story, but the most important characters must change.

2. Using poor transitions. When a scene change means we're in another country two years later, it must be done well, or you'll leave the audience perplexed. The play *Closer*, by Patrick Marber (made into a movie in 2004), follows four characters over the course of a few years, yet you never feel confused as to how much time has elapsed because the writing is good.

3. Beating the moral or message over the head of the audience. They're smarter than you think they are.

4. Using a cliché storyline. If you have a plot that's simple, such as a love story or a family member dying of cancer, it must have extraordinary characters and dialogue. Ask yourself: What makes your take on this story unique, different and special?

5. Not properly formatting your play, whether than means not including a cast of characters, not numbering pages, or simply not centering text that should be centered.

6. Being sloppy. Your text should have no typos, unless you're spelling out words phonetically for a reason. Make sure your submission is neat and professionally bound. If a contest turns down your submission and happens to send you the copy back, examine the play. If pages are bent and it's obvious that the play was indeed read, then don't send that same copy out again.

7. Creating too many long monologues. There are times and places for these, but four-page speeches don't often happen in real life.

8. Writing a conflict or scene a certain way "because it happened that way" in real life. A play must be entertaining to an audience, be it a drama or comedy. Writing about your own experiences is fine, as long as it's not simply a cathartic effort for you, but rather an entertaining play for the audience.

WHY WRITE PLAYS?

Playwriting is not an easy business by any means. First of all, money is scarce. There is a reason that community theaters close: Attendance is down. The ease of things such as DVR, Netflix and the Internet has provided even more reasons to stay in on the weekends rather than catch a show. After all, you can turn off a bad movie, but you can't turn off a bad play, which is perhaps why fewer people go to the theater. This is why plays must be good. They must be entertaining. They must pull you in through conflict, drama and emotion.

So if it's difficult and there's very little money if any, why do it? Because there's nothing like being behind the last row of audience seats (usually while pacing and biting fingernails)—and hearing a house laugh ripple through the venue. There's nothing like hearing a large crowd be dead silent at the exact moment where you hoped they would be.

Plays celebrate the written word, and quality is not just appreciated, but expected. With plays, the writer and his words truly reign.

Formatting Your Script

Make Your Work Look Professional

by Charles Galvin

The best part about writing a novel may be the simple formatting. It's all in block chunks, page after page. Easy peasy. Scripts, meanwhile, follow rigid guidelines when it comes to how things should appear on the page, and poorly formatted material is likely to be thrown in the trash.

You may be saying, "But a good story will see its way through." It may—but it's hard for your script to get read when it's in the recycle bin. Incorrect formatting of a screenplay or play is an obvious sign of an amateur. Producers and agents are used to reading scripts that follow the rules. It helps them read quicker—so make sure you follow them, too.

"If you want your script to stand out from the crowd in a good way, you want to make sure it doesn't stand out from the crowd just because of how it looks," says Gregory K. Pincus, a screenwriter (*Little Big League*) and TV writer. "If your script looks like you know what you're doing, you'll pass the first 'smell' test and, with luck, you can hook people with your story."

Don't skip a dream sequence just because you don't know how to write it. Don't avoid flashbacks because you're not sure if everything looks A-OK on the page. Tackle it all—by reading the guidelines below.

STARTING OFF

Title Page: Starting about a quarter from the top of the page is the title, centered and capitalized. A few lines below the title will be the credit line, centered, using both upper and lowercase. This line should simply say "By," or "A Screenplay by." A couple lines beneath the credit line should be your name, centered. In the bottom right hand corner of the page, be sure to include your contact information (address, phone number, e-mail, etc.). Many times, the contact will actually be your representation, so include that instead, if applicable.

Margins: Before you start, be sure to set the proper page margins. One inch from the top, bottom, and right, one and a half inches from the left. These criteria apply to all pages except the title page.

Font: The standard is Courier font, size 12. Filmmakers expect the same font in every screenplay they read, both for visual comfort and for the purpose of judging length. A different font is a quick way to irritate somebody who reads dozens of scripts a day, not to mention a sign of a writer's inexperience. Every page of text is usually translated to mean one minute of film. Changing the font will throw off the movie's estimated length.

CHARLES GALVIN is an assistant editor for *Screenwriter's & Playwright's Market*.

Formatting Screenplays

Use a header. Include your name, the script title, and the page number.

These slugs introduce the location and time of day.

Capitalize characters as they are introduced.

Center character names for dialogue.

Indent dialogue.

To specify emotions or specific actions while speaking, center it and use parentheses.

SAMBUCHINO/OCTOBER SURPRISE   25

EXT. POLICE PRECINCT—DAY

Civilians and police officers mill in and out. Down the street walks BILLY VAN RAYNE, 20s, tall, powerful—maybe even a bit dangerous. He looks at the police station, hesitating.

                    BILLY
        Now or never.

He pulls something out of his pocket. It's a HANDHELD TAPE RECORDER.

Capitalize key actions and objects.

                    VOICE (O.S.)
        Need some help?

Billy looks to see a BEAT COP, 30s, eyeing him suspiciously.

                    BILLY
        No thanks—I'm okay . . .

Billy walks up the steps toward the precinct front door.

INT. POLICE PRECINCT—DAY—CON'T

When one scene continues directly into another, use this abbreviation.

Billy enters. The first person he sees is an obese DESK SERGEANT, who is trying to answer questions from a Russian SKINHEAD.

                    DESK SERGEANT
        I don't know what else to tell you. You'll have to go to the courthouse for further instructions. After that—

                    SKINHEAD
                    (in Russian)
        I still cannot understand you!

                    DESK SERGEANT (CON'T)
        —we may be able to work something out. That's all I can tell you. As you can see, I'm very busy.
                    (calls out)
        Next!

INT. CAPTAIN RYBAN'S OFFICE—THAT MOMENT

                    RYBAN

You can use other slug variations besides "Night" and "Day," though don't get carried away. Common variations include "That Moment," "Early Morning," and "Dusk."

Don't leave "hangers."

Formatting Plays

Play formatting has its various little differences from screenplays. After the title page, you will want to include an informational page that contains the following:

1. **Characters**. Names of all characters with a one-sentence description, such as "Baby Joe's mother; a housekeeper who likes to keep things simple."

2. **Time**. How much time elapses during the course of the play? One night? Five years?

3. **Synopsis**. Keep this story summary as short as you can. Consider it a "logline."

4. **History**. Show the play's development. Was it read or workshopped yet? Has it had a production? If so, where?

This line designates the page, the act, and the scene (in that order).

The Snowflake Theory   *Page I—I—I*

ACT I
Scene 1

SETTING: MARGE's kitchen. Only a table and chairs are needed.
Tell what happens   On the table are two sets (different colors) of plastic
before the lights   unbreakable dishes and two sets of flatware. It's
come up.   Wednesday, Feb. 26, 2003.

BEFORE RISE: Sounds of MARGE removing dishes and flinging them
                 to the floor.

Explain what's
going on when the   AT RISE: Action continues. Nothing is breaking. MARGE
lights come up.   becomes more and more frustrated. She throws the
                                  flatware at the dishes. Finally, Marge gives up and sits.
Center character
names for
dialogue.   MARGE
You are where you are. That's what Manny always said.

Keep all dialogue
pushed left and
have it wrap all   Indent action and   (MARGE opens a garbage bag and
the way across.   stage directions.   starts throwing everything in.
                         Have it in   REBECCA enters in a coat.)
                         parentheses.

                                    REBECCA
It's not garbage night.

                                         Capitalize
                                         character
                                         names.

Tense: Other than dialogue, always write action and description in the present tense: "The bomb *explodes*. Jane *is* thrown from the passenger seat."

Page Numbers: Be sure to number all of your pages. This will help in determining screen time as well as serve as a reference for the reader. To be safe, also include a header, which will contain the film title and your last name.

GETTING INTO IT

"Fade In": The official beginning to each and every screenplay. This is probably one of the only—if not *the* only time—a screenwriter should include camera instruction in your writing. In fact, including camera directions, such as "zoom out," "dolly in" or "match cut," is a serious sign of a novice.

Scene Heading/Slug Line/Scene Slug: Each scene begins with basic information that is found in the heading. This part tells whether the scene is interior or exterior (INT. or EXT.), where the scene is taking place, and what time of day it is. All of this information should be left-justified and set in upper-case. The most traditional way to handle the time of day is simply stating "day" or "night." While other options are still acceptable, producers will often count the number of "day" scenes vs. "night" scenes to help estimate a budget, as shooting at night costs more money.

Scene Description: This information follows the scene heading. It is brief and written in sentence case. Don't get carried away here. Script readers like to see "white space" on a page—meaning that they don't want to read thick paragraphs of description and action. Keep it simple.

Dialogue: A character's dialogue is noted by centering the name in upper-case letters directly above their lines. In some cases, it is necessary to indicate how a line should be read using one or two descriptive adverbs. If necessary, these are placed in parentheses directly underneath the character's name, above their lines.

THE NITTY-GRITTY

Some screenwriting devices are not essential to writing a screenplay. In many cases, a writer can fall in love with things like montages or flashbacks. Overuse or misuse of certain techniques can detract from the screenplay, so if you are going to try something, make sure to do it the right way.

Montages, Dreams, Flashbacks, or Fantasy Sequences: Obviously, these are different elements in a screenplay, but they are introduced using the same method. For example, to indicate one of these sequences, write "BEGIN MONTAGE" in the scene heading. Any shots or descriptions to be included should be clear and concise. When finished, be sure to indicate "END MONTAGE."

Simultaneous or Dueling Dialogue: In scenes where two or more characters speak at the same time, their dialogue can be listed on the page next to each other. It is also acceptable to indicate in the scene description that they are both talking, and to place one dialogue above the other.

Phone Calls: Dialogue between characters on the phone can be showed in one of two ways. One way is to cut back and forth while each character speaks, showing both on the screen at different times (or even splitting the screen to show both characters at the same time). The other way is to show only one character on screen but still have the other character's voice heard through the phone. In this case, the character's name should be followed by a parenthetical indicating (ON PHONE) to specify that they can be heard but not seen.

V.O. and O.S.: In some cases, a character will not be onscreen yet will still be talking and a part of the scene, such as when a character is narrating. This is voiceover—and noted by writing (V.O.) next to the character's name above the dialogue. When a character offscreen is talking, use the notation (O.S.) next to their name.

Fading Out: You may have times at the end of a screenplay—or in the middle—where the screen fades to black. This is a common technique when large spans of time elapse. Avoid overusing fade-outs. Along with "fade to black," you can also "fade to white," such as at the end of *Total Recall* (so *was* it a dream?).

And the rest: Your title page should be on card stock—slightly thicker paper. Use card stock for the back page as well to give it a clear beginning and end. As with most submissions, only print on one side of the paper. Lastly, scripts are usually three-hole punched and bound by two brads.

Where to Read Scripts

The best way to see how the intricacies of a script are laid out and formatted is simply to look at other scripts. Here are some online locations where you can see professional scripts for free:

- Simply Scripts: www.simplyscripts.com
- Daily Script: www.dailyscript.com
- Drew's Script-o-Rama: www.script-o-rama.com
- The Internet Movie Database: www.imdb.com

Sitting Down to Write

On Dialogue

The How and When Concerning Spoken Words

by Charles Galvin and Chuck Sambuchino

There was a time when the only dialogue in movies was that of audience members talking to one another. Silent films in black and white attracted plenty of viewers before directors started experimenting with sound—first in the form of music, then eventually spoken lines by actors. Fast forward to the 21st century, where taglines by big time actors are selling points in trailers that can ultimately make or break a movie.

Dialogue is a large part of each and every script and ultimately has a big part in defining your voice as a writer. It's a tool you can use to wow producers and, ultimately, entertain an audience. "Dialogue not only creates space on the page, which is visually appealing, but it's also what brings characters to life in a story, which is emotionally appealing," says Gloria Kempton, in her book *Dialogue*. "The most effective way to reveal your characters' motives is through their own mouths."

So how can writers set their screenplay apart using dialogue? Here are some keys to follow, as well as some pitfalls to avoid.

THE IMPORTANCE OF DIALOGUE

Fundamentally, the reason writers use dialogue is to reveal information to the audience that cannot be conveyed on the screen with actions alone. This type of information usually consists of a characters thoughts, feelings, or emotions. Anything that a writer feels is necessary to tell the audience regarding what a character is thinking typically makes itself visible in the form of dialogue. Be careful using dialogue for this purpose, though. It's always a good idea to ask whether something can be shown through actions or without words. Consider a character who tells a woman he loves her and starts listing a number of reasons why, versus that same character simply holding the woman and kissing her passionately. Which image gets the point across more effectively? Perhaps more importantly, which do you think an audience would prefer to see?

In her book, Kempton lays out seven main purposes of dialogue:

- To characterize and reveal motives
- To set the mood in the story
- To intensify the story conflict
- To create tension and suspense

CHARLES GALVIN is the assistant editor of *Screenwriter's & Playwright's Market*. **CHUCK SAMBUCHINO** is the editor of *Screenwriter's and Playwright's Market*. **GLORIA KEMPTON**'s book, *Dialogue* (2004), is part of Writer's Digest Books' "Write Great Fiction Series."

- To speed up a scene
- To add bits of setting and background
- To communicate the theme

CRAFTING REALISTIC SPEECH

When dialogue is deemed necessary, it's important to make sure that a character's speech is realistic. Before you write any lines for your characters, consider filling out an interest or background inventory about them. Start with basic information, such as their name, age, and physical appearance—then add in deeper details. Where are they from? Are they educated? Have they been shaped by any profound life experiences, such as a near-death experience or a divorce? Who has influenced them? Answering these questions will make it easier for a screenwriter to fill in the blanks later.

Answering questions about your character's background can also lead to more complex questions about their dialogue. Where they are from geographically can lend a great deal of information regarding dialect or colloquialisms. The congressional hearings for baseball pitcher Roger Clemens provided a recent reminder of this, when an individual's answer of "It is what it is" proved to be a New Yorker's way of saying "It's true."

Consider a scene with two blue-collar electricians standing outdoors, discussing the hot weather. The dialogue would be completely different if you were in Jackson, Miss., than it would be in Philadelphia. Spending some time in a region your character is from can help you become more familiar with their native vocabulary and add some authenticity to the character's dialogue.

Concerning regional speech, don't overuse phonetic dialogue. For example, if a character speaks in a Southern accent, you don't need to spell out every word the exact way you feel it would be pronounced. Words here and there are fine, but an actor will do the rest of the work for you. Just make sure you say that the character speaks in a "distinct Georgia accent."

Stephen King said that good dialogue requires a certain degree of honesty—meaning that if a character's true nature is to say something unintelligent, racist, rude or naive, then you must stay true to the character. At the same time, consider this: Realistic dialogue doesn't mean boring. In the real world, people talk about mundane things, and most of what we say during lunch and over the phone is not movie-script-worthy. Just because pointless talk is a realistic aspect of life doesn't mean you need to make your script boring just to "truly capture it."

A UNIQUE VOICE

Voice. It's what everyone's looking for, and it's so very difficult to create. Having a unique voice means that the dialogue and narrative is fresh—told in a pacing and style all its own. Think of *Network*, *Pulp Fiction* and *Juno*. All are case studies in voice. *Juno* dealt with issues surrounding teenage pregnancy—a subject matter not exactly close to comedy. Narrated by protagonist Juno MacGuff, the teenage point of view does a good job of adding humor to what would conventionally be considered an uncomfortable topic for most viewers and their families. The language used in the film makes it more authentic, creating characters that younger audiences can relate to and empathize with. Look at this bit of dialogue from Diablo Cody's script, where the titular character explains how the cacti in her room are gifts from her estranged mother:

> JUNO (V.O.)
> Oh, and she inexplicably mails me a cactus
> every Valentine's Day. And I'm like, "Thanks
> a heap, Coyote Ugly. This cactus-gram stings
> even worse than your abandonment."

GRAMMAR TOOLS AT YOUR DISPOSAL

Don't limit yourself to "pristine" or "perfect" dialogue. In real life, people trail off, they interrupt one another, they misspeak, they stammer, they have a lot of "uh's" and "um's" that affect their speech.

All grammar tools, such as the dash, comma, semi-colon and ellipsis can and should be used when needed to emphasize how a sentence should be spoken. If you think a sentence must be paced a certain way to convey the meaning you have in mind, then write the sentence just how it should be spoken. For example, consider the scene in *American Beauty* when Kevin Spacey's character is working at a fast food restaurant and catches his wife with another man.

> CAROLYN
>
> Lester, just stop it!
>
> LESTER
>
> Unh-uh. You don't get to tell me what to
> do. Ever again.

The use of periods in the exchange above, especially, allows writer Alan Ball to sculpt a sentence exactly to his liking. Consider a different part of the same movie, where Wes Bentley's character asks her girlfriend, played by Thora Birch, to run away with him.

> RICKY
>
> If I had to leave tonight, would you come
> with me?
>
> JANE
>
> What?
>
> RICKY
>
> If I went to New York. To live. Tonight.
> Would you come with me?

Look below at this passage from the play, *Glengarry Glen Ross*. David Mamet's use of stammers, incomplete sentences and ellipses are some of the tools he uses to make his dialogue memorable and special.

> MOSS
>
> You don't ax your sales force.
>
> AARONOW
>
> No.
>
> MOSS
>
> You . . .
>
> AARONOW
>
> You . . .
>
> MOSS
>
> You build it!

AARONOW

That's what I . . .

MOSS

You fucking build it! Men come . . .

AARONOW

Men come work for you . . .

MOSS

. . . you're absolutely right.

VOICE OVER

You may remember Brian Cox in the film *Adaptation*. Portraying story guru Robert McKee, he bellows "And God help you if you use voice over in your work, my friends! God help you! That's flaccid, sloppy writing. Anybody can use voice over to show the thoughts of a character."

So it's settled, right? Voice over stinks.

But wait a minute. *Goodfellas. The Usual Suspects. Platoon. Little Children. American Beauty*. All amazing (some even Oscar-winning) scripts that used voice over.

Not so settled.

The bias against voice over is for just the reason said above: If overused, voice over becomes an awkward crutch—an easy way for a writer to tell, rather than show. Make sure there is a pertinent reason why you're using voice over before you start covering your script in interior monologue.

Chris Vogler

*A Master Storyteller Talks Character,
Craft, Pacing and Plot*

by Jenna Glatzer

Chris Vogler is a writer and story consultant. His book, *The Writer's Journey: Mythic Structure for Writers* is based on an influential memo he wrote while analyzing scripts for the Walt Disney Company in the 1980s. He was invited to consult on Disney animation projects including *Aladdin, The Lion King, Hercules*, and *Fantasia 2000*. His website for his consulting company, Storytech, is www.thewritersjourney.com.

Your book, *The Writer's Journey*, was inspired by Joseph Campbell's *The Hero with a Thousand Faces*. What drew you to his book?

As a young film student at USC, I was on a kind of vision quest, looking for guidance and a unifying system to organize the chaotic world of writing. I knew there had to be some order to it. I had already sensed some of the patterns in myth and movies when a film professor pointed me in the direction of Campbell's book. It was one of those life-changing experiences, hitting me like a bolt of lightning and completely re-organizing my brain. In that same semester, the first Star Wars movie was released, further clobbering me with the possibilities of Campbell's ideas.

Your book explores storytelling in terms of the "Hero's Journey." How do you answer critics who complain that writers should never follow formulas?

I agree with them. I hate formulaic movies, especially those that follow the Hero's Journey model formulaically. I don't see it or use it as a formula. It's not a cookbook recipe that you can follow to whip up a good screenplay. Instead, it's a map of the human territory that underlies storytelling, on which you can plan a unique journey that will follow a completely original path while still touching at the classic stations and crossing points that are present in any human experience.

I don't say it's the only way to tell a story or communicate with an audience. I do say that almost any story or work of art can be interpreted in the language of the Hero's Journey, because it's a universal description of just about anything that can happen to a human being.

How does your method differ from the traditional "three-act structure"?

My approach is based on the three-act model that Syd Field articulated and which is still the most practical way for filmmakers to communicate amongst themselves. The difference is

JENNA GLATZER (www.jennaglatzer.com) is a freelance writer of books, magazine articles and more. She is the founder of Absolute Write (www.absolutewrite.com).

that I see the long second act naturally breaking down into two distinct movements—one leading up to a central event or crisis (Syd Field's Midpoint, my Central Ordeal) and one trailing away from the central event. The first movement of Act II is the preparation for the Central Ordeal, and the second movement is the consequences of that central event. So you end up with a structure of four movements, Act I, Act IIa, Act IIb, and Act III.

Of course these are just conveniences—ways to talk generally about things that are never so neat and tidy in practice. The *story* tells you how many acts or movements it needs. Maybe you choose to think of it as one continuous, seamless flow of images; maybe you discover it needs 26 acts, movements, or chapters; maybe you don't spend one second thinking about how many acts it has. The best rule for structuring is "What happens next?" Your obligation is to be constantly, unrelentingly interesting—not perfectly structured.

How can a writer develop an anti-hero with whom audiences will empathize?

Just make them good characters, meaning they should have all the human equipment—hopes, dreams, fears, flaws, blessings, etc. Maybe they started out as optimists or innocents who got burned by life. They are wounded in some way. Maybe they had noble aspirations that got crushed or corrupted. They should have some flamboyant, colorful, flashy, charming, or skillful aspects. They can be appealing by their contempt for the hypocrisy of conventional heroes or society itself. They can be attractive because they get to express something the audience feels deeply and strongly. They fulfill some wish: to see the crushing authority of the world defied, to escape from social restrictions, to act on impulse without inhibition.

One of the key steps in the Hero's Journey is the "meeting with the mentor." Can you give us examples of characters who function as mentors?

Obvious mentors are benevolent guides and teachers like those in *Goodbye, Mr. Chips* and *Mr. Holland's Opus*, or the Jedi masters in the Star Wars series. The caddy in *The Legend of Bagger Vance* or Patrick Stewart's character in *X-Men* are mentors to their young heroes. Sometimes mentoring is less obvious and may be combined with other jobs like that of villain or antagonist, because we can learn a great deal from our opponents. That's the case in *Bedazzled*, where The Devil is trying to win the hero's soul but also serves as a teacher and guide for him, showing him in the long run what's really important in life. In romantic stories, you can look at the lovers as mentors for each other, each guiding the other to a deeper understanding.

How can a writer give enough backstory without stagnating the story?

Give the backstory in pieces as a series of reveals or surprises. Give it on the run, while people are *doing* something active, so the story doesn't stop. Let it come out of conflict, so that people blurt out backstory in the heat of an argument or have it pulled out of them with great difficulty. Use visuals, props, costumes, and sets to reveal backstory without words. A house full of trophies will tell us someone has a sports background without a word of dialogue.

Behavior can reveal backstory. It's especially effective if people refuse to answer questions, change the subject, or squirm when casual questions are asked about their backgrounds. Raise questions about background but leave some unanswered and let the audience do some of the work—they might fill in a more interesting backstory than can be provided with explanations and dialogue.

Must every script have external conflict, or can an entire script be based on the hero's internal conflict?

Even in the most internalized of stories, it's good to have some external sign of the inner turmoil, even if it's just a spilled coffee cup or a stuck window. It's just realistic that inner

conflict will find expression outside of the person in the form of disagreements, misunderstandings, and physical struggles. However, once in a while you might create an interesting contrast between a placid exterior environment and a raging inner conflict.

How can a hero prove his or her character arc is complete?

Character arc is another one of those convenient terms used to pummel writers in story meetings. Of course, you do have to demonstrate that a protagonist has learned a lesson, made a choice, or evolved to a new level, after passing through a series of logical, believable steps that evoke some conflict or emotion. One way to dramatize a character change is to show that the hero is able to do something at the end of the story that was impossible at the beginning (accept herself, forgive someone, be a team player, stand up for herself, find love, overcome an obstacle, defeat an opponent, reach a goal). You might ask: Has the hero gone through all the logical stages of learning about this problem? As a storyteller, have I explored all the possibilities inherent in this situation?

What are some of the most common mistakes you see new screenwriters make?

Over-explaining and over-writing. They give a lot of unnecessary detail because they are afraid their audience—the readers of the script—won't get it. We get it. Give your readers credit and let them participate. It's amazing what you can leave out and still achieve full communication.

On the other hand, some new writers take too much for granted, and don't spend enough time setting up and emphasizing their main character. Sometimes I don't know who the story is about for 40 or 50 pages because the characters are introduced with equal emphasis. Remember that writing is also directing—directing the audience's attention. "Look here. Now look here. Look at this—it's important."

In writing for Hollywood, is it ever advisable to write an open-ended story?

Hollywood favors "closed-loop" stories in which the loose ends are tied up and all plot threads are neatly resolved, like comforting fairy tales designed to reassure a child. However, Hollywood also adores novelty and variety, so a story that breaks the "rules" and isn't so neatly tied up may attract attention. You can be sure it will be severely tested in the much-hated development process, where all the conservative tendencies of the business will try to tack on a happy ending or a "satisfying" conclusion, but once in a while, the open ending works for Hollywood—especially in certain genres like horror, science fiction, or film noir where the whole concept may be to challenge conventional, comforting patterns of closure and resolution.

What are your responsibilities as a script consultant?

I have to read the script with an open mind, trying to evaluate it on its own terms. I try to think of what will bring out the writer's true intentions. Then I write notes or prepare for a meeting with the writer and producer, in which I look for a "big idea"—one unifying, overall insight that will bring the most positive development to the idea. Then, if the script is relatively close to production, I might go over it page by page to raise questions and make suggestions. I also evaluate the project—what's the best format for this story, novel, feature script, TV series, animation? What's the best path for getting it produced?

Anything further you'd like to add?

Adapt or die. Anybody wanting to keep working in this business should be very open-minded and adaptable. Screenwriting seems to be quickly dissolving and blending into other forms, such as writing for the Internet, creating computer game scenarios, and designing hybrids of movies and amusement park rides. A small number of people will be able to make their living entirely from writing Hollywood feature films; most writers will make a living by creating all sorts of things in all sorts of places. For example, designing Web sites is an infant art form, about where cinema was in 1900, and who knows what it will turn into? Some of my work lately has been in advising Web site and game designers on how to put the techniques of drama, myth, and film into the experiences they create.

The first generation of people who grew up in a world where computers were taken for granted may have new preferences in drama and entertainment. Screenwriters may have to adapt to their rhythms. Open-ended stories may become more popular. Young people may not be responding to movies as they used to simply because movies are finite, they go in one direction and they come to an end, whereas the possibilities of the computer are endless— literally something you can be immersed in all the time. Movies may evolve into much more complex, flexible, and open-ended forms, as is happening already with DVD versions that include alternate scenes and background material. We've always desired to see around the edges of the frame, to extend the movie experience and be able in some sense to live in that movie, and the future will allow us to indulge this even more.

Sitting Down to Write

Blake Snyder

*An Expert Storyteller's Advice
is Therapy for Screenwriters*

by Robin Mizell

When he was starting out as a screenwriter more than 20 years ago, Blake Snyder relied on the advice in the pages of *Writer's Digest*. Now, *he's* the professional giving instructions and providing moral support to aspiring writers and groups all over the world.

Snyder, a prolific scriptwriter, has spent two decades writing for Hollywood—a time during which he sold plenty of spec scripts, including the screenplay he co-wrote for Disney's *Blank Check* and an as-yet unproduced script called *Nuclear Family*, for which he signed a million-dollar deal with Steven Spielberg. Along the way, Snyder picked up tips and tricks from talented writers, and started enjoying the process of pitching a script. Possessed of an analytical mind and an intuitive understanding of audiences' instinctive reactions, he began to dissect what worked versus what was not effective in scripts, loglines, pitches, and the final product—movies. Before long, he'd codified each aspect of good screenwriting. "It just evolved sort of naturally," he explains. "People would ask me for advice on things, and I found myself giving the same advice again and again. So, I just put it down in a book."

The end result was a how-to book on screenwriting called *Save the Cat! The Last Book on Screenwriting You'll Ever Need*. The book focused on demystifying the storytelling process, and emphasized that structure and the initial idea are crucial in creating a successful script. The book went viral, becoming an underground hit as scriptwriters discovered it and began recommending it to other industry professionals, including managers, agents, and producers. By mid-2008, *Save the Cat!* was in its 12th printing and had sold more than 30,000 copies. "To me, it was just a labor of love," Snyder says, "and something that's really changed my life."

The book's success within the writing world allowed Snyder to connect with writing groups everywhere—online and in person—as he happily shares his tips on storytelling. Through his Web site and blog (www.blakesnyder.com), as well as his spin-off lectures and workshops, Snyder continues to give advice to film writers of all ages and skill levels. And *The Cat*'s popularity has even spawned more titles: "There's even a sequel to *The Last Book on Screenwriting You'll Ever Need*," says Snyder. His second book is *Save the Cat! Goes to the Movies*, and he plans at least two more in the series.

ROBIN MIZELL is the senior editor of *Screenwriter's & Playwright's Market*. To learn more about her and her writing, visit www.robinmizell.com.

WHAT'S *THE CAT* ABOUT?

Implicit in the iconic trade name, *Save the Cat!*, is the first lesson Snyder imparts to scriptwriters. "We have to like the guy we're following along," he explains. "The *Save the Cat!* moment is that moment when we meet the hero and he does something that makes us like him—such as saving a cat. It's remarkable how many times I've been in meetings at studios where executives say, 'Well, you know, it's a great script and everything, but I just don't like this guy.' " A sense of dissatisfaction occurs, according to Snyder, when an audience isn't given an excuse to take a liking to the protagonist. "You really need to put something in there that makes us want to root for him. Is that cheating? Is that not art? To me it's just good craft. It's just good storytelling."

Snyder resists referring to the method described in his books as a formula. "To me, this is just the essence of what makes good storytelling. I think the difference between how I wrote it out and told people about it and Aristotle's is this: I'm a slangy screenwriter." Snyder emphasizes that his recommendations can make the process of writing a salable script more comprehensible and systematic for working writers: "I'm a guy who's been in the trenches writing screenplays for a long time and just sort of distilled it down into a way that would be easy to understand. They're the same dynamics that have made storytelling work forever."

THE LOGLINE'S IMPORTANCE

Snyder devotes a lot of his energy and much of the first section of *Save the Cat!* to teaching screenwriters how to craft a logline. "Your pitch is your headline," he stresses. "Write a bad headline for a newspaper story, and we won't read it. Or a misleading headline, or a blurry headline, or a confusing headline. We won't read the article. And that applies to all kinds of things. What's your first point of contact with somebody who isn't standing in your shoes?"

Using what might seem like an unorthodox and counterintuitive strategy, Snyder recommends that screenwriters compose their loglines before beginning to write their scripts. "Just by reworking that one sentence, the entire complexion of the story changes. If you can write a better logline for your story, you can deliver a better story," he says.

It's remarkable what comes out of that exercise, he adds, when describing the four elements a truly effective logline must convey:

1. Irony
2. A compelling mental picture
3. Audience and production cost
4. A killer title

"What are you really trying to say?" Snyder continues. "What is the white-hot attraction of this particular idea? What does it boil down to at its essence? What's really cool about this? Figuring that out and then going on and exploiting it in the story really helps. It saves trees, by the way."

"BEAT IT OUT"

Using the "Blake Snyder Beat Sheet," writers are urged to outline 15 points of transition and the exact moments at which they occur in every successful movie. "I think some people didn't believe me—that it could be that simple," he says. "The other reaction is: 'If it *is* that simple, I don't want to do it. If it *is* that simple, it means I will be stifled creatively.' No, you won't! You need these tools to free yourself. Everything I talk about is about a kind of empowerment for writers."

Snyder had a personal motivation for creating the checklist for his beat sheet. He admits, "There were many scripts where I kind of ran out gas at page 50 and just couldn't finish."

Sitting Down to Write

He urges the timid, "You can do so much more than you thought. You can be so much more. I think some writers—I was one—are sort of held back by not daring to dream big enough. This is a freeing thing, if I can tell you, when you're having problems at the midpoint of your story, to check certain requirements of it."

Save the Cat! Goes to the Movies, Snyder's second book, is an effort to address the skepticism of those who suspected the beat sheet and storyboard concepts defined in his first book were too simplistic. Snyder's knack for detecting the 10 basic patterns underlying all great movie scripts didn't immediately convince everyone of the value of his methods. "I love finding this stuff," he says. "The reason for the second book is because so many people said, 'Oh, it's a formula,' or 'Oh, it just works for Hollywood movies and big studio movies.' The second book is showing how the beat sheet works in all movies, including independent and experimental films like *Open Water*, which is almost documentary in its feel and yet follows the beats of the beat sheet minute per minute. I think that second book really helped clarify what I meant."

NETWORKING FOR SCREENWRITERS

Looking back on his early career, Snyder says, "I felt very isolated. It was me and my agent, and that was about it. I never really networked with other writers. And yet the thing that I learned most and fastest from was working with partners—working with people who were better than me, frankly."

In Spain, the U.K., and Canada—and across the U.S.—Snyder encourages his workshop participants to form local *Cat!* groups and build on the networks they've established. He believes that adopting the jargon he employs and the methods he prescribes allows the members of the regional groups to understand and easily communicate with each other. *Cat!* groups ease writers into alliances Snyder hopes will help advance their careers. "My dream is to have these groups set up and, then, even help them market," he explains. "We send producers to some of these groups. We send managers and agents to these groups to hear what they're working on. We share resources. We pitch ideas back and forth to each other."

Ben Frahm, a middle school teacher who joined such a group, telephoned Snyder one day to announce he'd sold his first script, *Dr. Sensitive*, to Universal Studios for $300,000 up front, against a total deal of half a million dollars. Snyder's reaction? "I'm more excited for Ben than I was ever excited for myself."

Snyder wants screenwriters to understand that the Hollywood studios succeed because they deliver entertainment for the masses, and they do it using a time-honored method. "You don't have to reinvent the wheel to be creative. You can be creative by putting a fresh spin on something you already know," he says. "That's what the job is."

IT'S ALL ABOUT STORYTELLING

"All stories are about transformation," Snyder reminds writers. His background has made it easier for him to teach the concepts of catharsis and transformation. "I have had that transformative experience. I have been allowed to sort of have an Act Three in my life that I wasn't planning on."

Persistent in his search for life's hidden meaning, Snyder says, "For me personally, and for us as human beings, and I think for the heroes of all good stories, there's a point where the hero has a moment of clarity toward the end of the story, where he realizes what it has been about." He proposes, "That moment of clarity, for me, is touched by a higher power, touched by a sense of the divine. In movie after movie, story after story, the thing that gives us the chills, the thing that makes it work, is the subterranean story. It's the spiritual story."

When pressed to apply a character archetype to himself, something he frequently does with other people, Snyder laughs, "I'm the old soldier going back for one last mission—damaged, wounded, limping—but one last glorious mission."

Sitting Down to Write

Writing the TV Spec Script

Break In Using Existing Shows

by Ellen Sandler

Here's a truth: There is only one way to get a job writing television—and no, it's not by getting the right agent. The way to get work is by having something fresh and wonderful that people get excited about.

It's just that simple.

Simple, but not easy.

Because it's common, television is often dismissed as insignificant—unworthy of respect and care. Because it's pervasive, it's voracious. Television needs material, and it reproduces like an amoeba, constantly driving and replicating itself to fill the continuing void. Television needs more, and it needs it now. That's where you come in. Your job as a writer is to supply it with content. This leads to fast, which leads to sloppy, which leads to formulaic, writing.

In order to write for TV, you must get a job. In order to get a job, you must have material to show that you can write. Usually, that will be a spec script.

WHAT IS A SPEC SCRIPT?

A television spec script is an unsolicited, original episode written for an established TV show. No money, no contract, no guarantees. In all likelihood, a spec script will never be sold nor produced. What it will be is *read*. That's what you write it for: to be read by as many people connected to show business as you can get to. Everyone counts. You never know who knows someone who knows someone.

A television spec script is different than a film spec script. You don't write a TV spec with the expectation of selling it to the show. It could happen, but what's much more likely, and therefore what we'll be talking about, is that you'll write a spec TV episode to prove that you can do the work. It's a writing sample—a portfolio piece. In film, people are looking for a script, but in TV they are looking for a *writer*.

WHY WRITE FOR TV?

The only reason to write a television episodic spec script is: money. When I teach, I usually draw a big $ on the whiteboard and everybody laughs. I suppose because that's what they

ELLEN SANDLER (www.SandlerInk.com) received an Emmy nomination for her work as co-executive producer of "Everybody Loves Raymond." She has worked as a writer/producer for many other network television shows, including ABC's long-running series, "Coach." She has also created original series for numerous networks. This article reprinted with permission from *The TV Writer's Workbook: A Creative Approach to Television Scripts* (Delta Trade/ Random House, 2007).

were really thinking but were afraid to say. Or maybe they were even afraid to think it. Maybe they feel it's not a worthy reason to write. But the truth is that television is a commercial medium and you write it for money.

IS IT FORM OR FORMULA?

What writing for money means is that when you sit down to write, you have to follow the rules. By rules, I don't mean formula—*formula* is what makes a writer a hack, and leads to predictable, dull scripts that nobody wants to read past page eight. However, there is *form*— quite a different thing. Television scripts have a specific form, and you must follow it.

It doesn't matter if you think you know how to do it better or funnier than what's on the air. That's not your job when you're writing a spec script. You job is to do it exactly the way it's done and still be original. If you follow the rules without originality, your work will be okay but it will not distinguish itself as special.

Yes, you're writing for money, but you are not writing *only* for money. You must also put some art into your commercial product. It's very unlikely that you'll ever get to write for money if you don't put something of yourself into your script. The richest, most successful television writers I know have all written commercially savvy products from a personal point of view. Creative with the form? No. Creative with the content? Yes.

WHAT SHOW SHOULD YOU SPEC?

Write a show you love to watch. That, in my opinion, is the single most important factor in choosing a show to write. Don't write a spec of a show you don't like, even if someone in the industry has told you it's the hot show to write. When you get to pick, and your spec may be the only time you have that opportunity, by all means be picky. Only write a show that you relate to, a show you like to watch, with characters you care about. That is first and foremost—but it's not the only criterion.

Here are three other factors to keep in mind when choosing a show to write for.

1. The show must be on the air now

This is a rule. Don't write a "Friends" spec, even if you saw every episode and you have the greatest idea for a Rachel story ever. Anything that is off the air is an old show, even if reruns are playing every day.

In fact, any show that's been on the air more than five years is probably too old to write a spec for, even if it's not going off the air for a couple more seasons. If you're sending out an episode of an older show, the feeling is that you're not fresh, not current, not keeping up with the trends—and in TV, that is death.

2. It should be a hit

Here's why:

- A hit show is not likely to be canceled the day before you finish your spec.
- People who will be reading your spec will be familiar with the show and the characters.
- A hit is a hit because it works. A show that works will be easier to write and will make a much better sample.
- Hits are copied. There will be new shows like it on the air and those are shows that will be looking for staff. If you've written a spec of the show they've cloned, it will be an excellent sample to demonstrate how appropriate you would be for their show.

To be considered a "hit," a commercial network show should be in the top 25 to 30 on the list. Also consider critically acclaimed shows (think "Monk") that aren't necessarily a top-tier smash.

3. You have a connection

You went to acting school with someone in the cast; your roommate's buddy is an assistant editor on the show; your cousin knows a production assistant's life partner. If you have a genuine connection, no matter how minor, it could be a big help. For one thing, it will be easier to get scripts of the show to study. The most important advantage is the possibility of getting your spec read by a writer on the show and a chance for some professional feedback—and, who knows, maybe even a recommendation to that writer's agent or the showrunner. But don't expect that; just ask for feedback.

Stories to Avoid

When you do decide to sit down and write that glorious spec script, keep in mind these overused premises and steer clear of them.

Introducing an outside character

Writers may think they're showing how original they are, but what they're really showing is that they aren't excited enough by the show. A spec should show how you can color inside the lines and still make it fresh. In other words, that you can write for hire! And isn't that the point? The big exception here is for shows where the basic premise requires guest characters every week—medical shows have new patients, cop shows have new criminals and victims.

A famous guest star

It's called *stunt casting* and I know many shows do it, but it should be avoided in your spec; it says you're more interested in casting than in writing.

The past lover

Please don't write this as your spec script, especially if the ex-boy/girlfriend returns in a quirky, unexpected way. It seems like every third spec I read is a version of this story. It's just an overused idea.

The class reunion show

Besides being a much-used premise, which is reason enough to avoid it, anything involving the past history of your characters is shaky territory for a spec. It's really only appropriate for the show's creator to invent backstory, so leave the reunion show to him or her.

Trading places

I suggest you stay away from stories where the leads exchange roles. They can come across as contrived and gimmicky.

Trapped in an elevator/mountain cabin/bathroom, wherever

Dick Van Dyke got caught in a cabin in the snow and every sitcom since has done some version of this storyline. If you've got something that's fresh, okay—otherwise, come up with another idea.

More things to stay away from:

Animals and babies, flashbacks/fantasies/dream sequences, elaborate sets, exotic locations, and pop culture references.

ELEMENTS OF A SPEC SCRIPT STORY
1. Your story must revolve around the central character

So how do you know which character is the central character? If their name is in the title ("My Name is Earl"), then *that's* how you know. If the name of the central character and the name of the actor playing the character are one and the same—"Everybody Loves Raymond"—then you *really* know.

What it means for a story to revolve around the central character is:

a. The story must have an emotional conflict for the central character.
b. The central character drives the action; that is, his choices make the plot progress.
c. The central character resolves the problem.

In other words, the story is told from the central character's point of view. It happens to him; and even more important, he makes it happen.

If your show has two characters in the title, such as "Two and Half Men," examine which one of the leads often drives the story. For a spec script, it's probably a good idea to follow that pattern.

With a show like "Desperate Housewives" or "Entourage," the title tells you that you have an ensemble show, meaning a group of characters that are equally important, or nearly so. In a show like this, episodes often revolve around a theme with storylines for various characters.

Shows with no character names in the title, such as *CSI* and *Law & Order*, are shows where the *procedure* is primary; however, they still have central characters. Do some research. Which character is in the most scenes and how many? Which character solves the case? Is it the same in every episode? If these factors shift to different characters in different episodes, you have a choice of which character to feature in your script.

2. Your story must use all of the regular supporting characters

The regular characters are the ones featured in the opening credits. They appear in every episode, and therefore, they all must be in your spec script. Rule out ideas that create solitary confinement for the central character—lost at sea, home alone, etc.

3. Your story must respect the premise of the show

This means that if, for example, your show is about a married man whose parents live across the street, you don't choose a story for your spec script in which he files for divorce or moves to Vancouver. Create a story that illustrates the basic elements of the show as they exist in the premise. Your spec script is not an opportunity to demonstrate how much better the show would be if it were different. Your spec script is your opportunity to demonstrate how close you can come to exactly what the show is about and still be original, which, incidentally, is a much more difficult task.

Writing the TV Pilot

Three Rules for Doing It Right

by Chad Gervich

While the Writers Strike may have decimated 2007's pilot season, one thing it won't decimate is TV's continuing need for new show ideas. Now that the strike is over, networks and studios are looking for fresh shows and content. And fortunately, the market for spec pilots (pilots written without being first pitched and sold as ideas) has been surprisingly robust lately—with studios hungrier than usual to snatch up already-written scripts.

So as writers all across America work on their pilots, let's take a quick moment to discuss some of the vital elements that make pilots work.

First of all, let's answer this question, which a student in my "Writing the TV Pilot" class asked last month: What, exactly, is a pilot?

A pilot is most commonly thought of as the first episode of a television series—the first story in a series of many more stories. And while this is often the case, it's not entirely accurate.

The truth is: A pilot, whether in script form or actually produced, is a selling tool used to illustrate what the TV series is about and how it works. In other words, a pilot is designed to convince network or studio executives that this series a good investment of their money and airtime. Some pilots never even make it to air—they're simply used to get the series "picked up," then discarded.

When you begin looking at a pilot this way—as a selling tool, rather than just the first of many stories—you realize that pilots must accomplish certain things besides simply kicking off the series narratively. Thus, here are three important tips to think about as you craft your own TV pilots.

1. Pilots must prove your series has longevity.

TV series are designed to run not just for a few weeks, or even a few months. Successful TV series must run for years, which means your pilot needs to prove that this world can generate a nearly endless number of stories.

One way to do this is to base your series around a locale or occupation that organically

CHAD GERVICH (www.chadgervich.com) is a television producer, published author, and award-winning playwright. He has written, developed, or produced shows for Fox TV Studios, Paramount Television, NBC Studios, Warner Brothers, Fox Reality Channel, ABC Studios, E! Entertainment, and Twentieth Century Fox. Chad's book, *Small Screen, Big Picture: A Writer's Guide to the TV Business*, is currently available from www.mediabistro.com and Random House/Crown.

generates stories. Cop and detective shows, like *Bones* or *CSI*, never run out of stories; as long as the world has crimes, these shows have tales to tell. After all, every time the door of a police station or detective agency opens, in walks a case—which is a story.

Soaps, like *Brothers & Sisters* or even *Heroes*, never run out of stories because they're filled with incredibly deep, rich, and complex relationships. It's easy for an executive to see—in a world where people are constantly lying, cheating, sleeping with and backstabbing each other—how these relationships will generate many years of interesting stories.

Whether you're writing a mystery show, like *NCIS*, or a character-driven dramedy, like *Grey's Anatomy*, it's your pilot's job to prove this series can generate an endless number of stories.

2. Pilots must illuminate how every episode of the series will work.

Although a pilot is kicking off a new series, meaning it works a bit differently than subsequent stories and episodes, it must also demonstrate how the series' regular episodes will work the same on a regular basis. In other words, they must help buyers (executives and producers) understand exactly what it is they're buying. Does each episode tell a single, close-ended mystery, like *Law & Order: SVU*? Or will each episode deal with a particular issue about married life or relationships, a la *'Til Death* or *Rules of Engagement*?

While a pilot is indeed the catalyst that sparks the rest of the series, it must also work just like every other episode of the series. If your doctors will heal one patient per episode, let them heal a patient in the pilot. If your squabbling couple must solve a marital problem each week, let them do so in the pilot.

This is often a difficult tightrope to walk. How can a pilot be both the beginning of a long-running saga as well as an example of a prototypical episode? This, unfortunately, is the delicate artform of writing a pilot, and one of the reasons it often takes writers years of working in and developing TV before they get a series on the air.

"Your pilot should introduce all of your main characters and set the tone for the series," says Aury Wallington, a TV writer who's written pilots for USA, ABC and Sony. "The pilot is all about getting an audience invested in what's going to happen over the next 22 weeks."

3. Pilots must (usually) show us how/if episodes are repeatable.

Repeatability is the bread and butter of traditional television. This is because relatively little money is made off the "first run" of a TV episode; the real money comes when a series is sold into syndication (reruns on local stations or cable channels). But in order to be repeatable, episodes must function in specific ways. The most repeatable episodes are "stand-alone," meaning they tell a singular, close-ended story in each episode. Each week, the cops of *K-Ville* receive, investigate, and solve a completely new mystery. It begins and ends all in one episode, making it easy for audiences to watch a single episode—whether it's the show's first run or a rerun—and still understand what's going on.

Similarly, Justin and Raja in *Aliens In America* deal each week with a new problem in their friendship, school, or family—and it's solved that same episode. Standalone episodes not only make a series more repeatable, they make it easier for audiences to pop in and watch just one episode at a time. (It's pretty difficult to simply bounce in and watch a single third-season episode of *Lost*.)

If your series has repeatable episodes, it's infinitely more sell-able, and you need to show this in your pilot. Let your detectives begin and close a mystery in the pilot. Let your bickering best friends deal with an issue and resolve it.

On the flip side, if your show is highly serialized or soapy, like *24* or *Cane*, with stories spanning many weeks or months, let us see how this works as well. Use your pilot to show

how stories will play out over the course of an episode and then seduce us to come back the following week.

And always, follow the rules in terms of length, grammar and submissions. "If you're lucky enough to have a producer or agent read your script, you don't want to be rejected just because it doesn't look right or is the wrong length or format," Wallington says. "Your pilot script also needs to conform to all the rules of any other TV script. If it's a drama, it should be 60 pages long; comedies should be 30 pages. Unless you're envisioning it specifically for a network like HBO or FX, you should double-check your dialogue to make sure it's appropriate for television."

Remember: selling a TV series is like selling anything else, from vacuum cleaners to used cars. You job is to show your buyer what they're buying and how it will continue to work. This is the true purpose of a pilot.

Cut, Cut, Cut

*Rewrite and Revise your Script
Before It Hits the Streets*

by Emily Hoferer

You've finally done it. You have in your hands your finished script. The characters, plot and dialogue that you've been pouring over for months have finally culminated into a finished screenplay. Now you can send it off to a production company or script manager to begin the painstaking process of getting someone to pay you for it, right?

Well, not exactly. Before you lick the postage, there is one important process you are neglecting: rewriting.

Rewriting may not be the most enjoyable process; after all, not everyone likes to see their hard work drastically changed or have portions eliminated completely. But it's an essential tool in making your story better.

Not every change to a script is correcting a simple mistake or cutting out individual lines of dialogue. Rewriting also means adding or taking away things that are related to characters, plot and setting. "Cutting, shaping, adding, subtracting, working it, making it better—that's what real writing is all about," says James Scott Bell in his book, *Revisions and Self-Editing*. "That's how unpublished writers get published."

Each time you go through your draft to change or remove things, your script improves. "There's no piece of writing in the world that can't be shorter or better," says screenwriter Andrew Klavan, whose credits include *One Missed Call*.

So pick up your pen and take a deep breath. Rewriting is about to begin.

THE BASICS

The first and most important thing to do is check your script for simple mistakes in spelling and grammar. Once proofreading is complete, move on to the more complicated stuff. Do you have a sentence that's 20 words long that only needs to be 10? Don't be afraid to use words that pack a punch and get the meaning across. "Screenplays are like poetry in one sense—they're incredibly condensed," says Klavan. "Every word has to count."

One simple task to do early on is cut out excessive words that are overused in description, such as "very," "really," and "suddenly."

Character dialogue should move the plot forward

Sometimes the most difficult thing to do is cut dialogue between characters, especially when this dialogue is humorous or witty. But if you're looking at a long script with its fair share of slow scenes, dialogue that does not move the plot forward, however snappy and

EMILY HOFERER is an assistant editor for *Screenwriter's & Playwright's Market*.

Finding Zoetrope

Robb Lanum, a freelance TV writer for "Rugrats" and script coordinator for various other television shows, has this advice for writers seeking useful criticism of their work:

"How do you know when your script is ready? For writers without a network of other writers to help out with peer review, and even for writers with such a network, this is a big question. At some point, you want educated and credible feedback, but you don't want to waste a first impression with a production company or agency or pay money to enter a contest with an early draft that you're pretty sure needs some work. A writers' group or writing classmates are great, but these aren't always available.

So what do you do? I recommend www.Zoetrope.com. The Zoetrope site is part of Francis Ford Coppola's domain, and basically what you do is upload scripts for other people to read while you read other people's work in return. You read and give feedback on four or five scripts for each one you can upload, so usually you get at least three or four sets of comments on your work. Nobody sees the script comments except for the writer, and then you can e-mail the reviewer if you like, ask questions, even strike up a friendship. There is a real culture of helpfulness—there is nothing to gain from being snarky or mean—and all the readers are writers themselves. It is free."

crisp it may be, is not vital to the story and therefore can be nixed. Always ask yourself if the dialogue and actions are there for a necessity in plot progression or just there because you, the author, like it.

Cut out repetitive dialogue

Too often, dialogue is repetitive. Make sure that every line a character says is new and fresh and not echoing what another character previously said. Beware instances when one character gives a summary of an event that we, the audience, saw unfold in the previous scene. Don't underestimate your audience—they're smarter than you think they are.

"After I've finished a first draft, I do an edit check for the word 'remember,'" says Nancy Gall-Clayton, a Louisville playwright. "If it's in my play, I probably have two characters talking about something that both already know about. Such dialogue does not belong in a story unless it's motivated."

Avoid fluffy descriptions

Exposition should be scant. The trick is to define your characters and plot through action and dialogue. "So much can be explained in movies with a look or gesture or picture that most scenes where someone sits down and explains everything are unnecessary," Klavan says.

If you have lots of exposition that absolutely must be in the screenplay, think of a way to insert it so scenes don't get overloaded or boring. In *The Terminator*, a lot of exposition happens between two characters as they are in a car chase fleeing for their lives. The audience has to absorb plenty of information, but it's still exciting because of the visuals.

Plot basics

The overall plot should have the typical story arc of introduction, rising action, climax, falling action and resolution—and they typically go in that order. Deconstruct your script scene by scene and look at each scene in terms of plot. Does the scene move the plot forward? If it does, then it is important to the story. If not, cut it.

THE BIG STUFF

It's important to map out where your story is going and what the big emotional scenes are. Keeping a list of this information nearby as you write and rewrite will be helpful. Identify the big moments and look for ways that it could be more dramatic, intense or funny (depending on what you're going for). There is a purpose for each scene and you should never stray from its intent.

Information overload

While each scene should contain enough information for plot progression, be careful of unloading too much info too quick. Spread the information out to hold interest, but keep the plot going. Dropping heavy cargo all at once on a reader or audience will turn them off.

Evaluate subplots

While subplots add interest, depth and complexity to the plot, they are sometimes unnecessary. If a script is too long, think about eliminating an entire subplot. It's an alternate to chiseling off bits and pieces here and there to get to that desired page count.

Check again for camera cues

As you continue your rewrites, now is good a time as ever to make sure you're not inserting direction into your work. "Don't write a director's script," says Gena Ellis, a screenwriting

Hire a Script Doctor?

When your work is complete, it needs another pair (or many pairs) of eyes on it to get some feedback. One route to go is finding a freelance screenplay editor—or "script doctor"—who can pass on professional advice concerning structure and characters. Legitimate script doctors have roots in the screenplay industry and have probably made several sales, though some or none of those sales may have been produced, depending.

The benefit to a hiring a script doctor is that your work gets a thorough edit by someone who is knowledgeable about craft—and hopefully, has connections that you can utilize later. The danger is that you must make sure that you're getting a straight-up deal from someone who can indeed give you helpful criticism. A good script doctor is not cheap—and you'll end up paying anywhere from a few hundred bucks to more than $1,000. When you're talking with a stranger via e-mail, it's easy for them to embellish their credentials and accomplishments. Do your homework and take your time.

The best way to go with a script doctor is to get an excellent referral. Personally talk with someone who worked with a professional, and ask lots of questions. Then contact the editor and start a conversation; you can even ask for a free editing sample of a few pages to get a gist of their style.

instructor whose credits include the indie *Angela's Decision*. "Don't have scene numbers on the slug lines. Don't use 'Cut to' or 'Dissolve To' any more than you absolutely must. No camera angles. Try to keep the number of slug lines to 85-100, max. You are writing a submission script, not a final script."

Beginnings and endings

The beginning of the script should grab the interest of the reader or audience and set the stage to properly pull them through the story. Endings should tie up loose ends but also leave the audience with a feeling of completion that lies outside of the story.

A good rewriting process will result in a good screenplay. Remember that the process is not a lone man's task. Bounce ideas off of your friends and colleagues and always be on the lookout for a fresh perspective. Give your script to someone else to read and get feedback.

When you've finished that first draft, put your writing aside for a few days or weeks before coming back to it. You'll discover things that you missed as well as sections that seemed to work before but you now want to change. Consider a staged reading with professional actors. Although this process is more typical with stage plays, it's just as valuable with a screenplay.

The process may not be quick and easy, but don't get frustrated. Good scripts aren't written and rewritten in a day.

Queries and Synopses

Your First Contact with the Power Players

by Chuck Sambuchino

Before a manager or producer will read your work, you have to give them a reason to do so. Simply put, that means pitching your work through a query and synopsis and piquing enough interest to force them into demanding the full script. After all, Hollywood is famous for moving slowly. But how much slower would it move if everybody were reading every page of every script? That's a lot of text to slog through!

To combat the sheer volume of scripts waiting to be read, agents and producers want to see short versions of stories to judge whether time will be well spent further considering the project. And that's where queries and synopses come in handy.

QUERIES

A query is a one-page, single-spaced letter that quickly tells who you are, what the work is, and why the work is appropriate for the market in question. Just as queries are used as the first means of contact for pitching magazine articles and novels, they work just the same for scripts.

A well-written query is broken down into three parts.

Part I: Your reason for contacting/script details

Before even looking at the few sentences describing your story, a producer wants to see two other things:

1. What is it? State the title, genre, and whether it's a full-length script or a shorter one. This is also a place to include your logline if you've boiled it down to one sentence. (If it's more several sentences, there isn't much of a point, seeing as how the multi-sentence elevator pitch is to follow.)

2. Why are you contacting this market/person in particular? There are thousands of individuals who receive scripts. Why have you chosen this person to review the material? Is it because you met them in person and they requested to see your work? Have they represented writers similar to yourself? Did you read that they were actively looking for zombie comedies? Spelling out your reason upfront shows that you've done your research, and that's you're a professional.

CHUCK SAMBUCHINO is the editor of *Screenwriter's & Playwright's Market*. He is also the editor of *Guide to Literary Agents* (www.guidetoliteraryagents.com/blog) and assists in editing *Writer's Market*.

Sample Query Letter

Include all contact information— including phone and e-mail—as centered information at the top.

John Q. Writer
123 Main St.
Writerville, USA
(212)555-1234
johnqwriter@email.com

Date

Agent
JQA & Associates
678 Hollywood St.
Hollywood, CA 90210

Use proper greetings and last names.

Dear Mr./Ms. (Last Name):

Include a reason for contacting the reader.

My name is John Q. Writer and we crossed paths at the Writer's Digest Books Writers' Conference in Los Angeles in May 2008. After hearing the pitch for my feature-length thriller, *October Surprise*, you requested that I submit a query, synopsis and the first 10 pages of the script. All requested materials are enclosed. This is an exclusive submission, as you requested.

Try and keep the pitch to one paragraph.

U.S. Senator Michael Hargrove is breaking ranks with his own political party to endorse another candidate for President of the United States. At the national convention, he's treated like a rock star V.I.P.—that is, until, he's abducted by a fringe political group and given a grim ultimatum: Use your speech on live TV to sabotage and derail the presidential candidate you're now supporting, or your family back home will not live through the night.

Regarding your credentials, be concise and honest.

The script was co-written with my scriptwriting partner, Joe Aloysius. I am produced playwright and award-winning journalist. Thank you for considering *October Surprise*. I will be happy to sign any release forms that you request. May I send the rest of the full screenplay?

Best,

John Q. Writer

Part II: The Elevator Pitch

If you wrote the first paragraph correctly, you've got their attention, so pitch away. Explain what your story is about in 3-6 sentences. The point here is to intrigue and pique, only. Don't get into nitty-gritty details of any kind. Hesitate using a whole lot of character names or backstory. Don't explain how it ends or who dies during the climax or that the hero's father betrays him in Act II. Introduce us to the main character and his situation, then get to the key part of the pitch: the conflict.

Try to include tidbits here and there that make your story unique. If it's about a cop nearing retirement, that's nothing new. But if the story is about a retiring cop considering a sex change operation in his bid to completely start over, while the police union is threatening to take away his pension should he do this—*then* you've got something different that readers may want to see.

Part III: The Wrap-Up

Your pitch is complete. The last paragraph is where you get to talk about yourself and your accomplishments. If the script has won any awards or been a finalist in prominent competitions, this is the place to say so. Mention your writing credentials and experience. Obviously, any paid screenwriting experience is most valuable, but feel free to include other tidbits such as if you're a magazine freelancer or a published novelist.

Sometimes, there won't be much to say at the end of a query letter because the writer has no credits, no contacts and nothing to brag about. As your mother would tell you: If you don't have anything nice to say, don't say anything at all. Keep the last section brief if you must, rather than going on and on about being an ''active blogger'' (whatever that amounts to) or having one poem published in your college literary magazine.

Following some information about yourself, it's time to wrap up the query and propose sending more material. A simple way to do this is by saying: ''The script is complete. May I send you the full screenplay or perhaps some pages?''

SYNOPSES

If an agent or producer is intrigued by the super-condensed version of your story (in the query), their next step is to see your whole tale front to back in the form of a synopsis. A synopsis is a condensed summary of the entire story that showcases the central conflict of the story and the interlocking chain of events set off by that conflict. Unlike a query, a synopsis is designed to tell the *full* story, meaning the ending is revealed. Don't be coy or hold back information.

The challenge lies in telling your complicated and amazing story simply and briskly. You must introduce the protagonist, the antagonist, the love interest and the hook—and that's just the beginning! When in doubt, stick to the plot. If the character starts out lost in the Yukon, say so—but don't waste time talking about how remote and desolate and hopeless the area is. Keep moving! If you're stuck, try this: Sit down with a 10-year-old and give yourself two minutes or less to explain the entire story. You'll be forced to keep it simple and keep it moving.

The reason you have so little time is that a good screenplay synopsis should run approximately two full pages, double-spaced. ''Although writers may submit as long of a synopsis as they desire, ideally it should get to the point fairly quickly,'' says Margery Walshaw, script manager for Evatopia. ''In a sense, this is the writer's first test to see if they can get their point across in a concise manner that is also engaging.''

Do not intrude the narrative flow with authorial commentary, and do not let the underlying story framework show in your synopsis. Don't use phrases such as ''At the climax of the conflict . . .'' or ''Act II begins with . . .'' In short, do not let it read like a nonfiction outline.

Your goal is to entrance with the story itself and not to break the spell by allowing the supporting scaffolding to show.

Concerning the format, use a header and include page numbers. Make sure that you capitalize the names of all major characters as they are introduced. Double space the text and make sure your writing is in the present tense: "Michael wakes up to find that his family is gone."

FOLLOWING DIRECTIONS

When you submit your work to an agent or producer, remember to submit exactly what's asked. Send the materials in the requested manner, as well. If you got a request to submit materials and you're afraid your solicited script is just going to get tossed in with 400 others in the slush pile, put "Requested Material" on the envelope. Then, in the query's first paragraph, quickly explain when the material was requested to back up your claim.

You've spent months or years (or even decades) on that script, and so it may be frustrating to jump through the hoops of the submission process—but it's important. Don't give readers an excuse to ignore your work. You must craft a killer query and synopsis before the script gets its big shot. Compose them well, and you're on your way to selling that screenplay.

Working with Representation

Agents, Managers & Lawyers

by Robin Mizell

You've probably heard that finding the right professional representation will give your script the best chance of someday being made into a feature film, a television episode, or perhaps a video game. Persuading a studio or production company executive to give you a moment of attention can be torture. The task is made more complicated by contentious perspectives of which category of representative you should enlist to help you: an agent, a manager, or an attorney specializing in entertainment law. The debate about which type is most ethical, helpful, accessible, and cost-effective has been going on for years. How much of your projected income can you afford to pay for representation? Can you afford not to?

Throw out all the rhetoric. Toss the hyperbole. Disregard slick branding. Forget the snide remarks of disgruntled competitors. Regardless of title—agent, manager, or attorney-at-law—the person's skill, intelligence, and industry connections are what really matter. The good, the bad, and the worthless exist in all three categories. The less desperate and clueless you are, the better your chances of avoiding a ruthless opportunist who knows more about loopholes in labor laws than how to close deals in the entertainment industry.

Learn exactly what these different kinds of professionals can do to help advance your career, as well as what they don't do, and you'll avoid unrealistic expectations and enjoy a much better relationship with the one, or several, you choose to advise you.

THE DIFFERENCES ARE NOT JUST SEMANTIC

It's not always possible to tell by the business name whether a person is a manager, agent, packager, producer, or some combination thereof. Learn what the terms *should* mean, but remember they're often used loosely and interchangeably.

Agents

Agents that do business in California, New York, and other states with laws similar to California's Labor Code Sections 1700-1701 (commonly referred to as the Talent Agency Act) must be licensed by the state and bonded before they can procure work for writers. The Talent Agency Act also limits a talent agent's commission fee to 10 percent of a client's gross income, although provisions in the law permit an agent to recover from clients certain expenses related to postage, courier services, etc.

California law prohibits agents from collecting registration fees from clients. It also strictly

ROBIN MIZELL is the senior editor of *Screenwriter's & Playwright's Market*. To learn more about her and her writing, visit www.robinmizell.com.

regulates "advance-fee" agents and stipulates that clients of "advance-fee" agents be informed in writing of their right to cancel and their right to a prompt refund of fees paid in advance if they don't receive the services promised. This is a basic measure to help writers avoid scammers.

Agents can collect larger fees from studios and production companies for packaging talent. Packaging involves attaching several elements—maybe a script, an actor, and a producer—to one deal and then selling it to a buyer.

Agents whose clients are members of professional guilds, such the Writers Guild of America, West (WGAW), are also bound by guild regulations related to agencies, which are negotiated by the Association of Talent Agents (ATA). Agents can become franchised by a guild and are then referred to as guild signatories. One of the most significant of guild regulations is the stipulation that agents may not own any of their clients' work, which means they can't also serve as producers. For more detailed explanations, see the ATA's Web site, www.agentassociation.com, and the WGAW's Web site, www.wga.org.

Managers

Managers working in California are not currently required to be licensed, as long as they can demonstrate they are not "procuring work" for their clients. They typically charge writers 15 to 20 percent for their services.

There are many types of managers, including personal managers, business managers, and literary managers. The roles sometimes overlap, so it's important to understand the business model of the individual who offers to represent you. Managers consider their clients to be under contract, whether the contract is a written or oral agreement. Make sure you fully understand, in advance, the terms of the contract to which you'll be held, including the provisions for terminating it.

Managers differ from agents in that they have more time to work with new clients and shepherd material. "If you're indeed a newbie, try targeting managers," says Candy Davis, a screenwriter and freelancer. "A manager is someone who makes herself available to new talent and helps develop and polish a script. She's just as picky as any agent, and yes, she gets a bigger percentage of your take—somewhere around 15 percent. To the writer living outside Tinseltown, she's worth it. Managers nurture new talent with deft coaching, high expectations and a kick in the pants where needed."

Lawyers

Lawyers in the entertainment field are the easiest types of writers' representatives to identify. As you probably already know, possessing the professional law degree, Juris Doctor, doesn't automatically authorize an individual to practice law. Each state in the U.S. requires professionals with law degrees to be members of the state bar in order to practice law. On the other hand, power of attorney can be granted to anyone, including a manager or an agent. If the term "attorney" is being used to imply an authority of which you're uncertain, then check the individual's credentials through the American Bar Association's Web site, www.abanet.org.

Entertainment lawyers can charge hourly rates, flat fees for drafting or reviewing certain types of contracts, and percentages that are referred to as contingency fees. Some agents and managers have lawyers on staff or attorneys with whom they consult as needed. It's not unusual for an entertainment attorney to be able and willing to make the crucial connection between a scriptwriter and a studio or producer.

Because some experienced agents and managers review and negotiate hundreds of contracts, they can become just as adept as entertainment lawyers at interpreting rights agreements. Larger talent agencies and management companies often have in-house counsel; boutique businesses might engage a lawyer when needed. A scriptwriter who has an agent or manager can also pay for an entertainment attorney to conduct an independent review of a contract.

Know who your entertainment attorney's other clients are. Lawyers are not immune to conflicts of interest. In the event you're unhappy with your lawyer's services, you can dismiss him or her without difficulty.

WHICH ONE TO ENGAGE

Some agents, managers, and entertainment lawyers will agree to collaborate on the representation of a single scriptwriter. Others prefer to work independently to avoid inadvertent duplication of efforts. It would be unfortunate if two professionals representing the same writer unwittingly approached the same studio or producer separately to arrange a meeting. Clear and constant communication among the writer and his or her various representatives is imperative. Good relationships facilitate deals.

FLYING SOLO

Some studios are reluctant to arrange a sale or option agreement with a writer who isn't represented by an agent or a lawyer, just as judges are extremely cautious about allowing respondents or defendants represent themselves in court. To a production executive, it might not be worth the increased risk that an unrepresented writer will later claim a rights contract was confusing and unfair.

Furthermore, a glut of queries and submissions leaves everyone in the entertainment industry overworked. Studios contend with the heavy load by enabling agents and managers to act as gatekeepers, permitting only the most promising and commercially viable scripts through for their consideration.

PERSONALIZED CAREER DEVELOPMENT

You'll encounter claims that managers are hungrier for clients or that they devote more time to developing a writer's career and, therefore, are more willing to work with emerging talent. The same is said of agents who are new to the business, whether working independently or as junior associates at major talent agencies like the Creative Artists Agency, the William Morris Agency, and International Creative Management. Any writers' representative launching a new business will have more time for each client initially, before the business's client list expands.

The more working clients an agent, manager, or attorney has, the more money he or she can make. Naturally, you'd prefer undivided attention. That will happen only if your representative is a member of your family. If you can't swing such a beneficial arrangement, then find a representative who does a good job of balancing the client load, so you won't get lost in the crowd. If your phone calls or e-mail inquiries aren't answered promptly, if your questions are given short shrift, or if you don't feel a sense of partnership, then you won't be getting the service to which you're entitled.

You can certainly judge a business by the success of the clients it represents. A list of clients or their work is often published on an agency's or management company's Web site. If the information isn't provided, then don't hesitate to ask for it. Search the Web for any and all references to the business, as well as the individual manager or agent with whom you'll be dealing. Web sites devoted to exposing scams and frauds can help you avoid unnecessary expense and embarrassment, not to mention wasted time.

HOW DO YOU GET NOTICED?

You might meet script agents, managers, and entertainment lawyers at playwrights' or screenwriters' conferences or be introduced to them by other scriptwriters in your network of contacts. A personal meeting or introduction will help to distinguish you from other aspiring scriptwriters. If you don't already know someone who can recommend you to a representative, then start networking. Join a writers' group, post questions in an online forum devoted to the exchange of information among scriptwriters, apply for an internship, attend a workshop, or donate your time to a charity event at which professionals in the entertainment industry will be participating.

You'll still need to sell yourself with a query, samples of your work, and possibly a concise biography or résumé. Although everything hinges on the quality and variety of your sample scripts, your query will reveal a great deal about you. Professional agents and managers deal with such a high volume of inquiries that they can spot a high-maintenance, self-absorbed prospective client after reading the first sentence of a query letter. No agent or manager wants to sign the infamous 20 percent who take up 80 percent of a workday, no matter how talented.

The more appealing you are as a prospective client, the more choice you'll have in terms of who represents you. Give yourself an advantage by knowing what genres agents and managers are seeking and which ones they tend to avoid. Each representative has peculiar tastes. It's not unusual for them to specialize by focusing on niches where their experience and industry connections are best put to use. Don't risk annoying someone who isn't looking for the types of scripts you've written.

Have several spec or sample scripts already written when you submit your query. The more scripts you have to show, the greater the chance something you're offering will fit the specific needs of a buyer. You'll demonstrate that you're versatile and that you're not just dabbling or testing the waters—you're in the scriptwriting business for the long haul.

Position yourself as a professional who is not only talented but available and easygoing. Write a polished, high-concept script with a solid story that's fresh and marketable. Know the business, network and query persistently, and you'll earn your success.

Know Your Avenues

Begin with Realistic Goals

by Chuck Sambuchino and Vanessa Wieland

I f you're having trouble seeing your work come to life on the screen or the stage, perhaps the problem is as simple as aiming too high. Your first script doesn't have to wow Hollywood and generate Oscar buzz. Your first play probably won't win a Tony and make you oodles of money on Broadway. In any aspect of the writing business, scribes can always find happiness in knowing that one thing indeed leads to another. A play production at one location will greatly aid in getting another. Professional screenwriting credits, however small they are, will help show your skill and professionalism to key people.

There's no shame in setting realistic goals early on. Understandably, though, it can be confusing to a new writer when someone tells them to "simply start small and think local." That's why we've come up with several ways how new writers can jumpstart their career.

WRITE SHORT SCRIPTS

If you're stalling in the middle of a full-length work, look to shorter categories.

One-Act Plays

These plays range anywhere from 20 to 60 pages in length. One-acts are a good first step for a budding playwright, as the medium-sized length allows for things such as character arc, scene changes, and other aspects that are staples of a full-length work.

10-Minute Plays

Just what it sounds like, 10-minute plays run 10 pages and have a minimal plot with a minimal cast. There are plenty of contests looking for scripts of this length, and several winners are usually chosen each time. The goal is to have a small group of actors play all roles in all the winning plays.

Short Screenplays

A lot of contests exist for short screenplays running fewer than 60 pages. You can find plenty of them in this book.

CHUCK SAMBUCHINO is the editor of *Screenwriter's & Playwright's Market*. He is also the editor of *Guide to Literary Agents* (www.guidetoliteraryagents.com/blog) and assists in editing *Writer's Market*. **VANESSA WIELAND** is a staffer on the Writer's Digest Books editorial team.

Submitting Your Work

Online Script Warehouses

Script registries are Web sites where writers register their work to be viewed by prospective buyers. Sites such as InkTip and WriteSafe provide searchable databases allowing industry professionals to view thousands of loglines, synopses, treatments, and full scripts with the aim of purchasing the rights to create a play or film.

Registries are relatively new vehicles for marketing a script. The most obvious benefit is immediate accessibility to hundreds of industry professionals without having to query or find an agent. Once your script is uploaded to the site, anyone registered has immediate access to your work. If interested, they can then contact you to negotiate options or purchase your script. Another benefit: InkTip.com keeps records of the hits a logline or script has received. Knowing who is reading can be invaluable, and records are helpful in determining what captures attention versus what doesn't.

On the other hand, such Web sites create a risk of having work plagiarized or stolen and the creator receiving no credit—or money—for their efforts. WriteSafe.com cites this as the primary reason to register works with them. Not only does the work get presented to prospective buyers, the records showing when the work was created and who had access to viewing it offer some protection from theft. Yet proving intellectual property theft is neither easy, nor is it cheap, and ideas are not copyrightable. Anyone can look online, marvel at your concept, then put their own spin on the idea and turn it into a screenplay of their own.

Of course, like any warehouse, there is a lot to choose from—so will your script stand out? The advantage of a search engine is that the results are not only impartial, but tailored to the request. A search engine like InkTip's offers numerous methods for finding the right script: a simple title/author search, a keyword search, and an advanced search which pulls results based on up to 250 different options.

There is also the cost. Online registries make their money by being the middleman between you and potential buyers. Be sure that the service you're paying for will work for you and still be around in a few months' time. The ease of posting your work in one place may prove beneficial for getting you noticed but be sure that those wanting to buy are reputable. As always, be aware of potential frauds and predators. An online search brought up success stories—and a lot of warnings of shady behavior from "producers" who option scripts for little or no money.

According to InkTip President Jerrol LeBaron, the two common mistakes writers make when registering their works are: 1) writing loglines and synopses "that don't stand out," and 2) making typos and grammatical errors. "Experience has proven to [industry professionals] that writers who care about the professionalism of their work also care about structure, character, and have a much better understanding of development," he says.

Registry sites:

- Filmtracker (www.filmtracker.com)
- The Hollywood Script Readers Digest (www.screenscripts.com)
- InkTip (www.InkTip.com)
- The Screenplayers (www.screenplayers.net)
- The Screenwriters Market (www.screenwritersmarket.com)
- WriteSafe (www.writesafe.com)

THE 48-HOUR FILM PROJECT

A godsend to writers across the country, this annual contest pits film crews in cities across America against one another. The concept is simple: Teams comprised of writers, directors, actors and crew members are given 48 hours to write, shoot and edit a short film. Guidelines are provided at the last moment before the 48 hours begin, so that scripts cannot be written before the weekend starts. Naturally, each team needs a writer (or a team of writers) to compose their short script—and that's where you come in.

So where can you find a list of participating cities? Check out the official Web site (www.48hourfilm.com), as new locations are being added every year while others drop out. The list of cities ranges from the big (Chicago, Los Angeles, Philadelphia) to the small (Fargo, N.D.; Asheville, N.C.; Portland, Maine). The contest is also international, with participating cities overseas including Paris, Geneva, Athens and many more.

"The 48-Hour Film Project is a great reason for writers to get off the couch and start shooting. It's an adrenaline rush," says Liz Langston, co-founder of the project.

WORKING IN SCHOOL

If you're taking classes at a school (rather than online courses), see if there's a television department where you can get involved. Look for news shows where you can write copy and stories. Perhaps you're taking night classes at a university that has multiple original shows filmed by students. Get involved any way you can and pen some scripts to show to cast members.

"To get started on a local level, you just need to write something and then find someone to make it, if you can't make it yourself," says Clay Stafford, a Nashville-based screenwriter and playwright. "Production departments at universities are always looking for good short scripts—say around 20 minutes. If I wanted to see my work produced and I wanted to build some credits for myself, this is probably the route that I would take. It costs the writer nothing but the paper the script is printed on and the phone call."

COMMUNITY THEATERS

Writers living in Smalltown, Idaho, for example, have a good chance of finding a community theater group in the area—probably called something such as "The Smalltown Players." Local community theaters and groups are everywhere—so use them! Take your new play and ask them if they would ever consider producing a work from a local writer. Your script should get a quick read, and if it's good, you're in business. Newspapers love headlines like "Regional Theater Group Produces Work by Local Playwright." If the media can get behind it, that means butts in the seats.

In the same vein, look at local high schools as market possibilities. If you've written a play, ask your alma mater to perform a premiere. They may be excited to produce the work of one of their own. Schools of any kind are a great place to seek staged readings of your work. Younger actors are hungry for new material to test their chops, and it wouldn't be hard to gather a half dozen college actors together to read through your play so you can hear the words out loud.

Whether it's a local high school or community group that produces your work, you probably won't make much money. Funds will be a problem, so consider passing on any upfront fees and instead ask for a portion of the money made from ticket sales—a.k.a royalties. Eight percent is a safe bet.

Submitting Your Work

Screenwriting Contests

Enter Competitions without Fear of Scams

by Robin Mizell

If you're looking for a side door into Hollywood, look no further than screenplay competitions. Hundreds exist, and no matter what kind of story you've written—all genres and lengths included—you're likely to find a contest (or two or 50) to enter it in. It's common for competitions to have two main categories: feature length and short scripts.

Contests are valuable to writers for a number of reasons. Placing high in one—whether that means winning, being a finalist, or semi-finalist—proves your script's worth to producers and agents. It shows that your script is at least worth a look, and it helps set your work above the slush pile. Agents and producers judge competitions; naturally, they seek out winners of the most prestigious ones because the material may just be the next hot property around town.

But just as winning a contest can set you on the fast track to getting noticed, sending your work out blind may just leave you broke. Take a closer look at screenwriting competitions to see past scams, compare costs to benefits, and judge if the side door approach is the right one for you.

FIRST, BYPASS THE SCAMS

Before investing the money and effort to enter a scriptwriting contest, thoroughly investigate its legitimacy. Is the contest listed in the newest edition of *Writer's Market* or *Screenwriter's & Playwright's Market*, or have respected news outlets and industry periodicals such as *Script*, *Creative Screenwriting*, *MovieMaker*, and *Variety* published stories about the competition and its past winners? Be sure to distinguish among articles written by journalists and experts versus advertisements and advertorials paid for by contest organizers and sponsors. Advertorials can be written to look just like news stories, but, in truth, they're little more than press releases.

For published warnings about questionable scriptwriting contests, look to Web directories that provide resources and forums for writers. Absolute Write (www.absolutewrite.com), which offers message boards for screenwriters and also posts scam alerts called "bewares," can be searched through its index. Also check out other online resources, such as the Wordplay Forums (www.wordplay.com/forums/welcome.html) and Done Deal Professional (www.donedealpro.com).

Be alert for these indications that a scriptwriting contest might not be legitimate:

ROBIN MIZELL is the senior editor of *Screenwriter's & Playwright's Market*. To learn more about her and her writing, visit www.robinmizell.com.

- You're encouraged to pay for the services of a recommended editor, script doctor, or other consultant to make your submission more competitive.
- A workshop or online course, at an additional fee of course, is suggested to improve your chances of winning.
- Payments are requested for added features or services of doubtful value.
- Competition is ongoing year-round, and prizes are awarded indiscriminately.
- The contest is too comprehensive and submission guidelines are overly broad or vague.
- Submission guidelines, deadlines, rules, and any transfer of rights involved are not clearly published.
- Prizes are not guaranteed.
- Winners are obligated to sign a contract with a specific agent, manager, or production company.

A search engine can help you locate criticism of a scriptwriting contest that will never appear on the contest's official Web site. Take the time to sift through the information you can unearth online, including biographical profiles of the contest organizers and judges. People devoted to exposing fraud want to help you avoid making the same costly mistakes others have made.

If you do end up scouring message boards and forums while leaving opinions of your own, be careful not to disparage the contest in question or its sponsors unless you're speaking from firsthand experience and are willing to accept the repercussions. What you post online becomes part of a permanent record, even if you delete the post later. Discretion and self-restraint are highly desirable characteristics in a scriptwriter, because they demonstrate the capacity for collaboration. To agents, managers, producers, and other writers, your cooperative attitude is second in value only to your creativity as a storyteller.

COMPARE COSTS TO POTENTIAL BENEFITS

Next, try to ascertain how influential the scriptwriting contest is. Have any of the previous winning scripts been optioned or produced as films, television movies, TV shows, or video-games? Did the writers whose scripts reached the competition finals go on to land contracts with agents, managers, studios, or producers? Happy outcomes will be mentioned on the contests' Web sites or promotional literature.

When deciding whether a contest is worthwhile, compare the costs of participating to the potential benefits. Check for a contest entry fee, which can range from nothing to $100 or more. Keep in mind that if your script is optioned after you submit it to a competition and before the contest judging is completed, it will probably become ineligible to win.

To encourage submissions and help defray operating expenses, a contest might incorporate an added incentive for writers who think they stand little chance of winning. The BlueCat Screenplay Competition, for example, started with 384 entrants in 1999. In 2003, it began to offer very brief analyses of all submitted scripts, which made the $25 entry fee seem negligible. By 2007, contest entries numbered in the thousands. BlueCat's first winning screenplay to reach an audience, *Ball's Out: The Gary Houseman Story*, was scheduled for theatrical release in 2008.

Other screenwriting contests enlist agents and producers to judge submissions. These busy professionals aren't expected to provide constructive feedback to each and every entrant. The potential benefit of their participation in the judging is the discovery of new and talented writers to whom they can eventually offer contracts. In a business where professional connections and reputation matter as much as talent, getting your name and your material in front of the right people is invaluable.

A scriptwriting competition that attracts the notice of studio representatives and producers

A Judge's Perspective

Judges tend not to read scripts for commercial or production viability, or for its potential to attract big name talent (which is, conversely, exactly what production companies are looking for). This explains why many contest winners don't sell. Judges are looking for talent and craft, not commercial promise. In the past, the winners of many contests seemed to be dramas, historical dramas and melodramas. Perhaps this was due to the fact that many judges were from the "old school," when Hollywood was about big production and character-driven storytelling, and not about special effects and explosions. Dramas are better vehicles for delivery of emotions than the average shoot 'em up; they "fit" better with the judge's personal proclivities.

But that's changed. Scripts from all different genres win (although comedies tend not to). Perhaps this is because the next generation of Hollywood filmmakers are judging the contests now, or perhaps these other genres have evolved enough to break down the doors of institutional conventions. What counts now is *excellence*, regardless of genre (which is great for us sci-fi writers!). Still, be aware of what genres tend to do well in what contests, and plan accordingly.

I've been both the "front line," helping to discern what goes on to the second round, and I've been the "industry judge" who reads only the semifinalists and finalists. Here is what I've learned.

Getting through the first round

As a first-round judge, I had many, many scripts to read, and while I read them all start to finish, I could easily tell within the first 15 pages who was a contender. There is a typical laundry list of complaints that gets a script knocked out of contention:

1. **Format, format, format.** If your screenplay isn't properly formatted, save your entrance fee. An improperly formatted script means an inexperienced writer, which means poor quality of craft.

2. **Narrative.** If the narrative (you know—the stuff between the dialogue blocks) is too long, too wordy, or is written in style more appropriate to a novel, this again tells us the writer hasn't got his feet under him yet as a screenwriter.

3. **Dialogue.** Dialogue can save or kill a script. If narrative or story is weak, but the dialogue rocks, it's going to rise. If a script has an astonishingly great plot and the narrative is gripping, but the characters talk like wooden puppets, the script will sink. Why? Because the audience engages with the characters primarily through the dialogue, and readers know that.

Getting through the second round

As the finalist rounds judge, the criteria gets more obtuse and more sophisticated. At this level, the format is correct, the narrative and dialogue are going to be well crafted. Now it's about the deeper aspects of the craft:

1. **Concept.** Is the concept original? Did the writer do everything with it he could have?

2. **Story.** Bottom line: Does the story engage the audience (in this case, the reader)? Is it well plotted, with unique twists and turns? Did I see the ending coming from a mile away, and if so, was the execution good enough that I didn't care?

3 **Pace.** It is paced appropriately for its genre? Is the narrative, dialogue and average scene length, which all contribute to pacing, written appropriately for the genre?

4 **Tone.** Did the writer deliver a consistent tone? Are the narrative and dialogue right for the genre? Is the storyline appropriate?

5 **Characterization.** How well built are the characters? Was the hero a dud while the villain stole the show? Did the secondary characters feel real, and have purpose? Did the hero evolve?

6 **Veracity.** This is a little harder to define, but it essentially comes down to whether the script feels real. Does the world "hold," or does something unbelievable or off-tone happen that takes the reader out of the tale? Do the characters make believable decisions? Do they interact in a believable way?

7 **And finally, and most importantly, Voice.** Finding an original voice in screenwriting is a very exciting event for someone who reads a lot of screenplays. It's that indefinable element of a real writer doing their thing can carry a script past other problems. Because that is what it all comes down to: an original point of view. Hollywood regurgitates stories, but it sure loves to find someone doing something fresh to obsess over. It's also what makes a contest and its judges say, we stand by this writer because he or she will be someone to reckon with, someone who will go on to do great things.

Trai Cartwright (www.craftwrite.com) is a script consultant and contest judge who has had multiple scripts optioned. She now lives in Colorado.

is likely to be highly competitive and, therefore, more difficult to win. A startup contest that hasn't earned the reputation of a major screenwriting competition can be easier in terms of capturing an award, but it ultimately might attract nothing more than a smirk from a knowledgeable professional. In the end, regardless of the contest judges' stature or the dollar amount of the prize, the personal opinion and business needs of a producer to whom you hope to sell your work will outweigh any writing awards in your portfolio.

In addition to the networking opportunities, prizes for finalists in scriptwriting contests can include workshop tuition, film festival admission passes, critiques by noted professionals, a script's production by student filmmakers, or cash. It can be helpful to make a detailed list of costs and benefits before you immerse yourself in the process of entering a competition.

FILM FESTIVAL AND CONTESTS

Film festivals are everywhere, and most provide at least one competition for writers each year. Some festivals are regional, and only accept entries for a certain group of people—such as Wisconsin residents, for example. This means two things. First, entering such a contest can up your chances of winning outright; and second, always carefully read the entry guidelines to make sure you and your script are eligible.

Some highly regarded festivals and associated scriptwriting competitions that bring contest

Submitting Your Work

finalists and professional filmmakers together include: The Heart of Film Screenplay Competition (Austin Film Festival); The Cinequest Screenwriting Competition (Cinequest Film Festival); Showtime's Tony Cox Awards Screenplay Competition (Nantucket Film Festival); the Slamdance Writing Competition (Slamdance Film Festival); and the Tribeca/Sloan Screenplay Development Program (Tribeca Film Festival).

Keep in mind that although many contests are associated with festivals (as you will see when leafing through the listings), many aren't. Some may be independent competitions, while others are put on by magazines and studios. No matter what kind of organization is sponsoring the contest, the guidelines for protecting yourself remain the same.

DON'T SABOTAGE YOUR SCRIPT

Suppose you learn of a scriptwriting contest and, all things considered, it seems worth your effort to enter, but the deadline for submissions is only weeks away. Should you drop everything and rush to finish the script you started writing several years ago? After all, you perform best under the pressure of a deadline. It's easy to procrastinate when there's no prize in view.

Can you honestly say you're fully prepared to go up against the competition? Base your decision on these criteria:

1. Has your script been objectively critiqued, rewritten, and polished to perfection?
2. Is your script professionally and meticulously formatted?
3. Does your work meet all of the contest's guidelines for genre, word count, page length, running time, limits on entrants' prior income from scriptwriting, etc.?

It may come as a surprise to you that sloppy or nonstandard formatting is one of the first reasons scripts are eliminated during the preliminary rounds of reading submissions. Major contests employ script readers to process thousands of entries that are winnowed to quarter- and semi-finalists numbering in the hundreds, which are then judged by industry executives and professional filmmakers. The more scripts a reader can eliminate, the more time he or she will have for thorough consideration of scripts that meet all of the submission requirements. A poorly formatted screenplay is a sign of a writer who can't follow directions. Don't risk entering a script that will be instantly disqualified because of a technical flaw. Although most script readers and contest judges are given the latitude to overlook formatting errors, they're likely to be influenced by any signs of a lack of professionalism, inattention to detail, or downright disrespect.

There are lots of scriptwriting competitions. Don't rush. If a deadline comes and goes, there will be a call for submissions to another contest in a month or two.

VIEW A CONTEST WIN AS A BOOST

Scriptwriting contests are appealing because they guide entrants through the process with explicit submission guidelines. They entice participants with prizes and ceremonies attended by glamorous celebrities. The criteria on which winning scripts are scored may sometimes seem mysterious, but the step-by-step directions for getting onto the playing field are not. The outcome will eventually be announced, and the entrants can compare the winning efforts to their own.

In contrast to a screenwriting competition, selling your spec script directly to a buyer, or convincing an agent of your exceptional talent, requires considerably more effort, imagination, and persistent pitching. Scriptwriting contests ease business introductions and foster networking among professionals. They also make it possible for script buyers and agents to operate more efficiently by focusing only on the best scripts culled by reputable judges.

You might assume every prizewinning script is made into a film or television program. In reality, it's considered an excellent track record if even 10 percent of the scripts that win a contest are eventually produced. Winning can get you noticed; however, in order to make a career of scriptwriting, you'll still need to demonstrate that you're available, dependable, open to suggestions, and willing to collaborate.

Pitch Perfect

Learn How to Wow Producers in a Meeting

by Jonathan Koch and Robert Kosberg

Does the boardroom scare you? It shouldn't. Hollywood is looking for your script—you just have to know how to pitch it to them. Below are 12 dos and don'ts of pitch room etiquette. These tips will guide you in the conference room and give you the best possible chance of getting a producer to say yes.

THE DOS
Be on time
While obvious, it's still extremely important to be punctual. In Los Angeles, a five-mile journey might take you five and a half minutes, or it might take five and a half hours. Allow for extra time to get to your appointment. If you arrive early, run through your pitch, call to confirm other meetings, or grab a coffee. If you're running late, you must call the office. Let the assistant know that you'll be late and give her an approximate arrival time.

But please, do everything in your power to be on time. Remember that the producers and the execs with whom you're meeting are phenomenally busy. By being late, you risk messing with their schedules.

Sign the Studio Release Agreement
The Studio Release Agreement is a document that you might be asked to sign. Sign it. It's become somewhat of a standard in the industry, due to our hyper-litigious society. It states that you agree to not sue the company if it ends up producing a film or show that resembles yours.

Wait! Don't panic.

Your knee-jerk response to a legally binding document like this is probably shock and horror. We don't blame you. The agreement is a necessary evil for the studios. Lawsuits are as expensive as they are annoying. They require vast amounts of time, effort, money and emotion. Nobody wants them. This document discourages such suits. If a company steals your idea, you can still sue. It's possible to sue anyone for anything, after all.

Be aware of current projects and past successes
Research the studios and production companies you'll be contacting. Know their past and current projects; learn what's slated for production in the near future. Use your research to illustrate how your idea fits into a particular company's format, goals and timing. Being able to discuss

This article is excerpted *from Pitching Hollywood: How to Sell Your TV and Movie Ideas*, by **JONATHAN KOCH** and **ROBERT KOSBERG** with **TANYA MEURER NORMAN**. Used with permission of Quill Driver Books/Word Dancer Press.

this demonstrates to an exec you're professional enough to have done the proper research, you feel your idea is a good fit for his company and that you aren't just shooting blind.

Be enthusiastic and confident

You believe in your idea. You know it's going to make everyone involved a boatload of cash. Make sure everyone in the room understands this by conveying an air of excitement about your project. If you aren't thrilled with it, how can they possibly be? Your enthusiasm will fuel theirs. It's infectious.

Maintain eye contact. Smile. Enjoy your story as you tell it.

Read the room

At the same time, gauge the energy level in the room. If everyone else is calm and quiet and low-key but you're jumping around the room, you could come off looking like a circus performer. If this is the case, you won't appear enthusiastic— just kind of creepy.

Again, maintain eye contact. Talk to these people, not at them. You're confiding in them, not pontificating to them. Notice their body language. Are they open and attentive, or are they only marginally aware of your existence?

Maybe they're tired or hungry. Maybe the biggest deal they ever landed just went belly-up. Maybe they just aren't in the mood. If they seem unreceptive, you might need to dial your pitch down.

Conversely, if they're rolling with laughter and are thoroughly entertained by your pitch, run with that. Take advantage of the high energy and give your idea the hard sell.

Allow for collaboration

As you begin to pitch, the execs will listen. At a certain point in your pitch, the execs will "get" the concept and see where the plot or show is going. Once they get it, they'll most likely stop listening and start working through the idea in their minds. They think about commercial viability, timing, demographics, their other shows, how they'll pitch your idea "up the ladder." That glazed look might not mean that they're bored. It could, in fact, be a very good thing.

They might start to throw out ideas of their own, tweaking your idea. Stress not. This is a good thing. If they're personally vested in the idea, their enthusiasm for it will grow. If they're enthusiastic, they'll try harder to sell the idea to their higher-ups.

They might ask you leading questions: And does the terrible antagonist die a horrific, bloody death? Should the girl dump him for her professor? They might put a great new spin on the idea.

Be willing to morph your plot a bit. This doesn't mean you should completely abandon your original idea. Just aim to be the easiest person in the room. Flexibility is always an asset. Be open to another's thoughts. You may even like the revised idea better.

Be brief

You may be sick of hearing this, but it bears repeating. Pitch, thank them and get out. This brevity will read: I respect your time. It'll also convey that you're busy and have other meetings (which, of course, you do). Any lingering or small talk could easily damage your chances for future meetings. Keep in mind that you're building relationships. Always leave the room on an up note.

THE DON'TS:
Don't panic

Yes, the execs to whom you're pitching could launch your career and lead you to wealth beyond your wildest dreams. Odds are they won't, but the thought that they could is a bit unnerving. Don't panic. Everyone in that room is in the business of making money. They want to succeed. They want your idea to be fantastic, so they can get rich and famous—or richer and more famous.

Sure, they might ask you some tough questions about your idea, playing devil's advocate, looking to ferret out major holes in your idea. Don't be alarmed by this. You've asked these same questions while preparing this pitch (and if you haven't, then get back to the drawing board). It's their place to pick your concept apart and look at it from every angle. View this kind of probing as a compliment. If your idea weren't intriguing, they would quickly thank you and dismiss you.

Don't rush

While it's important to keep your meeting as brief as possible, never rush your pitch. Nervous energy will often cause pitchers to move through the necessary information far too quickly. Vital points in the pitch might be glossed over or dropped completely. Suddenly, the pitch that you worked and reworked makes no sense. Additionally, the increased speed can make it tough for those listening to hear and understand all of your words.

Plan ahead for this. Time your pitch so that you'll feel comfortable with its natural length and not feel the need to hurry through it. Practicing the pitch in front of strangers (the waiter, your doctor, your kid's soccer coach) will be helpful. You'll be surprised by how receptive people are to hearing ideas for Hollywood. Take the edge off the fear before your meetings begin.

Don't talk your way out of a sale

If they love your idea and want to buy it, take yes for an answer. The sale ends when the customer says "yes." At that point, stop talking and get out of the room quickly. You never know what might change their minds, so go home. Celebrate.

We once sold a show but had made the mistake of bringing its talkative creator to the meeting with us. After a fantastic pitch and an immediate offer to buy the concept, our guest felt compelled to start chatting. He began to explain his reasons for creating the idea, a TV show that lampooned all court shows. He went on to state the reasons that court shows were so bad and deserving of ridicule. He went on and on and on.

After several minutes of this, the execs began to squirm. Their network was currently airing several of these shows, and they started to wonder if it as a good idea to make fun of their own shows. What had been a fabulous idea only moments before now seemed horrible. They backed out of the sale.

Don't leave anything in writing

When you leave the room, you want to be sure that all of the questions have been asked and answered. Be sure that you've covered all of the reasons the idea is fabulous. If an exec wants further information, he can contact you.

The last thing you'd want is for him to sit alone, reading over your idea. The energy in a live pitch brings a concept to life in a way that printed words on a page cannot. The exec could be thrilled with the idea, then go back and reread it before pitching it up the ladder and find it not nearly as exciting as he remembered.

Or perhaps, while reading it, he comes up with reasons the show or film might not work. If you're not there to work with him, answer his questions and explain away his concerns, the idea could be abandoned.

Having said that, you'll find that some buyers will ask for a one-page treatment. If you say you don't have one with you, some execs will request that you get one to him. In these instances, send it.

Don't become discouraged

You might pitch an idea for the first time and make a sale. You might pitch it 10 or 20 times before someone shows interest. In this business, it's easy to feel your confidence slipping away. This loss of confidence can only hurt your chances of a sale. If you have a solid, commercially viable, high-concept idea, and you have a concise, enthusiastic pitch, eventually, you'll find a buyer.

Playwriting: The Next Steps

From Networking to Staged Readings

by Chuck Sambuchino

So you're wrapping up the latest draft of that masterpiece and hiding a small smile every time you read it because the second act is pretty darn good. You're on your way—but you're also wondering what happens now. Now it's time to plug yourself into the playwriting community and educate yourself as to how and why things work the way they do.

NETWORK

As is true in many things, whom you know in the business is of much importance. A glowing recommendation from the right person may be enough to see your play set in the fall schedule two years from now. With that in mind, don't be a shut-in! Get out and network with actors, directors, producers and everyone else who loves plays or knows someone who has power.

Consider working or volunteering at a local hall. Get to know the staff and how a production functions. Familiarize yourself with all things theater. Sooner or later, there will be a good moment to mention that you, too, write plays. "When a play is over, the principals, for the most part, all come out from backstage to mingle with the audience. Strike up a conversation with them," says Clay Stafford, a playwright and screenwriter based in Nashville. "Tell them you are a playwright and you would like them to consider reading it for the purpose of producing it. You would be amazed how many doors in Los Angeles or Anytown, USA, open simply because you walk up to a stranger and say, 'I'm a writer and I've got something I'd like you to read. How should I go about getting that to you?' "

Even try acting in some small productions and see how it feels. The more you know about how actors operate when delving into a character and moving around onstage, the better you can craft a play with their likings in mind. If you get ridiculously lucky, you can bump into an angel or two—a wealthy arts lover who takes on passionate causes and bankrolls projects. Also, you may even be able to build a relationship with a theater that agrees to premiere all of your plays. But you can't do any of that if you're always at the computer.

JOIN A GROUP

If there is a writing group near you solely dedicated to playwrights, you're lucky, so don't pass up the opportunity to join and schmooze. When I got out of college, I saw a small notice in the alternative weekly paper about a playwriting contest. I submitted a play and it was

CHUCK SAMBUCHINO is the editor of *Screenwriter's & Playwright's Market*. He is also the editor of *Guide to Literary Agents* (www.guidetoliteraryagents.com/blog) and assists in editing *Writer's Market*.

chosen as a finalist by the Cincinnati Playwrights Initiative—a wonderful resource that I didn't even know existed because I was too lazy to even Google the words "Cincinnati" and "playwrights."

Soon after being named a finalist, I was heavily involved with the group, having numerous plays read and workshopped while helping others do the same with their plays. Joining the organization also plugged me into the city's pool of talent: actors and directors. Without my peers telling me whom to call or offering casting suggestions, I don't know what I would have done when trying to get a play off the ground.

There may not be a specific playwriting group, though, and that's all right, too. Look for a general writers group in the area. Though not ideal, you will still be surrounded by peers who can help offer their ideas on storytelling. It's a good first step to finding other playwrights in the area and seeing how they achieved successes. Referrals are born from this.

KNOW A PLAY'S THREE STAGES

A new play typically won't be produced right off the bat. A play gets born in stages—and that happens for a reason. Usually, a work isn't pristine until it's been read aloud by actors and altered appropriately by the writer who now has heard different perspectives on what works and what doesn't. Here are the three stages that a play takes en route to success.

1. The Staged Reading

This is the first step for a newborn play, and allows the writer to hear the work spoken by acting professionals. A staged reading involves actors reading parts aloud while sitting down, scripts in hand (usually behind music stands). Stage directions, character descriptions, and act introductions are also simply read aloud, usually by a "narrator" who is also sitting behind a music stand.

Since the play is new, a staged reading is an easy way to "work out the kinks" and see how dialogue plays live. Phrases and sections that once seemed to flow so well on the page may seem very awkward when spoken aloud or performed with a thick German accent. As the writer, you sit in the crowd and take notes. Since the reading will likely have a few rehearsals, you can also make notes at that time—and even tweak dialogue prior to the actual event.

Actors may ask for a little room to improvise and change dialogue slightly, and it's up to you as to how much slack they have, if any. Staged readings will have a director, and it's not uncommon for a playwright to also act as the director, as duties are minimal.

Readings are commonly performed in front of an audience. This is done for two reasons. First, the audience will chime in with compliments and comments following the performance, once again giving the playwright feedback on what worked and what did not. Perhaps more important than audience feedback is the chance for producers and power players to be seated in the crowd.

The whole process works like this: You call up a theater and explain that you would like to use the venue on an upcoming night for a staged reading and ask to rent the space for a reasonable fee. Once a date is agreed upon, you start to assemble a cast and rehearse. Also in that timeframe, you should contact producers and other individuals who choose what plays to produce for their respective theaters and groups. Invite them free of charge to come see the staged reading, giving them a short synopsis of what the play is about. The goal here is simple: Get them in the seats and let them see your genius work performed live. That way, if any producer is intrigued, they can contact you about producing the work in the future.

2. The Developmental Workshop

The second stage of a play's life process is neither a reading nor a production but rather something in the middle: a workshop. This stage involves putting on a loose performance of the play to further see how it will work during a real show. Costumes are worn, some scenes blocked out, some lighting used, etc. Actors may have memorized some dialogue, but they're typically walking around with their scripts (going "on book").

A workshop may have anywhere from three to a dozen rehearsals, and the goal is to take the play as far as it can go in that limited amount of time. Be prepared to help out in any way necessary. Just like a staged reading, the writer must work out a location, assemble a crew, and try to get producers in the seats.

3. The Production

The real deal, just like the performances you've seen at theaters. A full production means that everything is in place—costumes, props, memorized scripts, promotion, lighting and everything else. The playwright is likely paid, and hopefully you can get reviewers to see the play. A favorable review can serve as a stepping-stone to getting a larger, more prominent theater to also consider producing the work.

Think about it: If you were to query a theater in San Jose about producing the work, wouldn't it be nice to be able to say how the play was recently performed in Tulsa, got rave reviews, and sold out almost every night? That way, the producer considering your script knows that the material is both battle-tested and a draw for getting butts in the seats. And, just maybe, his best friend is an angel who will take interest in your work.

Getting Serious with Playwriting

Evaluating Submissions, Theaters and Agents

by Jacqueline McMahon

You've spent months developing your ideas into the perfect play. You have revised, proofread and edited into the wee hours of the morning. You formatted your play with the latest software, then headed for the business supply store with the cheapest photocopying prices. You saved copies of your script on disk, on your computer and now, on paper. There is nothing more to do.

Wait a minute! Writing the play was only just the beginning. Unless you know of opportunities that come knocking on the doors of writers, you must now address the business side of playwriting.

MARKETS

Playwrights have several choices for getting their work out to the public: contests, theaters, publishers and residencies.

Contests: The book you hold in your hands, combined with any search engine, will provide playwrights with an incredible number of appropriate contests—some that do not even charge a fee. Obviously, the more prestigious and well known the contest, the more competition one will have and the harder it will be to win or even place as a finalist. Winning a contest can provide many different results, including prize money, a reading or production and even publication.

Warning: Follow the contest guidelines exactly as specified. Many wonderful plays will never be considered because the author did not comply with the complete submission guidelines.

Theaters: Theaters are always looking for new material for upcoming productions. It is always best to inquire before sending a script. Market listings will specify whether to query, send a synopsis or the complete manuscript and whether the theater accepts unsolicited submissions or only those from agents. Other information available to writers might be rights, compensation (i.e., royalties) and the theater's response time if they're interested. Working with a theater allows playwrights a chance to form contacts in the field, which could lead to further productions.

Sometimes newer playwrights will choose the option of self-production. They must be

JACQUELINE McMAHON runs a successful performing arts studio, "Slightly Off Broadway," with her best friend. See her Web site: www.slightlyoffbroadway.com. From 1998-2005, Jacqueline hosted Suite101's Performing and Writing Musical Theatre Web site. Today, she enjoys blogging at dramaquill.wordpress.com.

prepared to provide the financing, assemble the cast and crew and publicize the play—but for some, this may be a necessary step to becoming a recognized playwright.

Publishers: Many writers dream of having their work available in published form made possible through a professional company. For playwrights, having their works available in the catalogues of publishers such as Samuel French not only means recognition but potential financial rewards as well. Drama departments and theatre groups can order copies and pay royalties when doing productions or they may also purchase copies for their script libraries. Either way, the playwright stands to make some money when his materials are used by these groups.

These publisher Web sites are a great place to start:

- www.samuelfrench.com
- www.bakersplays.com
- www.playscripts.com
- www.lillenas.com/drama
- www.meriwetherPublishing.com
- www.dramatists.com/index.asp
- www.brookpub.com

Concerning self-publishing, the innovative playwrights of today are forming their own publishing companies and selling their scripts through their Web sites. Offering both electronic scripts and hard copies online can be quite an instrumental way of marketing to a broad customer base.

Residencies: Established playwrights may apply for a variety of "playwright in residence" positions at colleges and universities. Benefits may include opportunities to lecture, a stipend, an atmosphere conducive to writing and being involved in the rehearsals of one's own work.

HOW TO FIND OUT WHAT'S IN DEMAND

With so many market opportunities, finding the right place for one's work can be a daunting task. No matter how one seeks out opportunities, one standard remains: Do not send anything that does not fit the guidelines. Contests, theaters and publishers will all provide playwrights with their specific requirements in this regard. (See this article's sidebar for more on targeting markets.)

It has been my experience that most contests do not accept musicals, plays for children, or scripts with large casts and elaborate sets. Their resources simply cannot support such productions. That means that writers of these types of works must diligently seek out compatible markets for such projects. Writers of plays for children, for example, will find publishers and producers in *Children's Writer's & Illustrator's Market*. Similar books exist for writers of other markets. There are publishers who specialize in genre publishing (such as musicals, works for youth and other specialized markets) and larger firms who publish a great variety of genres.

HOW DOES THE PLAYWRIGHT MAKE ENDS MEET?

Unfortunately, unless your name is synonymous with theater, it is unlikely that your playwriting income will provide you with the equivalent of a full-time job salary. Playwrights often supplement their income by writing articles for magazines and e-zines or with jobs in the field, like teaching courses in playwriting and drama or even directing the works of others.

The main sources of income will come from performance royalties, script sales, and contest prize money. But most playwrights will tell you that it isn't the monetary rewards that keep them writing—it's seeing their words come to life in the ultimate reward: a production.

ORGANIZATIONS OF INTEREST TO PLAYWRIGHTS

There are many benefits to joining a nationwide playwrights' organization, such as informative newsletters and/or magazines, contacts in the business, Web listings to promote and sell your work, workshops/seminars/retreats, a place to meet and connect with other playwrights, and online resources such as forums/listserves/chats/links/articles (many of which can be utilized by anyone, not just members).

The following groups are among the best to be involved with:

- Dramatists Guild: www.dramatistsguild.org
- Theatre Communications Group: www.tcg.org
- Professional Organization of Canadian Theatres: www.pact.ca
- International Centre for Women Playwrights: www.netspace.org/ ~ icwp/index.html
- New Dramatists: www.newdramatists.org

Playwrights may also benefit from other writing organizations and Web resources. Although not a complete list, these are some of my favorites:

- National Association of Women Writers: www.naww.org
- Playwrights Union of Canada: www.puc.ca
- Virginia Commonwealth University's Playwriting Resource Page: www.vcu.edu/art web/playwriting/resources.html

Targeting a Market

With so many contests and theaters out there, where does a playwright begin when looking for a market? One play will not be a good fit everywhere; in fact, the more you research your options, the more tightly focused and shorter your list of markets will be. The good news is that markets will not only tell you exactly how to submit work, but they'll also tell you exactly what they're seeking.

For example, the Live Bait Theater is Chicago is upfront about their specifications: "We produce only new works by Chicago playwrights." Bingo—that's a key market for people in the region, but useless elsewhere. The Magic Theatre in San Francisco has an eye out for plays with "cutting-edge sociopolitical concerns." They are specific in their wants concerning subject and theme, but they will accept submissions from anyone anywhere.

If you're writing a play about a family that bravely escaped the Holocaust, look for theaters that seek works with Jewish themes. If your work has any multicultural aspect at all, for that matter—Latino themes, African-American themes, Native-American themes, etc.—then there are likely several theaters and contests that are specifically looking for works just like yours.

If you're writing something edgy, look for a local fringe festival that specializes in performing—you guessed it—edgy works. The first play I ever had professionally produced was a wacky comedy done through the local fringe festival. It was a perfect fit.

Identify what your play is. A comedy? Historical or contemporary? One-act or full length? Experimental? Deals with women's issues? Gay and lesbian themes? Mystery play? Has a Southern feel? Any or all of descriptive tidbits like these will help you target markets.

Submitting Your Work

IS IT TIME FOR AN AGENT YET?

Many playwrights believe that an agent is necessary for a successful writing career. Playwriting, however, differs in one very significant way from other media of writing. For most playwrights, it is the prospect of a staged reading or production that entices them to continue with their craft; rather than the continual quest for publication sought after by writers of articles, short stories and novels.

New writers of any genre will find it difficult to obtain representation until they have developed somewhat of a proven track record in the field. After all, an agent is looking to make money from his/her relationship with a writer and newcomers have not yet established themselves as worthwhile risks.

Cleveland-based playwright Linda Eisenstein has defied the odds surrounding the necessity of an agent to achieve success. With more than 100 productions, a large number of readings and many of her works in print, she is proving that tenacity and self-promotion are viable tools to a playwright's success. In fact, Linda would have the same take on marketing and making contacts even if she did have an agent: "Even playwrights with agents need to do a great deal of their own marketing," she says.

So is it unnecessary for playwrights to have agents? Absolutely not! In fact, an agent can open doors to larger, more prestigious markets, deal with contract negotiations and recommend scripts to contacts many playwrights would otherwise not have.

When you're ready to get serious and tackle the business of playwriting, make sure you immerse yourself in how things work. Identifying the best markets for yourself—whether contests or theaters or community groups—is a key and difficult step in the process, so do it right. That way, you'll make enough money to not have to look for the absolute cheapest copy center in town.

Mike Kuciak

A Script Manager Shares His Blunt Advice
with Screenwriters Eyeing the Prize

by Chuck Sambuchino

I first met Mike Kuciak at a writers' conference in Illinois, where he was sitting on a panel of publishing and entertainment professionals, listening to pitches from attendees in the crowd. Watching the panel in action, I was thinking probably the same thing the rest of the audience was thinking: Of the nine individuals onstage offering feedback, one in particular seems distinctly different from the rest—the guy on the end named Mike.

After Kuciak talked to another writer in the crowd and offered some blunt, honest, frank (did I mention blunt?) advice, the writer got quiet, and kind of half-nodded before sitting back down. Sensing that his honesty was perhaps not what audience members were accustomed to, Kuciak hid a smirk and explained why his thoughts were so unfiltered.

"I'm sorry, everyone. I'm from Hollywood," he said, shrugging.

More specifically, Kuciak is the senior vice president of development for AEI: Atchity Entertainment Inc., Motion Picture Production & Literary Management (www.aeionline.com) in Beverly Hills. That's a handful of words for a guy who likes to get to the point and talk about what needs talking about. That is, unless you want to talk about his favorite movies, like *Robocop* and *The Big Lebowski*. In that case, small talk is welcome.

Born on Chicago's north side, Kuciak grew up fascinated with both writing and music— penning articles for alternative weekly papers and jamming on the string bass with whatever band happened to be around. After working dozens of odd jobs on local film products in the Windy City area, Kuciak moved to Los Angeles in 2002 and interned at a literary agency, learning the ropes of the management business.

Following his internship, he faxed his résumé to agencies and management companies all over L.A. . . . and then he waited. Before long, a call came from Ken Atchity, founder of AEI, who asked Kuciak to come onboard their team to find, develop and sell TV and film properties. Say no more, Kuciak thought. He joined AEI that week.

Now, Kuciak spends his days seeking the next great script and developing film projects. When he gets out of the office, it's off to the movie theater, than back home to the screenwriting software, same as other writers in town. Several of his feature scripts are in preproduction around town, and he recently contributed a series of articles for *Scr(i)pt* magazine.

Lucky for us, Kuciak was happy to share some more of his frank advice about breaking into the business and what it takes to succeed in Hollywood. Here's what he had to say.

CHUCK SAMBUCHINO is the editor of *Screenwriter's & Playwright's Market*. He is also the editor of *Guide to Literary Agents* (www.guidetoliteraryagents.com/blog) and assists in editing *Writer's Market*.

Besides a concise pitch, what are you looking for when a writer talks to you in person or contacts you via a query?

Like everyone else in town, I'm looking for unique and commercial projects. You don't need bells and whistles, you just need a logline that'll get the buyers excited—and, by extension, something that will get reps and producers excited, as they make their living by bringing projects to the buyers.

On the flipside, a brilliant pitch won't help you with a project that reps can't sell and the studios don't want to make. Think of it like real estate: If you're trying to sell a house with three walls and no bathroom, it doesn't matter how you pitch it, you ain't gonna sell it, especially if there's a house with four walls and two baths for sale right down the street.

Concerning these ideas, can you tell us how you, personally, define the term "commercial"?

The definition is in constant flux, but I've seen two patterns emerge:

1) Scripts that have an obvious and proven wide appeal. For example, a high concept comedy with a star role—in which case it's "obvious" because the idea's funny, the script is funny, and it's written with a comedic star in mind. You can "see the movie," and the concept is "proven" by the track record of other high concept/star-driven comedies that have hit. It's something that the studios can open on 1,500 screens and market to a general audience. This is just one example; other genres have other criteria, and the criteria for all genres changes as film and culture evolve.

2) Scripts that are unique and brilliantly written, with amazing characters. "Unique" is hard to pin down. Everybody in town reads *a lot* of scripts. It's hard to impress the readers with something unique—they've likely already read five versions of your idea. But, every once in a while, something comes along that grabs people with the unique voice of the writing, the unique aspect of the story, and/or characters, etc. These scripts are of interest to the buyers because they feel like a "find." They tend to attract bankable elements willing to set aside a big paycheck in order to do something interesting—the "one for me, one for them" pattern. I could point to *Juno*, for example. It's not the first witty teen script ever written by any stretch of the imagination, but the quality and voice of the writing, characters and worldview make it unique, and thus commercial.

I'm referring to generalities, of course. There are always exceptions to everything.

Do you keep your eye on contests to read the winning scripts?

Absolutely. Placing well in a prominent contest is one of the best ways for beginning writers to generate interest in their work. I go after a lot of Nicholl semi- and quarter-finalists, though placing well in a contest doesn't automatically mean you'll get a rep and sell the script. The contests recognize well-written scripts, but they make little judgment on the commerciality.

Explain that more—the difference between a good contest script and a good commercial script.

There is a disconnect between scripts that do well in the contest world, which are judged on craft and writing, and scripts that do well in the real world, which are judged on their craft, writing, ability to attract elements and lay the blueprint for a movie the studios think the audience will want to see. This is why you'll sometimes meet a writer who has a script that's knockin' 'em dead in the contests, but can't get arrested when it comes to getting a rep and a sale.

Of course, the perfect storm is a script that is well written and catches the attention of the contests—and is a commercial high concept that fits what the buyers are looking for at the time. This is rare. James V. Simpson's *Armored* comes to mind as an example.

Noob writers don't understand the disconnect, because they think a script is a script is a script. "If X loved it, why don't Y and Z love it?" A script is a different thing to different people, depending on what they want and/or need. This is true for everybody, especially reps and producers. You can submit the exact same script to seven buyers, draw six passes and sell it to the seventh.

How do you handle a feature film writing sample that would be defined as "fan fiction"? If a buddy of yours called you up and said, "My friend has a script—will you read it?" You say yes, but the script is actually for *Wedding Crashers II*. How do you handle that? Even if you read it and it's good, can you pass material like that around town?

No. Do not write projects that are based on properties you don't control. You're wasting your time. Worse: you're proving to anybody you pitch it to that you can't come up with your own good ideas, and you don't understand the industry of which you're trying to become a part. If, using your example, I find out at the pitch it's *Wedding Crashers II*, I won't read it. If I start reading and realize it's *Wedding Crashers II*, I'll stop reading.

You've said before that one of the keys to success in Hollywood for writers is that they have to become students of writing. How does one become a student of writing?

Buy a stylebook and use it. Become an expert of grammar and spelling. Develop your craft every day. You should always be reading and watching. Read novels, nonfiction, magazines, graphic novels, comic books, newspapers, song lyrics, poetry and blogs. Watch old and new movies in every genre, watch television series, watch clips and Web series online. Play video games. Look at art of every kind; listen to music in every genre. Everything you watch, read, play and hear is like another word added to your vocabulary. Absorb the culture, stay on top of what's coming out and where we're going.

Live your life. Go places, do things, make mistakes, fall in love, dare yourself. The inherent job of a writer is to tell the truth about what it is to be a human. The more things you do with your life, the more emotions and situations you will be able to write about in a truthful manner, instead of regurgitating what you've encountered second-hand via media.

There are no guarantees for success in the film industry, for you or anybody. But there is a very distinct dividing line between people who fuck around and people who don't. If you don't fuck around—if you've made the conscious decision to become serious about your career and everything you do and say reflects that, other serious people in the industry will take you seriously. It can and probably will take years to break in and ascend to the next level but, if you're serious, you'll understand this career path is a marathon.

Do you have a final tip for writers trying to break in? Something you wish people would say to novice writers?

First, make the decision as to whether screenwriting is just a fun hobby you plan to dabble in, or if this is a serious career goal. If it's a hobby, write whatever you want, whenever you want, go with God and have fun. Maybe lightning will strike. Who knows?

If you're serious, you have to approach it with everything you have. Write every day, no excuses. Study the industry: read the trades every day; read magazines; read industry blogs; read interviews with writers, directors, producers and actors; read stories of how films came to be; read about the history of the film industry; but also read everything you can about emerging developments and trends. Film is collaborative by nature: Find out what it is to "play the other positions"—that is, educate yourself as to what agents, managers, studio execs, financers, directors, actors, marketers and physical production people do. Figure out "who you want to be" and emulate them; find out the paths they took, the choices they made. Take classes and read books, but keep your mind open and active, and don't take everything that's said at face value. Listen to everything, then make your own decisions.

Read a million screenplays.

Figure out what kind of projects the industry wants, and write them. But also write weird stuff that you just love. Follow the "one for me, one for them" paradigm. But whether it's a "commercial" script or a "personal" script, make it your own—find your voice. Figure out why you care about the characters and story. If you don't care, it'll show.

Richard Hatem

An Established TV Writer Looks Back At His Road to Success

by Chuck Sambuchino

Ask Richard Hatem about the first script he ever wrote, and the seasoned TV writer can't help but smile. "I was 16, a junior—it was March of 1983—and the first script I wrote was for 'The A-Team' " he says. The thought of being a teenager, sitting at home, and working on his mother's *IBM Selectric* typewriter is more than enough to get Hatem nostalgic and excited. A huge fan of Stephen J. Cannell shows such as "The Greatest American Hero," he fell in love with TV storytelling at a young age—gravitating toward material that was both exciting and smart. For Hatem, the plan at that age was simple: 1) Sell spec script. 2) Drop out of high school in East Los Angeles to join the writing staff of "The A-Team." 3) Move into cool apartment in Los Feliz. 4) Get girls.

Unfortunately, his spec script didn't sell—but Hatem was not deterred. As high school progressed, he pumped out more scripts—*a lot* more—for a dozen different shows. None of those additional episodes ever opened any doors, but they did teach him a lot about writing.

Now, Hatem is an experienced writing pro in Hollywood, passing on his knowledge to young scribes who also want to tell stories on the screen. Along with some screenwriting work, he's gathered an impressive number of TV writing credits—both as a writer and as a showrunner. He's even formed his own production company: Summerland Entertainment. And he's still in love with storytelling that challenges the minds of audience members, but entertains them at the same time.

Hatem sat down to talk with *Screenwriter's & Playwright's Market* about what it takes to make it as a writer out west. Here's what he said.

What was your first job in LA? How did you enter the entertainment business?

Well, my first *normal* job was busing tables at a public golf course dining room called Almansor Court in Alhambra. I waited tables there and at a place in Pasadena called Dodsworth that isn't there anymore, and then I spent years serving ribs at Tony Roma's. Plus, I did stand-up comedy and ended up teaching Comedy Traffic School for five years. So these were sort of "post-college, trying-to-survive" jobs while I tried to sell scripts.

CHUCK SAMBUCHINO is the editor of *Screenwriter's & Playwright's Market*. He is also the editor of *Guide to Literary Agents* (www.guidetoliteraryagents.com/blog) and assists in editing *Writer's Market*.

Your first major credit was a "story by" credit on *Under Siege 2: Dark Territory*. Were you commissioned to pen this script?

Under Siege 2: Dark Territory (US2DT) started out as a spec feature that Matt Reeves and I wrote in 1990, a couple years after college. (Matt and I became friends at USC film school.)

We wanted to write a big action movie, which they tell you never to do in film school. In film school, they really encourage you to write personal, idiosyncratic scripts that represent an original viewpoint and voice. Unfortunately, almost no one in film school, at age 19, has that. We were all a bunch of film and TV geeks that wanted to be Martin Scorsese or the Coen Brothers. We all wanted to be like the people we loved, so most of what we did was imitative, which is exactly appropriate—not only for that stage in our creative development, but also for the medium in question. It's much more valuable in the long run for a writer to be able to write a classically structured action movie or romantic comedy than to try to be the next Charlie Kaufman.

Anyway, Matt and I were hanging around in a video store trying to come up with an idea of something to write and we were talking about how great *Die Hard* was. And it was like, "Wouldn't it be fun to write a movie like that? What if it was like . . . 'Die Hard on a Train'?" So we decided to do that. And here's the thing; it wasn't cynical and we didn't think we were slumming or selling-out. We honestly thought—and still think—that *Die Hard* is a remarkably well-written, well-made movie. We were setting the bar high for ourselves in trying to build a machine that worked as well as *Die Hard*. So we did what all smart screenwriters *should* do—we took apart *Die Hard* the way a young inventor takes apart a toaster. We rented the video and paused after every scene and wrote down what the scene was and what it accomplished in terms of the over-all storytelling. And then we tried to write equivalent story and character beats in our own movie. I learned more about writing in the four months it took us to write *Dark Territory* than in my entire time at USC Film School.

We tried to sell *Dark Territory* in January of 1991—the week the first Gulf War started. It didn't sell. We did a few rewrites, and sent it out again under a different title and with our names replaced by pseudonyms so it would get a fresh read at all the same places. By then, a producer named Gary Goldstein was attached and he'd just had big success with *Under Siege* at Warner Bros. He saw an opportunity to present the script to WB as a possible sequel, and with that in mind, they bought it. It was an incredibly, impossibly lucky thing to have happen. Selling a script is one thing, but having a studio seriously want to make that film is another.

That's the hardest part of screenwriting—the realization that writing is only half of it. You have to be lucky and have a lot of things happen that you have *absolutely no control over*. You can write a fantastic script, but selling it is a crapshoot—always.

You didn't have another produced writing credit until your screenplay for *The Mothman Prophecies* seven years later. What did the experience of *US2DT* teach you about writing for Hollywood?

First, a few things I learned: Starting your writing career as half of a writing team, as I did (because *US2DT* was written by Matt Reeves and me) only really benefits you if you stay in that partnership. Soon after we sold the script, Matt began his feature directing career and I went back to writing alone, which is always how I'd done it before. But I had to establish myself all over again as a single writer, so a lot of the momentum from that first sale was blunted. It was like reaching the crest of Everest and then getting knocked halfway back down. Another thing I learned is that success is success, and work is work, and a credit is a credit—even if it's a sequel to a Steven Seagal movie. When Matt and I wrote that movie, we wanted Harrison Ford to star in it; we thought we had this classic underdog hero. The one thing we *didn't* want the movie to be was a sort of Arnold-Schwarzenegger-style thing where the poster would describe it as, you know, "Twelve terrorists pick the wrong train to hijack," where the hero is just picking them off one by one and never breaking a sweat. Which is, of course, exactly what it turned into. *Exactly.* Was it disappointing creatively? Sure. But it took me to the next step and I still get residual checks, so I'm not complaining. I've always figured it was up to me to determine the level of the stuff I write.

The year that *Under Siege 2: Dark Territory* came out—1995—I went out with another crime-thriller spec called *Truth or Consequences* that didn't sell. But that script, in a truly bizarre and fantastic coincidence, got me a shot to pitch a feature version of "The A-Team" that Universal was hot to make back then. So I got to pitch to my hero, Stephen J. Cannell, and I got the job. But—no big surprise by now, right?—the movie didn't get made. That was 12 years ago and, since then, at least five other writers have written five other versions and it still hasn't been made. And every one of those writers, including me, was very well paid to write those un-filmed drafts, so that's how most screenwriters make their living in between actual screen credits.

In 1997, I got it into my head to write a movie about paranormal phenomena. In another brilliantly well-timed coincidence, I happened across a book called *The Mothman Prophecies,* which captured exactly the sort of paranormal phenomena experiences I was interested in. I optioned the book myself for $2,500 and spent the summer and fall of 1997 writing a highly fictionalized spec script based on it. The script went out in November to every major studio in town. And it didn't sell. But what felt like failure at the time turned out to be another incredible stroke of luck. Because in January of 1998, it did sell, for a relatively small price, to Lakeshore Entertainment, a small, self-financed company that didn't buy dozens of scripts a year. They only bought one or two—*but they always made them.* It took a couple years to get all the elements into place—director, star—but once they did, they made the movie.

When I wrote *The Mothman Prophecies*, it was very unexpected because to the level I was known, I was known as an action writer. And changing genres is a big deal in movies and TV. Again, it's like starting your career over. So I couldn't just hope someone asked me to write a paranormal thriller. I had to spec one out (more on that later). And once it sold, paranormal thrillers were all I got offered. The final other big thing I learned is that, for most writers, there is no one big moment of success where you wake up one morning and you've "made it."

Finally, in the 12 months before *Mothman* came out, my TV career started.

Exactly. After *Mothman*, the floodgates started to open. You were writing for "Miracles," "Tru Calling," "The Insider." You were co-creator and showrunner in some instances. How did this happen so well so quickly?

The script for *Mothman* is what led to my first TV experience, which was the show "Miracles." Spyglass Entertainment and Touchstone TV (Now ABC TV Studios) contacted me because they had a feature film script that they felt might be the basis for a good TV show. The script was by a wonderful writer named Michael Petroni called "Miracles." It was sort of a romantic drama with supernatural overtones, about a young seminarian investigating miracles and sort of finding his own faith along the way. When I met with Megan Wolpert (Spyglass) and Suzanne Patmore (Touchstone), they told me that they'd like to take the idea of a young priest who investigates miracles and turn it into a sort of "spiritual *X-Files*." Our first meeting lasted three hours and I would say 95% of what the show turned out to be was developed in that meeting that day.

A quick word about TV development. There are *hundreds* of meetings just like this one taking place in offices all around town every day. The likelihood that any one of these conversations turns into a TV show you might ever see is very small. TV development is like any other elimination sport—you start with a very crowded field, and it keeps thinning out until just a few are left standing. Those are the shows that make it to the air—and then those start dropping like flies when no one watches. So any show you see on TV for more than a year is really like a lottery winner or an Olympic Gold medalist—maybe not in terms of quality, but certainly in terms of luck and odds.

So, over the summer and fall of 2001, I wrote the pilot for "Miracles" with a ton of help and direction from Spyglass and Touchstone, all in the hopes that ABC will like the script enough to actually film a pilot. Luckily—and this is not *nearly* always the case—Spyglass and Touchstone had a very clear idea of what ABC wanted, so we could tailor our script to their needs. (There's a much longer discussion here about how studios sell shows to networks, but suffice to say it really helps when the studio knows what the network wants. It helps even more if the *network* knows what the network wants.)

In January of 2002—the month *Mothman* came out in theaters—ABC decides to shoot the "Miracles" pilot. And they have this guy they want to direct it, a guy they love, the co-creator of "Felicity," which was a big hit for Touchstone. And they run his name past me to see if it's okay with me. It's Matt Reeves. My best friend who wrote *US2DT* with me. It was the single best, luckiest thing that's ever happened in my career. (Are you noticing how many times I've used the word "lucky" when describing my career success? Good.) So 15 years after Matt and I toiled away on our Super 8 film projects at USC and dreamed the impossible dream that maybe one day we'd have a career in Hollywood, here we are shooting a $3 million pilot with a real crew and a real cast and real free snacks. It was the greatest thing ever. Oh, and one other thing: It came out great.

Tell us about the transition from writer to showrunner. Is that a natural step all writers should be prepared for? What *weren't* you prepared for?

To the extent that I was a creator/showrunner of "Miracles," which was a *very* brief amount of time, I knew early on how I *didn't* want to do things. For instance, the people who work for you, various department heads and writers—they all kind of half-expect you to be a real jerk because most of them have worked for jerks in the past. So if you're not a jerk, they're ridiculously grateful and you end up getting great work from them. Someone told me early on that the way to get respect as a first-time showrunner was to walk onto the set the first day and fire someone. What bullshit. To me, that would be a display of massive insecurity. Some showrunners like to create a sense of competition among their writing staff so that everyone is trying to out-do or outmaneuver the other guy. Again, I think this is a huge mistake. I don't think most writers do their best work scared. I know I don't.

To be honest, I've always found the stress of working for someone else to be far greater than the stress of being the boss, because at least when you're the boss you know what you want, so you can just do it. Working for someone else, there's always a degree of guess work—"Is this what they want? Is *that* what they want? Am I doing this right?" And a lot of talented writers aren't particularly skilled at communicating to other writers what they want. Often it's because they don't *know* what they want until they're rewriting your script. It's only when the pages are running through *their* typewriter that they discover what it is they want, and by then it's very easy for them to think "Ah, I'm the *only* person in the world who can write this show. My staff sucks." However, if you know exactly what you want at the story-breaking stage or the outline stage, you can equip the writer with everything they need to turn in work that's going to please you.

One thing some people don't understand well is how much concern a writer should give whether a pilot is for FX, or HBO, or Disney the networks, or . . .? Can you give some advice on learning what networks air what shows and how that will come in handy during pitch time?

If you're doing face-to-face pitching and you have an agent, you can reasonably expect your agent to have a sense of what the various networks might be looking for. Even better, if you are working with a production company that has some TV credits, they, too, should know the landscape and can help strategize. But really, the best advice is simply this: Pitch everywhere. Pitch your show to the networks, to the cable channels—just pitch it everywhere, because you never know who might love it.

Let's say you're talking to someone who is trying to break in, and has some spec scripts ready. They say to you "I'm thinking about writing an original, but I don't think it'll really matter much." What do you say?

Right now is a very good time to have an original spec TV pilot. It's always been a good way of demonstrating your own voice, but now, much more than any time I've been in the business, spec TV pilots are actually selling. There are a lot of networks, cable and otherwise, looking for signature shows to distinguish their "brand," so there's a greater openness to considering new concepts from unknown writers.

How do you decide if an idea you have is best fit for TV versus the big screen?

Here's a stupid but honest answer: Some ideas just *feel* like movies, whereas others *feel* like TV shows. If an idea is "event-based," it's probably a movie. For instance, "Someone is trying to kill the president," or "One day, a monster comes out of the water in New York harbor and starts stomping around." You're examining one incident in great detail, so that feels like a movie. However, an idea that is more about characters and settings probably feels more like a TV show. For example, "Three competitive brothers open a private golf course in Beverly Hills," or "A neurotic, control-freak New Yorker inherits a small-town newspaper in Nevada." These are "characters in a setting" ideas and they can be explored from many angles over a long period of time. Character-based movies like "The Odd Couple" make great TV shows. Same thing with "setting-based" movies like "M*A*S*H."

I've heard that composing bibles early on is a waste of time. True?

Yeah, I'd say this is true. If you're pitching a new series or writing a spec pilot, it's good to have general idea about where the show might go, but it's probably not important to write out a detailed bible or even detailed episode ideas. The time will come for that sort of work after the pilot has been sold. (Often, it's after the pilot has been shot and you want to make sure the network has every reason to pick up the show to series.)

What other advice can you throw writers on anything we've missed?

If you want to write for movies and television, you should move to Los Angeles. Take classes at UCLA Extension, AFI, USC and get to know the people. (This is that "networking" thing you've heard about.) Chances are you'll meet people who work at small production companies—or even large agencies—and they will have ideas and advice about how to get your script into the right hands. More important, the people you meet are your peers. They are struggling right along with you. Some of the people you meet in the first few months you live here will turn into lifelong friends. Short of that, they will be the future writers/producers/ executives/agents/studio chiefs you'll be working with for the balance of your career.

Most new writers on network and/or cable shows are former writer's assistants. A writer's assistant is someone who takes notes in the writer's room on any given series. They usually get this job as a promotion from office assistant in the production company that produces the show. Or sometimes they start as the personal assistant to one of the writer-producers. The reason these people get promoted onto a writing staff is because they are a familiar face to all the current writers, so they don't frighten or threaten them as much. They're already a member of the family.

I happily and confidently urge you to keep pushing forward and never give up. There are plenty of people warning you about long odds and low pay and lack of respect and sleazy producers. So gently set all that good advice aside and remind yourself of one persistent, undeniable little fact: *Every night, somewhere in Hollywood, a new writer is celebrating their first big sale. Every. Single. Night.*

But Will It Get Produced?

Don't Write with Red Carpets in Mind

by Chuck Sambuchino

If you want to be a screenwriter, you must love writing. When it comes down to it, that's all you're guaranteed—time sitting down cranking out scenes and getting paid for it. If your ultimate goal is something other than to make a living writing scripts, then you may be in trouble. Below you will find four classic bad ideas that novice script scribes may think about as they begin their voyage to screenwriter superstardom. Avoid them like the Blob— or Keyser Soze.

BAD IDEA NO. 1: WRITE FOR A TREND

At a recent writers' conference in Los Angeles, a panel of script managers sat down to answer audience questions on screenwriting. Invariably, an attendee stood up and asked about "what's hot," bringing up the topic of trends. Wisely, instead of answering the question, the script managers refused to expound on the topic, saying that writers shouldn't write to trends.

The reasoning behind this is two-fold. First, a writer will likely be too late to capitalize on an existing trend. At the time of the conference, the latest Indiana Jones film was released, stirring up much interest in adventure-type films with treasures and hidden places. But there was no point in trying to follow the trend, because Hollywood was flooded by Indiana Jones rip-offs well before the film hit theaters.

In an absolute best-case scenario, a film may hit theaters two years after a writer starts writing the script. That takes into consideration everything at every stage going perfect. But, more than likely, it will be several years from writing to fruition, thereby ruining any chance screenwriters have to capitalize on a trend.

The second reason to avoid trends is because a writer's best writing will show up where the writer is passionate. If vampire flicks are hot right now and you try to craft tale about the undead, but you don't really know or care about the subject matter, then your best work will not land on the page.

To be fair, trends may come into play for you down the road. If you have an agent and you inquire one day as to what studios are looking for, he may say "a space opera fantasy." At that point, you'll be ahead of the trend, and may be able to talk your way into a writing (or rewriting) assignment for a space opera fantasy that's in development somewhere. Perhaps you have a completed script around that you could rewrite and see if excellence develops. If it does, give it to your agent to make some rounds.

CHUCK SAMBUCHINO is the editor of *Screenwriter's & Playwright's Market*. He is also the editor of *Guide to Literary Agents* (www.guidetoliteraryagents.com/blog) and assists in editing *Writer's Market*.

BAD IDEA NO. 2: COMPROMISE YOUR QUALITY FOR SALABILITY

Yes, ideally you want to write something that will sell and land you a hefty paycheck. But the truth is: post-strike boom aside, spec scripts are a tough sell. Studios have already spent oodles of money acquiring all kinds of properties that are now in development. It's in their best interest to get those projects moving, not buy something completely new that has no built-in fan base.

The goal is to write to your passions and create a writing sample so astounding that power players of the film business will want you to work on other projects. The spec script you write serves as a wonderful way to get your foot in the door and land you assignments. Like manager Ken Sherman of Ken Sherman Associates says: "What I'm looking for, and what every producer, studio, network and agent I know is looking for, is a killer writing sample—meaning something that we can send out in one day to 30 producers and have them say 'This may not be exactly the story I'm looking for, but I need to know this writer.' (That way), they will meet with the writer and talk about other projects because that writer has a unique voice."

Screenwriter Zak Penn, scribe of *X-Men 3: The Last Stand* and *The Incredible Hulk*, says a great example of how to break into the business correctly was his friend, Marc Hyman. According to Penn, Hyman wrote a spec script that was an animation comedy starring fish. The script was extremely funny, but at the same time, would be a difficult project to produce and turn a profit on. The fish project never materialized, but producers knew Hyman's name and his humor skills because his script proved he was a formidable writer. Years later, when an animation comedy called *Osmosis Jones* was materializing, the studio needed a funny writer who could deal with animation. They called Hyman.

Mission accomplished.

BAD IDEA NO. 3: GET REALLY UPSET IF YOUR WORK ISN'T PRODUCED

If you're like me (i.e., if you're a writer with a heartbeat), you love bylines. Getting an assignment is a jolt. Writing the piece is fun. Getting my check in the mail is awesome. And lastly, seeing my work in print gives me the final thrill, as well as something else: closure. The process I just described is how a typical magazine writing assignment goes. If a magazine contracts and purchases an article from me, they will print it somewhere, many more times than not. If a writer sells a novel, it, too, will likely see the light of day, as the publishing house has paid you for it and they want to put the content in print and use it. It's in this regard that screenwriting stands alone. In Hollywood, much more material is written and optioned and passed around town than will ever come to life. There's so much money flying around, that it's hardly uncommon to see a studio pay $1 million for a dynamite new script and $250,000 for a rewrite of another, with neither project ever hitting the big screen.

It all adds up to this: If you want to be a career screenwriter, you must enjoy the actual duty of screenwriting. We all picture our stories on the big screen, envisioning ourselves looking smashingly handsome (or stunning glamorous) at a red carpet premiere. But that's not likely to happen. There will be meetings, assignments, and nice paychecks, but production is another monster altogether. If the thought of your work never coming to life sounds maddening, then you'll definitely want to write a lot of magazine articles on the side to scratch that itch.

BAD IDEA NO. 4: JUST WRITE ONE SCREENPLAY

Don't put all your eggs in one basket. Agents all say the same thing: They represent careers, not projects. A manager may not even send you out to a pitch meeting until you have several projects up your sleeve. Having multiple scripts in your arsenal allows you to be more valuable, and shows that you're a dedicated writer who actually does what they should—writes!

Contracts and Rights

Making Sense of Copyright and Lingoese

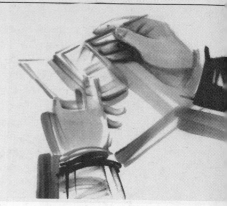

by Robin Mizell

I f you're an aspiring scriptwriter who has yet to meet the requirements for joining a guild or other professional writers' association, you can attempt to break into the business by speculating. By drafting an original script, you will have a means of attracting the interest of an agent, manager, or producer. Before you begin writing a spec script, however, you must understand the provisions of copyright, defamation, and privacy laws—both to protect your investment in your work and to avoid infringing on the rights of others.

COPYRIGHT

Story ideas, basic plots, concepts, facts, and information commonly known cannot be protected by copyright. That said, the expression of your story or idea in a fixed form such as your script, book, or film—including any original, well-defined character that is part of your work product—*is* subject to copyright. As soon as the tangible work is created, it becomes the property of the author. The copyright notice does not need to appear on the work for copyright law to apply.

Until you agree to sell your script, you possess the copyright. When you enter into a purchase agreement with a buyer—once the expressed terms of the contractual agreement are met, the ownership of the script is transferred to the purchaser, and the copyright is transferred along with the script. This gives the purchaser the ability to modify the script, sometimes extensively, to suit a project. Often, this means another writer will eventually be hired to revise portions of your work.

Registration is not required for copyright law to cover your script. However, the relatively minor cost of registering your script with the U.S. Copyright Office in Washington, D.C., does help you to establish ownership as of a specific date. You can save money by using the electronic registration option at www.copyright.gov. It's possible to register your work at any time during the decades of copyright's duration. However, if you wait to do so after being accused of copyright infringement, you will no longer be entitled to the full extent of the law's provisions. For a similar fee, you can record ownership and the date of your script's creation by registering it with the Writers Guild of America Registration Office, even if you are not a guild member.

It's important to understand that any dramatic work you create in the regular course of your employment is considered the property of your employer. Absent a contractual agree-

---

ROBIN MIZELL is the senior editor of *Screenwriter's & Playwright's Market*. To learn more about her and her writing, visit www.robinmizell.com.

ment to the contrary, your employer legally becomes the work's author as well as the copyright holder. The same is true of a commissioned script you are under contract to write, otherwise known as work-for-hire. The company or individual that commissioned the work holds the copyright.

You might find yourself inspired by material to which you do not possess the copyright, such as a song, book, poem or video recording. In order to use even small excerpts from the work of others in your script, you must incorporate the required attribution and the material must be in the public domain, out-of-copyright, or licensed appropriately. Some versions of the Creative Commons license permit derivative works under certain conditions. It's also possible to use portions of another person's material, with specifications, if you obtain authorization from the copyright holder, although it can sometimes be an expensive proposition. Whenever you are given permission to use someone else's material, be extremely careful to retain documentation of the licensing, authorization and all correspondence that will protect you in the event of future claims of infringement. You must also correctly acknowledge the originator of the material to avoid allegations of plagiarism.

DEFAMATION AND PRIVACY LAWS

It's common to base a script on the lives of real people, actual events, or your own experiences. Even when a story is fictionalized, if the individual on whom you based one of your characters can be identified, you can be accused of defamation or invasion of privacy. Obtaining a written release from the person whose story you intend to use offers you only partial protection. You must be extremely cautious about portraying falsely or in an unflattering manner any character based on a real person, living or deceased. You should also think twice about revealing intimate personal details the average person would consider private.

Any works you create based on real circumstances, individuals, or events require the added protection of an errors and omissions (E&O) policy to insure you against any resulting claims by injured parties. The studio or purchaser that acquires your script should provide this coverage, and the specific clause requiring the E&O insurance policy must be included in the purchase agreement.

SUBMISSION AGREEMENTS

A detailed discussion of copyright could make you hesitate to pitch a mere idea or concept to a producer or agent for consideration. If your idea isn't protected by copyright, then how can you prevent someone from taking it without compensating you? Perhaps the best solution is to submit a complete treatment or a draft of your script, which is covered by copyright.

Some producers will ask you to sign a submission agreement that, for your protection, should include a clause specifying your material will not be used unless you are compensated. Unfortunately, the submission agreement will also spell out the very real possibility that a similar treatment or script might be submitted by another writer. Ultimately, the safest course of action is to deal only with established studios and producers whose honorable reputations are known to you, your agent, or your attorney.

CONTRACTS: OPTION AGREEMENTS FOR SPEC SCRIPTS

A producer is usually not in a position to set up a project immediately upon entering negotiations to purchase your script. Instead, the producer is likely to pay a relatively small amount of money in exchange for the option to purchase the script in the future. Optioning a script takes it off the market for a specified length of time, usually one or two years, after which the producer must exercise the option to proceed with a purchase agreement or lose the contractual right to do so. Option prices are applicable to, or in other words, deductible from, the purchase price—something of a rent-to-own strategy. Producers sometimes attempt to option scripts for free.

The Writers Guild Agreement prohibits a producer from submitting a script to studios or other buyers for consideration unless there is a written agreement with the scriptwriter. This protects Guild members from the occasional unscrupulous producer who would shop a script around during ongoing negotiations for an option rather than after the option has been purchased.

RIGHTS

As the creator of an original script, copyright law establishes your rights of reproduction, adaptation, and public distribution, performance, and display. You can separate these rights and sell them individually or in groups. You can also negotiate to retain some of them. Although your agent and attorney should guide the process, it doesn't hurt to know they will often be able to negotiate for you to reserve these and other specific rights to your work:

- Novelization and other types of publication
- Radio and live television performance
- Stage production
- Sequels or series
- Merchandising

COLLABORATION AGREEMENTS

After you've experienced one contract negotiation, you'll have a better perspective of the potential pitfalls of collaborating with another writer on a spec script. If you decide to work with another writer, each of you will need to agree to the terms of any option or purchase agreement. It's best to have a written agreement with the other writer before work on the script begins.

A collaboration agreement should specify what percentage of the material is owned by each writer; otherwise, it will be assumed each person is entitled to 50 percent ownership and compensation. The writers' collaboration agreement should also include the minimum acceptable terms for the sale of the script and for any subsequent writing assignments. Collab-

Professional Associations

These associations' Web sites are excellent sources of information about industry standards and minimum compensation for scriptwriters in various markets.

- **Writers Guild of America**, West, www.wga.org
- **Writers Guild of America**, East, www.wgaeast.org
- **Screenwriters Federation of America**, www.screenwritersfederation.org
- **American Screenwriters Association**, www.asascreenwriters.com
- **The Dramatists Guild of America**, www.dramatistsguild.com
- **Writers Guild of Canada**, www.writersguildofcanada.com
- **The Writers' Guild of Great Britain**, www.writersguild.org.uk

Perspectives

oration complicates the sale of a script, especially when one of the writers is also a producer or when the writers' contributions to the work are unequal.

CONTRACTS: WORK-FOR-HIRE

When you are commissioned to write a script, you will sign an agreement to provide your writing services, almost always exclusively, to the studio or buyer to which you are under contract. You will be given a contractual deadline for submitting your first draft and often the right to perform a single rewrite as well. A bonus payment may be stipulated if you receive a writing credit. You can also be hired to revise another scriptwriter's work, in which case you might, in certain circumstances, be entitled to a writing credit and the related bonus.

Under work-for-hire agreements, you are likely to be paid half at the beginning of a project and the balance upon completion of it. The Writers Guild Agreement establishes industry minimum standards for scriptwriters' financial compensation. If you are engaged as a writer with a television series production and are considered indispensable, it's possible to negotiate a percentage of profits. More often, the producer is looked upon as a vital component of the production, while the writer is viewed as replaceable. It's a competitive business.

Nancy Gall-Clayton

An Up-And-Coming Playwright Speaks Out

by Chuck Sambuchino

Nancy Gall-Clayton is a quintessential example of an up-and-coming playwright—neither uber-popular nor utterly unknown. Her 13 years in the playwriting world have given her the chance to do it all—write commissioned works, see her full-length works produced, pen plenty of 10-minute plays, get paid four figures for a world premiere, and more.

A staple in the Louisville playwriting community, Gall-Clayton's first play came to life simply by chance. "My first play was a finalist for the Heideman Prize at Actors Theatre of Louisville. I had no idea what I'd done right, but with recognition like that, I decided playwriting was easy and took up my pen again," she says. Surprised and buoyed by her first success, she quickly penned a second play, only to realize it wasn't nearly as good as the first. That second play ended up in the shredder instead of onstage, but the fate of her sophomore work wasn't really important. What *was* important was that this new medium allowed Gall-Clayton to write about complicated subjects where she had a passionate opinion. "Members of the audience may not agree with my take on genetic engineering, sweet potato pie, or interfaith marriage, but if I do my job right, the audience will think about the issue and probably in a new way," she says.

During the past decade, more than 40 of Gall-Clayton's works have come to life on the stage, and several of said works were produced in numerous locations. Now battle-tested and wise in the ways of stage plays, Gall-Clayton is a great resource for fellow playwrights who are trying to get produced and build a portfolio.

Nancy, why write plays? What draws you to playwriting?

It's harder to get poetry and fiction published, and then if you do reach print, you will probably be read once—and only once—by the subscribers of one literary journal. If you are unknown and write a book, it's difficult to have it published, and then if it is published, it's difficult to have it reviewed, and then if it is reviewed but not enthusiastically, it's difficult to sell it. A well-written play can and will reach many stages and many people over time.

I am drawn to playwriting because theater is collaborative. I create the characters and the plot, and I write the words, but the director, actors and designers bring their expertise and experience to the play. Playwriting is different from all other writing. The story is told exclusively in dialogue and exclusively in the present tense. If these criteria are not met, the result is not a play, at least not in any traditional sense. I love the challenge of telling a story in dialogue and the fact that each time it is presented, it's as if the story is unfolding afresh.

CHUCK SAMBUCHINO is the editor of *Screenwriter's & Playwright's Market*. He is also the editor of *Guide to Literary Agents* (www.guidetoliteraryagents.com/blog) and assists in editing *Writer's Market*.

You have memberships in some writing and playwriting groups. What do these groups offer for a writer?

I belong to a few groups, each of which serves a different purpose in my literary life. I have a sense of camaraderie with other writers, playwrights, and artists and a feeling that we understand one another better than non-artists.

At some point, every serious playwright needs to join the Dramatists Guild of America. Regardless of your level of success, the guild has lots to offer, including free contract templates and legal advice as well as a bimonthly publication where you can publicize your latest shows and awards and a directory of theaters, competitions, residencies, and other opps for playwrights.

You seem to tap into a lot of your own life and its themes when writing plays—such as being a mother, being involved in social justice themes, being Jewish. Do you feel this allows you to dig deeper into subjects?

I start with what I know and what concerns me and interests me, but I don't feel I'm going deeper or less deep when I go beyond the immediate. I disagree with the idea "Write only what you know." It's exciting to explore.

When you sit down to flesh out a character, what are some steps you take?

With full-length plays, I create timelines of major events (9/11, JFK assassination, Katrina, etc.) and personal events in the characters' lives (father died, dropped out of college, met future spouse). This work is tedious at times, but just as we are influenced by the events large and small around us, so are our characters. If I'm stuck, I go back to the timeline (it's not static, I work on it off and on while creating the play) to help me figure out who the character really is and how they would respond, act, and so on. I also make sure no two characters are alike or nearly alike, from speech to views.

I saw one of your plays at a staged reading and it was a series of monologues, which are not an easy thing to write. What's your advice for composing a monologue?

I recommend holding off on writing monologues . . . On the other hand, I think it's very helpful to write monologues for characters in plays when these monologues are strictly for you the writer to gain insight. For example, imagine your character is walking toward you across a field. She has something in her hand. When she finally gets to you, she says, "There's something you need to know." Write the rest of her speech to you.

After you're done, what is your rewriting process like?

I'm never done. I have plays in print that I'm rewriting. If a play is produced or read nearby, I go to every performance with a notepad. I sit in the back and watch when people get restless. I listen intently. I try to make lines actor- and director-proof, meaning the dialogue does it all. No one can misunderstand or misinterpret.

Looking at your accomplishments, you have a large amount of 10-minute plays in your repertoire. What draws you to this form?

I work full time and have the usual busy life everyone else has. It takes me at least a year to write a full-length and two years if it's based on a historical person or time. A 10-minute play should have all the same elements of a full-length, so writing them keeps me in practice. I can respond to all sorts of things going on in the world—and then be done with it. Also, it was *Special Delivery*, a 10-minute play, that was a finalist at Actors Theatre of Louisville for their annual contest that draws as many as 2,500 entries. If a theater like Actors is interested in 10-minute plays, so am I. A literary manager visited a playwriting workshop I was in this winter and indicated that the 10-minute play competition allows the theater to "meet" writers they may want to know better.

When you sit down to write a 10-minute play, what are your goals?

My goals for a 10-minute play are the same as my goals for any play. For a first attempt at a 10-minute play, I recommend three characters as well as times within the play that allow for each combination—these two, those two, and all three. All of us act differently depending on who is around.

1. Decide what the main character really, really wants—it can be serious or silly: to work up the courage to propose, to quit a job to paint, to dye one's hair, to get his teenager to mow the grass.

2. Now figure out what obstacles the protagonist is facing—someone else has just proposed to her on a billboard, no less; you support yourself, so you gotta work; your children will think you've gone nuts if you become a redhead; there has never been a way to motivate your teen to do anything.

3. Who's the third character? Someone else with a stake one way or another: the intended bride or groom, the boss or your painting instructor; the clerk who will sell you the dye; the teen's other parent.

4. Place these people anywhere but the living room, and keep it simple. No scene changes, no fancy props. Think of places where interesting things happen that also allow movement.

5. Don't write with the ending in mind. Put these people together and get into each of their heads as you write. About the bottom of page nine, draw things to a close. When a play is done, it's really done.

When you write a full-length drama, are you shooting for a particular length? Or do you just write?

I think "full-length" but not necessarily X number of pages. I think mine range from 90 to 110 pages. I don't worry about details until the first draft is done, and I don't do huge amounts of revision while I'm working since the ending or the decisions a character makes may change as I write.

You have all of your scripts available online on your Web site to order for a nominal fee. Would you suggest others do it?

I'm in eight or 10 anthologies, and I do hear from people who saw an excerpt or a monologue and want the whole play. Usually, these are students or people auditioning for a part, and they like using material that's not being done by half the competition. I do license productions at very modest fees. I even offer a rebate if they send me flyers about a show I license them to perform. I'm not interesting in posting whole scripts on the web, but I love hearing from people who are interested in my work.

In a circumstance where a theater or group contacts you and wants to do a play, how do you negotiate price and royalties?

I have set rates for most work. I expect more for a premiere because many competitions don't want work that has been performed. For a full-length, I always want a written contract, though I use a very short one-pager from the Dramatists Guild if I am able to supply it.

How loose are you with your text? Do you allow actors some slack in changing the pace and wording to suit them?

I am not loose at all. No one has the right to change a word of my script without my permission. However, if it's a new play and I am at the rehearsal, I love hearing ideas from the actors and director, and I often agree, but it's strictly my call. Some years ago, I had a $1,000 prize for a full-length play that was produced and changed radically. I wasn't happy and realized as I was sitting there cringing at the premiere that we had not entered a contract. Something about that $1,000 check blinded me temporarily, but no more.

What's the most times you've had to submit a play to various markets before it was awarded or picked up?

I'm not at home with my records, so I can't swear to a number, but I've had way over 40 submissions on a few plays.

Talk to me about how a play gets produced. You finish a full-length work and it's polished. Now what?

After at least one informal reading and usually two, I put it on the list to market. When a play is brand new, I'm very particular about where to send it since so many competitions and theaters want to do premieres. I definitely spend a lot of time marketing. I learn about opportunities from the International Centre for Women Playwrights, from Dramatists Guild's *Resource Directory*, from the TCG publication *Dramatist's Sourcebook*, from Googling at times if I have a play that seems to fit a very specific market, and from playwright friends who see an opp that seems right for me.

I also submit to theaters that have produced or read me before. They obviously already like my work, and I've had second experiences because of that.

Do you have any relationships with theaters where they agree to debut some of your work?

Yes, several. My relationships are local and were built around them not just knowing my work, but knowing me. I'm not a hothead and I play well with others. In a collaborative venture like theater, there is no room for prima donnas, and theaters appreciate having someone involved who wants to be a team player.

Do you enter a lot of contests? What are some guidelines you adhere to when doing so?

I do not pay submission fees. I'm with the Guild on this.

I follow the guidelines very, very carefully and follow them precisely. I make sure my play fits their solicitation. I try to submit at least a little before the deadline. I make sure everything I send looks professional. I never send postage-paid envelope for return of a rejected script. It's too much work for the theater or they'll overlook it or by the time they think of it, the postage rates will have gone up. Or the post office will mangle it and it can't be sent out again. And of course, in my case, I will have revised the play before it is returned.

I don't mark my calendar up awaiting a response. Some never reply. I've got 50+ scripts in circulation, and it's highly unlikely I will remember what I sent to whom. The acceptance by a theater in the Northwest last spring truly puzzled me. It turns out they accepted my 2004 submission in 2008 without even mentioning the name of the play in the acceptance letter. A friend in the area eyeballed the theater, and I decided to (say no).

Do you still find yourself having to be a huge marketer and advocate for your work?

Yes. Even friends with agents find they are their own best advocate.

Thinking over all you've said so far, let's say you sit down with a writer who says they have a good story, but are unsure if a play is the correct medium for it. You say, "You've got to ask yourself some questions before you know if it's a play." He asks, "What questions?" You say:

First and foremost: Is there conflict? A mentor of mine says, "Nothing is more boring on stage than nice people being nice to each other."

How much time is covered? The longer the time period covered in a play, the harder it is to write well. The story of someone's life, no matter how engaging, should—if on stage—focus on one moment in that person's life.

How many issues are there? Plays work best when they focus on one issue or question or problem.

Is there a main character in this story? The best plays focus on one central character and that character's desire and the roadblocks to that desire.

In your mind's eye, do you need "close ups" of your characters' faces or quick costume changes or many scene changes? Stage plays aren't the best vehicle for stories that need these things.

From Script to Career

Find More Work and Negotiate Deals

by Susan Kouguell

They like you! They really like you! And why do they like you? You've rewritten your spec script to perfection. You've written an attention-getting query and a stunning synopsis. You've delivered the perfect pitch. You've persevered. You didn't give up, no matter how many rejections you received. Now, if luck continues to stay on your side, one of two things may happen: They'll want to buy your script. (Your script will be optioned.) Or, they'll want to hire you to write a script for them. (You enter into a development deal.)

This is the moment you've been striving for. You've arrived! Now what?

THE OPTION AGREEMENT

If a company is interested in producing your spec script, its first step will usually be an offer to option your script. An option agreement means that the producer or production entity is buying the exclusive rights to purchase your script within a specified period of time and for a specified price.

Option fees

There is no standard option fee; fees are negotiable. It can be a token fee of one dollar or a more substantial fee of $1,000 to $10,000 or more. The amount depends on the type of script (high-concept/mainstream or art house) and the producer or production entity's economic backing (independent production company or studio). Often the option fee is 10 percent of the purchase price. For example, if your script is optioned for $5,000, then the purchase price of your script will be $50,000.

If at the end of the option period (which can be anywhere from six to 18 months, depending on the deal), the producer has raised the financing to produce your script, and exercises the option, you will receive the balance of $45,000. Or, if the option period ends and no financing has been secured, you can keep the initial option fee of $5,000 and you may enter into a new deal with a new producer or production entity.

The purchase price

The purchase price is the fee that you will receive for your spec script. Like option fees, purchase prices are negotiable. Generally, the purchase price is between two and five percent of the film's budget.

This article excerpted with permission from *The Savvy Screenwriter* (St. Martin's Griffin, 2006). **SUSAN KOUGHELL** (www.su-city-pictures.com) is an award-winning screenwriter and filmmaker and associate producer. As chairperson of Su-City Pictures East, she works as a screenplay and post-production consultant with a client base of more than 1,000 writers, filmmakers, production companies, agents and studios.

If you are a member of the WGA or if the producer is signatory to the WGA, Basic Agreement for union-mandated minimums applies. The WGA Schedule of Minimums can be found at www.wga.org. If you are not a WGA member, try to negotiate a purchase price comparable to the one WGA members receive.

The option period

During the option period, the producer or production entity will try to secure financing, attach talent to the film, and possibly arrange domestic and foreign presales. Additionally, you may be asked to do rewrites, which you may or may not be paid for, depending on your contract.

Since the producer/production entity now has the exclusive rights to your spec script, you may not have this script optioned by another producer during the option period.

Option extensions

In your option agreement, there may be a renewal or extension clause, which means that you agree to the producer's right to renew his or her option for a specified amount of time for an additional payment should the producer need more time to secure financing. Usually the option extension payment is not applied against the purchase price, which means that it is not deducted from the payment you will receive from the sale of your spec script.

"Exercising the option"

This means the producer/production entity that has optioned your spec script is now going to buy it. The ownership rights of your spec script will be transferred from you, the writer, to the producer/production entity, and you will be paid the purchase price. Once the option is exercised, you can no longer option or sell this script to anyone else.

YOUR OPTION AGREEMENT CONTRACT

Under no circumstances should you negotiate your own contract. If you don't have an agent, hire an experienced entertainment attorney to negotiate your contract.

What to ask for:

Credit: Be sure that you are properly credited for your work. If you are a WGA member or the producer/production entity is a WGA signatory, the WGA will determine your credit. Generally, the credit will be the same size on the screen as the director's and will appear before the director's credit in the main titles of the film. Additionally, credits should appear in all advertising and on the DVD and/or video box. If this is not a WGA agreement, then your credit will be negotiated.

Exclusivity: Your goal is to be the sole screenwriter of the film. Getting exclusivity may be difficult unless you are an established writer, but it's worth negotiating.

Rewrites: There are two main points to consider when negotiating your rewrite fee: (1) Be sure that the expected number of rewrites is clearly stated in your contract, otherwise you may be doing endless rewrites without compensation; (2) your rewrite fees should be separate from the purchase price, otherwise you will earn less money.

Percentage of profits: It is reasonable for a writer to seek a percentage of the profits. Generally, asking for 2 to 5 percent of the net is acceptable. However, it's unlikely that you will ever see any percentage of the profits due to the unfortunate fact that the production companies and studios often hide the true profits behind false production expenses—often referred to as "creative accounting."

Sequels: You may want to negotiate to write any sequels to your original script. You may ask for the "first right of refusal," which means that you will be the first writer to be offered the job of writing the sequel, but you will have the right to turn it down. Additionally, you may negotiate a fee or percentage of the profits from any sequels if you are not the writer.

Spin-off's, series episodes, and remakes: You may negotiate a fee or a percentage for each of these three items.

Ancillary rights: If the film becomes a hit like *Shrek* or *Toy Story* (usually this applies to kids' films or animated films), then lunchboxes, records, toys, books, and such will be manufactured. It's important to negotiate a percentage of the profits from sales of these items.

THE DEVELOPMENT DEAL

Generally, a producer or production entity, after reading your spec script (as a writing sample) or hearing your outstanding pitch, will offer you a development deal. They will pay you a fee to write a screenplay for them, which they own all rights to.

You are essentially a hired gun—an employee of the producer. It is your job to translate the ideas of the person hiring you onto the page and into a great script. This may be quite a challenge. Ultimately, it is the person hiring you who will make the final script decisions, so remember to be diplomatic when you suggest ideas or try to make changes.

Writers are usually presented with a step deal. You will be paid in stages against the total purchase price of your script. These stages may include: (1) an advance payment before you begin work; (2) payment for your treatment; (3) payment for a first draft; (4) payment for a second draft; and (5) final payment for a polish. (Often, a writer can negotiate a bonus payment if the film is produced.) The downside of this deal is that at any time during this process you can be eliminated from the project.

And yes, Virginia, there really is a Development Hell, and it is comprised of endless rewrites and changes and tweaks to the script you have been hired to write. What they loved yesterday, they hate today. Or a producer's mother just read the new draft and didn't like the main female teen character and thinks this character should be changed to a gay, male, senior citizen. You get the picture.

LIFE AS A WRITER-FOR-HIRE

Whether you've been hired to write or rewrite a script, you must understand the director and/or producer's goals for the project:

- Ask what initially inspired the story (was it a news story? a person? a dream?) and thoroughly research all aspects of the material, such as setting and time period.
- If this is a writing assignment, ask specific questions, such as (1) What is the story that you want to tell? (2) Who do you see as the main characters, and what are the major obstacles they must overcome? (3) What is the genre?
- If this is a rewriting assignment, come to an agreement as to what exactly needs to be done. For example: (1) Do the characters need to be fleshed out? (2) Does the story structure need to be reworked or tightened? (3) Does the dialogue need fine-tuning?
- After these questions are agreed upon, submit an outline to confirm that you're all literally on the same page.

KEYS TO AUTHOR COLLABORATION

Coauthoring and collaborating can be very exasperating if you're not in sync with your writing partner or with the person who hired you.

Put Your Cards on the Table

Doing this from the onset of the collaboration avoids hurt egos and surprises later on.

1. Clearly express your expectations and goals for the script and your collaboration, and ask what the other person has in mind.
2. Explain your writing process and work habits, and ask what your collaborator's process and work habits are.

Keep Your Goals in Mind

You want a great script. This sounds obvious, but when tensions run high (almost inevitable at some point in the collaborative process), keep your eye on the prize—the great, finished script.

Be Willing to Compromise and Listen

Compromising does not mean that you're selling out; it means that you are open to new ideas. You may discover that your partner has great ideas and inspiring suggestions that you never even considered or initially thought were terrible. Keep the lines of communication open to avoid any conflicts during this process.

Perspectives

Hollywood Pet Peeves

Avoid These Peeves and Get Work Read

by Chuck Sambuchino

Here's a secret many writers don't know about managers and producers. When they tackle the slush pile (much like when readers review entries in a writing contest), they are flooded with hundreds, sometimes thousands, of submissions. With such an overwhelming volume of potential scripts to consider, producers are looking for reasons *not* to choose a particular script. They're looking for any sign of weakness in your writing or professionalism that will justify rejecting your work and making their huge stack of scripts decrease by one. That's why your work must be as perfect as it can be. And before an agent even reads your work, you've got to do something more important: Avoid Hollywood pet peeves.

There's a scene in the television show "Arrested Development" where the character Tobias Fünke, an aspiring actor, starts packaging his headshot to send out to different casting directors in Hollywood. Each headshot is placed in a decorative bag filled with glitter, candy and a note saying, "I know where you live, ha ha." We then see a casting director struggling to open one of these glittery bags, then looking at the headshot and telling herself aloud never to hire Tobias Fünke. This is a quintessential example of an amateur implementing gimmicks to get their work noticed—and remember, gimmicks and "cute" don't work. In fact, they're huge Hollywood pet peeves.

Glitter and unfunny notes aren't the only dislikes in the movie world—there's plenty more. Keep your work concise and professional to help avoid annoying possible representatives for your work. Below you'll find a series of tips and need-to-know facts that will help your work get a fair read by the people in power. Study them well.

REGARDING SUBMISSIONS

- Any type of misspelling or gross formatting error will make an agent grimace, and likely reject your query.
- No matter how much you want to woo a specific manager or production company, never submit a work to a market that doesn't accept the genre in question—you're just showing you can't follow directions (and wasting postage).
- Don't embellish your accomplishments; that just leads to a very awkward moment later when you have to explain yourself. If you get caught in a lie, it's likely people will start to wonder what else you were untruthful about.

CHUCK SAMBUCHINO is the editor of *Screenwriter's & Playwright's Market*. He is also the editor of *Guide to Literary Agents* (www.guidetoliteraryagents.com/blog) and assists in editing *Writer's Market*.

- Don't mention ideas for your movie's poster design or possible casting. If you have suggestions, let that conversation happen naturally down the road. Likely, such decisions will be out of your hands, and offering your input too soon (or even at all) makes you look amateurish. This brings up another point: Know when to work your tail off, and when to step away and let other people operate.
- Single-space your query letters.
- Managers and agents may assist with rewriting suggestions, but they're not there to act as the world's editors. If your query or pitch has a sentence such as "Act III needs a little tweaking," then you should never have pitched in the first place.
- Don't submit a query that's written in the voice of your lead character.
- Don't submit your query in script format.
- Make sure you always provide what's asked of you.

REGARDING APPEARANCE

- Avoid letterhead or logos on your work. Remember: Always avoid "cute."
- Keep things short (e.g., query letters should be one page). You may go long because you feel that your plot can't properly be condensed into just one or two paragraphs. This leads to a larger problem: If you can't summarize your work with a short explanation or a concise logline, then the manager won't be able to summarize the work when talking to production companies who may consider the project. You put him at a disadvantage in selling your work.
- Format your materials and always use a standard font.
- Use no graphics or art (or worse: Clip Art).
- Take dates off your script and don't say that this is "Draft 5."

REGARDING THE SCRIPT

- Don't mention who you think should play a character in the role, and don't include pictures of actors.
- Don't turn in a super long script. Especially with spec scripts, less is more. Aim for approximately 110 pages.
- Don't awkwardly staple or bind your script together. The standard format of two brads is chosen because it's easy for readers, and easy to undo should copies be needed.
- Beware including music cues in your work. Yes, Queen's "Bohemian Rhapsody" would really be great in that scene you're writing, but a director will have a much better sense of movie music.

ON ETIQUETTE

- Act with humility always, whether when writing your query or speaking with a producer in person. If you can show someone that you deeply respect their time, you've shown them that you're a professional and courteous writer, which ups your value as a potential client.
- Don't write an exec and tell her she's an idiot for not signing you. Let's say someone sends you a form rejection letter and you've got an inkling that they gave your script a quick read let alone any true consideration at all. You're frustrated. Sending an angry letter giving your candid thoughts is not the answer. The letter isn't likely to make someone change their submission review procedures, and a worse scenario is that person contacting fellow professionals and warning them against taking you on as a client.
- Mentioning how much money your project will make is a big no-no. Writers, many of which are very proud of their work, will often compare their script to a current blockbuster. It's best to not even joke about these clichés.

Perspectives

- Don't say your family members or writing group liked your work. Their opinion, though kind, means nothing to agents. And because professionals think that writers should know these opinions are worthless, they'll look down on writers who mention such statements.
- Take no chances when addressing a person whose gender is ambiguous (e.g., Pat or Alex). Call up the studio and ask the person who picks up whether Pat/Alex is male or female.
- Don't demand a cameo (or worse—a starring role) in your script should it get produced. You're a writer, so write.

ON CONTACTING

- Though it's been said before, it bears repeating: Personalize your queries.
- If you receive a rejection letter, you likely won't get any personal feedback on your work. If this happens, don't contact that manager after a rejection and ask her for feedback, or a specific reason as to why you received only a generic rejection letter. I know you're thinking that you're entitled to a reason as to why your work was rejected (and perhaps you are), but reps are too busy to give personal feedback to everyone. Instead of contacting the agent, get feedback from where it would logically come—peers in a writing group.
- Never ask an agent if she charges fees. Use Internet forums, blogs and this book to weed out inappropriate agencies before pitching, then you'll know you're dealing with someone legitimate.
- Don't refer to yourself as "a screenwriter." That's obvious, no?
- Don't submit your script with two additional scripts for your proposed sequels.

ON FOLLOWING UP AND MOVING ON

- Beware calling without a request. I know this is tempting because you may actually get a live person on the end of the phone, but it provides for a massively awkward situation with agents as they're requested to explain why they haven't gotten back to you yet. The last thing an agent wants is to have that awkward moment on the phone.
- If a representative takes you on, make sure you don't clamor for an unrealistic payday. If you've done your homework, you should know what a logical payout for a script/series will be.
- Don't be a blowhard. Your work will get rewritten and some of your ideas may be stolen. Such is the nature of Hollywood. Kicking and screaming will do no good.

Navigating Hollywood requires a careful balance of what to do and what not to do, but the basics will always be the same: Be professional, write well and always follow directions. Avoid the pet peeves and ensure that your work ends up in the hands of a big-time power player, not a recycle bin.

Agents & Managers

This section contains agents and managers who represent feature film scripts, television scripts and theatrical stage plays. Many of the script agents listed here are signatories to the Writers Guild of America (WGA) Artists' Manager Basic Agreement. They have paid a membership fee and agree to abide by the WGA's standard code of behavior.

It's a good idea to register your script before sending it out, and the WGA offers a registration service to members and nonmembers alike. Membership in the WGA is earned through the accumulation of professional credits and carries a number of significant benefits.

A few of the listings in this section are actually management companies. The role of managers is quickly changing in Hollywood. Actors and the occasional writer were once the only ones to use them. Now many managers are actually selling scripts to producers.

Like the literary agents listed in this book, some script agencies ask that clients pay for some or all of the office fees accrued when sending out scripts. Always have a clear understanding of any fee an agent asks you to pay.

SUBHEADS

Each listing is broken down into subheads to make locating specific information easier. In the first section, you'll find contact information for each agency. You'll also learn if the agent is a WGA signatory or a member of any other professional organizations. Other information provided indicates the agency's size, its willingness to work with a new or unpublished writer, and a percentage breakdown of the general types of scripts the agency will consider.

Member Agents: Agencies comprised of more than one agent list member agents and their individual specialties to help you determine the person to whom you should send your query letter.

Represents: In this section, agents specify what type of scripts they represent. Make sure you query only agents who represent the type of material you write.

☛ Look for the key icon to quickly learn an agent's areas of specialization. In this portion of the listing, agents mention the specific subject areas they're currently seeking, as well as those subject areas they do not consider.

How to Contact: Most agents open to submissions prefer an initial query letter that briefly describes your work. Script agents usually discard material sent without a SASE. In this section, agents also mention if they accept queries by fax or e-mail; if they consider simultaneous submissions; and how they prefer to solicit new clients.

Recent Sales: Reflecting the different ways scriptwriters work, agents list scripts optioned or sold and scripting assignments procured for clients. The film industry is very secretive about sales, but you may be able to get a list of clients or other references upon request—especially if the agency is interested in representing your work.

Terms: Most agents' commissions range from 10-15 percent, and WGA signatories may not earn more than 10 percent from WGA members.

Writers' Conferences: A great way to meet an agent is at a writers' conference. Here agents list the conferences they usually attend. For more information about a specific conference, check the Conferences section starting on page 253.

Tips: In this section, agents offer advice and additional instructions for writers seeking representation.

SPECIAL INDEXES

Agents Specialties Index: This index (page 372) organizes agencies according to the subjects they are interested in receiving. This index should help you compose a list of agents specializing in your areas. Cross-referencing categories and concentrating on agents interested in two or more aspects of your manuscript might increase your chances of success.

Agents Index: This index (page 386) provides a list of agents' names in alphabetical order along with the name of the agency for which they work. Find the name of the person you would like to contact, and then check the agency listing.

General Index: This index (page 395) lists all agencies, theaters, production companies, contests and conferences appearing in the book.

Quick Reference Icons

At the beginning of some listings, you will find one or more of the following symbols:

N Agency new to this edition

Canadian agency

International agency

Agency actively seeking clients

Agency seeking both new and established writers

Agency seeking mostly established writers through referrals

Agency specializing in certain types of work

Agency not currently seeking new clients

Find a pull-out bookmark with a key to symbols on the inside cover of this book.

A.P. WATT, LTD

20 John St., London England WC1N 2DR, United Kingdom. (44)(207)405-6774. Fax: (44)(207)831-2154. E-mail: apw@apwatt.co.uk. Web site: www.apwatt.co.uk. **Contact:** Caradoc King, Derek Johns, Georgia Garrett, Kevin Conroy Scott (Literary Fiction, General Nonfiction, Narrative Nonfiction and Children's Authors); Linda Shaughnessy (Translation Rights, Literary Estates); Natasha Fairweather (Nonfiction, Young Novelists); Sheila Crowley (Women's Commercial Fiction, Thrillers, Children's Fiction and Mass Market Nonfiction); Christine Glover, Rob Kraitt (Scripts, Screenplays and Play-wrighting); Teresa Nicholls (foreign Rights).

Represents Nonfiction books, feature film, TV scripts, TV movie of the week, stage plays. **Considers these fiction areas:** Juvenile; literary; Commercial.

   ○━ No poetry considered.

How to Contact Send query letter.

Recent Sales Other clients include Tony Parsons, Dame Ellen MacArthur, Rudyard Kipling, John Creed, Michael Innes and Camille Griffin, Robert Heller, Mick Jackson, James Robertson, Elaine Showalter and Zadie Smith.

A&B PERSONAL MANAGEMENT LTD

162-168 Regent St., Suite 330 Linen Hall, London England W1B 5TD, United Kingdom. (44)(207)434-4262. Fax: (44)(207)038-3699. E-mail: billellis@aandb.co.uk. **Contact:** R.W. Ellis. Estab. 1982.

Represents Nonfiction books, novels, movie scripts, feature film, TV scripts, episodic drama, sitcom, stage plays.

◖ ABOVE THE LINE AGENCY

468 N. Camden Drive, #200, Beverly Hills CA 90210. (310)738-4730. Fax: (310)859-6119. Web site: www.anet.net/users/rima/web/agency.html. **Contact:** Bruce Bartlett; Rima Bauer Greer, owner. Estab. 1994. Signatory of WGA. Represents 35 clients. 10% of clients are new/unpublished writers. Currently handles: 100% movie scripts.

   ● Prior to opening her agency, Ms. Greer served as president of Writers & Artists Agency.

Represents Feature film. **Considers these script subject areas:** Cartoon/animation.

   ○━ "We are rarely accepting new clients."

How to Contact This agency accepts clients by referral only and does not guarantee a response.

Recent Sales *The Great Cookie Wars*, by Greg Taylor and Jim Strain (Fox); *Velveteen Rabbit*, by Greg Taylor (Disney); *Wing and a Prayer*, by David Engelbach and John Wolff (Franchise).

Terms Agent receives 10% commission on domestic sales; 10% commission on foreign sales.

◖ ABRAMS ARTISTS AGENCY

Theatrical and Literary Agency, 275 Seventh Ave., 26th Floor, New York NY 10001. Web site: www.abramsartists.com/.

Represents Stage plays, screenplays, books. **Considers these script subject areas:** Action/adventure; biography/autobiography; comedy; contemporary issues; detective/police/crime; ethnic; experimental; family saga; fantasy; feminist; gay/lesbian; glitz; historical; horror; juvenile; mainstream; multicultural; multimedia; mystery/suspense; psychic/supernatural; regional; religious/inspirational; romantic comedy; romantic drama; science fiction; sports; teen; thriller; western/frontier.

O→ This agency specializes in musicals and stage plays.

How to Contact Query with SASE. Prefers to read materials exclusively. Referrals needed for new materials. *No unsolicited mss.* No e-mail or fax queries.

⬤ ACME TALENT & LITERARY

4727 Wilshire Blvd., Suite #333, Los Angeles CA 90010. (323)602-0330. Fax: (323)954-2262. E-mail: mickeyasst@acmeagents.com. Web site: www.acmetalentandliterary.com. **Contact:** Mickey Frieberg, head of literary division. Estab. 1993. Signatory of WGA. Represents 50 clients.

Member Agents Mickey Freiberg (books, film scripts).

Represents Movie scripts, TV scripts, video game rights. **Considers these script subject areas:** Action/adventure; biography/autobiography; cartoon/animation; comedy; contemporary issues; detective/police/crime; erotica; ethnic; experimental; family saga; fantasy; feminist; gay/lesbian; glitz; historical; horror; juvenile; mainstream; multicultural; multimedia; mystery/suspense; psychic/supernatural; regional; religious/inspirational; romantic comedy; romantic drama; science fiction; sports; teen; thriller; western/frontier.

O→ This agency specializes in feature films and completed specs or pitches by established/produced writers and new writers. Actively seeking great feature scripts. Does not want to receive unsolicited screenplays.

How to Contact Only query through the mail with an SASE and a brief synopsis. Referrals and recommendations highly recommended. No e-mail or fax queries. Obtains most new clients through recommendations from established industry contacts, production companies of note and reputable entertainment attorneys.

Recent Sales Film rights to *Flags of Our Fathers*, by Ron Powers.

Terms Agent receives 10% commission on domestic sales; 15% commission on foreign sales. Offers written contract, binding for 2 years.

⬤ AEI: ATCHITY EDITORIAL/ENTERTAINMENT INTERNATIONAL, INC. MOTION PICTURE PRODUCTION & LITERARY MANAGEMENT

9601 Wilshire Blvd., Box #1202, Beverly Hills CA 90210. (323)932-0407. Fax: (323)932-0321. E-mail: submissions@aeionline.com. Web site: www.aeionline.com. **Contact:** Jennifer Pope. Estab. 1995. Member of Producers Guild of America. Represents 65 clients. 50% of clients are new/unpublished writers. Currently handles: 25% nonfiction books; 25% novels; 5% juvenile books; 40% movie scripts; 5% TV scripts.

Member Agents Ken Atchity (books and film); Chi-Li Wong (TV and film); Brenna Lui (books); Mike Kuciak (films and TV); Greg F. Dix (uplifting stories, inspirational, faith-based work).

Represents Nonfiction books, novels, juvenile books, animation, miniseries, Web sites, games for dramatic exploitation. **Considers these nonfiction areas:** Animals; biography/autobiography; business/economics; computers/electronic; current affairs; ethnic/cultural interests; government/politics/law; health/medicine; history; how-to; humor/satire; memoirs; military/war; money/finance; nature/environment; popular culture; psychology; religious/inspirational; science/technology; self-help/personal improvement; translation; true crime/investigative; women's issues/studies. **Considers these fiction areas:** Action/adventure; confession; detective/police/crime; ethnic; family saga; fantasy; historical; horror; humor/satire; juvenile; literary; mainstream/contemporary; mystery/suspense; religious/inspirational; science fiction; thriller; westerns/frontier; young adult; African-American, ethnic, psychic/supernatural. **Considers these script subject areas:** Action/adventure; biography/autobiography; cartoon/animation; comedy; contemporary issues; detective/police/crime; fantasy; horror; juvenile; mainstream; mystery/suspense; psychic/supernatural; religious/inspirational; romantic comedy; teen; thriller.

    ⊶ "We've developed the niche of focusing on storytellers instead of 'projects' or 'writers,' and helping them tell their stories (whether fiction or nonfiction) for all possible markets (book, film, Web, etc.). Actively seeking young adult novels, nonfiction, mom lit, minority lit, action screenplays, broad comedy screenplays. Does not want to receive poetry, children's books or photo books.

How to Contact Query with SASE, submit proposal package, synopsis. Accepts e-mail queries. No fax queries. Considers simultaneous queries. Responds in 2-4 weeks to queries; 4-6 weeks to mss. Returns materials only with SASE. Obtains most new clients through recommendations from others, solicitations, conferences, referrals from our books, Web site.

Recent Sales Sold 10 titles and sold 5 scripts in the last year. *Demon Keeper*, by Royce Buckingham (Putnam/Fox 2000); *Dark Gold*, by David Angsten (Thomas Dunne); *Arm Bone Flute*, by Alaya Johnson (Agate).

Terms Agent receives 15% commission on domestic sales; 30% commission on foreign sales. Offers written contract, binding for 1 year; 30-day notice must be given to terminate contract. Agency charges for misc. expenses, but costs not to exceed $500 from any publication advance, with the balance recoupable from other gross proceeds.

Writers' Conferences Santa Barbara Writers' Conference; Midwest Literary Festival; Pacific Northwest Writers' Conference.

Tips "Respect what we do as story merchants, and treat us, from the beginning, as business partners who can help you build the creative life of your dreams. Find out who we are and know what we like and believe in even before you approach us. It's all on our Web site. Most of all, think outside the box and take an entrepreneurial approach to both your career and your relationship with us."

◎ AFFINITY MODELS & TALENT AGENCY

5724 W. 3rd St., #511, Los Angeles CA, 90036. (323)525-0577. Fax: (323)843-9696. E-mail: info@affinitytalent.com. Web site: www.affinitytalent.com. **Contact:** Literary Division / Ross Grossman.

How to Contact Send e-query with logline and synopsis. No fax queries.

Tips "Please be sure to indicate if any other parties are looking at the query, any significant individuals already attached or involved. No phone calls or packages please! Please title your e-mail 'LITERARY DEPARTMENT QUERY LETTER' (your name/city/state/phones)."

AGENCY FOR THE PERFORMING ARTS

APA, 405 South Beverly Drive, Beverly Hills California 90212. (310)888-4200. Fax: (310)888-4242. Web site: www.apanewyork.com. 250 West 57th Street, Suite 1701, New York, NY 10107 and 3017 Poston Avenue, Nashville, TN 37203.

Represents Nonfiction books, novels, movie scripts, feature film, TV scripts, Reality TV.

    ⊶ "APA's literary department boasts an impressive roster of established screenwriters, directors, show creators, and novelists. We pride ourselves on working as a team that is as passionate about our clients' material as they are about it themselves. This shared camaraderie and dedication drive us to sell screenplays, novels, scripted and reality television shows and to obtain employment for writers and directors in both the feature and television worlds. As a cohesive unit we easily cross motion picture clients into television, television clients into features, and novelists into both worlds.''

THE AGENCY, LTD.

24 Pottery Lane, Holland Park, London England W11 4LZ, United Kingdom. E-mail: info@theagency. co.uk. Web site: www.theagency.co.uk. Estab. 1995. Currently handles: movie scripts; TV scripts; stage plays; Radio Scripts.

Member Agents Partners: Stephen Durbridge, Leah Schmidt, Julia Kreitman, Bethan Evans, Norman North, and Anna Cameron. Directors: Hilary Delamere and Katie Haines Associates: Nick Quinn, Faye Webber, Fay Davies, Ian Benson, and Jago Irwin. Hilary Delamere represents children's authors and illustrators.

Represents Juvenile books, movie scripts, feature film, TV scripts.

How to Contact All unsolicited mss returned unopened.

◎ AIM

Associated International Management, Fairfax House, Fulwood Place, London England WC1V 6HU, United Kingdom. (44)(207)831-9709. Fax: (44)(207)242-0810. E-mail: email@aimagents.com. Web site: www.aimagents.com/. Member of Personal Managers Association.

Member Agents Derek Webster, Stephen Gittins, and Lisa-Marie Assenheim.

How to Contact Query with SASE, submit résumé, SASE. No e-mail or fax queries.

Recent Sales Other clients include David Bartlett; Peter Cregeen; John Davies; Ken Russell; Carol Wilks.

AIMEE ENTERTAINMENT AGENCY

15840 Ventura Blvd., Suite 215, Encino CA 91436. (818)783-3831. Fax: (818)783-4447. E-mail: info@aimeeentertainment.com. Web site: www.aimeeentertainment.com/. **Contact:** Sharif Ali. Estab. 1962.

Member Agents Sharif Ali (scriptwriters and book authors); George Salinas, junior agent.

Represents Movie scripts, feature film, book-length works.

    ☐ ''Aimee Entertainment Agency was formed with the specific goal of becoming a personalized boutique agency, where clients, agents and sponsors could always rely on an open-door policy. Based on ethics, integrity and good and fair business practices, combined with years of experience as a performer as well as a sub agent with other agencies, Joyce Aimee sought to fill a void left by the high-powered, mega agencies with their impersonal booking styles and minimal attention to their clients' aspirations. Aimee Entertainment believes in building careers for artists, and listening carefully to the needs of casting directors, producers and bookers.''

☑ THE ALPERN GROUP

15645 Royal Oak Road, Encino CA 91436. (818)528-1111. E-mail: mail@alperngroup.com. **Contact:** Jeff Alpern. Estab. 1994. Represents 50 clients. 10% of clients are new/unpublished writers. Currently handles: 30% movie scripts; 60% TV scripts; 10% stage plays.

• Prior to opening his agency, Mr. Alpern was an agent with William Morris.

Member Agents Jeff Alpern, president; Elana Trainoff; Jeff Aghassi.

Represents Movie scripts, feature film, TV scripts, TV movie of the week, episodic drama, miniseries.
Considers these script subject areas: Action/adventure; biography/autobiography; comedy; contemporary issues; detective/police/crime; ethnic; fantasy; feminist; gay/lesbian; horror; juvenile; mainstream; multicultural; mystery/suspense; regional; romantic comedy; science fiction; teen; thriller; family; supernatural.

How to Contact Query with SASE or via e-mail. Only responds to e-mail queries if interested. Responds to all mail queries that include a SASE. Responds in 1 month to queries.

Terms Agent receives 10% commission on domestic sales. Offers written contract.

AMSEL, EISENSTADT & FRAZIER

AEF Talent, 5757 Wilshire, #510, Los Angeles CA 90036. (323)939-1188. Web site: www.aeftalent. com/.

MARCIA AMSTERDAM AGENCY

41 W. 82nd St., Suite 9A, New York NY 10024-5613. (212)873-4945. **Contact:** Marcia Amsterdam. Estab. 1970. Signatory of WGA. Currently handles: 15% nonfiction books; 70% novels; 5% movie scripts; 10% TV scripts.

• Prior to opening her agency, Ms. Amsterdam was an editor.

Represents Novels, feature film, sitcom. **Considers these fiction areas:** Action/adventure; detective/police/crime; horror; mainstream/contemporary; mystery/suspense; romance (contemporary, historical); science fiction; thriller; young adult. **Considers these script subject areas:** Comedy; romantic comedy.

How to Contact Query with SASE. No e-mail or fax queries. Responds in 1 month to queries.

Recent Sales *Hidden Child*, by Isaac Millman (FSG); *Lucky Leonardo*, by Jonathan Canter (Sourcebooks).

Terms Agent receives 15% commission on domestic sales; 20% commission on foreign sales; 10% commission on dramatic rights sales. Offers written contract, binding for 1 year. Charges clients for extra office expenses, foreign postage, copying, legal fees (when agreed upon).

Tips "We are always looking for interesting literary voices."

ANCHORAGE PRESS PLAYS

617 Baxter Ave., Louisville KY 40204-1105. (502)583-2288. Fax: (502)583-2288. E-mail: applays@bell south.net. Web site: www.applays.com. P.O. Box 2901, Louisville, KY 40201-2901 **Contact:** Marilee Hebert Miller, publisher. Estab. 1935.

Represents Stage plays (for children and young people).

How to Contact Submit Review sheet, SASE. Submit complete manuscript. No e-mail or fax queries.

ANCO ENTERTAINMENT THEATER PRODUCTIONS

Zijperstraat 41, Alkmaar 1823 CX, The Netherlands. E-mail: info@toneelwerken.nl. Web site: www. toneelwerken.nl/.

DARLEY ANDERSON LITERARY, TV & FILM AGENCY

Estelle House, 11 Eustace Rd., London England SW6 1JB, United Kingdom. (44)(207)385-6652. Fax: (44)(207)386-5571. E-mail: enquiries@darleyanderson.com. Web site: www.darleyanderson.com. **Contact:** Darley Anderson (Crime and Thrillers); Julia Churchill (Children's Books); Lucie Whitehouse (Women's Fiction); Zoe King (Nonfiction). Estab. 1988.

Represents Sitcom. **Considers these nonfiction areas:** Animals; biography/autobiography; child guidance/parenting; cooking/foods/nutrition; memoirs; popular culture; religious/inspirational; self-help/personal improvement; sports; Finance, Children's nonfiction. **Considers these fiction areas:** Action/adventure; confession; erotica; ethnic; family saga; fantasy; gay/lesbian; historical; horror; juvenile; mainstream/contemporary; mystery/suspense; picture books; regional; religious/inspirational; romance; science fiction; sports; thriller; young adult; Women's 'Chick Lit'. **Considers these script subject areas:** Action/adventure; biography/autobiography; cartoon/animation; comedy; contemporary issues; detective/police/crime; ethnic; family saga; glitz; psychic/supernatural.

How to Contact Submit synopsis. Send query letter with SAE. Accepts query letters by phone. Submit first 3 chapters.

ANGEL CITY TALENT

4741 Laurel Canyon Blvd., #101, Valley Village CA 91607. (818)760-9980. Web site: angelcitytalent. biz/.

Member Agents Mimi Mayer (adult theatrical agent); Katie Johnson (adults, teen and youth commercial agent), Gwen Davis (teen and youth theatrical agent).

   ○━ This agency prides itself on representing theatrical, print and literary works for children and adults. It does handle some literary representation, but more so handles actors.

How to Contact Query with SASE. Literary submissions are currently being accepted via snail mail, Attn: Literary Department. No e-mail or fax queries.

ANONYMOUS CONTENT

588 Broadway, Suite 308, New York NY 10012. (212)925-0055. Fax: (212)925-5030. E-mail: info@anonymouscontent.com. Web site: www.anonymouscontent.com/. Los Angeles Office: 3532 Hayden Ave., Culver City, CA 90232, (310)558-3667 / (310)558-4212 fax; London Office: 7 / 8 Bourlet Close, London, UK W1W 7BW (44)(207)927-9400 / (44)(207)927-9401 fax. Estab. 1999.

Member Agents Paul Muniz and Lisa Sabatino—East Coast; David Wagner—Midwest; Michael Di Girolamo—West; Dave Morrison—Commercials.

Represents Movie scripts, feature film, TV scripts, TV movie of the week.

How to Contact Query with SASE.

◎ DENCH ARNOLD AGENCY

10 Newburgh St., London England W1F 7RN, United Kingdom. (44)(207)437-4551. Fax: (44)(207)439-1355. E-mail: contact@dencharnold.com. Web site: www.dencharnold.co.uk.

Member Agents Elizabeth Dench, Michelle Arnold, and Matthew Dench.

Represents Movie scripts, feature film, TV scripts.

How to Contact Query with SASE.

Recent Sales Other clients include Joe Ainsworth; Jan Bauer; Maurice Bessman; Karen Brown; Peter Chelsom & Adrian Dunbar; Greg Cruttwell; Eric Deacon; Matthew Faulk & Mark Skeet; Lucy Flannery;

Ellis Freeman; Ted Gannon; Robert Golden; Henrique Goldman; Steve Gough; Jeff Gross; Robert Hammond; Malcolm Kohll; Anna Kythreotis; Sarah Lambert; Paul Makin; Kevin Molony; Grant Morris; Matthew Newman; Omid Nooshin; Phil O'Shea; Dave Simpson; Roger Tucker; Alan Whiting; Kate Wood; Heather Dixon; Nick Stevens; Luke Watson; Anthony Alleyne; Peter Briggs; Jim Davies; Tiffany Freisberg; Mark Anthony Galluzzo; Liam Gavin; Jo Ho; Julian Kemp; Seth Linder; Dominic Macdonald; Steve McAteer; Bob McCabe & Rob Churchill; Abigail Abban-Mensah; Katie Newman; Junior Rhone.

MARILYN ATLAS MANAGEMENT

8899 Beverly Blvd., Suite 704, Los Angeles CA 90048. (310)278-5047.

Represents Movie scripts, feature film.

➤ Seeking writers with at least 4 scripts done. Does not want to receive sci-fi or horror.

How to Contact Query with SASE.

Recent Sales Movie of the week ''Bitteroot'' to Hallmark; ''Ivy League Posse'' pilot to ABC Family; ''Real Women Have Curves'' (HBO).

◎ AURA-PONT

Veslarsky ostrov 62, Podoli 147 00 Praha 4, Czech Republic. E-mail: aura-pont@aura-pont.cz. Web site: www.aura-pont.cz/en/. Estab. 1990.

Member Agents Petra Markova, head of the Theatre Department; Zuzana Jezkova, foreign rights; Anna Pychova, foreign rights; Jitka Sloupova, literary manager; Michal Kotrous, literary manager, distribution of texts and archive.

➤ The agency represents dramatists, writers, and translators.

◎ AURORA ARTISTS

19 Wroxeter Ave., Toronto ON M4K 1J5, Canada. (416)463-4634. Fax: (416)463-4889. E-mail: aurora. artists@sympatico.ca. **Contact:** Janine S. Cheeseman. Estab. 1990.

Member Agents Janine S. Cheeseman, principal agent; Tracy Essex-Simpson, associate agent.

Represents Movie scripts, TV scripts, stage plays.

How to Contact Query with SASE, submit synopsis, publishing history, author bio, up to 3 pages of a screenplay, SASE. Accepts e-mail queries. No fax queries.

AUTHOR LITERARY AGENTS

53 Talbot Rd., Highgate, London England N64QX, United Kingdom. (44)(208)341-0442. Fax: (44)(208)341-0442. E-mail: agile@authors.co.uk. **Contact:** John Havergal. Estab. 1997. **Considers these nonfiction areas:** Agriculture/horticulture; animals; anthropology/archaeology; art/architecture/design; biography/autobiography; business/economics; child guidance/parenting; computers/electronic; cooking/foods/nutrition; education; history; humor/satire; language/literature/criticism; music/dance; nature/environment; psychology; religious/inspirational; science/technology; sociology; true crime/investigative; Crafts & Hobbies, Film. **Considers these fiction areas:** Action/adventure; confession; detective/police/crime; experimental; family saga; fantasy; historical; juvenile (literary); literary; mainstream/contemporary; mystery/suspense; picture books; religious/inspirational; romance; science fiction; thriller; young adult. **Considers these script subject areas:** Action/adventure; biography/autobiography; cartoon/animation; contemporary issues; detective/police/crime; experimental; family saga.

How to Contact Query with SASE, outline, synopsis, 1st sample chapter(s), author bio. Accepts e-mail and fax queries.

DON BAKER ASSOCIATES

25 Eley Dr., Rottingdean, East Sussex England BN2 7FH, United Kingdom. **Contact:** Director: Donald Baker; Director: Katy Quayle. Estab. 1996.

Represents Movie scripts, TV scripts, stage plays.

How to Contact Send query letter with SAE.

◙ BASKOW AGENCY

2948 E. Russell Road, Las Vegas NV 89120. (702)733-7818. Fax: (702)733-2052. E-mail: jaki@baskow .com. Web site: www.baskow.com. **Contact:** Jaki Baskow. Estab. 1976. Represents 8 clients. 40% of clients are new/unpublished writers. Currently handles: 5% nonfiction books; 5% novels; 20% movie scripts; 70% TV scripts.

Member Agents Jaki Baskow (true life stories and comedies).

Represents Feature film, TV movie of the week, episodic drama, sitcom, documentary, miniseries, variety show. **Considers these script subject areas:** Action/adventure; biography/autobiography; comedy; contemporary issues; family saga; glitz; mystery/suspense; religious/inspirational; romantic comedy; romantic drama; science fiction (juvenile only); thriller.

> ⚬⟋ Actively seeking unique scripts, all-American true stories, kids' projects, and movies of the week. Looking for light, comedic and family-oriented work. Does not want to receive scripts with heavy violence or scripts that require animation.

How to Contact Query with SASE, submit outline, proposal, treatments. Accepts e-mail and fax queries. Responds in 1 month to queries; 60 days to mss. Obtains most new clients through recommendations from others.

Recent Sales Sold 3 movie/TV MOW scripts in the last year. *Dying to be Young*, by Eric Katlan (Nightengale Books); *Malpractice*, by Larry Leirketen (Blakely); *Angel of Death* (CBS). Other clients include Cheryl Anderson, Camisole Prods, Michael Store.

Terms Agent receives 10% commission on domestic sales; 10% commission on foreign sales. Offers written contract.

MARC BASS AGENCY, INC.

9255 Sunset Blvd., Suite 727, Los Angeles CA 90069, USA. (310)278-1900. Fax: (310)281-0900. E-mail: mlbass@mba-agency.com. Web site: www.mba-agency.com.

> ⚬⟋ This agency has affiliates all over the country and the world.

How to Contact Use a referral to break into this selective agency.

◙ BEACON ARTISTS AGENCY, INC.

120 E. 56th St., Suite 540, New York NY 10022. (212)736-6630. Fax: (212)868-1052. **Contact:** Patricia McLaughlin. Member of AAR. Represents 20-25 clients.

Represents Movie scripts, TV movie of the week, episodic drama, stage plays. **Considers these script subject areas:** Mainstream.

> ⚬⟋ "We are not seeking new clients at this time. We handle playwrights and screenwriters, as well as some TV and the occasional book. We are a small agency with very personal service."

Terms Agent receives 10% commission on domestic sales; 15-20% commission on foreign sales. Offers written contract, binding for 2-3 years (renewable). Client pays own legal fees and any extraordinary office costs.

BENDERSPINK

6735 Yucca Street, Hollywood CA 90028. E-mail: info@benderspink.com. Web site: www.benderspin k.com/. Estab. 1998.

Represents Feature film, TV scripts, TV movie of the week.

    ○┰ "Our company's focus is on 'breaking' new talent and constantly discovering, creating and developing unique and interesting material." Actively seeking writers with a distinct voice.

How to Contact Submit synopsis, query. Accepts e-mail queries. No fax queries.

Recent Sales *Just Friends* (2005).

◖ BICOASTAL TALENT

210 North Pass Ave., Suite 204, Burbank CA 91505. (818)845-0150. Fax: (818)845-0152. E-mail: literary@bicoastaltalent.com. Web site: www.bicoastaltalent.com/. Estab. 2001.

Member Agents Liz and Greta Hanley.

    ○┰ Writers of feature-length screenplays should submit queries only. The agency does not represent authors of self-published or unpublished manuscripts, treatments, concepts, or TV pilots.

How to Contact Query with SASE, submit synopsis, list of at least three completed screenplays including title and genre. All unsolicited mss returned unopened. One-paragraph synopses.

BLACKWOOD COMPANY

8306 Wilshire Boulevard, Suite 1724, Beverly Hills CA 90211. (310)295-0111. Fax: (310)295-0110. E-mail: horacio@blackwoodcompany.com, raquel@blackwoodcompany.com. Web site: www.black woodcompany.com/.

Represents Movie scripts, feature film.

How to Contact Query with SASE, submit logline with query letter. Accepts e-mail queries. No fax queries.

BETH BOHN MANAGEMENT, INC.

2658 Griffith Park Blvd., Suite 508, Los Angeles CA 90039. (323)664-2658. Signatory of WGA.

◖ THE BOHRMAN AGENCY

8899 Beverly Blvd., Suite 811, Los Angeles CA 90048. **Contact:** Michael Hruska, Caren Bohrman. Signatory of WGA.

Represents Novels, feature film, TV scripts. **Considers these script subject areas:** Action/adventure; biography/autobiography; cartoon/animation; comedy; contemporary issues; detective/police/crime; erotica; ethnic; experimental; family saga; fantasy; feminist; gay/lesbian; glitz; historical; horror; juvenile; mainstream; multicultural; multimedia; mystery/suspense; psychic/supernatural; regional; religious/inspirational; romantic comedy; romantic drama; science fiction; sports; teen; thriller; western/frontier.

How to Contact *Absolutely no unsolicited mss.* Query only by U.S. Mail with an accompanying self-addressed, stamped postcard. No phone calls. Obtains most new clients through recommendations from others.

Recent Sales This agency prefers not to share information on specific sales.

☾ ALAN BRODIE REPRESENTATION LTD.

Fairgate House, 78 New Oxford St., Sixth Floor, London England WC1A 1HB, United Kingdom. Web site: www.alanbrodie.com. Member of PMA. 10% of clients are new/unpublished writers.

Member Agents Alan Brodie; Sarah McNair; Lisa Foster.

Represents Theater, television, film, new media, radio.

　　⚷ Does not want to receive fiction, nonfiction or poetry.

How to Contact Does not accept unsolicited mss. North American writers accepted only in exceptional circumstances. Accepts e-mail and fax queries. Responds in 3 months to queries. Returns materials only with SASE. Obtains most new clients through recommendations from others.

Recent Sales See this agency's Web site for clients and sales.

Terms Charges clients for photocopying.

Tips "Biographical details can be helpful. Generally only playwrights whose work has been performed will be considered, provided they come recommended by an industry professional. Please be aware that all submissions are treated as strictly confidential. Be advised: From time to time, two writers will come up with very similar ideas; this is the nature of the business and is purely coincidence. In submitting your material to us you are relying on our professional integrity."

MARCUS BRYAN & ASSOCIATES INC. LITERARY AGENCY

1500 Skokie Blvd., Suite 310, Northbrook IL 60068. (847)412-9394. Fax: (847)412-9394. E-mail: mba3308@aol.com. Web site: marcusbryan.com/. Signatory of WGA.

　　⚷ "We are always happy to take query letters from screenwriters as well as Book Authors. We pride ourselves in trying our best to help new writers as well as those of you that have been writing for years. Everyone needs a little help now and then."

☾ DON BUCHWALD & ASSOCIATES, INC.

6500 Wilshire Blvd., 22nd Floor, Los Angeles CA 90048. (323)655-7400. Fax: (323)655-7470. Web site: www.donbuchwald.com. Estab. 1977. Signatory of WGA. Represents 50 clients.

Represents Movie scripts, feature film, TV scripts, TV movie of the week, episodic drama, sitcom, documentary, miniseries.

How to Contact See the Web site and secure a good referral before contacting this agency. Considers simultaneous queries. Obtains most new clients through recommendations from others.

☾ KELVIN C. BULGER AND ASSOCIATES

4540 W. Washington Blvd., Suite 101, Chicago IL 60624. (312)218-1943. E-mail: kcbwoi@aol.com. Web site: bulgerandassociates.biz/profile.html. **Contact:** Kelvin Bulger. Estab. 1992. Signatory of WGA. Represents 25 clients. 90% of clients are new/unpublished writers. Currently handles: 75% movie scripts; 25% TV scripts.

Represents Feature film, TV movie of the week, documentary, syndicated material. **Considers these script subject areas:** Action/adventure; cartoon/animation; comedy; contemporary issues; ethnic; family saga; religious/inspirational.

How to Contact Query with SASE, submit 1-page logline, 1-page plot synopsis (beginning/middle/end), first 10 pages of screenplay. Accepts e-mail and fax queries. Considers simultaneous queries. Responds in 3 weeks to queries; 2 months to mss. Returns materials only with SASE. Obtains most new clients through recommendations from others, solicitations.

Recent Sales *Severed Ties*, by David Johnson (Maverick Entertainment).

Terms Agent receives 10% commission on domestic sales; 10% commission on foreign sales. Offers written contract, binding for 6-12 months.

Tips "Proofread before submitting to an agent. We only reply to letters of inquiry if a SASE is enclosed."

CANTON SMITH AGENCY

E-mail: cantonsmithagency@cantonsmithagency.com. Web site: www.cantonsmithagency.com. **Contact:** Eric Smith, senior partner (esmith@cantonsmithagency.com); Chamein Canton, partner (chamein@cantonsmithagency.com); Netta Beckford, associate (nettab@cantonsmithagency.com). Estab. 2001. Represents 28 clients. 100% of clients are new/unpublished writers.

- Prior to becoming agents, Mr. Smith was in advertising and bookstore retail; Ms. Canton was a writer and a paralegal.

Member Agents Chamein Canton, managing partner, chamein@cantonsmithagency (women's fiction, chick-lit, business, how to, fashion, romance, erotica, African American, Latina, women's issues, health, relationships, decorating, cookbooks, lifestyle, literary novels, astrology, numerology, New Age) Eric Smith, senior partner, ericsmith@cantonsmithagency.com (science fiction, sports, literature); James Weil, reviewer, jamesw@cantonsmithagency.com.

Represents Nonfiction books, novels, juvenile books, scholarly books, textbooks, movie scripts. **Considers these nonfiction areas:** Art/architecture/design; business/economics; child guidance/parenting; cooking/foods/nutrition; education; ethnic/cultural interests; health/medicine; history; how-to; humor/satire; language/literature/criticism; memoirs; military/war; music/dance; photography; psychology; sports; translation; women's issues/studies. **Considers these fiction areas:** Fantasy; humor/satire; juvenile; multicultural; romance; young adult; Latina fiction; chick lit; African-American fiction; entertainment. **Considers these script subject areas:** Action/adventure; comedy; romantic comedy; romantic drama; science fiction.

"We specialize in helping new and established writers expand their marketing potential for prospective publishers. We are currently focusing on women's fiction (chick lit), Latina fiction, African American fiction, multicultural, romance, memoirs, humor and entertainment, in addition to more nonfiction titles (cooking, how to, fashion, home improvement, etc)."

How to Contact Only accepts e-queries. Send a query, not sample chapters and/or proposals, unless specifically requested. Considers simultaneous queries. Responds in 5 months to queries; 5 months to mss. Obtains most new clients through recommendations from others.

Recent Sales Sold 7 titles in the last year. Clients include Robert Koger, Olivia, Jennifer DeWit, Sheila Smestad, James Weil, Jaime Nava, JC Miller, Diana Smith, Robert Beers, Marcy Gannon, Keith Maxwell, Dawn Jackson, Jeannine Carney, Mark Barlow, Robert Marsocci, Anita Ballard Jones, Deb Mohr, Seth Ahonen, Melissa Graf, Robert Zavala, Cliff Webb, John and Carolyn Osborne.

Terms Agent receives 15% commission on domestic sales; 20% commission on foreign sales. Offers written contract; 2-month notice must be given to terminate contract.

Tips "Know your market. Agents, as well as publishers, are keenly interested in writers with their finger on the pulse of their market."

CAPEL & LAND LTD

29 Wardour St., London England W1D 6PS, United Kingdom. (44)(207)734-2414. Fax: (44)(207)734-8101. E-mail: georgina@capelland.co.uk. Web site: www.capelland.com. **Contact:** Director: Georgina Capel (ALiterary); Director: Anita Land (TV/Radio); Matilda Cooke (Corporate, Film & TV rights, TV/Radio); Phillipa Brewster, Abi Fellows, Rosie Apponyi (Literary). Estab. 2000.

Represents Nonfiction books, movie scripts, feature film, TV scripts. **Considers these nonfiction areas:** Biography/autobiography; history. **Considers these fiction areas:** Literary; General.

How to Contact Submit synopsis, 3 sample chapter(s), Query letter with SAE.

Recent Sales Other clients include Kohn Bew, Matthew Dennison, Julie Burchill, Andrew Greig, Eammon Holmes, Liz Jones, Dr. Tristram Hunt, Stella Rimington, Jeremy Paxman, Fay Weldon and Greg Woolf.

CASAROTTO RAMSAY & ASSOCIATES LIMITED

Waverley House, 7-12 Noel Street, London W1F 8GQ, United Kingdom. E-mail: info@casarotto.co.uk. Web site: www.casarotto.co.uk/. Estab. 1989. Currently handles.

Member Agents Jenne Casarotto, (Film and TV, Represents Writers and Directors); Tom Erhardt (Theatrical); Mel Kenyon (Theatrical); Ruth Arnaud (Amateurs and Stock Rights); Kirsty Coombs (Stage Directors).

Represents Movie scripts, feature film, TV scripts, TV movie of the week, theatrical stage play, stage plays, Radio Scripts.

How to Contact Query with SASE. Other clients include J.G. Ballard, Howard Brenton, Simon Callow, Caryl Churchill, David Hare, Nick Hornby, Bob Hoskins, Terry Jones, Dominic Minghella, Frank McGuinness, Ian Hislop, Nick Newman.

CATALYST AGENCY

12400 Wilshire Blvd., Los Angeles CA 90025. (818)597-8335. Fax: (818)597-1443. E-mail: catalyst@catalystagency.com. Web site: www.catalystagency.com/. **Contact:** Harvey E. Harrison. Estab. 1996.

Represents Movie scripts, feature film, TV scripts, animation, Video and New Media.

Tips "We do not accept or review query or literary material except by known referral."

◪ CEDAR GROVE AGENCY ENTERTAINMENT

P.O. Box 1692, Issaquah WA 98027-0068. (425)837-1687. Fax: (425)391-7907. E-mail: cedar groveagency@msn.com. **Contact:** Samantha Powers. Estab. 1995. Member of Cinema Seattle. Represents 7 clients. 100% of clients are new/unpublished writers. Currently handles: 90% movie scripts; 10% TV scripts.

● Prior to becoming an agent, Ms. Taylor worked for Morgan Stanley Dean Witter.

Member Agents Amy Taylor, senior vice president of motion picture division; Samantha Powers, executive vice president of motion picture division.

Represents Feature film, TV movie of the week, sitcom. **Considers these script subject areas:** Action/adventure; biography/autobiography; comedy; detective/police/crime; family saga; juvenile; mystery/suspense; romantic comedy; science fiction; sports; thriller; western/frontier.

o⊸ Cedar Grove Agency Entertainment was formed in the Pacific Northwest to take advantage of the rich and diverse culture, as well as the many writers who reside there. Does not want to receive period pieces, horror writing, children's scripts dealing with illness, or scripts dealing with excessive substance abuse.

How to Contact Submit 1-page synopsis via mail with SASE or via e-mail (no attachments). No phone calls, please. Responds in 10 days to queries; 2 months to mss. Obtains most new clients through referrals, Web site.

Recent Sales This agency prefers not to share information on specific sales.

Terms Agent receives 10% commission on domestic sales. Offers written contract, binding for 6-12 months; 30-day notice must be given to terminate contract.

Tips "We focus on finding that rare gem, the undiscovered, multi-talented writer, no matter where they live. Write, write, write! Find time every day to write. Network with other writers when possible, and write what you know. Learn the craft through books. Read scripts of your favorite movies. Enjoy what you write!"

☑ THE CHARACTERS TALENT AGENCY

8 Elm St., Toronto ON M5G 1G7 Canada. (416)964-8522. Fax: (416)964-6349. E-mail: clib5@aol.com. Web site: www.thecharacters.com. **Contact:** Carl Liberman. Estab. 1969; Signatory of WGC. Represents 1,000 clients (writers, actors, directors). 5% of clients are new/unpublished writers.

• Before becoming an agent, Mr. Liberman was an advertising executive, writer and actor.

Member Agents Brent Jordan Sherman (film/TV writers and directors); Geoff Brooks (animation, children's writers); Ben Silverman (writers).

Represents Movie scripts, feature film, TV scripts, TV movie of the week, episodic drama, sitcom, animation, documentary, miniseries, soap opera, syndicated material. **Considers these script subject areas:** Action/adventure; biography/autobiography; cartoon/animation; comedy; contemporary issues; detective/police/crime; erotica (no porn); ethnic; family saga; fantasy; feminist; gay/lesbian; glitz; historical; horror; juvenile; mainstream; mystery/suspense; psychic/supernatural; romantic comedy; romantic drama; science fiction; sports; teen; thriller; western/frontier.

o⊸ Actively seeking romantic comedy features, comedy features, family comedy features, and strong female leads in thrillers (MOW/features). Does not want to receive stage plays.

How to Contact Query with SASE. include a 1-page synopsis. Accepts e-mail and fax queries. Considers simultaneous queries. Responds in 2 days to queries if by e-mail; 60 days to ms if query is accepted. Obtains most new clients through recommendations from others.

Recent Sales *Ada*, by Ronalda Jones (Milagro Films); *13th Apostle*, by Paul Margolis (Stallion Films); *Drake Diamond: Exorcist for Hire*, by Arne Olsen (Montecito Pictures); *Grounded in Eire*, by Ralph Keefer (Amaze Film & TV).

Terms Agent receives 10% commission on domestic sales; 10% commission on foreign sales. No written contract.

Tips "To reach or get information about each individual agent, please call for an e-mail address. All agents are based in Toronto, except one in Vancouver."

☑ THE CHASIN AGENCY

8899 Beverly Blvd., #716, Los Angeles CA 90048. **Contact:** Scott.

Member Agents Tom Chasin (actors) while Scott Penney (writers).

☑ CIRCLE OF CONFUSION

Fax: (212)572-8304 or (212)975-7748. E-mail: queries@circleofconfusion.com. Web site: www.circleofconfusion.com. Estab. 1990.

Represents Movie scripts. **Considers these script subject areas:** Action/adventure; fantasy; horror; science fiction; thriller.

> ○┭ This agency specializes in comic books, video games and screenplays (science fiction, action, fantasy, thrillers, urban, horror).

How to Contact Submit query and brief synopsis via e-mail. Obtains most new clients through recommendations from others, writing contests, queries.

Recent Sales *Movie/TV MOW script(s) optioned/sold: The Matrix*, by Wachowski Brothers (Warner Brothers); *Reign of Fire*, by Chabot/Peterka (Dreamworks); *Mr. & Mrs. Smith*, by Simon Kinberg.

Terms Agent receives 10% commission on domestic sales; 10% commission on foreign sales. Offers written contract, binding for 1 year.

Tips "We look for writing that shows a unique voice, especially one which puts a fresh spin on commercial Hollywood genres."

◎ JONATHAN CLOWES, LTD

10 Iron Bridge Rd., Bridge Approach, London England NW1 8BD, United Kingdom. (44)(207)722-7674. Fax: (44)(207)722-7677. **Contact:** Jonathan Clowes. Estab. 1960.

Represents Nonfiction books. **Considers these fiction areas:** Literary. **Considers these script subject areas:** Comedy.

> ○┭ Does not want to receive textbooks or children's works.

How to Contact Submit Query letter & SAE.

◎ ELSPETH COCHRANE PERSONAL MANAGEMENT

16 Old Town, Clapham, London England SW4 0JY, United Kingdom. (44)(207)819-4297. Fax: (44)(207)819-4297. E-mail: elspeth@elspethcochrane.co.uk. **Contact:** Elspeth Cochrane. Estab. 1960.

Represents Nonfiction books, movie scripts, TV scripts, Radio Scripts. **Considers these nonfiction areas:** Biography/autobiography.

> ○┭ Does not want to receive self-help, memoirs, poetry or children's fiction.

How to Contact Submit synopsis, Query letter with SAE.

Recent Sales Other clients include Alex Jones, Dominic Leyton, Royce Ryton, F.E. Smith and Robert Tannitch.

ROSICA COLIN, LTD.

1 Clareville Grove Mews, London England SW7 5AH, United Kingdom. (44)(207)370-1080. Fax: (44)(207)244-6441. **Contact:** Director Joanna Marston. Estab. 1949.

Represents Movie scripts, TV scripts, stage plays, Radio Scripts.

How to Contact Submit synopsis, query letter with SAE.

COLLECTIVE, THE

9100 Wilshire Blvd., 700W, Beverly Hills CA 90212. (310)288-8181. Fax: (310)888-1555. Web site: www.thecollective-la.com/.

Member Agents Jeff Golenberg; Michael Green; Sam Maydew; Aaron Ray.

Represents Movie scripts, feature film, TV scripts. Other clients include the entire RKO studio and Steve Jackson Games.

CORALIE JR. THEATRICAL AGENCY

907 S. Victory Blvd., Burbank CA 91502. (818)842-5513. Signatory of WGA.
Represents Theatrical stage play, stage plays.
How to Contact Query with SASE.

☑ THE CORE GROUP TALENT AGENCY, INC.

89 Bloor St. W., Suite 300, Toronto ON M5S 1M1 Canada. (416)955-0819. Fax: (416)955-0825. E-mail: literary@coregroupta.com; info@coregroupta.com. Web site: www.coregroupta.com. **Contact:** Charles Northcote, literary agent/co-owner. Estab. 1989. Member of WGC. Represents 60 clients. 10% of clients are new/unpublished writers. Currently handles: 25% movie scripts; 25% TV scripts; 50% stage plays.

Represents Movie scripts, feature film, TV scripts, TV movie of the week, episodic drama, sitcom, animation, documentary, miniseries, soap opera, stage plays. **Considers these script subject areas:** Action/adventure; biography/autobiography; cartoon/animation; comedy; contemporary issues; detective/police/crime; erotica; ethnic; experimental; family saga; fantasy; feminist; gay/lesbian; glitz; historical; horror; juvenile; mainstream; multicultural; mystery/suspense; psychic/supernatural; regional; romantic comedy; romantic drama; sports; teen; thriller; western/frontier.

   O⊸ Seeks previously-produced writers with Canadian status. Does not want queries from international writers without Canadian status.

How to Contact Query with SASE. Responds in 1 week to queries. Returns materials only with SASE.
Terms Agent receives 10% commission on domestic sales. Offers written contract, binding for 1 year; 60-day notice must be given to terminate contract.

☑ CREATIVE ARTISTS AGENCY

CAA, 2000 Avenue of the Stars, Los Angeles CA 90067. (424)288-2000. Fax: (424)288-2900. Web site: www.caa.com/. Other offices in New York, Nashville, London, Beijing, St. Louis, Calgary, Stockholm.

☑ CREATIVE CONVERGENCE, INC.

E-mail: query@creative-convergence.com. Web site: www.creativecvg.com/. Estab. 2004.
Member Agents Philippa Burgess and Bradley D. Kushner.
Represents Movie scripts, feature film, TV scripts.

   O⊸ "Creative Convergence Inc. is a multi-faceted entertainment company based in Los Angeles encompassing Literary Management, Film & TV Production, and Entertainment Consulting."

How to Contact Your query should include a logline and all needed contact info.
Writers' Conferences San Francisco Writers' Conference; Santa Barbara Writers' Conference, Screenwriting Expo; Jack London Writers Conference.
Tips "Creative Convergence is always seeking dynamic new writers who have the skills, imagination and talent to succeed and thrive in the Entertainment Industry. Please be aware that as we receive hundreds of new requests each month from writers seeking representation, we typically only respond to the handful of queries that we are serious about considering."

◎ CREATIVE MEDIA MANAGEMENT

Ealing Studios, Ealing Green, 3b Walpole Court, London England W5 5EP, United Kingdom. (44)(208)584-5363. Fax: (44)(208)566-5554. E-mail: enquiries@creativemediamanagement.com. Web site: www.creativemediamanagement.com/. **Contact:** Paul Usher. Estab. 1999.

- "With a scriptwriter for a father and an agent and film producer for a mother, perhaps it was inevitable that Jacqui would end up in the 'business.' She produced many award-winning commercials and had her own music library company prior to becoming an agent in 1992 when she joined KCPM. She was joint-managing director when she left to start Creative Media Management."

Member Agents Writers' submissions should be made to Paul Usher.

Represents Movie scripts, feature film, TV scripts, episodic drama, sitcom, Radio.

How to Contact Query with SASE.

◎ CREATIVE REPRESENTATION

274 Brunswick St., 2nd Floor, Fitzroy VIC 3065, Australia. E-mail: agents@creativerep.com.au. Web site: www.creativerep.com.au. P.O. Box 108 Estab. 2004.

Member Agents Jacinta Waters; Helen Townshend; Katherine Dodd.

Represents Movie scripts, TV scripts, stage plays.

How to Contact Query with SASE. Other clients include Tim Robertson; Adam Richard; Paul McCarthy; Alan Hopgood; Ryan Shelton; Richard Marsland; Lech Mackiewicz; Edward White.

◎ CAMERON CRESWELL

61 Marlborough St., Surry Hills NSW 2010, Australia. E-mail: info@cameronsmanagement.com.au. Web site: www.cameronsmanagement.com.au/. Estab. 1976.

Member Agents Jane Cameron; Sadie Chrestman; Sue Muggleton; Anthony Blair; Sophie Hamley; Siobhan Hannan.

Represents Nonfiction books, movie scripts, feature film, TV scripts, stage plays. **Considers these nonfiction areas:** Health/medicine; history; memoirs; psychology; sex; sociology; spirituality; sports; travel.

- ⚷ "We are not currently accepting submissions of fiction and children's manuscripts. Any unsolicited submissions received before the next round will not be read or replied to. It is likely that submissions for these manuscripts will reopen in September or October 2008."

How to Contact E-mail submissions only. Accepts e-mail queries. No fax queries. Responds in 1 year to mss.

Recent Sales Other clients include Craig Pearce; Don Watson; David Williamson; Bob Ellis; John Alsop; Pip Karmel.

CRITERION GROUP, INC.

4842 Sylmar Avenue, Sherman Oaks CA 91423. (818)995-1485. E-mail: info@criterion-group.com. Web site: www.criterion-group.com/. **Contact:** Susan Wright; Julie Fitzgerald. Estab. 2002. Signatory of WGA.

Represents Movie scripts, feature film, theatrical stage play, stage plays.

How to Contact Query with SASE. All unsolicited mss returned unopened.

Recent Sales Other clients include Charles Daniels; Proctor/Hirsch; Mark Reese; Dave Richards.

JUDY DAISH ASSOCIATES, LTD

2 St. Charles Place, London England W10 6EG, United Kingdom. (44)(208)964-8811. Fax: (44)(208)964-8966. **Contact:** Judy Daish; Howard Gooding; Tracey Elliston. Estab. 1978. **Represents** Movie scripts, TV scripts.

0→ Books will not be considered.

How to Contact Submit Query letter.

DEITER LITERARY AGENCY

6207 Fushsimi Court, Burke VA 22015-3451. **Contact:** Mary A. Deiter. Estab. 1995. Signatory of WGA. Represents 12 clients.

Member Agents Mary A. Deiter (general fiction, general nonfiction, general interest screenplays).

Represents Nonfiction books, novels, movie scripts.

0→ This is a small agency with a set list of clients. While the agency will consider new work, Ms. Deiter is very selective.

How to Contact Query with SASE, submit synopsis, publishing history, author bio. No e-mail or fax queries. Returns materials only with SASE. Offers written contract.

Tips "We usually don't take on TV writers because it's a hard sell, but if the work is good, we will consider it."

THE DENCH ARNOLD AGENCY

10 Newburgh St., London England W1F 7RN, United Kingdom. (44)(207)437-4551. Fax: (44)(207)439-1355. E-mail: contact@dencharnold.co.uk. Web site: www.dencharnold.co.uk. **Contact:** Elizabeth Dench, Michelle Arnold, Matthew Dench, Fiona Grant, Louise Jordan. Estab. 1972.

Represents Nonfiction books, movie scripts, TV scripts. **Considers these fiction areas:** General.

How to Contact Query with SASE, submit author bio, Sample of work for scripts. SAE. Other clients include Karen Brown, Lucy Flannery, Jeff Gross, Michael Hines, Phil O'Shea and Julian Kemp.

DIVERSE TALENT GROUP

1925 Century Park East, Suite 880, Los Angeles CA 90067. (310)201-6565. Fax: (310)201-6572. Web site: www.diversetalentgroup.com/.

0→ This selective agency specializes in talent and literary representation. Query with a referral.

DRAMATIC PUBLISHING

311 Washington St., Woodstock IL 60098. (815)338-7170. Fax: (815)338-8981. E-mail: plays@dramat icpublishing.com. Web site: www.dramaticpublishing.com. **Contact:** Linda Habjan. Estab. 1885. Currently handles: 2% textbooks; 98% stage plays.

Represents Stage plays.

0→ This agency specializes in a full range of stage plays, musicals, adaptations and instructional books about theater.

How to Contact Query with SASE, submit complete ms, SASE. Reports in 10-12 weeks to mss.

Recent Sales This agency prefers not to share information on specific sales.

DRAMATISTS PLAY SERVICE, INC.

440 Park Avenue South, New York New York 10016. (212)683-8960. Fax: (212)213-1539. E-mail: postmaster@dramatists.com. Web site: www.dramatists.com. Estab. 1936.

Member Agents Stephen Sultan, President (sultan@dramatists.com); Elisa Nikoloulias, Assistant (nikoloulias@dramatists.com); Stephen Sultan (sultan@dramatists.com); Tamra Feifer, Director of Operations (feifer@dramatists.com).

Represents Stage plays.

How to Contact Query with SASE.

Tips Other clients represented include *August: Osage County* by Tracy Letts; *Rabbit Hole* by David Lindsay-Abaire; *Doubt, A Parable* by John Patrick Shanley; *I Am My Own Wife* by Doug Wright.

BRYAN DREW, LTD

Quadrant House, 80-82 Regent St., London England W1B 5AU, United Kingdom. (44)(207)437-2293. Fax: (44)(207)437-0561. E-mail: bryan@bryandrewltd.com. **Contact:** Literary Manager: Bryan Drew. Estab. 1962.

Represents Nonfiction books, movie scripts, feature film, TV scripts. **Considers these nonfiction areas:** Biography/autobiography.

How to Contact Query with SASE, submit synopsis, 2-3 sample chapter(s), Query letter with SAE/IRC.

☑ THE E S AGENCY

6612 Pacheco Way, Citrus Heights CA 95610. (916)723-2794. Fax: (916)723-2796. E-mail: edley07@cs.com. **Contact:** Ed Silver, president. Estab. 1995. Signatory of WGA. Represents 50-75 clients. 70% of clients are new/unpublished writers. Currently handles: 50% nonfiction books; 25% novels; 25% movie scripts.

  • Prior to becoming an agent, Mr. Silver was an entertainment business manager.

Represents Nonfiction books, novels, movie scripts, feature film, TV movie of the week. **Considers these nonfiction areas:** General nonfiction. **Considers these fiction areas:** Action/adventure; detective/police/crime; erotica; experimental; historical; humor/satire; literary; mainstream/contemporary; mystery/suspense; thriller; young adult. **Considers these script subject areas:** Action/adventure; comedy; contemporary issues; detective/police/crime; erotica; ethnic; experimental; family saga; mainstream; mystery/suspense; romantic comedy; romantic drama; sports; thriller.

  ⊶ This agency specializes in theatrical screenplays, MOW, and miniseries. Actively seeking anything unique and original. Does not want to receive horror, sci-fi, mob, or Vietnam stories.

How to Contact Query with SASE. Send a one-page pitch. If the pitch is liked, they will ask for a beat sheet and then coverage before requesting the full script. Considers simultaneous queries. Returns materials only with SASE. Obtains most new clients through recommendations from others, queries from WGA agency list.

Terms Agent receives 15% commission on domestic sales; 20% commission on foreign sales; 10% commission on dramatic rights sales. Offers written contract; 30-day notice must be given to terminate contract.

ENCORE ARTISTS MANAGEMENT

3815 West Olive Ave., Suite 101, Burbank CA 91505. (818)955-8821. E-mail: literary@encorela.com. Web site: www.encorela.com. **Contact:** Lin Bickelmann. Estab. 1996.

● Lin Bickelmann holds a bachelor's degree in sociology from Oakland University in Rochester, Mich. His business and technology experiences include SPSS, tax preparation, financial planning, building computers, and developing Web sites. After successfully guiding his daughter's career, he was encouraged to become an agent.

How to Contact Query with SASE, submit outline, synopsis, all coverage reports. All unsolicited mss returned unopened. Only send materials that are registered with the WGA's Intellectual Property Registry or The Library of Congress, U.S. Copyright Office.

THE ENDEAVOR AGENCY

9601 Wilshire Blvd., 3rd Floor, Beverly Hills CA 90210. (310)248-2000. **Contact:** Tom Strickler; Ari Emanuel; Rick Rosen. Estab. 1995. Signatory of WGA.

Represents Movie scripts, feature film, TV scripts, video games.

How to Contact All unsolicited mss returned unopened. Query with a referral.

Recent Sales Other clients include Aaron Sorkin ("The West Wing"); Tina Fey ("30 Rock").

ENERGY ENTERTAINMENT

999 N. Doheny Dr., #711, Los Angeles CA 90069. (310)274-3440. Fax: info@energyentertainment.net. Web site: www.energyentertainment.net/. Estab. 2001.

● Prior to their current positions, Brooklyn Weaver worked at Endeavor, Adam Marshall worked for Brillstein-Grey Entertainment, and Jake Wagner was in series production at MTV.

○⇥ Energy has two divisions: a management division comprised of writers and actors—and a production division. This agency specializes in discovering new edgy screenwriters.

How to Contact All unsolicited mss returned unopened. Query only!

Recent Sales *The Low Dweller*, by Brad Ingelsby.

⊘ EVATOPIA, INC.

8447 Wilshire Blvd., Ste. 401, Beverly Hills CA 90211. E-mail: submissions@evatopia.com. Web site: www.evatopia.com. **Contact:** Margery Walshaw. Estab. 2004. Represents 15 clients. 85% of clients are new/unpublished writers. Currently handles: 100% movie scripts.

● Prior to becoming an agent, Ms. Walshaw was a writer and publicist for the entertainment industry.

Member Agents Mary Kay (story development); Stacy Glenn (story development); Jamie Davis (story assistant); Jill Jones (story editor).

Represents Movie scripts. **Considers these script subject areas:** Action/adventure; biography/autobiography; cartoon/animation; comedy; contemporary issues; detective/police/crime; ethnic; family saga; fantasy; historical; horror; juvenile; mainstream; mystery/suspense; psychic/supernatural; romantic comedy; romantic drama; science fiction; sports; teen; thriller.

○⇥ "We specialize in promoting and developing the careers of first-time screenwriters. All of our staff members have strong writing and entertainment backgrounds, making us sympathetic to the needs of our clients." Actively seeking dedicated and hard-working writers.

How to Contact Submit via online submission form. Considers simultaneous queries. Responds in 2 weeks to queries; 3 weeks to mss. Returns materials only with SASE. Obtains most new clients through recommendations from others, solicitations.

Terms Agent receives 15% commission on domestic sales; 15% commission on foreign sales. Offers written contract, binding for up to 2 years; 30-day notice must be given to terminate contract.

Tips "Remember that you only have one chance to make that important first impression. Make your loglines original and your synopses concise. The secret to a screenwriter's success is creating an original story and telling it in a manner that we haven't heard before."

JANET FILLINGHAM ASSOCIATES

52 Lowther Rd., London England SW13 9NU, United Kingdom. (44)(208)748-5594. Fax: (44)(208)748-7374. E-mail: info@janetfillingham.com. Web site: www.janetfillingham.com. **Contact:** Director: Janet Fillingham. Estab. 1992.

Represents Feature film, TV scripts, stage plays.

How to Contact Query with SASE.

Recent Sales Other clients include Esther May Campbell, Clive Endersby, Nick Gleaves, Christopher Green, Steve Griffiths, Charles McKeown, Dale Overton, Tina Pepler, Allan Plenderleith, Robert Rigby, Robert Rohrer & Frances Tomelty.

FILM RIGHTS, LTD

Mezzanine, Quadrant House, 80-82 Regent St., London England W1B 5AU, United Kingdom. (44)(207)734-9911. Fax: (44)(207)734-0044. E-mail: information@filmrights.ltd.uk. Web site: www. filmrights.ltd.uk. **Contact:** Director: Brendan Davis; Director: Joan Potts. Estab. 1932.

⚬➤ Considers scripts for Adults and Children.

How to Contact Query with SASE.

⊘ FILMWRITERS LITERARY AGENCY

4932 Long Shadow Drive, Midlothian VA 23112. (804)744-1718. **Contact:** Helene Wagner. Signatory of WGA.

● Prior to opening her agency, Ms. Wagner was director of the Virginia Screenwriters' Forum for 7 years and taught college-level screenwriting classes. "As a writer myself, I have won or been a finalist in most major screenwriting competitions throughout the country and have a number of my screenplays optioned. Through the years, I have enjoyed helping and working with other writers. Some have gone on to have their movies made, their work optioned, and won national contests."

Represents Feature film, TV movie of the week, miniseries. **Considers these script subject areas:** Action/adventure; comedy; contemporary issues; detective/police/crime; historical; juvenile; mystery/suspense; psychic/supernatural; romantic comedy; romantic drama; teen; thriller.

⚬➤ This agency does not accept unsolicited queries and is currently not accepting new clients.

How to Contact No e-mail or fax queries. Obtains most new clients through recommendations from others.

Recent Sales *Woman of His Dreams*, by Jeff Rubin (Ellenfreyer Productions).

Terms Agent receives 10% commission on domestic sales; 10% commission on foreign sales. Offers written contract. Charges clients for photocopying and postage. Writers are reimbursed for office fees after the sale of the ms.

Tips "Professional writers should wait until they have at least 4 drafts done before they send out their work. Show me something I haven't seen before with characters that I care about and that jump off the page. I not only look at a writer's work, I look at the writer's talent. If I believe in a writer, even though a piece may not sell, I'll stay with the writer and help nurture that talent, which a lot of the big agencies won't do."

LAURENCE FITCH, LTD.

Mezzanine, Quadrant House, 80-82 Regent St., London England W1B 5AU, United Kingdom. (44)(207)734-9911. Fax: (44)(207)734-0044. E-mail: information@laurencefitch.com. Web site: www.laurencefitch.com. **Contact:** Brendan Davis, director. Estab. 1952. **Considers these script subject areas:** Juvenile; mainstream.

How to Contact Submit proposal package, synopsis, query letter with SAE, sample chapters & 3 sample scenes/screens.

Recent Sales Other clients include Dave Freeman, Ray Cooney, Walter Greenwood, Ronald Gow, Edward Taylor, John Graham.

JILL FOSTER, LTD

9 Barb Mews, Brook Green, London England W6 7PA, United Kingdom. (44)(207)602-1263. Fax: (44)(207)602-9336. E-mail: agents@jfagency.com. **Contact:** Jill Foster, Alison Finch, Simon Williamson, Dominic Lord, Gary Wild. Estab. 1976.

Represents Movie scripts, TV scripts.

○► No books, poetry or short stories considered.

How to Contact Include query letter with submission.

FOURSIGHT ENTERTAINMENT

8840 Wilshire Blvd., 2nd Floor, Beverly Hills CA 90211. (310)358-3150. E-mail: info@foursight.com. Web site: www.foursight.com/. Estab. 1999.

Member Agents Jeremy Bell; George Heller; Michael Lasker; Brent Lilley.

○► "Foursight Entertainment is a management/production company comprised of writers, directors, and actors with a concentration on young professionals and new voices. Based in Los Angeles, Foursight represents filmmakers, properties, and talent in motion pictures and television."

How to Contact Submit queries by e-mail.

☑ ROBERT A. FREEDMAN DRAMATIC AGENCY, INC.

1501 Broadway, Suite 2310, New York NY 10036. (212)840-5760. Fax: (212)840-5776. **Contact:** Robert A. Freedman. Estab. 1928. Member of AAR; signatory of WGA.

● Mr. Freedman has served as vice president of the dramatic division of AAR.

Member Agents Robert A. Freedman, president; Selma Luttinger, senior vice president; Robin Kaver, vice president (movie/TV scripts); Marta Praeger, agent (stage plays).

Represents Movie scripts, TV scripts, stage plays.

○► This agency works with both new and established authors who write plays and movie and TV scripts.

How to Contact Query with SASE. All unsolicited mss returned unopened. Responds in 2 weeks to queries; 3 months to mss.

Recent Sales "We will speak directly with any prospective client concerning sales that are relevant to his/her specific script."

Terms Agent receives 10% commission on domestic sales. Charges clients for photocopying.

☙ SAMUEL FRENCH, INC.

45 W. 25th St., New York NY 10010-2751. (212)206-8990. Fax: (212)206-1429. E-mail: info@samuel french.com. Web site: samuelfrench.com. **Contact:** Lawrence Harbison, senior editor. Estab. 1830. Member of AAR.

Member Agents Leon Embry.

Represents Theatrical stage play, musicals. **Considers these script subject areas:** Comedy; contemporary issues; detective/police/crime; ethnic; fantasy; horror; mystery/suspense; thriller.

   O⊸ This agency specializes in publishing plays which it also licenses for production.

How to Contact Query with SASE, or submit complete ms to Lawrence Harbison. Accepts e-mail and fax queries. Considers simultaneous queries. Responds in 2-8 months to mss. Responds immediately to queries.

Recent Sales This agency prefers not to share information on specific sales.

Terms Agent receives variable commission on domestic sales.

⬛ FUTERMAN, ROSE & ASSOCIATES LITERARY AGENTS

FRA, 91 St. Leonards Road, London SW14 7BL, United Kingdom. (44)(208)255-7755. Fax: (44)(208)286-4860. E-mail: enquiries@futermanrose.co.uk. Web site: www.futermanrose.co.uk. Estab. 1984. Member of The Authors' Agents Association. Currently handles: nonfiction books; novels; movie scripts; TV scripts.

Member Agents Guy Rose, senior agent.

   O⊸ Does not want to receive poetry, science-fiction, children's books, or educational textbooks

How to Contact Submit synopsis, first two sample chapter(s), SASE. No e-mail or fax queries.

⬛ THE GAGE GROUP

14724 Ventura Blvd., Suite 505, Sherman Oaks CA 91403. (818)905-3800. Fax: (818)905-3322. Estab. 1976. Member of DGA; signatory of WGA.

Member Agents Jonathan Westover (feature, television); Joshua Orenstein (TV).

Represents Movie scripts, feature film, TV scripts, theatrical stage play.

   O⊸ Considers all script subject areas.

How to Contact Snail mail queries preferred. Accepts e-mail queries. No fax queries. Considers simultaneous queries. Responds in 1 month to queries; 1 month to mss.

Recent Sales This agency prefers not to share information on specific sales.

Terms Agent receives 10% commission on domestic sales; 10% commission on foreign sales. This agency charges clients for photocopying.

◎ NOEL GAY

19, Denmark St., London England WC2H 8NA, United Kingdom. (44)(207)836-3941. E-mail: info@ noelgay.com. Web site: www.noelgay.com. Estab. 1938.

Member Agents Alex Armitage, CEO; Nick Ranceford-Hadley, Managing Director; Jane Compton, Assistant Agent; Jessica Williamson, Assistant Agent; Claire King, Agent.

O→ Noel Gay has a long established reputation as a leading theatrical management company in the West End. It managed the hugely successful *Me And My Girl* at the Adelphi Theatre and supervised more than a dozen other productions of the show around the world.

How to Contact Query with SASE.

ERIC GLASS, LTD

25 Ladbroke Crescent, London England W11 1PS, United Kingdom. (44)(207)229-9500. Fax: (44)(207)229-6220. E-mail: eglassltd@aol.com. **Contact:** Janet Glass. Estab. 1932.

Represents Nonfiction books, movie scripts, TV scripts, Radio Scripts.

O→ Does not want to receive short stories, poetry, or children's titles.

How to Contact Query letter with SAE. Send the entire ms, if requested.

Recent Sales Other clients include Herbert Appleman, Henry Fleet and Alan Melville.

GLICK AGENCY, LLC

1250 Sixth Street, Suite 100, Santa Monica CA 90401. (310)593-6500. Web site: www.glickagency. com/. **Contact:** Steve Glick. Estab. 2006. Signatory of WGA.

● Prior to his current position, Steve Glick worked at ICM.

Represents Movie scripts, feature film, TV scripts.

▣ GRAHAM AGENCY

311 W. 43rd St., New York NY 10036. E-mail: grahamacynyc@aol.com. **Contact:** Earl Graham. Estab. 1971. Represents 40 clients. 30% of clients are new/unpublished writers.

Represents Theatrical stage play, musicals.

O→ This agency specializes in playwrights. "We're interested in commercial material of quality." Does not want to receive one-acts or material for children.

How to Contact Query with SASE. No e-mail or fax queries. Responds in 3 months to queries; 6 weeks to mss. Obtains most new clients through recommendations from others, solicitations.

Recent Sales This agency prefers not to share information on specific sales.

Terms Agent receives 10% commission on dramatic rights sales.

Tips "Write a concise, intelligent letter giving the gist of what you are offering."

LARRY GROSSMAN & ASSOCIATES

2129 Ridge Drive, Los Angeles CA 90049. (310)550-8127. Signatory of WGA.

◎ GRUENBERG FILM

Blankenburger Chaussee 84, Berlin D-13125, Germany. E-mail: info@gruenbergfilm.de. Web site: www.gruenbergfilm.com/.

Represents Movie scripts, feature film. **Considers these script subject areas:** Action/adventure; horror; mystery/suspense; romantic comedy; thriller.

O→ While concentrating on producing films, the agency manages a few writers and has sold scripts to production companies. Actively seeking script and project synopses

How to Contact Query with SASE. Send loglines and synopses first.

Recent Sales Sold 2 scripts in the last year. *Movie/TV MOW script(s) optioned/sold:* In 2006 the agency sold *A Girl Named Freedom*, written by Ed Dawson, to an Irish production company. It also handled the negotiations for the option to *Castle Stalker*, which was renewed in December 2007.

◖ THE SUSAN GURMAN AGENCY, LLC

865 West End Ave., # 15A, New York NY 10025. (212)749-4618. Fax: (212)864-5055. E-mail: susan@gurmanagency.com. Web site: www.gurmanagency.com. Estab. 1993. Signatory of WGA.
Represents Playwrights, directors, composers, lyricists.
How to Contact Obtains new clients by referral only. No e-mail or fax queries.

THE ROD HALL AGENCY

6th Floor, Fairgate House, 78 New Oxford St., London England WC1A 1HB, United Kingdom. (44)(207)079-7987. Fax: (44)(845)638-4094. E-mail: office@rodhallagency.com. Web site: www.rodhallagency.com. **Contact:** Company Director: Charlotte Mann; Tanya Tillet (Submissions, Amateur & Play Leasings, Foreign Rights, General Inquiries); Emily Hayward (Film, TV & Theatre). Estab. 1997.
• Charlotte Mann has worked extensively in theatre, while Tanya Tillet's experience lies in film & TV development & production. Emily Hayward studied drama before working as an agent at both PFD and Sheil Land Associates.
Represents Most categories of scripts & screenplays.
○┅ No writing partnerships or soap writers considered.
How to Contact Submit outline, author bio, CV. Send query with SAE.
Recent Sales Other clients include Hassan Abdulrazzak; Lydia Adetunji; Yousaf Ali Khan; Samina Baig; Simon Beaufoy; Simon Bennett; Alecky Blythe; Oliver Bosman; Harriet Braun; Jeremy Brock; Sean Buckley; Jane Carter Woodrow; Suzette Coon; Nick Cohen; Marco Crivellari; Loughlin Deegan; David Dipper; Clare Duffy; Matthew Dunster; Janet Eisenstein; Ben Ellis; Jane Elson; Susan Everett; Tom Farrelly; Robert Farquhar; Brian Fillis; Josh Freedman Berthoud; Simon Judd; Tom Fry; Patrick Gale; Bettina Gracias; Helen Greaves; David Hale; Simon Harris; Dan Hine; Chris Sussman; The Estate of Arthur Hopcraft; Anto Howard; David Hunt; John Jackson; Curtis Jobling; Gareth Lewis; Bernard Kops; Michael Kustow; John Langridge; Dominic Leyton; Catherine Linstrum; Terry Loane; Liz Lochhead; Tara Maria Lovett; Jacqueline McCarrick; Martin McDonagh and more.

ROGER HANCOCK, LTD

4 Water Lane, London England NW1 8NZ, United Kingdom. (44)(207)267-4418. Fax: (44)(207)267-0705. E-mail: info@rogerhancock.com. Web site: www.rogerhancock.com. **Considers these script subject areas:** Comedy; drama & light entertainment scripts.

◎ RICHARD HATTON, LTD

29 Roehampton Gate, London England SW15 5JR, United Kingdom. (44)(208)876-6699. **Contact:** Richard Hatton.
Represents Movie scripts, TV scripts, Radio Scripts.
How to Contact Send query letter with SAE.

DAVID HIGHAM ASSOCIATES LTD

5-8 Lower John St., Golden Square, London England W1F 9HA, United Kingdom. (44)(207)434-5900. Fax: (44)(207)437-1072. E-mail: dha@davidhigham.co.uk. Web site: www.davidhigham.co.uk. **Con-**

tact: Anthony Goff, Alice Williams, Bruce Hunter, Lizzy Kremer, Veronique Baxter (Fiction, Nonfiction, Children); Caroline Walsh (Fiction, Children, Illustrators); Georgia Glover, Jacqueline Korn (Fiction, Nonfiction); Gemma Hirst, Georgia Ruffhead, Jessica Cooper, Nicky Lund (Script Writing & Drama); Ania Corless (Translation). Estab. 1935.

Represents Nonfiction books, movie scripts, feature film, TV scripts. **Considers these fiction areas:** Juvenile; Adult.

O→ Actively seeking good commercial and literary fiction, and general nonfiction.

How to Contact Submit outline, synopsis, 3 sample chapter(s), author bio. Send query letter with SAE.

Recent Sales Other clients include Chinua Achebe, J.M. Coetzee, Roald Dahl, Anne Fine, F. Scott Fitzgerald, James Herbert, John le Carré, Penelope Lively, Mervyn Peake, Alice Sebold, Gertrude Stein and Alice Walker.

◎ HOFRA THEATRICAL AND LITERARY AGENCY

Budapest H-1061, Hungary. E-mail: info@hofra.hu. Web site: www.hofra.hu. **Contact:** Judit Zádori (judit@hofra.hu); Virág Katalin Balogh (virag@hofra.hu); Hajnalka Ihárosi (hajnalka@hofra.hu); Ági Obinger (agi@hofra.hu).

O→ The agency represents Hungarian writers with several years of experience.

How to Contact Make an appointment or stop in the office. Do not send queries if you live outside the country.

◖ ◎ HOHMAN MAYBANK LIEB

9229 Sunset Blvd., Suite 700, Los Angeles CA 90069. (310)274-4600. Fax: (310)274-4741. E-mail: info@hmllit.com. Web site: www.hmllit.com/.

Member Agents Bob Hohman; Bayard Maybank; Devra Lieb; Trish Connery; Andy Tunnicliffe.

Represents Movie scripts, feature film, TV scripts.

O→ This agency specializes in representing screenwriters.

How to Contact Send queries only with a strong referral.

Tips Query with a referral.

HOLLYWOOD VIEW

5255 Veronica Street, Los Angeles CA 90008. **Contact:** David Freedman. Signatory of WGA. **Considers these fiction areas:** Thriller (low budget).

O→ This agency is not interested in representing writers who live outside of LA.

How to Contact Query when you have multiple scripts written and polished.

Terms Agent receives 10% commission on domestic sales; 10% commission on foreign sales.

VALERIES HOSKINS ASSOCIATES LTD

20 Charlotte St., London England W1T 2NA, United Kingdom. (44)(207)637-4490. Fax: (44)(207)637-4493. E-mail: vha@vhassociates.co.uk. **Contact:** Valerie Hoskins, Rebecca Watson. Estab. 1983.

Represents Nonfiction books, movie scripts, TV scripts, animation, Radio Scripts.

How to Contact Query with SAE.

☑ AMANDA HOWARD ASSOCIATES LTD.

AHA, 21 Berwick Street, London W1F 0PZ, United Kingdom. (44)(207)287-9277. Fax: (44)(207)287-7785. E-mail: mail@amandahowardassociates.co.uk. Web site: www.amandahowardassociates.co.uk.

Member Agents Amanda Fitzalan Howard; Kate Haldane; Mark Price; Kirsten Wright; Darren Rugg; Chloe Brayfield.

> ⚬ₓ Popular non-fiction, humour, manuals, and memoir. The agency will not take on a new client who resides outside the UK and Ireland. It does not represent poetry.

How to Contact Submit outline, synopsis, author bio, SASE. Do not send full manuscript. No e-mail or fax queries. Other clients include Niall Ashdown; Julie Balloo; Michael Begley; Simon Blackwell; Andrew Collins; Trevor Dann; Susie Donkin; Rufus Jones; Stuart Maconie; Phelim McDermott; Charlotte McDougall; Jim Miller; Iain Pattinson; David Quantick; Carrie Quinlan; Jan Ravens; Tom Robinson; Catherine Shepherd; Adam Smith; Justin Spear; Adam Tandy; John Tiffney; Jonny Trunk.

◎ HUDSON AGENCY

3 Travis Lane, Montrose NY 10548. (914)739-4668. Web site: www.hudsonagency.net. Estab. 1994. Signatory of WGA. Represents 20 clients. Currently handles: 100% movie scripts.

Member Agents Sue Giordano (Partner/Producer); Pat Giordano (Partner/Producer); Kelly Olenik (Creative).

Represents Feature film, TV movie of the week, animation, miniseries. **Considers these script subject areas:** Action/adventure; cartoon/animation; comedy; contemporary issues; detective/police/crime; family saga; fantasy; juvenile; mystery/suspense; romantic comedy; romantic drama; teen; western/frontier.

> ⚬ₓ "Originally launched as a motion picture agency, we quickly expanded into television and developed a strong talent base of children's television writers. Feeling a responsibility to influence the world in a beneficial way through entertainment, and with over a thousand contacts in the business, we have earned the reputation of being hard working, pleasantly persistent agents who follow through."

How to Contact Query with SASE. Considers simultaneous queries. Returns materials only with SASE. Obtains most new clients through recommendations from others.

Terms Agent receives 10% commission on domestic sales; 10% commission on foreign sales.

INNOVATIVE ARTISTS

1505 Tenth Street, Santa Monica CA 90401. (310)656-0400. **Contact:** Scott Harris. Signatory of WGA.

Represents Movie scripts, feature film. **Considers these script subject areas:** Romantic comedy; thriller.

How to Contact Snail mail queries preferred.

INTERNATIONAL ARTISTES LTD.

4th Floor, Holborn Hall, 193-197 High Holborn, London England WC1V 7BD, United Kingdom. (44)(207)025-0600. Fax: (44)(207)404-9865. Web site: intart.co.uk/. Estab. 1946.

Member Agents Malcolm Browning; Michael Cronin; Phil Dale, assisted by Lucy Saunders; Emma Engers; Laurie Mansfield, assisted by Keely Gilbert; Mich_le Milburn, assisted by Tara Lynch; Robert Voice, assisted by Nicola Hobbs; Mandy Ward, assisted by Kirsty Lloyd-Jones.

Represents Movie scripts, feature film, TV scripts, theatrical stage play, stage plays.
How to Contact Query with SASE.

◎ INTERNATIONAL ARTS ENTERTAINMENT

8899 Beverly Blvd., Suite 800, Los Angeles CA 90048. (310)550-6760. Fax: (310)550-8839. Web site: www.internationalartsentertainment.com/. **Contact:** Alan Greenspan.

INTERNATIONAL SCRIPTS

1a Kidbrooke Park Rd., London England SE3 0LR, United Kingdom. (44)(208)319-8666. Fax: (44)(208)319-0801. E-mail: internationalscripts@btinternet.com. **Contact:** H.P. Tanner; J. Lawson. Estab. 1979.
Represents Nonfiction books, movie scripts, TV scripts. **Considers these nonfiction areas:** Biography/autobiography; business/economics. **Considers these fiction areas:** Detective/police/crime. **Considers these script subject areas:** Contemporary issues; women's/chick lit.
   o→ Does not want to receive short stories, poetry or articles.
How to Contact Send query letter with SAE.
Recent Sales Other clients include Jane Adams, Ashleigh Bingham, Dr. James Fleming, Trevor Lummis, Chris Pascoe, Anne Spencer.

◪ JARET ENTERTAINMENT

6973 Birdview Ave., Malibu CA 90265. (310)589-9600. Fax: (310)589-9602. Web site: www.jaretentertainment.com. **Contact:** Seth Jaret. Represents 20 clients. 10% of clients are new/unpublished writers. Currently handles: 75% movie scripts; 25% TV scripts.
Represents Movie scripts, TV scripts, books.
Considers these script subject areas Action/adventure; comedy; horror; romantic comedy; science fiction; thriller.
   o→ This management company specializes in creative, out-of-the-box thinking. "We're willing to take a chance on well-written materials." Actively seeking high concept action and comedies. Does not want westerns, serial killer, black comedy, or period pieces.
How to Contact Accepts fax queries only. Discards unwanted material. Obtains most new clients through recommendations from others.
Recent Sales Sold 5 scripts in the last year. *Bumper to Bumper* (Fox); *The Fraud Prince* (Warner Brothers); *The Path*; *The Cold*; *Girl in the Curl* (Paramount).
Terms Agent receives 10% commission on domestic sales. Offers written contract, binding for 2 years.

JKA TALENT & LITERARY AGENCY

James Kellem & Associates, Inc., Talent & Literary Agency, 8033 Sunset Blvd., Suite 115, Los Angeles CA 90046. (818)980-2093. Fax: (818)980-4092. E-mail: jkatalentagency@aol.com. Signatory of WGA.

◎ KAPLAN STAHLER GUMER BRAUN AGENCY

KSGB Agency, 8383 Wilshire Blvd., Suite 923, Beverly Hills CA 90211. (323)653-4483. Fax: (323)653-4506. E-mail: info@ksgbagency.com. Web site: www.ksgbagency.com/.

- "Mitchell Kaplan got his start in the William Morris Agency mailroom along with agency co-founder Elliot Stahler."

Member Agents Mitchell Kaplan; Elliot Stahler; Robert Gumer; Alan Braun; Bradley Stewart Glenn; Gordon Hvolka; Sean Zeid; Dino Carlaftes; Zac Simmons.

Represents Movie scripts, feature film, TV scripts, reality TV.

How to Contact Query with SASE.

MICHELLE KASS ASSOCIATES

85 Charing Cross Road, London England WC2H 0AA, United Kingdom. (44)(207)439-1624. Fax: (44)(207)734-3394. E-mail: office@michellekass.co.uk. **Contact:** Michelle Kass. Estab. 1991.

Represents Movie scripts. **Considers these script subject areas:** Drama & literary fiction.

How to Contact All unsolicited mss returned unopened. Contact by phone before submitting mss.

ⓘ KAUFMANN, FEINER, YAMIN, GILDIN & ROBBINS LLP

Kaufmann Feiner, 777 Third Ave., New York NY 10017. (212)755-3100. Fax: (212)755-3174. E-mail: dakufmann@kfygr.com. Web site: www.kaufmannfeiner.com. Estab. 1928.

Member Agents David A. Cannon; Ronald E. Feiner; Daniel Gildin; Pamela M Golinski; David J Kaufmann; Susan H. Morton; David W. Oppenheim; Christianna M.L. Reed; David E. Robbins; Kevin M. Shelley.

Represents Movie scripts, feature film, TV scripts, theatrical stage play, stage plays. Other clients include John Gray; John Leguizamo; James McBride; Glyn O'Malley.

ⓘ CHARLENE KAY AGENCY

901 Beaudry St., Suite 6, St.Jean/Richelieu QC J3A 1C6 Canada. E-mail: lmchakay@hotmail.com. **Contact:** Louise Meyers, director of development. Estab. 1992. Member of BMI; signatory of WGA. 50% of clients are new/unpublished writers. Currently handles: 50% movie scripts; 50% TV scripts.

- Prior to opening her agency, Ms. Kay was a screenwriter.

Member Agents Louise Meyers; Karen Forsyth.

Represents Feature film, TV scripts, TV movie of the week, episodic drama, sitcom. **Considers these script subject areas:** Action/adventure; biography/autobiography; family saga; fantasy; psychic/supernatural; romantic comedy; romantic drama; science fiction.

> ⚬╌ This agency specializes in teleplays and screenplays. "We seek stories that are out of the ordinary, something we don't see too often. A well-written and well-constructed script is important." Does not want to receive thrillers, barbaric/erotic films, novels, books or mss.

How to Contact Query with SASE, submit outline/proposal. Does not return materials. Rejected mss are shredded. Responds in 1 month to queries; 10 weeks to mss.

Recent Sales This agency prefers not to share information on specific sales.

Terms Agent receives 10% commission on domestic sales; 10% commission on foreign sales. Offers written contract, binding for 1 year.

Tips "This agency is on the WGA lists, and query letters arrive by the dozens every week. As our present clients understand, success comes with patience. A sale rarely happens overnight, especially when you are dealing with totally unknown writers. We are not impressed by the credentials of a writer, amateur or professional, or by his/her pitching techniques, but by his/her story ideas and ability to build a well-crafted script."

CARY KOZLOV LITERARY REPRESENTATION

16000 Ventura Blvd., Suite 1000, Encino CA 91436. (818)501-6622. Signatory of WGA.

Represents Movie scripts, feature film.

How to Contact Query with SASE.

✂ ◎ EDDIE KRITZER PRODUCTIONS

1112 Montana Ave., Suite 449, Santa Monica CA 90403. E-mail: producedby@aol.com. Web site: www.eddiekritzer.com. **Contact:** Executive Story Editor. Estab. 1974.

Member Agents Eddie Kritzer (producer who also secures publishing agreements).

Represents Nonfiction books, movie scripts, feature film, TV scripts, TV movie of the week.

How to Contact Query with SASE. Prefers to read materials exclusively. Discards unwanted queries and mss. Obtains most new clients through recommendations from others, solicitations.

Recent Sales *Gmen & Gangsters* (Seven Locks Press/in development at Mandeville Films); *The Practical Patient* (Seven Locks Press); *The Making of a Surgeon in the 21st Century*, by Craig Miller (Blue Dolphin Press); *Kids Say the Darndest Things*, by Art Linkletter (Ten Speed Press/produced by Nick@Nite); *Live Ten Years Longer*, by Clarence Agrees (Ten Speed Press); *Take Back a Scary Movie* (currently at auction).

Terms Agent receives 15% commission on domestic sales; 20% commission on foreign sales. Offers written contract.

Tips "Contact by e-mail. I am only looking for the most compelling stories. Be succinct, but compelling."

◎ KUBLER AUCKLAND MANAGEMENT

KAM, P.O. Box 1064, Double Bay NSW 1360, Australia. E-mail: Sydney@KublerAuckland.com. Web site: www.KublerAuckland.com. Alternate address: P.O. Box 1062, Milton, Qld 4064

Represents Theatrical stage play, stage plays. **Considers these fiction areas:** Plays.

   o→ The agency represents playwrights throughout Australia.

How to Contact Do not send queries from North America.

Recent Sales Other clients include Buck Buckingham; Adam Couper; Stephen Davis; Philip Dean; Rowan Ellis Michael; Margery Forde; Michael Futcher; Helen Howard; Elise Greig; Marjean Holden; Sally McKenzie; Danny Murphy; Matthew Ryan; Kier Shorey; Sven Swenson.

◙ THE CANDACE LAKE AGENCY

10677 Somma Way, Los Angeles CA 90077. (310)476-2882. Fax: (310)476-8283. E-mail: candace@lakeliterary.com. **Contact:** Candace Lake. Estab. 1977; Signatory of WGA, DGA. 50% of clients are new/unpublished writers. Currently handles: 80% movie scripts; 20% TV scripts.

Member Agents Candace Lake, president; Richard Ryba, agent; Ryan Lewis, agent.

Represents Novels, feature film, TV movie of the week, episodic drama. **Considers these script subject areas:** Action/adventure; comedy; contemporary issues; detective/police/crime; fantasy; historical; horror; mainstream; mystery/suspense; psychic/supernatural; romantic comedy; romantic drama; science fiction; teen; thriller.

   o→ This agency specializes in screenplay and teleplay writers.

How to Contact *No unsolicited material.* Obtains most new clients through recommendations from others.

Recent Sales This agency prefers not to share information on specific sales.

Terms Agent receives 10% commission on domestic sales; 10% commission on foreign sales. Offers written contract, binding for 2 years.

☑ THE LANTZ OFFICE

200 W. 57th St., Suite 503, New York NY 10019. (212)586-0200. Fax: (212)262-6659. E-mail: rlantz@lantzoffice.com; tlo@lantzoffice.com. Web site: www.lantzoffice.com. **Contact:** Robert Lantz. Member of AAR.

Represents Movie scripts, feature film, theatrical stage play.

How to Contact As of July 2008, the Lantz Office was closed to new clients. Check the Web site periodically to see if this policy has changed. Obtains most new clients through recommendations from others.

Terms Agent receives 10% commission on domestic sales; 10% commission on foreign sales.

Tips This is a very selective agency.

☑ LARCHMONT LITERARY AGENCY

444 N. Larchmont Blvd., Suite 200, Los Angeles CA 90004. (323)856-3070. Fax: (323)856-3071. Web site: www.larchmontlit.com. Estab. 1998.

- Prior to becoming an agent, Mr. Millner attended NYU Film School and participated in The William Morris agent training program.

Represents Novels, movie scripts, feature film. **Considers these script subject areas:** Action/adventure; biography/autobiography; cartoon/animation; comedy; contemporary issues; detective/police/crime; fantasy; historical; horror; mainstream; mystery/suspense; psychic/supernatural; romantic comedy; romantic drama; science fiction; sports; thriller.

- This agency specializes in feature writers and feature writer/directors. "We maintain a small, highly selective client list and offer a long-term career management style of agenting that larger agencies can't provide."

How to Contact Query with SASE. Prefers to read materials exclusively. Responds in 2 weeks to queries. Obtains most new clients through recommendations from others. This agency prefers not to share information on specific sales.

Terms Agent receives 10% commission on domestic sales. No written contract.

Tips "Please do not send a script until it is in its best possible draft."

MIKE LEIGH ASSOCIATES

37 Marylebone Lane, London England W1U 2NW, United Kingdom. Web site: www.mikeleighassoc.com.

Represents TV scripts, TV movie of the week, radio scripts, commercials.

How to Contact Query through online form. Other clients include Neil Cole; Iain Coyle; Dominik Diamond; Chas Early; Paolo Hewitt; Dominic Holland; Marianne Levy; Neil Sean; Paul Simper; Dave Skinner; Richard Thomson; Christos Tolera; Phil Whelans.

◎ LENHOFF & LENHOFF

830 Palm Ave., West Hollywood CA 90069. (310)855-2411. Fax: (310)855-2412. E-mail: charles@lenhoff.com or lisa@lenhoff.com. Web site: www.lenhoff.com/. Estab. 1991.

● Charles Lenhoff formerly co-owned the Lenhoff/Robinson Talent & Literary Agency, was a literary agent with the Gray/Goodman Agency, and worked in production management at Metromedia-Mediasync Producers in New York City. Lisa Helsing Lenhoff was previously a literary agent at Susan Smith & Associates and at ICM.

Member Agents Charles Lenhoff; Lisa Helsing Lenhoff.

How to Contact All unsolicited mss returned unopened. Use a referral or meet these agents at a conference.

◎ JACK LENNY ASSOCIATES

9454 Wilshire Blvd., Suite 600, Beverly Hills CA 90212. (310)271-2174. Signatory of WGA.

Represents Feature film.

How to Contact This is a very selective representative company that should only be queried through a referral, or if your work was solicited.

Terms Agent receives 10% commission on domestic sales; 10% commission on foreign sales.

⬛ PAUL S. LEVINE LITERARY AGENCY

1054 Superba Ave., Venice CA 90291-3940. (310)450-6711. Fax: (310)450-0181. E-mail: pslevine@ix. netcom.com. Web site: www.paulslevine.com. **Contact:** Paul S. Levine. Estab. 1996. Member of the State Bar of California. Represents over 100 clients. 75% of clients are new/unpublished writers. Currently handles: 30% nonfiction books; 30% novels; 10% movie scripts; 30% TV scripts.

Represents Nonfiction books, novels, movie scripts, feature film, TV scripts, TV movie of the week, episodic drama, sitcom, animation, documentary, miniseries, syndicated material. **Considers these nonfiction areas:** Art/architecture/design; biography/autobiography; business/economics; child guidance/parenting; computers/electronic; cooking/foods/nutrition; crafts/hobbies; current affairs; education; ethnic/cultural interests; gay/lesbian issues; government/politics/law; health/ medicine; history; how-to; humor/satire; interior design/decorating; language/literature/criticism; memoirs; military/war; money/finance; music/dance; nature/environment; New Age/metaphysics; photography; popular culture; psychology; religious/inspirational; science/technology; self-help/ personal improvement; sociology; sports; theater/film; true crime/investigative; women's issues/ studies; creative nonfiction. **Considers these fiction areas:** Action/adventure; comic books/cartoon; confession; detective/police/crime; erotica; ethnic; experimental; family saga; feminist; gay/ lesbian; glitz; historical; humor/satire; literary; mainstream/contemporary; mystery/suspense; regional; religious/inspirational; romance; sports; thriller; westerns/frontier. **Considers these script subject areas:** Action/adventure; biography/autobiography; cartoon/animation; comedy; contemporary issues; detective/police/crime; erotica; ethnic; experimental; family saga; feminist; gay/ lesbian; glitz; historical; horror; juvenile; mainstream; multimedia; mystery/suspense; religious/ inspirational; romantic comedy; romantic drama; sports; teen; thriller; western/frontier.

⚬⚈ Actively seeking commercial fiction and nonfiction. Also handles children's and young adult fiction and nonfiction. Does not want to receive science fiction, fantasy, or horror.

How to Contact Query with SASE. Accepts e-mail and fax queries. Considers simultaneous queries. Responds in 1 day to queries; 2 months to mss. Returns materials only with SASE. Obtains most new clients through conferences, referrals, listings on various Web sites and in directories.

Recent Sales Sold 25 titles in the last year. This agency prefers not to share information on specific sales.

Terms Agent receives 15% commission on domestic sales; 20% commission on foreign sales. Offers written contract. Charges clients for messengers, long distance calls, postage (only when incurred). No advance payment necessary.

Writers' Conferences California Lawyers for the Arts Workshops; Selling to Hollywood Conference; Willamette Writers Conference; and many others.

MICHAEL LEWIS & ASSOCIATES

2506 Fifth St., Suite 100, Santa Monica CA 90405. (310)399-1999. Fax: (310)399-9104. E-mail: mlewis2506@aol.com. Signatory of WGA.

Represents Feature film.

☑ THE LUEDTKE AGENCY

1674 Broadway, Suite 7A, New York NY 10019. (212)765-9564. Fax: (212)765-9582. **Contact:** Penny Luedtke.

- Prior to becoming an agent, Ms. Luedtke was in classical music management.

Represents Movie scripts, TV scripts (pilots), stage plays, musicals.

- ⚷ Actively seeking well-written material with originality. Works closely with writers and offers editorial assistance, if desired. Does not want to receive any project with graphic or explicit violence.

How to Contact Query with SASE. No e-mail or fax queries. Considers simultaneous queries. Returns materials only with SASE. Obtains most new clients through recommendations from others, workshops.

Recent Sales This agency prefers not to share information on specific sales.

Terms Agent receives 10% commission on domestic sales; 15% commission on foreign sales. Offers written contract.

MACFARLANE CHARD ASSOCIATES LIMITED

33 Percy Street, London W1T 2DF, United Kingdom. (44)(207)636-7750. Fax: (44)(207)636-7751. E-mail: enquiries@macfarlane-chard.co.uk. Web site: www.macfarlane-chard.co.uk. Estab. 1994.

MACNAUGHTON LORD 2000 LTD.

ML2000, 19 Margravine Gardens, London W6 8RL, United Kingdom. Web site: www.ml2000.org.uk. Estab. 1967.

Member Agents Patricia Macnaughton; Gavin Plumley.

- ⚷ Musical theatre

◎ THE MANAGEMENT CO.

1337 Ocean Ave., Suite F, Santa Monica CA 90401. **Contact:** Tom Klassen. Represents 18 clients.

- Prior to starting his agency, Mr. Klassen was an agent with International Creative Management (ICM).

Member Agents Tom Klassen; Steve Gamber; Helene Taber; Paul Davis.

Represents Feature film (scripts), TV scripts, Internet scripts, computer game scripts.

- ⚷ Actively seeking studio-quality, action-drama scripts and really good comedies. Does not want to receive horror scripts.

How to Contact Submit e-queries only with the e-mail subject line saying "Query: (Title)" Accepts e-mail queries. No fax queries. Responds in 2-3 weeks to queries. Returns materials only with SASE. Obtains most new clients through recommendations from others, conferences.

Recent Sales Sold 14 scripts in the last year.

Terms Agent receives 10% commission on domestic sales; 10% commission on foreign sales. Offers written contract, binding for 2 years.

Writers' Conferences Sundance Film Festival; film festivals in New York, Telluride, Atlanta, Chicago, Austin, Minnesota.

Tips "We only accept e-mail queries. Send only what is requested. If you have a 1-2 page synopsis, say so and we may request it, but do not send it with the initial qery. We only respond if interested. Be sure to send your phone number(s) as we generally call if interested. We rarely take on non-referred material, but have done very well with those we have taken on."

ANDREW MANN, LTD

1 Old Compton St., London England W1D 5JA, United Kingdom. (44)(207)734-4751. Fax: (44)(207)287-9264. E-mail: manuscript@onetel.com. **Contact:** Anne Dewe, Tina Betts, Sacha Elliot. Estab. 1975.

Represents Nonfiction books, movie scripts, feature film, TV scripts, Radio plays. **Considers these fiction areas:** Juvenile; young adult.

   Oⁿ No poetry considered.

How to Contact Submit synopsis, 3 sample chapter(s), SAE.

⬤ MARJACQ SCRIPTS, LTD

34 Devonshire Place, London England W1G 6JW, United Kingdom. (44)(207)935-9499. Fax: (44)(207)935-9115. E-mail: philip@marjacq.com; luke@marjacq.com. Web site: www.marjacq.com. **Contact:** Philip Patterson (literary); Luke Speed (film). Estab. 1974. Represents 80 clients. 40% of clients are new/unpublished writers. Currently handles: 10% nonfiction books; 40% novels; 5% juvenile books; 20% movie scripts; 25% TV scripts.

   • Prior to becoming an agent, Mr. Patterson was a film, TV and theatre agent at Curtis Brown and sold rights at HarperCollins; Mr. Speed worked in film production with Civilian Content and worked at Saatchi and Saatchi.

Member Agents Philip Patterson, literary agent; Luke Speed, film/TV agent.

   Oⁿ "We are a young and vibrant agency always looking for clients. We handle all rights—print publishing, film, TV, radio, translation and intellectual property." Actively seeking quality fiction, nonfiction, children's books and young adult books. Does not want to receive plays, poetry or short stories.

How to Contact Submit outline, synopsis, 3 sample chapters, bio, covering letter, SASE. Do not bother with fancy bindings and folders. Keep synopses, bio and covering letter short. Accepts e-mail queries via Word attachment. Considers simultaneous queries. Responds in 3 days to queries; 4-6 weeks to mss. Returns materials only with SASE. Obtains most new clients through recommendations from others, solicitations, conferences.

Recent Sales Sold 40 titles in the last year. *Second Time Round,* by Sophie King (Hodder & Stoughton); 3-book deal for Stuart MacBride (HarperCollins UK); 3-book deal for Catrin Collier (Orion Books); 2-book deal for Jack Sheffield (Transworld); 2-book deal for John Connor (Orion Books). Other clients include Katherine John, Rosie Goodwin, R.D. Wingfield, Christopher Goffard, Giulio Leoni, Ben Pastor, James Follett, George Markstein, Richard Lambert, Michael Taylor, Pat Mills, Graham Oakley, Richard Craze, Ros Jay, Richard Asplin, Stewart Hennessey, Claes Johansen, David Clayton.

Terms Agent receives 10% commission on domestic sales; 20% commission on foreign sales. Offers written contract. Charges for bank fees for money transfers.

Tips "Keep trying! If one agent rejects you, that is his/her opinion. Perseverance and self-belief are important. Listening to constructive criticism is good, but be warned, few agents will give you advice. We just don't have the time. Be aware of what is being published. If you show awareness of what others writers are doing in your field/genre, you might be able to see how your book fits in and why an editor/agent might be interested in taking it on. Take care with your submissions. Research the agency and pay attention to presentation. Join writers groups. Sharing your work is a good way to get constructive criticism. If you know anyone in the industry, use your contacts. A personal recommendation will get more notice than cold calling."

⊘ THE MARTON AGENCY, INC.

One Union Square W., Suite 815, New York NY 10003-3303. Fax: (212)691-9061. E-mail: info@martonagency.com. Web site: www.martonagency.com. **Contact:** Tonda Marton. Member of AAR.
Member Agents Tonda Marton; Anne Reingold.

    ⊶ This agency specializes in foreign-language licensing.

◎ MBA LITERARY AGENTS, LTD

62 Grafton Way, London England W1T 5DW, United Kingdom. (44)(207)387-2076. Fax: (44)(207)387-2042. E-mail: firstname@mbalit.co.uk. Web site: www.mbalit.co.uk. **Contact:** Managing Dir. & Lit. Agent: Diana Tyler; Dir.: John Richard Parker (Fiction/Nonfiction, Science Fiction & Fantasy); Dir.: Meg Davis (Scriptwriters/Authors all genres); Dir.: Laura Longrigg (Fiction/Nonfiction); David Riding & Jean Kitson (Film, TV, Theatre, Radio Scripts). Estab. 1971.

Represents Movie scripts, Broadcast Scripts. **Considers these nonfiction areas:** Biography/autobiography; history; memoirs; popular culture; self-help/personal improvement; travel. **Considers these fiction areas:** Fantasy; literary; science fiction; Commercial.

How to Contact Submit proposal package, 3 sample chapter(s), Query letter, SAE.

Recent Sales *The Tenderness of Wolves*, by Stef Penney; *Warprize*, by Elizabeth Vaughan; *Hideous Absinthe*, by Jad Adams; *A Fete Worse than Death*, by Iain Aitch. Other clients include Robert Jones, Nick Angel, Dr. Mark Atkinson, Anila Baig, Rob Bailey, Ed Hurst, Christopher Bird, Vivienne Bolton, Audrey & Sophie Boss, Martin Buckley, Debbie Cash, Vic Darkwood, Sarah Ash, Michael Cobley, Murray Davis, Alan Dunn & Stef Penney.

◢ MCINTOSH & OTIS

353 Lexington Ave., 15th Floor, New York NY 10016. E-mail: info@mcintoshandotis.com. Web site: www.mcintoshandotis.net/. Member of AAR.

Member Agents Eugene H. Winick; Elizabeth Winick (literary fiction, women's fiction, historical fiction, and mystery/suspense, along with narrative nonfiction, spiritual/self-help, history and current affairs. Elizabeth represents numerous New York T); Edward Necarsulmer IV; Rebecca Strauss (nonfiction, literary and commercial fiction, women's fiction, memoirs, and pop culture); Cate Martin; Ina Winick (psychology, self-help, and mystery/suspense); Ian Polonsky (Film/TV/Stage/Radio).

Represents Nonfiction books, novels, movie scripts, feature film. **Considers these script subject areas:** General.

How to Contact Send a query, synopsis, two sample chapters, and SASE by regular mail. For nonfiction, include bio and outline. For screenplays, send a query letter, synopsis, and SASE by regular mail. Responds in 8 weeks to queries.

Recent Sales Paperback rights to Donald J. Sobol's Encyclopedia Brown series (Puffin).

Tips "Please send a query letter, synopsis, two sample chapters, and SASE by regular mail. For nonfiction, please include a biography and outline as well. For screenplays, please send a query letter, synopsis, and SASE by regular mail. No phone calls please."

BILL MCLEAN PERSONAL MANAGEMENT, LTD

23b Deodar Road, London England SW15 2NP, United Kingdom. (44)(208)789-8191. Estab. 1972.

Represents Movie scripts, feature film, TV scripts, stage plays, Radio. **Considers these nonfiction areas:** Theater/film.

O→ Does not accept books.

How to Contact Send letter with SAE.

☑ THE STUART M. MILLER CO.

11684 Ventura Blvd., #225, Studio City CA 91604-2699. (818)506-6067. Fax: (818)506-4079. E-mail: smmco@aol.com. **Contact:** Stuart Miller. Estab. 1977; Signatory of WGA, DGA. Currently handles: 50% movie scripts; 10% multimedia; 40% books.

Represents Nonfiction books, novels, movie scripts. **Considers these nonfiction areas:** Biography/autobiography; computers/electronic; current affairs; government/politics/law; health/medicine; history; how-to; memoirs; military/war; self-help/personal improvement; true crime/investigative. **Considers these fiction areas:** Action/adventure; detective/police/crime; historical; literary; mainstream/contemporary; mystery/suspense; science fiction; sports; thriller. **Considers these script subject areas:** Action/adventure; biography/autobiography; cartoon/animation; comedy; contemporary issues; detective/police/crime; family saga; historical; mainstream; multimedia; mystery/suspense; romantic comedy; romantic drama; science fiction; sports; teen; thriller.

How to Contact For screenplays, query with SASE, narrative outline (2-3 pages). For books, submit narrative outline (5-10 pages). Accepts e-mail and fax queries. Considers simultaneous queries. Responds in 3 days to queries. Responds in 4-6 weeks to screenplays and mss. Returns materials only with SASE.

Recent Sales This agency prefers not to share information on specific sales.

Terms Offers written contract, binding for 2 years. Agent receives 10% commission on screenplay sales; 15% commission on motion picture/TV rights sales for books and other non-screenplay literary properties.

Tips "Always include an SASE, e-mail address or fax number with query letters. Make it easy to respond."

MKS & ASSOCIATES

8675 W. Washington Blvd., Suite 203, Culver City CA 90232. (310)838-1200. Fax: (310)838-1245. Web site: www.mksagency.com/.

◐ MONTEIRO ROSE DRAVIS AGENCY, INC.

17514 Ventura Blvd., Suite 205, Encino CA 91316. (818)501-1177. Fax: (818)501-1194. E-mail: monro se@monteiro-rose.com. Web site: www.monteiro-rose.com. **Contact:** Candy Monteiro. Estab. 1987. Signatory of WGA. Represents 50 clients. Currently handles: 40% movie scripts; 20% TV scripts; 40% animation.

Member Agents Candace Monteiro; Fredda Rose; Milissa Brockish; Jason Dravis.

Represents Feature film, TV movie of the week, episodic drama, animation. **Considers these script subject areas:** Action/adventure; cartoon/animation; comedy; contemporary issues; detective/police/crime; ethnic; family saga; historical; juvenile; mainstream; mystery/suspense; psychic/supernatural; romantic comedy; romantic drama; science fiction; teen; thriller.

> ⚬⚬ The Monteiro Rose Agency represents live _action and animation writers for children's television, features, home video, and interactive markets, and has done so for more than 15 years. We invite you to contact us and discuss your needs. We would be happy to work with you to select the best scriptwriters for your projects from our multi-talented, award-winning list of clients.

How to Contact Query with SASE. Accepts e-mail and fax queries. Responds in 1 week to queries; 2 months to mss. Returns materials only with SASE. Obtains most new clients through recommendations from others, solicitations.

Recent Sales This agency prefers not to share information on specific sales.

Terms Agent receives 10% commission on domestic sales. Offers written contract, binding for 2 years; 3-month notice must be given to terminate contract. Charges for photocopying.

Tips "We prefer to receive inquiries by e-mail, although snail mail is OK with a SASE. We do not return manuscripts. We suggest that all feature manuscripts be no longer than 120 pages."

WILLIAM MORRIS AGENCY (UK), LTD

Centrepoint Tower, 103 Oxford St., London England WC1A 1DD, United Kingdom. (44)(207)534-6800. Fax: (44)(207)534-6900. Web site: www.wma.com. **Contact:** CEO: Jim Wiatt; Chairman: Norman Brokaw. Estab. 1965.

Represents Nonfiction books, novels, movie scripts, TV scripts.

How to Contact Query with SASE, submit synopsis, up to 50 sample pages. SAE.

THE NARROW ROAD COMPANY

182 Brighton Rd., Coulsden Surrey CR2 2NF, United Kingdom. (44)(208)763-9695. Fax: (44)(208)763-9329. E-mail: narrowroad@freeuk.com. Web site: www.narrowroad.co.uk.

Represents Broadcast Scripts.

> ⚬⚬ Does not want to receive novels or poetry.

How to Contact Submit author bio, query letter, SASE.

◪ THE NASHVILLE AGENCY

P.O. Box 110909, Nashville TN 37222. (615)263-4143. Fax: (866)333-8663. E-mail: info@nashvilleage ncy.com; submissions@nashvilleagency.com. Web site: www.nashvilleagency.com. **Contact:** Taylor Joseph. Estab. 2002. Represents 18 clients. 50% of clients are new/unpublished writers. Currently handles: 40% nonfiction books; 15% novels; 5% novellas; 40% juvenile books.

Member Agents Tim Grable (business books); Jonathan Clements (nonfiction, juvenile); Taylor Joseph (fiction, novels, memoirs).

Represents Nonfiction books, novels, novellas, juvenile books, scholarly books, movie scripts, documentary. **Considers these nonfiction areas:** Biography/autobiography; business/economics; child guidance/parenting; cooking/foods/nutrition; crafts/hobbies; current affairs; education; history; how-to; humor/satire; juvenile nonfiction; memoirs; military/war; music/dance; popular culture; religious/inspirational; self-help/personal improvement; sports; true crime/investigative; women's issues/studies. **Considers these fiction areas:** Action/adventure; fantasy; historical; humor/satire; juvenile; literary; mainstream/contemporary; mystery/suspense; regional; religious/inspirational; thriller; young adult; women's. **Considers these script subject areas:** Action/adventure; contemporary issues.

○┰ "Our agency looks not as much for specific genres or stylings. Rather, we look for far-reaching potentials (i.e., brands, properties) to branch outside a token specific market." Actively seeking novels, nonfiction, religious/spiritual material. Does not want to receive poetry, stage plays or textbooks.

How to Contact Query with SASE, submit proposal package, synopsis, publishing history, author bio, Description of how your relationship with The Nashville Agency was initiated. Query via e-mail. No fax queries. Considers simultaneous queries. Responds in 3 weeks to queries; 3 months to mss. Returns materials only with SASE. Obtains most new clients through recommendations from others.

Recent Sales This agency prefers not to share information on specific sales.

Terms Agent receives 15% commission on domestic sales; 20% commission on foreign sales. Offers written contract, binding for 5 years; 30-day notice must be given to terminate contract. This agency charges for standard office fees.

Writers' Conferences Blue Ridge Writers' Conference.

NATURAL TALENT, INC.

3331 Ocean Park Blvd., Suite 203, Santa Monica CA 90405. (310)450-4945. E-mail: info@naturaltalentinc.com. Web site: naturaltalentinc.com/. **Contact:** Will Swift. Signatory of WGA.

Represents Animation, comics, video games. **Considers these script subject areas:** Cartoon/animation.

○┰ Specializing in the consultation and representation of creative talent and intellectual properties in the converging markets of animation, comics, and video games.

◙ NIAD MANAGEMENT

15030 Ventura Blvd., Bldg. 19 #860, Sherman Oaks CA 91403. (818)505-1272. Fax: (818)505-1637. E-mail: queries@niadmanagement.com. Web site: www.niadmanagement.com. Estab. 1997. Represents 20 clients. Currently handles: 1% novels; 99% movie scripts.

Represents Movie scripts, feature film, TV movie of the week, miniseries, stage plays. **Considers these nonfiction areas:** Biography/autobiography. **Considers these fiction areas:** Action/adventure; detective/police/crime; family saga; literary; mainstream/contemporary; multicultural; mystery/suspense; psychic/supernatural; romance; thriller. **Considers these script subject areas:** Action/adventure; biography/autobiography; comedy; contemporary issues; detective/police/crime; ethnic; family saga; historical; horror; mainstream; multicultural; mystery/suspense; psychic/supernatural; romantic comedy; romantic drama; sports; teen; thriller.

How to Contact Query with SASE. Responds to queries only if interested,. Accepts e-mail and fax queries. Considers simultaneous queries. Responds in 1 week to queries; 3 months to mss. Returns materials only with SASE. Obtains most new clients through recommendations from others.

Recent Sales *MacGyver* (the feature film), by Lee Zlotoff; *Moebius*, by Neil Cohen (Mandate); *Winter Woke Up*, by Aaron Garcia and Melissa Emery; *Under the Bed*, by Susan Sandler (Caldwell Theater).

Terms Offers written contract, binding for 1 year; 30-day notice must be given to terminate contract. Agent receives 15% commission on all gross monies received.

NORDISKA ApS

International Performing Rights Agency, 457 West 57th St., Suite 1109, New York NY 10019, USA. (212)247-1680. Fax: (212)247-1775. E-mail: info@nordiska.dk. Web site: www.nordiska.dk. **Contact:** David Coffman. Estab. 1988.

Represents Theatrical stage play, stage plays, Musicals. **Considers these nonfiction areas:** Theater/film.

> o→ International plays and musicals in Scandinavia, Finland, and Iceland and Danish and Scandinavian authors and composers worldwide.

How to Contact Accepts e-mail and fax queries.

☑ OMNIQUEST ENTERTAINMENT

1416 N. La Brae Ave., Hollywood CA 90028. Fax: (303)802-1633. E-mail: info@omniquestmedia.com. Web site: www.omniquestmedia.com. **Contact:** Michael Kaliski. Estab. 1997. Currently handles: 10% novels; 5% juvenile books; 40% movie scripts; 20% TV scripts; 10% multimedia; 15% stage plays.

Member Agents Michael Kaliski; Traci Belushi.

Represents Screenwriters, established playwrights. **Considers these script subject areas:** Action/adventure; biography/autobiography; comedy; contemporary issues; detective/police/crime; experimental; family saga; fantasy; historical; mainstream; multimedia; mystery/suspense; psychic/supernatural; romantic comedy; romantic drama; science fiction; thriller.

> o→ Does not accept unsolicited material at this time.

How to Contact Obtains most new clients through recommendations from others.

Recent Sales This agency prefers not to share information on specific sales.

Terms Agent receives 15% commission on domestic sales; 15% commission on foreign sales. Offers written contract.

ORIGINAL ARTISTS

9465 Wilshire Blvd., Suite 324, Beverly Hills CA 90212. (310-)275-6765. Fax: (310)275-6725. E-mail: matt@original-artists.com. Web site: www.original-artists.com/. **Contact:** Matt Leipzig; Jordan Bayer. Estab. 1993. Signatory of WGA.

> • Mr. Bayer began his career at the William Morris Agency. Mr. Leipzig broke into the entertainment industry at New Horizons Pictures.

Represents Movie scripts, TV scripts.

> o→ "Original Artists writer clients have sold over 100 spec screenplays and pitches and dozens of television pilots."

☺ DOROTHY PALMER TALENT AGENCY, INC.

235 W. 56 St., New York NY 10019. (212)765-4280. Fax: (212)977-9801. Web site: www.dorothypalm
ertalentagency.com/. Estab. 1968 (talent agency); 1990 (literary agency). Signatory of WGA. Represents 12 clients. Currently handles: 70% movie scripts; 30% TV scripts.

• In addition to being a literary agent, Ms. Palmer has worked as a talent agent for 36 years.

Represents Feature film, TV movie of the week, episodic drama, sitcom, miniseries, independent
films. **Considers these script subject areas:** Action/adventure; comedy; contemporary issues; detec-
tive/police/crime; family saga; feminist; horror; mainstream; mystery/suspense; romantic comedy;
romantic drama; thriller.

    ⊶ This agency specializes in screenplays and TV. Actively seeking successful, published writers
       (screenplays only). Does not want to receive work from new or unpublished writers.

How to Contact Query with SASE. Prefers to read materials exclusively. Returns materials only with
SASE. Obtains most new clients through recommendations from others.

Recent Sales This agency prefers not to share information on specific sales.

Terms Agent receives 10% commission on domestic sales; 10% commission on foreign sales. Offers
written contract, binding for 1 year. Charges clients for postage and photocopies.

Tips ''Do not telephone. When I find a script that interests me, I call the writer.''

◎ PARADIGM TALENT AND LITERARY AGENCY

360 N. Crescent Drive, Beverly Hills 90210. (310)288-8000. Fax: (310)288-2000. Web site: www.paradi
gmla.com.

Member Agents Lydia Wills, others.

Represents Movie scripts, feature film, TV scripts, theatrical stage play, stage plays.

    ⊶ ''Paradigm Talent and Literary Agency is an Los-Angeles-based talent agency with an addi-
       tional office in New York City. The firm acquired Writers & Artists Group International in
       2004. The acquisition of WAGI added both talent and agents to Paradigm's roster, bolstering
       its New York office with legit agents, representing playwrights and theatre directors.

How to Contact Query with SASE.

Recent Sales *Outside In*, by Courtney Thorne-Smith (Broadway); *What Pets Eat*, by Marion Nestle
and Malden Nesheim (Harcourt).

PEAKE ASSOCIATES

14 Grafton Crescent, London England NW1 8SL, United Kingdom. (44)(207)482-0609. Fax:
(44)(870)141-0447. E-mail: tony@tonypeake.com. Web site: www.tonypeake.com. **Contact:** Tony
Peake.

• Tony Peake has spent time as a theatre production manager, model, actor & film distributor.

Represents Movie scripts, TV scripts. **Considers these fiction areas:** Poetry; General fiction. Other
clients include Johnathon Coe, Steven Kelly, David Reynolds & Alison Fell.

☑ BARRY PERELMAN AGENCY

1155 N. La Cienega Blvd., Suite 412, W. Hollywood CA 90069. (310)659-1122. Fax: (310)659-1122.
E-mail: barry_perelman@hotmail.com. Estab. 1982; Signatory of WGA, DGA. Represents 40 clients.
15% of clients are new/unpublished writers. Currently handles: 100% movie scripts.

Agents & Managers

• Prior to forming his own agency, Mr. Perelman was with William Morris and ICM.

Member Agents Barry Perelman.

Represents Movie scripts, TV scripts, reality shows. **Considers these script subject areas:** Action/adventure; biography/autobiography; contemporary issues; detective/police/crime; historical; horror; mystery/suspense; romantic comedy; romantic drama; science fiction; thriller.

Oᴙ This agency specializes in motion pictures/packaging.

How to Contact Query with SASE, proposal package, outline. Responds in 1 month to queries. Obtains most new clients through recommendations from others, solicitations.

Recent Sales This agency prefers not to share information on specific sales.

Terms Agent receives 10% commission on domestic sales; 10% commission on foreign sales. Offers written contract, binding for 1-2 years. This agency charges clients for postage and photocopying.

STEPHEN PEVNER, INC.

382 Lafayette St., Eighth Floor, New York NY 10003. (212)674-8403. Fax: (212)529-3692. E-mail: spevner@aol.com. **Contact:** Stephen Pevner.

Represents Nonfiction books, novels, feature film, TV scripts, TV movie of the week, episodic drama, animation, documentary, miniseries. **Considers these nonfiction areas:** Biography/autobiography; ethnic/cultural interests; gay/lesbian issues; history; humor/satire; language/literature/criticism; memoirs; music/dance; New Age/metaphysics; photography; popular culture; religious/inspirational; sociology; travel. **Considers these fiction areas:** Comic books/cartoon; erotica; ethnic; experimental; gay/lesbian; glitz; horror; humor/satire; literary; mainstream/contemporary; psychic/supernatural; thriller; urban. **Considers these script subject areas:** Comedy; contemporary issues; detective/police/crime; gay/lesbian; glitz; horror; romantic comedy; romantic drama; thriller.

Oᴙ This agency specializes in motion pictures, novels, humor, pop culture, urban fiction, and independent filmmakers.

How to Contact Query with SASE, submit outline/proposal. Prefers to read materials exclusively. No e-mail or fax queries. Responds in 2 weeks to queries; 1 month to mss. Obtains most new clients through recommendations from others.

Terms Agent receives 15% commission on domestic sales; 20% commission on foreign sales. Offers written contract, binding for 1 year; 6-week notice must be given to terminate contract. 100% of business is derived from commissions on ms sales.

Tips "Be persistent, but civilized."

PLAYMARKET

P.O. Box 9767, Te Aro Wellington, New Zealand. E-mail: info@playmarket.org.nz. Web site: www.playmarket.org.nz. Level 2, 16 Cambridge Terrace **Contact:** Katrina Chandra (agency@playmarket.org.nz). Estab. 1973.

Oᴙ This agency specializes in New Zealand plays and Maori and Pacific Island playwrights in the Auckland region.

How to Contact Only residents of the New Zealand area should query.

PMA LITERARY AND FILM MANAGEMENT, INC.

45 West 21st St., Suite 4SW, New York NY 10010. (212)929-1222. Fax: (212)206-0238. E-mail: queries @pmalitfilm.com. Web site: www.pmalitfilm.com. Address for packages is P.O. Box 1817, Old Chel-

sea Station, New York NY 10113 **Contact:** Kelly Skillen. Represents more than 100 clients. 50% of clients are new/unpublished writers. Currently handles: 40% nonfiction books; 30% novels; 5% juvenile books; 25% movie scripts.

● In his time in the literary world, Mr. Miller has successfully managed more than 1,000 books and dozens of motion picture and television properties. He is the author of *Author! Screenwriter!*; Ms. Skillen was previously in the restaurant and nightclub industry.

Member Agents Peter Miller (''big'' nonfiction, business, true crime, religion); Kelly Skillen, kelly@p malitfilm.com (literary fiction, narrative nonfiction, pop culture); Adrienne Rosado (literary and commercial fiction, young adult).

Represents Nonfiction books, novels, juvenile books, movie scripts, TV scripts, TV movie of the week. **Considers these nonfiction areas:** Biography/autobiography; business/economics; child guidance/ parenting; cooking/foods/nutrition; current affairs; ethnic/cultural interests; humor/satire; memoirs; money/finance; popular culture; religious/inspirational; self-help/personal improvement; sports; true crime/investigative. **Considers these fiction areas:** Action/adventure; detective/police/crime; erotica; ethnic; experimental; gay/lesbian; historical; humor/satire; juvenile; literary; mainstream/contemporary; mystery/suspense; psychic/supernatural; religious/inspirational; romance; thriller; young adult; women's. **Considers these script subject areas:** Action/adventure; comedy; mainstream; romantic comedy; romantic drama; thriller.

○━ ''PMA believes in long-term relationships with professional authors. We manage an author's overall career—hence the name—and have strong connections to Hollywood.'' Actively seeking new ideas beautifully executed. Does not want to receive poetry, stage plays, picture books and clichés.

How to Contact Query with SASE, submit publishing history, author bio. Send no attachments or mss of any kind unless requested. Accepts e-mail queries. No fax queries. Considers simultaneous queries. Responds in 4-6 weeks to mss. 5-7 days for e-mail queries; six months for paper submissions. Returns materials only with SASE. Obtains most new clients through recommendations from others, solicitations, conferences.

Recent Sales *For the Sake of Liberty,* by M. William Phelps (Thomas Dunne Books); *The Haunting of Cambria*, by Richard Taylor (Tor); *Cover Girl Confidential*, by Beverly Bartlett (5 Spot); *Ten Prayers God Always Says Yes To!*, by Anthony DeStefano (Doubleday); *Miss Fido Manners: The Complete Book of Dog Etiquette*, by Charlotte Reed (Adams Media); film rights to *Murder in the Heartland*, by M. William Phelps (Mathis Entertainment); film rights to *The Killer's Game*, by Jay Bonansinga (Andrew Lazar/Mad Chance, Inc.).

Terms Agent receives 15% commission on domestic sales; 25% commission on foreign sales. Offers written contract; 30-day notice must be given to terminate contract. This agency charges for approved expenses, such as photocopies and overnight delivery.

Writers' Conferences A full list of Mr. Miller's speaking engagements is available online.

Tips ''Don't approach agents before your work is ready, and always approach them as professionally as possible. Don't give up.''

FRED R. PRICE LITERARY AGENCY

14044 Ventura Blvd., Suite 201, Sherman Oaks CA 91423. (818)763-6365. Signatory of WGA.

◎ SHELDON PROSNIT AGENCY

800 S. Robertson Blvd., Suite 6, Los Angeles CA 90035. 310-652-8778. E-mail: rebecca@lspagency.net. Web site: www.lspagency.net/. **Contact:** Robin Sheldon. Signatory of WGA. Currently handles: movie scripts; TV scripts; Commercials.

Represents Movie scripts, TV scripts, commercials.

How to Contact This agency is very selective, as writers are only one of many types of creative artists they rep. Seek a referral.

PTI TALENT AGENCY

14724 Ventura Blvd., Penthouse Suite, Sherman Oaks CA 91403. (818)386-1310. Fax: (818)386-1311. Web site: www.ptitalentagency.com/. **Contact:** Sheryl Abrams.

QUALITA DELL' ARTE

6303 Owensmouth Ave., 10th Floor, Woodland Hills CA 91367. 818-598-8073. Signatory of WGA.

◎ THE QUILLCO AGENCY

3104 W. Cumberland Court, Westlake Village CA 91362. (805)495-8436. Fax: (805)373-9868. E-mail: quillco2@aol.com. **Contact:** Sandy Mackey. Estab. 1993. Signatory of WGA. Represents 7 clients.

Represents Feature film, TV movie of the week, animation, documentary.

How to Contact Prefers to read materials exclusively. Not accepting query letters at this time.

Recent Sales This agency prefers not to share information on specific sales.

Terms Agent receives 10% commission on domestic sales; 10% commission on foreign sales.

READ. A LITERARY & TALENT AGENCY

8033 Sunset Blvd., Suite 937, Los Angeles CA 90046. (323)876-2800. E-mail: melissa@readagency.net. **Contact:** Melissa Read. Signatory of WGA. Other clients include Courtney Rundell.

REAL CREATIVES WORLDWIDE

14 Dean St., London England W1D 3RS, United Kingdom. (44)(207)437-4188. E-mail: malcolm.rasa la@realcreatives.com. **Contact:** Malcolm Rasala, Mark Maco. Estab. 1984.

Represents Episodic drama, Technology, Science & General entertainment scripts. **Considers these nonfiction areas:** Science/technology.

How to Contact Query with SASE.

REBEL ENTERTAINMENT PARTNERS, INC.

5700 Wilshire Blvd., Suite 456, Los Angeles CA 90036. (323)935-1700. Fax: (323)932-9901. E-mail: inquiry@reptalent.com. Web site: www.reptalent.com/. Signatory of WGA.

Member Agents Philip Irven; Seth Lawrence; Jason Egenberg; David Olsen.

◙ REDHAMMER MANAGEMENT, LTD.

186 Bickenhall Mansions, London England W1U 6BX, United Kingdom. (44)(207)487-3465. E-mail: info@redhammer.info. Web site: www.redhammer.info. **Contact:** Peter Cox, managing director. Estab. 1999. Represents 24 clients. 65% of clients are new/unpublished writers. Currently handles: 40% nonfiction books; 10% novels; 30% juvenile books; 10% movie scripts; 10% TV scripts.

- Prior to becoming an agent, Mr. Cox was a bestselling author. He was also the managing director of an advertising agency.

Represents Nonfiction books, novels, juvenile books, movie scripts, TV scripts, TV movie of the week, documentary. **Considers these nonfiction areas:** Biography/autobiography; business/economics; current affairs; gay/lesbian issues; government/politics/law; health/medicine; history; how-to; humor/satire; language/literature/criticism; memoirs; military/war; money/finance; music/dance; nature/environment; popular culture; psychology; religious/inspirational; science/technology; self-help/personal improvement; sociology; sports; true crime/investigative. **Considers these fiction areas:** Action/adventure; erotica; family saga; feminist; gay/lesbian; historical; horror; humor/satire; juvenile; literary; mainstream/contemporary; mystery/suspense; romance; science fiction; sports; thriller; young adult; women's/chick lit. **Considers these script subject areas:** Action/adventure; biography/autobiography; comedy; contemporary issues; detective/police/crime; fantasy; glitz; historical; horror; juvenile; mainstream; mystery/suspense; romantic comedy; romantic drama; science fiction; thriller.

- ○━ "We handle a small number of clients and give them unparalleled attention, help them plan their writing careers, fulfill their goals and dreams, and leverage maximum value out of all aspects of their creative output." Actively seeking committed, top-flight authors with distinctive voices and extraordinary talent. Does not want to receive bulk e-mail submissions. "Read our Web site if you are serious about submitting work to us."

How to Contact See the Web site for submission information. Considers simultaneous queries. Responds in 6 weeks to queries; 6 weeks to mss. Returns materials only with SASE.

Recent Sales Sold 20 titles and sold 4 scripts in the last year. *Jack Flint and the Redthorn Sword*, by Joe Donnelly (Orion Children's Books); *Perfect Hostage*, by Justin Wintle (Hutchinson); *Dave Allen: The Biography*, by Carolyn Soutar (Orion); *The God Effect*, by Brian Clegg (St. Martin's Press). Other clients include Martin Bell, Nicolas Booth, John Brindley, Audrey Eyton, Maria Harris, U.S. Sen. Orrin Hatch, Amanda Lees, Nicholas Monson, Michelle Paver, Donald Trelford, David Yelland.

Terms Agent receives 17.5% commission on domestic sales; 20% commission on foreign sales. Offers written contract; 90-day notice must be given to terminate contract. "We charge reimbursement for couriers and FedEx but these fees are applied only once the writer has started earning royalty."

REISLER, AGENCE

Reisler Talent, c.p. 55067 csp Fairmount, Montreal Quebec H2T 3E2, Canada. (514)843-4551. Fax: (866)906-6106. Web site: www.reisler.ca/. Estab. 1981. Member of WGC.

Member Agents Mollye Reisler, Tania Giampetrone

Represents Movie scripts, TV scripts, animation, stage plays, Commercials.

How to Contact Query with SASE.

Recent Sales Other clients include Don Druick, Mark Blutman.

RESULT TALENT GROUP

RTG, 468 N. Camden Drive, Suite 300J, Beverly Hills CA 90210. (310)601-3186. Fax: (310)388-3121. E-mail: newfaces@rtgtalent.com. Web site: www.rtgtalent.com. **Contact:** Darren VanCleave, darren @rtgtalent.com.

Represents Movie scripts, feature film, TV scripts.

o→ "We are a full service Production and Talent Management Company representing a strong film slate and an impressive array of working actors and celebrities. RTG manages the careers of artists with extensive experience and undiscovered talented actors that need hands on development to get to the next level. The RTG management team has successfully managed Fortune 500 Companies, private enterprises, and careers of professionals for over 25 years."

◎ RGM ASSOCIATES

Robyn Gardiner Management, 64-76 Kippax Street, Level 2, Suite 202, Surry Hills NSW 2010, Australia. E-mail: info@rgm.com.au. Web site: www.rgm.com.au/. **Contact:** Lisa Scott or Dayne Kelly. Estab. 1982.

Represents Theatrical stage play, stage plays.

o→ "RGM Artist Group is one of Australia's leading theatrical management agencies, representing a number of great plays which are available for amateur and professional production. At rgm.com.au you can read a synopsis of each play, find out cast size and gender divisions, and learn about the playwrights."

How to Contact All unsolicited mss returned unopened.

Recent Sales Other clients include Hilary Bell; Paul Brown; Matt Cameron; Raimondo Cortese; Wesley Enoch; Louise Fox; Jonathan Gavin; Alma De Groen; Trudy Hellier; Ned Manning; Suzie Miller; Justin Monjo; Tee O'Neill; Debra Oswald; Suneeta Peres da Costa; Andrew Upton; Alana Valentine; Catherine Zimdahl.

THE LISA RICHARDS AGENCY

108 Upper Leeson St., Dublin Republic of Ireland 4, Ireland. (03)(531)637-5000. Fax: (03)531)667-1256. E-mail: info@lisarichards.ie. Web site: www.lisarichards.ie. **Contact:** Chairman: Alan Cook; Managing Director: Miranda Pheifer, Fergus Cronin, Patrick Sutton; Actors' Agents: Lisa Cook, Richard Cook, Jonathan Shankey, Lorraine Cummins: Comedy Agents: Caroline Lee, Christine Dwyer; Literary Agent: Faith O'Grady; Voice Overs & Corp. Bookings: Eavan Kenny. Estab. 1989.

Represents Movie scripts, TV scripts, Broadcast. **Considers these nonfiction areas:** Biography/auto-biography; current affairs; history; memoirs; popular culture; travel; Politics. **Considers these fiction areas:** General fiction titles. **Considers these script subject areas:** Comedy; general scipts.

How to Contact Submit proposal package, synopsis, 2-3 sample chapter(s), query letter with SAE.

Recent Sales Other clients include Denise Deegan, Arlene Hunt, Roisin Ingle, Declan Lynch, Jennifer MacCann, Sarah O'Brien, Kevin Rafter.

⊘ RIPPLE EFFECT MANAGEMENT

468 N. Camden Drive, 2nd Floor, Beverly Hills CA 90210. E-mail: contact@rippleeffectmanagement. com. Web site: www.rippleeffectmanagement.com/. Currently handles: movie scripts.

Represents Feature film.

How to Contact This agency is not seeking new clients at this time. No e-mail or fax queries. Obtains most new clients through they will find writers.

◪ LESLIE RIVERS, INTERNATIONAL (LRI)

P.O. Box 940772, Houston TX 77094-7772. (281)493»5822. Fax: (281)493»5835. E-mail: LRivers@Les lieRivers.com. Web site: www.leslierivers.com. **Contact:** Judith Bruni. Estab. 2005; adheres to AAR's canon of ethics. Represents 20 clients. 80% of clients are new/unpublished writers. Currently handles: 15% nonfiction books; 70% novels; 5% scholarly books.

Member Agents Judith Bruni, literary agent and founder; Mark Bruni, consulting editor.

Represents Nonfiction books, novels, scholarly books, movie scripts, TV scripts, stage plays. **Considers these nonfiction areas:** Open to all genres, as long as the author is established with a platform. **Considers these fiction areas:** All fiction genres, but no children's fiction. **Considers these script subject areas:** Considers all script genres.

> ⊶ LRI collaborates with creative professionals and offers a customized, boutique service, based on the client's individual requirements. Send only your finest work. Actively seeking fiction— all subgenres. Does not want to receive children's books or poetry.

How to Contact Query with SASE, submit synopsis, author bio, 3 chapters or 50 pages, whichever is longer. Prefers an exclusive read, but will consider simultaneous queries. Accepts e-mail queries. No fax queries. Responds in 2 months to queries; 2 months to mss. Returns materials only with SASE. Obtains most new clients through recommendations from others, solicitations.

Terms Agent receives 15% commission on domestic sales; 25% commission on foreign sales. Offers written contract; 90-day notice must be given to terminate contract. This agency charges for postage, printing, copying, etc. If no sale is made, no charges are enforced.

⦾ MICHAEL D. ROBINS & ASSOCIATES

23241 Ventura Blvd., #300, Woodland Hills CA 91364. (818)343-1755. Fax: (818)343-7355. E-mail: mdr2@msn.com. **Contact:** Michael D. Robins. Estab. 1991. Member of DGA; signatory of WGA.

> ● Prior to opening his agency, Mr. Robins was a literary agent at a mid-sized agency.

Represents Nonfiction books, novels, movie scripts, feature film, TV scripts, TV movie of the week, episodic drama, animation, miniseries, stage plays.

How to Contact Query with SASE. Accepts e-mail and fax queries. Considers simultaneous queries. Obtains most new clients through recommendations from others.

Recent Sales This agency prefers not to share information on specific sales.

Terms Agent receives 10% commission on domestic sales; 10% commission on foreign sales. Offers written contract.

MAGGIE ROIPHE AGENCY

1721 S. Garth Ave., Los Angeles CA 90035. (310)876-1561. Signatory of WGA. Represents 25 clients.

> ● Maggie Roiphe graduated from Oberlin College.

Represents Movie scripts, feature film. **Considers these script subject areas:** Action/adventure; comedy; horror; romantic comedy; thriller.

> ⊶ "Actively seeking high concept comedies, urban comedies, thrillers—especially psychological thrillers, action, horror, a really good romantic comedy." Other things of importance include "originality. Strong concept, characters and dialogue. The writing cannot be not oblivious to the marketplace."

How to Contact This agency likes writers who contact through a referral.

BRANT ROSE AGENCY

6671 Sunset Blvd., Suite 1584-B, Los Angeles CA 90028. (323)460-6464. Estab. 2001. Signatory of WGA.

• Brant Rose began his career as an agent at UTA in 1994. Before that, he worked at Procter & Gamble in brand management. He graduated from Dartmouth College.

Represents Movie scripts, TV scripts.

How to Contact Query with SASE.

☑ THE ROTHMAN BRECHER AGENCY

9250 Wilshire Blvd., Penthouse, Beverly Hills CA 90212. (310)247-9898. E-mail: reception@rothman brecher.com. **Contact:** Andrea Kavoosi. Signatory of WGA.

Represents Movie scripts, feature film, TV scripts.

THE SARNOFF COMPANY, INC.

10 Universal City Plaza, 20th Floor, Universal City CA 91608. (818)753-2377. **Contact:** Jim Sarnoff. Estab. 2000. Signatory of WGA.

Represents Movie scripts.

☑ SAYLE SCREEN, LTD

11 Jubilee Place, London England SW3 3TD, United Kingdom. (44)(207)823-3883. Fax: (44)(207)823-3363. E-mail: info@saylescreen.com. Web site: www.saylescreen.com. Estab. 1952. Represents 100+ clients. 5% of clients are new/unpublished writers. Currently handles: 50% movie scripts; 50% TV scripts.

Member Agents Toby Moorcroft; Jane Villiers; Matthew Bates.

Represents Movie scripts, TV scripts, episodic drama, sitcom. **Considers these script subject areas:** Action/adventure; comedy; contemporary issues; detective/police/crime; ethnic; experimental; fantasy; horror; mainstream; mystery/suspense; psychic/supernatural; romantic comedy; romantic drama; teen; thriller.

  ⚘ Actively seeking writers and directors for film and TV.

How to Contact Query with synopsis, bio, SASE. No e-mail or fax queries. Responds in 2-3 months to queries; 2-3 months to mss. Returns materials only with SASE. Obtains most new clients through recommendations from others.

Recent Sales *Curious Incident of the Dog in the Nighttime*, by Mark Haddon (Warner Brothers); *Night Watch*, by Sarah Waters (BBC); *Dog Called Cork*, by Josie Doder (Xingu); *Dreamer*, by David Hilton (Rocket/Silver Creek).

Terms Agent receives 10% commission on domestic sales; 15% commission on foreign sales. Offers written contract; 1-month notice must be given to terminate contract.

SCHIOWITZ CONNOR ANKRUM WOLF, INC.

1680 Vine St., Suite 1016, Los Angeles CA 90028. (323)463-8355. Fax: (323)463-7355.

KATHLEEN SCHULTZ ASSOCIATES

Dade/Schultz Associates, 6442 Coldwater Canyon, Suite 206, Valley Glen CA 91606. (818)760-3100. Fax: (818)760-3125. E-mail: KschultzAssoc@aol.com. Signatory of WGA.

Represents Movie scripts, feature film.

DAVID SHAPIRA & ASSOCIATES

193 N. Robertson Blvd., Beverly Hills CA 90211. (310)967-0480. Signatory of WGA.
Member Agents David Shapira; Mark Scroggs; Ryan Karvola.
Represents Theatrical stage play, stage plays.

O→ "We are a boutique, theatrical talent agency that represent actors and writers."

FRANK ELLIOTT SHAPIRO AGENCY

5522 Lemona Ave., Sherman Oaks CA 91411. (818)376-1583. Signatory of WGA.
Represents Movie scripts.

⊘ MARTY SHAPIRO MANAGEMENT

1333 Beverly Green, Los Angeles CA 90035. (310)859-8877. Fax: (310)276-0630. **Contact:** Martin Shapiro. Estab. 1969.
Represents Nonfiction books, novels, novellas, feature film, TV movie of the week, episodic drama, sitcom, animation (movie/TV), miniseries, soap opera, variety show.

O→ Does not accept unsolicited material. Represents work from published authors only.
How to Contact Obtains most new clients through recommendations from others.
Recent Sales This agency prefers not to share information on specific sales.
Terms Agent receives 10% commission on domestic sales; 20% commission on foreign sales. Offers written contract.

SHAPIRO-WEST & ASSOCIATES

141 El Camino Drive, Suite 205, Beverly Hills CA 90212. (310)278-8896. Fax: (310)278-7238. **Contact:** Howard West, president. Estab. 1973.
Member Agents Howard West; George Shapiro; Diane Barnett Shapiro.
Represents Theatrical stage play, stage plays.

◎ THE SHARLAND ORGANISATION

The Manor House, Manor Street, Raunds Northamptonshire NN96JW, United Kingdom. E-mail: info@sharlandorganisation.co.uk. Web site: www.sharlandorganisation.co.uk/. **Contact:** Mike Sharland, Alice Sharland. Estab. 1988.

● Before becoming an agent, Mike Sharland started in the film industry and became a writer on more than 600 TV shows. He is a past chair of the Writers Guild of Great Britain.
Represents Movie scripts, feature film, TV scripts, soap opera, theatrical stage play, stage plays, Radio Scripts.
How to Contact Query with SASE.
Recent Sales Other clients include David Conville; David Gooderson; Brian McAvera; Anthony Marriott; Alistair Foot; Mike Coleman.

SHEIL LAND ASSOCIATES, LTD

43 Doughty St., London England WC1N 2LS, United Kingdom. (44)(207)405-9351. Fax: (44)(207)831-2127. E-mail: info@sheilland.co.uk. **Contact:** Sonia Land, Vivien Green, Ben Mason, Emily Hayward (Film Theatre & TV); Sophie Janson (Film, Theatre & TV); Gaia Banks (Foreign Rights). Estab. 1962.
Represents Movie scripts, Braodcast Scripts. **Considers these nonfiction areas:** Biography/autobiog-

raphy; cooking/foods/nutrition; gardening; history; humor/satire; military/war; travel; Politics. **Considers these fiction areas:** Detective/police/crime; literary; romance; thriller; Drama.

o— No science fiction, fantasy, children's or poetry considered.

How to Contact Submit proposal package, synopsis, 2-3 sample chapter(s), author bio, SAE.

Recent Sales Other clients include Peter Ackroyd, Hugh Bicheno, Melvyn Bragg, David Cohen, Anna del Conte, Seamus Dean, Bonnie Greer, Susan Hill, Richard Holmes, HRH The Prince of Wales, Mark Irving, Richard Mabey.

⬤ KEN SHERMAN & ASSOCIATES

9507 Santa Monica Blvd., Beverly Hills CA 90210. (310)273-8840. Fax: (310)271-2875. **Contact:** Ken Sherman. Estab. 1989. Member of BAFTA, PEN International; signatory of WGA, DGA. Represents approximately 35 clients. 10% of clients are new/unpublished writers.

● Prior to opening his agency, Mr. Sherman was with The William Morris Agency, The Lantz Office and Paul Kohner, Inc. He has taught "The Business of Writing For Film and Television and The Book Worlds" at UCLA and USC. He is currently a commissioner of arts and cultural affairs in the city of West Hollywood, and is on the international advisory board of the Christopher Isherwood Foundation.

Represents Nonfiction books, novels, movie scripts, TV scripts (not episodic), teleplays, life rights, film/TV rights to books. **Considers these nonfiction areas:** Agriculture/horticulture; americana; animals; anthropology/archaeology; art/architecture/design; biography/autobiography; business/economics; child guidance/parenting; computers/electronic; cooking/foods/nutrition; crafts/hobbies; current affairs; education; ethnic/cultural interests; gardening; gay/lesbian issues; government/politics/law; health/medicine; history; how-to; humor/satire; interior design/decorating; language/literature/criticism; memoirs; military/war; money/finance; multicultural; music/dance; nature/environment; New Age/metaphysics; philosophy; photography; popular culture; psychology; recreation; regional; religious/inspirational; science/technology; self-help/personal improvement; sex; sociology; software; spirituality; sports; theater/film; translation; travel; true crime/investigative; women's issues/studies; young adult; creative nonfiction. **Considers these fiction areas:** Action/adventure; comic books/cartoon; confession; detective/police/crime; erotica; ethnic; experimental; family saga; fantasy; feminist; gay/lesbian; glitz; gothic; hi-lo; historical; horror; humor/satire; literary; mainstream/contemporary; military/war; multicultural; multimedia; mystery/suspense; New Age; occult; picture books; plays; poetry; poetry in translation; psychic/supernatural; regional; religious/inspirational; romance; science fiction; short story collections; spiritual; sports; thriller; translation; westerns/frontier; young adult. **Considers these script subject areas:** Action/adventure; biography/autobiography; cartoon/animation; comedy; contemporary issues; detective/police/crime; erotica; ethnic; experimental; family saga; fantasy; feminist; gay/lesbian; glitz; historical; horror; mainstream; multicultural; multimedia; mystery/suspense; psychic/supernatural; regional; religious/inspirational; romantic comedy; romantic drama; science fiction; sports; teen; thriller; western/frontier.

How to Contact Contact by referral only. Reports in approximately 1 month to mss. Obtains most new clients through recommendations from others.

Recent Sales Sold more than 20 scripts in the last year. *Back Roads*, by Tawni O'Dell (Dreamworks); *Priscilla Salyers Story*, produced by Andrea Baynes (ABC); *Toys of Glass*, by Martin Booth (ABC/Saban Entertainment); *Brazil*, by John Updike (film rights to Glaucia Carmagos); *Fifth Sacred Thing*, by Starhawk (Bantam); *Questions From Dad*, by Dwight Twilly (Tuttle); *Snow Falling on Cedars*, by

David Guterson (Universal Pictures); *The Witches of Eastwick—The Musical*, by John Updike (Cameron Macintosh, Ltd.).

Terms Agent receives 15% commission on domestic sales; 15% commission on foreign sales; 10-15% commission on dramatic rights sales. Offers written contract. Charges clients for reasonable office expenses (postage, photocopying, etc.).

Writers' Conferences Maui Writers' Conference; Squaw Valley Writers' Workshop; Santa Barbara Writers' Conference; Screenwriting Conference in Santa Fe; Aspen Summer Words Literary Festival.

⦿ MICHAEL SIEGEL & ASSOCIATES

8330 West Third St., Los Angeles CA 90048. (323)658-8600. Fax: (323)658-6262. E-mail: inquiries@msalit.com. Web site: www.msalit.com/.

Tips Not much info is available about this selective agency. Use a referral to break in.

BLAIR SILVER & COMPANY LLC

P.O. Box 3188, Manhattan Beach CA 90266. (310)546-4669. E-mail: blairsilver@aol.com. Web site: www.blairsilver.com/.

Represents Movie scripts, TV scripts, multimedia, video games.

○⚊ This agency reps Actors, Animators, Athletes, Comedians, Directors, Models, Multimedia Artists, Music Professionals, Producers, Screenwriters, Television Writers and Video Game Professionals.

How to Contact Query with a referral.

THE SUSAN SMITH COMPANY

1344 N. Wetherly Drive, Los Angeles CA 90069. (310)276-4224. E-mail: susan@susansmithco.com. Web site: www.susansmithco.com. Signatory of WGA.

SPICER PRODUCTIONS, DAVID

274 Military Road, Dover Heights NSW 2030, Australia. E-mail: david@davidspicer.com. Web site: www.davidspicer.com/. **Contact:** David Spicer.

● The agency was launched when David Spicer began researching a book and was asked by composer Bernard J. Taylor to be his agent. David Spicer also works as a TV news reporter for the Australian Broadcasting Corporation in Sydney.

Represents Stage plays, Musicals, Operetta, Pantomimes.

○⚊ Musicals, operetta, plays, and pantomimes for professional, amateur, and school productions.

STARS: THE AGENCY

23 Grant Avenue, 4th Floor, San Francisco CA 94108. (415)421-6272. Fax: (415)421-7620. E-mail: connieh@starsagency.com. Web site: starsagency.com/. **Contact:** Connie Hall, Literary Agent. Estab. 1986. Member of ATA; signatory of WGA.

Member Agents Kristin Claxon Stinnett; Connie Hall.

Represents Movie scripts.

○⚊ This focuses mostly on onscreen talent, but does handle screenplays as well.

How to Contact Query with SASE.

◎ STARWIL PRODUCTIONS

433 N. Camden Drive, 4th Floor, Beverly Hills CA 90210. (818)761-3213. **Contact:** A. Starwil.

Represents Movie scripts, feature film, TV scripts, TV movie of the week.

How to Contact Please query this company by referral only. No fax queries.

ELAINE STEEL

110 Gloucester Ave., London England NW1 8HX, United Kingdom. (44)(208)348-0918. Fax: (44)(208)341-9807. E-mail: ecmsteel@aol.com. **Contact:** Elaine Steel. Estab. 1986.

Represents Nonfiction books, feature film, TV scripts. **Considers these fiction areas:** General.

How to Contact Send query letter with SAE.

STEIN AGENCY

5125 Oakdale Ave., Woodland Hills CA 91364. (818)594-8990. Fax: (818)594-8998. E-mail: mail@th esteinagency.com. Web site: www.thesteinagency.com. **Contact:** Mitchel Stein. Estab. 2000. Signatory of WGA. Represents 60 clients. Currently handles: 20% movie scripts; 80% TV scripts.

Represents Movie scripts, TV scripts, episodic drama, sitcom.

How to Contact Query with SASE. Discards material without SASE. Accepts e-mail and fax queries. Considers simultaneous queries. Responds in 1 week to queries. Returns materials only with SASE. Obtains most new clients through recommendations from others. Sold 4 scripts in the last year. This agency prefers not to share information on specific sales.

Terms Agent receives 10% commission on domestic sales; 10% commission on foreign sales. Offers written contract.

◎ MICHELINE STEINBERG ASSOCIATES

104 Great Portland St., London England W1W 6PE, United Kingdom. (44)(207)631-1310. Fax: (44)(207)631-1146. E-mail: info@steinplays.com. Web site: www.steinplays.com/. Estab. 1985. Currently handles: movie scripts; TV scripts; stage plays; Radio Scripts.

Represents Movie scripts, feature film, TV scripts, animation, theatrical stage play, stage plays, Radio Scripts. **Considers these script subject areas:** Action/adventure; biography/autobiography; cartoon/animation; comedy; contemporary issues; detective/police/crime; erotica; ethnic; experimental; family saga; fantasy; feminist; gay/lesbian; glitz; historical; horror; juvenile; mainstream; multicultural; mystery/suspense; psychic/supernatural; regional; religious/inspirational; romantic comedy; romantic drama; science fiction; sports; teen; thriller; western/frontier.

    ◦ₐ The agency represents writers and writer-directors for stage, television, film, radio, and animation.

How to Contact Query via e-mail first. Accepts e-mail queries. No fax queries.

ROCHELLE STEVENS & CO.

2 Terretts Place, Upper Street, London England N1 1QZ, United Kingdom. (44)(207)359-3900. Fax: (44)(207)354-5729. E-mail: info@rochellestevens.com. **Contact:** Founder: Rochelle Stevens; Agents: Frances Arnold, Lucy Fawcett. Estab. 1984.

Represents Movie scripts, TV scripts, stage plays, radio scripts.

How to Contact Submit author bio, query letter with SAE.

STONE MANNERS AGENCY

6500 Wilshire Blvd., Suite 550, Los Angeles CA 90048. (323)655-1313. E-mail: postmaster@stoneman ners.com. Estab. 1982. Signatory of WGA.

Represents Movie scripts, TV scripts.

How to Contact Query with SASE. Accepts e-mail queries. No fax queries.

Recent Sales This agency prefers not to share information on specific sales.

Terms Agent receives 10% commission on domestic sales; 10% commission on foreign sales.

MITCHELL K. STUBBS & ASSOCIATES

8695 W. Washington Blvd., Suite 204, Culver City CA 90232. (310)838-1200. Fax: (310)838-1245. Web site: www.mksagency.com/. Signatory of WGA.

SUITE A MANAGEMENT TALENT & LITERARY AGENCY

120 El Camino Drive, Suite 202, Beverly Hills CA 90212. (310)278-0801. Fax: (310)278-0807. E-mail: suite-a@juno.com. **Contact:** Lloyd Robinson. Estab. 1996; Signatory of WGA, DGA. Represents 76 clients. 10% of clients are new/unpublished writers. Currently handles: 15% novels; 40% movie scripts; 40% TV scripts; 5% stage plays.

• Prior to becoming an agent, Mr. Robinson worked as a manager.

Member Agents Lloyd Robinson (adaptation of books and plays for development as features or TV MOW); Kevin Douglas (scripts for film and TV); Judy Jacobs (feature development).

Represents Feature film, TV movie of the week, episodic drama, documentary, miniseries, variety show, stage plays, CD-ROM. **Considers these script subject areas:** Action/adventure; cartoon/animation; comedy; contemporary issues; detective/police/crime; erotica; ethnic; experimental; family saga; fantasy; mainstream; mystery/suspense; psychic/supernatural; religious/inspirational; romantic comedy; romantic drama; science fiction; sports; teen; thriller; western/frontier.

○┬ "We represent screenwriters, playwrights, novelists, producers and directors."

How to Contact Submit synopsis, outline/proposal, logline. Obtains most new clients through recommendations from others.

Recent Sales This agency prefers not to share information on specific sales or client names.

Terms Agent receives 10% commission on domestic sales; 10% commission on foreign sales. Offers written contract, binding for minimum 1 year. Charges clients for photocopying, messenger, FedEx, postage.

Tips "We are a talent agency specializing in the copyright business. Fifty percent of our clients generate copyright (screenwriters, playwrights and novelists). Fifty percent of our clients service copyright (producers and directors). We represent produced, published, and/or WGA writers who are eligible for staff TV positions, as well as novelists and playwrights whose works may be adapted for film or TV."

SUMMIT TALENT & LITERARY AGENCY

9454 Wilshire Blvd., Suite 203, Beverly Hills CA 90212. 310-205-9730. **Contact:** Sanford. Estab. 2000. Signatory of WGA.

THE SWETKY AGENCY

2150 Balboa Way, No. 29, St. George UT 84770. E-mail: fayeswetky@amsaw.org. Web site: www.am saw.org/swetkyagency/index.html. **Contact:** Faye M. Swetky. Estab. 2000. Member of American Society of Authors and Writers. Represents 40+ clients. 80% of clients are new/unpublished writers. Currently handles: 30% nonfiction books; 30% novels; 20% movie scripts; 20% TV scripts.

• Prior to becoming an agent, Ms. Swetky was an editor and corporate manager. She has also raised and raced thoroughbred horses.

Represents Nonfiction books, novels, short story collections, juvenile books, movie scripts, feature film, TV scripts, TV movie of the week, sitcom, documentary. **Considers these nonfiction areas:** All major nonfiction genres. **Considers these fiction areas:** All major fiction genres. **Considers these script subject areas:** Action/adventure; biography/autobiography; cartoon/animation; comedy; contemporary issues; detective/police/crime; erotica; ethnic; experimental; family saga; fantasy; feminist; gay/lesbian; glitz; historical; horror; juvenile; mainstream; multicultural; multimedia; mystery/suspense; psychic/supernatural; regional; religious/inspirational; romantic comedy; romantic drama; science fiction; sports; teen; thriller; western/frontier.

O— "We handle only book-length fiction and nonfiction and feature-length movie and television scripts. Please visit our Web site before submitting. All agency-related information is there, including a sample contract, e-mail submission forms, policies, clients, etc." Actively seeking young adult material. Do not send unprofessionally prepared mss and/or scripts.

How to Contact See Web site for submission instructions. Accepts e-mail queries only. Considers simultaneous queries. Response time varies. Obtains most new clients through queries.

Recent Sales *Zen and the Art of Pond Building*, by J.D. Herda (Sterling); *Solid Stiehl*, by D.J. Herda (Archebooks); *24/7*, by Susan Diplacido (Zumaya Publications); *House on the Road to Salisbury*, by Lisa Adams (Archebooks). ***Movie/TV MOW script(s) optioned/sold:*** *Demons 5*, by Jim O'Rear (Katzir Productions); *Detention* and *Instinct Vs. Reason*, by Garrett Hargrove (Filmjack Productions).

Terms Agent receives 15% commission on domestic sales; 20% commission on foreign sales; 20% commission on dramatic rights sales. Offers written contract, binding for 1 year; 30-day notice must be given to terminate contract.

Tips "Be professional. Have a professionally prepared product."

☑ TALENT SOURCE

1711 Dean Forest Road, Suite H, Savannah GA 31408. E-mail: michael@talentsource.com. Web site: www.talentsource.com/literary.html. **Contact:** Michael L. Shortt. Estab. 1991. Signatory of WGA. 35% of clients are new/unpublished writers. Currently handles: 85% movie scripts; 15% TV scripts.

• Prior to becoming an agent, Mr. Shortt was a TV program producer/director.

Represents Feature film, TV movie of the week. **Considers these script subject areas:** Comedy; contemporary issues; detective/police/crime; erotica; family saga; juvenile; mainstream; romantic comedy; romantic drama; teen.

O— Actively seeking character-driven stories (e.g., *Sling Blade* or *Sex, Lies, and Videotape*). Does not want to receive science fiction or scripts with big budget special effects.

How to Contact Send a cover letter (query) with SASE, synopsis. Reports on queries in 10-12 weeks. No e-mail or fax queries. Obtains most new clients through recommendations from others.

Recent Sales This agency prefers not to share information on specific sales.

Terms Agent receives 10% commission on domestic sales; 15% commission on foreign sales. Offers written contract.

Tips "See the literary button on our Web site for complete submissions details. No exceptions."

THE TENNYSON AGENCY

10 Cleveland Ave., London England SW20 9EW, United Kingdom. (208)543-5939. E-mail: submission s@tenagy.co.uk. Web site: www.tenagy.co.uk. **Contact:** Christopher Oxford (Film, Theatre & TV scripts); Adam Sheldon (Arts & Humanities); Jane Hutchinson. Estab. 2001. **Considers these nonfiction areas:** Popular culture; Arts & Humanities. **Considers these fiction areas:** General fiction.

o━ Does not want to receive poetry, short stories, science fiction, fantasy or children's titles.

How to Contact Submit proposal package, synopsis, author bio, details of any previously published work. SAE.

Recent Sales *Billy's Day Out*, by Anthony Mann; *Helen's Story*, by Ken Ross; *Lighthouse*, by Graeme Scarfe; *The Hammer*, by Jonathan Holloway. Other clients include Vivienne Allen, Tony Bagley, Kristina Bedford, Alastair Cording, Caroline Coxon, Iain Grant, Philip Hurd-Wood, Joanna Leigh, Steve MacGregor, John Ryan, Walter Saunders, Diane Speakman, Diana Ward, and the estate of Julian Howell.

◎ 3SG TALENT MANAGEMENT

45 Charles Street East, LL7, Toronto Ontario M4Y 1S2, Canada. (416)925-9009. E-mail: info@3sg.ca. Web site: www.3sg.ca. Estab. 2001. Member of TAMAC.

• Catherine Knights, founder of 3SG, is a graduate of York University and has been a professional agent in Toronto since 1998. Mary Swinton has worked in the Canadian entertainment industry for 35 years. She was a member in good standing of ACTRA and Actor's Equity from 1971 to 1990, before she became a talent agent. She spent two years at the Edward G. Talent Agency and 15 years with the Core Group Talent Agency Inc., where she represented clients for film, television, theatre, voiceovers, commercials, industrials, and print as well as creating the company's children's division.

Represents Theatrical stage play, stage plays, Commercials.

Recent Sales Other clients include Wendy Lill.

◎ J.M. THURLEY MANAGEMENT

Archery House, 33 Archery Square, Walmer, Deal, Kent England, UK. Estab. 1976. **Considers these script subject areas:** General/commercial.

o━ Does not want to receive short stories, poetry, articles, fantasy or play scripts.

How to Contact Submit query letter & SAE.

TV WRITERS, LTD

74 The Drive, Fulham Rd., London England SW6 6JH, United Kingdom. (44)(207)371-8474. Fax: (44)(207)371-8474. E-mail: tvwriters@gmail.com. **Contact:** Company Director: Marie-Louise Hogan. Estab. 2005. **Considers these script subject areas:** Comedy; drama and factual scripts.

How to Contact Query with SASE.

Recent Sales Other clients include Ali Crockatt, Lee Stuart Evans and Jez Stevenson.

◎ JULIA TYRRELL MANAGEMENT, LTD.

57 Greenham Road, London N10 1LN, United Kingdom. (44)208)374-0575. E-mail: julia@jtmanagem ent.co.uk. Web site: www.jtmanagement.co.uk. **Contact:** Abigail Hedderwick. Estab. 2005.

• Following a career as a dancer, Julia Tyrrell started at Noel Gay Organization as an assistant to literary agent Pauline Asper and production secretary for Noel Gay Theatre. After 10 years at Hamilton Asper, she joined MacFarlane Chard Associates before starting her own agency.

Represents Movie scripts, feature film, TV scripts, TV movie of the week, theatrical stage play, stage plays, radio.

How to Contact Query with SASE, submit sample chapter(s), SASE. No e-mail or fax queries.

⊘ UNITED TALENT AGENCY, INC.

UTA, 9560 Wilshire Blvd., Suite 500, Beverly Hills CA 90212-2401. (310)273-6700. Fax: (310)247-1111. Web site: www.unitedtalent.com/. Signatory of WGA.

Represents Nonfiction books, novels, movie scripts, feature film, TV scripts, animation, stage plays, Video Games, Commercials.

How to Contact All unsolicited mss returned unopened. No e-mail or fax queries.

Tips This agency operates exclusively by referral.

⊘ ANNETTE VAN DUREN AGENCY

11684 Ventura Blvd., #235, Studio City CA 91604. (818)752-6000. Fax: (818)752-6985. **Contact:** Annette Van Duren. Estab. 1985. Signatory of WGA. Represents 12 clients.

Represents Feature film, TV movie of the week, episodic drama, sitcom, animation.

   o┐ Not accepting new clients.

Recent Sales This agency prefers not to share information about specific sales.

Terms Agent receives 10% commission on domestic sales. Offers written contract, binding for 2 years.

WARDEN, WHITE & ASSOCIATES

8444 Wilshire Blvd., 4th Floor, Beverly Hills CA 90211. 323-852-1028. **Contact:** Dave Warden. Signatory of WGA.

   o┐ Actively seeking writers who have several screenplays and many treatments ready to pitch. Other clients include the writers of *Sleepless in Seattle, Meet Joe Black* and *Enemy of the State.*

CECILY WARE LITERARY AGENTS

19C John Spencer Square, London England N1 2LZ, United Kingdom. (44)(207)359-3787. Fax: (44)(207)226-9828. E-mail: info@cecilyware.com. **Contact:** Cecily Ware, Warren Sherman, Gilly Schuster. Estab. 1972. **Considers these script subject areas:** Comedy; family saga; juvenile; drama, adaptations, series/serials.

How to Contact Query with SAE.

WASHINGTON SQUARE ARTS & FILMS

310 Bowery, 2nd Floor, New York NY 10012. (212)253-0333. Fax: (212)253-0330. E-mail: production @wsfilms.com. Web site: www.washingtonsquarearts.com.

Represents Feature film, TV scripts, documentary, miniseries, theatrical stage play, stage plays, Musicals.

How to Contact Query only. Do not send unsolicited work.

Recent Sales *Adrift in Manhattan, Sweet Flame, Old Joy,* and *Love Ludlow.* Other clients include Johanna Baldwin, Richard Gray, Chris Jeffries, David Bar Katz, Suzanne Maynard Miller, Kelly Younger.

ANN WAUGH TALENT AGENCY

4741 Laurel Canyon Blvd., Suite 200, N. Hollywood CA 91607. (818)980-0141. Signatory of WGA.
Member Agents John Hugh; Ann Waugh; Connie Hamilton; Shelley Pang; Larry Benedict.

◙ WESTWOOD CREATIVE ARTISTS, LTD.

94 Harbord St., Toronto Ontario M5S 1G6, Canada. (416)964-3302. Fax: (416)975-9209. E-mail:
wca_office@wcaltd.com. Web site: www.wcaltd.com. Represents 200+ clients.
Member Agents Deborah Wood, book-to-film agent; Aston Westwood, book-to-film agent; Linda
McKnight, literary agent; Jackie Kaiser, literary agent; Hilary McMahon, literary agent; John Pearce,
literary agent; Natasha Daneman, subsidiary rights director; Michael Levine, film & TV agent.
Represents Canadian literary fiction and nonfiction.
How to Contact Query with SASE. Use a referral to break into this agency. Accepts e-mail queries.
No fax queries. Considers simultaneous queries.
Recent Sales A biography of Richard Nixon, by Conrad Black (Public Affairs); *The New Cold War:
Revolutions, Rigged Elections and Pipeline Politics in the Former Soviet Union*, by Mark MacKinnon
(Carroll & Graf).

◙ PEREGRINE WHITTLESEY AGENCY

279 Central Park W., New York NY 10024. (212)787-1802. Fax: (212)787-4985. E-mail: pwwagy@aol.
com. **Contact:** Peregrine Whittlesey. Estab. 1986. Signatory of WGA. Represents 30 clients. 50% of
clients are new/unpublished writers. Currently handles: 1% movie scripts; 99% stage plays.
   ⚷ This agency specializes in playwrights who also write for screen and TV.
How to Contact Query with SASE. Prefers to read materials exclusively. Accepts e-mail and fax
queries. Responds in 1 week to queries; 1 month to mss. Obtains most new clients through recommen-
dations from others.
Recent Sales Sold 20 scripts in the last year. Scripts sold to Actors Theatre of Louisville's Humana
Festival, South Coast Repertory, Stratford Festival, Ontario Canada, Alabama Shakespeare Festival,
ACT Seattle, Seattle Rep, Arena Stage, City Theatre Pittsburgh, Repertorio Espanol and producers in
England, Germany and Spain.
Terms Agent receives 10% commission on domestic sales; 15% commission on foreign sales. Offers
written contract, binding for 2 years.

◙ WILL ENTERTAINMENT

1228 Romulus Drive, Glendale CA 91205. (818)389-6895. Fax: (818)246-4520. E-mail: info@willenter
tainment.com. Web site: www.willentertainment.com. **Contact:** Garrett Hicks. Estab. 2003. Represents 20 clients. 30% of clients are new/unpublished writers. Currently handles: 30% juvenile books;
30% movie scripts; 40% TV scripts.
   ● Prior to becoming a literary and script manager, Mr. Hicks was a development executive for
   Disney Animation.
Represents Juvenile books, movie scripts, feature film, TV scripts. **Considers these script subject
areas:** Action/adventure; cartoon/animation; comedy; fantasy; juvenile; mainstream; romantic comedy; teen.
   ⚷ Specializes in children's book authors and illustrators, especially those crossing over from
      film, TV and animation. Juvenile, picture books and young adult.

How to Contact Query with SASE, submit synopsis. Accepts e-mail queries. No fax queries. Considers simultaneous queries. Responds in 2 weeks to queries; 2 weeks to mss. Obtains most new clients through recommendations from others.

Recent Sales Sold 2 titles and sold 5 scripts in the last year. *Hot Sour Salty Sweet*, by Sherri Smith (Delacorte); *Flygirl*, by Sherri Smith (Putnam); *Patty Dolan is Dead*, by Patrick O'Connor (FP Prods/Disney); *Hopeville*, TV pilot by Howard Nemetz (Fox).

Terms Agent receives 15% commission on domestic sales; 15% commission on foreign sales. Offers written contract; 60-day notice must be given to terminate contract.

Tips Mr. Hicks is a manager.

⊘ WRITERS' PRODUCTIONS LITERARY AGENCY

P.O. Box 630, Westport CT 06881-0630. (203)227-8199. E-mail: dlm67@mac.com. **Contact:** David L. Meth. Estab. 1982. Currently handles: 40% novels; 60% drama.

Represents Drama for theater, TV, films and novels (literary fiction).

   o⊸ "We are not accepting new clients at this time."

How to Contact Contact by e-mail, if your work was asked for. No e-mail or fax queries. Obtains most new clients through recommendations from others. This agency prefers not to share information on specific sales.

Terms Agent receives 15% commission on domestic sales; 25% commission on foreign sales. Offers written contract. Charges clients for land-line transmissions.

Tips "We are not taking on new clients."

◻ ZEBRA AGENCY

Broadland House, 1 Broadland, Shevington Lancashire WN6 8DH, United Kingdom. E-mail: admin@zebraagency.co.uk. Web site: www.zebraagency.co.uk/.

Represents TV scripts, Film.

   o⊸ This film and literary Agency represents writers as well as many other groups of performers. Your first contact should be a query letter that tells about your project and publishing history. No phone calls or submissions by fax or e-mail. International letters should have an IRC, not a SASE.

Contests

The contests and awards listed in this section are arranged by alphabetical order.

New contests and awards are announced in various writer's publications nearly every day. However, many lose their funding or fold—and sponsoring magazines go out of business just as often. We have contacted the organizations whose contests and awards are listed here with the understanding that they are valid through 2009. **Contact names**, **entry fees**, and **deadlines** have been highlighted and set in bold type for your convenience.

To make sure you have all the information you need about a particular contest, always send a SASE to the contact person in the listing before entering a contest. The listings in this section are brief, and many contests have lengthy, specific rules and requirements that we could not include in our limited space. Often a specific entry form must accompany your submission.

When you receive a set of guidelines, you will see that some contests are not applicable to all writers. The writer's age, previous publication, geographic location, and length of the work are common matters of eligibility. Read the requirements carefully to ensure you don't enter a contest for which you are not qualified. You should also be aware that every year, more and more contests are charging entry fees.

Winning a contest or award can launch a successful writing career. The power players in Hollywood often look at who's placing well in contests around town and around the country.

AAA SCREENPLAY CONTEST

AAA Screenplay Contest % Creative Screenwriting, 6404 Hollywood Blvd., Suite 145, Los Angeles CA 90028. E-mail: aaacontest@creativescreenwriting.com. Web site: www.creativescreenwriting.com/aaa/index.html. **Contact:** Pasha McKenley, contest coordinator. "We encourage submissions from any and all genres, from comedy to horror to science fiction to drama and everything in between. As in real life, we never know what's going to happen—no particular genre has an edge. Our winner may be a horror movie about mutant hedgehogs or a biopic on the life of Ivan the Terrible. What our judges are looking for is a great story, compelling characters, and sharp dialogue. We want your best work without regard to genre or budget. In fact, the new Special Jury Prize, "Suzanne's Prize for Best Love Story" specifically says genre is wide open." "Because the contest is geared toward offering access into the world of screenwriting, we do have to limit applicants to those who have made less than $8,000 on feature options or sales." Annually. **Deadline: June 11. June 25.** Guidelines for SASE. **Charges $30-$40.** Prize: $5,000. Open to any writer.

Tips "Do not send or try to submit scripts to our e-mail address. They will be deleted."

ACCLAIM FILM

300 Central Ave., Suite 501, St. Petersburg FL 33701. (727)502-9049. E-mail: acclaimtv@go.com. Web site: www.acclaimtv.netfirms.com. Affiliated production companies consider scripts from film and TV contests. **Deadline: February 8. March 19.** Guidelines for SASE. **Charges $45-$60.** Prize: Cash prize up to $1,000. Open to any writer.

ACCOLADE COMPETITION

P.O. Box 9117, La Jolla CA 92038. (858)454-9868. E-mail: info@accoladecompetition.org. Web site: www.accoladecompetition.org. Annually. **Deadline: August.** Guidelines for SASE. **Charges $50.** Prize: Best of Show, Awards of Excellence, & Honorable Mention. Open to any writer.

ACTORS' CHOICE AWARDS

The Screenwriting Conference in Santa Fe, P.O. Box 29762, Santa Fe NM 87592. (866)424-1501. Fax: (505)424-8207. E-mail: writeon@scsfe.com. Web site: www.scsfe.com. **Deadline: April 28.** Guidelines for SASE. **Charges $25.** Prize: Software. In addition, scripts are forwarded to producers attending Producers Seminar. Open to any writer.

ACTORS' THEATRE FULL-LENGTH PLAY CONTEST

Actors' Theatre, 1001 Center St., Santa Cruz CA 95060. (831)425-1003. Web site: www.sccat.org/contests.htm. Annually, Must Be Unpublished. **Deadline: October.** Guidelines for SASE. **Charges $15.** Prize: $200 and possible staged reading in 2009. "It is highly suggested that the submitting playwright be available to attend & participate in the discussion of his/her play." Open to any writer.

ACTORS' THEATRE TEN-MINUTE PLAY CONTEST

Actors' Theatre, 1001 Center St., Santa Cruz CA 95060. (831)425-1003. Web site: www.sccat.org/contests.htm. Annually, Must Be Unpublished. **Deadline: July.** Guidelines for SASE. **Charges $10.** Prize: "The 8 winning plays will receive a fully staged production in the sell-out 'Eight Tens @ Eight' Ten Minute Play Festival opening in January 2009." Open to any writer.

ACTORS' THEATRE YOUNG PLAYWRIGHTS' CONTEST

Actors' Theatre, 1001 Center St., Santa Cruz CA 95060. Web site: www.sccat.org/contests.htm. 3 categories considered: Short Shorts (5 minutes or less); 10 Minute Plays (no more than 10 pages long); & One-Act Plays (30 minutes or less). Annually, Must Be Unpublished. **Deadline: December.** Guidelines for SASE. **Charges $5.** Prize: Winning plays will have staged readings in April, 2009 at the Young Writers' Festival Weekend. Judged by Blind judging. Writers must be between the ages of 16 and 19.

AFC STORYTELLING INTERNATIONAL SCREENWRITING COMPETITION

African Film Commission, 8306 Wilshire Boulevard #330, Beverly Hills CA 90211, USA. (310)770-6246. E-mail: info@africanfilmcommission.org. Web site: www.africanfilmcommission.org. Scripts must have African content and themes. **Deadline: March.** Guidelines for SASE. **Charges $30.** Prize: $5,000 and a trip to Hollywood. Open to any writer.

ALBERTA PLAYWRITING COMPETITION

Alberta Playwrights' Network, 2633 Hochwald Ave. SW, Calgary AB T3E 7K2, Canada. (403)269-8564. Fax: (403)265-6773. Web site: www.albertaplaywrights.com. Offered annually for unproduced plays with full-length and Discovery categories. Discovery is open only to previously unproduced playwrights. Open only to residents of Alberta. **Deadline: March 31. Charges $40 fee (Canadian).** Prize: Full length: $3,500 (Canadian); Discovery: $1,500 (Canadian); plus a written critique, workshop of winning play, and reading of winning plays at a Showcase Conference.

ALL ACCESS SCREENWRITING COMPETITION

13428 Maxella Ave., #501, Los Angeles CA 90292. (310)577-3181. E-mail: questions@soyouwannasellascript.com. Web site: www.soyouwannasellascript.com. **Deadline: July 31. November 15.** Guidelines for SASE. **Charges $40-$50.** Prize: First place is a cash prize of $2,000. Second place is $300. Third place is $100. Open to any writer.

ALL STUDENT SCREENPLAY CONTEST

Brown University, Genesis Literary Agency, 75 Waterman St., Box 1930 Brown University, Providence RI 02912. (401)867-4977. E-mail: screenplay@ivyfilmfestival.com. Web site: www.ivyfilmfestival. com. Entries can be short films or feature length. Guidelines for SASE. **Charges $20-$45.** Judged by Agents from Genesis Literary Agency.

AMERICA'S BEST WRITING COMPETITION

3936 S. Sermon Blvd., Ste. 368, Orlando FL 32822. (407)894-9001. Fax: (407)894-5547. E-mail: info@writersfoundation.com. Web site: www.writersfoundation.com. Actively seeking screenplays, TV scripts, sitcom scripts. **Deadline: Takes submissions throughout the year.** Guidelines for SASE. **Charges up to $35.** Prize: Varies by category (TV, feature film, etc.) Screenplay contest top prize is $10,000. Open to any writer.
Tips You must have an online account to submit material. Getting an account is not difficult.

AMERICAN ACCOLADES TV & SHORTS COMPETITION

2118 Wilshire Blvd., Suite 160B, Santa Monica CA 90403. E-mail: info@americanaccolades.com. Web site: www.americanaccolades.com. **Deadline: November 13.** Guidelines for SASE. **Charges $55.**

Prize: Grand Prize ($2,000), plus $500 for 1st Place in Genre. First Place in each genre wins $500 and more. Open to any writer.

AMERICAN GEM SHORT CONTEST

FilmMakers Magazine, American Gem Short Screenplay Contest, P.O. Box 4678, Mission Viejo CA 92690. Web site: www.filmmakers.com/contests/short/index.htm. Contest is held annually. Short scripts only. **Deadline: March 15.** Guidelines for SASE. **Charges $29-$65.** Open to any writer.

AMERICAN SCREENWRITERS ASSOCIATION INTERNATIONAL SCREENPLAY COMPETITION

269 S. Beverly Drive, Ste. 2600, Beverly Hills, CA 90212-3807. (866)265-9091. E-mail: asa@goasa.com. Web site: www.goasa.com/competition.shtml. Open to all genres. Annually. **Deadline: October 31. November 30.** Guidelines for SASE. **Charges $25-50.** Prize: "Our winner receives $10,000 plus all finalists receive a cash award as well. We promote the winners in a number of ways including an ad in the *Hollywood Reporter*; an international press release; direct mailings to more than 6,500 studios and production companies; and the presentation of awards at the ASA Screenwriting Hall of Fame Awards during the San Diego Film Festival / ASA International Screenwriters Conference. Finalists receive a full script consultation or script critique from a top Hollywood consultant; the winner receives a script development trip to Hollywood; and we get the winning scripts into the hands of Hollywood decision makers from studios to production companies, and agents to managers. Every quarterfinalist receives a professional script critique." Open to any writer.

Tips "Please do not send us unsolicited scripts. We do not act as an agent, manager, referral source or clearinghouse for scripts. All unsolicited scripts received will be destroyed without opening. Note: Scripts being submitted for our screenplay competitions must be sent to the address listed in our most current competition guidelines, which will be published on our web site during active months for the competition."

AMERICAN ZOETROPE SCREENPLAY CONTEST

American Zoetrope, 916 Kearny Street, San Francisco CA 94133, USA. E-mail: contests@zoetrope.com. Web site: www.zoetrope.com/contests. Scripts must be between 87 to 130 pages in standard screenplay format. The writer must own all rights to the work. The writer must be at least 18 years old and have never have made more than $5,000 as a screen- or television-writer. The contest's aim is to seek out and encourage compelling film narratives, and to introduce the next generation of great screenwriters to today's leading production companies and agencies. Annually. **Deadline: August 1-September 2.** Guidelines for SASE. **Charges $35.** Prize: The grand prize-winner receives $5,000. The winner and top-ten finalists will be considered for representation by icm, uta, paradigm, william morris independent, the gersh agency, caa, exile entertainment, the schiff company, and the firm. Their scripts will be considered for film option and development by leading production companies, including: American Zoetrope, Samuel Goldwyn Films, Fox Searchlight, Sony Pictures Classics, IFC Entertainment, Paramount Classics, Icon Pictures, Working Title, Dimension Films, Antidote Films, Bull's Eye Entertainment, C/W Productions, The Film Department, First Look, Frelaine, Greenestreet Films, Matinee Pictures, Michael London Productions, Number 9 Films, Phoenix Pictures, Pretty Pictures, This is That, Roserock Films, Benderspink, Room 9 Entertainment, Industry Entertainment, Ovie Entertainment, Nine Yards Entertainment, and Ziskin Productions. Open to any writer.

THE ANNUAL BLANK THEATRE COMPANY YOUNG PLAYWRIGHTS FESTIVAL

The Blank Theatre Co., 1301 Lucile Ave., Los Angeles CA 90026-1519. (323)662-7734. Fax: (323)661-3903. E-mail: info@theblank.com. Web site: www.youngplaywrights.com; www.theblank.com. "Offered annually for unpublished work to encourage young writers to write for the theater by presenting their work as well as through our mentoring programs." Open to all writers 19 or younger on the submission date. **Deadline: March 15.** Prize: Workshop of the winning plays by professional theater artists.

ANNUAL DREAM GRANT

The Hobson Foundation, P.O. Box 2551, McKinleyville CA 95519. E-mail: writers@hobsonfoundation .com. Web site: www.hobsonfoundation.com. **Contact:** Cyndy Phillips, director. "Our Dream Grant, modeled after the MacArthur Fellows Program, is not a reward for past accomplishment, but rather an investment in potential; it is a 'no strings attached' award in support of writers' dreams. The foundation is primarily interested in knowing how a particular writing project can help our world." Annually. **Deadline: June 1. Charges $20 processing fee.** Prize: up to $800 for the grant winner, as well as the winners' grant idea displayed on our Web site along with the author's contact information. Judged by a panel of professional writers and writing professors. Open to any writer.

ANNUAL NATIONAL PLAYWRITING COMPETITION

Wichita State University, School of Performing Arts, 1845 Fairmount, Wichita KS 67260-0153. (316)978-3368. Fax: (316)978-3202. E-mail: steve.peters@wichita.edu. **Contact:** Dr. Steven J. Peters, contest director. Offered annually for full-length plays (minimum of 90 minutes playing time), or 2-3 short plays on related themes (minimum of 90 minutes playing time). **Deadline: February 15.** Guidelines for SASE. Prize: Production by the Wichita State University Theatre. Winner announced April 15. No plays returned after February 15. Open to all undergraduate and graduate students enrolled at any college or university in the US (indicate school affiliation).

ANNUAL ONE-ACT PLAYWRITING CONTEST

TADA!, 15 W. 28th St., 3rd Floor, New York NY 10001. (212)252-1619, ext. 17. Fax: (212)252-8763. E-mail: jgreer@tadatheater.com. Web site: www.tadatheater.com. **Contact:** Joanna Greer, associate artistic director. Offered annually to encourage playwrights to develop new plays for teen and family audiences. Call or e-mail for guidelines. **Deadline: April 25.** Prize: Cash award and staged readings.

ANOTHER SLEEPLESS NIGHT SCREENWRITING COMPETITION

℅ Marissa Commerville, 256 S. Robertson Blvd. #405, Beverly Hills CA 90211. (858)829-6394. E-mail: anothersleeplessnight@hotmail.com. Web site: www.anothersleeplessnight.com. Guidelines for SASE. **Charges $30-$50.** Prize: Up to $1,000 and consideration of review by studios. Open to any writer.

ANY GENRE SHORT SCRIPT COMPETITION

Yoot Music & Films, Inc, PMB# 53 5576 Norbeck Road, Suite A, Rockville MD 20853. Web site: www.yootfilms.org/ShortScriptCompetition.html. "Can you write a short script that deserves to be made? If you think you can, we'd like to read it. The grand prize winner will receive $2,500 and consideration by Yoot Music & Films to make the winning script into a film. All submissions are required to be submitted in a professional Hollywood format. Your script can be in any genre." Guidelines for SASE. **Charges $50.** Open to any writer.

APPALACHIAN FESTIVAL OF PLAYS & PLAYWRIGHTS

Barter Theatre, Box 867, Abingdon VA 24212-0867. (276)619-3314. Fax: (276)619-3335. E-mail: apfestival@bartertheatre.com. Web site: www.bartertheatre.com. **Contact:** Nick Piper. "With the annual Appalachian Festival of New Plays & Playwrights, Barter Theatre wishes to celebrate new, previously unpublished/unproduced plays by playwrights from the Appalachian region. If the playwrights are not from Appalachia, the plays themselves must be about the region." **Deadline: April 23.** Guidelines for SASE. Prize: $250, a staged reading performed at Barter's Stage II theater, and some transportation compensation and housing during the time of the festival. There may be an additional award for the best staged readings. Judged by the Barter Theatre's artistic director and associate director.

APPALACHIAN FILM FESTIVAL SCREENPLAY CONTEST

Appalachian Film Festival, % Huntington Regional Film Commission, P.O. Box 347, Huntington WV 25708. E-mail: appyfilmfest@gmail.com. Web site: www.appyfilmfest.com/pages/pdfs/2008forms/2008ScreenEntry.pdf. "Screenwriters must have resided during either of the last 2 years (or been a full-time student attending a college) in any of the 13 states that make up the Appalachian region—WV, OH, KY, NY, PA, MD, VA, TN, SC, GA, AL and MS." Scripts may not exceed 130 pages. Guidelines for SASE. **Charges $35.** Prize: Up to $1,000.

APPLAUSE SCREENWRITING COMPETITION

P.O. Box 3098, Rocklin CA 95677. (916)435-9862. E-mail: aplcontest@comcast.net; applause4you@bvunet.net. Web site: www.applause4you.com/. Annually. Guidelines for SASE. **Charges $50-55.** Prize: Up to $1,000. Judged by "All judges are well known screenwriting instructors and/or Hollywood industry professionals. Not too many screenwriting competitions have judges the stature of Lew Hunter (Emeritus Chair of the UCLA Screenwriting Program, arguably the best in the world) and other excellent judges." Open to any writer.
Tips To see the contest's previous winners, look online.

ARIZONA SCREENPLAY SEARCH

Phoenix Film Foundation, 1700 N. Seventh Ave., Suite 250, Phoenix AZ 85007. (602)955-6444. Web site: www.phxfilm.com. This contest is actually multiple contests in one. One contest only accepts scripts where the plot happens in the state. The other contest is open to all plots. Annually. Guidelines for SASE. **Charges fee varies by year.** Prize: Cash prizes offered. Open to any writer.

ART WITHIN LABS

Art Within, 1225 Johnson Ferry Rd., Suite 230, Marietta GA 30068. E-mail: labs@artwithin.org. Web site: www.artwithinlabs.org. An annual program for the next great screenwriters of faith. **Deadline: November.** Held annually, but deadline does change. Guidelines for SASE. **Charges $30.** Open to any writer.

ARTS & LETTERS PRIZES

Arts & Letters Journal of Contemporary Culture, Campus Box 89, GC&SU, Milledgeville GA 31061. (478)445-1289. E-mail: al@gcsu.edu. Web site: al.gcsu.edu. **Contact:** The Editors. Offered annually for unpublished work. **Deadline: March 15 (postmarked). Charges $15/entry (payable to GC&SU), which includes a 1-year subscription to the journal.** Prize: $1,000 for winners in fiction, poetry, creative nonfiction and drama (one-act play). Fiction and poetry winners will attend a weekend program in the fall, and the creative nonfiction and drama winner will attend a Spring program that includes readings and a production of the prize-winning play. Judged by editors (initial screening); see Web site for final judges and further details about submitting work. Open to any writer.

THE ARTS CENTRE SHORT + SWEET

The Arts Centre, P.O. Box 7585, St. Kilda Road VIC 8004, Australia. E-mail: shortandsweet@thearts centre.net.au. Web site: www.assets.theartscentre.net.au/shortandsweet/index.htm. Annually. **Deadline: August.** Guidelines for SASE. **Charges $15 (AUS).** Prize: "Should your script be selected for the competition, it will be transformed into a production and performed at the Short + Sweet competition the Arts Centre, Fairfax Studio. The plays selected for the competition will be in the running to grab a share of $20,000 in cash prizes for Best Overall Production, Best Drama Writing, Best Comedy Writing, People's Choice and many others." Australian residents only.

ASA INTERNATIONAL SCREENPLAY COMPETITION

American Screenwriters Association & Gotham Writers' Workshop, 555 8th Ave., Suite 1402, New York NY 10018-4358. (866)265-9091. Fax: (513)321-2989. E-mail: asa@apasa.com, screenplay@ write.org. Web site: www.asascreenwriters.com/. Annually. Guidelines for SASE. **Charges $60 (non-ASA member, Nov. deadline, discounts for early entry & membership).** Prize: $10,000 cash, industry recognition, writer development. Open to any writer.

ASHEVILLE FILM FESTIVAL SCREENPLAY COMPETITION

City of Asheville Parks and Recreation, 70 Court Plaza, Asheville NC 28801. (828)259-5800. Fax: (828)259-5606. Web site: www.mountainx.com/images/filmfest/AFF08ScreenplayContestApplicati on.pdf. Applicants may submit more than one script. Must Be Unpublished, July. Guidelines for SASE. **Charges $25-30.** Prize: $1,000+. All scripts reviewed by the Asheville Film Festival Staff. Open to any writer.

Tips 2008 is the contest's first year.

ATLANTA FILM FESTIVAL SCREENPLAY COMPETITION

Atlanta Film Festival, 535 Means St., Atlanta GA 30318. (404)352-4225. Fax: (404)352-0173. Web site: www.imagefv.org/image_services_SCREENCOMP.html. "The Atlanta Film Festival Screenplay Competition looks to discover high quality screenplays and then help the writer further develop and refine their script through an intensive workshop retreat with professional writers and filmmakers. The Atlanta Film Festival Screenplay Competition will provide travel from within the U.S., Canada, or Mexico as well as room and board for one for the retreat." Accepts short screenplays and feature-length work. For an extra fee, professional script coverage also available. Must Be Previously Published. Guidelines for SASE. **Charges $25-180, depending on date submitted and coverage.** Open to any writer.

AUSTIN FILM FESTIVAL SCREENPLAY COMPETITION

1604 Nueces, Austin TX 78701. (512)478-4795. Fax: (512)478-6205. E-mail: info@austinfilmfestival. com. Web site: www.austinfilmfestival.com. **Deadline: May 15. June 1.** Guidelines for SASE. **Charges**

$30-$40. Prize: Cash prizes. Some of the contest winning scripts, such as *Excess Baggage*, have gone on to be not only bought, but produced. Open to any writer.

BALTIMORE FILM OFFICE SCREENWRITING COMPETITION

Baltimore Office of Promotion & The Arts, 7 E. Redwood St. Suite 500, Baltimore MD 21202. (410)752-8632. Fax: (410)385-0361. Web site: www.baltimorefilm.com/index.cfm?page=screenwriting_com petition. Guidelines for SASE. Prize: Multiple cash prizes, up to $1500. Open to any writer.

BAY AREA PLAYWRIGHTS FESTIVAL

Produced by Playwrights Foundation, 131 10th St., 3rd Floor, San Francisco CA 94103. E-mail: literary @playwrightsfoundation.org. Web site: www.playwrightsfoundation.org. **Contact:** Jonathan Spector; jonathan@playwrightsfoundation.org. Offered annually for unpublished plays by established and emerging theater writers to support and encourage development of a new work. Unproduced full-length play only. **Deadline: January 15 (postmarked). Charges $20.** Prize: Small stipend and in-depth development process with dramaturg and director, and a professionally staged reading in San Francisco. Open to any writer.

Tips Guidelines on Web site.

BEA FESTIVAL OF MEDIA ARTS FACULTY SCRIPTWRITING COMPETITION

POB 1053, Dunedin FL 34697-1053. (607)262-0904. E-mail: cynsava@aol.com. Web site: www.beafe stival.org/facultyscript.html. **Contact:** Cynthia Savaglio, faculty competition Chair. Annually. Guidelines for SASE. **Charges $35.** Prize: Cash prizes. Open to any writer.

Tips There is specific submission instructions that are in flux each year. Look online to see how to submit. Scripts are reviewed blindly.

BEA FESTIVAL OF MEDIA ARTS STUDENT SCRIPTWRITING COMPETITION

340 Moore Hall, Central Michigan University, Mt. Pleasant MI 48859. E-mail: corbe1kj@cmich.edu. Web site: www.beafestival.org/student.html. **Contact:** Kevin Corbett, PhD, associate professor, School of Broadcast and Cinematic Arts. Guidelines for SASE. Prize: The first place winner in each category will receive Final Draft Software, and a book from Michael Weise Productions. All second and third Place winners will also get software. "Each entrant must be a registered student, either full- or part-time, either graduate or undergraduate, in any U.S. college, university, or community/technical college, or in any BEA member institution anywhere in the world, in calendar year 2007. Student entrants must either be individual BEA members OR their institutions must be BEA Institutional Members. Membership forms and information on BEA Institutional Members may be found on the BEA Web site, www.beaweb.org."

Tips Specific submission instruction is in flux year to year and is online. See it before submitting. Each category will be judged by at least two independent judges.

BEVERLY HILLS FILM FESTIVAL SCREENPLAY COMPETITION

Beverly Hills Film Festival, 9663 Santa Monica Blvd, Suite 777, Beverly Hills CA 90210. (310)779-1206. E-mail: info@beverlyhillsfilmfestival.com. Web site: www.beverlyhillsfilmfestival.com/. "Please indicate if the submission is complete, or work in progress. Also include 1) Synopsis of the Script (in English); 2) A statement from the writer on the script; 3) Biography of the writer; 4) Stills if any; 5) Poster and/or press booklet.'' Guidelines for SASE. **Charges $35.** Open to any writer.

Tips Space is limited. Dates subject to change. No refunds.

BIENNIAL PROMISING PLAYWRIGHT CONTEST

Colonial Players, Inc., 108 East St., Annapolis MD 21401. (410)268-7373. E-mail: cpartisticdir@yahoo
.com. Web site: www.cplayers.com. Offered every 2 years for unproduced full-length plays and one-
acts with 10 actor or fewer. Musicals are not eligible. Open to any aspiring playwright residing in West
Virginia, Washington DC, or any of the states descendant from the original 13 colonies (Connecticut,
Delaware, Georgia, Maryland, Massachusetts, New Hampshire, New Jersey, New York, North Carolina, Pennsylvania, Rhode Island, South Carolina, and Virginia). Next contest runs September 1-
December 1, 2008. Guidelines available online beginning summer 2008. Prize: $1,000, a weekend
workshop, and a public reading.

BIG BEAR LAKE SCREENWRITING COMPETITION

P.O. Box 1981, Big Bear Lake CA 92315-1981. (909)866-3433. E-mail: BigBearFilmFest@aol.com.
Web site: www.bigbearfilmfestival.com. Annually. **Deadline: May 1. May 30.** Guidelines for SASE.
Charges $40. Prize: No confirmed money prizes, but winners receive software and their script submit-
ted to studios. Open to any writer.

BIG BREAK INTERNATIONAL SCREENWRITING COMPETITION

Final Draft, Inc., 26707 W. Aguora Rd., Suite 205, Calabasas CA 91302. (800)231-4055. Fax: (818)995-
4422. Web site: www.bigbreakcontest.com. Estab. 2000. Annual global screenwriting competition
designed to promote emerging creative talent. Guidelines online or for SASE. **Deadline: Febraury 1-
June 15. Charges $40-60, depending on entry date.** Judged by industry professionals. Open to any
writer.

BLUECAT SCREENPLAY COMPETITION

P.O. Box 2630, Hollywood CA 90028. E-mail: info@bluecatscreenplay.com. Web site: www.bluecats
creenplay.com/. ''We are a writing competition founded in 1998 by a writer and judged by the same
writer for its entire history. We're not a film festival, an agency or media corporation, or the arm of
a corporate studio. We are for screenwriters only!'' ''Past and present scripts consulted on through
Gordy Hoffman's screenplay consultation service are not eligible. Scripts must be between 80 and
145 pages.'' Annually. **Deadline: April 1.** Guidelines for SASE. Prize: Winner receives $10,000. Four
finalists receive $1500. Every writer receives a written script analysis of their screenplay. Open to any
writer.

Tips A list of past winners and their coverage is available online.

BREAKTHROUGH WITH A SCREAM

% Marissa Sommerville, 256 S. Robertson Blvd. #405, Beverly Hills CA 90211. (858)829-6394. E-
mail: anothersleeplessnight@hotmail.com. Web site: www.anothersleeplessnight.com/. Looking for
science fiction and horror scripts. This is the second of two scriptwriting contests put on by Another
Sleepless Night. Annually. Guidelines for SASE. **Charges $30-50.** Prize: Cash prizes offered, as well
as submissions to interested studios. Open to any writer.

THE BRITISH SHORT SCREENPLAY COMPETITION

% Pinewood Film Studios, Pinewood Road, Iver Heath, Buckinghamshire SL0 0NH, United Kingdom. E-mail: info@kaosfilms.co.uk. Web site: www.kaosfilms.co.uk/rules/. "The British Short Screenplay Competition is open to writers of any nationality from any country. The entered screenplay must not have been previously optioned, sold or produced. Screenplays must be written in English language. The screenplay must be no less than five-minutes and no more than fifteen minutes screen time." Guidelines for SASE. **Charges 25-35 British pounds.** Open to any writer.

BURNABY WRITERS' SOCIETY CONTEST

E-mail: info@bws.bc.ca. Web site: www.bws.bc.ca. **Contact:** Eileen Kernaghan. Offered annually for unpublished work. Open to all residents of British Columbia. Categories vary from year to year. Send SASE for current rules. Purpose is to encourage talented writers in all genres. **Deadline: May 31. Charges $5 fee.** Prize: 1st Place: $200; 2nd Place: $100; 3rd Place: $50; and public reading.

CAA CAROL BOLT AWARD FOR DRAMA

Canadian Authors Association with the support of the Playwrights Guild of Canada and Playwrights Canada Press, 320 S. Shores Rd., P.O. Box 419, Campbellford ON K0L 1L0, Canada. (705)653-0323 or (866)216-6222. Fax: (705)653-0593. E-mail: admin@canauthors.org. Web site: www.canauthors.org. **Contact:** Alec McEachern. Annual contest for the best English-language play for adults by an author who is Canadian or a landed immigrant. Obtain form from contact name or download from Web site. **Deadline: December 15; plays published or performed in December are due January 15. Charges $35 (Canadian funds).** Prize: $1,000 and a silver medal. Judged by a trustee for the award (appointed by the CAA). The trustee appoints up to 3 judges. The identities of the trustee and judges are confidential. Short lists are not made public. Decisions of the trustee and judges are final, and they may choose not to award a prize.

CALIFORNIA YOUNG PLAYWRIGHTS CONTEST

Playwrights Project, 2356 Moore St., #204, San Diego CA 92110-3019. (619)239-8222. Fax: (619)239-8225. E-mail: write@playwrightsproject.org. Web site: www.playwrightsproject.org. **Contact:** Cecelia Kouma, managing director. Offered annually for previously unpublished plays by young writers to stimulate young people to create dramatic works, and to nurture promising writers. Scripts must be a minimum of 10 standard typewritten pages; send 2 copies. Scripts will *not* be returned. If requested, entrants receive detailed evaluation letter. Writers must be California residents under age 19 as of the deadline date. Guidelines available online. **Deadline: June 1.** Prize: Professional production of 3-5 winning plays at a professional theatre in San Diego, plus royalty.

CENTURY CITY CELL PHONE FESTIVAL

P.O. Box 67132, Century City CA 90067. (310)652-0271. Web site: centurycitycellphonefest.com/. This contest is for movies that are made to be filmed and played directly on cell phones. Entries should be 15 seconds to 3 minutes. Guidelines for SASE. Prize: Cash prizes and introduction to studio representatives. Open to any writer.

Tips There are specific technical requirements to this contest, such as the method of delivery and format (e.g., Mp4). Look online for more information.

JANE CHAMBERS PLAYWRITING AWARD

The Women and Theatre Program of the Association for Theatre in Higher Education, Department of Theatre, Southern Methodist University, P.O. Box 750356, Dallas TX 75275-0356. E-mail: gesmith@ mail.smu.edu. Web site: www.womenandtheatre.com/contest. **Contact:** Gretchen E. Smith. Estab. 1983. Offered annually to recognize a woman playwright who has written a play with a feminist perspective, a majority of roles for women, and which experiments with the dramatic form. Guidelines online or for SASE. **Deadline: February 15.** Prize: $1,000 and a staged reading during the ATHE conference.

CHICANO/LATINO LITERARY CONTEST

Dept. of Spanish and Portuguese, University of California-Irvine, 322 Humanities Hall, Irvine CA 92697-5276. (949)824-5443. Fax: (949)824-2808. E-mail: cllp@uci.edu. Web site: www.hnet.uci.edu/ spanishandportuguese/contest.html. **Contact:** Evelyn Flores. Estab. 1974. Offered annually to promote the dissemination of unpublished Chicano/Latino literature in Spanish or English, and to encourage its development. The call for entries will be genre specific, rotating through 4 categories: drama (2006), novel (2007), short story (2008), and poetry (2009). The contest is open to all US citizens and permanent residents. **Deadline: June 1.** Prize: 1st Place: $1,000, publication, and transportation to the award ceremony; 2nd Place: $500; 3rd Place: $250.

CHRISTIAN SCREENWRITE

P.O. Box 447, Bloomfield NJ 07003. (859)579-6064. E-mail: info@christianscreenwrite.com. Web site: www.christianscreenwrite.com. Contemporary Christian screenplays only. The contest is looking for films that spread the messages and principles and Christianity. **Deadline: June 1. August 1.** Guidelines for SASE. **Charges $30.** Prize: Cash prizes offered for top three winners. Open to any writer.

CINEQUEST FILM FESTIVAL SCREENPLAY COMPETITION

Cinequest Film Festival, 22 N. Almaden Ave., San Jose CA 95110. (408)295-3378(FEST). Fax: (408)995-5713. E-mail: info@cinequest.org. Web site: www.cinequest.org/sp_agent.php. "All genres and lengths of screenplays (up to 125 pages) are accepted, from low-budget Indie dramas to mega-money flicks." Must Be Unpublished. Guidelines for SASE. **Charges $35-40.** Prize: Multiple prizes, with a $5,000 grand prize. Winning scripts will be passed on to moviemakers. Open to any writer.

CITA PLAY DEVELOPMENT CONTEST

Christians in Theatre Arts, P.O. Box 26471, Greenville SC 29616. (864)679-1898. Fax: (864)679-1899. E-mail: admin@cita.org. Web site: www.cita.org. Competition encourages and equips CITA members by providing the winner with a high-quality intensive dramaturgical experience. Plays must be full-length (75 minutes or more) and reflect the author's Judeo-Christian worldview. Musicals must include a tape/CD. See Web site for guidelines. **Deadline: March 15.** Guidelines for SASE. **Charges $20/entry.** Prize: The winning playwright will work with 2 dramaturgs at the national conference with the rewritten result being presented at a staged reading. The winning playwright will also be awarded free conference registration, but is responsible for travel, food, and accommodations. Open to any writer.

THE CITY OF VANCOUVER BOOK AWARD

Office of Cultural Affairs, 453 W. 12th Ave., Vancouver BC V5Y 1V4, Canada. (604)871-6434. Fax: (604)871-6005. E-mail: marnie.rice@vancouver.ca. Web site: www.vancouver.ca/culture. Offered annually for books published in the previous year which exhibit excellence in the categories of content, illustration, design, and format. The book must contribute significantly to the appreciation and understanding of the city of Vancouver and heighten awareness of 1 or more of the following: Vancouver's history, the city's unique character, or achievements of the city's residents. The book may be fiction, nonfiction, poetry, or drama written for adults or children, and may deal with any aspects of the city—history, geography, current affairs, or the arts. Guidelines online. Prize: $2,000.

CITA SKETCH WRITING AND PLAY CONTEST

Christians in Theatre Arts, P.O. Box 26471, Greenville SC 29616. (864)679-1898. Fax: (864)679-1899. E-mail: admin@cita.org. Web site: www.cita.org. Annual sketch contest for CITA members: to encourage excellence in theatrical sketch writing, focusing on material created to minister in worship services, evangelistic outreach, street theatre, or educational, amateur, or professional theatre performance. Sketches must in some way reflect Christian truth, values, or questions. Sketches may be presentational, slice-of-life, monologue, mime, or any combination of forms. See Web site for guidelines. Annual play contest: The goal of this competition is to encourage CITA playwrights by providing the competition winner with exposure and connection with organizations related to CITA which may then consider it for further development and/or production. **Deadline: February 1.** Guidelines for SASE. **Charges $10/entry.** Prize: Winners of Drama and Comedy categories will receive a plaque at a general session of the CITA National Conference in June. Staged readings/productions of these works may also be a part of the conference at the discretion of the judges. Works may be published in the CITA magazine, *Christianity and Theatre*, with the author's permission. All further production rights will be reserved by the author. Open to any writer.

THE CLAYMORE DAGGER AWARD

Killer Nashville, P.O. Box 680686, Franklin TN 37068-0686. (615)599-4032. E-mail: contact@killernashville.com. Web site: www.killernashville.com. **Contact:** Clay Stafford, Event Producer. The Claymore Dagger Award is Killer Nashville's award for the best opening for an unpublished ms. submitted to the judging committee. Annually. **Deadline: 4 mos. prior to the Killer Nashville conference. Charges $25.** Prize: An engraved dagger as well as consideration for publication by the judging publisher. Judged by a committee of experienced, dedicated readers and writers including past and current Killer Nashville attendees will review all submissions. They will recommend and submit 10 mss to our sponsor publisher, whose editors will make the final decision and award the Claymore Dagger to the winning author. All decisions are final and at the sole discretion of the publisher. Although anyone with an unpublished ms is eligible to submit, the award would best benefit authors who have not been previously published, and published authors who are "between publishers" and would like to get some buzz about their new works. We don't want to exclude anyone, though, so if you're a published author with an unpublished ms you'd like to enter, please be our guest.

COE COLLEGE PLAYWRITING FESTIVAL

Coe College, 1220 First Ave. NE, Cedar Rapids IA 52402-5092. (319)399-8624. Fax: (319)399-8557. E-mail: swolvert@coe.edu. Web site: www.theatre.coe.edu. **Contact:** Susan Wolverton. Estab. 1993.

Offered biennially for unpublished work to provide a venue for new works for the stage. "We are interested in full-length productions, not one-acts or musicals. There are no specific criteria although a current résumé and synopsis is requested." Open to any writer. **Deadline: November 1, even years. Notification: January 15, odd years.** Guidelines for SASE. Prize: $500, plus 1-week residency as guest artist with airfare, room and board provided.

THE COMPLETE SCRIPTDOCTOR'S OPEN SCREENPLAY COMPETITION

ScriptDoctor, 555 E. Limberlost Dr., Suite 1067, Tucson AZ 85705. E-mail: thedoc@scriptdoctor.com. Web site: www.scriptdoctor.com. **Contact:** Howard Allen. No entry may have earned money or other consideration for more than $5,000. Annually. Guidelines for SASE. **Charges $50.** Must be at least 18 years of age.

CONTEST OF WINNERS

ScriptDoctor, 555 E. Limberlost Dr., Suite 1067, Tucson AZ 85705. E-mail: thedoc@scriptdoctor.com. Web site: www.scriptdoctor.com. **Contact:** Howard Allen. For screenplays that have placed as a finalist or won a contest in the past 5 years. Annually. **Deadline: December.** Guidelines for SASE. **Charges $55.** Prize: Cash $1,000 and notes from a ScriptDoctor partner. Must be at least 18 years of age.

CREATIVE WORLD AWARD (CWA) SCREENWRITING COMPETITION

P.O. Box 10699, Marina del Rey CA 90295. E-mail: info@creativeworldawards.com; submissions@ creativeworldawards.com. Web site: www.creativeworldawards.com/. **Contact:** Marlene Neubauer. "What sets this screenwriting contest apart is the fact that our winning screenplays will not only be sent to top agencies, major film studios, managers, producers, and international financers, but outside of the judging review process and the usual post award circulation, this screenwriting competition its first year out has secured an unprecedented amount of commitments from prominent companies to take first looks at our top three finalists." Each writer or writing team's total earnings from all film screenwriting may not exceed $5,000. We will accept collaborative work, but by no more than two authors. Each writer, however, must fill out and sign the online entry application and release form individually. If selected as a winner, the prize money will be split equally between them. All screenplays must be between 90-120 pages and in standard spec screenplay format, fastened with 2-3 brads. See our Basic FAQ page for allowed exceptions to length. The writer's name, address, phone number and email address should appear ONLY on the title page, and not on any other page of the script. If the script is based on a true story, it should be noted on the title page. Short screenplays are not accepted. Annually. **Deadline: August.** Guidelines for SASE. **Charges $45-65.** Prize: Multiple prizes, with a grand prize of $5,000. Open to any writer.

THE CUNNINGHAM COMMISSION FOR YOUTH THEATRE

The Theatre School at DePaul University, 2135 N. Kenmore, Chicago IL 60614-4111. (773)325-7938. Fax: (773)325-7920. E-mail: aables@depaul.edu. Web site: theatreschool.depaul.edu/ special_programs_cunningham_commission.html. **Contact:** Cunningham Commission Selection Committee. Chicago-area playwrights only. Commission will result in a play for younger audiences that affirms the centrality of religion, broadly defined, and the human quest for meaning, truth, and community. Guidelines for SASE or online. **Deadline: December 1.** Prize: $6,000—$2,500 when commission is contracted; $1,000 if script moves to workshop; $2,500 as royalty if script is produced by The Theatre School. Open to writers whose primary residence is in the Chicago area.

CWW ANNUAL AWARDS COMPETITION

Council for Wisconsin Writers, Web site: www.wisconsinwriters.org/index.htm. Offered annually for work published by Wisconsin writers the previous calendar year. Ten awards: major/life achievement; short fiction; short nonfiction; nonfiction book; poetry book; fiction book; children's literature; Lorine Niedecher Poetry Award; outstanding service to Wisconsin writers. Open to Wisconsin residents. Guidelines on Web site. **Deadline: January 31. Charges $10 nonrefundable fee.** Prize: $500 and a certificate.

DAYTON PLAYHOUSE FUTUREFEST

The Dayton Playhouse, 1301 E. Siebenthaler Ave., Dayton OH 45414-5357. (937)424-8477. Web site: www.daytonplayhouse.org. **Contact:** Adam J. Leigh, executive director. Three plays selected for full productions, 3 for readings at July FutureFest weekend. The 6 authors will be given travel and lodging to attend the festival. Professionally adjudicated. Guidelines for SASE or online. **Deadline: October 31.** Prize: $1,000; $100 goes to the other 5 playwrights.

DC SHORTS SCREENWRITING COMPETITION

DC Shorts Film Festival, 1317 F Street, NW, Ste 920, Washington DC 20004. (202)393-4266. **Contact:** Jon Gann. "DC Shorts is proud to present a different kind of screenwriting competition. A panel of judges consisting of filmmakers, screenwriters and critics will review and provide condensed coverage (feedback) for scripts of 15 pages or less. A set of finalists (no more than 7) will be selected to be featured during the festival weekend, which the screenwriters are invited to attend, and cast a live reading of the script from a bank of actors and directors. The live readings will be performed in front of an audience, who will vote on their favorite. These votes, along with the scores of the judges, will determine a competition winner." Annually. Guidelines for SASE. Prize: One script will receive $1,000 up front, plus a $1,000 upon completion of the final film. The final film is guaranteed entry into DC Shorts 2009. Open to any writer.

DOWNBEACH FILM FESTIVAL SCREENPLAY COMPETITION

Downbeach Film Festival, Margate Performing Arts Center, C/O Eugene A. Tighe School, 7804 Amherst Avenue, Margate NJ 08402. (609)823-9159. E-mail: director@downbeachfilmfestival.org. Web site: www.downbeachfilmfestival.org. W. Sokolic, Executive Director. Both short scripts and feature length scripts are considered. Annually, Must Be Unpublished. Guidelines for SASE. **Charges $25 for short scripts fewer than 60 pages. $30 for features.** Prize: Multiple prizes up to $500. Open to any writer.
Tips Some of this festival's contests have a "Surf & Turf" theme with a given logline.

DRURY UNIVERSITY ONE-ACT PLAY CONTEST

Drury University, 900 N. Benton Ave., Springfield MO 65802-3344. E-mail: msokol@drury.edu. **Contact:** Mick Sokol. Offered in even-numbered years for unpublished and professionally unproduced plays. One play/playwright. Guidelines for SASE or by e-mail. **Deadline: December 1.**

DUBUQUE FINE ARTS PLAYERS ANNUAL ONE-ACT PLAY CONTEST

Dubuque Fine Arts Players, 1686 Lawndale, Dubuque IA 52001. E-mail: gary.arms@clarke.edu. **Contact:** Gary Arms. "We select 3 one-act plays each year. We award cash prizes of up to $600 for a winning entry. We produce the winning plays in August." Offered annually for unpublished work. Guidelines and application form for SASE. **Deadline: January 31. Charges $10.** Prize: 1st Place: $600; 2nd Place: $300; 3rd Place: $200. Judged by 3 groups who read all the plays; each play is read at least twice. Plays that score high enough enter the second round. The top 10 plays are read by a panel consisting of 3 directors and 2 other final judges. Open to any writer.

EERIE HORROR FILM FESTIVAL SCREENPLAY COMPETITION

P.O, Box 98, Edinboro PA 16412. E-mail: info@eeriehorrorfest.com. Web site: www.eeriehorrorfilmf estival.com/. There is also a student contest for ages 12-17. Entries must be in the horror film genre. There are contests for features as well as short scripts. Only Horror, Sci-fi, supernatural, and suspense genres will be considered. Annually, Must Be Unpublished. Guidelines for SASE. **Charges $20-$65.** Open to any writer.

EMERGING PLAYWRIGHT'S AWARD

Urban Stages, 17 E. 47th St., New York NY 10017-1920. (212)421-1380. Fax: (212)421-1387. E-mail: sonia@urbanstages.org. Web site: www.urbanstages.org. **Contact:** Sonia Kozlova, managing director. Estab. 1986. Submissions must be unproduced in New York City. Prefers full-length plays; subject matter and charager variations are open (no translations or adapatations). Cast size is limited to 9 actors. Send script, bio, production history, character breakdown, synopsis, and SASE. Submissions are accepted year-round and plays are selected in the spring. **Deadline: Ongoing.** Prize: $500 (in lieu of royalties), and a staged production of winning play in New York City. Open to US residents only.

ESHAY.COM SCRIPT WRITING COMPETITION

258 Harvard St. #361, Brookline MA 02446-2904. (877)706-8869. E-mail: info@eshay.com. Web site: www.eshay.com. Guidelines for SASE. **Charges $25.** Open to any writer.

ESSENTIAL THEATRE PLAYWRITING AWARD

The Essential Theatre, P.O. Box 8172, Atlanta GA 30306. (404)212-0815. E-mail: pmhardy@aol.com. Web site: www.essentialtheatre.com. **Contact:** Peter Hardy. Offered annually for unproduced, full-length plays by Georgia resident writers. No limitations as to style or subject matter. **Deadline: April 23.** Prize: $500 and full production.

THE LOUIS ESSON PRIZE FOR DRAMA

Victorian Premier's Literary Awards, State Library of Victoria, 328 Swanston St., Melbourne VIC 3000 Australia. (61)(3)8664-7277. E-mail: pla@slv.vic.gov.au. Web site: www.slv.vic.gov.au/pla. **Contact:** Awards Coordinator. Prize for theatre or radio scripts produced between May 1 and April 30. The State Library of Victoria reserves the right to place a copy of all nominated works in its collection. Further copyright remains with the author. **Deadline: May 4.** Guidelines for SASE. Prize: $15,000. Open to Australian citizens or permanent residents.

FADE IN AWARDS SCREENWRITING CONTEST

287 S. Robertson Blvd., #467, Beverly Hills CA 90211. (310)275-0287. Web site: www.fadeinonli ne.com/Contests/Fade_In_Awards/. "The Fade In Awards were established in 1996 to assist talented new writers and writer/directors in getting recognized within the Hollywood community in order to begin a career as a working filmmaker." Annually. Guidelines for SASE. Prize: Cash prizes offered, and scripts presented to studios. Open to any writer.

Tips You can enter the contest online or mail in a submission.

FEATURE LENGTH SCREENPLAY COMPETITION

Austin Film Festival, 1604 Nueces St., Austin TX 78701. (512)478-4795. Fax: (512)478-6205. E-mail: info@austinfilmfestival.com. Web site: www.austinfilmfestival.com. Offered annually for unpublished screenplays. The Austin Film Festival is looking for quality screenplays which will be read by industry professionals. Two competitions: Adult/Family Category and Comedy Category. Guidelines for SASE or call (800)310-3378. The writer must hold the rights when submitted; it must be original work. The screenplay must be 90-130 pages and it must be in industry standard screenplay format. **Deadline: May 15 (early); June 1 (late). Charges $40/early entry; $50/late entry.** Prize: $5,000 in each category.

A FEEDING FRENZY

AMLC Productions, 703 Pier Ave., Suite B #687, Hermosa Beach CA 90254. E-mail: amlcprods@afree dingfrenzy.com. Web site: www.afeedingfrenzy.com/. This contest prides itself on being not only a contest, but also a place where writers can get feedback on their work. Guidelines for SASE. Prize: Top 3 Finalists: Loglines and scripts distributed to top production companies and industry contacts—see Sponsors. Top 3 & Top 10 Finalists: Loglines will be posted on our Web site and in industry newsletters. InkTip.com will email an announcement to 6,500 film industry professionals and snail-mail loglines to 5,000 film industry professionals in its printed publication. Open to any writer.

FEMALE EYE FILM FESTIVAL SCREENPLAY ENTRY

50 Wallace St., Woodbridge ON L4L 2P3, Canada. (905)264-7731. E-mail: info@femaleeyefilmfestival .com. Web site: www.femaleeyefilmfestival.com. **Contact:** Leslie Ann Coles, program director. Annually. **Deadline: October (late: December).** Guidelines for SASE. **Charges $25 ($50 late).** Open to any writer.

SHUBERT FENDRICH MEMORIAL PLAYWRITING CONTEST

Pioneer Drama Service, Inc., P.O. Box 4267, Englewood CO 80155. (303)779-4035. Fax: (303)779-4315. E-mail: submissions@pioneerdrama.com. Web site: www.pioneerdrama.com. **Contact:** Lori Conary, assistant editor. Offered annually for unpublished, but previously produced, submissions to encourage the development of quality theatrical material for educational and community theater. Rights acquired only if published. Authors already published by Pioneer Drama are not eligible. Contest submissions must also meet standard submission guidelines. **Deadline: December 31 (postmarked).** Guidelines for SASE. Prize: $1,000 royalty advance and publication.

FESTIVAL OF NEW AMERICAN PLAYS

Firehouse Theatre Project, 1609 W. Broad St., Richmond VA 23220. (804)355-2001. E-mail: info@fi rehousetheatre.org. Web site: www.firehousetheatre.org. **Contact:** Carol Piersol, artistic director. Annual contest designed to support new and emerging American playwrights. Scripts must be full-length and previously unpublished/unproduced. (Readings are acceptable if no admission was charged.) Submissions should be mailed in hard copy form and accompanied by a letter of recommendation from a theater company or individual familiar with your work. **Deadline: July 31.** Annual deadline is adjusted depending on the volume of plays received. Prize: 1st Place: $1,000 and a staged reading; 2nd Place: $500 and a staged reading. All plays are initially read by a panel of individuals with experience in playwriting and literature. Previous judges have included Lloyd Rose (former *Washington Post* theatre critic), Bill Patton (frequent Firehouse director), Richard Toscan (dean of the Virginia Commonwealth University School for the Arts), and Israel Horovitz (playwright). All finalists are asked to sign a contract with the Firehouse Theatre Project that guarantees performance rights for the staged reading in January and printed credit for Firehouse Theatre Project if the play is produced/published in the future. All American playwrights are welcome to submit their work.

FILMMAKERS INTERNATIONAL SCREENWRITING AWARDS

P.O. 4678, Mission Viejo CA 92690, USA. E-mail: info@filmmakers.com. Web site: www.filmmakers.com. **Deadline: April 30. May 31.** Guidelines for SASE. **Charges $49-$65.** Open to any writer.

FIND THE FUNNY SCREENPLAY CONTEST

2600 W. Vanowen St., Burbank CA 91505. (818)845-6405. E-mail: screenplaycontest@findthefunny.com. Web site: www.findthefunny.com. Comedy scripts only. Annually. **Deadline: November 15. January 31.** Guidelines for SASE. Open to any writer.

FIREHOUSE THEATRE PROJECT NEW PLAY COMPETITION

The Firehouse Theatre Project, 1609 W. Broad St., Richmond VA 23220. (804)355-2001. Web site: www.firehousetheatre.org. **Contact:** Literary Manager FTP. Calls for previously unpublished full-length works with non-musical and non-children's themes. Submissions must be in standard play format. Scripts should be accompanied by a letter of recommendation from a company or individual familiar with your work. Submissions must be unpublished. Visit Web site for complete submission guidelines. "We're receptive to unusual, but well-wrought works." **Deadline: June 30.** Prize: 1st Prize: $1,000; 2nd Prize: $500. Judged by a committee selected by the executive board of the Firehouse Theatre Project. Acquires the right to produce the winning scripts in a staged reading for the FTP Festival of New American Plays. Following the Festival production dates, all rights are relinquished to the author. Open to US residents only.

FROM SCREENPLAY TO PRODUCTION FILM FESTIVAL

Boston International Film Festival, P.O. Box 240023, Dorchester MA 02124. (617)482-3900. Fax: (617)482-3903. E-mail: info@bifilmfestival.com. Web site: www.bifilmfestival.com/biffscreenplaycontest.html. "BIFF Screenplay to Production Contest (BIFF SPC) offers an opportunity for under-represented screenwriters and filmmakers to produce a film entirely from Pre-Production, Production, Post-Production to a completed finished project on High Definition Format only. Selected Projects may be produced anywhere in the United States." Winning scripts are produced. Annually, Must Be Unpublished. Guidelines for SASE. **Charges $55-75.** Prize: Production. Open to any writer.
Tips There are multiple categories with this contest—short submissions and feature submissions.

GARDEN STATE FILM FESTIVAL SCREENPLAY COMPETITION

P.O. Box 751, Asbury Park NJ 07712. E-mail: info@gsff.org. Web site: www.gsff.org. **Contact:** Diane Raver, executive director. This contest is designed to introduce audiences to the cinematic arts and assist in the revitalization of Asbury Park by filling a cultural void. Entered screenplays must not have been previously optioned, sold, or produced. All screenplays should be registered with the WGA and/or a Library of Congress copyright. Screenplays must be the original work of the writer. If based on another person's life story, a statement attesting to the rights obtained must be attached. No adaptations of other written work will be accepted. Multiple entries are accepted. A separate entry form and fee must accompany each script. Screenplays containing multiple writers are also accepted. Include two cover pages with each screenplay. One that only contains the screenplay's title. A second one that contains all contact information (name, address, phone, and email and Withoutabox tracking number). The writer's name must not appear any where inside the body of the screenplay. All screenplays must abide by proper industry format. All screenplays must be in English, with numbered, plain-write pages. All screenplay MUST be bound with two or three brads. No substitutions of new drafts, or corrected pages, for any screenplay, for any reason, will be accepted after the initial submission. Please enter the draft you are most confident about. No individual feedback or coverage will be made available pertaining to submitted screenplays. Annually. **Deadline: December.** Guidelines for SASE. **Charges $45.** Prize: The winner receives a live staged reading with a professional director and professional actors in a seated venue to kick off the festival. Open to any writer.

JOHN GASSNER MEMORIAL PLAYWRITING COMPETITION

New England Theatre Conference, 215 Knob Hill Dr., Hamden CT 06158. Fax: (203)288-5938. E-mail: mail@netconline.org. Web site: www.netconline.org. Offered annually to unpublished full-length plays and scripts. Open to New England residents and NETC members. Playwrights living outside New England may participate. **Deadline: April 15.** Guidelines for SASE. **Charges $10 fee.** Prize: 1st Place: $1,000; 2nd Place: $500.

GIDEON MEDIA ARTS CONFERENCE & FILM FESTIVAL ORIGINAL/ADAPTATION SCREENPLAY CONTEST

P.O. Box 5, Ridgecrest NC 28770. (828)768-3070. E-mail: rtmarett@charter.net. Web site: www.gideonfilmfestival.com. **Contact:** Lori Marett or Rodney Marett, co-Directors. "Spread the message of Jesus Christ through quality screenplays and films." **Deadline: January.** Guidelines for SASE. **Charges $35.** Open to any writer.

GIDEON MEDIA ARTS CONFERENCE & FILM FESTIVAL SHORT FILM CONTEST

P.O. Box 5, Ridgecrest NC 28770. (828)768-3070. E-mail: rtmarett@charter.net. Web site: www.gideonfilmfestival.com. **Contact:** Lori Marett or Rodney Marett, co-Directors. "Original, un-produced, un-optioned." "Spread the message of Jesus Christ through quality screenplays and films." Must Be Unpublished. **Deadline: January.** Guidelines for SASE. **Charges $35 ($30 before Dec. 31, 2008).** Judges to be announced. Entrants retain all rights. Must be at least 18 years old. Must be biblically based.

GIMME CREDIT SCREENPLAY COMPETITION

4470 W. Sunset Boulevard, #278, Los Angeles CA 90027. (310)499-1475. E-mail: submissions@gimmecreditcompetition.com. Web site: www.gimmecreditcompetition.com/. Short (30 pages) scripts only. ''Only short screenplays of up to thirty (30) pages for submissions to the short category and five (5) pages for the super short category, not including the cover page, will be accepted. All live action genres, including short plays and original teleplays, are acceptable. Variety is encouraged. Screenplays must not have been previously sold, optioned or produced in any form. In the event an entry is sold, optioned or produced after being received, the author(s) must notify us IMMEDIATELY.'' **Deadline: June 16. October 6.** Guidelines for SASE. **Charges $14-$50.** Judged by ''Screenplays are evaluated based on the following criteria: story and structure, dialogue, character, feasibility and their ending. During the second round of judging, a script's feasibility is examined further, along with an emphasis on originality and marketability.'' Open to any writer.

GLOBAL ART FILM FESTIVAL SCREENPLAY COMPETITION

Gaffers, 2020 Arliss Way, Sacramento CA 95822. (916)804-7333. E-mail: contact@gaffers.org. Web site: www.gaffers.org. **Contact:** Loren Reed. Writers can download an entry form online and should include a logline. Scripts should be 125 pages or fewer. Adaptations written by someone other than the original author are not acceptable. **Deadline: April.** Guidelines for SASE. **Charges $25-35.** Prize: Up to $500. Open to any writer.

SAMUEL GOLDWYN WRITING AWARDS COMPETITION

Awards Coordinator, UCLA School of Theater, Film and Television, 103 E. Melnitz Hall, Box 951622, Los Angeles CA 90095. (310)206-6154. E-mail: chernand@tft.ucla.edu. Students from any campus of the University of California are eligible. **Deadline: May 30.** Guidelines for SASE. Prize: First place is $10,000. Second is $5,000. Third is $3,000. Honorable mentions receive a money prize.

GOTHAM SCREEN FILM FESTIVAL AND SCREENPLAY CONTEST

Screenplay Submissions, P.O. Box 250862, New York NY 10025. E-mail: info@gothamscreen.com. Web site: www.gothamscreen.com/. The contest is open to anyone. ''Feature length screenplays should be properly formatted and have an approximate length of 80-120 pages. On the cover page, please put the title, the writer's name(s) and the contact details.'' **Deadline: September.** Guidelines for SASE. **Charges $35-50.** Prize: ''The 2008 Screenplay Contest comes new with a $2,500 cash prize for the winning screenplay! In addition, excerpts from selected contest entries will be performed live by professional actors at a staged reading during the festival.'' Open to any writer.
Tips Include an e-mail address to be notified.

GOVERNOR GENERAL'S LITERARY AWARD FOR DRAMA

Canada Council for the Arts, 350 Albert St., P.O. Box 1047, Ottawa ON K1P 5V8, Canada. (613)566-4414, ext. 5573. Fax: (613)566-4410. Web site: www.canadacouncil.ca/prizes/ggla. Offered for the best English-language and the best French-language work of drama by a Canadian. **Deadline: March 15 or August 7, depending on the book's publication date.** Prize: Each laureate receives $25,000; nonwinning finalists receive $1,000.

GREAT LAKES FILM ASSOCIATION ANNUAL SCREENPLAY CONTEST

6851 Rt. 6N West, Edinboro PA 16412. (814)873-5069. E-mail: screenplays@greatlakesfilmfest.com. Web site: www.greatlakesfilmfest.com. ''The annual Scriptwriting Competition is a way for new and veteran scriptwriters to possibly get the break they need. Each year we are contacted by many agents and production companies and have launched the careers of many budding scriptwriters while giving new exposure to veteran scriptwriters.'' The entered script must not be or previously been optioned, sold, or produced. Scripts entered in the teleplay contest must be original material and not based on existing shows. Must Be Unpublished. Guidelines for SASE. **Charges $25-$45.** Prize: $500. Open to any writer.

GREAT PLAINS SCREENWRITING CONTEST

313 N. 13th St., P.O. Box 880253, Lincoln NE 68588-0253. (402)472-5353. Fax: (402)472-2576. E-mail: help@nebraskascreenwriter.com. Web site: www.theross.org/. Annually. Guidelines for SASE. **Charges $30.** Prize: Cash prizes. Open to any writer.

Tips This contest is only looking for scripts that can be filmed and produced in Nebraska (the great plains area). Special preference will be given to films that highlight the diverse community in the plains area.

THE GREEN GLOBE CONTEST: SHORT ENVIRONMENTAL SCREENPLAY COMPETITION

Sour Entertainment, 455 N. College Ave., Bloomington In 47404. Web site: www.sourentertainment. com. **Contact:** Dmitrii Gabrielov. Scripts must be 5-15 pages with an environmental overview. Guidelines for SASE. Open to any writer.

GRIFFIN AWARD

Griffin Theatre Company, 13 Craigend St., Kings Cross NSW 2011 Australia. (61)(2)9332-1052. Fax: (61)(2)9331-1524. E-mail: info@griffintheatre.com.au. Web site: www.griffintheatre.com.au. Annual award for a script that has not been produced or commissioned. Guidelines for SASE. Prize: $5,000. Judged by panel of theatre professionals, including Griffin's artistic director. Open to anyone over age 18.

AURAND HARRIS MEMORIAL PLAYWRITING AWARD

The New England Theatre Conference, Inc., 215 Knob Hill Dr., Hamden CT 06518. Fax: (203)288-5938. E-mail: mail@netconline.org. Web site: www.netconline.org. Offered annually for an unpublished full-length play for young audiences. Guidelines for SASE. ''No phone calls, please.'' Open to New England residents and/or members of the New England Theatre Conference. **Deadline: May 1.** Guidelines for SASE. **Charges $20 fee.** Prize: 1st Place: $1,000; 2nd Place: $500. Open to any writer.

HENRICO THEATRE COMPANY ONE-ACT PLAYWRITING COMPETITION

Henrico Recreation & Parks, P.O. Box 27032, Richmond VA 23273. (804)501-5138. Fax: (804)501-5284. E-mail: per22@co.henrico.va.us. Web site: www.co.henrico.va.us/rec. **Contact:** Amy A. Perdue. Offered annually for previously unpublished or unproduced plays or musicals to produce new dramatic works in one-act form. Scripts with small casts and simpler sets given preference. Controversial themes and excessive language should be avoided. **Deadline: July 1.** Guidelines for SASE. Prize: $300; Runner-Up: $200. Winning entries may be produced; videotape sent to author.

HIV SHORT SCRIPT COMPETITION

Yoot Music and Films, Inc., PMB# 53 5576 Norbeck Road, Suite A, Rockville MD 20853. Web site: www.yootfilms.org/HIVShortScriptCompetition.html. This is a contest for short screenplays dealing with stopping the spread of HIV in the African-American community. Guidelines for SASE. **Charges $50.** Prize: $2,000 and production of the script. Open to any writer.

HOLIDAY SCREENPLAY CONTEST

P.O. Box 450, Boulder CO 80306. (303)629-3072. E-mail: Cherubfilm@aol.com. Web site: www.s creenplaycontests.com/holiday/index.html. Scripts must be centered on a holiday. The screenplay must be centered around one Holiday (New Year's Day, President's Day, Valentine's Day, St. Patrick's Day, April Fool's Day, Easter, 4th of July, Halloween, Thanksgiving, Hanukkah, Christmas, Kwanzaa, or any other world holiday you would like to feature). This contest is limited to the first 300 entries. Screenplays must be in English. Screenplays must not have been previously optioned, produced, or purchased prior to submission. Multiple submissions are accepted but each submission requires a separate online entry and separate fee. Screenplays must be between 90—125 pages. **Deadline: November.** Guidelines for SASE. **Charges $30.** Prize: Up to $500. Open to any writer.

HOLLYWOOD BLACK FILM FESTIVAL STORYTELLER COMPETITION

8306 Wilshire Blvd., Suite 2057, Beverly Hills CA 90211. (310)407-3596. E-mail: info@hbff.org; story teller@hbff.org. Web site: www.hbff.org. This is a contest for African-American filmmakers. "We accept full-length features, shorts, and teleplays. Scripts must arrive meeting industry standards. They must be 3-hole punched, with brass brads in the top and bottom holes, and a cover. Be sure to choose brads that aren't too small and pop out of the script when it's being read. All scripts must be formatted properly (see The Complete Guide to Standard Script Formats, by Cole/Haag). HBFF suggests Courier 12-point or the closest you can find to typewriter print. Feature length screenplays should be between 70 and 110 pages, shorts between 5 and 50 pages. We will not consider any script beyond 140 pages. Pages must be numbered. Any script that does not at least meet the basic industry standards mentioned here will not be read or returned. DO NOT include your name, WGA number, or contact information on the cover or anywhere in the script. It is also not necessary to include a printout of your withoutabox confirmation." **Deadline: February 15. February 22.** Guidelines for SASE. **Charges $45-$65.** Prize: Prizes include scriptwriting software, script consultations, screenwriting workshops, and the opportunity to have your script read by leading motion picture studio and production company development executives. Open to African-Americans.

HOLLYWOOD SCREENPLAY AWARDS

433 N. Camden Dr., Suite 600, Beverly Hills CA 90210. (310)288-3040. Fax: (310)288-0060. E-mail: hollyinfo@hollywoodnetwork.com. Web site: www.hollywoodawards.com. Annual contest that bridges the gap between writers and the established entertainment industry and provides winning screenwriters what they need most: access to key decision-makers. Only non-produced, non-optioned screenplays can be submitted. **Deadline: March 31.** Guidelines for SASE. **Charges $55 fee.** Prize: 1st Prize $1,000; 2nd Prize $500; 3rd Prize $250. Scripts are also introduced to major studios and winners receive 2 VIP passes to the Hollywood Film Festival. Judged by reputable industry professionals (producers, development executives, story analysts). Open to any writer.

HOLLYWOOD SCRIPTWRITING CONTEST

1605 Cahuenga Blvd., Dept. A, Hollywood CA 90028-6201. (800)727-4787. E-mail: info@moviewritin g.com; hwdscreen@aol.com. Web site: www.moviewriting.com/contest.html. The screenplay competition is open to writers who have not earned money writing for television or film. Submissions must be full length feature films or one hour teleplays. Screenplays or teleplays must not have been optioned or sold at the time of submission but may be submitted to other people thereafter. This is a monthly contest. Guidelines for SASE. **Charges $50.** Open to any writer.

HORROR CREEK'S FESTIVAL OF FEAR SCREENPLAY COMPETITION

R E Stull Production, P.O. Box 1793, Glen Burnie MD 21060. E-mail: restull@aol.com. Web site: www.myspace.com/horrorcreekfestivaloffear. **Contact:** "Only Horror, Sci-fi, supernatural, and suspense genres will be considered." Feature length scripts should be 70 pages or more. "Multiple authorship is allowed. If such a screenplay wins, the prize will be split between the writers. Multiple entries are allowed, but each entry must be accompanied by their own completed entry form and their own appropriate entry fee. You are allowed to mail them to us in one package to save on postage. No corrected pages or additional pages will be accepted after the screenplay has been entered. PLEASE be sure you double check your screenplay for errors, blank pages, etc., before mailing them to us!" Must Be Unpublished. Guidelines for SASE. **Charges $20-35.** Open to any writer.

HORROR SCREENPLAY CONTEST

Cherub Productions, P.O. Box 540, Boulder Co 80306. (303)629-3072. E-mail: Cherubfilm@aol.com. Web site: www.screenplaycontests.com/horror/. This contest is looking for horror scripts. This contest is limited to the first 500 entries. Screenplays must be between 90—125 pages. Must Be Unpublished. Guidelines for SASE. **Charges $25-35.** Prize: More than $5000 in cash and prizes. Open to any writer.

ILLINOIS SCREENWRITING COMPETITION

Chicago Film Office, 121 N. LaSalle, Room 806, Chicago IL 60602. (312)814-8711. E-mail: rmoskal@cityofchicago.org. Web site: www.cityofchicago.org/filmoffice. Guidelines for SASE. Open to any writer.

IMPRACTICAL VENTURES SCREENWRITING COMPETITION

333 Washington Blvd., P.O. Box 330, Marina Del Rey CA 90292. E-mail: impventures@yahoo.com. Web site: www.geocities.com/impventures/contest.html. The frequency of this contest varies. The Web site will have all updates when a new contest is announced. Guidelines for SASE. Prize: Cash prizes up to $500. Open to any writer.

INDEPENDENT BLACK FILM FESTIVAL SCREENPLAY CONTEST

P.O. Box 18914, Atlanta GA 31126. (404)468-3013. Fax: (404)627-4634. E-mail: indieblackfilm@yahoo.com. Web site: www.indieblackfest.org/. Guidelines for SASE. This contest is for African-Americans.
Tips This contest is part of the film festival.

INDEPENDENT PILOT COMPETITION

New York Television Festival, P.O. Box 627, Planetarium Station, New York NY 10024-0627. (718)350-8519. Web site: www.nytvf.com/2008_ipc.htm. Pilots should be between 4 and 22 minutes. Programs created or funded by broadcast networks, cable networks or major production studios are ineligible to compete in the Independent Pilot Competition but may be submitted to the NYTVF for consideration as a specialty screening. Entrants must be 18 years of age or older. If under the age of 18, entries must include written parental consent. Programs for the Independent Pilot Competition must not have been publicly broadcast on television (except for previous broadcast on college campus television) prior to the Festival. Foreign language programs must have English subtitles or be dubbed in English. "There is no better way for independent television creators to get their work noticed by the industry. Winners in previous years have sold to major networks such as NBC Universal Television Studios and A&E. In 2005, the winner of the Audience Award and Best Reality Pilot, *Off the Hook*, was developed and aired as a series on the Versus network." **Deadline: June.** Guidelines for SASE. **Charges $25-50.** Open to any writer.

INDIEFEST SCREENWRITING COMPETITION AND MARKET

P.O. Box 148849, Chicago IL 60614. (312) 226-3838. E-mail: info@indiefestchicago.com. Web site: www.indiefestchicago.com. **Contact:** Executive Director Cynthia Castillo-Hill, cynthia@indiefestchicago.com. Guidelines for SASE. Open to any writer.

INDIVIDUAL PROJECT GRANTS

Rhode Island State Council on the Arts, One Capitol Hill, 3rd Floor, Providence RI 02908. (401)222-3880. Fax: (401)222-3018. E-mail: cristina@arts.ri.gov. Web site: www.arts.ri.gov. **Contact:** Cristina DiChiera, director of individual artist & public art programs. "Request for Proposal grants enable an artist to create new work and/or complete works-in-progress by providing direct financial assistance. By encouraging significant development in the work of an individual artist, these grants recognize the central contribution artists make to the creative environment of Rhode Island." Guidelines online. Open to Rhode Island residents age 18 or older; students not eligible. **Deadline: October 1 and April 1.** Prize: Nonmatching grants typically under $5,000.

INTERNATIONAL FAMILY FILM FESTIVAL

P.O. Box 801507, Valencia CA 91380-1507. (661)257-3131. Fax: (661)257-8989. E-mail: info@iffilmfest.org. Web site: www.iffilmfest.org. IFFF advocates, promotes and encourages excellence in films produced for a general audience by emerging screenwriters, filmmakers and studios worldwide. Short screenplays and feature screenplays reviewed. Features should be fewer than 120 pages, and shorts should be fewer than 45 pages. With entry form, you will need to include a 50-word synopsis as well as character descriptions. **Deadline: January.** Guidelines for SASE. **Charges $30 (short); $60 (full).** Open to any writer.

INTERNATIONAL HORROR AND SCI-FI FILM FESTIVAL SCREENPLAY CONTEST

Phoenix Film Festival, (602)955-6444. E-mail: info@HorrorSciFi.com. Web site: www.horrorscifi.com/screenplays.html. "Our organization is dedicated to organizing and perpetuating a World-class event that creates a community of horror and sci-fi fans and filmmakers who encourage and educate the world about horror and sci-fi filmmaking. Our aim is to promote independent filmmaking, with a spotlight on films in the horror and sci-fi genre." Annually, Must Be Unpublished. Guidelines for SASE. Prize: "Screenplay winners not only win cash prizes but also get the opportunity to have their screenplays reviewed by major entertainment companies." Open to any writer.

KAIROS PRIZE FOR SPIRITUALLY UPLIFTING SCREENPLAYS

5620 Paseo de Norte, #127C-308, Carlsbad CA 92008. Web site: www.kairosprize.com. For screenplays that are spiritually uplifting and inspirational. Annually. **Deadline: October 27. December 1.** Guidelines for SASE. **Charges $50-$75.** Prize: More than $50,000 in cash and prizes, with a $25,000 grand prize. Open to any writer.

KANSAS ARTS COMMISSION ARTIST FELLOWSHIPS AND EMERGING ARTIST AWARDS

Kansas Arts Commission, 700 SW Jackson St., Suite 1004, Topeka KS 66603-3761. (785)296-3335. Fax: (785)296-4989. E-mail: kac@arts.ks.us. Web site: arts.ks.us. **Contact:** Christine Dotterweich Bial. Offered annually for Kansas artists, both published and unpublished. Fellowships and awards are offered in 10 artistic disciplines, rotating 5 disciplines every other year, and are awarded based on artistic merit. The artistic disciplines are: music composition; choreography; film/video; interdisciplinary/performance art; playwriting; fiction; poetry; 2-dimensional visual art; 3-dimensional visual art; and crafts. Guidelines available online. Open to Kansas residents only. **Deadline: Varies.** Prize: Fellowship: $5,000; Mid-Career Artist Fellowships: $750; Emerging Artist Awards: $250. Open to Kansas residents only.

THE KAUFMAN & HART PRIZE FOR NEW AMERICAN COMEDY

Arkansas Repertory Theatre, P.O. Box 110, Little Rock AR 72201. (501)378-0445. Web site: www.ther ep.org. **Contact:** Brad Mooy, literary manager. Offered every 2 years for unpublished, unproduced, full-length comedies (no musicals or children's plays). Scripts may be submitted with the recommendation of an agent or theater professional only. Must be at least 65 pages, with minimal set requirements and a cast limit of 12. One entry/playwright. Open to US citizens only. **Deadline: February 1.** Prize: $10,000, a staged reading, and transportation.

KUMU KAHUA/UHM THEATRE DEPARTMENT PLAYWRITING CONTEST

Kumu Kahua Theatre, Inc./University of Hawaii at Manoa, Dept. of Theatre and Dance, 46 Merchant St., Honolulu HI 96813. (808)536-4222. Fax: (808)536-4226. E-mail: kumukahuatheatre@verizon.net. Web site: www.kumukahua.com. **Contact:** Harry Wong III, artistic director. Offered annually for unpublished work to honor full-length and short plays. Guidelines available every September. First 2 categories open to residents and nonresidents. For Hawaii Prize, plays must be set in Hawaii or deal with some aspect of the Hawaiian experience. For Pacific Rim prize, plays must deal with the Pacific Islands, Pacific Rim, or Pacific/Asian-American experience—short plays only considered in 3rd category. **Deadline: January 2.** Prize: Hawaii: $600; Pacific Rim: $450; Resident: $250.

L.A. DESIGNERS' THEATRE-COMMISSIONS

L.A. Designers' Theatre, P.O. Box 1883, Studio City CA 91614-0883. (323)650-9600 or (323)654-2700 T.D.D. Fax: (323)654-3210. E-mail: ladesigners@juno.com. **Contact:** Richard Niederberg, artistic director. Quarterly contest "to promote new work and push it onto the conveyor belt to filmed or videotaped entertainment." All submissions must be registered with copyright office and be unpublished. Material will not be returned. "Do not submit anything that will not fit in a #10 envelope. No rules, guidelines, fees, or entry forms. Just present an idea that can be commissioned into a full work." Proposals for uncompleted works are encouraged. Unpopular political, religious, social, or other themes are encouraged; 'street' language and nudity are acceptable. Open to any writer. **Dead-**

line: **March 15, June 15, September 15, December 15.** Prize: Production or publication of the work in the Los Angeles market. "We only want 'first refusal.' "

LAS VEGAS INTERNATIONAL FILM FESTIVAL SCREENPLAY COMPETITION

Las Vegas International Film Festival, 10300 W. Charleston Blvd., Las Vegas NV 89135. (502)371-8037. E-mail: info@lvfilmfest.com. Web site: www.lvfilmfest.com/Filmmakers/Screenplay_Competition.aspx. "This annual screenplay competition was created to help aspiring screenwriters break into the entertainment industry as well as to support emerging new talent." "Scripts may be submitted via hardcopy or electronic file. Scripts should be no longer than 180 pages." Must Be Unpublished. Guidelines for SASE. **Charges $30.** Prize: Cash prizes are awarded to the First, Second, and Third place winners. Open to any writer.

LATINO SCREENPLAY COMPETITION

Tica Productions, 13700 Marina Pointe Drive #1620, Marina del Rey CA 90292. 310.574.8422. E-mail: info@latinoscreenplaycompetition.com. Web site: www.latinoscreenplaycompetition.com/. "The Latino Screenplay Competition (LSC) was conceived by Tica Productions to cultivate a greater interest in Latino-themed stories in popular cinema. The objective of the Latino Screenplay Competition is to promote talented screenwriters of Latino-themed screenplays, as well as encourage a demand for Latino-themed stories in the American film market. Both feature-length screenplays, as well as short screenplays will be awarded. It is not a requirement of the LSC that the screenwriters of Latino-themed screenplays be of Latino descent or speak a Latino language as his/her primary language. It is also not a requirement that the Latino-themed screenplays be written in a Latino language." Feature scripts must be more than 80 pages. Short scripts must be fewer than 30 pages. "Screenplays must be original screenplays. Adaptations will only be accepted if author possesses rights to adapt original work. Writer(s) may be asked to provide written and executed proof of their right to adapt the previously published work to screenplay form or to prove the original work is indisputably in public domain. If proof of rights cannot be provided, LSC reserves right to disqualify entry." Must Be Unpublished. Guidelines for SASE. **Charges $35-50.** Prize: "Winners selected by the LSC will be considered for both monetary prizes, as well as prizes provided by LSC Sponsors. The LSC will offer awards in several screenplay divisions, including but not limited to 'Best Latino-Themed Dramatic Feature' and 'Best Latino-Themed Short Screenplay.' " Open to any writer.

BRENDA MACDONALD RICHES FIRST BOOK AWARD

Saskatchewan Book Awards, Inc., 205B-2314 11th Ave., Regina SK S4P 0K1, Canada. (306)569-1585. Fax: (306)569-4187. E-mail: director@bookawards.sk.ca. Web site: www.bookawards.sk.ca. **Contact:** Glenda James, executive director. Offered annually for work published September 15 of year past to September 14 of current year. This award is presented to a Saskatchewan author for the best first book, judged on the quality of writing. Books from the following categories will be considered: children's; drama; fiction (short fiction by a single author, novellas, novels); nonfiction (all categories of nonfiction writing except cookbooks, directories, how-to books, or bibliographies of minimal critical content); poetry. **Deadline: First deadline: July 31; Final deadline: September 14.** Guidelines for SASE. **Charges $20 (Canadian).** Prize: $2,000.

MAXIM MAZUMDAR NEW PLAY COMPETITION

Alleyway Theatre, 1 Curtain Up Alley, Buffalo NY 14202. (716)852-2600. Fax: (716)852-2266. E-mail: newplays@alleyway.com. Web site: www.alleyway.com. **Contact:** Literary Manager. Estab. 1989. Annual competition. Full Length: Not less than 90 minutes, no more than 10 performers. One-Act: Less than 20 minutes, no more than 6 performers. Musicals must be accompanied by audio CD. Finalists announced October 1; winners announced November 1. Playwrights may submit work directly. There is no entry form. Writers may submit once in each category, but pay only 1 fee. Please specify if submission is to be included in competition. Alleyway Theatre must receive first production credit in subsequent printings and productions. **Deadline: July 1. Charges $25.** Prize: Full length: $400, production, and royalties; One-act: $100, production, and royalties. Open to any writer.

MCKNIGHT ADVANCEMENT GRANT

The Playwrights' Center, 2301 Franklin Ave. E., Minneapolis MN 55406-1099. (612)332-7481, ext. 10. Fax: (612)332-6037. Web site: www.pwcenter.org. Estab. 1981. Offered annually for either published or unpublished playwrights to recognize those whose work demonstrates exceptional artistic merit and potential and whose primary residence is in the state of Minnesota. The grants are intended to significantly advance recipients' art and careers, and can be used to support a wide variety of expenses. Applications available December 1. Guidelines for SASE. Additional funds of up to $2,000 are available for workshops and readings. The Playwrights' Center evaluates each application and forwards finalists to a panel of 3 judges from the national theater community. Applicant must have been a citizen or permanent resident of the US and a legal resident of the state of Minnesota since July 1, 2004. (Residency must be maintained during fellowship year.) Applicant must have had a minimum of 1 work fully produced by a professional theater at the time of application. **Deadline: February 3.** Prize: $25,000 which can be used to support a wide variety of expenses, including writing time, artistic costs of residency at a theater or arts organization, travel and study, production, or presentation.

MCLAREN MEMORIAL COMEDY PLAY WRITING COMPETITION

Midland Community Theatre, 2000 W. Wadley, Midland TX 79705. (432)682-2544. Fax: (432)682-6136. Web site: www.mctmidland.org. Estab. 1990. Offered annually in 2 divisions: one-act and full-length. All entries must be comedies for adults, teens, or children; musical comedies are *not* accepted. Work must have never been professionally produced or published. See Web site for competition guidelines and required entry form. **Deadline: Jan. 1-Feb. 28. Charges $15/script.** Prize: $400 for winning full-length play; $200 for winning one-act play; staged readings for full length finalist.

MEXICO INTERNATIONAL FILM FESTIVAL SCREENPLAY COMPETITION

Mexico International Film Festival, 20058 Ventura Blvd., Suite 123, Woodland Hills CA 91364. E-mail: info@mexicofilmfestival.com. Web site: www.mexicofilmfestival.com/Filmmakers/Screen play_Competition.aspx. Annually. Guidelines for SASE. **Charges $30.** Judged by Awards are based solely on overall merits of the screenplays. Open to any writer.

MINNESOTA STATE ARTS BOARD ARTIST INITIATIVE GRANT

Minnesota State Arts Board, Park Square Court, Suite 200, 400 Sibley St., St. Paul MN 55101-1928. (651)215-1600 or (800)866-2787. Fax: (651)215-1602. E-mail: erin.mclennon@arts.state.mn.us. Web site: www.arts.state.mn.us. **Contact:** Erin McLennon. The grant is meant to support and assist artists at various stages in their careers. It encourages artistic development, nurtures artistic creativity, and recognizes the contributions individual artists make to the creative environment of the state of Minnesota. Literary categories include prose, poetry, playwriting, and screenwriting. Open to Minnesota residents. Prize: Bi-annual grants of $2,000-6,000.

THE W.O. MITCHELL LITERARY PRIZE

The Writers' Trust of Canada, 90 Richmond St. E., Suite 200, Toronto ON M5C 1P1, Canada. (416)504-8222. Fax: (416)504-9090. E-mail: info@writerstrust.com. Web site: www.writerstrust.com. **Contact:** James Davies. Offered annually to a writer who has produced an outstanding body of work and has acted during his/her career as a "caring mentor" for other writers. They must also have published a work of fiction or had a new stage play produced during the 3-year period for each competition. Every third year the W.O. Mitchell Literary Prize will be awarded to a writer who works in French. Prize: $15,000. Open to Canadian residents only.

MONTEREY SCREENPLAY COMPETITION

Monterey County Film Commission, 801 Lighthouse Ave, Suite 104, Monterey CA 93940. (831)646-0910. Fax: (831) 655-9250. E-mail: info@filmmonterey.org. Web site: www.filmmonterey.org/sw_contest.htm. Feature scripts must be between 90 and 120 pages. "A completed and signed Entry Form and Entry Fee must accompany each submission. The act of signing and submitting the form constitutes acceptance without reservation of all rules and requirements of the Monterey Screenplay Competition and all decisions rendered by its judges." Annually, Must Be Unpublished. **Deadline: May 19. July 31.** Guidelines for SASE. **Charges $40-$50.** Open to any writer.

MOONDANCE INTERNATIONAL FILM FESTIVAL

970 Ninth St., Boulder CO 80302. (303)545-0202. E-mail: info@moondancefilmfestival.com. Web site: www.moondancefilmfestival.com. WRITTEN WORKS SUBMISSIONS: feature screenplays, short screenplays, feature & short musical screenplays, feature & short screenplays for children, 1, 2 or 3-act stageplays, mini-series for TV, television movies of the week, television pilots, libretti, musical film scripts, short stories, radio plays & short stories for children. **Deadline: April 1. May 1.** Guidelines for SASE. **Charges $50-$75.** Open to any writer.

MOVIE SCRIPT CONTEST (FEATURE & SHORT)

P.O. Box 6336, Burbank CA 91510-6336. Fax: (818)688-3990. E-mail: info@moviescriptcontest.com. Web site: www.moviescriptcontest.com. **Contact:** Jason Zimmatore, Contest Coordinator. "To discover & promote new writing talent." Annually, Must Be Unpublished. **Deadline: July.** Guidelines for SASE. Prize: "$1,000 for 1st Place Winners in each category, and the top 10 loglines are read by our producer partners." Open to any writer.

MOVING ARTS PREMIERE ONE-ACT COMPETITION

Moving Arts, P.O. Box 481145, Los Angeles CA 90048. (213)622-8906. Fax: (213)622-8946. E-mail: info@movingarts.org. Web site: www.movingarts.org. **Contact:** Trey Nichols. Offered annually for unproduced one-act plays in the Los Angeles area (single set; maximum cast of 8 people). All playwrights are eligible except Moving Arts resident artists. Send 5-70 pages, cover letter, and SASE.

Guidelines online, for SASE, or by e-mail. **Deadline: November 1-February 1 (postmarked). Charges $10 fee/script.** Prize: 1st Place: $200, plus a full production with a 4-8 week run; finalists get program mention and possible production.

MUSICAL STAIRS

West Coast Ensemble, P.O. Box 38728, Los Angeles CA 90038. (323)876-9337. Fax: (323)876-8916. **Contact:** Les Hanson. Offered annually for unpublished writers to nurture, support, and encourage musical creators. Permission to present the musical is granted if work is selected as finalist. **Deadline: June 30.** Prize: $500 and presentation of musical.

NANTUCKET FILM FESTIVAL SCREENPLAY COMPETITION

Nantucket Film Festival, 1633 Broadway, suite 15-333, New York NY 10019. (212)708-1278. Fax: (212)708-7490. E-mail: info@nantucketfilmfestival.org. Web site: www.nantucketfilmfestival.org/ ScreenplayApplication.php. Screenplays must be standard feature film length (90-130 pages) and standard U.S. format only. Guidelines for SASE. **Charges $50.** Open to any writer.

NASHVILLE FILM FESTIVAL NAFF AWARDS

P.O. Box 24330, Nashville TN 37202. (615)742-2500. Fax: (615)742-1004. E-mail: info@nashvillefilmf estival.org. Web site: www.nashvillefilmfestival.org. This contest seeks film submissions less than 40 minutes in length, as well as full-length features and documentaries. **Deadline: October (late: December).** Guidelines for SASE. **Charges $25+.** Prize: There are numerous awards: press/industry screenings, $1,000 and option of international representation for one year. Open to any writer.

NATIONAL AUDIO DRAMA SCRIPT COMPETITION

National Audio Theatre Festivals, 115 Dikeman St., Hempstead NY 11150. (516)483-8321. Fax: (516)538-7583. Web site: www.natf.org. **Contact:** Sue Zizza. Offered annually for unpublished radio scripts. ''NATF is particularly interested in stories that deserve to be told because they enlighten, intrigue, or simply make us laugh out loud. Contemporary scripts with strong female roles, multicultural casting, and diverse viewpoints will be favorably received.'' Preferred length is 25 minutes. Guidelines available online. Open to any writer. NATF will have the right to produce the scripts for the NATF Live Performance Workshop; however, NATF makes no commitment to produce any script. The authors will retain all other rights to their work. **Deadline: November 15. Charges $25 (US currency only).** Prize: $800 split between 2-4 authors and free workshop production participation.

NATIONAL CANADIAN ONE-ACT PLAYWRITING COMPETITION

Ottawa Little Theatre, 400 King Edward Ave., Ottawa ON K1N 7M7, Canada. (613)233-8948. Fax: (613)233-8027. E-mail: olt@on-aibn.com. Web site: www.ottawalittletheatre.com. **Contact:** Elizabeth Holden, office administrator. Estab. 1913. Purpose is to encourage literary and dramatic talent in Canada. Guidelines for #10 SASE with Canadian postage or #10 SAE with 1 IRC. **Deadline: August 31.** Prize: 1st Place: $1,000; 2nd Place: $700; 3rd Place: $500.

NATIONAL CHILDREN'S THEATRE FESTIVAL

Actors' Playhouse at the Miracle Theatre, 280 Miracle Mile, Coral Gables FL 33134. (305)444-9293, ext. 615. Fax: (305)444-4181. E-mail: maulding@actorsplayhouse.org. Web site: www.actorsplay

house.org. **Contact:** Earl Maulding. Offered annually for unpublished musicals for young audiences. Target age is 4-12. Script length should be 45-60 minutes. Maximum of 8 actors to play any number of roles. Prefer settings which lend themselves to simplified scenery. Bilingual (English/Spanish) scripts are welcomed. Call or visit Web site for guidelines. Open to any writer. **Deadline: April 1. Charges $10 fee.** Prize: $500 and full production.

Tips Travel and lodging during the festival based on availability.

NATIONAL LATINO PLAYWRIGHTS AWARD

Arizona Theatre Co., 343 S. Scott Ave, Tucson AZ 85701. (520)884-8210. Fax: (520)628-9129. E-mail: eromero@arizonatheatre.org. Web site: www.aztheatreco.org. **Contact:** Elaine Romero, playwright-in-residence. Offered annually for unproduced, unpublished plays over 50 pages in length. Plays may be in English, bilingual, or in Spanish (with English translation). The award recognizes exceptional full-length plays by Latino playwrights on any subject. Open to Latino playwrights currently residing in the US, its territories, and/or Mexico. Guidelines online or via e-mail. **Deadline: Dec. 31.** Prize: $1,000.

NATIONAL PLAYWRITING COMPETITION

Young Playwrights, Inc., P.O. Box 5134, New York NY 10185. (212)594-5440. Fax: (212)594-5441. E-mail: literary@youngplaywrights.org. Web site: youngplaywrights.org. **Contact:** Literary Department. Offered annually for stage plays of any length (no musicals, screenplays, or adaptations). Writers ages 18 or younger (as of deadline) are invited to send scripts. **Deadline: January 2.** Prize: Invitation to week-long writers' conference in New York City (all expenses paid) and off-Broadway presentation.

NATIONAL TEN-MINUTE PLAY CONTEST

Actors Theatre of Louisville, 316 W. Main St., Louisville KY 40202-4218. (502)584-1265. Web site: www.actorstheatre.org. Offered annually for previously (professionally) unproduced 10-minute plays (10 pages or less). "Entries must *not* have had an Equity or Equity-waiver production." One submission/playwright. Scripts are not returned. Please write or call for submission guidelines. Open to US residents. **Deadline: November 1 (postmarked).** Prize: $1,000.

LARRY NEAL WRITERS' COMPETITION

DC Commission on the Arts and Humanities, 1371 Harvard St. N.W., Washington DC 20009. (202)724-5613. Fax: (202)727-4135. Web site: http://dcarts.dc.gov. **Contact:** Lisa Richards, arts program coordinator. Offered annually for unpublished poetry, fiction, essay, and dramatic writing. Call or visit Web site for current deadlines. Open to Washington DC residents only. Prize: Cash awards.

NEVADA FILM OFFICE SCREENWRITER'S COMPETITION

555 E. Washington Ave., Ste. 5400, Las Vegas NV 89101. 1-877-NEV-FILM. Web site: www.nevadafilm.com/screenwriters.php. At least 75% of the locations in the script must be filmable in Nevada. **Deadline: August 1.** Guidelines for SASE. **Charges $15 or $30.** Open to any writer.

NEW AMERICAN COMEDY WORKSHOP

Ukiah Players Theatre, 1041 Low Gap Rd., Ukiah CA 95482. (707)462-9226. Fax: (707)462-1790. E-mail: info@ukiahplayerstheatre.org. Web site: ukiahplayerstheatre.org. **Contact:** Kate Magruder, executive director. Offered every 2 years to playwrights seeking to develop their unproduced, full-length comedies into funnier, stronger scripts. Two scripts will be chosen for staged readings; 1 of these may be chosen for full production. Guidelines for SASE or online. **Deadline: November 30 of odd-numbered years.** Prize: Playwrights chosen for readings will receive a $25 royalty/performance. The playwright chosen for full production will receive a $50 royalty/performance, travel (up to $500) to Ukiah for development workshop/rehearsal, lodging, and per diem.

NEW JERSEY FEATURE SCREENPLAY COMPETITION

New Jersey State Film Festival / Cape May Film Society, P.O. Box 595, Cape May NJ 08204. E-mail: info@njstatefilmfestival.com. Web site: www.njstatefilmfestival.com/screenplay.htm. **Contact:** William Sokolic, chair New Jersey Screenplay Competition at bsaks47@comcast.net or (609) 823.9159. "The contest is open to residents and non-residents. The one caveat: those outside New Jersey must use the state as the principal setting. Features must be between 80 and 120 pages. All scripts need to be in standard screenplay format." **Deadline: Nov. 1.** Guidelines for SASE. **Charges $24.** Prize: "In addition to admission to this year's Cape May New Jersey State Film Festival, potential prizes include software from Write Brothers. Decision by the judges will be final." Open to any writer.

NEW JERSEY SHORT SCREENPLAY COMPETITION

New Jersey State Film Festival / Cape May Film Society, PO 595, Cape May NJ 08204. (609)823-9159. E-mail: bsaks47@comcast.net. Web site: www.njstatefilmfestival.com/screenplay.htm. **Contact:** William Sokolic, chair. "For talented screenwriters from New Jersey looking to enter the industry, the lack of a venue left a void we are determined to fill. The initial emphasis on short films also speaks to an avenue ignored by most screenplay competitions, which tend to favor features. Who is eligible: all New Jersey residents; students at New Jersey colleges; anyone else who uses New Jersey as the principal setting for the script." Short scripts should be 12 pages or fewer. **Deadline: November.** Guidelines for SASE. **Charges $12.**

NEW JERSEY STATE COUNCIL ON THE ARTS FELLOWSHIP PROGRAM

P.O. Box 306, Trenton NJ 08625-0306. (609)292-6130. Fax: (609)989-1440. Web site: www.njartscouncil.org. Offered in even numbered years. Writers may apply in either poetry, prose or playwriting. Fellowship awards are intended to provide support for the artist during the year to enable them to continue producing new work. Guidelines and application available on line at: www.midatlanticarts.org after May 1 of even numbered years. Must be New Jersey resident; may not be high school, undergraduate or graduate matriculating student. **Deadline: July 15 of even numbered years.** Prize: $6,500-$12,000.

NEW WORKS FOR THE STAGE

COE College Theatre Arts Department, 1220 First Ave. NE, Cedar Rapids IA 52402. (319)399-8624. Fax: (319)399-8557. E-mail: swolvert@coe.edu. Web site: www.public.coe.edu/departments/theatre. **Contact:** Susan Wolverton. Offered in odd-numbered years to encourage new work, to provide an interdisciplinary forum for the discussion of issues found in new work, and to offer playwright contact with theater professionals who can provide response to new work. Full-length, original, unpublished and unproduced scripts only. No musicals, adaptations, translations, or collaborations. Submit 1-

page synopsis, résumé, and SASE if the script is to be returned. **Deadline: November 1 even years.** Prize: $500, plus travel, room and board for residency at the college.

NEW YORK FOUNDATION FOR THE ARTS ARTISTS' FELLOWSHIPS

New York Foundation for the Arts, 155 Avenue of the Americas, 6th Floor, New York NY 10013-1507. (212)366-6900. E-mail: fellowships@nyfa.org. Web site: www.nyfa.org. Estab. 1985. Fellowships are awarded in 16 disciplines on a biannual rotation made to individual originating artists living and working in the State of New York. Awards are based upon the recommendations of peer panels and are not project support. The Fellowships may be used by each recipient as she/he sees fit. **Deadline: October 3.** Prize: Grants of $7,000. All applicants must be 18 years of age, and a New York resident for 2 years prior to the time of application.

DON AND GEE NICHOLL FELLOWSHIPS IN SCREENWRITING

Academy of Motion Picture Arts & Sciences, 1313 N. Vine St., Hollywood CA 90028-8107. (310)247-3010. E-mail: nicholl@oscars.org. Web site: www.oscars.org/nicholl. Estab. 1985. Offered annually for unproduced screenplays to identify talented new screenwriters. **Deadline: May 1. Charges $30 fee.** Prize: Up to five $30,000 fellowships awarded each year. Open to writers who have not earned more than $5,000 writing for films or TV.

THE NICHOLL FELLOWSHIP IN SCREENWRITING

1313 Vine St., Hollywood CA 90028-8107. (310)247-3010. E-mail: nicholl@oscar.org. Web site: www.oscars.org/nicholl/index.html. "No applicant may have earned (or during this competition shall earn) money or other consideration as a screenwriter for theatrical films or television, or for the sale of, or sale of an option to, any original story, treatment, screenplay or teleplay for more than $5,000. An entrant's total earnings from all film and television screenwriting may not exceed $5,000. Applicants may not have received a screenwriting fellowship or prize for more than $5,000 that includes a "first look" clause, an option or any other quid pro quo involving the writer's work. Members and employees of the Academy of Motion Picture Arts and Sciences and their immediate families are not eligible, nor are competition judges and their immediate families." **Deadline: May 1.** Guidelines for SASE. **Charges $30.** Judged by The first and quarterfinal rounds are judged by industry professionals who are not members of the Academy. The semifinal round is judged by Academy members drawn from across the spectrum of the motion picture industry. The finalist scripts are judged by the Nicholl Committee. Open to any writer.

NICKELODEON WRITING FELLOWSHIP

Nickelodeon, 231 W. Olive Ave., Burbank CA 91502. (818)736-3663. E-mail: info.writing@nick.com. Web site: www.nickwriting.com. This contests looks for scripts written for half-hour TV. Animation stories are OK. "Due to the nature of the Fellowship Program, we are unable to sponsor individuals for United States work visas to participate in the Fellowship Program. In order to be eligible for the Fellowship Program, an applicant must possess and present evidence of identity and United States employment eligibility (valid for the duration of the Fellowship Program). The Fellowship is a full-time position with an expected one-year duration; however, employment is on an "at will" basis. Due to the intensive nature of the Fellowship Program, you may not hold other employment or be enrolled in school on a full-time basis during the Fellowship period if it will interfere with any aspect of or time commitment to the Program. **Deadline: February 2.** Guidelines for SASE. Open to any writer.

Tips "If you have previously applied to the program and have not been selected as a fellow, you are welcomed and encouraged to apply again, however you are required to submit a different spec script for each new submission period."

OGLEBAY INSTITUTE TOWNGATE THEATRE PLAYWRITING CONTEST

Oglebay Institute, Stifel Fine Arts Center, 1330 National Rd., Wheeling WV 26003. (304)242-7700. Fax: (304)242-7747. Web site: www.oionline.com. **Contact:** Kate H. Crosbie, director of performing arts. Estab. 1976. Offered annually for unpublished works. All full-length nonmusical plays that have never been professionally produced or published are eligible. Open to any writer. **Deadline: January 1; winner announced May 31.** Guidelines for SASE. Prize: cash award & production. In the event that no entry is deemed to meet our established standards no winner will be declared.

OHIO INDEPENDENT SCREENPLAY AWARDS

Ohio Independent Film Festival, 1392 West 65th Street, Cleveland OH 45102. (216)651-7315. Fax: (216)696-6610. E-mail: OhioIndieFilmFest@juno.com. Web site: www.ohiofilms.com/. **Contact:** Jen O'Neal, coordinator. Scripts must be 80-120 pages. Must Be Unpublished. Guidelines for SASE. **Charges $55-75.** Prize: In addition to the top prize, there is a prize for the best script set in Northern Ohio. Open to any writer.

ONE ACT MARATHON

Attic Theatre Ensemble, 5429 W. Washington Blvd., Los Angeles CA 90016-1112. (323)525-0600. E-mail: info@attictheatre.org. Web site: www.attictheatre.org. **Contact:** Literary Manager. Offered annually for unpublished and unproduced work. Scripts should be intended for mature audiences. Length should not exceed 45 minutes. Guidelines for SASE or online. **Deadline: December 31. Charges $15.** Prize: 1st Place: $300; 2nd Place: $100.

ONE IN TEN SCREENPLAY CONTEST

Cherub Productions, P.O. Box 540, Boulder CO 80306. E-mail: Cherubfilm@aol.com. Web site: www. screenplaycontests.com/oneinten/contact.html. Scripts that provide a positive potrayal of gays and lesbians. "A requirement of the competition is that at least one of the primary characters in the screenplay be gay or lesbian (bisexual, transgender, questioning, and the like) and that gay and lesbian characters must be portrayed positively. All writers are encouraged to enter!" **Deadline: September 1.** Guidelines for SASE. **Charges $45.** Prize: $1,000. Open to any writer.

ONE PAGE SCREENPLAY COMPETITION

80 St. Clair Ave., Ste. 2309, Toronto ON M4T 1N6, Canada. E-mail: wildsoundreadingseries@simpatico.ca. Web site: www.wildsound-filmmaking-feedback-events.com/index.html. This is a contest seeking submissions of films, TV pilots, spec scripts and screenplays. "Write a 1 page script. Any script longer than one page is disqualified. Please include title page with full contact information. (Title page does not include the 1 page script). Script must be presented in proper screenplay format." **Deadline: September.** Guidelines for SASE. **Charges $10.** Prize: The winning script is filmed and will be screened at festivals. "The TOP 10 Finalists will have their 1 page scripts read at our November

2008 event. The audience will then vote on their favorite one page script and the winner will then have their 1 page script produced using the top cast/crew in Toronto." Open to any writer.

OPEN CURTAIN SCREENWRITING CONTESTS

Open Curtain Productions, LLC, P.O. Box 3278, Reno NV 89505. (775)842-6832. E-mail: dsanders@opencurtainprod.com. Web site: www.opencurtainprod.com/contest.html. Full-length & Short categories are accepted in this contest. **Deadline: January through September**—see guidelines. Guidelines for SASE. **Charges $35 (full-length), $25 (short).** Prize: Grand Prize (Full-Length): $1,000; 2nd Prize: $300; 3rd Prize: $200. Grand Prize (Short): $500; 2nd Prize: $350; 3rd Prize: $200. Open to any writer.

PACIFIC NORTHWEST WRITERS CONFERENCE LITERARY CONTEST

P.O. Box 2016, Edmonds WA 98020-9516. (452)673-2665. E-mail: pnwa@pnwa.com. Web site: www.pnwa.org. The contest is part of the Pacific Northwest Writers Conference, occurring in Edmonds, WA, each summer. **Deadline: February 22, 2008.** Guidelines for SASE. **Charges $35-$50.** Open to any writer.

PAGE INTERNATIONAL SCREENWRITING AWARDS

7510 Sunset Blvd., #610, Hollywood CA 90046. E-mail: info@internationalscreenwritingawards.com. Web site: internationalscreenwritingawards.com/. Feature length, short film and TV pilots for drama or sitcom scripts accepted. Short film script submissions must be fewer than 40 pages. TV pilots must be 30-70 pages. Adaptations of books, plays, or other source material written by another author are not eligible under any circumstances; nor are scripts adapted from books, plays, or other source material written by you if your source material has been sold, produced, or is currently under option to any third party. Scripts adapted from your own self-published books, plays, or other source material are eligible if you have retained all rights to your work. **Deadline: April 15.** Guidelines for SASE. **Charges $39-$59.** Prize: "The winners of our screenplay contest will receive over $30,000 in cash and prizes, including a $10,000 GRAND PRIZE. Most importantly, each year dozens of top producers, agents, and development execs ask to read the winning scripts. As a result, many of our past winners have landed writing assignments, secured representation, and signed option agreements on their work, and several now have movies in various stages of production and release." Open to any writer.

THE PAGE INTERNATIONAL SCREENWRITING AWARDS

The PAGE Awards Committee, 7510 Sunset Blvd., #610, Hollywood CA 90046-3408. E-mail: info@internationalscreenwritingawards.com. Web site: www.internationalscreenwritingawards.com. **Contact:** Jennifer Berg, administrative director. Annual competition to discover the most talented new screenwriters from across the country and around the world. Each year, awards are presented to 31 screenwriters in 10 different categories: action/adventure, comedy, drama, family film, historical film, science fiction/fantasy, thriller/horror, short film script, 1-hour TV pilot, and half-hour TV pilot. Guidelines and entry forms are online. **Deadline: January 31 (early); March 15 (regular); April 30 (late). Charges $39 (early); $49 (regular); $59 (late).** Prize: "Each year we present more than $30,000 in cash and prizes, including a $10,000 grand prize, plus gold, silver, and bronze prizes in all 10 categories. Most importantly, the award-winning writers receive extensive publicity and industry exposure." Judging is done entirely by Hollywood professionals, including industry script readers, consultants, agents, managers, producers, and development executives. Entrants retain all rights to their work. The contest is open to all writers 18 years of age and older who have not previously earned more than $25,000 writing for film and/or television. Please visit contest Web site for a complete list of rules and regulations.

MILDRED & ALBERT PANOWSKI PLAYWRITING AWARD

Forest Roberts Theatre, Northern Michigan University, Marquette MI 49855-5364. (906)227-2559. Fax: (906)227-2567. Web site: www.nmu.edu/theatre. **Contact:** Award Coordinator. Estab. 1977. Offered annually for unpublished, unproduced, full-length plays. Guidelines and application for SASE. **Deadline: July 15-October 31.** Prize: $2,000, a summer workshop, a fully-mounted production, and transportation to Marquette to serve as Artist-in-Residence the week of the show.

PEACE WRITING INTERNATIONAL WRITING AWARDS

Peace and Justice Studies Association and Omni: Center for Peace, Justice & Ecology, 2582 Jimmie, Fayetteville AR 72703-3420. (479)442-4600. E-mail: jbennet@uark.edu. Web site: www.omnicenter. org. **Contact:** Dick Bennett. Offered annually for unpublished books. PeaceWriting encourages writing about war and international nonviolent peacemaking and peacemakers. PeaceWriting seeks book manuscripts about the causes, consequences, and solutions to violence and war, and about the ideas and practices of nonviolent peacemaking and the lives of nonviolent peacemakers. Three categories: Nonfiction Prose (history, political science, memoirs); Imaginative Literature (novels, plays, collections of short stories, collections of poetry, collections of short plays); and Works for Young People. Open to any writer. **Deadline: December 1.** Prize: $500 in each category.

PEN CENTER USA ANNUAL LITERARY AWARDS

PEN Center USA, 400 Corporate Pointe, Culver City CA 90230. E-mail: awards@penusa.org. Web site: www.penusa.org. **Contact:** Literary Awards Coordinator. Estab. 1982. Offered annually for fiction, nonfiction, poetry, children's literature, or translation published January 1-December 31 of the current year. Open to authors west of the Mississippi River. Guidelines for SASE or online. **Deadline: December 16 (book categories); January 31 (nonbook categories). Charges $35 fee.** Prize: $1,000.

PEN CENTER USA LITERARY AWARDS

PEN Center USA, 400 Corporate Pointe, Culver City CA 90230. (310)862-1555. E-mail: awards@penusa.org. Web site: www.penusa.org. **Contact:** Literary Awards Coordinator. Offered for work published or produced in the previous calendar year. Open to writers living west of the Mississippi River. Award categories: drama, screenplay, teleplay, journalism. Guidelines for SASE or download from Web site. **Deadline: 4 copies must be received by January 31. Charges $35.** Prize: $1,000.

THE PEN IS A MIGHTY SWORD

The Virtual Theatre Project, 1901 Rosalia Rd., Los Angeles CA 90027. (877)787-8036. Fax: (323)660-5097. E-mail: pen_sword2008@yahoo.com. Web site: www.virtualtheatreproject.org. **Contact:** Whit Andrews. Annual contest open to unproduced plays written specifically for the stage. Plays should be bold, compelling, and passionate. Guidelines for SASE or online. **Deadline: June 30. Charges $25.** Prize: 1st Place: $2,000 and full, 6-week premiere production; 2nd Place: $1,000 and a staged reading; 3rd Place: $500 and a reading. In addition, up to 7 honorable mentions receive $100 each. Judged by a panel of professional writers, directors, and producers. Open to any writer.

PEN WRITING AWARDS FOR PRISONERS

PEN American Center, 588 Broadway, Suite 303, New York NY 10012. Web site: www.pen.org. Offered annually to the authors of the best poetry, plays, short fiction, and nonfiction received from prison writers in the U.S. **Deadline: Submit January 1-September 1.** Guidelines for SASE. Prize: 1st Place: $200; 2nd Place: $100; 3rd Place: $50 (in each category).

PEOPLE'S PILOT COMPETITION

Cloud Creek Institute for the Arts, 3767 MC 5026, St. Joe AZ 72675. Web site: www.tvwriter.com/contests/peoples/about.htm. For TV scripts only. **Deadline: February 1. August 1.** Guidelines for SASE. **Charges $40.** Open to any writer.

PEW FELLOWSHIPS IN THE ARTS

Philadelphia Center for Arts & Heritage, 1608 Walnut St., 18th Floor, Philadelphia PA 19103. (267)350-4920. Fax: (267)350-4997. Web site: www.pewarts.org. **Contact:** Melissa Franklin, director. Estab. 1991. Offered annually to provide financial support directly to artists so that they may have the opportunity to dedicate themselves wholly to the development of their artwork for up to 2 years. Areas of interest have included fiction, creative nonfiction, poetry, playwriting, and screenwriting. Call for guidelines or view from the Web site. Entrants must be Pennsylvania residents of Bucks, Chester, Delaware, Montgomery, or Philadelphia counties for 2 years or longer. Current students are not eligible. **Deadline: December.** Prize: $60,000 fellowship.

JAMES D. PHELAN LITERARY AWARD

The San Francisco Foundation, Intersection for the Arts, 446 Valencia St., San Francisco CA 94103. (415)626-2787. E-mail: kevin@theintersection.org. Web site: www.theintersection.org. **Contact:** Kevin B. Chen, program director. Estab. 1935. Offered annually for unpublished, work-in-progress fiction, nonfiction, short story, poetry, or drama by a California-born author age 20-35. **Deadline: March 31.** Guidelines for SASE. Prize: Three awards of $2,000.

ROBERT J. PICKERING AWARD FOR PLAYWRITING EXCELLENCE

Coldwater Community Theater, % 89 Division, Coldwater MI 49036. (517)279-7963. Fax: (517)279-8095. **Contact:** J. Richard Colbeck, committee chairperson. Estab. 1982. Contest to encourage playwrights to submit their work and to present a previously unproduced play in full production. Must be previously unproduced monetarily. Submit script with SASE. "We reserve the right to produce winning script." **Deadline: December 31.** Guidelines for SASE. Prize: 1st Place: $300; 2nd Place: $100; 3rd Place: $50.

PILGRIM PROJECT GRANTS

156 Fifth, #400, New York NY 10010. (212)627-2288. Fax: (212)627-2184. E-mail: davida@firstthings.com. **Contact:** Davida Goldman. Grants for a reading, workshop production, or full production of plays that deal with questions of moral significance. **Deadline: Ongoing.** Guidelines for SASE. Prize: Grants of $1,000-7,000.

PLAYING BY THE LAKE SCRIPTWRITING CONTEST

Lake County Repertory Theater, P.O. Box 4388, Clearlake CA 95422. E-mail: ljaltman2@mchsi.com. Web site: lcrt_festival.home.mchsi.com/homepage.htm. **Contact:** Linda J. Altman, contest coordinator.

Award offered every even-numbered year for unproduced scripts to help new playwrights and bring original theater to local audiences. Guidelines and entry form for SASE or online. **Deadline: January 1-April 15. Charges $10.** Prize: $300, full production by LCRT, video of performance, and consideration by a major play publisher. Judged by a panel of professional writers, actors, directors, and teachers. Open to any writer.

PLAYS FOR THE 21ST CENTURY

Playwrights Theater, P.O. Box 395, Four Oaks NC 27524. Web site: www.playwrightstheater.org. Annual contest for unpublished or professionally unproduced plays (at time of submission). To provide playwrights an opportunity for exposure of their work and to provide guidance through our careful constructive comments for each play. **Deadline: March 22. Charges $20.** Prize: $1,500 first prize; $500 each for second and third prizes. First prize receives a rehearsed reading. The judges decide on readings for second and third prizes. "Winners and their bios and contact info are posted on our Web site with a 15-page sample of the play (with playwright's permission)." All rights remain with the author. Judged by an outside panel of 3 theater professionals. The judges are different each year. Open to any writer.

PLAYWRIGHTS/SCREENWRITERS FELLOWSHIPS

NC Arts Council, MSC #4632, Dept. of Cultural Resources, Raleigh NC 27699-4632. (919)807-6512. Fax: (919)807-6525. E-mail: debbie.mcgill@ncmail.net. Web site: www.ncarts.org. **Contact:** Deborah McGill, literature director. Offered every even year to support the development and creation of new work. See Web site for guidelines and other elegibility requirements. Offered to support the development and creation of new work. **Deadline: November 1.** Prize: $8,000 grant. Judged by a panel of film and theater professionals (playwrights, screenwriters, directors, producers, etc.). Artists must be current North Carolina residents who have lived in the state for at least 1 year as of the application deadline. Grant recipients must maintain their North Carolina status during the grant year and may not pursue academic or professional degrees during that period.

PNWA LITERARY CONTEST

Pacific Northwest Writers Association, PMB 2717-1420 NW Gilman Blvd, Ste, Issaquah WA 98027. (425)673-2665. Fax: (425)771-9588. E-mail: pnwa@pnwa.org. Web site: www.pnwa.org. **Contact:** Kell Liddane. Annual contest for unpublished writers. Over $12,000 in prize monies. Categories include: Mainstream; Inspirational; Romance; Mystery/Thriller/Horror; Science Fiction/Fantasy; Young Adult Novel; Nonfiction Book/Memoir; Screenwriting/Playwriting; Poetry; Adult Short Story; Children's Picture Book/Short Story/Chapter Book; Adult Short Topics. Each entry receives 2 critiques. Guidelines online. **Deadline: February 22. Charges $35/entry (members); $50/entry (nonmembers).** Prize: 1st Place: $600; 2nd Place: $300; 3rd Place: $150. Each prize is awarded in all 12 categories. Judged by industry experts. Open to any writer.

POPPY JASPER FILM FESTIVAL SCRIPT COMPETITION

Poppy Jasper Film Festival, P.O. Box 1028, Morgan Hill CA 95038-1028. (408)782-8087. E-mail: info@poppyjasperfilmfest.org. Web site: www.poppyjasperfilmfest.org. Estab. 2004. This contest in California looks for short scripts. Guidelines for SASE. Prize: Up to $250. Open to any writer.

PRAXIS FALL SCREENWRITING COMPETITION

Praxis Centre for Screenwriters, 515 W. Hastings St., Suite 3120, Vancouver BC V6B 5K3, Canada. (778)782-7880. Fax: (778)782-7882. E-mail: praxis@sfu.ca. Web site: www.praxisfilm.com/en/com petitions/fallscreenwriti/default.aspx. ''We are looking for feature film scripts of any genre. Each writer remains anonymous to the jury until a short list has been identified.'' Annually. **Deadline: June.** Guidelines for SASE. **Charges $75.** Must be Canadian citizens or landed immigrants.

PRINCESS GRACE AWARDS PLAYWRIGHT FELLOWSHIP

Princess Grace Foundation—USA, 150 E. 58th St., 25th Floor, New York NY 10155. (212)317-1470. Fax: (212)317-1473. E-mail: pgfusa@pgfusa.com. Web site: www.pgfusa.com. **Contact:** Christine Giancatarino, grants coordinator. Offered annually for unpublished, unproduced submissions to support playwright-through-residency program with New Dramatists, Inc., located in New York City. Entrants must be US citizens or have permanent US status. Guidelines for SASE or on Web site. **Deadline: March 31.** Prize: $7,500, plus residency with New Dramatists, Inc., in New York City, and representation/publication by Samuel French, Inc.

PULITZER PRIZES

The Pulitzer Prize Board, Columbia University, 709 Journalism Building, 2950 Broadway, New York NY 10027. (212)854-3841. E-mail: pulitzer@www.pulitzer.org. Web site: www.pulitzer.org. **Contact:** Sig Gissler, administrator. Estab. 1917. Journalism in US newspapers (published daily or weekly), and in letters, drama, and music by Americans. **Deadline: January 15 (music); February 1 (journalism); June 15 and October 15 (letters); December 31 (drama). Charges $50.** Prize: $10,000.

QUEENS INTERNATIONAL FILM FESTIVAL SCREENPLAY COMPETITION

Queens International Film Festival, 64-00 Saunders St., #4G, Rego Park NY 11374. (347)439-6592. E-mail: infoqueensfilmfestival.com. Web site: www.queensfilmfestival.com/submit/. Scripts should be 90-130 pages. Annually, Must Be Unpublished. Guidelines for SASE. **Charges $40/feature, $20/short.** Open to any writer.
Tips The 2007 winning scripy was *Hunchback of Notre Dame*, by Julio Ponce Palmieri & Max Ryan.

RANDOM HOUSE, INC. CREATIVE WRITING COMPETITION

1745 Broadway, New York NY 10019. E-mail: creativewriting@randomhouse.com. Web site: www. randomhouse.com/creativewriting. Offered annually for unpublished work to NYC public high school seniors. Four categories: poetry, fiction/drama, personal essay and graphic novel. **Deadline: February 1.** Guidelines for SASE. Prize: Awards range from $500-10,000. Applicants must be seniors (under age 21) at a New York high school. No college essays or class assignments will be accepted.

REEL WOMEN SCRIPT COMPETITION

Reel Women International Film Festival, 1317 N. San Fernando Blvd. # 340, Burbank CA 91504. (818)749-6162. E-mail: dmeans25@yahoo.com. Web site: reelwomenfest.com/. **Deadline: June.** Guidelines for SASE. **Charges $35-55.** Prize: Prizes are sponsored, and change from year to year.

REGENT UNIVERSITY'S ANNUAL ONE-ACT PLAY COMPETITION

Regent University, 1000 Regent University Dr., Virginia Beach VA 23464. (757)226-4237. E-mail: theatre@regent.edu. Web site: www.regent.edu/theatre. Annual contest to encourage new, unpublished playwrights who address the hope and creativity of the Judeo-Christian worldview. **Deadline: September 1.** Prize: 1st Place: $250, and play is eligible for production during the one-act play festival in March; 2nd Place: Honorable mention and play is eligible for production during the festival. Judged by Regent University MFA in Script and Screenwriting faculty. Open to any writer.

REGINA BOOK AWARD

Saskatchewan Book Awards, Inc., 205B-2314 11th Ave., Regina SK S4P 0K1, Canada. (306)569-1585. Fax: (306)569-4187. E-mail: director@bookawards.sk.ca. Web site: www.bookawards.sk.ca. **Contact:** Glenda James, executive director. Offered annually for work published September 15 of year past to September 14 of current year. In recognition of the vitality of the literary community in Regina, this award is presented to a Regina author for the best book, judged on the quality of writing. Books from the following categories will be considered: children's; drama; fiction (short fiction by a single author, novellas, novels); nonfiction (all categories of nonfiction writing except cookbooks, directories, how-to books, or bibliographies of minimal critical content); poetry. **Deadline: First deadline: July 31; Final deadline: September 14.** Guidelines for SASE. **Charges $20 (Canadian).** Prize: $2,000.

REPPED SCREENPLAY COMPETITION

Repped Management, % Slamster, LLC, 1400 W. Olympic Blvd., 4th Floor, Los Angeles CA 90064. Fax: (323)395-0569. E-mail: submit@reppedscreenplay.com/info@reppedscreenplay.com. Web site: www.reppedscreenplay.com. To offer exposure and representation to script writers. Must Be Unpublished. **Deadline: August.** Guidelines for SASE. **Charges $45; $55 for late entry.** Prize: Representation by Repped Management, referrals to Hollywood literary agencies, meetings with some of the executives or producers from major studios. Must be 18 years of age or older.

RHODE ISLAND ARTIST FELLOWSHIPS AND INDIVIDUAL PROJECT GRANTS

Rhode Island State Council on the Arts, One Capitol Hill, 3rd Floor, Providence RI 02908. (401)222-3880. Fax: (401)222-3018. E-mail: cristina@arts.ri.gov. Web site: www.arts.ri.gov. **Contact:** Cristina DiChiera, director of individual artist & public art programs. Annual fellowship competition is based upon panel review of mss for poetry, fiction, and playwriting/screenwriting. Project grants provide funds for community-based arts projects. Must Be Unpublished. **Deadline: April 1 and October 1. Charges $40.** Prize: Fellowship awards: $5,000 and $1,000. Grants range from $500-10,000 with an average of around $3,000. Rhode Island artists may apply without a nonprofit sponsor. Applicants for all RSCA grant and award programs must be at least 18 years and not currently enrolled in an arts-related degree program.

RHODE ISLAND INTERNATIONAL FILM FESTIVAL FEATURE SCREENPLAY COMPETITION

P.O. Box 162, Newport RI 02840. (401)861-4445. Fax: (401)861-7590. E-mail: adams@film-festival. org. Web site: www.film-festival.org/enterasscreenplay.php. Scripts not to exceed 130 pages. ''The purpose of the contest is to promote, embolden and cultivate screenwriters in their quest for opportunities in the industry.'' Submit a logline. Annually, Must Be Unpublished. **Deadline: July 5.** Guidelines for SASE. Judged by ''Screenplays will be judged on creativity, innovation, vision, originality and the use of language. The key element is that of communication and how it complements and is transformed by the language of film.'' Open to any writer.

RHODE ISLAND INTERNATIONAL FILM FESTIVAL SHORT SCREENPLAY COMPETITION

P.O. Box 162, Newport RI. (401)861-4445. Fax: (401)490-6735. E-mail: adams@film-festival.org. Web site: www.film-festival.org/enterascreenplay.php. This second contest for the festival looks for short scripts (fewer than 40 pages) and short teleplays. "The purpose of the contest is to promote, embolden and cultivate screenwriters in their quest for opportunities within the industry." Annually, Must Be Unpublished. Guidelines for SASE. Open to any writer.

RIVERRUN INTERNATIONAL FILM FESTIVAL SCREENPLAY CONTEST

RiverRun International Film Festival, 870 W. 4th St., Winston-Salem NC 27101. (336)724-1502. Fax: (336)724-1112. E-mail: margaret@riverrunfilm.com. Web site: www.riverrunfilm.com. "RiverRun's Story to Screenplay Adaptation Competition is open to any original, feature-length screenplay adapted from one or more short stories. Short stories eligible for this competition must be written in English, and can be either published or unpublished, and must be submitted with the short story author's permission. There are no genre categories (comedy, drama, etc.); the only criterion is a compelling screenplay." Guidelines for SASE. Prize: "The screenwriting finalists, as selected by industry professional judges, will be complimentary guests of the 2009 RiverRun International Film Festival 2009. The finalists will be introduced and the winner will be announced at the RiverRun Awards ceremony in April 2009." Open to any writer.

RICHARD RODGERS AWARDS IN MUSICAL THEATER

American Academy of Arts and Letters, 633 W. 155th St., New York NY 10032-7599. (212)368-5900. Fax: (212)491-4615. Web site: www.artsandletters.org. **Contact:** Jane E. Bolster. Estab. 1978. The Richard Rodgers Awards subsidize full productions, studio productions, and staged readings by non-profit theaters in New York City of works by composers and writers who are not already established in the field of musical theater. Authors must be citizens or permanent residents of the US. Guidelines and application for SASE or online. **Deadline: November 1.**

SAN DIEGO SCREENWRITING CONTEST

San Diego Film Foundation Screenplay Contest, P.O. Box 16396, Beverly Hills CA 90209. (619)582-2368. Fax: (619)286-8384. E-mail: info@sdff.org. Web site: www.sdff.org/. This contest is associated with the San Diego Film Festival. **Deadline: April 15.** Guidelines for SASE. **Charges $50.** Prize: Recognition at the SDFF. Open to any writer.

SASKATCHEWAN BOOK OF THE YEAR AWARD

Saskatchewan Book Awards, Inc., 205B, 2314 11th Ave., Regina SK S4P OK1, Canada. (306)569-1585. Fax: (306)569-4187. E-mail: director@bookawards.sk.ca. Web site: www.bookawards.sk.ca. **Contact:** Glenda James, executive director. Offered annually for work published September 15-September 14 annually. This award is presented to a Saskatchewan author for the best book, judged on the quality of writing. Books from the following categories will be considered: children's; drama; fiction (short fiction by a single author, novellas, novels); nonfiction (all categories of nonfiction writing except cookbooks, directories, how-to books, or bibliographies of minimal critical content); poetry. Visit Web site for more details. **Deadline: First deadline: July 31; Final deadline: September 14.** Guidelines for SASE. **Charges $20 (Canadian).** Prize: $3,000.

SASKATOON BOOK AWARD

Saskatchewan Book Awards, Inc., Box 1921, Regina SK S4P 3E1, Canada. (306)569-1585. Fax: (306)569-4187. E-mail: director@bookawards.sk.ca. Web site: www.bookawards.sk.ca. **Contact:** Glenda James, executive director. Offered annually for work published September 15-September 14. In recognition of the vitality of the literary community in Saskatoon, this award is presented to a Saskatoon author for the best book, judged on the quality of writing. Books from the following categories will be considered: children's; drama; fiction (short fiction by a single author, novellas, novels); nonfiction (all categories of nonfiction writing except cookbooks, directories, how-to books, or bibliographies of minimal critical content); poetry. **Deadline: First deadline: July 31; Final deadline: September 14.** Guidelines for SASE. **Charges $20 (Canadian).** Prize: $2,000.

CAROL SAUTTER MEMORIAL TELEVISION OUTREACH PROGRAM

The Scriptwriters Network, 6404 Wilshire Blvd., No 1640, Los Angeles CA 90048. E-mail: info@script writersnetwork.org. Web site: www.scriptwritersnetwork.org. **Contact:** Diane House, (503)913-3870, dkhouse7@gte.net. Include three copies of each script. You can submit up to three different scripts for consideration. Complete and sign the entry/release form. Writers should not put their name anyway on the script, as they are judged blindly. Scripts must not have been sold or produced. Annually. **Deadline: July.** Guidelines for SASE. **Charges $40-60.** Judged by All screening is anonymous. Readers will give feedback on submitted scripts. No scripts will be returned. Winning scripts are judged on story, originality, structure, character, dialogue and format/punctuation. Open to any writer.

SCR(I)PT MAGAZINE OPEN DOOR CONTEST

Open Door Contest, Scr(i)pt Magazine, 5638 Sweet Air Road, Baldwin MD 21013. (410)592-3466. Fax: (410)592-8062. Web site: www.scriptmag.com. **Deadline: Quarterly.** Guidelines for SASE. **Charges $45.** Prize: The winner receives $3,000, consideration for literary representation, Final Draft screenwriting software, a $200 gift certificate from The Writers Store, a two-year membership to Script P.I.M.P.'s Writer's Database, and a copy of "Dr. Format Answers Your Questions." Open to any writer.

SCREENPLAY FESTIVAL

11693 San Vicente Blvd., Ste. 806, Los Angeles CA 90046. (310)801-7896. Fax: (310)820-2303. E-mail: info@screenplayfestival.com. Web site: www.screenplayfestival.com. Entries in the feature-length competition must be more than 60 pages; entries in the short screenplay contest must be fewer than 60 pages. "The Screenplay Festival was established to solve two major problems: Problem Number One: It is simply too difficult for talented writers who have no 'connections' to gain recognition and get their material read by legitimate agents, producers, directors and investors. Problem Number Two: Agents, producers, directors, and investors complain that they cannot find any great material, but they will generally not accept 'unsolicited material.' This means that unless the script comes from a source that is known to them, they will not read it. Screenplay Festival was established to help eliminate this 'chicken and egg' problem. By accepting all submitted screenplays and judging them based upon their quality—not their source or their standardized formatting or the quality of the brads holding them together—Screenplay Festival looks to give undiscovered screenwriters an opportunity to rise above the crowd. Annually, Must Be Unpublished. **Deadline: August 1. October 1.** Guidelines for SASE. **Charges $40-$50.** Open to any writer.

THE SCREENWRITER'S PROJECT

Indiefest: Film Festival & Market, P.O. Box 148849, Chicago IL 60614-8849. (773)665-7600. Fax: (773)665-7660. E-mail: info@indiefestchicago.com. Web site: www.indiefestchicago.com. Offered annually to give both experienced and first-time writers the opportunity to begin a career as a screenwriter. **Deadline: January 1; March 1; April 1.** Guidelines for SASE. **Charges $40-100.** Prize: Various cash awards and prizes.

SCREENWRITING EXPO SCREENPLAY COMPETITION

6404 Hollywood Blvd., Ste 415, Los Angeles CA 90028. (323)957-1405. Fax: (323)957-1406. E-mail: contests@screenwritingexpo.com. Web site: www.screenwritingexpo.com. **Contact:** Jim Mercurio, contest coordinator. Writers must be at least 18 years old and have not earned more than $8,000 for writing services in film or television. Submitted screenplays must be the unproduced, unoptioned, and wholly original work of the writer(s). There must be no dispute about the ownership of submitted screenplays or the writers, right to submit screenplay. Submitted teleplays will adhere to the industry "spec script" practice of being a derivative work based on a pre-existing television series, however submitted teleplays must contain original story and dialogue. For teleplays, any characters created by the writer(s) must be wholly original work. Pilots for unproduced television shows or episodes of an unproduced series will not be accepted. Must Be Unpublished. **Deadline: multiple deadlines.** Guidelines for SASE. **Charges $45-55.** Prize: $20,000 grand prize, a trip to LA for the Expo, and four genre prizes totaling $10,000. Open to any writer.

SCRIPT PIMP SCREENWRITING COMPETITION

Script P.I.M.P., 8033 Sunset Blvd., Hollywood CA 90046. (310)401-1155. Fax: (310)564-2021. E-mail: comp@scriptpimp.com. Web site: scriptpimp.com. **Contact:** Chadwick Clough. Annual international competition open to all original English-written feature film screenplays that have yet to be produced, optioned, or sold. "We're looking for the best stories told by the best screenwriters demonstrating the best craft." The awards ceremony gathers hundreds of film industry professionals who meet with the finalists to provide advice and potential leads. Guidelines available for SASE or online. **Deadline: May 1. Charges $40.** Prize: Four grand-prize winners will each receive $2,500. In addition to mentor meetings, each of the 20 finalists will be guaranteed circulation of their script to over 20 companies, free 5-year memberships to Script P.I.M.P.'s Writers Database, and featured posting of their script in the Script Pimp Finalist listing on InkTip. Judged by a panel of working literary agents, literary managers, and development directors from the film industry. Each screenplay is guaranteed 2 reads from the panel of judges. Script P.I.M.P. does not acquire any rights to materials submitted through the contest. Open to writers 18 years and older who are the exclusive owner of all rights, titles, and interest in the script. Entrants must not have received sole or shared writing, directing, or producing credit on any film, series, or episode that has been produced for presentation in theatres or on TV. Individuals who have sold or optioned any screenplay for $15,000 or more are ineligible.

SCRIPTAPALOOZA SCREENWRITING COMPETITION

Supported by Writers Guild of America West and sponsored by Write Brothers, Inc., 7775 Sunset Blvd., PMB #200, Hollywood CA 90046. (323)654-5809. E-mail: info@scriptapalooza.com. Web site: www.scriptapalooza.com. Annual competition for unpublished scripts from any genre. Open to any writer, 18 or older. Submit 1 copy of a 90- to 130-page screenplay. Body pages must be numbered, and scripts must be in industry-standard format. All entered scripts will be read and judged by more than 60 production companies. **Deadline: Early Deadline: January 7; Deadline: March 5; Late Deadline: April 15.** Guidelines for SASE. **Charges $40 (early); $45 (regular deadline); $50 (late).** Prize: 1st Place: $10,000 and software package from Write Brothers, Inc; 2nd Place, 3rd Place, and 10 Runners-Up: Software package from Write Brothers, Inc. The top 13 scripts will be considered by over 60 production companies.

SCRIPTAPALOOZA TELEVISION WRITING COMPETITION

7775 Sunset Blvd., PMB #200, Hollywood CA 90046. (323)654-5809. E-mail: info@scriptapalooza. com. Web site: www.scriptapaloozatv.com. Biannual competition accepting entries in 4 categories: reality shows, sitcoms, original pilots, and 1-hour dramas. There are more than 25 producers, agents, and managers reading the winning scripts. Two past winners won Emmys because of Scriptapalooza and 1 past entrant now writes for Comedy Central. **Deadline: October 15 and April 15.** Guidelines for SASE. **Charges $40.** Prize: 1st Place: $500; 2nd Place: $200; 3rd Place: $100 (in each category). Open to any writer.

SCRIPTSHARK INSIDER SCREENWRITING COMPETITION

3415 S. Sepulveda Blvd, Suite 200, Los Angeles CA 90034. (310)482-3434. Fax: (310)482-3300. E-mail: scriptshark@blssi.com. Web site: www.scriptshark.com/insider/Home.asp. Estab. 2004. ''We've found that so many screenwriting competitions stop at the basic award itself. That's just part of our goal. The ScriptShark Insider, however, is looking to discover a new talent and break them into the industry itself. Using the winning screenplay as the measuring stick, the winner of the contest will work with a successful representative to develop an original idea into a workable pitch and 'shop' it to the town. Not only will you have the opportunity to get a screenplay into the hands of people that really matter, but you will have a shot to get in a room and do what professional writers do— pitch your idea.'' Guidelines for SASE. Prize: $15,000 in total prizes, as well as a chance for the winner to come to LA and pitch professionals. Open to any writer.
Tips ''Material must NOT be published, produced, sold, or under option at the time of submission. Personal information should only be included on the entry form. Must be between 70-140 pages in length. All pages must be numbered, and no writing is permitted on the spine of the script.''

ROD SERLING CONFERENCE SHORT FEATURE SCRIPTWRITING COMPETITION

3800 Barham Blvd., Suite 305, Los Angeles CA 90068. (607)274-3079. Fax: (607)274-1108. E-mail: stropiano@ithaca.edu. Web site: www.ithaca.edu/rhp/serling/script.html. **Contact:** Steve Tropiano, coordinator. ''Each script must be written in the same genre and style that would have been suitable to conform with episodes for either The Twilight Zone or Night Gallery. More specifically this means displaying traits of either a horror or a science fiction genre, while exhibiting strong social themes. An example of a script has been posted for your reference. It is a script from a Night Gallery episode that aired in September, 1971. Entitled Class of '99, it is available here for information purposes only. It is copyrighted material not intended for reproduction purposes. Each script must be written in English. Each script must be between 10 to 20 pages in length. No exceptions. Scripts that do not conform to the above page limit will be disqualified. Each script must be written in Master Scene Format, the accepted industry standard for motion pictures. All scripts must use standard industry script binding: three-hole punched with brass brads in the top and bottom holes.'' **Deadline: Febru-**

ary. Guidelines for SASE. **Charges $20.** Prize: 1st Place: $250; 2nd Place: $150; 3rd Place: $100. Judged by Carol Serling judges the top 5 finalists. "Non-produced, or non-optioned writers only." Script must be registered with the Writer's Guild of America Script Registry at http://wga.org/.

SET IN PHILADELPHIA SCREENPLAY CONTEST

Greater Philadelphia Film Office, 100 S. Broad Street, Suite 600, Philadelphia PA 19110. (215)686-2668. Fax: (215)686-3659. E-mail: mail@film.org. Web site: www.film.org. "Screenplays must be set primarily in the Greater Philadelphia area (includes the surrounding counties). All genres and storytelling approaches are acceptable. Screenplays must be between 85-130 pages in length." There are different awards, such as an award for the best script for writers under 25, as well as the best script for a regional writer. See the Web site for full details. Annually. Guidelines for SASE. **Charges $45-65.** Prize: $10,000 grand prize, with other prizes offered. Open to any writer.

REVA SHINER FULL-LENGTH PLAY CONTEST

Bloomington Playwrights Project, 107 W. 9th St., Bloomington IN 47404. E-mail: bppwrite@new plays.org. Web site: www.newplays.org. **Contact:** Literary Manager. Annual award for unpublished/unproduced plays. The Bloomington Playwrights Project is a script-developing organization. Winning playwrights are expected to become part of the development process, working with the director in person or via long-distance. **Deadline: October 31.** Guidelines for SASE. **Charges $10 reading fee.** Prize: $500, a reading, and possible production. Judged by the literary committee of the BPP. Open to any writer.

SHORT GRAIN WRITING CONTEST

Grain Magazine, Box 67, Saskatoon SK S7K 3K1, Canada. (306)244-2828. Fax: (306)244-0255. E-mail: grainmag@sasktel.net. Web site: www.grainmagazine.ca. Offered annually for unpublished dramatic monologues, postcard stories (narrative fiction) and prose (lyric) poetry, and nonfiction creative prose. Maximum length for short entries: 500 words. Entry guidelines online. All entrants receive a 1-year subscription to *Grain Magazine. Grain* purchases first Canadian serial rights only. Open to any writer. No fax or e-mail submissions. **Deadline: January 31. Charges $28 fee for 2 entries; $8 for 3 additional entries; US and international entries $28, plus $6 postage in US funds.** Prize: $6,000; 3 prizes of $500 in each category.

SHRIEKFEST HORROR/SCI-FI FILM FESTIVAL & SCREENPLAY COMPETITION

P.O. Box 920444, Sylmar CA 91392. E-mail: shriekfest@aol.com. Web site: www.shriekfest.com. **Contact:** Denise Gossett/Todd Beeson. "We accept award winning screenplays, no restrictions as long as it's in the horror/thriller or sci-fi/fantasy genres. We accept shorts and features. No specific lengths. Our awards are to help screenwriters move their script up the ladder and hopefully have it made into a film. Our winners take that win and parlay it into agents, film deals, and options." Annual. **Deadline: May 24th. June 28.** Guidelines for SASE. **Charges $25-$55.** Prize: This consists of trophies, product awards, usually cash. "Our awards are updated all year long as sponsors step onboard. The winners go home with big bags of stuff though. We have at least 15-20 judges and they are all in different aspects of the entertainment industry such as producers, Directors, writers, actors, agents. We don't use loglines anywhere, we keep your script private." Open to any writer.

SIENA COLLEGE INTERNATIONAL PLAYWRIGHTS COMPETITION

Siena College Theatre Program, 515 Loudon Rd., Loudonville NY 12211-1462. (518)783-2381. Fax: (518)783-2381. E-mail: maciag@siena.edu. Web site: www.siena.edu/theatre. **Contact:** Gary Maciag, director. Offered every 2 years for unpublished plays to allow students to explore production collaboration with the playwright. In addition, it provides the playwright an important development opportunity. Plays should be previously unproduced, unpublished, full-length, nonmusicals, and free of copyright and royalty restrictions. Plays should require unit set, or minimal changes, and be suitable for a college-age cast of 3-10. There is a required 4-6 week residency. Guidelines for SASE. Guidelines are available after November 1 in odd-numbered years. Winning playwright must agree that the Siena production will be the world premiere of the play. **Deadline: February 1-June 30 in even-numbered years.** Prize: $2,000 honorarium, up to $2,000 to cover expenses for required residency, and full production of winning script.

THE SILVER FALCHION AWARD

Killer Nashville, P.O. Box 680686, Franklin TN 37068-0686. (615)599-4032. E-mail: contact@killernashville.com. Web site: www.killernashville.com. **Contact:** Clay Stafford. Previously published entries must have appeared in print between the previous conference and the current conference. The purpose of the Silver Falchion Award is to recognize the best publishing achievement by a Killer Nashville attendee published during the current or previous calendar year, as voted upon by Killer Nashville conference attendees. Annually, Must Be Previously Published. **Deadline: 2 weeks prior to conference, usually around Aug. 1.** Guidelines for SASE. Prize: A plaque with the Silver Falchion emblem stating the Killer Nashville year of receipt. Judged by Voted on by Killer Nashville attendees of the current year. Open to any writer.

DOROTHY SILVER PLAYWRITING COMPETITION

The Jewish Community Center of Cleveland, 26001 S. Woodland, Beachwood OH 44122. (216)831-0700. Fax: (216)831-7796. E-mail: dbobrow@clevejcc.org. Web site: www.clevejcc.org. **Contact:** Deborah Bobrow, competition coordinator. Estab. 1948. All entries must be original works, not previously produced, suitable for a full-length presentation, and directly concerned with the Jewish experience. **Deadline: December 31.** Prize: Cash award and a staged reading.

SLAMDANCE SCREENPLAY COMPETITION

WGA-West/*Script Magazine*/Final Draft/Writers Bootcamp, 5634 Melrose Ave., Los Angeles CA 90038. (323)466-1786. E-mail: screenplay@slamdance.com. Web site: www.slamdance.com/screencomp. **Contact:** John Stoddard. Annual competition to discover and support emerging screenwriting talent. Entrants must be first-time writers and cannot submit material that has been previously optioned, purchased, or produced by non-indepenedent means. Entrants cannot have won awards from other competitions, nor can they have any previously produced/distributed projects. Applications are available online. **Deadline: June 2. Charges $40.** Prize: $7,000, Writers Bookcamp certificates, Final Draft software, *Script Magazine* subscription, Slamdance Film Festival passes, staged reading in Los Angeles, and elgibility for membership in the WGA's Independent Writers Caucus. No rights are required—register your work before entering the competition. Judged by Slamdance alumni screenwriters, filmmakers, professional writers, journalists, playwrights, and readers with a background in development/production.

SLAMDANCE SHORT SCREENPLAY COMPETITION

5634 Melrose Ave., Los Angeles CA 90038. (323)466-1786. Fax: (323)466-1784. E-mail: screenplay@s lamdance.com. Web site: www.slamdance.com/writing/short.html. Entries must be 40 pages or fewer. Screenplays must not have been previously optioned, purchased or produced. Screenplays must not have received awards from other competitions over $500. Annually. **Deadline: March 31. June 2.** Guidelines for SASE. **Charges $30.** Open to any writer.

Tips Some discounts exist on the entry fee, such as a cheaper price for students.

KAY SNOW WRITING AWARDS

Willamette Writers, 9045 SW Barbur Blvd., Suite 5A, Portland OR 97219. (503)452-1592. Fax: (503)452-0372. E-mail: wilwrite@willamettewriters.com. Web site: www.willamettewriters.com. Contest offered annually to "offer encouragement and recognition to writers with unpublished submissions." Acquires right to publish excerpts from winning pieces 1 time in their newsletter. **Deadline: April 23.** Guidelines for SASE. **Charges $15 fee; no fee for student writers.** Prize: 1st Place: $300; 2nd Place: $150; 3rd Place: $50; excerpts published in Willamette Writers newsletter, and winners acknowledged at banquet during writing conference. Student writers win $50 in categories for grades 1-5, 6-8, and 9-12. $500 Liam Callen Memorial Award goes to best overall entry.

Tips This contest has many different categories, including film scripts.

SOUND HERITAGE NATIONAL SCREENPLAY CONTEST

P.O. Box 1020, Winchester CA 92596. (951)926-6765. E-mail: soundheritage@soundheritageproducti on.com. Web site: www.soundheritageproduction.com/screenplaycontest.html. Scripts must be 85 to 135 pages. Annually, Must Be Unpublished. **Deadline: April.** Guidelines for SASE. **Charges approx. $50.** Open to any writer.

Tips Writers seeking a full story analysis can do so for an additional $120.

SOUTHEASTERN CREATIVE MEDIA COMPETITION

GAMMA, P.O. Box 50238, Summerville SC 29485. (843)276-1875. E-mail: gammamotionpictures@ya hoo.com. Web site: www.festivalfocus.org/festival-view.php?uid=291. **Contact:** Kirk and Kelly Lowe. Annual competition to promote and encourage media development in the Charleston, S.C. area, the southeastern US, and the world. Categories include: motion picture (short), motion picture (feature), screenplay, and music (includes music video). **Deadline: September 15. Charges $8-10.** Prize: $100 for the best entry in each category. Non-cash awards (certificates) will also be given for the best in each genre/style under each category. Judged by the general partners of GAMMA and other drama/media-related volunteers.

SOUTHEASTERN THEATRE CONFERENCE NEW PLAY PROJECT

Department of Theatre & Dance, Southeast Missouri State University, 1 University Plaza: MS 2800, Cape Girardeau MO 63701. E-mail: kstilson@semo.edu. Web site: www.setc.org. **Contact:** Kenn Stilson. Annual award for full-length plays. No musicals or children's plays. Submissions must be unproduced/unpublished. Submit application, synopsis, and 1 copy of script on CD or as an e-mail attachment (preferred). Send SASE or visit Web site for application. **Deadline: June 1.** Prize: $1,000 and a staged reading.

SOUTHEASTERN THEATRE CONFERENCE SECONDARY SCHOOL PLAY CONTEST

The Walker School, 700 Cobb Parkway N., Marietta GA 30062. E-mail: wattsk@thewalkerschool.org. Annual contest for unpublished one-act plays (no musicals) on any subject. Visit Web site or send SASE for application. **Deadline: December 1.** Prize: $250 and a staged reading.

SOUTHERN PLAYWRIGHTS COMPETITION

Jacksonville State University, 700 Pelham Rd. N., Jacksonville AL 36265-1602. (256)782-5414. Fax: (256)782-5441. E-mail: jmaloney@jsu.edu; swhitton@jsu.edu. Web site: www.jsu.edu/depart/en glish/southpla.htm. **Contact:** Joy Maloney, Steven J. Whitton. Estab. 1988. Offered annually to identify and encourage the best of Southern playwriting. Playwrights must be a native or resident of Alabama, Arkansas, Florida, Georgia, Kentucky, Louisiana, Missouri, North Carolina, South Carolina, Tennessee, Texas, Virginia, or West Virginia. **Deadline: February 15.** Guidelines for SASE. Prize: $1,000 and production of the play.

SOUTHWEST WRITERS

3721 Morris N.E., Albuquerque NM 87111. (505)265-9485. Fax: (505)265-9483. E-mail: contactus@ southwestscreenwriters.com. Web site: www.southwestwriters.com. "The SouthWest Writers Writing Contest encourages and honors excellence in writing. In addition to competing for cash prizes and the coveted Storyteller Award, contest entrants may receive an optional written critique of their entry from a qualified contest critiquer." Submit first 20 pages and 1 page synopsis (using industry-standard formatting, Courier font, brad-bound). Annually, Must Be Unpublished. **Deadline: May 1. May 15.** Guidelines for SASE. Prize: Up to $1,000 grand prize. Judged by "All manuscripts will be screened by a panel and the top 10 in each category will be sent to appropriate editors or literary agents to determine the final top 3 places. The top 3 winners will also receive a critique from the judging editor or literary agent. Contacting any judge about an entry is an automatic disqualification. 12. Entrants retain all rights to their entries. By entering this contest, you agree to abide by the rules, agree that decisions by the judges are final, and agree that no refunds will be awarded." Open to any writer.

SPEC SCRIPTACULAR COMPETITION

Cloud Creek Institute for the Arts, Cloud Creek Ranch, 3767 MC 5026, St. Joe AZ 72675. (805)495-3659. E-mail: info@specscriptacular.com. Web site: www.specscriptacular.com. **Deadline: February.** Guidelines for SASE. **Charges $40.** Prize: $10,000 in prizes. Open to any writer.
Tips "The Sitcom category is for spec episodes of current (or very recent) broadcast and cable network sit-coms, which are usually (but not necessarily) half-hour shows. The Action/Drama category is for spec episodes of current (or very recent) broadcast and cable network action or dramatic shows— including sci-fi shows, medical shows, cop shows, lawyer shows, dramedies, et al. These are usually one-hour shows, but this is also the proper category in which to enter any current half-hour action or drama series. The Pilot/MOW/Special category is for pilots of any length that you have written for your own prospective series regardless of genre, for any and all original spec TV movies, and for any and all original spec specials regardless of length. The People's Pilot has shown us that many of you have already written or are eager to write pilots for your own ideas. This is the contest and category in which to enter those pilots. And we know that many of you have already written or are writing feature screenplays that can fit into the MOW mold. This is the contest and category in which to enter

those screenplays. Teleplays from all current and recent series airing in all English-speaking countries now are eligible for the Spec Scriptacular. This means series airing on U.S. broadcast and cable networks, Canadian broadcast and cable networks, United Kingdom broadcast and cable networks, Australian broadcast and cable networks, South African broadcast and cable networks, and in first run syndication in the U.S., Canada, UK, Australia and South Africa. In addition, teleplays for all current and recent series being presented via cell phone, ITunes, YouTube, and any and all entertainment Web sites available online in the English language are eligible in the New Media category.''

STANLEY DRAMA AWARD

Dept. of Theatre, Wagner College, One Campus Rd., Staten Island NY 10301. (718)420-4036. Fax: (718)390-3323. **Contact:** Dr. Felicia J. Ruff, director. Offered for original full-length stage plays, musicals, or one-act play sequences that have not been professionally produced or received trade book publication. **Deadline: November 1.** Guidelines for SASE. **Charges $20 submission fee.** Prize: $2,000.

STRAIGHT TWISTED: FIRST ANNUAL HORROR SCREENPLAY CONTEST

Hollywood Query, E-mail: support@hollywoodquery.com. Web site: www.hollywoodquery.com/horror/. ''The Compeition has been established by an alliance of Hollywood producers, agents, and development executives. Our goal: to discover the most horrific new scripts by up-and-coming writers from across the country and around the world.'' The sponsoring company is looking to produce horror scripts in the future and hopes to find worthy material. Guidelines for SASE. Prize: $5,000 grand prize; $16,000 in total prizes. Open to any writer.

Tips 2008 is this contest's first year.

THE STEPHEN SUSCO SCREENWRITING MENTORSHIP COMPETITION

The Writers Room of Bucks County, 4 W. Oakland Ave., Doylestown PA 18901. (215)348-1663. Fax: (215)348 8137. E mail: info@writersroom.net. Web site: www.writersroom.net. **Contact:** Jill Sherer. Launched in January 2005, this contest will give three budding screenwriters a chance to be personally mentored for one year on the business and craft of screenwriting by Stephen Susco, author of the hit movie ''The Grudge'' and one of Hollywood's hottest young screenwriters. The goal is to give new writers an opportunity to write and sell a winning screenplay, and raise funds for the Writers Room of Bucks County—a not-for-profit writers' center providing workshops, and publishing and editorial services. **Deadline: April 30. Charges $45.** Prize: One year of personal one-on-one mentoring by Stephen Susco and the opportunity to document your experiences in a blog on writersroom.net and in the literary publication *Bucks County Writer*. Judged by Applicants are narrowed to 36 by Writers Room professionals before being submitted to a panel of three industry judges: Ian Abrams, Alan Hines, and Mark Rosenthal. Open to any writer.

Tips ''We don't know of any other competition that doesn't require a finished screenplay to enter and gives multiple winners the chance to study with a master. Whether you've written a book you think would make a great film, been toying with screenwriting, or been at it for years, the winners will be judged on the strength of their basic idea and the way they pitch it.''

SYRACUSE INTERNATIONAL FILM FESTIVAL SCREENPLAY COMPETITION

Syracuse International Film Festival, Syracuse University, 216 HB Crouse Hall, Syracuse NY 13244. (315)443-8826. E-mail: manager@syrfilm.com. Web site: www.syrfilm.com/screenplay.html. ''To produce and present year-round, community wide programs of newly made, independent, international film and video for the purpose of exploring diversity and promoting a dialogue on shared issues and solutions through the universal artistic language of the cinema. Knowledge (insights) incites change." Guidelines for SASE. Prize: Cash prizes go up to $5,000. Open to any writer.

TAHOE RENO INTERNATIONAL FILM FESTIVAL

Tahoe Reno International Film Festival, 948 Incline Way, Incline Village NV 89451. (775)298-0018. Fax: (775)298-0019. E-mail: tahoefilmfest@aol.com. Web site: www.t-riff.org. Guidelines for SASE. Open to any writer.

TELEPLAY COMPETITION

Austin Film Festival, 1604 Nueces St., Austin TX 78701. (512)478-4795. Fax: (512)478-6205. E-mail: info@austinfilmfestival.con. Web site: www.austinfilmfestival.com. Offered annually for unpublished work to discover talented television writers and introduce their work to production companies. Categories: drama and sitcom (must be based on current television program). Contest open to writers who do not earn a living writing for television or film. **Deadline: June 1.** Guidelines for SASE. **Charges $30.** Prize: $1,000 in each category.

10-MINUTE PLAY FESTIVAL

Fire Rose Productions & International Arts Group, 11246 Magnolia Blvd., NoHo Theatre & Arts District CA 91601. (818)766-3691. E-mail: info@fireroseproductions.com. Web site: www.fireroseproductions.com. **Contact:** Kaz Matamura, director. Contest is offered twice a year for unpublished and unproduced plays that are 8-12 minutes long. Fire Rose Productions & International Arts Group are nonprofit organizations that are committed to discovering new playwrights and giving them opportunities to work with directors and producers. **Deadline: March 31.** Guidelines for SASE. **Charges $5; $2/ additional submission.** Prize: 1st Place: $250; 2nd Place: $100; profesionally mounted production for winners and semi-finalists. Guest judges are entertainment professionals including writers, producers, directors, and agents. Fire Rose Productions does the first evaluation. Acquires right to produce and mount the plays if chosen as festival finalists or semi-finalists. No royalties are gathered for those performances. Open to any writer.

Tips Download the application online.

TENNESSEE SCREENWRITING ASSOCIATION SCRIPT COMPETITION

P.O. Box 40194, Nashville TN 37204-0194. (615)316-9448. E-mail: info@tennscreen.com. Web site: www.tennscreen.com. **Deadline: Aug. 1.** Guidelines for SASE. **Charges $30.** Prize: Multiple prizes include up to $1,000.

THEATRE BC'S ANNUAL CANADIAN NATIONAL PLAYWRITING COMPETITION

Theatre BC, P.O. Box 2031, Nanaimo BC V9R 6X6, Canada. (250)714-0203. Fax: (250)714-0213. E-mail: pwc@theatrebc.org. Web site: www.theatrebc.org. **Contact:** Robb Mowbray, executive director. Offered annually to unpublished plays to promote the development and production of previously unproduced new plays (no musicals) at all levels of theater. Categories: Full Length (75 minutes or longer); One-Act (less than 75 minutes); and an open Special Merit (juror's discretion). Guidelines for SASE or online. Winners are also invited to New Play Festival: Up to 16 hours with a professional dramaturg, registrant actors, and a public reading in Kamloops (every Spring). Production and publishing rights remain with the playwright. Open to Canadian residents. All submissions are made under pseudonyms. E-mail inquiries welcome. **Deadline: Fourth Monday in July. Charges $40/ entry; optional $25 for written critique.** Prize: Full Length: $1,000; One-Act: $750; Special Merit: $500.

THEATRE CONSPIRACY ANNUAL NEW PLAY CONTEST

Theatre Conspiracy, 10091 McGregor Blvd., Ft. Myers FL 33919. (239)936-3239. Fax: (239)936-0510. E-mail: info@theatreconspiracy.org. **Contact:** Bill Taylor, artistic director. Offered annually for full-length plays that are unproduced or have received up to 3 productions with 8 or less characters and simple to moderate production demands. No musicals. One entry per year. Send SASE for contest results. **Deadline: March 30. Charges $5 fee.** Prize: $700 and full production. Open to any writer.

THEATRE IN THE RAW ONE-ACT PLAY WRITING CONTEST

Theatre In the Raw, 3521 Marshall St., Vancouver BC V5N 4S2, Canada. (604)708-5448. E-mail: theatreintheraw@hotmail.com; titraw@vcn.bc.ca. Web site: www.theatreintheraw.ca. **Contact:** Artistic Director. Biennial contest for an original one-act play, presented in proper stage-play format, that is unpublished and unproduced. The play (with no more than 6 characters) cannot be longer than 25 double-spaced, typed pages equal to 30 minutes. **Deadline: December 31. Charges $25 entry fee, $40 for 2 plays (payable to Theatre In the Raw).** Prize: 1st Place: $150, at least 1 dramatic reading or staging of the play at a Theatre In the Raw Cafe/Venue, or as part of a mini-tour program for the One-Act Play Series Nights; 2nd Place: $50; 3rd Place: $40. Winners announced March 31.

THEATRE OXFORD'S ANNUAL TEN MINUTE PLAY CONTEST

Theatre Oxford, P.O. Box 1321, Oxford MS 38655. E-mail: 10-minute-plays@live.com. Web site: www .10minuteplays.com. **Contact:** Melissa Kuhl, Contest Director. Annually, Must Be Unpublished. **Deadline: February.** Guidelines for SASE. **Charges $10.** Prize: 5 winners are chosen. Grand prize will receive L.W Thomas Award, $1,000 and a production of the winning script. Open to any writer.

THEATRE PUBLICUS PRIZE FOR DRAMATIC LITERATURE

Media Darlings Literature, Art & Sound, 5201 Great America Parkway, Suite 320, Santa Clara CA 95054. E-mail: dropbox@mediadarlings.org. Web site: www.mediadarlings.org/publicus. Annual competition to recognize the work of emerging playwrights and to provide promotional and financial support to innovative new talent who may be overlooked by mainstream literary or theater circles. Submissions are accepted regardless of content, genre, or theme. No musicals, please. **Deadline: August 31.** Guidelines for SASE. **Charges $10/one-act plays; $20/full-length plays.** Prize: $200 for jury prize (best overall); $150 each for best one-act and full-length plays. Judged by the staff of Media Darlings Literature, Art & Sound—an arts collective based in the San Francisco Bay area. The staff includes published fiction writers, editors, and former industry professionals. Open to all American and Canadian playwrights over the age of 18 who have completed a one-act or full-length play since 2003.

THEATREPEI NEW VOICES PLAYWRITING COMPETITION

P.O. Box 1573, Charlottetown PE C1A 7N3, Canada. (902)894-3558. Fax: (902)368-7180. E-mail: theatre@isn.net. Web site: theatrepei.org. **Contact:** Dawn Binkley, general manager. Offered annually. Open to individuals who have been residents of Prince Edward Island for 6 months preceding the deadline for entries. Guidelines online or for SASE. **Deadline: February 14. Charges $5 fee.** Prize: Full-length Plays—1st Place: $500; 2nd Place: $300. One-Act Plays—1st Place: $200; 2nd Place: $100. High School Entries—Winning English-language play: $100; Winning French-languagle play: $100.

THUNDERBIRD FILMS SCREENPLAY COMPETITION

214 Riverside Drive, Ste. 112, New York NY 10025. E-mail: estannard@dekker.com. Web site: ho me.att.net/~thunderbirdfilms/contest.htm. Estab. 1997. **Deadline: March 3.** Guidelines for SASE. **Charges $40.** Prize: $2,000 first prize. Open to any writer.

TRILLIUM BOOK AWARD/PRIX TRILLIUM

Ontario Media Development Corp., 175 Bloor St. E., SouthTower, Suite 501, Toronto ON M4W 3R8, Canada. (416)314-6698. Fax: (416)314-6876. E-mail: jhawkins@omdc.on.ca. Web site: www.omd c.on.ca. **Contact:** Janet Hawkins. Estab. 1987. Offered annually for books of any genre. Publishers submit titles on behalf of authors. Authors must have been Ontario residents 3 of the last 5 years. Guidelines online or for SASE. **Deadline: December 9 for titles published between January and October; January 9 for books published in November and December.** Prize: The winning author in each category (English and French) receives $20,000; the winning publisher in each category receives $2,500. Judged by a jury of writers, poets, and other members of the literary community.

TRUSTUS PLAYWRIGHTS' FESTIVAL

Trustus Theatre, Box 11721, Columbia SC 29211-1721. (803)254-9732. Fax: (803)771-9153. E-mail: trustus@trustus.org. Web site: www.trustus.org. **Contact:** Jon Tuttle, literary manager. Offered annu- ally for professionally unproduced full-length plays; cast limit of 8. Prefers challenging, innovative dramas and comedies. No musicals, plays for young audiences, or ''hillbilly'' southern shows. Send SASE or consult Trustus Web site for guidelines and application. Festival for 2009 has been suspended for production of in-house play. **Deadline: for 2010 festival: December 1, 2008-February 28, 2009.** Prize: $500 and a 1-year development period with full production and travel/accommodations to attend the public opening.

TURKS & CAICOS INTERNATIONAL FILM FESTIVAL & SCREENWRITING COMPETITION

27 Third Avenue, No. 302, New York NY 10016. (212)591-2823. E-mail: tcifilmfestival@yahoo.com. Web site: www.turksandcaicosfilmfestival.com. **Contact:** Festival Executive Director: Geoffrey Wil- liams. ''The Turks & Caicos International Film Festival & Screenwriting Competition invites filmmak- ers and screenwriters from around the world to submit completed films and scripts to its inaugural event on the island of Providenciales in Turks & Caicos, British West Indies, which is fast becoming the 'Sun, Sand, Sea, and Cinema' capital of the Caribbean.'' Guidelines for SASE. Open to any writer.

TVWRITER.COM SPEC SCRIPTACULAR

Cloud Creek Institute for the Arts, Cloud Creek Ranch, 3767 MC 5026, St. Joe AZ 72675. (805)495- 3659. E-mail: info@specscriptacular.com. Web site: www.specscriptacular.com. TVwriter.com helps to get your spec episodes and pilots read by those who can purchase them or hire you. **Deadline: August 1.** Guidelines for SASE. **Charges $40.** Prize: The Grand Prize is awarded to the best entry regardless of category and its recipient is chosen from the three category Winners. The Grand Prize

Winner will receive: $500 from Cloud Creek Institute For The Arts, Special 1 Week Writing Retreat at Cloud Creek Institute For The Arts ($2500 value), free admission to the next TV Writer.Com Summer Intensive Seminar ($400 value), free admission to the Action/Cut Filmmaking Seminar of your choice ($375 value), 1 month (4 weeks) of weekly mentorship (by phone, e-mail, or on the Cloud Creek Institute For The Arts premises) with producer-writer Larry Brody of TV Writer.Com & Cloud Creek Institute For The Arts ($800 value), a copy of FinalDraft Scriptwriters' Suite Software, courtesy of FinalDraft ($299 value), a free featured creator page at WriteSafe.Com, one of the most respected intellectual property registration sites on the web ($250 value), Five Free Creative Work Registrations at WriteSafe.Com ($75), 1 year of Gold Plan Spotlighted Screenplay Posting service at Screenwriter Showcase.Com ($84 value), Submission of winning material for consideration for purchase and/or representation by the members of the Cloud Creek Institute For The Arts Board of Advisors (priceless), inclusion in the vaunted TV Writer.Com List of Recommended Writers (almost as priceless). See other prizes (for category winners) online. Open to any writer.

20/20 SCREENWRITING CONTEST
3639 Malibu Vista Drive, Malibu CA 90265. (310)454-0971. Fax: (310)573-3868. E-mail: info@lets-do-lunch.com. Web site: www.lets-do-lunch.com. Send in the first 20 pages of your script for the first round and then go from there. **Deadline: June 20.** Guidelines for SASE. **Charges $20-$40.** Prize: You will win a WGA-signatory, veteran agent. In addition, winners have their choice of either a pass to the next Screenwriters Expo, or a four DVDs from past Expo speakers. Open to any writer.

UCROSS FOUNDATION RESIDENCY
30 Big Red Lane, Clearmont WY 82835. (307)737-2291. Fax: (307)737-2322. E-mail: info@ucross.org. Web site: www.ucrossfoundation.org. Eight concurrent positions open for artists-in-residence in various disciplines (includes writers, visual artists, music, humanities, natural sciences) extending from 2 weeks to 2 months. No charge for room, board, or studio space. **Deadline: March 1 and October 1. Charges $20 application fee.**

UNICORN THEATRE NEW PLAY DEVELOPMENT
Unicorn Theatre, 3828 Main St., Kansas City MO 64111. (816)531-7529, ext. 22. Fax: (816)531-0421. Web site: www.unicorntheatre.org. **Contact:** Herman Wilson, literary assistant. Offered annually to encourage and assist the development of an unpublished and unproduced play. "We look for nonmusical, issue-oriented, thought-provoking plays set in contemporary times (post 1950s) with a cast limit of 10." Submit cover letter, brief bio/résumé, short synopsis, complete character breakdown, complete ms, SASE. Does not return scripts. **Deadline: Ongoing.** Guidelines for SASE.

UNITED HOLLYWOOD SHORT FILM CONTEST
United Hollywood, Web site: fairdeal4writers.com/. Estab. 2007. Videos can be up to, but no more than, four minutes long. There is no minimum length. Nothing obscene or illegal will be accepted. SAG Members: may only work in these productions if you have signed the Screen Actors Guild Internet Agreement. Special arrangements have been made with Screen Actors Guild to make it easy—please call (323) 549-6007, mention the Fair Deal for Writers competition and the agreement will be emailed to you. The short films are designed to exhibit a message of unity between writers. Guidelines for SASE. Open to any writer.

VAIL FILM FESTIVAL SCREENPLAY COMPETITION

Vail Film Institute, P.O. Box 747, Vail CO 81657. (970)476-1092. Fax: (646)349-1767. E-mail: info@ vailfilmfestival.org. Web site: www.vailfilmfestival.org/screenplay.shtml. Feature Scripts must be between 70-125 pages in length. Short Scripts must be between 3-45 pages in length. Must Be Unpublished. Guidelines for SASE. **Charges $35-65.** Prize: "2 Filmmaker Passes to the 2009 Vail Film Festival, 1 domestic air ticket to Denver, 3 night hotel accomodations in Vail, screenplay read by established film production companies. Staged reading of excerpt of winning screenplay during the Vail Film Festival." Open to any writer.

VENANGO DIGITAL FILM FESTIVAL SCRIPT COMPETITION

Venango Film Festival, P.O. Box 1082, Franklin PA 16323. E-mail: thelatonia@verizon.net. Web site: www.joannwheelerfineart.com/html/vdfa/scriptcompetition.htm. This contest seeks original 10-minute screenplays of any genre on a given theme. Check the Web site to learn more about the current "theme." **Deadline: August.** Guidelines for SASE. **Charges $25.** Prize: Two winning scripts will be produced by local crews. Winners have the option of directing their own films. Open to any writer.

VERMONT ARTS COUNCIL

136 State St., Drawer 33, Montpelier VT 05633-6001. (802)828-5425. Fax: (802)828-3363. E-mail: srae@vermontartscouncil.org. Web site: www.vermontartscouncil.org. **Contact:** Sonia Rae. Offered twice a year for previously published or unpublished works. Opportunity Grants are for specific projects of writers (poetry, playwriters, fiction, nonfiction) as well as not-for-profit presses. Also available are Artist Development funds to provide technical assistance for Vermont writers. Write or call for entry information. Open to Vermont residents only. Prize: $250-5,000.

VERMONT PLAYWRIGHT'S AWARD

The Valley Players, P.O. Box 441, Waitsfield VT 05673. (802)583-6767. E-mail: valleyplayer@madriver.com. Web site: www.valleyplayers.com. **Contact:** Sharon Kellerman. Offered annually for unpublished, nonmusical, full-length plays suitable for production by a community theater group to encourage development of playwrights in Vermont, New Hampshire, and Maine. **Deadline: February 1.** Prize: $1,000.

THE VILLAGE ROADSHOW PRIZE FOR SCREEN WRITING

Victorial Premier's Literary Awards, State Library of Victoria, 328 Swanston St., Melbourne VIC 3000 Australia. (61)(3)8664-7277. E-mail: pla@slv.vic.gov.au. Web site: www.slv.vic.gov.au/pla. **Contact:** Awards Coordinator. Prize for a screenplay of a feature-length film. The State Library of Victoria reserves the right to place a copy of the shortlisted works in its collection. Further copyright remains with the author. **Deadline: May 5.** Guidelines for SASE. Prize: $15,000. Open to Australian citizens or permanent residents.

VIRGINIA GOVERNOR'S SCREENWRITING COMPETITION

901 E. Byrd St., Richmond VA 23219-4048. (804)371-8204. E-mail: vafilm@virginia.org. Web site: film.virginia.org/for_virginians/screenwriting_comp.aspx. Virginia writers are able to submit a full-length screenplay or television script to a panel of Virginia judges. Virginia writers only. **Deadline: May 23.** Guidelines for SASE. Prize: Three $1,000 cash awards. Writers in the commonwealth are eligible.

THE HERMAN VOADEN NATIONAL PLAYWRITING COMPETITION

Drama Department, Queen's University, Kingston ON K7L 3N6, Canada. (613)533-2104. E-mail: han naca@post.queensu.ca. Web site: www.queensu.ca/drama. **Contact:** Carol Anne Hanna. Offered every 2 years for unpublished plays to discover and develop new Canadian plays. See Web site for deadlines and guidelines. Open to Canadian citizens or landed immigrants. **Charges $30 entry fee.** Prize: $3,000, $2,000, and 8 honorable mentions. 1st- and 2nd-prize winners are offered a 1-week workshop and public reading by professional director and cast. The 2 authors will be playwrights-in-residence for the rehearsal and reading period.

WASHINGTON STATE SCREENPLAY COMPETITION

Northwest Film Forum, 1515 12th Ave., Seattle WA 98122. 206.329.2629. E-mail: screenplay@nwfilmforum.com. Web site: www.nwfilmforum.com. Guidelines for SASE. **Charges $35-50.** Prize: Grand prize includes ''1) Announcement as winner in display ad in *Variety* and *Hollywood Reporter*, along with publicity releases to film industry and script-related publications, 2) Staged script reading with a cast of talented Seattle actors at the 11th annual Local Sightings Film Festival, NWFF's October 2008 festival of Northwest film and video, 3) One year membership to NWFF and NWSG, and 4) Save The Cat bundle (both books and software).'' Open to any writer.
Tips ''Screenplays must meet ONE of the following criteria: a) Written by a resident of Washington State, b) 50% set in Washington State, c) Able to be filmed in Washington State.

WATERFRONT FILM FESTIVAL AND INDIE SCREENPLAY COMPETITION

P.O. Box 387, Saugatuck MI 49453. 269) 857-8351. E-mail: screenplay@waterfrontfilm.org. Web site: www.waterfrontfilm.org. Films must be able to be shot in Michigan for less than $5 million. The contest is now accepting entries from writers in any state. Previously, the contest was only for local writers. Scripts must be 80-130 pages in length. Annually. **Deadline: April 1.** Guidelines for SASE. **Charges $40.** Open to any writer.

PATRICK WHITE PLAYWRIGHTS' AWARD

Sydney Theatre Company, P.O. Box 777, Millers Point NSW 2000, Australia. (61)(2)9250-1700. Fax: (61)(2)9251-3687. E-mail: mail@sydneytheatre.com.au. Web site: www.sydneytheatre.com.au. **Contact:** Jane FitzGerald. Annual contest for a full-length unproduced play by an Australian age 19 and up. Guidelines for SASE. Prize: $20,000 and a reading at the Sydney Writers' Festival. Open to any writer.

WHITE RIVER INDIE FILMS SCREENWRITING CONTEST

White River Indie Films, P.O. Box 101, White River Junction VT 05001. (802)738-5550. E-mail: info@wrif.org. Web site: www.wrif.org/screenplay.php. ''WRIF is seeking submissions from Vermont and New Hampshire residents, student or professional. They may be on any subject. All scripts must be original and submitted in English. Feature scripts should be 95-120 pages in length and in proper screenplay format, preferably on three-hole punch paper and bound with appropriate paper fasteners. Short scripts may be up to 25 pages long.'' **Deadline: August.** Guidelines for SASE. **Charges $25; $15 for students.** Prize: Up to $250. Open to any writer.
Tips Submission address varies from film commission address above. Submit scripts to Bill Phillips, Film and Media Studies, Hinman Box 6194, Dartmouth College, Hanover, NH 03755.

WHITING WRITERS' AWARDS

Mrs. Giles Whiting Foundation, 1133 Avenue of the Americas, 22nd Floor, New York NY 10036-6710. Web site: whitingfoundation.org. Estab. 1985. ''The Foundation gives annually $35,000 each to up to 10 writers of poetry, fiction, nonfiction, and plays. The awards place special emphasis on exceptionally promising emerging talent.'' Direct applications and informal nominations are not accepted by the Foundation. Literary professionals are contacted by the foundation to make nominations. Judged by 6-7 writers of distinction and accomplishment.

WICHITA STATE UNIVERSITY PLAYWRITING COMPETITION

School of Performing Arts, Wichita State University, 1845 N. Fairmount, Campus Box 153, Wichita KS 67260-0153. (316)978-3368. Fax: (316)978-3202. E-mail: jeannine.saunders@wichita.edu. Web site: webs.wichita.edu/?u = FA_PERFORMINGARTS&p = /pa_contest/. **Contact:** Drew Tombrello, director. Estab. 1974. Offered for unpublished, unproduced (a) Full-length plays in one or more acts should be a minimum of 90 minutes playing time; (b) Two or three short plays on related themes by the same author will be judged as one entry. The total playing time should be a minimum of 90 minutes; (c) Musicals should be a minimum of 90 minutes playing time and must include a CD of the accompanying music. Contestants must be graduate or undergraduate students in a US college or university. **Deadline: February 15.** Guidelines for SASE. Prize: Production of winning play (ACTF). Judged by Judged by a panel of faculty.

WINFEMME MONTHLIES

Women's Image Network, 2118 Wilshire Boulevard, Suite 144, Santa Monica CA 90403. (310)229-5365. E-mail: info@winfemme.com. Web site: www.winfemme.com. Scripts may be TV specs, TV movies, feature film scripts, theatre plays and/or novellas. Category one: Films/videos created by both men and women, ''Which Tell A Woman's Story.'' These stories will feature female protagonists. Category two: Films with a lesbian story. Category three: Films directed and/or produced by a woman that tell either a man's or a woman's story. **Deadline: Last day of each month.** Guidelines for SASE. **Charges $50.** Prize: Festival award. Open to any writer.

WISCONSIN SCREENWRITERS FORUM CONTEST

P.O. Box 7395, Madison WI 53707. E-mail: memberservices@wiscreenwritersforum.org. Web site: www.wiscreenwritersforum.org/contests.html. Guidelines for SASE. Open to any writer.

WOODS HOLE FILM FESTIVAL SCREENWRITING COMPETITION

Woods Hole Film Festival, P.O. Box 624, Woods Hole MA 02543. E-mail: info@woodsholefilmfestival.org. Web site: www.woodsholefilmfestival.org/pages/CFE-screenplaycomp.php. Ideally, scripts are works-in-progress, but anything unsold and unproduced may be submitted. **Deadline: May.** Guidelines for SASE. **Charges $10-35.** Judged by ''an independent, non-HSSW/WHFF panel with blind scripts (no names).'' Open to any writer.

WORLDFEST-HOUSTON INDEPENDENT INTERNATIONAL FILM FESTIVAL

9898 Bissonnet St., Suite 650, Houston TX 77036. (713)965-9955. Fax: (713)965-9960. E-mail: entry@worldfest.org. Web site: www.worldfest.org. **Contact:** Entry Coordinator. Genre categories. Annually,

Must Be Unpublished. **Deadline: December.** Guidelines for SASE. **Charges $85.** Prize: Cash Prizes, Options, Production Deals, & Seminars. Open to any writer.

WRITE A PLAY! NYC

Young Playwrights, Inc., P.O. Box 5134, New York NY 10185. (212)594-5440. Fax: (212)684-4902. Web site: youngplaywrights.org. **Contact:** Literary Department. Offered annually for plays by NYC elementary, middle, and high school students only. **Deadline: April 11.** Prize: Varies.

WRITEMOVIES AND TALENTSCOUT MANAGEMENT INTERNATIONAL WRITING CONTEST

11444 Washington Blvd, Suite C-227, Los Angeles CA 90066. (310)276-5160. Fax: (310)276-5134. E-mail: admin@writemovies.com. Web site: www.writemovies.com/writingcontest.html. "Only 1,000 entries will be accepted. Enter early and save! Out of close to three hundred 'contest sites,' WriteMovies is one of only a handful that has produced movies from winning projects. 'The List,' was written by WriteMovies winner Marcus Folmar. In addition, former winner Jon Rosten has parlayed his success in the contest into getting his project, 'Valley of Angels' produced last December. Hundreds of others have had their scripts optioned and bought and have found representation. Several novels have also been published and plays produced. Production companies, studios and agencies contact us all the time about our winners! The founder of the company discovered Andrew Niccol, who wrote and produced 'The Truman Show' among others. We succeed when you succeed." Annual. **Deadline: Early February 20. March 15.** Guidelines for SASE. **Charges $29-$49.** Prize: Grand Prize: $3,000 in cash and guaranteed representation. Up to $1 million in option monies from the A-List producers we work with. If a studio/production company wishes to option the script, we will fly the winner to Los Angeles and pay (up to $4,000) for their accommodation. We will submit the top three projects to relevant production companies (such as Neal Moritz Productions, Bruckheimer Films, Scott Rudin Prods.) networks (FOX, ABC, CBS, etc.) and studios (Paramount, Warner Bros, NBC Universal, etc.). You keep ALL the option/sales money. The Grand Prize winner is also submitted to several literary agencies and management companies as well as non-US companies to increase the chances of a sale. We will pitch your script to companies such as ICM, William Morris, Endeavor, ACME, The Gage Group, etc. The names of the top five winners and their projects are mentioned in press releases and on the web. The Grand Prize winner will receive $1,000 in free script consulting to develop the winning script. Courtesy of Final Draft, the top winners will receive their award-winning screenwriting software. Courtesy of Filmstew, the Grand Prize winner will also receive 1 year free access to Filmstew's new service, Project Tracker. The four runners up will also receive 1 month free access. Courtesy of Click&Copyright, the top three winners will receive a free Complete Copyright Package, that will enable them to protect their winning project or a future project of their choosing." Open to any writer.

WRITER'S DIGEST WRITING COMPETITION

Writer's Digest, a publication of F + W Media, Inc., 700 E. State Street, Iola WI 54990. (513)531-2690, ext. 1328. E-mail: writing-competition@fwpubs.com. Web site: www.writersdigest.com. **Contact:** Nicki Florence. Writing contest with 10 categories: Inspirational Writing (spiritual/religious, maximum 2,500 words); Memoir/Personal Essay (maximum 2,000 words); Magazine Feature Article (maximum 2,000 words); Short Story (genre, maximum 4,000 words); Short Story (mainstream/literary, maximum 4,000 words); Rhyming Poetry (maximum 32 lines); Nonrhyming Poetry (maximum 32 lines); Stage Play (first 15 pages and 1-page synopsis); TV/Movie Script (first 15 pages and 1-page

Contests

synopsis). Entries must be original, in English, unpublished/unproduced (except for Magazine Feature Articles), and not accepted by another publisher/producer at the time of submission. *Writer's Digest* retains one-time publication rights to the winning entries in each category. **Deadline: June 1. Charges $10/first poetry entry; $5/additional poem. All other entries are $15/first ms; $10/additional ms.** Prize: Grand Prize: $2,500 and a trip to New York City to meet with editors and agents; 1st Place: $1,000, ms critique and marketing advice from a *Writer's Digest* editor, commentary from an agent, and $100 of Writer's Digest Books; 2nd Place: $500 and $100 of Writer's Digest Books; 3rd Place: $250 and $100 of Writer's Digest Books; 4th Place: $100 and a subscription to *Writer's Digest*; 5th Place: $50 and a subscription to *Writer's Digest*.

WRITERS GUILD OF ALBERTA AWARDS

Writers Guild of Alberta, Percy Page Centre, 11759 Groat Rd., Edmonton AB T5M 3K6, Canada. (780)422-8174. Fax: (780)422-2663. E-mail: mail@writersguild.ab.ca. Web site: www.writersguild.ab.ca. **Contact:** Executive Director. Offers the following awards: Wilfred Eggleston Award for Non-fiction; Georges Bugnet Award for Novel; Howard O'Hagan Award for Short Fiction; Stephan G. Stephansson Award for Poetry; R. Ross Annett Award for Children's Literature; Gwen Pharis Ringwood Award for Drama; Jon Whyte Memorial Essay Competition. Eligible entries will have been published anywhere in the world between January 1 and December 31 of the current year; the authors must have been residents of Alberta for at least 12 of the 18 months prior to December 31. Unpublished mss, except in the Drama and Essay categories, are not eligible. Anthologies are not eligible. Anthologies are not eligible. Works may be submitted by authors, publishers, or any interested parties. **Deadline: December 31.** Guidelines for SASE. Prize: Winning authors receive $1,000; Jon Whyte Memorial Essay Prize offers one prize of $1,000 and two prizes of $500. Other awards: Isabel Miller Young Writers Award. Authors must be 12-18 years of age and a resident of Alberta. Deadline: May 1.

THE WRITERS NETWORK SCREENPLAY & FICTION COMPETITION

287 South Robertson Blvd. #467, Beverly Hills CA 90211. (800)646-3896. E-mail: writersnet@aol.com. Web site: www.fadeinonline.com. The Writers Network Screenplay & Fiction Competition is a unique program, co-sponsored by WGA Signatory Literary Agencies in Los Angeles and New York, designed to give new and talented writers across the country the chance to pursue careers in film, television and/or publishing. **Deadline: May 29. June 15.** Guidelines for SASE. **Charges $35-$45.** Prize: More than $10,000 in cash and prizes. Open to any writer.

WRITERS ON THE STORM SCREENPLAY COMPETITION

Coverage, Ink., P.O. Box 899, Venice CA 90294. (310)582-5880. E-mail: writerstorm@gmail.com. Web site: www.writerstorm.com. "We're all about empowering the writer, because we ARE writers. Yes, you read that right. A contest that's actually by writers, for writers. Our prizes are deliberately development-heavy because we believe knowledge is power." **Deadline: July.** Guidelines for SASE. **Charges $40.** Prize: $22,000 in prizes. Must be 18 years of age or older. Open to anyone who has earned less than $10,000 career earnings as a screenwriter.

THE WRITERS PLACE SCREENPLAY CONTEST

311 North Robertson Blvd., #336, Beverly Hills CA. (310)429-5181. E-mail: contact2@thewritersplace.org. Web site: www.thewritersplace.org. **Deadline: May 15th and November 15th.** Guidelines for SASE. **Charges $10.** Open to any writer.

WRITESAFE PRESENT-A-THON

422 W. Carlisle Road, Westlake Village CA 91361. (805)495-3659. E-mail: admin@writesafe.com. Web site: www.writesafe.com/wscontest.html. A quarterly contest with these deadlines: The first Present-A-Thon of each year starts January 1 and ends March 31. The second Present-A-Thon of each year starts April 1 and ends June 30. The third Present-A-Thon of each year starts July 1 and ends September 30. The fourth Present-A-Thon of each year starts October 1 and ends December 31. **Deadline: March 31, June 30, September 30 and December 31.** Guidelines for SASE. Prize: First Prize is consideration for publication, production, or representation by a panel of experts. Second Prize is consideration for publication, production, or representation. More prizes awarded. Open to any writer.

YEAR END SERIES (YES) NEW PLAY FESTIVAL

Dept. of Theatre, Nunn Dr., Northern Kentucky University, Highland Heights KY 41099-1007. (859)572-6362. Fax: (859)572-6057. E-mail: forman@nku.edu. **Contact:** Sandra Forman, project director. Receives submissions from May 1-October 1 in even-numbered years for the festivals which occur in April of odd-numbered years. Open to all writers. **Deadline: October 1.** Guidelines for SASE. Prize: $500 and an expense-paid visit to Northern Kentucky University to see the play produced.

YOUNG ARTS

National Foundation for Advancement in the Arts, 444 Brickell Ave., Suite P-14, Miami FL 33131. (305)377-1140 or (800)970-ARTS. Fax: (305)377-1149. Web site: www.youngARTS.org. **Contact:** Roberta Behrend Fliss. Estab. 1981. For high school seniors in cinematic arts, dance, music, jazz, photography, theater, visual art, voice, and writing. Applications available on Web site or by phone request. **Deadline: Early: June 2 ($25 fee); regular: October 1 ($35 fee).** Prize: Individual awards range from $250-10,000 in an awards package totalling $900,000—$3 million in scholarship opportunities and the chance to be named Presidential Scholars in the Arts.

YOUNG PLAYWRIGHTS FESTIVAL NATIONAL PLAYWRITING COMPETITION

Young Playwrights, Inc., P.O. Box 5134, New York NY 10185. (212)594-5440. Fax: (212)594-5441. E-mail: admin@youngplaywrights.org. Web site: youngplaywrights.org. The Young Playwrights Festival National Playwriting Competition is offered annually to identify talented American playwrights aged 18 or younger. Please include your address, phone number, and date of birth on the title page. **Deadline: December 1 (postmarked).** Guidelines for SASE. Prize: Winners receive an invitation to New York City for the annual Young Playwrights, Inc. Writers Conference and a professionally staged reading of their play. Several of the winners will be offered a full Off-Broadway production or workshop in the Young Playwrights Festival. Entrants retain all rights to their work. Open to US residents only.

ANNA ZORNIO MEMORIAL CHILDREN'S THEATRE PLAYWRITING COMPETITION

University of New Hampshire, Dept. of Theatre and Dance, PCAC, 30 College Rd., Durham NH 03824-3538. (603)862-3044. E-mail: mike.wood@unh.edu. Web site: www.unh.edu/theatre-dance/zornio.html. **Contact:** Michael Wood. Offered every 4 years for unpublished well-written plays or musicals appropriate for young audiences with a maximum length of 60 minutes. May submit more than 1 play, but not more than 3. All plays will be performed by adult actors and must be appropriate for a children's audience within the K-12 grades. Guidelines and entry forms available as downloads on the Web site. **Deadline: March.** Prize: $1,000. The play is also produced and underwritten as part of the 2009-2010 season by the UNH Department of Theatre and Dance. Winner will be notified in November 2008. Open to all playwrights in US and Canada. All ages are invited to participate.

Theaters

Where TV and movies have a diminished role for writers in the collaboration that produces the final product, whether a show or a film, theater places a very high value on the playwright. This may have something to do with the role of the scripts in the different settings.

Screenplays are often in a constant state of "in progress," where directors make changes; producers make changes; and even actors and actresses make changes throughout the filming of the TV show or movie. Plays, on the other hand, must be as solid as a rock, because the script must be performed live night after night.

As a result, playwrights tend to have more involvement in the productions of their scripts, a power screenwriters can only envy. Counterbalancing the greater freedom of expression are the physical limitations inherent in live performance: a single stage, smaller cast, limited sets and lighting, and, most importantly, a strict, smaller budget. These conditions not only affect what but also how you write.

Listings

The following listings include contact information, submission details, current needs, and other helpful tips to help you find a home for your finished and polished play. As with any market, it is advised that after you pinpoint a listing that you then follow up with them to find out their most current submission policy and to ask who you should address your submission. This might seem like a lot of work, but writing plays is a competitive business. Your professionalism will go a long way in separating you from other "wannabe" playwrights.

For more information

To find out more about writing and submitting plays, contact the Dramatists Guild (www.dramaguild.com) and the Writers Guild of America (www.wga.org). Both organizations are great for networking and for learning the basics needed to build a successful career crafting plays.

ABINGDON THEATRE CO.

312 W. 36th St., 6th Floor, New York NY 10018. (212)868-2055. Fax: (212)868-2056. E-mail: literary@ abingdontheatre.org. Web site: www.abingdontheatre.org. Artistic Director: Jan Buttram. **Contact:** Literary Manager: Kim T. Sharp. Estab. 1993. **Produces 2-3 Mainstage and 2-3 Studio productions/ year.** Professional productions for a general audience. Submit full-length script in hard copy, cast breakdown, synopsis and development history, if any. No one-act. Responds in 4 months. Buys variable rights. **Payment is negotiated.** Include SASE for return of manuscript.

Needs All scripts should be suitable for small stages. No musicals where the story line is not very well-developed and the driving force of the piece.

Tips Check Web site for updated submission guidelines.

ACT II PLAYHOUSE

P.O. Box 555, Ambler PA 19002. (215)654-0200. Fax: (215)654-9050. Web site: www.act2.org. **Contact:** Stephen Blumenthal, literary manager. Estab. 1998. **Produces 5 plays/year.** Query and synopsis. Responds in 1 month. **Payment negotiable.**

Needs Contemporary comedy, drama, musicals. Full length. 6 character limitation; 1 set or unit set. Does not want period pieces. Limited number of scenes per act.

ACTORS THEATRE OF LOUISVILLE

316 W. Main St., Louisville KY 40202-4218. (502)584-1265. Fax: (502)561-3300. E-mail: awegener@ actorstheatre.org. Web site: www.actorstheatre.org. **Contact:** Amy Wegener, literary manager. Estab. 1964. **Produces approximately 30 new plays of varying lengths/year.** Professional productions are performed for subscription audience from diverse backgrounds. Agented submissions only for full-length plays, will read 10-page samples of unagented full-length works. Open submissions to National Ten-Minute Play Contest (plays 10 pages or less) are due November 1. Responds in 9 months to submissions, mostly in the fall. Buys variable rights. **Offers variable royalty.**

Needs "We are interested in full-length, one-act and 10-minute plays and in plays of ideas, language, humor, experiment and passion."

ALLEYWAY THEATRE

1 Curtain Up Alley, Buffalo NY 14202. (716)852-2600. Fax: (716)852-2266. E-mail: newplays@alley way.com. Web site: www.alleyway.com. **Contact:** Literary Manager. Estab. 1980. **Produces 4-5 full-length, 6-12 one-act plays/year.** Submit complete script; include CD for musicals. Responds in 6 months. Seeks first production rights. **Pays 7% royalty.**

- Alleyway Theatre also sponsors the Maxim Mazumdar New Play Competition. See the Contest & Awards section for more information.

Needs Wants works written uniquely for the theatre. Theatricality, breaking the fourth wall, and unusual settings are of particular interest. "We are less interested in plays which are likely to become TV or film scripts."

ALLIANCE THEATRE

1280 Peachtree St. NE, Atlanta GA 30309. (404)733-4650. Fax: (404)733-4625. Web site: www.alli ancetheatre.org. **Contact:** Literary Intern. Estab. 1969. **Produces 11 plays/year.** Professional production for local audience. Query with synopsis and sample or submit through agent. Enclose SASE. Responds in 9 months.

Needs Full-length scripts and scripts for young audiences no longer than 60 minutes.

Tips "As the premier theater of the southeast, the Alliance Theatre sets the highest artistic standards, creating the powerful experience of shared theater for diverse people. Please submit via snail mail."

☑ AMERICAN CONSERVATORY THEATER

30 Grant Ave., 6th Floor, San Francisco CA 94108-5800. (415)834-3200. Web site: www.act-sf.org. Artistic Director: Carey Perloff. **Contact:** Pink Pasdar, associate artistic director. Estab. 1965. **Produces 8 plays/year.** Plays are performed in Geary Theater, a 1,000-seat classic proscenium. No unsolicited scripts.

APPLE TREE THEATRE

1850 Green Bay Rd., Suite 100, Highland Park IL 60035. (847)432-8223. Fax: (847)432-5214. E-mail: info@appletreetheatre.com. Web site: www.appletreetheatre.com. Artistic Director: Eileen Boevers. **Contact:** Eileen Boevers. Estab. 1983. **Produces 4 plays/year.** "Professional productions intended for an adult audience mix of subscriber base and single-ticket holders. Our subscriber base is extremely theater-savvy and intellectual." Rights obtained vary. **Pays variable royalty.** Return SASE submissions only if requested.

Needs "We produce a mixture of musicals, dramas, classical, contemporary, and comedies. Length: 90 minutes-2½ hours. Small space, unit set required. No fly space, theatre in the round. Maximum actors 5.

Tips "No farces or large-scale musicals. Theater needs small shows with 1-unit sets due to space and financial concerns. Also note the desire for nonlinear pieces that break new ground. *Please do not submit unsolicited manuscripts—send letter and description along with tapes for musicals*; if we want more, we will request it."

☑ ARENA STAGE

1101 6th St. SW, Washington DC 20024. (202)554-9066. Fax: (202)488-4056. Web site: www.arenastage.org. Artistic Director: Molly Smith. **Contact:** Mark Bly, senior dramaturg. Estab. 1950. **Produces 8 plays/year.** Only accepts scripts from writers with agent or theatrical representation.

Needs Plays about the diverse voices in America (racial, cultural, political). Plays that provoke thought about the individual and collective American consciousness (past, present, and future). Seeks only full-length plays and musicals in all genres.

ARIZONA THEATRE CO.

P.O. Box 1631, Tucson AZ 85702. (520)884-8210. Fax: (520)628-9129. Web site: arizonatheatre.org. **Contact:** Literary Department. Estab. 1966. **Produces 6-8 plays/year.** Arizona Theatre Company is the State Theatre of Arizona and plans the season with the population of the state in mind. Only Arizona writers may submit unsolicited scripts, along with production history (if any), brief bio, and SASE. Out-of-state writers can send a synopsis, 10-page sample dialogue, production history (if any), brief bio, and SASE. Responds in 4-6 months. **Payment negotiated.**

Needs Full length plays of a variety of genres and topics and full length musicals. No one-acts.

Tips "Please include in the cover letter a bit about your current situation and goals. It helps in responding to plays."

ART STATION THEATRE

5384 Manor Dr., Stone Mountain GA 30083. (770)469-1105. E-mail: info@artstation.org. Web site: www.artstation.org. **Contact:** Jon Goldstein, program manager. Estab. 1986. **Produces 3 plays/year.** "ART Station Theatre is a professional theater located in a contemporary arts center in Stone Mountain, GA, which is part of Metro Atlanta." Audience consists of middle-aged to senior, suburban patrons. Query with synopsis and writing samples. Responds in 1 year. **Pays 5-7% royalty.**

Needs Full length comedy, drama and musicals, preferably relating to the human condition in the contemporary South. Cast size no greater than 6.

ARTISTS REPERTORY THEATRE

1515 SW Morrison, Portland OR 97205. (503)241-1278. Fax: (503)241-8268. Web site: www.artistsrep .org. Estab. 1982. **Produces.** Plays performed in professional theater with a subscriber-based audience. Send synopsis, résumé, and sample (maximum 10 pages). No unsolicited mss accepted. Responds in 6 months. **Pays royalty.**

Needs Full-length, hard-hitting, emotional, intimate, actor-oriented shows with small casts (rarely exceeds 10-13, usually 2-7). Language and subject matter are not a problem. No one-acts or children's scripts.

ASIAN AMERICAN THEATER CO.

55 Teresita Blvd., San Francisco CA 94127. E-mail: aatcspace@gmail.com. Web site: www.asianamer icantheater.org. **Contact:** Artistic Director. Estab. 1973. **Produces 4 plays/year.** Produces professional productions for San Francisco Bay Area audiences. Submit complete script. **Payment varies.**

Needs The new voice of Asian American theater. No limitations in cast, props or staging.

Tips Looking for plays from the new Asian American theater aesthetic—bold, substantive, punchy. Scripts from Asian Pacific Islander American women and under-represented Asian Pacific Islander ethnic groups are especially welcome.

☑ ASOLO THEATRE CO.

5555 N. Tamiami Trail, Sarasota FL 34234. (941)351-9010. Fax: (941)351-5796. Web site: www.aso lo.org. Estab. 1960. **Produces 7-8 plays/year.** A LORT theater with 2 intimate performing spaces. **Negotiates rights and payment.**

• Not currently accepting new scripts.

Needs Play must be full length. "We operate with a resident company in rotating repertory."

ATTIC THEATRE & FILM CENTRE

5429 W. Washington Blvd., Los Angeles CA 90016-1112. (323)525-0600. Web site: www.atticthea tre.org. Artistic Director: James Carey. **Contact:** Literary Manager. Estab. 1987. **Produces 4 plays/ year.** "We are based in Los Angeles and play to industry and regular Joes. We use professional actors; however, our house is very small, and the salaries we pay, including the royalties are very small because of that." Send query and synopsis or check out Web site. Responds in 4 months. Buys first producer rights. **Payment is negotiated on a case by case basis.**

Needs "We will consider any type of play except musicals and large cast historical pieces with multiple hard sets." Must be original 1-act plays no longer than 45 minutes in length. "Plays featuring elderly casts cannot be done because of our acting ages."

Tips "Please send an SASE and read our guidelines on the Web site. Follow all the directions."

BAILIWICK REPERTORY

Bailiwick Arts Center, 1229 W. Belmont Ave., Chicago IL 60657-3205. (773)883-1090. Fax: (773)883-2017. E-mail: bailiwick@bailiwick.org. Web site: www.bailiwick.org. **Contact:** David Zak, artistic director. Estab. 1982. **Produces 5 mainstage plays (classic and newly commissioned) each year; 12 one-acts in annual Directors Festival.** Pride Performance Series (gay and lesbian), includes one-acts, poetry, workshops, and staged adaptations of prose. Submit year-round. One-act play fest runs July-August. Responds in 9 months for full-length only. **Pays 6% royalty.**

Needs "We need daring scripts that break the mold. Large casts or musicals are OK. Creative staging solutions are a must."

Tips "Know the rules, then break them creatively and boldly! Please send SASE for manuscript submission guidelines *before you submit* or get manuscript guidelines at our Web site."

BAKER'S PLAYS PUBLISHING CO.

45 W. 25th St., New York NY 10010. E-mail: publications@bakersplays.com. Web site: www.bakersplays.com. **Contact:** Managing Editor. Estab. 1845. **Publishes 20-30 straight plays and musicals. Works with 2-3 unpublished/unproduced writers annually. 80% freelance written. 75% of scripts unagented submissions.** Plays performed by amateur groups, high schools, children's theater, churches and community theater groups. Submit complete script with news clippings, résumé, production history. Submit complete cd of music with musical submissions. See our Web site for more information about e-submissions. Responds in 3-6 months. **Pay varies; negotiated royalty split of production fees; 10% book royalty.**

Needs "We are finding strong support in our new division—plays from young authors featuring contemporary pieces for high school production."

Tips "We are particularly interested in adaptation of lesser-known folk tales from around the world. Also of interest are plays which feature a multicultural cast and theme. Collections of one-act plays for children and young adults tend to do very well. Also, high school students: Write for guidelines (see our Web site)for information about our High School Playwriting Contest."

MARY BALDWIN COLLEGE THEATRE

Mary Baldwin College, Staunton VA 24401. Fax: (540)887-7139. Web site: www.mbc.edu/theatre/. **Contact:** Terry K. Southerington, professor of theater. Estab. 1842. **Produces 5 plays/year.** 10% of scripts are unagented submissions. Works with up to 1 unpublished/unproduced writer annually. An undergraduate women's college theater with an audience of students, faculty, staff and local community (adult, conservative). Query with synopsis. Responds in 1 year. Buys performance rights only. **Pays $10-50 per performance.**

Needs Full-length and short comedies, tragedies, and music plays geared particularly toward young women actresses, dealing with women's issues both contemporary and historical. Experimental/ studio theater not suitable for heavy sets. Cast should emphasize women. No heavy sex; minimal explicit language.

Tips "A perfect play for us has several roles for young women, few male roles, minimal production demands, a concentration on issues relevant to contemporary society, and elegant writing and structure."

BARTER THEATRE

P.O. Box 867, Abingdon VA 24212-0867. (276)628-2281. Fax: (276)619-3335. E-mail: dramaturge@ bartertheatre.com. Web site: www.bartertheatre.com. **Contact:** Catherine Bush, dramaturge. Estab. 1933. **Produces 17 plays/year.** Plays performed in residency at 2 facilities, a 500-seat proscenium theater and a smaller 167-seat flexible theater. "Our plays are intended for diversified audiences of all ages." Submit synopsis and dialogue sample only with SASE. Responds in 9 months. **Pays negotiable royalty.**

• Barter Theatre often premieres new works.

Needs "We are looking for good plays, comedies and dramas that entertain and are relevant; plays that examine in new and theatrical ways the human condition and contemporary issues. We prefer casts of 4-12, single or unit set. Strong language may lessen a play's appeal for Barter audiences."

Tips "We are looking for material that appeals to diverse, family audiences."

BLOOMSBURG THEATRE ENSEMBLE

226 Center St., Bloomsburg PA 17815. E-mail: jsatherton@bte.org. Web site: www.bte.org. Ensemble Director: Daniel Roth. **Contact:** J. Scott Atherton, manager of administration and development. Estab. 1979. **Produces 6 plays/year.** Professional productions for a non-urban audience. Query and synopsis. Responds in 9 months. Buys negotiable rights **Pays 6-9% royalty. Pays $50-70 per performance.** "Because of our non-urban location, we strive to exposé our audience to a broad range of theatre—both classical and contemporary. We are drawn to language and ideas and to plays that resonate in our community. We are most in need of articulate comedies and cast sizes under 6."

Tips "Because of our non-urban setting we are less interested in plays that focus on dilemmas of city life in particular. Most of the comedies we read are cynical. Many plays we read would make better film scripts; static/relationship-heavy scripts that do not use the 'theatricality' of the theatre to an advantage."

BOARSHEAD THEATER

425 S. Grand Ave., Lansing MI 48933. (517)484-7800. Fax: (517)484-2564. Web site: www.boarshead. org. **Contact:** Kristine Thatcher, artistic director. Estab. 1966. **Produces 8 plays/year (6 mainstage, 2 Young People's Theater productions inhouse), 4 or 5 staged readings.** Mainstage Actors' Equity Association company; also Youth Theater—touring to schools by our intern company. Submit synopsis, character breakdown, 20 pages of sample dialogue, bio, production history (if any) via mail or e-mail. **Pays royalty for mainstage productions, transport/per diem for staged readings.**

Needs Thrust stage. Cast usually 8 or less; occasionally up to 20; no one-acts and no musicals considered. Prefers staging which depends on theatricality rather than multiple sets. "Send materials for full-length plays (only) to Kristine Thatcher, artistic director. For Young People's Theater, send one-act plays (only); 4-5 characters."

Tips "Plays should not have multiple realistic sets—too many scripts read like film scripts. Focus on intelligence, theatricality, crisp, engaging humorous dialogue. Write a good play and prove it with 10 pages of great, precise dialogue."

BROADWAY PLAY PUBLISHING

56 E. 81st St., New York NY 10028-0202. (212)772-8334. Fax: (212)772-8358. E-mail: sara@broad wayplaypubl.com; broadwaypl@aol.com. Web site: www.broadwayplaypubl.com. This publisher does not read play mss. It will only publish a play if the playwright is an American-born resident; the play is not in print elsewhere; the play is full-length (at least 1 hour); the play has contemporary subject matter; the play is for at least 2 actors; the play has been professionally produced for at least 12 pefromances; there is acceptable color artwork for the cover; there are a few sentences from print media complimenting the play.

CELEBRATION THEATRE

7985 Santa Monica Blvd., #109-1, Los Angeles CA 90046. Fax: (323)957-1826. E-mail: celebrationth tr@earthlink.net. Web site: www.celebrationtheatre.com. Artistic Director: Michael Matthews. **Contact:** Literary Management Team. Estab. 1983. **Produces 4 plays/year.** Performed in a small theatre in Los angeles. For all audiences, but with gay and lesbian characters at the center of the plays. Query and synopsis. Responds in 5 months. **Pays 6-7% royalty.**

Needs Produce works with gay and lesbian characters at the center of the narrative. There aren't any limitations, but simple productions work best. Don't send coming-out plays/stories.

CHAMBER THEATRE

158 N. Broadway, Milwaukee WI 53202. (414)276-8842. Fax: (414)277-4477. E-mail: mail@chamber-theatre.com. Web site: www.chamber-theatre.com. **Contact:** C. Michael Wright, artistic director. Estab. 1975. **Produces 5 plays/year.** Plays produced for adult and student audience. Query and synopsis. Responds in 3 months. **Pays royalty.**

Needs Produces literary, thought-provoking, biographical plays. Plays require small-unit settings. No plays for a large cast.

CHILDSPLAY, INC.

P.O. Box 517, Tempe AZ 85280. (480)350-8101. Fax: (480)350-8584. E-mail: info@childsplayaz.org. Web site: childsplayaz.org. **Contact:** Artistic Director. Estab. 1978. **Produces 5-6 plays/year.** "Professional touring and in-house productions for youth and family audiences." Submit synopsis, character descriptions and 7- to 10-page dialogue sample. Responds in 6 months. **Pays royalty of $20-35/ performance (touring) or pays $3,000-8,000 commission. Holds a small percentage of royalties on commissioned work for 3-5 years.**

Needs Seeking theatrical plays on a wide range of contemporary topics. "Our biggest market is K-6. We need intelligent theatrical pieces for this age group that meet touring requirements and have the flexibility for in-house staging. The company has a reputation, built up over 30 years, of maintaining a strong aesthetic. We need scripts that respect the audience's intelligence and support their rights to dream and to have their concerns explored. Innovative, theatrical and small is a constant need." Touring shows limited to 5 actors; in-house shows limited to 6-10 actors.

Tips No traditionally-handled fairy tales. "Theater for young people is growing up and is able to speak to youth and adults. The material must respect the artistry of the theater and the intelligence of our audience. Our most important goal is to benefit children. If you wish your materials returned send SASE."

CIRCUIT PLAYHOUSE/PLAYHOUSE ON THE SQUARE

51 S. Cooper, Memphis TN 38104. (901)725-0776. **Contact:** Jackie Nichols, artistic director. **Produces 16 plays/year. 100% of scripts unagented submissions. Works with 1 unpublished/unproduced writer/year**. Professional plays performed for the Memphis/Mid-South area. Member of the Theatre Communications Group. Contest held each fall. Submit complete script. Responds in 6 months. Buys percentage of royalty rights for 2 years. **Pays $500.**

Needs All types; limited to single or unit sets. Casts of 20 or fewer.

Tips "Each play is read by 3 readers through the extended length of time a script is kept. Preference is given to scripts for the southeastern region of the US."

I.E. CLARK PUBLICATIONS

P.O. Box 246, Schulenburg TX 78956-0246. E-mail: email@ieclark.com. Web site: www.ieclark.com. Estab. 1956. Publishes 10-15 plays/year for educational theater, children's theater, religious theater, regional professional theater and community theater. Publishes unagented submissions. Catalog on-line. Writer's guidelines for #10 SASE. Submit complete script, 1 at a time with SASE. Responds in 6 months. Buys all available rights; "We serve as an agency as well as a publisher." **Pays standard book and performance royalty, amount and percentages dependent upon type and marketability of play.**

• "One of our specialties is "Young Adult Awareness Drama"—plays for ages 13 to 25 dealing with sex, drugs, popularity, juvenile, crime, and other problems of young adults. We also need plays for children's theatre, especially dramatizations of children's classic literature."

Needs "We are interested in plays of all types—short or long. Audiotapes of music or videotapes of a performance are requested with submissions of musicals. We require that a play has been produced (directed by someone other than the author); photos, videos and reviews of the production are helpful. No limitations in cast, props, staging, etc. Plays with only one or two characters are difficult to sell. We insist on literary quality. We like plays that give new interpretations and understanding of human nature. Correct spelling, punctuation and grammar (befitting the characters, of course) impress our editors."

Tips Publishes plays only. "Entertainment value and a sense of moral responsibility seem to be returning as essential qualities of a good play script. The era of glorifying the negative elements of society seems to be fading rapidly. Literary quality, entertainment value and good craftsmanship rank in that order as the characteristics of a good script in our opinion. 'Literary quality' means that the play must—in beautiful, distinctive, and un-trite language—say something; preferably something new and important concerning man's relations with his fellow man or God; and these 'lessons in living' must be presented in an intelligent, believable and creative manner. Plays for children's theater are tending more toward realism and childhood problems, but fantasy and dramatization of fairy tales are also needed."

Ⓐ CLEVELAND PLAY HOUSE

8500 Euclid Ave., Cleveland OH 44106. E-mail: sgordon@clevelandplayhouse.com. Web site: www.clevelandplayhouse.com. Artistic Director: Michael Bloom. **Contact:** Seth Gordon, associate artistic director. Estab. 1915. **Produces 10 plays/year.** "We have five theatres, 100-550 seats." Submit 10-page sample with synopsis. Responds in 6 months. **Payment is negotiable.**

Needs All styles and topics of new plays.

COLONY THEATRE CO.

555 N. Third St., Burbank CA 91502. (818)558-7000. Fax: (818)558-7110. E-mail: colonytheatre@colo
nytheatre.org. Web site: www.colonytheatre.org. **Contact:** Michael David Wadler, literary manager.
Produces 6 plays/year. Professional 276-seat theater with thrust stage. Casts from resident company
of professional actors. Query and synopsis. Negotiated rights. **Pays royalty for each performance.**
Needs Full length (90-120 minutes) with a cast of 4-12. Especially interested in small casts of 4 or
fewer. No musicals or experimental works.
Tips "We seek works of theatrical imagination and emotional resonance on universal themes."

ⒶA CONTEMPORARY THEATRE

700 Union St., Seattle WA 98101. (206)292-7660. Fax: (206)292-7670. Web site: www.acttheatre.org.
Estab. 1965. **Produces 5-6 mainstage plays/year.** "ACT performs a subscription-based season on 3
stages: 2 main stages (a thrust and an arena) and a smaller, flexible 99-seat space. Although our focus
is towards our local Seattle audience, some of our notable productions have gone on to other venues
in other cities." *Agented submissions only* or through theatre professional's recommendation. Query
and synopsis only for Northwest playwrights. Responds in 6 months. **Pays 5-10% royalty.**
Needs "ACT produces full-length contemporary scripts ranging from solo pieces to large ensemble
works, with an emphasis on plays that embrace the contradictions and mysteries of our contemporary
world and that resonate with audiences of all backgrounds through strong storytelling and compelling
characters."
Tips "ACT is looking for plays that offer strong narrative, exciting ideas, and well-drawn, dimensional
characters that will engage an audience emotionally and intellectually. These may sound like obvious
prerequisites for a play, but often it seems that playwrights are less concerned with the story they
have to tell than with the way they're telling it, emphasizing flashy, self-conscious style over real
substance and solid structure."

CREEDE REPERTORY THEATRE

P.O. Box 269, Creede CO 81130-0269. (719)658-2541. E-mail: mo@creederep.com. Web site: www.
creederep.org. **Contact:** Maurice LaMee, artistic director. Estab. 1966. **Produces 6 plays/year.** Plays
performed for a smaller audience. Query and synopsis. Responds in 1 year. **Royalties negotiated
with each author—paid on a per performance basis.**
Needs One-act children's scripts. Special consideration given to plays focusing on the cultures and
history of the American West and Southwest.
Tips "We seek new adaptations of classical or older works as well as original scripts."

DALLAS CHILDREN'S THEATER

Rosewood Center for Family Arts, 5938 Skillman, Dallas TX 75231. E-mail: artie@dct.org. Web site:
www.dct.org. **Contact:** Artie Olaisen, associate artistic director. Estab. 1984. **Produces 11 plays/year.**
Professional theater for family and student audiences. Query with synopsis, number of actors required,
any material regarding previous productions of the work, and a demo tape or lead sheets (for musicals). Responds in 8 months. Rights negotiable. **Pays negotiable royalty.** No materials will be returned
without a SASE included.
Needs Substantive material appropriate for youth and family audiences. Most consideration given to
full-length, non-musical works, especially classic and contemporary adaptations of literature. Also

interested in social, topical, issue-oriented material. Very interested in scripts which enlighten diverse cultural experiences, particularly Hispanic and African-American experiences. Prefers scripts with no more than 15 cast members; 6-12 is ideal.

Tips ''No adult experience material. We are a family theater. Not interested in material intended for performance by children or in a classroom. Productions are performed by professional adults. Children are cast in child-appropriate roles. We receive far too much light musical material that plays down to children and totally lacks any substance. Be patient. We receive an enormous amount of submissions. Most of the material we have historically produced has had previous production. We are not against perusing non-produced material, but it has rarely gone into our season unless we have been involved in its development.''

DARLINGHURST THEATRE COMPANY

19 Greenknowe Ave., Potts Pointe NSW 2011, Australia. (61)(2)9331-3107. E-mail: theatre@darlingh ursttheatre.com. Web site: www.darlinghursttheatre.com. Submission period ends September 15. Seeks to exposé the audience to a diverse range of work, included narratives, non-narratives, Australian content, and international work. Classics are not excluded, though work new to Sydney is encouraged. Financial issues are a part of the selection process, so discuss your proposal with Glenn Terry before submitting. If asked, send complete ms or outline. See Web site for more submission details.

DETROIT REPERTORY THEATRE

13103 Woodrow Wilson, Detroit MI 48238-3686. (313)868-1347. Fax: (313)868-1705. **Contact:** Barbara Busby, literary manager. Estab. 1957. **Produces 4 plays/year.** Professional theater, 194 seats operating on A.E.A. SPT contract Detroit metropolitan area. Submit complete ms in bound folder, cast list, and description with SASE. Responds in 6 months. **Pays royalty.**

Needs Wants issue-oriented works. Cast limited to no more than 7 characters. No musicals or one-act plays.

DIVERSIONARY THEATRE

4545 Park Blvd., Suite 101, San Diego CA 92116. (619)220-6830. E-mail: dkirsch@diversionary.org. Web site: www.diversionary.org. **Contact:** Dan Kirsch, executive director. Estab. 1986. **Produces 5-6 plays/year.** Non-professional full-length productions of gay, lesbian, bisexual and transgender content. Ideal cast size is 2-6. Submit application and 10-15 pages of script. Responds in 6 months.

DIXON PLACE

258 Bowery, 2nd Floor, New York NY 10012. (212)219-0736. Fax: (212)219-0761. Web site: www.dix onplace.org. **Contact:** Leslie Strongwater, artistic director. Estab. 1986. **Produces 12 plays/year.** Submit full script. Does not accept submissions from writers outside the NYC area. **Pays flat fee.**

• Looking for new work, not already read or workshopped in full in New York.

Needs Particularly interested in non-traditional, either in character, content, structure and/or themes. ''We almost never produce kitchen sink, soap opera-style plays about AIDS, coming out, unhappy love affairs, getting sober or lesbian parenting. We regularly present new works, plays with innovative structure, multi-ethnic content, non-naturalistic dialogue, irreverent musicals and the elegantly bizarre. We are an established performance venue with a very diverse audience. We have a reputation for bringing our audience the unexpected. Submissions accepted year-round.''

Ⓐ DORSET THEATRE FESTIVAL

Box 510, Dorset VT 05251-0510. (802)867-2223. Web site: www.dorsettheatrefestival.org. Estab. 1976. **Produces 5 plays/year (1 a new work).** "Our plays will be performed in our Equity theater and are intended for a sophisticated community." Agented submissions only. **Rights and compensation negotiated.**

Needs Looking for full-length contemporary American comedy or drama. Limited to a cast of 6.

Tips "Language and subject matter must be appropriate to general audience."

DRAMATIC PUBLISHING

311 Washington St., Woodstock IL 60098. (800)448-7469. Fax: (800)334-5302. Web site: www.dramaticpublishing.com. **Contact:** Linda Habjan, submissions editor. **Publishes 40-50 titles/year.** Publishes paperback acting editions of original plays, musicals, adaptations, and translations. **Receives 250-500 queries and 600 mss/year.** Catalog and script guidelines free. **Pays 10% royalty on scripts; performance royalty varies.**

Needs Interested in playscripts appropriate for children, middle and high schools, colleges, community, stock and professional theaters. Send full ms.

Tips "We publish all kinds of plays for the professional, stock, amateur, high school, elementary and children's theater markets: full lengths, one acts, children's plays, musicals, adaptations."

DRAMATICS MAGAZINE

2343 Auburn Ave., Cincinnati OH 45219. (513)421-3900. Fax: (513)421-7077. E-mail: dcorathers@edta.org. Web site: www.edta.org. **Contact:** Don Corathers, editor. Estab. 1929. **Publishes 7 plays/year.** For high school theater students and teachers. Submit complete script. Responds in 3 months. Buys first North American serial rights only.

Needs "We are seeking one-acts to full-lengths that can be produced in an educational theater setting."

Tips "No melodrama, musicals, farce, children's theater, or cheap knock-offs of TV sitcoms or movies. Fewer writers are taking the time to learn the conventions of theater—what makes a piece work on stage, as opposed to film and television—and their scripts show it. We're always looking for good interviews with working theatre professionals."

EAST WEST PLAYERS

120 N. Judge John Aiso St., Los Angeles CA 90012. (213)625-7000. Fax: (213)625-7111. E-mail: jliu@eastwestplayers.org. Web site: www.eastwestplayers.org. Artistic Director: Tim Dang. **Contact:** Jeff Liu, literary manager. Estab. 1965. **Produces 5 plays/year.** Professional 240-seat theater performing under LOA-BAT contract, presenting plays which explore the Asian-Pacific or Asian-American experience. Submit ms with title page, résumé, cover letter, and SASE. Responds in 3-9 months. **Pays royalty against percentage of box office.**

Needs "Whether dramas, comedies, performance art or musicals, all plays must either address the Asian-American experience or have a special resonance when cast with Asian-American actors."

Tips "We are especially looking for comedies."

ELDRIDGE PUBLISHING CO.

P.O. Box 14367, Tallahassee FL 32317. (800)447-8243. Fax: (800)453-5179. E-mail: editorial@histage.com. Web site: www.histage.com. Managing Editor: Nancy Vorhis. **Contact:** Editor: Susan Shore.

Estab. 1906. **Publishes 65 new plays/year for junior high, senior high, church, and community audience.** Query with synopsis (acceptable). Please send CD with any musicals. Responds in 1-2 months. Buys all dramatic rights. Buys All rights. **Pays 50% royalties for amateur productions, 80% for professional productions and 10% copy sales in general market. Makes outright purchase of $100-600 in religious market.**

Needs "We are most interested in full-length plays and musicals for our school and community theater market. Nothing lower than junior high level, please. We always love comedies but also look for serious, high caliber plays reflective of today's sophisticated students. We also need one-acts and plays for children's theater. In addition, in our religious market we're always searching for holiday plays." No plays which belong in a classroom setting as part of a lesson plan. Unless it is for Christmas, no other religious musicals considered.

Tips "Please have your work performed, if at all possible, before submitting. The quality will improve substantially."

THE ENSEMBLE STUDIO THEATRE

549 W. 52nd St., New York NY 10019. (212)247-4982. Fax: (212)664-0041. E-mail: firman@ensembl estudiotheatre.org. Web site: www.ensemblestudiotheatre.org. Artistic Director: William Carden. **Contact:** Linsay Firman, artistic director. Estab. 1972. **Produces 250 projects/year for off-off Broadway developmental theater in a 100-seat house, 60-seat workshop space.** Do not fax mss or résumés. Submit complete ms. Responds in 10 months.

Needs Full-length plays with strong dramatic actions and situations and solid one-acts, humorous and dramatic, which can stand on their own. Special programs include Going to the River Series, which workshops new plays by African-American women, and the Sloan Project, which commissions new works on the topics of science and technology. Seeks "original plays with strong dramatic action, believable characters and dynamic ideas. We are interested in writers who respect the power of language." No verse-dramas or elaborate costume dramas. Accepts new/unproduced work only.

ENSEMBLE THEATRE OF CINCINNATI

1127 Vine St., Cincinnati OH 45248. (513)421-3555. Fax: (513)562-4104. E-mail: lynn.meyers@cincy etc.com. Web site: cincyetc.com. **Contact:** D. Lynn Meyers, producing artistic director. Estab. 1987. **Produces 12 plays/year, including a staged reading series.** Professional year-round theater. Query with synopsis, submit complete ms or submit through agent. Responds in 6 months. **Pays 5-10% royalty.**

Needs Dedicated to good writing of any style for a small, contemporary cast. Small technical needs, big ideas.

THE ESSENTIAL THEATRE

P.O. Box 8172, Atlanta GA 30306. (404)212-0815. E-mail: pmhardy@aol.com. Web site: www.essenti altheatre.com. **Contact:** Peter Hardy, artistic director. Estab. 1987. **Produces 3 plays/year.** "Professional theatre on a small budget, for adventurous theatregoers interested in new plays." Submit complete script by regular mail, or e-mail in Word format to: pmhardy@aol.com. Responds in 10 months. Include SASE for return of submission.

Needs Accepts unproduced plays of any length by Georgia writers only, to be considered for Essential Theatre Playwriting Award.

Tips Submission deadline: April 23

THE FOOTHILL THEATRE CO.

P.O. Box 1812, Nevada City CA 95959. (530)265-9320. Fax: (530)265-9325. E-mail: info@foothillthea tre.org. Web site: www.foothilltheatre.org. Artistic Director: Carolyn Howarth. **Contact:** Literary Manager. Estab. 1977. **Produces 6-9 plays/year.** "We are a professional theater company operating under an Actors' Equity Association contract for part of the year, and performing in the historic 246-seat Nevada Theatre (built in 1865) and at an outdoor amphitheatre on the north shore of Lake Tahoe. We also produce a new play development program called New Voices of the Wild West that endeavors to tell the stories of the non-urban Western United States." The audience is a mix of locals and tourists. Query by e-mail. Responds in 6 months-1 year. Buys negotiable rights. **Payment varies.**

Needs "We are most interested in plays which speak to the region and its history, as well as to its current concerns. No melodramas. Theatrical, above all."

Tips "At present, we're especially interested in unproduced plays that speak to the rural and semi-rural American West for possible inclusion in our new play reading and development program, New Voices of the Wild West. History plays are okay, as long as they don't sound like you wrote them with an encyclopedia open in your lap. The best way to get our attention is to write something we haven't seen before, and write it well."

FOUNTAIN THEATRE

5060 Fountain Ave., Los Angeles CA 90029. (323)663-2235. Fax: (323)663-1629. E-mail: ftheatre@aol .com. Web site: fountaintheatre.com. Artistic Directors: Deborah Lawlor, Stephen Sachs. **Contact:** Simon Levy, dramaturg. Estab. 1990. Produces both a theater and dance season. Produced at Fountain Theatre (99-seat equity plan). *Professional recommendation only.* Query with synopsis to Simon Levy, producing director/dramaturg. Responds in 6 months. Rights acquired vary. **Pays royalty.**

Needs Original plays, adaptations of American literature, material that incorporates dance or language into text with unique use and vision.

THE FREELANCE PRESS

P.O. Box 548, Dover MA 02030-2207. (508)785-8250. Fax: (508)785-8291. **Contact:** Narcissa Campion, managing director. Estab. 1984. Submit complete ms with SASE. Responds in 4 months. **Pays 70% of performance royalties to authors. Pays 10% script and score royalty.**

Needs "We publish original musical theater to be performed by young people, dealing with issues of importance to them. Also adapt 'classics' into musicals for 8- to 16-year-old age groups to perform." Large cast, flexible.

SAMUEL FRENCH, INC.

45 W. 25th St., New York NY 10010. (212)206-8990. Fax: (212)206-1429. E-mail: publications@sa muelfrench.com. Web site: www.samuelfrench.com. **Contact:** Editorial Department. Estab. 1830. **Publishes 50-60 titles/year.** Publishes paperback acting editions of plays. Receives 1,500 submissions/year, mostly from unagented playwrights. 10% of publications are from first-time authors; 20%

from unagented writers. **Pays 10% royalty on retail price, plus amateur and stock royalties on productions.**

Needs Comedies, mysteries, children's plays, high school plays.

Tips "Broadway and Off-Broadway hit plays, light comedies and mysteries have the best chance of selling to our firm. Our market is comprised of theater producers—both professional and amateur—actors and students. Read as many plays as possible of recent vintage to keep apprised of today's market; write plays with good female roles; and be 100% professional in approaching publishers and producers. We recommend (not require) that submissions be in the format used by professional playwrights in the US, as illustrated in *Guidelines*, available for $4 (postpaid)."

WILL GEER THEATRICUM BOTANICUM

P.O. Box 1222, Topanga CA 90290. (310)455-2322. Fax: (310)455-3724. Web site: www.theatricum.com. **Contact:** Ellen Geer, artistic director. Estab. 1973. **Produces 3 classical and 1 new play if selected/year.** Professional productions for summer theater. "Botanicum Seedlings" new plays selected for readings and one play each year developed. Contact: Jennie Webb. Send synopsis, sample dialogue and tape if musical. Responds in 6 months. **Pays 6% royalty or $150 per show.**

Needs Socially relevant plays, musicals; all full-length. Cast size of 4-10 people. "We are a large outdoor theatre—small intimate works could be difficult."

Tips "September submissions have best turn around for main season; year-round for 'Botanicum Seedlings.' "

⊘ GEORGE STREET PLAYHOUSE

9 Livingston Ave., New Brunswick NJ 08901. (732)246-7717. Web site: www.georgestplayhouse.org. Artistic Director: David Saint. **Contact:** Literary Associate. **Produces 6 plays/year.** Professional regional theater (LORT C). Proscenium/thurst stage with 367 seats. *No unsolicited scripts. Agent or professional recommendation only.*

Tips "It is our firm belief that theater reaches the mind via the heart and the funny bone. Our work tells a compelling, personal, human story that entertains, challenges and stretches the imagination."

GEVA THEATRE CENTER

75 Woodbury Blvd., Rochester NY 14607. (585)232-1366. **Contact:** Marge Betley, literary manager. **Produces 7-11 plays/year.** Professional and regional theater, modified thrust, 552 seats; second stage has 180 seats. Subscription and single-ticket sales. Query with sample pages, synopsis, and résumé. Responds in 3 months.

Needs Full-length plays, translations, and adaptations.

THE GOODMAN THEATRE

170 N. Dearborn St., Chicago IL 60601-3205. (312)443-3811. Fax: (312)443-3821. E-mail: artistic@ goodman-theatre.org. Web site: www.goodman-theatre.org. **Contact:** Tanya Palmer, literary manager. Estab. 1925. **Produces 9 plays/year.** "The Goodman is a professional, not-for-profit theater producing a series in both the Albert Theatre and the Owen Theatre, which includes an annual New Play Series. The Goodman does not accept unsolicited scripts, nor will it respond to synopsis of plays submitted by playwrights unless accompanied by a stamped, self-addressed postcard. The Goodman may request plays to be submitted for production consideration after receiving a letter of inquiry or

telephone call from recognized literary agents or producing organizations." Responds in 6 months. Buys variable rights. **Pays variable royalty.**

Needs Full-length plays, translations, musicals; special interest in social or political themes.

Ⓐ GRETNA THEATRE

P.O. Box 578, Mt. Gretna PA 17064. Fax: (717)964-2189. E-mail: larryfrenock@gretnatheatre.com. Web site: www.gretnatheatre.com. **Contact:** Larry Frenock, producing director. Estab. 1927. "Plays are performed at a professional equity theater during summer." Agent submissions only. **Pays negotiable royalty (6-12%).**

Needs "We produce full-length plays for a summer audience—subject, language and content are important." Prefer "package" or vehicles which have "star" role.

Tips "No one-acts. Given that we re a summer stock theatre, the chances of producing a new play are extremely remote, though we have produced play readings in the past."

GRIFFIN THEATRE COMPANY

13 Craigend St., Kings Cross NSW 2011, Australia. (61)(2)9332-1052. Fax: (61)(2)9331-1524. Web site: www.griffintheatre.com.au. Gives consideration and feedback if the author has had a play professionally produced, has an agent, has been shortlisted for the Griffin Award, or has had a play workshopped at Griffin. "If you don't meet these requirements, you may still send a 1-page outline and a 10-page sample. If interested, we will request the full manuscript."

Ⓐ HARTFORD STAGE CO.

50 Church St., Hartford CT 06103. (860)525-5601. Fax: (860)525-4420. Web site: www.hartfordstage.org. Estab. 1963. **Produces 6 plays/year.** Regional theater productions with a wide range in audience.

Needs Classics, new plays, musicals. *Agented submissions only.* No queries or synopses.

HORIZON THEATRE CO.

P.O. Box 5376, Atlanta GA 31107. (404)523-1477. Fax: (404)584-8815. Web site: www.horizontheatre.com. **Contact:** Lisa and Jeff Adler, artistic directors. Estab. 1983. **5+ plays/year, and workshops 6-10 plays as part of New South Playworks Festival.** Professional productions. Accepts unsolicited résumés, samples, treatments, and summaries with SASE. Responds in 1 year. Buys rights to produce in Atlanta area.

Needs "We produce contemporary plays that seek to bridge cultures and communities, utilizing a realistic base but with heightened visual or language elements. Particularly interested in comedy, satire, plays that are entertaining and topical, but thought provoking. Also particular interest in plays by women, African-Americans, or that concern the contemporary South." No more than 8 in cast.

ILLINOIS THEATRE CENTRE

371 Artists' Walk, P.O. Box 397, Park Forest IL 60466. (708)481-3510. Fax: (708)481-3693. E-mail: ilthctr@sbcglobal.net. Web site: www.ilthctr.org. Estab. 1976. **Produces 8 plays/year.** Professional Resident Theatre Company in our own space for a subscription-based audience. Query with synopsis or agented submission. Responds in 2 months. Buys casting and directing and designer selection rights. **Pays 7-10% royalty.**

Needs All types of 2-act plays, musicals, dramas. Prefers cast size of 6-10.

Tips Always looking for mysteries and comedies. "Make sure your play arrives between November and January when play selections are made."

INDIANA REPERTORY THEATRE

140 W. Washington St., Indianapolis IN 46204-3465. (317)635-5277. E-mail: rroberts@irtlive.com. Web site: www.irtlive.com. Artistic Director: Janet Allen. Dramaturg: Richard Roberts. Modified proscenium stage with 600 seats; thrust stage with 300 seats. Send synopsis with résumé via e-mail to the dramaturg. No unsolicited scripts. Submit year-round (season chosen by January). Responds in 6 month.

Needs Full-length plays, translations, adaptations, solo pieces. Also interested in adaptations of classic literature and plays that explore cultural/ethnic issues with a midwestern voice. Special program: Discovery Series (plays for family audiences with a focus on youth). Cast size should be 6-8.

Tips "The IRT employs a playwright-in-residence from whom the majority of our new work is commissioned. We occasionally place other subject-specific commissions."

INTERACT THEATRE CO.

The Adrienne, 2030 Sansom St., Philadelphia PA 19103. (215)568-8077. Fax: (215)568-8095. E-mail: pbonilla@interacttheatre.org. Web site: www.interacttheatre.org. **Contact:** Peter Bonilla, literary associate. Estab. 1988. **Produces 4 plays/year.** Produces professional productions for adult audience. Query with synopsis and bio. No unsolicited scripts. Responds in 6 months. **Pays 2-8% royalty or $25-100/performance.**

Needs Contemporary dramas and comedies that explore issues of political, social, cultural or historical significance. "Virtually all of our productions have political content in the foregound of the drama." Prefer plays that raise interesting questions without giving easy, predictable answers. "We are interested in new plays." Limit cast to 8. No romantic comedies, family dramas, agit-prop.

Ⓐ INTIMAN THEATRE

201 Mercer St., Seattle WA 98109. (206)269-1901. Fax: (206)269-1928. E-mail: literary@intiman.org. Web site: www.intiman.org. Artistic Director: Bartlett Sher. **Contact:** Sheila Daniels. Estab. 1972. **Produces 6 plays/year.** LORT C Regional Theater in Seattle. Best submission time is October through March. *Agented submissions only* or by professional recommendation. Responds in 8 months.

Needs Well-crafted dramas and comedies by playwrights who fully utilize the power of language and character relationships to explore enduring themes. Prefers nonnaturalistic plays and plays of dynamic theatricality.

JEWEL BOX THEATRE

3700 N. Walker, Oklahoma City OK 73118-7099. (405)521-1786. Fax: (405)525-6562. **Contact:** Charles Tweed, production director. Estab. 1956. **Produces 6 plays/year.** Amateur productions. 3,000 season subscribers and general public. **Pays $500 contest prize.**

Needs Annual Playwriting Competition: Send SASE in September-October. Deadline: mid-January.

JEWISH ENSEMBLE THEATRE

6600 W. Maple Rd., West Bloomfield MI 48322. (248)788-2900. E-mail: e.orbach@jettheatre.org. Web site: www.jettheatre.org. **Contact:** Evelyn Orbach, artistic director. Estab. 1989. **Produces 4-6 plays/**

year. Professional productions at the Aaron DeRoy Theatre (season), The Detroit Institue of Arts Theatre, and Scottish Rite Cathedral Theatre (schools), as well as tours to schools. Submit complete script. Responds in 1 year. "Obtains rights for our season productions and staged readings for festival." **Pays 6-8% royalty for full production or honorarium for staged reading—$100/full-length play.**

Needs "We do few children's plays except original commissions; we rarely do musicals." Cast limited to a maximum of 8 actors.

Tips "We are a theater of social conscience with the following mission: to produce work on the highest possible professional level; to deal with issues of community & humanity from a Jewish perspective; to provide a platform for new voices and a bridge for understanding to the larger community."

KITCHEN DOG THEATER

3120 McKinney Ave., Dallas TX 75204. (214)953-2258. Fax: (214)953-1873. **Contact:** Chris Carlos, co-artistic director. Estab. 1990. **Produces 5 plays/year.** Kitchen Dog has two performance spaces: a 100-seat black box and a 150-seat thrust. Submit complete manuscript with SASE. Each year the deadline for submissions is March 1 (received by). Writers are notified by May 15. Buys rights to full production. **Pays $1,000 for winner of New Works Festival.**

Needs "We are interested in experimental plays, literary adaptations, historical plays, political theater, gay and lesbian work, culturally diverse work, and small musicals. Ideally, cast size would be 1-5, or more if doubling roles is a possibility." No romantic/light comedies or material that is more suited for television than the theater.

Tips "We are interested in plays that are theatrical and that challenge the imagination—plays that are for the theater, rather than TV or film."

KUMU KAHUA

46 Merchant St., Honolulu HI 96813. (808)536-4222. Fax: (808)536-4226. E-mail: kumukahuathea tre@hawaiiantel.net. Web site: kumukahua.org. **Contact:** Artistic Director. Estab. 1971. **Produces 5 productions, 3-4 public readings/year.** "Plays performed at new Kumu Kahua Theatre, flexible 120-seat theater, for community audiences." Submit complete script. Responds in 4 months. **Pays royalty of $50/performance; usually 20 performances of each production.**

Needs "Plays must have some interest for local Hawai'i audiences."

LILLENAS PUBLISHING CO.

P.O. Box 419527, Kansas City MO 64141-6527. (816)931-1900. Fax: (816)412-8390. Web site: www.lil lenasdrama.com. **Contact:** Kim Messer, product manager. Estab. 1926. "We publish on 2 levels: 1) Program Builders—seasonal and topical collections of recitations, sketches, dialogues, and short plays; 2) Drama Resources which assume more than 1 format: a) full-length scripts; b) one-acts, shorter plays, and sketches all by 1 author; c) collection of short plays and sketches by various authors. All program and play resources are produced with local church and Christian school in mind. Therefore there are taboos." Queries are encouraged, but synopses and complete scripts are read. Responds in 3 months. "First rights are purchased for Program Builders scripts. For Drama Resources, we purchase all print rights." **Drama Resources are paid on a 12% royalty, whether full-length scripts, one-acts, or sketches. No advance.**

- This publisher is interested in collections of and individual sketches. There is also a need for short pieces that are seasonal and on current events.

Needs 98% of Program Builders materials are freelance written. Scripts selected for these publications are outright purchases; verse is minimum of 25¢/line, prose (play scripts) are minimum of $5/double-spaced page. "Lillenas Drama Resources is a line of play scripts that are, for the most part, written by professionals with experience in productions as well as writing. While we do read unsolicited scripts, more than half of what we publish is written by experienced authors whom we have already published."

Tips "All plays need to be presented in standard play script format. We welcome a summary statement of each play. Purpose statements are always desirable. Approximate playing time, cast and prop lists, etc., are important to include. Contemporary settings generally have it over Biblical settings. Christmas and Easter scripts must have a bit of a twist. Secular approaches to these seasons (Santas, Easter bunnies, and so on), are not considered. We sell our product in 10,000 Christian bookstores and by catalog. We are in the forefront as a publisher of religious drama resources. Request a copy of our newsletter and/or catalog."

Ⓐ Ⓞ LONG WHARF THEATRE

222 Sargent Dr., New Haven CT 06511. (203)787-4284. Fax: (203)776-2287. Web site: www.long wharf.org. **Contact:** Literary Department. Estab. 1965. **Produces 6-8 plays/year.** Professional regional theater. *Agented submissions only.*

Needs Full-length plays, translations, adaptations. Special interest: Dramatic plays and comedies about human relationships, social concerns, ethical and moral dilemmas.

Tips "We no longer accept queries."

LOS ANGELES DESIGNERS' THEATRE

P.O. Box 1883, Studio City CA 91614-0883. E-mail: ladesigners@juno.com. **Contact:** Richard Niederberg, artistic director. Estab. 1970. **Produces 8-20 plays/year.** Professional shows/industry audience. Submit proposal only (i.e., 1 page in #10 SASE). Reports in 3 months (minimum) to submission. Purchases rights by negotiation, first refusal for performance/synchronization rights only. **Payment varies.**

- "We want highly commercial work without liens, 'understandings,' or promises to anyone."

Needs All types. No limitations—"We seek design challenges." No boring material. Shorter plays with musical underscores are desirable; nudity, street language, and political themes are OK."

MAGIC THEATRE

Fort Mason Center, Bldg. D, 3rd Floor, San Francisco CA 94123. (415)441-8001. Fax: (415)771-5505. E-mail: info@magictheatre.org. Web site: www.magictheatre.org. Artistic Director: Chris Smith. **Contact:** Mark Routhier, director of artistic development. Estab. 1967. **Produces 6 mainstage plays/year, plus monthly reading series and several festivals each year which contain both staged readings and workshop productions.** Regional theater. Bay area residents can send complete ms or query with cover letter, résumé, 1-page synopsis, SASE, dialogue sample (10-20 pages). Those outside the Bay area can query or submit through an agent. Responds in 6-8 months. **Pays royalty or per performance fee.**

Needs Plays that are innovative in theme and/or craft, cutting-edge sociopolitical concerns, intelligent comedy. Full-length only, strong commitment to multicultural work.

Tips "Not interested in classics, conventional approaches and cannot produce large-cast (over 10) plays. Send query to Mark Routhier, literary manager."

MALTHOUSE THEATRE

113 Sturt St., Southbank VIC 3006, Australia. (61)(3)9685-5100. Fax: (61)(3)9685-5111. E-mail: admin@malthousetheatre.com.au. Web site: www.malthousetheatre.com.au. **Contact:** Michael Kantor, artistic director. "We are dedicated to contemporary Australian theatre." Writers should have had at least 1 professional production of their work. Proposals are called for on March 1, July 1, and October 1. Mail 1-page synopsis, brief author bio, and 10-page sample. Responds in 3 months if interested.

Ⓐ Ø MANHATTAN THEATRE CLUB

311 W. 43rd St., 8th Floor, New York NY 10036. (212)399-3000. Fax: (212)399-4329. E-mail: questions @mtc-nyc.org. Web site: www.mtc-nyc.org. Director of Artistic Development: Paige Evans. **Contact:** Raphael Martin, literary manager. **Produces 7 plays/year.** 1 Broadway and 2 Off-Broadway theatres, using professional actors. *Solicited and agented submissions only.* No queries. Responds within 6 months.

Needs "We present a wide range of new work, from this country and abroad, to a subscription audience. We want plays about contemporary concerns and people. All genres are welcome. MTC also maintains an extensive play development program."

Ⓐ MCCARTER THEATRE

91 University Place, Princeton NJ 08540. E-mail: literary@mccarter.org. Web site: www.mccarter.org. Artistic Director: Emily Mann. **Contact:** Literary Manager. **Produces 5 plays/year; 1 second stage play/year.** Produces professional productions for a 1,077-seat and 360-seat theaters. Agented submissions only. Responds in 4-6 months. **Pays negotiable royalty.**

Needs Full length plays, musicals, translations.

MELBOURNE THEATRE COMPANY

129 Ferrars St., Southbank VIC 3006, Australia. (61)(3)9684-4500. Fax: (61)(3)9696-2627. E-mail: info@mtc.com.au. Web site: www.mtc.com.au. **Contact:** Simon Phillips, artistic director. "We are interested in timeless classics, modern classics, and the best new plays from Australia and overseas. Victorian work is given emphasis." Submissions are accepted February-October. Unsolicited scripts are only accepted if they satisfy 2 of these requirements: the author has had 1 script professionally produced or workshopped, the script is submitted by an agent, or the script is recommended by a professional theatre company or script development agency. Responds in 3 months.

MERIWETHER PUBLISHING, LTD.

885 Elkton Dr., Colorado Springs CO 80907-3557. Fax: (719)594-9916. E-mail: merpcds@aol.com. Web site: www.meriwether.com. President: Mark Zapel. Associate Editor: Arthur L. Zapel. **Contact:** Ted Zapel, associate editor. Estab. 1969. "We publish how-to theatre materials in book and video formats. We are interested in materials for middle school, high school, and college-level students only." Query with synopsis/outline, résumé of credits, sample of style, and SASE. Catalog available

for $2 postage. Responds in 1 month to queries; 2 months to full-length mss. **Offers 10% royalty.**

Needs Musicals for a large cast of performers, one-act or two-act comedy plays with large casts, and book mss on theatrical arts subjects. "We are now looking for scenebooks with special themes: scenes for young women, comedy scenes for 2 actors, etc. These need not be original, provided the compiler can get letters of permission from the original copyright owner. We are interested in all textbook candidates for theater arts subjects. Christian children's activity book manuscripts also accepted. We will consider elementary-level religious plays, but no elementary-level children's secular plays."

Tips "We publish a wide variety of speech contest materials for high-school students. We are publishing more full-length play scripts and musicals parodies based on classic literature or popular TV shows. Our educational books are sold to teachers and students at college and high-school levels. Our religious books are sold to youth activity directors, pastors, and choir directors. Another group of buyers is the professional theater, radio, and TV category. We will be especially interested in full-length (two- or three-act) plays with name recognition (either the playwright or the adaptation source)."

Ⓐ ⊘ METROSTAGE

1201 N. Royal St., Alexandria VA 22314. (703)548-9044. Fax: (703)548-9089. Web site: www.metros tage.org. **Contact:** Carolyn Griffin, producing artistic director. Estab. 1984. **Produces 5-6 plays/year.** Professional productions for 130-seat theatre, general audience. Agented submissions only. Responds in 3 months. **Pays royalty.**

Needs Contemporary themes, small cast (up to 6 actors), unit set.

Tips "Plays should have *already* had readings and workshops before being sent for our review. Do not send plays that have never had a staged reading."

NEBRASKA THEATRE CARAVAN

6915 Cass St., Omaha NE 68132. Fax: (402)553-6288. E-mail: info@omahaplayhouse.com. Web site: www.omahaplayhouse.com. Artistic Director: Carl Beck. **Contact:** Alena Furlong, development director. Estab. 1976. **Produces 4-5 plays/year.** "Nebraska Theatre Caravan is a touring company which produces professional productions in schools, arts centers, and small and large theaters for elementary, middle, high school and family audiences." Query and synopsis. Responds in 3 weeks. Negotiates production rights "unless the work is commissioned by us." **Pays $20-50 per performance.**

Needs "All genres are acceptable bearing in mind the student audiences. We are truly an ensemble and like to see that in our choice of shows; curriculum ties are very important for elementary and hich school shows; 75 minutes for middle/high school shows. No sexually explicit material."

Tips "We tour eight months of the year to a variety of locations. Flexibility is important as we work in both beautiful performing arts facilities and school multipurpose rooms."

THE NEW GROUP

410 W. 42nd St., New York NY 10036. (212)244-3380. Fax: (212)244-3438. E-mail: info@thenew group.org. Web site: www.thenewgroup.org. Artistic Director: Scott Elliott. **Contact:** Ian Morgan, associate artistic director. Estab. 1991. **Produces 4 plays/year.** Off-Broadway theater. Submit 10-page sample, cover letter, résumé, synopsis, and SASE. Responds in 9 months to submissions. **Pays royalty. Makes outright purchase.**

● No submissions that have already been produced in NYC.

Needs "We produce challenging, character-based scripts with a contemporary sensibility." Does not want to receive musicals, historical scripts or science fiction.

NEW JERSEY REPERTORY CO.

179 Broadway, Long Branch NJ 07740. (732)229-3166. Fax: (732)229-3167. Web site: www.njrep.org. Artistic Director: SuzAnne Barabas. **Contact:** Literary Manager. Estab. 1997. **Produces 6 plays/year and 25 script-in-hand readings.** Professional productions year round. Previously unproduced plays and musicals only. Submit script with SASE. Responds in 1 year. Rights negotiable.

Needs Full-length plays with a cast size no more than 5. Unit or simple set.

NEW PLAYS, INC.

P.O. Box 5074, Charlottesville VA 22905. (434)823-7555. E-mail: pat@newplaysforchildren.com. Web site: www.newplaysforchildren.com. **Contact:** Patricia Whitton Forrest, publisher. Estab. 1964. **Publishes 3-6 plays/year.** Publishes for children's or youth theaters. Submit complete script. Attempts to respond in 2 months, sometimes longer. Buys all semi-professional and amateur rights in US and Canada. **Pays 50% royalty on productions, 10% on sale of books.**

Needs "I have eclectic taste—plays must have quality and originality in whatever genres, topics, styles or lengths the playwright chooses."

Tips "No adaptations of stuff that has already been adapted a million times, i.e., *Tom Sawyer*, *A Christmas Carol*, or plays that sound like they've been written by the guidance counselor. There will be more interest in youth theater productions with moderate to large casts (15 people). Plays must have been produced and directed by someone other than the author or author's spouse. People keep sending us material suitable for adults—this is not our market. Read our online catalog."

NEW REPERTORY THEATRE

200 Dexter Ave., Waterton MA 02472. (617)923-7060. Fax: (617)923-7625. E-mail: artistic@newrep.org. Web site: www.newrep.org. **Contact:** Rick Lombardo, producing artistic director. Estab. 1984. **Produces 5 plays/year.** Professional theater, general audience. Query with synopsis and dialogue sample. Buys production and subsidiary rights. **Pays 5-10% royalty.**

Needs Idea laden, all styles, full-length only. New musicals.

Tips No sitcom-like comedies. Incorporating and exploring styles other than naturalism.

NEW STAGE THEATRE

1100 Carlisle, Jackson MS 39202. (601)948-3533. Fax: (601)948-3538. E-mail: mail@newstagetheatre.com. Web site: www.newstagetheatre.com. **Contact:** Artistic Director. Estab. 1965. **Produces 8 plays/year.** "Professional productions, 8 mainstage, 1 in our 'second space.' We play to an audience comprised of Jackson, the state of Mississippi and the Southeast." Query and synopsis. Exclusive premiere contract upon acceptance of play for mainstage production. **Pays 5-8% royalty. Pays $25-60 per performance.**

Needs Southern themes, contemporary issues, small casts (5-8), single set plays.

NEW THEATRE

4120 Laguna St., Coral Gables FL 33146. (305)443-5373. Fax: (305)443-1642. E-mail: tvodihn@new-theatre.org. Web site: www.new-theatre.org. **Contact:** Tara Vodihn, literary manager. Estab. 1986.

Produces 7 plays/year. Professional productions. Submit query and synopsis. Responds in 3-6 months. Rights subject to negotiation. **Payment negotiable.**

Needs Interested in full-length, non-realistic, moving, intelligent, language-driven plays with a healthy dose of humor. No musicals or large casts.

Tips "No kitchen sink realism. Send a simple query with synopsis. Be mindful of social issues."

NEW THEATRE

542 King St., Newtown NSW 2042, Australia. (61)(2)9519-3403. Fax: (61)(2)9519-8960. E-mail: new theatre@bigpond.com. Web site: www.newtheatre.org.au. **Contact:** Administrator. Estab. 1932. "We welcome the submission of new scripts." Submissions are assessed by playreaders and the artistic director. Submit complete ms and SASE.

NEW YORK STATE THEATRE INSTITUTE

37 First St., Troy NY 12180. (518)274-3200. Fax: (518)274-3815. E-mail: nysti@capital.net. Web site: www.nysti.org. **Contact:** Patricia DiBenedetto Snyder, producing artistic director. **Produces 6 plays/ year.** Professional regional productions for adult and family audiences. Query and synopsis. Responds in 6 weeks. **Payment varies.**

Needs "We are not interested in material for 'mature' audiences. Submissions must be scripts of substance and intelligence geared to family audiences."

Tips Do not submit complete script unless invited after review of synopsis.

NEW YORK THEATRE WORKSHOP

83 E. 4th St., New York NY 10003. Fax: (212)460-8996. Web site: nytw.org. Artistic Director: James C. Nicoloa. **Contact:** Literary Department. Estab. 1979. **Produces 6-7 full productions and approximately 50 readings/year.** Plays are performed off-Broadway. Audience is New York theater-going audience and theater professionals. Query with cover letter, synopsis, 10-page dialogue sample, 2 letters of recommendation. Include tape/CD/video where appropriate. Responds in 6-10 months.

Needs Full-length plays, translations/adaptations, music theater pieces; proposals for performance projects. Socially relevant issues, innovative form, and language.

Tips "No overtly commercial and conventional musicals or plays."

NORTH SHORE MUSIC THEATRE AT DUNHAM WOODS

P.O. Box 62, Beverly MA 01915. (978)232-7200. Fax: (978)921-7874. Web site: www.nsmt.org. Estab. 1955. **Produces 8 plays/year.** Plays are performed at Arena theater for 27,500 subscribers. Submit letter of interest, synopsis, production details, music tape/CD, SASE. Responds in 4 months. Rights negotiable. **Payment negotiable.**

Needs Musicals only (adult and children's), with cast size under 20.

Tips No straight plays, opera.

NORTHLIGHT THEATRE

9501 Skokie Blvd., Skokie IL 60077. (847)679-9501. Fax: (847)679-1879. Web site: www.northlight. org. **Contact:** Meghan Beals McCarthy, dramaturg. Estab. 1975. **Produces 5 plays/year.** "We are a professional, equity theater, LORT C. We have a subscription base of over 8,000 and have a significant number of single ticket buyers." Query with 10-page dialogue sample, synopsis, résumé/bio, and

SASE/SASPC for response. Responds in 3-4 months. Buys production rights, plus royalty on future mountings. **Pays royalty.**

Needs "Full-length plays, translations, adaptations, musicals. Interested in plays of 'ideas'; plays that are passionate and/or hilarious; accessible plays that challenge, incite, and reflect the beliefs of our society/community. Generally looking for cast size of 6 or fewer, but there are exceptions made for the right play."

Tips "As a mainstream regional theater, we are unlikely to consider anything overtly experimental or absurdist. We seek good stories, vivid language, rich characters, and strong understandings of theatricality."

THE O'NEILL PLAYWRIGHTS CONFERENCE

305 Great Neck Rd., Waterford CT 06385. (860)443-5378. Fax: (860)443-9653. E-mail: info@theoneil l.org; playwrights@theoneill.org. Web site: www.theoneill.org. **Contact:** Jill Mauritz, general manager. Estab. 1964. **Produces 7-8 plays/year.** The O'Neill Center theater is located in Waterford, Connecticut, and operates under an Equity LORT contract. There are 4 theaters: Barn—250 seats, Edith Oliver Theater—150 seats, Dina Merrill—188 seats. "Please send #10 SASE for guidelines in the fall, or check online." Decision by late April. We accept submissions September 1-October 1 of each year. Conference takes place during June/July each summer. Playwrights selected are in residence for one month and receive a four-day workshop and two script-in-hand readings with professional actors and directors. **Pays stipend plus room, board and transportation.**

EUGENE O'NEILL THEATER CENTER, O'NEILL MUSIC THEATER CONFERENCE

305 Great Neck Rd., Waterford CT 06385. (860)443-5378. Fax: (860)443-9653. Web site: www.oneill theatercenter.org. **Contact:** Jill A. Mauritz, general manager. Developmental process for new music theater works. Creative artists are in residence with artistic staff and equity company of actors/singers. Public and private readings, script in hand, piano only. For guidelines and application deadlines, send SASE to address above. **Pays stipend, room and board.**

ODYSSEY THEATRE ENSEMBLE

2055 S. Sepulveda Blvd., Los Angeles CA 90025. (310)477-2055. Fax: (310)444-0455. **Contact:** Sally Essex-Lopresti, director of literary programs. Estab. 1969. **Produces 9 plays/year.** Plays performed in a 3-theater facility. "All 3 theaters are Equity 99-seat theater plan. We have a subscription audience of 4,000 for a nine-play main season, and they are offered a discount on our rentals and co-productions. Remaining seats are sold to the general public." No unsolicited material. Query with résumé, synopsis, 10 pages of sample dialogue, and cassette if musical. Responds in 2 weeks. Buys negotiable rights. **Pays 5-7% royalty.** Does not return scripts without SASE.

Needs "Full-length plays only with either an innovative form and/or provocative subject matter. We desire highly theatrical pieces that explore possibilities of the live theater experience. We are not reading one-act plays or light situation comedies."

OMAHA THEATER CO./ROSE THEATER

2001 Farnam St., Omaha NE 68102. (402)345-9718. E-mail: jlarsonotc@msn.com. Web site: www.ro setheater.org. **Contact:** James Larson, artistic director. **Produces 6-10 plays/year.** "Our target audience is children, preschool-high school and their parents." Query and synopsis. Responds in 9 months. **Pays royalty.**

Needs "Plays must be geared to children and parents (PG rating). Titles recognized by the general public have a stronger chance of being produced." Cast limit: 25 (8-10 adults). No adult scripts.

Tips "Unproduced plays may be accepted only after a letter of inquiry (familiar titles only!)."

ONE ACT PLAY DEPOT

Box 335, Spiritwood Saskatchewan S0J 2M0, Canada. E-mail: submissions@oneactplays.net. Web site: oneactplays.net. Accepts unsolicited submissions only in February of each year. Submit complete script by mail or via e-mail as a plaintxt file or pasted into the body of the message.

Needs Interested only in one-act plays. Does not want musicals or farces. Do not mail originals. "Our main focus will be black comedy, along with well-written dramatic and comedic pieces."

Ⓐ Ⓞ OREGON SHAKESPEARE FESTIVAL

15 S. Pioneer St., Ashland OR 97520. Fax: (541)482-0446. Web site: www.osfashland.org. Artistic Director: Bill Rauch. **Contact:** Director of Literary Development and Dramaturgy. Estab. 1935. **Produces 11 plays/year.** OSF directly solicits playwright or agent, and does not accept unsolicited submissions.

PERTH THEATRE COMPANY

P.O. Box 3514, Adelaide Terrace, Perth WA 6832, Australia. (61)(8)9323-3433. Fax: (61)(8)9323-3455. E-mail: frontdesk@perththeatre.com.au. Web site: www.perththeatre.com.au. **Contact:** Alan Becher, artistic director. Estab. 1983. Seeks to develop new West Australian theatre and provide opportunities to talented local artists. Develops most of its scripts through the Writer's Lab program. Do not send an unsolicited ms unless it is submitted by or accompanied by a letter of recommendation from a writer's agency, script development organization, or professional theatre company. Make sure to include a SASE.

Ⓐ Ⓞ PHILADELPHIA THEATRE CO.

230 S. Broad St., Suite 1105, Philadelphia PA 19102. (215)985-1400. Fax: (215)985-5800. Web site: www.philadelphiatheatrecompany.org. **Contact:** Literary Office. Estab. 1974. **Produces 4 plays/year.** Agented submissions only. No e-mail submissions, letter of inquiry, summaries or excerpts please.

Needs Philadelphia Theatre Company produces contemporary American plays and musicals.

Tips "Our work is challenging and risky—look to our history for guidance."

PIONEER DRAMA SERVICE, INC.

P.O. Box 4267, Englewood CO 80155-4267. (303)779-4035. Fax: (303)779-4315. E-mail: submissions @pioneerdrama.com. Web site: www.pioneerdrama.com. Publisher: Steven Fendrich. **Contact:** Lori Conary, submissions editor. Estab. 1963. **Publishes 30 to 40 plays/year.** Plays are performed by schools, colleges, community theaters, recreation programs, churches, and professional children's theaters for audiences of all ages. Query or submit complete ms. Responds in about 2 weeks to queries; 4-6 months to submissions. Retains all rights. Buys All rights. **Pays royalty.**

● All submissions automatically entered in Shubert Fendrich Memorial Playwriting Contest.

Needs Comedies, mysteries, dramas, melodramas, musicals and children's theater. Two-acts up to 90 minutes; children's theater (1 hour); one-acts no less than 20 minutes. Prefers large ensemble casts with many female roles, simple sets, and costumes. Plays need to be appropriate for amateur groups and family audiences. Interested in adaptations of classics of public domain works appropriate for children and teens. Also plays that deal with social issues for teens and preteens.

Tips "Check out our Web site to see what we carry and if your material would be appropriate for our market. Make sure to include proof of productions and a SASE if you want your material returned."

PITTSBURGH PUBLIC THEATER

621 Penn Ave., Pittsburgh PA 15222. (412)316-8200. Fax: (412)316-8216. Web site: www.ppt.org. Artistic Director: Ted Pappas. **Contact:** Dramaturg. Estab. 1975. **Produces 7 plays/year.** O'Reilly Theater, 650 seats, thrust seating. Submit full script through agent, or query with synopsis, cover letter, 10-page dialogue sample, and SASE. Responds in 4 months.

Needs Full-length plays, adaptations and musicals.

PLAYSCRIPTS, INC.

325 W. 38th St., Suite 305, New York NY 10018. E-mail: submissions@playscripts.com. Web site: www.playscripts.com. Estab. 1998. Audience is professional, community, college, high school and children's theaters worldwide. See Web site for complete submission guidelines. Response time varies. Buys exclusive publication and performance licensing rights. **Pays negotiated book and production royalties.**

Needs "We are open to a wide diversity of writing styles and content. Musicals are not accepted."

Tips "Playscripts, Inc. is a play publishing company dedicated to new work by established and emerging playwrights. We provide all of the same licensing and book production services as a traditional play publisher, along with unique promotional features that maximize the exposure of each dramatic work. Be sure to view our guidelines before submitting."

PLAYWRIGHTS HORIZONS

416 W. 42nd St., New York NY 10036. (212)564-1235. Fax: (212)594-0296. Web site: www.playwright shorizons.org. Artistic Director: Tim Sanford. **Contact:** Adam Greenfield, literary manager (plays); send musicals Attn: Christie Evangelisto, Director of Musical Theater. Estab. 1971. **Produces 6 plays/ year.** Plays performed off-Broadway for a literate, urban, subscription audience. Submit complete ms with author bio; include CD for musicals. Responds in 6-8 months. Negotiates for future rights. **Pays royalty. Makes outright purchase.**

Needs "We are looking for new, full-length plays and musicals by American authors."

Tips "No adaptations, children's theater, one-person shows, biographical or historical plays. We dislike synopses because we accept unsolicited manuscripts. We look for plays with a strong sense of language and a clear dramatic action that truly use the resources of the theater."

ⒶPLAYWRIGHTS THEATRE OF NEW JERSEY

P.O. Box 1295, Madison NJ 07940-1295. (973)514-1787. Fax: (973)514-2060. Web site: www.ptnj.org. Artistic Director: John Pietrowski. **Contact:** Alysia Souder, director of program development. Estab. 1986. **Produces 3 plays/year.** "We operate under a Small Professional Theatre Contract (SPT), a development theatre contract with Actors Equity Association. Readings are held under a staged reading code." Responds in 1 year. "For productions we ask the playwright to sign an agreement that gives us exclusive rights to the play for the production period and for 30 days following. After the 30 days we give the rights back with no strings attached, except for commercial productions. We ask that our developmental work be acknowledged in any other professional productions.'' **Makes outright purchase of $750.**

- 10-page submission program has been discontinued. Accepts agented submission only.

Needs Any style or length; full length, one acts, musicals.

Tips ''We are looking for American plays in the early stages of development—plays of substance, passion, and light (comedies and dramas) that raise challenging questions about ourselves and our communities. We prefer plays *that can work only on the stage* in the most theatrical way possible— plays that are not necessarily 'straight-on' realistic, but rather ones that use imagery, metaphor, poetry and musicality in new and interesting ways. Plays can go through a 3-step development process: A roundtable, a concert reading, and then a workshop production.''

THE PLAYWRIGHTS' CENTER'S PLAYLABS

2301 Franklin Ave. E., Minneapolis MN 55406. (612)332-7481. Fax: (612)332-6037. E-mail: info@pw center.org. Web site: www.pwcenter.org. Producing Artistic Director: Polly K. Carl. Estab. 1971. ''PlayLabs is a 2-week developmental workshop for new plays. The program is held in Minneapolis and is open by script competition. Up to 5 new plays are given reading performances and after the festival, a script sample and contact link are posted on the Center's Web site. Announcements of playwrights by May 1. Playwrights receive honoraria, travel expenses, room and board.

Needs ''We are interested in playwrights with ambitions for a sustained career in theater, and scripts that could benefit from development involving professional dramaturgs, directors, and actors.'' US citizens or permanent residents only. Participants must attend entire festival. Submission deadline in October; see Web site for application and exact deadline. No previously produced materials.

PLAYWRIGHTS' PLATFORM

398 Columbus Ave., #604, Boston MA 02116. Web site: www.playwrightsplatform.org. **Contact:** Jerry Bisantz, producing director. Estab. 1972. **Produces approximately 50 readings/year.** Plays are read in staged readings at Hovey Players on Spring St. (Walthan MA). Accepts scripts on a face-to-face basis. Submit script and SASE (or e-mail or hand deliver). Responds in 2 months.

Needs Any types of plays. ''We will not accept scripts we think are sexist or racist.'' Massachusetts residents only. There are no restrictions on length or number of characters, but it's more difficult to schedule full-length pieces.

Ⓐ PLOWSHARES THEATRE CO.

2870 E. Grand Blvd., Suite 600, Detroit MI 48202-3146. (313)872-0279. Fax: (313)872-0067. Web site: www.plowshares.org. **Contact:** Gary Anderson, producing artistic director. Estab. 1989. **Produces 5 plays/year.** Professional productions of plays by African-American writers for African-American audience and those who appreciate African-American culture. *Agented submissions only.* Responds in 8 months.

Tips ''Submissions are more likely to be accepted if written by an African-American with the willingness to be developed. It must also be very good, and the writer should be ready to make a commitment.''

PORTLAND STAGE CO.

P.O. Box 1458, Portland ME 04104. (207)774-1043. Fax: (207)774-0576. E-mail: info@portlandsta ge.com. Web site: www.portlandstage.com. Artistic Director: Anita Stewart. **Contact:** Daniel Burson, literary manager. Estab. 1974. **Produces 7 plays/year.** Professional productions at Portland Stage Company. Send first 10 pages with synopsis. Responds in 3 months. Buys 3- or 4-week run in Maine. **Pays royalty.**

Needs Developmental Staged Readings: Little Festival of the Unexpected.

Tips "Work developed in Little Festival generally will be more strongly considered for future production."

ⓐ PRIMARY STAGES CO., INC.

131 W. 45th St., 2nd Floor, New York NY 10036. (212)840-9705. Fax: (212)840-9725. **Contact:** Tessa LaNeve, literary manager. Estab. 1985. **Produces 4 plays/year.** All plays are produced professionally off-Broadway at 59E59 Theatres' 199 seat theatre. Agented submissions only. **Pays flat fee.** Guidelines online.

Needs Full-length plays, small cast (6 or fewer) musicals. New York City premieres only. Small cast (1-6), unit set or simple changes, no fly or wing space.

Tips Best submission time: September-June. Chances: Over 1,000 scripts read, 4-5 produced. Women and minorities encouraged to submit.

PRINCE MUSIC THEATER

100 S. Broad St., Suite 650, Philadelphia PA 19110. (215)972-1000. Fax: (215)972-1020. Web site: www.princemusictheater.org. **Contact:** Marjorie Samoff, producing artistic director. Estab. 1984. **Produces 4 musicals/year.** Professional musical productions. Send synopsis and sample audio tape with no more than 4 songs. Responds in 6 months. **Pays royalty.**

Needs Song-driven music theater, varied musical styles. Nine in orchestra, 10-14 cast, 36x60 stage.

Tips Innovative topics and use of media, music, technology a plus. Sees trends of arts in technology (interactive theater, virtual reality, sound design); works are shorter in length (1-1 & ½ hours with no intermissions or 2 hours with intermission).

PRINCETON REP COMPANY

44 Nassau St., Suite 350, Princeton NJ 08542. E-mail: prcreprap@aol.com. Web site: www.princeton rep.org. **Contact:** New Play Submissions. Estab. 1984. Plays are performed in site-specific venues, outdoor amphitheatres, and indoor theatres with approximately 199 seats. "Princeton Rep Company works under Actors' Equity contracts, and its directors are members of the SSDC." Query with synopsis, SASE, résumé, and 10 pages of sample dialogue. Responds in up to 2 years. Rights are negotiated on a play-by-play basis. **Payment negotiated on a play-by-play basis.**

Needs Stories that investigate the lives of middle and working class people. Love stories of the rich, famous, and fatuous. "If the play demands a cast of thousands, please don't waste your time and postage." No drama or comedy set in a prep school or ivy league college.

THE PUBLIC THEATER

425 Lafayette St., New York NY 10003. (212)539-8500. Web site: www.publictheater.org. Artistic Director: Oskar Eustis. **Contact:** Literary Department. Estab. 1964. **Produces 6 plays/year.** Profes-

sional productions. Query with synopsis,10-page sample, letter of inquiry, cassette with 3-5 songs for musicals/operas. Responds in 1 month.

Needs Full-length plays, translations, adapatations, musicals, operas, and solo pieces. All genres, no one-acts.

☑ PULSE ENSEMBLE THEATRE

266 W. 36th St., 22nd Floor, New York NY 10018. (212)695-1596. Fax: (212)594-4208. E-mail: theatre @pulseensembletheatre.org. Web site: www.pulseensembletheatre.org. **Contact:** Brian Richardson. Estab. 1989. **Produces 3 plays/year.** No unsolicited submissions. Only accepts new material through the Playwright's Lab. Buys variable rights. **Usually pays 2% of gross.**

Needs Meaningful theater. No production limitations. Does not want to see fluff or vanity theater.

THE PURPLE ROSE THEATRE CO.

137 Park St., Chelsea MI 48118. (734)433-7782. Fax: (734)475-0802. Web site: www.purplerosethea tre.org. **Contact:** Guy Sanville, artistic director. Estab. 1990. **Produces 4 plays/year.** PRTC is a regional theater with an S.P.T. equity contract which produces plays intended for Midwest/Middle American audience. Query with synopsis, character breakdown, and 10-page dialogue sample. Responds in 9 months. **Pays 5-10% royalty.**

Needs Modern, topical full length, 75-120 minutes. Prefers scripts that use comedy to deal with serious subjects. 8 cast maximum. No fly space, unit set preferable. Intimate 168 seat ¾ thrust house.

QUEENSLAND THEATRE COMPANY

P.O. Box 3310, South Brisbane QLD 4101, Australia. (61)(7)3010-7600. Fax: (61)(7)3010-7699. E-mail: mail@qldtheatreco.com.au. Web site: www.qldtheatreco.com.au. **Contact:** Michael Gow, artistic director. Seeks timeless classics, modern classics, and new plays from Australia and overseas. Only considers unsolicited scripts if the playwright has had at least 1 play professionally produced, or if the script has been workshopped, submitted by an agent, or recommended by a professional theatre company or script development agency. Responds in 3 months.

Needs Works specifically aimed at child/youth audiences are less likely to be considered.

RED LADDER THEATRE CO.

3 St. Peter's Buildings, York St., Leeds LS9 1AJ, United Kingdom. (44)(113)245-5311. E-mail: ro d@redladder.co.uk. Web site: www.redladder.co.uk. **Contact:** Rod Dixon, artistic director. Estab. 1969. **Produces 2 plays/year.** "Our work tours nationally to young people, aged 13-25, in youth clubs, community venues and small scale theatres." Query and synopsis. Responds in 6 months. **Offers ITC/Equity writers contract.**

Needs One hour in length for cast size no bigger than 5. Work that connects with a youth audience that both challenges them and offers them new insights. "We consider a range of styles and are seeking originality." Small scale touring. Does not want to commission single issue drama. The uses of new technologies in production (DVD, video projection). Young audiences are sophisticated.

Tips "Please do not submit full length plays. Get in touch with us first. Tell us about yourself and why you would like to write for Red Ladder. We like to hear about ideas you may have in the first instance."

RESOURCE PUBLICATIONS

160 E. Virginia St., Suite 290, San Jose CA 95112-5876. (408)286-8505. Fax: (408)287-8748. E-mail: editor@rpinet.com. Web site: www.resourcepublications.com. Estab. 1973. Audience includes laity and ordained seeking resources (books/periodicals/software) in Christian ministry, worship, faith formation, education, and counseling (primarily Roman Catholic, but not all). Submit query and synopsis via e-mail. Responds in 3 months.

Needs Needs materials for those in pastoral ministry, faith formation, youth ministry, and parish administration. No fiction, children's books, or music.

ROUND HOUSE THEATRE

P.O. Box 30688, Bethesda MD 20824. (240)644-1099. Fax: (240)644-1090. Web site: www.round housetheatre.org. Producing Artistic Director: Blake Robison. **Contact:** Danisha Crosby, associate producer. **Produces 5-7 plays/year.** Professional AEA Theatre. Query with synopsis; no unsolicited scripts accepted. Responds in 2-12 months. **Pays negotiated percentage for productions.**

SALTWORKS THEATRE CO.

569 N. Neville St., Pittsburgh PA 15213. (412)621-6150. Fax: (412)621-6010. E-mail: nalrutz@saltwor ks.org. Web site: www.saltworks.org. **Contact:** Norma Alrutz, executive director. Estab. 1981. **Produces 8-10 plays/year.** Query and synopsis. Responds in 2 months. Obtains regional performance rights for educational grants. **Pays $25 per performance.**

Needs Wants plays for children, youth, and families that address social issues like violence prevention, sexual responsibility, peer pressures, tobacco use, bullying, racial issues/diversity, drug and alcohol abuse (grades 1-12). Limited to 5 member cast, 2 men/2 women/1 either.

Tips "Check Web site for current play contest rules and deadlines."

SEATTLE REPERTORY THEATRE

P.O. Box 900923, Seattle WA 98109. E-mail: bradena@seattlerep.org. Web site: www.seattlerep.org. Artistic Director: David Esbjornson. **Contact:** Braden Abraham, literary manager. Estab. 1963. **Produces 8 plays/year.** Send query, résumé, synopsis and 10 sample pages. Responds in 6 months. Buys percentage of future royalties. **Pays royalty.**

Needs "The Seattle Repertory Theatre produces eclectic programming. We welcome a wide variety of writing."

SECOND STAGE THEATRE

307 W. 43rd St., New York NY 10036. (212)787-8302. Fax: (212)397-7066. **Contact:** Sarah Bagley, literary manager. Estab. 1979. **Produces 6 plays/year.** Professional off-Broadway productions. Adult and teen audiences. Query with synopsis and 10-page writing sample or agented submission. Responds in 6 months. **Payment varies.**

Needs "We need socio-political plays, comedies, musicals, dramas—full lengths for full production."

Tips "No biographical or historical dramas, or plays in verse. Writers are realizing that audiences can be entertained while being moved. Patience is a virtue but persistence is appreciated."

SHAW FESTIVAL THEATRE

P.O. Box 774, Niagara-on-the-Lake ON L0S 1J0, Canada. (905)468-2153. Fax: (905)468-7140. Web site: www.shawfest.com. **Contact:** Jackie Maxwell, artistic director. Estab. 1962. **Produces 12 plays/**

year. "Professional theater company operating 3 theaters (Festival: 869 seats; Court House: 327 seats; Royal George: 328 seats). Shaw Festival presents the work of George Bernard Shaw and his contemporaries written during his lifetime (1856-1950) and in 2000 expanded the mandate to include contemporary works written about the period of his lifetime." Query with SASE or SAE and IRC's, depending on country of origin. "We prefer to hold rights for Canada and northeastern US, also potential to tour." **Pays 5-10% royalty.**

Needs "We operate an acting ensemble of up to 75 actors; and we have sophisticated production facilities. During the summer season (April-November) the Academy of the Shaw Festival organizes workshops of new plays commissioned for the company."

SOUTH COAST REPERTORY

P.O. Box 2197, Costa Mesa CA 92628-2197. (714)708-5500. Fax: (714)545-0391. Web site: www.scr.org. Artistic Directors: Martin Benson and David Emmes. **Contact:** Megan Monaghan, literary manager. Estab. 1964. **Produces 14 plays/year.** Professional nonprofit theater; a member of LORT and TCG. "We operate in our own facility which houses the 507-seat Segerstrom stage and 336-seat Julianne Argyros stage. We have a combined subscription audience of 18,000." Query with synopsis and 10 sample pages of dialogue, and full list of characters. Responds in 2-3 months on queries; 9-12 months on full scripts. Acquires negotiable rights. **Pays royalty.**

Needs "We produce full-length contemporary plays, as well as theatre for young audiences scripts with a running time of approximately 65 minutes. We prefer plays that address contemporary concerns and are dramaturgically innovative. A play whose cast is larger than 15-20 will need to be extremely compelling, and its cast size must be justifiable."

Tips "We don't look for a writer to write for us—he or she should write for him or herself. We look for honesty and a fresh voice. We're not likely to be interested in writers who are mindful of any trends. Originality and craftsmanship are the most important qualities we look for."

SOUTHERN APPALACHIAN REPERTORY THEATRE (SART)

Mars Hill College, P.O. Box 1720, Mars Hill NC 28754. (828)689-1384. E-mail: sart@mhc.edu. Managing Director: Rob Miller. Estab. 1975. **Produces 5-6 plays/year.** Since 1975 the Southern Appalachian Repertory Theatre has produced over 50 world premieres in the 166-seat Owen Theatre on the Mars Hill College campus. SART is a professional summer theater company whose audiences range from students to senior citizens. SART also conducts an annual playwrights conference in which 4-5 playwrights are invited for a weekend of public readings of their new scripts. The conference is held in March or May each year. Submissions must be postmarked by September 30. If a script read at the conference is selected for production, it will be given a fully-staged production in the following summer season. Playwrights receive honorarium and housing. Enclose SASE for return of script.

Needs Comedies, dramas and musicals. No screenplays, translations, or adaptations. Please send complete scripts of full-length plays and musicals, synopsis, and a recording of at least 4 songs (for musicals). Include name and contact information only on a cover sheet. New plays are defined as those that are unpublished and have not received a fully-staged professional production. "Workshops and other readings do not constitute a fully-staged production."

STAGE LEFT THEATRE

3408 N. Sheffield, Chicago IL 60657. (773)883-8830. E-mail: scripts@stagelefttheatre.com. Web site: www.stagelefttheatre.com. **Contact:** Kevin Heckman, producing artistic director. Estab. 1982. **Pro-**

duces 3-4 plays/year. Professional productions (usually in Chicago), for all audiences (usually adult). Submit script through an agent or query with cover letter, 10-page excerpt, 1-page synopsis, SASE, supporting material, and résumé. Responds in 3 months. **Pays 6% royalty.**

Needs "Any length, any genre, any style that fits the Stage Left mission—to produce plays that raise debate on political and social issues. We do have an emphasis on new work."

STAMFORD THEATRE WORKS

307 Atlantic St., Stamford CT 06901. (203)359-4414. Fax: (203)356-1846. E-mail: stwct@aol.com. Web site: www.stamfordtheatreworks.org. **Contact:** Steve Karp, producing director. Estab. 1988. **Produces 4-6 plays/year.** Professional productions for an adult audience. *Agented submissions* or queries with a professional recommendation. Responds in 3 months. **Pays 5-8% royalty.** Include SASE for return of submission.

Needs Plays of social relevance; contemporary work. Limited to unit sets; maximum cast of about 8.

STEPPENWOLF THEATRE CO.

758 W. North Ave., 4th Floor, Chicago IL 60610. (312)335-1888. Fax: (312)335-0808. Web site: www.steppenwolf.org. Artistic Director: Martha Lavey. **Contact:** Edward Sobel, director of new play development. Estab. 1976. **Produces 9 plays/year.** 500-, 250- and 100-seat performance venues. Many plays produced at Steppenwolf have gone to Broadway. "We currently have 20,000 savvy subscribers." Agented submissions only with full scripts. Others please check our Web site for submission guidelines. Unrepresented writers may send a 10-page sample along with cover letter, bio, and synopsis. Responds in 6-8 months. Buys commercial, film, television, and production rights. **Pays 5% royalty.**

Needs "Actor-driven works are crucial to us, plays that explore the human condition in our time. We max at around 10 characters."

Tips No musicals, one-person shows, or romantic/light comedies. Plays get produced at STC based on ensemble member interest.

STONEHAM THEATRE

395 Main St., Stoneham MA 02180. E-mail: weylin@stonehamtheatre.org. Web site: www.stoneham theatre.org. **Contact:** Weylin Symes, artistic director. Estab. 1999. **Produces 7 plays/year.** "Plays will be produced on-stage in our 350-seat SPT-7 theater—either as part of the Mainstage Season or our Emerging stages series of new works." Submit complete script via mail or e-mail. Responds in 3 months. Rights acquired varies according to script. **Pays royalty.**

Needs "Anything of quality will be considered. We look for exciting new work with a fresh voice, but that can still appeal to a relatively mainstream audience." Does not want anything with a cast size over 18 for a musical or 9 for a play.

STUDIO ARENA THEATRE

710 Main St., Buffalo NY 14202. (716)856-8025. E-mail: jblaha@studioarena.com. Web site: www.studioarena.org. **Contact:** Jana Blaha, executive assistant. Estab. 1965. **Produces 6-8 plays/year.** Professional productions. Agented submissions only.

Needs Full-length plays. No fly space.

Tips "Do not fax or send submissions via the Internet. Submissions should appeal to a diverse audience. We do not generally produce musicals. Please send a character breakdown and 1-page synopsis for a faster reply."

TADA!

15 W. 28th St., 3rd Floor, New York NY 10001. (212)252-1619. Fax: (212)252-8763. E-mail: jgreer@ta datheater.com. Web site: www.tadatheater.com. **Contact:** Literary Manager. Estab. 1984. **Produces 3 musical plays/year.** "TADA! produces original musicals performed by children and teens, ages 8-18. Productions are for family audiences." Submit a brief summary of the musical, 10 pages from the scripts, and a CD or cassette with songs from the score. Responds in 2-3 months. **Pays 5% royalty. Commission fee.**

- TADA! also sponsors an annual one-act playwriting contest for their Spring Staged Reading Series. Works must be original, unproduced and unpublished one-acts. Plays must be geared toward teen audiences. Call or e-mail for guidelines.

Needs Generally pieces run 1 hour long. Must be enjoyed by children and adults and performed by a cast of children ages 8-18.

Tips "No redone fairy tales or pieces where children are expected to play adults. Plays with animals and non-human characters are highly discouraged. Be careful not to condescend when writing for children's theater."

TEATRO VISIÓN

1700 Alum Rock Ave., Suite 265, San Jose CA 95116. (408)272-9926. Fax: (408)928-5589. E-mail: elisamarina@teatrovision.org. Web site: www.teatrovision.org. **Contact:** Elisa Marina Alvarado, artistic director. Estab. 1984. **Produces 3 plays/year.** Professional productions for a Latino population. Query with synopsis or submit complete ms. Responds in 6 months.

Needs "We produce plays by Latino playwrights—plays that highlight the Chicano/Latino experience."

THE TEN-MINUTE MUSICALS PROJECT

P.O. Box 461194, West Hollywood CA 90046. E-mail: info@tenminutemusicals.org. Web site: www. tenminutemusicals.org. **Contact:** Michael Koppy, producer. Estab. 1987. **Produces 1-10 plays/year.** "Plays performed in Equity regional theaters in the US and Canada." Deadline August 31; notification by November 30. Submit complete script, lead sheets and, cassette/CD. Buys first performance rights. **Pays $250 royalty advance upon selection, against equal share of performance royalties when produced.**

Needs Looking for complete short stage musicals lasting 7-14 minutes. Limit cast to 10 (5 women, 5 men).

THEATER AT LIME KILN

P.O. Box 1244, Lexington VA 24450. Web site: www.theateratlimekiln.com. Estab. 1984. **Produces 3 (1 new) plays/year.** Outdoor summer theater (May through October) and indoor space (October through May, 144 seats). Query and synopsis. Responds in 3 months. Buys performance rights. **Pays $25-75 per performance.**

Needs Plays that explore the history and heritage of the Appalachian region. Minimum set required.

Tips "Searching for plays that can be performed in outdoor space. Prefer plays that explore the cultural and/or history of the Appalichian region."

THEATER BY THE BLIND

306 W. 18th St., New York NY 10011. (212)243-4337. Fax: (212)243-4337. E-mail: gar@nyc.rr.com. Web site: www.tbtb.org. **Contact:** Ike Schambelan, artistic director. Estab. 1979. **Produces 2 plays/ year.** "Off Broadway, Theater Row, general audiences, seniors, students, disabled. If play transfers, we'd like a piece." Submit complete script. Responds in 3 months. **Pays $1,000-1,500/production. Needs** Genres about blindness.

THEATRE BUILDING CHICAGO

1225 W. Belmont Ave., Chicago IL 60657. (773)929-7367 ext. 222. Fax: (773)327-1404. E-mail: jsparks co@aol.com. Web site: www.theatrebuildingchicago.org. **Contact:** John Sparks, artistic director. **Produces mostly readings of new works, 4 skeletal productions, and Stages Festival.** "Mostly developed in our workshop. Some scripts produced are unagented submissions. Plays performed in 3 small off-Loop theaters are seating 148 for a general theater audience, urban/suburban mix." Submit synopsis, sample scene, CD or cassette tape and piano/vocal score of three songs, and author bios. Responds in 3 months.

Needs Musicals *only.* "We're interested in all forms of musical theater including more innovative styles. Our production capabilities are limited by the lack of space, but we're very creative and authors should submit anyway. The smaller the cast, the better. We are especially interested in scripts using a younger (35 and under) ensemble of actors. We mostly look for authors who are interested in developing their scripts through workshops, readings and production." No one-man shows or 'single author' pieces.

Tips "We would like to see the musical theater articulating something about the world around us, as well as diverting an audience's attention from that world." Offers Script Consultancy—A new program designed to assist authors and composers in developing new musicals through private feedback sessions with professional dramaturgs and musical directors. For further info contact (773)929-7367, ext. 222.

THEATRE IV

114 W. Broad St., Richmond VA 23220. (804)783-1688. Fax: (804)775-2325. E-mail: j.serresseque@ theatreivrichmond.org. Web site: www.theatreiv.org. **Contact:** Janine Serresseque. Estab. 1975. **Produces approximately 20 plays/year.** National tour of plays for young audiences—maximum cast of 5, maximum length of an hour. Mainstage plays for young audiences in 600 or 350 seat venues. Query and synopsis. Responds in 1 month. Buys standard production rights. **Payment varies.**

Needs Touring and mainstage plays for young audiences. Touring—maximum cast of 5, length of 60 minutes.

THEATRE THREE

P.O. Box 512, 412 Main St., Port Jefferson NY 11777-0512. (631)928-9202. Fax: (631)928-9120. Web site: www.theatrethree.com. **Contact:** Jeffrey Sanzel, artistic director. Estab. 1969. "We produce an Annual Festival of One-Act Plays on our Second Stage." Deadline for submission is September 30.

Send SASE for festival guidelines or visit Web site. Responds in 6 months. "We ask for exclusive rights up to and through the festival." **Pays $75 for the run of the festival.**

Needs One-act plays. Maximum length: 40 minutes. "Any style, topic, etc. We require simple, suggested sets and a maximum cast of 6. No adaptations, musicals or children's works."

Tips "Too many plays are monologue-dominant. Please—reveal your characters through action and dialogue."

Ⓐ THEATRE THREE

2800 Routh St., #168, Dallas TX 75201. (214)871-3300. Fax: (214)871-3139. E-mail: admin@theatre3dallas.com. Web site: theater3dallas.com. **Contact:** Jac Alder, executive producer-director. Estab. 1961. **Produces 7 plays/year.** Professional regional theatre, in-the-round. Audience is college age to senior citizens. Query with synopsis; agented submissions only. Responds in 6 months. **Contractual agreements vary.**

Needs Musicals, dramas, comedies, bills of related one-acts. Modest production requirement; prefer casts no larger than 10. Theatre Three also produces in a studio theatre (its former rehearsal hall) called Theatre Too. The space is variously configured according to demands of the show. Shows in that space include cabaret type revues, experimental work, dramas with small casts and staged readings or concert versions of musicals.

Tips No parodies or political commentary/comedy. Most produced playwrights at Theatre Three (to show "taste" of producer) are Moliere, Sondheim, Ayckbourne, Miller, Stoppard, Durang (moralists and irony-masters).

THEATRE WEST

3333 Cahuenga Blvd. W., Hollywood CA 90068-1365. (323)851-4839. Fax: (323)851-5286. E-mail: theatrewest@theatrewest.org. Web site: www.theatrewest.org. **Contact:** Chris DiGiovanni and Doug Haverty, moderators of the Writers Workshop. Estab. 1962. "99-seat waiver productions in our theater. Audiences are primarily young urban professionals." Residence in Southern California is vital as it's a weekly workshop. Submit script, résumé and letter requesting membership. Responds in 4 months. Contracts a percentage of writer's share to other media if produced on MainStage by Theatre West. **Pays royalty based on gross box office.**

Needs Full-length plays only, no one-acts. Uses minimalistic scenery, no fly space.

Tips "Theatre West is a dues-paying membership company. Only members can submit plays for production. So you must first seek membership to the Writers Workshop. We accept all styles of theater writing, but theater only—no screenplays, novels, short stories or poetry will be considered for membership."

THEATREWORKS

P.O. Box 50458, Palo Alto CA 94303. (650)463-1950. Fax: (650)463-1963. E-mail: kent@theatreworks.org. Web site: www.theatreworks.org. **Contact:** Kent Nicholson, new works director. Estab. 1970. **Produces 8 plays/year.** Specializes in development of new musicals. Plays are professional productions intended for an adult audience. Submit synopsis, 10 pages of sample dialogue, and SASE. Responds in 6-8 months. Buys performance rights. **Payment varies per contract.**

Needs TheatreWorks has a high standard for excellence. "We prefer well-written, well-constructed plays that celebrate the human spirit through innovative productions and programs inspired by our exceptionally diverse community. There is no limit on the number of characters, and we favor plays with multi-ethnic casting possibilities. We are a LORT C company. Plays are negotiated per playwright." Does not want one-acts, plays with togas. "We are particularly interested in plays with musical elements."

Tips "Guidelines are online—check out our Web site for Submission Checklist Request and the New Works Program under New Works."

⊘ THEATREWORKS/USA
151 W. 26th St., 7th Floor, New York NY 10001. (212)647-1100. Fax: (212)924-5377. Web site: www.twusa.org. Estab. 1961. **Produces 3-4 plays/year.** Professional equity productions for young audiences. Weekend series at Equitable Towers, NYC. Also, national and regional tours of each show. Submit query and synopsis only. *No unsolicited submissions.* Responds in 1 month. Obtains performing rights. **Pays 6% royalty.**

UNICORN THEATRE
3828 Main St., Kansas City MO 64111. (816)531-7529 ext. 23. Fax: (816)531-0421. Web site: www.unicorntheatre.org. Producing Artistic Director: Cynthia Levin. **Contact:** Herman Wilson, literary assistant. **Produces 6-8 plays/year.** "We are a professional Equity Theatre. Typically, we produce plays dealing with contemporary issues." Send complete script (to Herman Wilson) with brief synopsis, cover letter, bio, character breakdown. Send #10 SASE for results. Does not return scripts. Responds in 4-8 months.

Needs Prefers contemporary (post-1950) scripts. Does not accept musicals, one-acts, or historical plays. A royalty/prize of $1,000 will be awarded the playwright of any play selected through this process, The New Play Development Award. This script receives production as part of the Unicorn's regular season.

URBAN STAGES
17 E. 47th St., New York NY 10017. (212)421-1380. Fax: (212)421-1387. E-mail: urbanstage@aol.com. Web site: www.urbanstages.org. **Contact:** Frances Hill. Estab. 1986. **Produces 2-4 plays/year.** Professional productions off Broadway throughout the year. General audience. Submit complete script. Responds in 4 months. If produced, option for 1 year. **Pays royalty.**

- Enter Emerging Playwright Award competition. There is a reading fee of $10 per script. Prize is $1,000, plus NYC production.

Needs Full-length; generally 1 set or styled playing dual. Good imaginative, creative writing. Cast limited to 3-6.

Tips "We tend to reject 'living-room' plays. We look for imaginative settings. Be creative and interesting. No one acts. No e-mail submissions, scripts are not returned."

UTAH SHAKESPEAREAN FESTIVAL
New American Playwright's Project, 351 W. Center St., Cedar City UT 84720-2498. (435)586-7884. Fax: (435)865-8003. Founder/Executive Producer Emeritus: Fred C. Adams. **Contact:** Charles Metten, director. Estab. 1993. **Produces 9 plays/year.** Travelling audiences ranging in ages from 6-80. Programming includes classic plays, musicals, new works. Submit complete script; no synopsis. No musicals. Responds in 3-4 months. **Pays travel, housing, and tickets for USF productions only.**

Needs The USF is only interested in material that explores characters and ideas that focus on the West and our western experience, spirit, and heritage. Preference is given to writers whose primary residence is in the western United States. New plays are for staged readings only. These are not fully mountable productions. Cast size is a consideration due to the limited time of rehearsal and the actors available during the USF production period. Does not want plays that do not match criteria or plays longer than 90 pages.

Tips "We want previously unproduced plays with western themes by western playwrights."

WALNUT STREET THEATRE

Ninth and Walnut Streets, Philadelphia PA 19107. (215)574-3550. Fax: (215)574-3598. Producing Artistic Director: Bernard Havard. **Contact:** Literary Office. Estab. 1809. **Produces 10 plays/year.** "Our plays are performed in our own space. WST has 3 theaters—a proscenium (mainstage), 1,052 seats; and 2 studios, 79-99 seats. We have a subscription audience—the largest in the nation." Query with synopsis, 10-20 pages of dialogue, character breakdown, and bio. Include SASE for return of materials. Responds in 5 months. Rights negotiated per project. **Pays negotiable royalty or makes outright purchase.**

Needs Full-length dramas and comedies, musicals, translations, adaptations, and revues. The studio plays must have a cast of no more than 4 and use simple sets.

Tips "Bear in mind that on the mainstage we look for plays with mass appeal, Broadway-style. The studio spaces are our off-Broadway. No children's plays. Our mainstage audience goes for work that is entertaining and light. Our studio season is where we look for plays that have bite and are more provocative."

WILLOWS THEATRE CO.

1425 Gasoline Alley, Concord CA 94520. (925)798-1824. Fax: (925)676-5726. Web site: www.willows theatre.org. Artistic Director: Richard Elliott. **Produces 6 plays/year.** "Professional productions for a suburban audience." Accepts new manuscripts in March and April only; accepts queries year-round. Responds in 6-12 months to scripts. **Pays standard royalty.**

Needs "Commercially viable, small-medium size musicals or comedies that are popular, rarely produced, or new. Certain stylized plays or musicals with a contemporary edge to them (e.g., *Les Liasons Dangereuses, La Bete, Candide*)." No more than 15 actors. Unit or simple sets with no fly space, no more than 7 pieces. "We are not interested in 1-character pieces."

Tips "Our audiences want light entertainment, comedies, and musicals. Also, have an interest in plays and musicals with a historical angle." Submission guidelines are on Web site.

ⓐ THE WILMA THEATER

265 S. Broad St., Philadelphia PA 19107. (215)893-9456. Fax: (215)893-0895. E-mail: wcb@wilma theater.org. Web site: www.wilmatheater.org. **Contact:** Walter Bilderback, dramaturg and literary manager. Estab. 1980. **Produces 4 plays/year.** LORT-C 300-seat theater, 7,500 subscribers. *Agented submissions only* for full mss. Accepts queries with cover letter, résumé, synopsis, and sample if recommended by a literary manager, dramaturg, or other theater professional. Responds in 6 months.

Needs Full-length plays, translations, adaptations, and musicals from an international repertoire with emphasis on innovative, bold staging; world premieres; ensemble works; works with poetic dimension; plays with music; multimedia works; social issues, particularly the role of science in our lives. Prefers maximum cast size of 12. Stage 44′ × 46′.

Tips "Before submitting any material to The Wilma Theater, please research our production history. Considering the types of plays we have produced in the past, honestly assess whether or not your play would suit us. In general, I believe researching the various theaters to which you send your play is important in the long and short run. Different theaters have different missions and therefore seek out material corresponding with those goals. In other words, think through what is the true potential of your play and this theater, and if it is a compatible relationship."

WOMEN'S PROJECT AND PRODUCTIONS

55 West End Ave., New York NY 10023. (212)765-1706. Fax: (212)765-2024. Web site: www.womens project.org. **Contact:** Megan E. Carter, Associate Artistic Director. Estab. 1978. **Produces 3 plays/ year.** Professional Off-Broadway productions. Please see Web site for submission guidelines.

Needs "We are looking for full-length plays written by women."

Ⓐ WOOLLY MAMMOTH THEATRE CO.

641 D St. NW, Washington DC 20004. (202)289-2443. E-mail: elissa@woollymammoth.net. Web site: www.woollymammoth.net. Artistic Director: Howard Shalwitz. **Contact:** Elissa Goetschius, literary manager. Estab. 1980. **Produces 5 plays/year.** Produces professional productions for the general public. Solicited submissions only. Responds in 6 months to scripts; very interesting scripts often take much longer. Buys first- and second-class production rights. **Pays variable royalty.**

Needs "We look for plays with a distinctive authorial voice. Our work is word and actor driven. One-acts and issue-driven plays are not used." Cast limit of 5.

Production Companies

Writers do not often get into screenwriting for the fame. Most of the glory shines on the directors, actors and actresses. But every great movie and TV show relies upon a great script that was crafted by a screenwriter.

Writing for TV

To break into TV you must have spec scripts—work written for free that serves as a calling card and gets you in the door. A spec script showcases your writing abilities and gets your name in front of influential people. Whether a network has invited you in to pitch some ideas, or a movie producer has contacted you to write a first draft for a feature film, the quality of writing in your spec script got their attention and that may get you the job.

Writing for the movies

An original movie script contains characters you have created, with story lines you design, allowing you more freedom than you have in TV. However, your writing must still convey believable dialogue and realistic characters, with a plausible plot and high-quality writing carried through roughly 120 pages.

Many novice screenwriters tend to write too many visual cues and camera directions into their scripts. Your goal should be to write something readable, like a "compressed novella." Write succinct resonant scenes and leave the camera technique to the director and producer.

+ENTERTAINMENT
468 N. Camden Drive, Suite 250, Beverly Hills CA 90210. Web site: www.plusent.com. Distribution credits include *Mexican Bloodbath*, *Zoo Safari*, *Three Cultures of Appalachia: Women of These Hills II*.

@RADICAL.MEDIA
435 Hudson Street, New York NY 10014. (212)462-1500. Fax: (212)462-1600. Web site: www.radicalmedia.com.

100% TERRY CLOTH
421 Waterview Street, Playa Del Ray CA 90293. (310)823-3432. Fax: (310)861-9093. E-mail: TM@terencemichael.com. Web site: www.terencemichael.com.

1492 PICTURES
4000 Warner Blvd., Bldg. 139, Room 118, Burbank CA 91522. (818)954-4929.

2929 PRODUCTIONS
9100 Wilshire Blvd., Beverly Hills CA 90212. (310)309-5200. Fax: (310)309-5716. E-mail: kkelly@2929entertainment.com. Web site: www.2929productions.com.

3 ARTS ENTERTAINMENT
9460 Wilshire Blvd., 7th Floor, Beverly Hills CA 90212. (310)888-3200. Fax: (310)888-3210. Production credits include *I Am Legend*, *The Onion Movie*, ''The Starter Wife.''

3 BALL PRODUCTIONS
1600 Rosecrans Ave., Bldg. 7, 2nd Floor, Manhattan Beach CA 90266. (310)727-3337. Fax: (310)727-3339. Web site: www.3ballproductions.com.

3 RING CIRCUS FILMS
1040 N. Sycamore Ave., Hollywood CA 90038. (323)466-5300. Fax: (323)466-5310. E-mail: info@3ringcircus.tv. Web site: www.3ringcircus.tv. Production credits include *One*, *Cherish*, *Dream With the Fishes*.

3AM PICTURES
P.O. Box 639, San Gabriel CA 91778. (626)285-0005. Web site: www.3ampictures.com.

3N1 ENTERTAINMENT
11726 San Vicente Blvd., Suite 360, Los Angeles CA 90049. (310)773-1147. Fax: (310)571-9216. E-mail: info@3n1ent.com. Web site: www.3n1ent.com.

40 ACRES & A MULE FILMWORKS
75 S. Elliot Place, Third Floor, Brooklyn NY 11217. (718)624-3703. This production company is run by filmmaker Spike Lee. It has been in operation since the early 1990s.

44 BLUE PRODUCTIONS

4040 Vineland Ave., Suite 105, Studio City CA 91604. (818)760-4442. Fax: (818)760-1509. E-mail: reception@44blue.com. Web site: www.44blue.com.

4KIDS ENTERTAINMENT, INC.

1414 Avenue of the Americas, New York NY 10019. Web site: www.4kidsentertainmentinc.com. This company focuses on material for kids and youngsters.

○━ This market acquires properties that entertain and inform kids.

51 MINDS ENTERTAINMENT

6565 Sunset Blvd., Suite 301, Los Angeles CA 90028. (323)466-9200. E-mail: info@51minds.com. Web site: www.51minds.com.

57TH & IRVING PRODUCTIONS

645 Madison Ave., Suite 9B, New York NY 10022. (212)995-0057. E-mail: info@57irving.com. Web site: www.57irving.com.

72 PRODUCTIONS

8332 Melrose Avenue, 2nd Floor, Los Angeles CA 90069. (323)651-1511. Fax: (323)651-1555. Web site: www.72productions.com.

9.14 PICTURES

No public address available. (215)238-0707. Fax: (215)238-0663. E-mail: info@914pictures.com. Web site: www.914pictures.com.

900 FILMS

1203 Activity Dr., Vista CA 92081. (760)477-2470. Fax: (760)477-2478. E-mail: irene@900films.com. Web site: www.900films.com.

A BAND APART

7966 Beverly Blvd., Los Angeles CA 90048. (323)951-4600. Web site: www.dsire.com/archive/aba/swf/Base.html. *Kill Bill: Vol. 2* and *Dirty Dancing: Havana Nights*. This is the production company for Writer/Director Quentin Tarantino.

A&E TELEVISION NETWORKS

235 E. 45th St., New York NY 10017. (212)210-1400. Web site: www.aetv.com/.

ABANDON ENTERTAINMENT

135 W. 50th St., Ste 2305, New York NY 10020. (212)246-4445. Web site: www.abandonent.com/. **Contact:** Marcus Ticotin. Credits include *Oxygen*.

ABERRATION FILMS

311 N. Robertson Blvd., #737, Beverly Hills CA 90211. (310)385-0585. E-mail: aberrationfilms@yahoo.com. Web site: www.aberrationfilms.com.

ACAPELLA PICTURES

8271 Melrose Ave., Ste. 101, Los Angeles CA 90046. (323)782-8200. Fax: (323)782-8210. Credits include *The Brave* and *The House of Mirth*.

ACORN ENTERTAINMENT

5777 W. Century Blvd., Los Angeles CA 90045. (818)340-5272. E-mail: info@acornentertainment. com. Web site: www.acornentertainment.com.

ACT III PRODUCTIONS

100 N. Crescent Dr., Ste. 250, Beverly Hills CA 90210. (310)385-4111. Fax: (310)385-4148. Credits include *Fried Green Tomatoes* and *704 Hauser*. This is the production company for producer Norman Lear.

ACTUAL REALITY PICTURES

6725 W. Sunset Blvd., Suite 350, Los Angeles CA 90028. (310)202-1272. Fax: (310)202-1502. E-mail: questions@arp.tv. Web site: www.actualreality.tv.

ADAM PRODUCTIONS

11777 San Vincente Blvd., Ste. 880, Los Angeles CA 90040. (310)442-3580.

ADIRONDACK PICTURES

267 W 17th Street, 2nd Floor, New York NY 10011. (212)343-2405. E-mail: info@adirondackpics.com. Web site: www.adirondackpics.com.

AEI—ATCHITY ENTERTAINMENT INTERNATIONAL, INC.

518 S. Fairfax Avenue, Los Angeles CA 90036. (323)932-0407. E-mail: submissions@aeionline.com. Web site: www.aeionline.com.

AFTERBURNER FILMS, INC.

No public address available. (818)980-0488. Fax: (818)980-0489. E-mail: info@afterburnerfilms.com. Web site: www.afterburnerfilms.com.

AGAMEMNON FILMS INC.

650 N. Bronson Ave., Ste. B-225, Los Angeles CA 90004. (323)960-4066. Credits include *Treasure Island* and *The Bible*.

ALCHEMY TELEVISION GROUP

8530 Wilshire Blvd., Suite 400, Beverly Hills CA 90211. (310)289-7766. Fax: (310)289-7833. E-mail: sales@alchemy.tv. Web site: www.alchemy.tv.

ALCON ENTERTAINMENT

10390 Santa Monica Blvd., Ste. 250, Los Angeles CA 90025. (310)789-3040. Fax: (310)789-3060. Credits include *My Dog Skip* and *Insomnia*.

ALL GIRL PRODUCTIONS

10153 Riverside Dr., Ste. 249, Toluca Lake CA 91602. (818) 358-4100. Fax: (818) 358-4119. Credits include *Beaches* and *Divine Secrets of the Ya-Ya Sisterhood*. This is the production company for actress Bette Midler.

ALLIANCE ATLANTIS COMMUNICATIONS CORPORATION

808 Wilshire Blvd., Ste. 300, Santa Monica CA 90401. (310)899-8000. Fax: (310)899-8100. E-mail: info@allianceatlantis.com. Web site: www.allianceatlantis.com/motionpictures. Credits include *Formula 51* and *Joan of Arc*.

⊘ ALLIANCE FILMWORKS

9595 Wilshire Blvd., Suite 900, Beverly Hills CA 90212. Web site: www.alliancefilmworks.com. Estab. 2001. Produces 3 movies/year. *Alliance is not accepting unsolicited TV or film submissions, screenplays, pitches, log lines or treatments at this time.* **Pays option; makes outright purchase.**

⎯ Produces all genres. Budgets are $1.5 million +.

ALLIED ARTISTS, INC.

9360 W. Flamingo Rd., Unit 110-189, Las Vegas NV 89147. (702)991-9011. E-mail: query@alliedartistsonline.com. Web site: www.alliedartistsonline.com. Estab. 1990. Produces material for broadcast and cable television, home video, and film. **Buys 3-5 script(s)/year. Works with 10-20 writer(s)/year.** Buys first or all rights. Accepts previously produced material. Submit synopsis, outline. Responds in 2 months to queries; 3 months to scripts. **Pays in accordance with WGA standards.**

Needs Films, videotapes, social issue TV specials (30-60 minutes), special-interest home video topics, positive values feature screenplays.

Tips "We are looking for positive, uplifting dramatic stories involving 'real people' situations. Future trend is for more reality-based programming, as well as interactive television programs for viewer participation. Send brief e-mail query only. Do not send scripts or additional material until requested. No phone pitches accepted."

ALLIED ENTERTAINMENT GROUP

8899 Beverly Blvd., Ste. 911, West Hollywood CA 90048. (310)271-0703. Fax: (310)271-0706. E-mail: info@alliedentertainment.com. Web site: www.alliedentertainment.com/screencaps/baron-index.php.

ALPHAVILLE

5555 Melrose Ave., DeMille Bldg., Hollywood CA 90038. (323)956-4803. Credits include *Rat Race* and *The Mummy*. This is the production company for Sean Daniel and Jim Jacks.

ALTITUDE ENTERTAINMENT

No public address available. (323)230-9539. E-mail: kyle@altitudeentertainment.com. Web site: www.altitudeentertainment.com.

ALTURAS REDFISH FILMS

1617 Broadway 2nd Floor, Santa Monica CA 90404. (310)401-6200. Fax: (310)822-7565. E-mail: info@alturasfilms.com. Web site: www.alturasfilms.com.

AM PRODUCTIONS & MANAGEMENT

8899 Beverly Blvd., Ste. 713, Los Angeles CA 90048. (310)275-9081. Fax: (310)275-9082. Credits include *Any Given Sunday* and *Driven*. This is the production company for actors Ann-Margret and Burt Reynolds.

AMBUSH ENTERTAINMENT

7364½ Melrose Ave, Los Angeles CA 90046. (323)951-9197. Fax: (323)951-9998. E-mail: info@ambus hentertainment.com. Web site: www.ambushentertainment.com.

AMEN RA

520 Washington Blvd., #813, Marina del Rey CA 90292. (310)246-6510. Fax: (310)550-1932. Credits include *Blade: The Bloodhunt* and *The Art of War*. This is the production company for actor Wesley Snipes.

AMERICAN BLACKGUARD, INC.

P.O. Box 680686, Franklin TN 37068. (615)599-4032. E-mail: contact@americanblackguard.com. Web site: www.americanblackguard.com.

AMERICAN CINEMA INTERNATIONAL

15363 Victory Blvd., Van Nuys CA 91406. (818)907-8700. Fax: (818)907-8719. E-mail: Laura@aci-americancinema.com. Web site: aci-americancinema.com/main.htm. **Contact:** Laura Voros. Credits include *The Accidental Witness* and *The Boxer*.

AMERICAN EMPIRICAL PRODUCTIONS

36 E. 23rd St., 6th Fl., New York NY 10010. (212)475-1771. Credits include *The Royal Tennenbaums* and *Rushmore*. This is the production company for writer/director Wes Anderson.

AMERICAN ENTERTAINMENT CO.

5225 Wilshire Blvd., #615, Los Angeles CA 90036. (323)939-6746. Fax: (323)939-6747. Credits include *Frailty*. This is the production company for actor Bill Paxton.

AMERICAN WORLD PICTURES, INC.

16027 Ventura Blvd., Suite 320, Encino CA 91436. (818)380-9100. Fax: (818)380-0050. E-mail: jaso n@americanworldpictures.com. Web site: www.americanworldpictures.com. **Contact:** Jason Corey, acquisitions. **Buys 4 script(s)/year. Works with 5 writer(s)/year.** Buys all rights. Accepts previously produced material. Query. Responds in 2 months to queries; 3 months to scripts. **Pays only $15,000 for scripts. Do not contact if price is more than that.**

☌ Needs feature-length films. Send DVD/VHS to the Acquisitions Department.

Tips "Use strong characters and strong dialogue."

AMERICAN ZOETROPE

916 Kearny St., San Francisco CA 94133. Web site: www.zoetrope.com.

AMSELL ENTERTAINMENT

12001 Ventura Pl., Ste. 404, Studio City CA 91604. (818)766-8500. Fax: (818)766-7873. E-mail: amsellent@sbcglobal.net. Web site: www.amsellentertainment.com/contact.htm. Credits include numerous action, martial arts, and horror films.

CRAIG ANDERSON PRODUCTIONS

444 N. Larchmont Blvd., Suite 109, Los Angeles CA 90004. (323)463-2000. Fax: (323)463-2022. E-mail: www.cappix.com. Web site: info@cappix.com.

ANGEL ARK PRODUCTIONS

12711 Ventura Blvd., Ste. 330, Studio City CA 91604. (818)508-3338. Fax: (818)508-2009. Credits include *Shallow Hal* and *Agent Cody Banks*. This is the production company for actor Jason Alexander.

ANGEL/BROWN PRODUCTIONS

1416 N. La Brea, Bldg. E, 2nd Fl., Hollywood CA 90028. (323)802-1535. Credits include *X-Files* and *Battlestar Galactica*.

ANGRY DRAGON ENTERTAINMENT

10202 Washington Blvd., Culver City CA 90232. (310)244-6996. **Contact:** Dean Cain. This is the production company for Dean Cain. Credits include *Ripley's Believe It Or Not* and *Dragon Fighter*.

ANGRY FILMS, INC.

10202 Washington Blvd., Poitier 3206, Culver City CA 90232. (310)244-7590. Fax: (310)244-2060. **Contact:** Don Murphy, Producer. Credits include *The League of Extraordinary Gentlemen* and *Shoot 'em Up*.

ANIMUS FILMS

914 Hauser Boulevard, Los Angeles CA 90036. (323)571-3302. Fax: (323)571-3361. E-mail: info@animusfilms.com. Web site: www.animusfilms.com.

ANTIDOTE FILMS

200 Varick Street, Suite 502, New York NY 10014. (646)486-4344. Fax: (646)486-5885. E-mail: info@antidotefilms.com. Web site: www.antidotefilms.com.

APATOW PRODUCTIONS

2900 W. Olympic Blvd., Ste. 141, Santa Monica CA 90404. (310)255-7026. Fax: (310)255-7025. Credits include *Forgetting Sarah Marshall*, *Talladega Nights: the Ballad of Ricky Bobby*, and *The 40-Year-Old Virgin*.

APOSTLE

568 Broadway, Suite 301, New York NY 10012, United States. (212)541-4323. Fax: (212)541-4330. Web site: www.apostlenyc.com.

APOSTLE PICTURES
The Ed Sullivan Theater, 1697 Broadway, Ste. 906, New York NY 10019. (212)541-4323. E-mail: apostlepix@aol.com. This is the production company of actor Denis Leary. Credits include *Blow*, *Monument Avenue*, and *Rescue Me*.

APPLESEED ENTERTAINMENT
9801 Amestay Ave., Los Angeles CA 91325. (818)718-6000. Fax: (818)993-8720. E-mail: films@apple seedent.com. Web site: www.appleseedent.com. Credits include *Good Morning, Vietnam* and *Hope Ranch*.

APRIL FILMS
725 Arizona Ave., Suite 200, Santa Monica CA 90401. (310)394-1000. E-mail: info@aprilfilms.com. Web site: www.aprilfilms.com.

ARAMA ENTERTAINMENT, INC.
18034 Ventura Blvd., Ste. 435, Encino CA 91316. (818)788-6400. Fax: (818)990-9344. E-mail: ara maent@aol.com. **Contact:** Shimon Arama. Credits include *The Heist*, *Black Eagle* and *Triumph of the Spirit*.

ARCLIGHT FILMS
9229 Sunset Blvd., Suite 705, Los Angeles CA 90069. (310)777-8855. E-mail: info@arclightfilms.com. Web site: www.arclightfilms.com.

ARDEN ENTERTAINMENT
12034 Riverside Drive, Suite 200, N. Hollywood CA 91607. (818)985-4600. Fax: (818)985-3021. E-mail: chris@ardenentertainment.com. Web site: www.ardenentertainment.com.

ARLINGTON ENTERTAINMENT
9200 Sunset Blvd., Ste. 1209, Los Angeles CA 90069. (310) 247-1863. Fax: (310) 247-1864. Credits include *Masks of Death* and *Murder Elite*.

ARROW FILMS INTERNATIONAL
57 W. 38th St., Ste. 302, New York NY 10036. (212) 719-4548. Fax: (212) 719-4549. Credits include *Restless*, *Day at the Beach*.

ARS NOVA
511 West 54th Street, New York NY 10019, United States. (212)489-9800. Fax: (212)489-1908. E-mail: info@arsnovanyc.com. Web site: www.arsnovanyc.com.

ARTICLE 19 FILMS
247 Centre Street, 7th Floor, New York NY 10013. (212)777-1987. Fax: (212)777-2585. E-mail: in fo@article19films.com. Web site: www.article19films.com.

ARTISAN ENTERTAINMENT

2700 Colorado Ave., 2nd Fl., Santa Monica CA 90404. (310)449-9200. Web site: www.artisanent.com. Credits include *Requiem for a Dream*, *The Blair Witch Project* and *Buena Vista Social Club*.

ARTIST VIEW ENTERTAINMENT

4425 Irvine Ave., Studio City CA 91602. (818)752-2480. Fax: (818)752-9339. E-mail: info@artistvie went.com. Web site: www.artistviewent.com. Credits include *13th Child—Legend of the Jersey Devil*, *48 Angels* and *Arizona Summer*.

THE ARTISTS' COLONY

256 S. Robertson Blvd., Ste. 1500, Beverly Hills CA 90211. (310) 720-8300. E-mail: mail@theartistsco lony.com. **Contact:** David Donnelly. Credits include *12*, *Solid Ones*, and *Snow Falling on Cedars*.

ASCENDANT PICTURES

406 Wilshire Blvd., Santa Monica CA 90401. (310)288-4600. Fax: (310)288-4601. E-mail: info@ascen dantpictures.com. Web site: www.ascendantpictures.com.

ASGAARD ENTERTAINMENT

9320 Wilshire Blvd., Ste. 202, Beverly Hills CA 90212. (310)246-0942. Fax: (310)774-3919. E-mail: info@asgaardentertainment.com. Web site: www.asgaardentertainment.com.

ASIS PRODUCTIONS

200 N. Larchmont Blvd., Ste. 2, Los Angeles CA 90004. (323)871-4290. Fax: (323)871-4847. This is the production company of actor Jeff Bridges. Credits include *American Heart* and *Hidden in America*.

ASSOCIATED TELEVISION INTERNATIONAL

4401 Wilshire Blvd., Los Angeles CA 90010. (323)556-5600. Fax: (323)556-5610. E-mail: sales@ati.la. Web site: www.associatedtelevision.com. Credits include *The Curse of the Black Dahlia*, *The Trip*, and *The Lost Samurai*.

ASYLUM ENTERTAINMENT

7920 Sunset Blvd., Second Floor, Los Angeles CA 90046. (310)696-4600. Fax: (310)696-4891. Web site: www.asylument.com.

ATELIER PICTURES

280 S. Beverly Dr. #500, Beverly Hills CA 90212. E-mail: atelierpictures@yahoo.com. Web site: ww w.atelierpix.com. Credits include *Please Don't Walk Around in the Nude*, *Starfish*, *Everyman*.

ATLANTIC STREAMLINE

1323-A Third St., Santa Monica CA 90401. (310)319-9366. E-mail: info@atlanticstreamline.com. Cred its include *Igby Goes Down*, *The Thirteenth Floor*, *All the Queen's Men*.

ATLAS ENTERTAINMENT

9169 Sunset Blvd., Los Angeles CA 90069. (310)724-7350. Fax: (310)724-7345. Producer: Charles Roven. Credits include *12 Monkeys*, *Three Kings*, *Scooby Doo 2: Monsters Unleashed*.

ATLAS MEDIA CORPORATION

242 West 36th Street, New York NY 10018. (212)714-0222. Fax: (212)714-0240. E-mail: info@atlasmediacorp.com. Web site: www.atlasmediacorp.com.

ATMAN ENTERTAINMENT

7966 Beverly Blvd., 3rd Fl., Los Angeles CA 90048. (323)951-4600. E-mail: mail@atmanentertainment.com. Web site: www.atmanentertainment.com. **Contact:** Ross Grayson Bell. Credits include *Fight Club* and *Under Suspicion*.

ATMOSPHERE ENTERTAINMENT MM, LLC

9200 Sunset Blvd., 5th Fl., Los Angeles CA 90069. (310)860-5451. Fax: (310)860-0410. Web site: www.atmospheremm.com. **Contact:** Mark Canton. Credits include *300*, *The Spiderwick Chronicles*, *Land of the Dead*.

ATTRACT MEDIA

133 Wagstaff Ln., Jacksdale, Nottingham NG16 5JN England. E-mail: scripts@attract.co.uk.

AURORA PRODUCTIONS

8642 Melrose Ave., Ste. 200, Los Angeles CA 90069. (310)854-6900. Fax: (310)854-0583. Credits include *The Secret of NIMH*, *Eddie & the Cruisers*, *Heart Like a Wheel*.

AUTOMATIC PICTURES

5225 Wilshire Blvd., Ste. 525, Los Angeles CA 90036. (323)935-1800. Fax: (323)935-8040. E-mail: azentertainment@hotmail.com. Web site: www.automaticpictures.net. **Contact:** Frank Beddor, producer. Credits include *There's Something About Mary* and *Wicked*.

   ⚊ Looking for comedy, horror, or romantic comedy.

AVALANCHE! ENTERTAINMENT

506 Santa Monica Blvd., Ste. 322, Santa Monica CA 90401. (310)395-3660. Fax: (310)395-8322.

AVENUE PICTURES

11111 Santa Monica Blvd., Suite 525, Los Angeles CA 90025. (310)996-6800. Fax: (310)473-4376. Credits include *The Player*, *Wit*, and *Path to War*.

AVNET-KERNER COMPANY

3815 Hughes Ave., Culver City CA 90232-2715. (310)838-2500. Fax: (310)204-4208. Credits include *D2: The Mighty Ducks*.

AXIAL ENTERTAINMENT

20 W. 21st St., 8th Fl., New York NY 10010. Web site: www.axialentertainment.com. Credits include *Ultimates* (2006) (TV), *Why Can't I Be You?*, *Into Character*.

THE BADHAM COMPANY

360 North Crescent Drive, Beverly Hills CA 90210. Web site: www.badhamcompany.com. **Contact:** John Badham, director. Credits include *The Jack Bull*, *My Brothers Keeper*, *Obsessed*, *The Shield*.

BAER ANIMATION COMPANY

7743 Woodrow Wilson Dr., Los Angeles CA 90046. (818)558-3518. Credits include *Roger Rabbit*, *The Prince & the Pauper*, *Annabelle's Wish*.

BAKULA PRODUCTIONS, INC.

% Paramount Pictures, 5555 Melrose Ave., Los Angeles CA 90038. (323)956-3030. Production company of actor Scott Bakula. Credits include *What Girls Learn*, *Papa's Angels*, *Mr. & Mrs. Smith* (13 TV episodes).

BALDWIN ENTERTAINMENT GROUP

3000 West Olympic Blvd., Suite 200, Santa Monica CA 90404. (310)453-9277. E-mail: erin@baldwi nent.com. Web site: www.baldwinent.com.

BALLPARK PRODUCTIONS

P.O. Box 508, Venice CA 90294. (310)827-1328. Fax: (310)577-9626. Credits include *The Four Feathers*, *Crimson Tide*, *Very Bad Things*.

BALLYHOO, INC.

6738 Wedgewood Pl., Los Angeles CA 90068. (323)874-3396. Credits include *Seven Years in Tibet*, *Bounce*, *About Schmidt*.

BALTIMORE/SPRING CREEK PICTURES, LLC

4000 Warner Blvd., Burbank CA 91522-0768. Web site: www.levinson.com. **Contact:** Production company of Barry Levinson and Paula Weinstein. Credits include *Analyze This*, *Liberty Heights*, *The Perfect Storm*.

BANDEIRA ENTERTAINMENT

8447 Wilshire Blvd., Suite 212, Beverly Hills CA 90211. (323)866-3535. Credits include *Bubble Boy*, *Guinevere*, *Life During Wartime*.

BARNSTORM FILMS

73 Market St., Venice CA 90291. (310)396-5937. Fax: (310)450-4988. **Contact:** Tony Bill, president. Credits include *Taxi Driver*, *Untamed Heart*, *My Bodyguard*.

BARWOOD FILMS

330 W. 58th St., New York NY 10019. (212)765-7191. Fax: (212)765-6988. Production company of Barbara Streisand, actress/director/producer. Credits include *Prince of Tides*, *Yentl*, *Reels Models: The 1st Women in Film*.

BASE CAMP FILMS

3000 31st Street, Suite D, Santa Monica CA 90405. (310)-450-5300. Fax: (310)450-3805. E-mail: info@ basecampfilms.com. Web site: www.basecampfilms.com.

CAROL BAUM PRODUCTIONS

8899 Beverly Blvd., Suite 721, Los Angeles CA 90048. (310)550-4575. Fax: (310)550-2088. Credits include *Fly Away Home*, *Father of the Bride*, *Kicking and Screaming*.

BAUMGARTEN/PROPHET ENTERTAINMENT

1640 S. Sepulveda Blvd., Suite. 218, Los Angeles CA 90025. (310)455-1601. Fax: (310)996-1892. Production company of Craig Baumgarten and Melissa Prophet. Credits include *Love Stinks*, *Cold Around the Heart*.

BAY FILMS

2110 Broadway, Santa Monica CA 90404. (310)829-7799. Fax: (310)829-7099. Production company of director Michael Bay. Credits include *Pearl Harbor*, *Armageddon*, *The Rock*.

BEACON PICTURES

120 Broadway #200, Santa Monica CA 90401. (310)260-7000. Fax: (310)260-7050. Credits include *For Love of the Game*, *Commitments*, *Air Force One*.

BEDFORD FALLS COMPANY

409 Santa Monica Blvd., PH, Santa Monica CA 90401. (310)394-5022. Fax: (310)394-5825. Director: Ed Zwick. Credits include *Traffic*, *Shakespeare in Love*, *Legends of the Fall*.

BEDLAM PICTURES

3000 W. Olympic Blvd., Bldg. 4, Suite 2204, Santa Monica CA 90404. (310)315-4764. Fax: (310)315-4757.

BEECH HILL FILMS

443 Greenwich St., Suite 5A, New York NY 10013. (212)226-3331. Fax: (212)226-2179.

BEL-AIR ENTERTAINMENT

4000 Warner Blvd., Bldg. 66, Burbank CA 91522. (818)954-4040. Fax: (818)954-2838. **Contact:** Steve Reuther. Credits include *Pay It Forward*, *Sweet November*, *Collateral Damage*.

BENDERSPINK

6735 Yucca St., Hollywood CA 90028. (323)845-1640. Fax: (323)845-5347. **Contact:** Chris Bender, J.C. Spink. Credits include *American Pie* franchise, *Cats & Dogs*, *The Ring*.

BERG ENTERTAINMENT

7421 Beverly Blvd., Los Angeles CA 90036. (323)930-9935. Fax: (323)930-9934. **Contact:** Peter Berg, actor/producer/director. Credits include *Very Bad Things*, *Welcome to the Jungle (The Rock)*, *Friday Night Lights*.

RICK BERMAN PRODUCTIONS

5555 Melrose Ave., Suite 232, Los Angeles CA 90038. (323)956-5037. Fax: (323)862-1076. Credits include *Star Trek: The Next Generation*, *Star Trek: Insurrection*, *Star Trek: Deep Space Nine*.

JAY BERNSTEIN PRODUCTIONS

P.O. Box 1148, Beverly Hills CA 90213. (310)858-1485. Fax: (310)858-1607. Credits include *Murder Takes All*, *Mike Hammer*, *Double Jeopardy*.

BEYOND FILMS, LTD.

8642 Melrose Ave., Suite 200, Los Angeles CA 90069. (310)358-9494. Fax: (310)358-9393. Web site: www.beyond.com.au.

BIG EVENT PICTURES

3940 Laurel Canyon Blvd., #1137, Studio City CA 91604. E-mail: bigevent1@bigeventpictures.com. **Contact:** Michael Cargile, president. Produces G, PG, and R-rated feature films for theaters, cable TV, and home video. Query by e-mail. Producers will respond if interested.

Needs All film genres.

Tips "Interesting query letters intrigue us—and tell us something about the writer. Query letter should include a short log line or pitch encapsulating what this story is about and should be no more than 1 page in length. We look for unique stories with strong characters and would like to see more action and science fiction submissions. We make movies that we would want to see. Producers are known for encouraging new/unproduced screenwriters and giving real consideration to their scripts."

BIG TOWN PRODUCTIONS

6201 Sunset Blvd., Suite 80, Los Angeles CA 90028. (323)962-8099. Fax: (323)962-8029. This is actor Bill Pullman's company. Credits include *The Virginian*.

BIGEL ENTERTAINMENT

9701 Wilshire Blvd., Suite 1100, Beverly Hills CA 90212. (310)278-9400. Fax: (310)278-2220. E-mail: info@bigelentertainment.com. Web site: www.bigelentertainment.com.

BIZAZZ MEDIA

8964 Oso Ave., Chatsworth CA 91311. (818)407-2208. E-mail: rupert@bizazzmedia.com. Web site: www.bizazzmedia.com.

SAM BLATE ASSOCIATES, LLC

10331 Watkins Mill Dr., Montgomery Village MD 20886-3950. (301)840-2248. Fax: (301)990-0707. E-mail: info@writephotopro.com. Web site: www.writephotopro.com. **Contact:** Sam Blate, CEO. Produces educational and multimedia for marine, fishing, boating, business, education, institutions and state and federal governments. **Works with 2 local writers/year on a per-project basis—it varies as to business conditions and demand.** Buys first rights when possible. Query with writing samples and SASE for return. Responds in 1 month to queries. **Payment depends on contact with client. Pays some expenses.**

Needs Scripts on technical, business, and outdoor subjects.

Tips "Writers must have a strong track record of technical and aesthetic excellence."

BLEIBERG ENTERTAINMENT, INC.

9454 Wilshire Blvd., Suite 200, Beverly Hills CA 90212. (310)273-0003. Fax: (310)273-0007. E-mail: info@bleibergent.com. Web site: www.bleibergent.com.

BLINDING EDGE PICTURES

100 Four Falls Corporate Center, Suite 102, Conshohocken PA 19428. (610)251-9200. Fax: (610)251-9200. Credits include: *Unbreakable*, *Signs*, *The Happening*. Owned by Writer/Director: M. Night Shyamalan.

BLUE BAY PRODUCTIONS

1119 Colorado Ave., Suite 100, Santa Monica CA 90401. (310)440-9904. Credits include: *Big Momma's House*, *Wild Things*, *Dunston Checks In*. Producer: Rod Liber.

BLUE RELIEF

1438 N. Gower St., Bldg 35, Suite 551, Hollywood CA 90028. (323)860-7565. Fax: (310)860-7497. This is actress Diane Keaton's company. Credits include *Hanging Up*, *Northern Lights*, *Crossed Over*.

BLUE RIDER PICTURES

2801 Ocean Park Blvd., Suite 193, Santa Monica CA 90405. Web site: www.blueriderpictures.com. Production credits include *Shergar*, *The Call of the Wild*, *Holes*.

BLUE SKY STUDIOS

44 South Broadway, White Plains NY 10601. (914)259-6500. Fax: (914)259-6499. E-mail: info@blueskystudios.com. Web site: www.blueskystudios.com.

BLUE TULIP PRODUCTIONS

1708 Berkeley St., Santa Monica CA 90404. (310)582-1587. Fax: (310)582-1597. E-mail: info@bluetulippprod.com. Production credits include: *Speed, Twister, Minority Report, Equilibrium*. Director: Jan De Bont.

BLUE TURTLE, INC.

1740 Clear View Dr., Beverly Hills CA 90210. (310)276-4994. Fax: (310)276-4997. Production credits include: *Teknolust, Pontiac Moon, Diggstown*.

BLUEPRINT ENTERTAINMENT

1801 Century Park East, Suite 1910, Los Angeles CA 90067. (310)407-0960. Fax: (310)407-0961. E-mail: info@blueprint-corp.com.

BOB & ALICE PRODUCTIONS

11693 San Vicente Blvd., Los Angeles CA 90049. (310)449-3858. Production credits include *Return to Me*, *Life With Bonnie*. This is the production company of actress Bonnie Hunt.

BODEGA BAY PRODUCTIONS, INC.

P.O. Box 17338, Beverly Hills CA 90209. (310)273-3157. Fax: (310)271-5581. This is the production company of Michael Murphy. Credits include *Celebrity Island Videos*, *Bill & Ted's Excellent Adventure*.

BOLD FILMS

6464 Sunset Blvd., Suite 800, Los Angeles CA 90028. (323)769-8900. Fax: (323)769-8954. E-mail: info@boldfilms.com. Web site: www.boldfilms.com.

BONA FIDE PRODUCTIONS

8899 Beverly Blvd., Suite 804, Los Angeles CA 90048. (310)273-6782. Fax: (310)273-7821. Production credits include *Pumpkin*, *Jack the Bear*, *King of the Hill*, *Election*.

BOXING CAT PRODUCTIONS

11500 Hart St., North Hollywood CA 91605. (818)765-4870. Fax: (818)765-4975. This is actor Tim Allen's production company. Credits include *Joe Somebody*, *The Santa Clause*, *Jungle 2 Jungle*.

BOX PRODUCTIONS

1632 N. Sierra Bonita Ave., Los Angeles CA 90046-2816. (323)876-3232. Fax: (323)876-3231. "This is Director/Producer Bo Zenga's company."

BRAVERMAN PRODUCTIONS

3000 Olympic Blvd., Santa Monica CA 90404. (310)264-4184. Fax: (310)388-5885. E-mail: info@braverman.com. Web site: www.bravermanproductions.com.

BREGMAN-IAC PRODUCTIONS

9100 Wilshire Blvd., Suite 401E, Beverly Hills CA 90212. (818)954-9988. "This is the company of Producers/Directors Martin/Michael Bregman; credits include *Carolina*."

BRILLSTEIN ENTERTAINMENT PARTNERS, LLC

9150 Wilshire Blvd., Suite 350, Beverly Hills CA 90212. (310)275-6135. Fax: (310)275-6180. Production credits include *Just Shoot Me*, *The Steve Harvey Show*, *The Sopranos*.

BRISTOL BAY PRODUCTIONS

1888 Century Park E., 14th Floor, Los Angeles CA 90067. (310)887-1000. Fax: (310)887-1001. E-mail: info@bristolbayproductions.com. Web site: www.crusaderentertainment.com. This company was formerly known as Crusader Entertainment. Production credits include: *Sahara*, *Ray*, *Amazing Grace*.

BRITISH LION FILMS

Los Angeles CA. (818)990-7750. Fax: (818)789-2901. E-mail: petersnell@britishlionfilms.com. Web site: www.britishlionfilms.com.

BROADWAY VIDEO ENTERTAINMENT

1619 Broadway, New York NY 10019. (212)265-7600. Fax: (212)713-1535. Web site: www.broadwayvideo.com.

BROOKSFILMS, LTD.

9336 W. Washington Blvd., Culver City CA 90232. (310)202-3292. Fax: (310)202-3225. This is the production company of Mel Brooks, writer/director/producer; credits include *Spaceballs*, *Robin Hood: Men in Tights*, *Elephant Man*, *The Producers*.

BROOKWELL MCNAMARA ENTERTAINMENT

1600 Rosecrans Blvd., Raleigh Studios Manhattan Beach, Building 6a, 3rd Floor, North Wing, Manhattan Beach CA 90266. (310)-727-3353. Fax: (310)-727-3354. E-mail: laurie@bmetvfilm.com. Web site: www.bmetvfilm.com.

BROWNHOUSE PRODUCTIONS

1 William Morris Pl., Beverly Hills CA 90212. (323)650-2670. "This is actress Whitney Houston's production company. Credits include *The Bodyguard*, *The Preacher's Wife*, *Waiting to Exhale*, *The Princess Diaries*, *The Cheetah Girls.*"

JERRY BRUCKHEIMER FILMS

1631 10th St., Santa Monica CA 90404. (310)664-6260. Production credits include "CSI:Miami", "The Amazing Race," *Remember the Titans*, *Top Gun*.

THE BUBBLE FACTORY

8840 Wilshire Blvd., 3rd Floor, Beverly Hills CA 90211. (310)358-3000. Fax: (310)358-3299. Production credits include *A Simple Wish*, *For Richer or Poorer*, *Player's Mona Lisa*, *McHale's Navy*.

BUNGALOW 78 PRODUCTIONS

5555 Melrose Ave., Lasky Bldg., Suite 200, Los Angeles CA 90038. (323)956-4440. Fax: (323)862-2090. Production credits include *Catch Me If You Can*, *Romy and Michelle's High School Reunion*, *Patch Adams*.

BURRUD PRODUCTIONS, INC.

468 N. Camden Drive, 2nd Floor, Beverly Hills CA 90210. (310)860-5158. Fax: (562)494-6419. E-mail: info@burrud.com. Web site: www.burrud.com.

BUSHWOOD PICTURES

320 S. Irving Blvd., Los Angeles CA 90020. (323)936-1659. Fax: (323)936-1977.

BUTCHERS RUN FILMS

8978 Norma Place, W. Hollywood CA 90069. (310)246-4630. Fax: (310)246-1033. Production company of actor Robert Duvall; credits include *A Family Thing*, *The Man Who Captured Eichmann*, *The Apostle*.

C-2 PICTURES

2308 Broadway, Santa Monica CA 90404. (310)315-6000. Fax: (310)828-0443. E-mail: development@cinergyprod.com. Production credits include: *Evita*, *Die Hard 3*, *Star Gate*.

C/W PRODUCTIONS

5555 Melrose Ave., Hollywood CA 90038. (323)956-8150. Fax: (323)862-1250. This is Tom Cruise's production company. Credits include: *Missions Impossible* (1 & 2), *The Others*, *Vanilla Sky*.

CALICO WORLD ENTERTAINMENT

10200 Riverside Dr., N. Hollywood CA 91602. (818)755-3800. Produces animation.

CAMELOT ENTERTAINMENT GROUP

130 Vantis, Suite 140, Aliso Viejo CA 92656. (949)334-2950. Web site: www.camelotfilms.com.

CAMELOT PICTURES

9255 Sunset Blvd., Suite 711, Los Angeles CA 90069. (310)288-3000. Fax: (310)288-3054. E-mail: info@camelot-pictures.com. Web site: www.camelot-pictures.com.

CAMERA MARC

4605 Lankershim Blvd., Suite 201, N. Hollywood CA 91602. (818)753-9901.

CANAL+

301 N. Canon Dr., Suite 228, Beverly Hills CA 90210. (310)247-0994. Fax: (310)247-0998.

CANNELL STUDIOS

7083 Hollywood Blvd., Suite 600, Hollywood CA 90028. (323)465-5800. Fax: (323)856-7390. This is Stephen J. Cannell's production company; credits include *21 Jump Street*, *A-Team*, *Greatest American Hero*, *Wiseguy*.

THE CANTON COMPANY

Warner Bros., 4000 Warner Blvd., Bldg. 81, Suite 200, Burbank CA 91522. (818)954-2130. Fax: (818)954-2967.

CAPELLA INTERNATIONAL, INC.

9242 Beverly Blvd., Suite 280, Beverly Hills CA 90210-3710. (310)247-4700. Fax: (310)247-4701. Production credits include *The Adventures of Rocky & Bullwinkle*.

CAPITAL ARTS ENTERTAINMENT

233151 Clifton Pl., Valencia CA 91354. (310)581-3020. Fax: (310)581-3023. Production credits include *Casper Meets Wendy*, *Richie Rich*, *Addams Family Reunion*.

CAPSTONE PICTURES

1990 S. Bundy Dr., Suite 370, Hollywood CA 90025. (310)571-9211. Fax: (310)481-6242. Production credits include *The Raffle*, *Local Boys*, *The Endless Summer II*, *The Monk*.

CARLTON INTERNATIONAL MEDIA, INC.

12711 Ventura Blvd., Suite 300, Studio City CA 91604. (818)753-6363. Fax: (818)753-6388. E-mail: enquiries@carltonint.co.uk. Production credits include *Danger Beneath the Sea*, *Rough Air: Danger on Flight 534*, *Rudy: The Rudy Giuliani Story*.

CARLYLE PRODUCTIONS & MANAGEMENT

2050 Laurel Canyon Rd., Los Angeles CA 90046. (323)848-4960. Fax: (323)650-8249. E-mail: carly le@earthlink.net. **Contact:** Phyllis Carlyle, manager/producer. Production credits include *Seven*, *The Accidental Tourist*, *Mean Streak*.

CARRIE PRODUCTIONS

4444 Riverside Dr., Suite 110, Burbank CA 91505. (818)567-3292. Fax: (818)567-3296. This is actor Danny Glover's production company; credits include *Buffalo Soldiers*, *Freedom Song*, *America's Dream*, *Just a Dream*.

THE THOMAS CARTER COMPANY

3000 W. Olympic Blvd., Bldg. 5, Suite 1100, Santa Monica CA 90404. (310)586-7600. Fax: (310)586-7607. Production credits include *Save the Last Dance*, *Don King: Only in America*, *Ali: An American Hero*.

CARTOON NETWORK

1050 Temple Dr., Atlanta GA 30318. (404)885-2263. Produces animation; production credits include *The Powerpuff Girls Movie*.

CARTOON NETWORK STUDIOS

300 N. Third St., Burbank CA 91502. (818)729-4000. Produces animation.

CASTLE HILL PRODUCTIONS INC./CINEVEST

1414 Avenue of the Americas, 15th Floor, New York NY 10019. (212)888-0080. Fax: (212)644-0956.

CASTLE ROCK ENTERTAINMENT

335 N. Maple Dr., Suite 135, Beverly Hills CA 90210. (310)285-2300. Fax: (310)285-2345. Credits include *Miss Congeniality*, *A Few Good Men*, *City Slickers*, *The Shawshank Redemption*, *Seinfeld*.

CATALAND FILMS

555 West 25th St., New York NY 10001. (212)989-5995. Fax: (212)989-5505. E-mail: richp@cataland. com. Web site: www.cataland.com.

CATFISH PRODUCTIONS

23852 Pacific Coast Hwy., Suite 313, Malibu CA 90265. (310)456-7365. Fax: (310)264-9148. Production company of actors James Keach and Jane Seymour; credits include *The Absolute Truth*, *A Passion for Justice*, *Dr. Quinn (The Movie)*.

CECCHI GORI GROUP

11990 San Vicente Blvd., Suite 200, Los Angeles CA 90049. (310)442-4777. Fax: (310)442-9507. E-mail: msalvo@earthlink.net. Production credits include *La Vita Bella (Life Is Beautiful)*, *A Bronx Tale*, *House of Cards*.

CFP PRODUCTIONS

5555 Melrose Ave., Lucy Bungalow 105, Hollywood CA 90038. (323)956-8866. Fax: (323)862-2445. Web site: www.cfpproductions.com.

CHANCELLOR ENTERTAINMENT

10600 Holman Ave., Suite 1, Los Angeles CA 90024. (310)470-4521. Fax: (310)470-9273. Web site: www.chancellorentertainment.com. Production credits include *Sing Out, The Idolmaker, The Razor's Edge, Letter to Three Wives.*

CHARTOFF PRODUCTIONS

1250 6th St., Suite 101, Santa Monica CA 90401. (310)319-1960. Fax: (310)319-3469. Production credits include *Rocky* Series, *Raging Bull, Straight Talk, The Right Stuff.*

CHEYENNE ENTERPRISES

406 Wilshire Blvd., Santa Monica CA 90401. (310)455-5000. Fax: (310)688-8000. E-mail: info@rifkin-eberts.com. Web site: www.rifkin-ebertsproductions.com. Production company of actor Bruce Willis; credits include *Bandits, Hart's War, Timber Falls.*

CHIODO BROS. PRODUCTIONS, INC.

110 W. Providencia Ave., Burbank CA 91502. (818)842-5656. Fax: (818)848-0891. E-mail: klown s@chiodobros.com. Web site: www.chiodobros.com.

CINE EXCEL ENTERTAINMENT

1219 W. El Segundo Blvd., Gardena CA 90247-1521. (323)754-5500. Fax: (818)848-1590. E-mail: cineexcel@msn.com. Web site: www.cineexcel.com. Credits include *Reptilicant, Carnival Evil.*

CINE MOSAIC

130 West 25th St., 12th Fl., New York NY 10001. (212)625-3797. Fax: (212)625-3571. E-mail: info@ci nemosaic.net. Web site: www.cinemosaic.net.

CINEMA ELECTRIC

16030 Ventura Blvd., Suite 460, Encino CA 91436. E-mail: info@cinemaelectric.com. Web site: www.c inemaelectric.com.

CINEMA EPOCH

10940 Wilshire Blvd., 16th Fl., Los Angeles CA 90024. (310)443-4244. E-mail: info@cinemaepoch. com. Web site: www.cinemaepoch.com.

CINEMA LIBRE STUDIO

8328 De Soto Ave., Canoga Park CA 91304. (818)349-8822. Fax: (818)349-9922. E-mail: info@cinema librestudio.com. Web site: www.cinemalibrestudio.com.

CINERGI PICTURES

2308 Broadway, Santa Monica CA 90404-2916. (310)315-6000. Fax: (310)828-0443. Credits include *Die Hard With a Vengeance, Evita, Tombstone.*

CINETEL FILMS, INC.

8255 W. Sunset Blvd., Los Angeles CA 90046-2432. (323)654-4000. Fax: (323)650-6400. Production credits include *Judgment Day*, *Carried Away*, *The Pandora Project*.

CINEVILLE, INC.

3400 Airport Ave., Suite 10, Santa Monica CA 90405. (310)397-7150. Fax: (310)397-7155. Web site: www.cineville.com. Production credits include *Hurly Burly*, *Swimming With Sharks*, *Mi Vida Loca*.

CITY LIGHTS MEDIA GROUP

6 East 39th St., New York NY 10016. (646)519-5200. Fax: (212)679-4481. Web site: www.citylightsmedia.com.

CLARITY PICTURES

1107 Fair Oaks Ave., Suite 155, South Pasadena CA 91030. (877)868-8298. E-mail: info@claritypictures.net. Web site: www.claritypictures.net.

DICK CLARK PRODUCTIONS

2900 Olympic Blvd., Santa Monica CA 90404. (310)255-4600. Web site: www.dickclarkproductions.com.

CLASSIC FILMS

6427 Sunset Blvd., Hollywood CA 90028. (323)962-7855. Fax: (323)962-8028. Production credits include *James and the Giant Peach*, *FernGully: The Last Rainforest*, *FernGully: The Magical Rescue*.

CLEAN BREAK PRODUCTIONS

14046 Aubrey Rd., Beverly Hills CA 90210. (818)995-1221. Fax: (818)995-0089. Production company of actor Tom Arnold; credits include ''The Tom Show.''

CODE ENTERTAINMENT

9229 Sunset Blvd., Suite 615, Los Angeles CA 90069. (310)772-0008. Fax: (310)772-0006. E-mail: contact@codeentertainment.com. Web site: www.codeentertainment.com.

CODEBLACK ENTERTAINMENT

1560 Ventura Boulevard, Suite 840, Sherman Oaks CA 91403. E-mail: info@codeblack.com. Web site: www.codeblackentertainment.com.

COHEN PICTURES

8439 Sunset Blvd., Los Angeles CA 90069. (323)822-4100. Production credits include *The Cider House Rules*, *Rounders*, *View from the Top*.

COLLABORATIVE ARTISTS

445 S. Beverly Dr., Suite 100, Beverly Hills CA 90212. (310)274-4800. Fax: (310)274-4803. E-mail: collaborative@sbcglobal.net. Production credits include *The Season: Red Storm Rising*.

COLLISION ENTERTAINMENT

445 S. Beverly Dr., Suite 310, Beverly Hills CA 90212. (310)785-0425. Fax: (310)785-0463. Production credits include *Venom*.

COLOMBY/KEATON PRODUCTIONS

2110 Main St., Suite 302, Santa Monica CA 90405. (310)432-2000. Fax: (310)392-1323. Actor Michael Keaton's production company; credits include *Body Shots*.

COMIC BOOK MOVIES, LLC

333 Crestmont Road, Cedar Grove NJ 07009. (973)857-6172. Fax: (973)857-6174. E-mail: info@comic bookmovies.net. Web site: www.comicbookmovies.net.

COMMOTION PICTURES

301 N. Canon Dr., Suite 324, Beverly Hills CA 90210. (310)432-2000. Fax: (310)432-2001. Production credits include *Green Day: International Supervideos!*, *The Big Clock*.

COMPANY FILMS

2601 2nd St., Santa Monica CA 90405. (310)399-2500. Fax: (310)399-2583.

CONCEPT ENTERTAINMENT

334$\frac{1}{2}$ N. Sierra Bonita Ave., Los Angeles CA 90036. E-mail: enquiries@conceptentertainment.biz. Web site: www.conceptentertainment.biz.

CONCORDE-NEW HORIZONS CORP.

11600 San Vincente Blvd., Los Angeles CA 90049. (310)820-6733. Fax: (310)207-6816.

CONQUISTADOR ENTERTAINMENT

131 Green St., Suite 4A, New York NY 10012. (212)353-1696. Fax: (212)353-1497.

CONSTANTIN FILM DEVELOPMENT, INC.

9200 Sunset Blvd., Suite 730, Los Angeles CA 90069. (310)247-0305. Fax: (310)247-0305. Production credits include *Smilla's Sense of Snow*, *House of the Spirits*, *Resident Evil*.

CONTEMPTIBLE ENTERTAINMENT

% USA Films, 9333 Wilshire Blvd., Beverly Hills CA 90210. (310)385-4183. Fax: (310)385-6633. Production company of actor/director Neil Labute. Credits include *Your Friends & Neighbors*, *In the Company of Men*, *Nurse Betty*.

CONTENTFILM

1337 Third Street Promenade, Suite 302, Santa Monica CA 90401. (310)576-1059. Fax: (310)576-1859. E-mail: la@contentfilm.com. Web site: www.contentfilm.com.

CONUNDRUM ENTERTAINMENT

325 Wilshire Blvd., Suite 201, Santa Monica CA 90401. (310)319-2800. Fax: (310)310-319-2808. This is the production company of writers/directors Bobby and Peter Farrelly. Credits include *Shallow Hal*, *Me, Myself & Irene*; *There's Something About Mary*.

COOKIE JAR ENTERTAINMENT INC.

4500 Wilshire Blvd., 1st Floor, Los Angeles CA 90010, United States. (323)-937-6244. E-mail: info@ thecookiejarcompany.com. Web site: www.cookiejarentertainment.com.

COOPER'S TOWN PRODUCTIONS

302A W. 12th St. #214, New York NY 10014. (212)255-7566. Fax: (212)255-0211. E-mail: info@coop erstownproductions.com. Web site: www.cooperstownproductions.com.

CORNER OF THE SKY ENTERTAINMENT

1635 N Cahuenga Blvd., Los Angeles CA 90028. (323)860-1572. Fax: (323)860-1574. E-mail: Dus tin@cornersky.com. Web site: www.cornersky.com.

CORNICE ENTERTAINMENT

190 N. Canon Dr., Beverly Hills CA 90210. (310)777-0200. Fax: (310)777-0357. Production credits include *Highwaymen*.

CORNUCOPIA PICTURES

10989 Bluffside Dr., Suite 3414, Studio City CA 91604. (818)985-2720. Production credits include: *Rain Man*, *Switched at Birth*, *Gross Point Blank*.

CINDY COWAN ENTERTAINMENT

8265 Sunset Blvd., Suite 205, Los Angeles CA 90046. (323)822-1082. E-mail: info@cowanent.com. Web site: www.cowanent.com.

CRAVE FILMS

3312 Sunset Blvd., Los Angeles CA 90026. (323)669-9000. Fax: (323)669-9002. Web site: www.cravefil ms.com.

WES CRAVEN FILMS

11846 Ventura Blvd., Suite 208, Studio City CA 91604. (818)752-0197. Fax: (818)752-1789. Production credits include: *Scream (1-3)*, *Music of the Heart*.

CREANSPEAK PRODUCTIONS, LLC

120 El Camino Drive, Suite 100, Beverly Hills CA 90212. (310)273-8217. E-mail: info@creanspeak. com. Web site: www.creanspeak.com.

CREATIVE CAPERS ENTERTAINMENT

2233 Honolulu Ave., 2nd Floor, Montrose CA 91020. (818)658-7120. Fax: (818)658-7123. E-mail: admin@creativecapers.com. Web site: www.creativecapers.com.

CREATIVE DIFFERENCES

11846 Ventura Blvd., Suite 204, Studio City CA 91604. (818)432-4200. Fax: (818)763-2485. Web site: www.creatvdiff.com.

CREATIVE LIGHT WORLDWIDE

8383 Wilshire Blvd., Beverly Hills CA 90211. (323)658-9166. Fax: (323)658-9169. Web site: www.crea tivelightworldwide.com. **Contact:** Scott Zakari. Creative Light Worldwide is a global theatrical, video, television distribution and sales company.

CROWN INTERNATIONAL PICTURES, INC.

8701 Wilshire Blvd., Beverly Hills CA 90211. (310)657-6700. Fax: (310)657-4489. E-mail: crown@ crownintlpictures.com. Web site: www.crownintlpictures.com. Productions credits include: *My Mom's a Werewolf, My Tutor, My Chauffeur.* Does not accept unsolicited screenplays via email.

CRYSTAL SKY, LLC

1901 Avenue of the Stars, Suite 605, Los Angeles CA 90067. (310)843-0223. Fax: (310)553-9895. Production credits include: *Baby Geniuses I, II, Murder in a Small Town, Unleashed.*

CUNNINGHAM PRODUCTIONS, INC.

4420 Hayvenhurst Ave., Encino CA 91436. (818)995-1585. This is Producer Sean S. Cunningham's company. Production credits include: *Terminal Invasion, Deep Star Six, Friday the 13th.*

CURB ENTERTAINMENT INTERNATIONAL

3907 W. Alameda Ave., Burbank CA 91505. (818)843-8580. Fax: (818)566-1719. E-mail: info@curbe ntertainment.com. Web site: www.curbentertainment.com. Production credits include: *Tough Luck, Pipe Dream, Zoe.*

DANAMATION STUDIOS

1007 Montana Ave., Suite 404, Santa Monica CA 90403. (310)317-517. This is an animation studio.

LEE DANIELS ENTERTAINMENT

315 W. 36th St., Suite 1002, New York NY 10018. (212)334-8110. Fax: (212)334-8290. E-mail: info@ leedanielsentertainment.com. Web site: www.leedanielsentertainment.com. **Contact:** VP of Development. "We work in all aspects of entertainment, including film, television, and theater." All nonagency scripts must be accompanied by a signed copy of the submission release form, which can be downloaded from the Web site. All scripts should be registered or copyrighted for your protection. All scripts should be in standard screenplay format. Include a synopsis, logline, and character breakdown (including lead and supporting roles). Do not send any extraneous materials.

Tips Lee Daniels produced *Monster's Ball* and *The Woodsman*, and produced/directed *Shadowboxer.* He is the first African-American sole producer of an Academy-Award-winning film.

DANJAQ, INC.

2401 Colorado Ave., Suite 330, Santa Monica CA 90404. (310)449-3185. Fax: (310)449-3189. Production credits include: The James Bond Films; *Chitty Chitty Bang Bang.*

DARK HORSE ENTERTAINMENT

421 S. Beverly Dr., Beverly Hills CA 90212. (310)789-4751. Web site: www.dhentertainment.com. Production credits include: *Hellboy, The Mask, Mystery Men, Time Cop.*

DARKWOODS PRODUCTIONS

1041 N. Formosa Ave. SME, Suite 108, W. Hollywood CA 90046. (323)850-2497. Fax: (323)850-2491. Production credits include: *The Green Mile, The Salton Sea, The Majestic.* Director: Frank Darabont.

DAVIS ENTERTAINMENT CO.

2121 Avenue of the Stars, Suite 2900, Los Angeles CA 90067. (310)556-3550. **Contact:** John Davis, director. Production credits include: *Behind Enemy Lines, Dr. Doolittle, The Firm.*

DINO DE LAURENTIIS COMPANY

100 Universal City Plaza, Bungalow 5195, Universal City CA 91608. (818)777-2111. Fax: (818)866-5566. Web site: www.ddlc.net. Production credits include: *Hannibal Rising, U-571, Red Dragon.*

DE LINE PICTURES

Paramount Pictures, 5555 Melrose Ave., Los Angeles CA 90038. (323)956-3200. Fax: (323)862-1301.

DEE GEE ENTERTAINMENT

368 N. La Cienega Blvd., Los Angeles CA 90048. (310)652-0999. Fax: (310)652-0718. Production credits include: *Ricochet River* (tv), *The Wedding Planner.*

DEEP RIVER PRODUCTIONS

100 N. Crescent Dr., Suite 350, Beverly Hills CA 90210. (310)432-1800. Fax: (310)432-1801. Production credits include: *Dr. Dolittle, Courage Under Fire, Big Momma's House.*

DEJA VIEW PRODUCTIONS

7603 Atron Ave., West Hills CA 91304. (818)704-9185. Fax: (818)704-6001. Production credits include: *The Flintstones in Viva Rock Vegas, Eraser, Pacific Heights.*

DELAWARE PICTURES

650 N. Brosnan Ave., Suite B120, Hollywood CA 90004. (323)960-4552. Fax: (323)960-4556. E-mail: info@delawarepictures.net. Web site: www.delawarepictures.net. **Contact:** J. Patrick Leny. Production credits include: *Pretty Boy Floyd, Universal Soldiers.*

DEREKO ENTERTAINMENT

9663 Santa Monica Blvd., Suite 722, Beverly Hills CA 90210. (310)706-3600, ext. 6280. Web site: www.derekoent.com.

DESTINATION FILMS

1299 Ocean Ave., 5th Fl., Santa Monica CA 90401. (310)434-2700. Fax: (310)434-2701. Production credits include: *The Good Night, Glass House: The Good Mother, The Squid & the Whale.*

DESTINY FORCE PRODUCTIONS

233 Wilshire Blvd., Suite 400, Santa Monica CA 90401. (310)449-0076. Fax: (310)734-1822.

DI NOVI PICTURES

3110 Main St., Suite 220, Santa Monica CA 90405. (310)581-1355. Fax: (310)399-0499. Production credits include: *Sisterhood of the Traveling Pants*, *Practical Magic*, *A Walk To Remember*.

DIC ENTERTAINMENT

303 N. Glenoaks Blvd., Burbank CA 91502. (818)955-5400. Fax: (818)955-5696. **Contact:** Brad Brooks, president. (Animation).

DIMENSION FILMS

% Miramax Films, 375 Greenwich St., New York NY 10013. (212)941-3800/(323)951-4200. Fax: (212)941-3949. Production credits include: *The Others*, *Scream*, *Spy Kids*.

DINAMO ENTERTAINMENT

1537 Pontius Ave., 2nd Fl., Los Angeles CA 90025. (310)473-1311. Fax: (310)473-8233. Production credits include: *Lost & Found*, *Suicide Kings*, *The Substitute*.

DISTANT HORIZON, LTD.

8282 Sunset Blvd., Suite A, Los Angeles CA 90046. (323)848-4140. Fax: (323)848-4144. E-mail: la@distant-horizon.com; london@distant-horizon.com. Web site: www.distant-horizon.com. Production credits include: *Sarafina!*, *Cry, the Beloved Country*, *Theory of Flight*.

DIVERSA FILMS

7974 Mission Bonita Dr., San Diego CA 92120, USA. E-mail: karl.kozak@home.com. Web site: www.diversafilms.com. **Contact:** Karl Kozak. Production credits include: *To Hell With Love*, *Out of the Black*.

MAUREEN DONLEY PICTURES

914 Westwood Blvd., Suite 591, Los Angeles CA 90024. (310)441-0834. Fax: (310)441-1595. Production credits include: *The Little Mermaid*, *Anastasia*.

THE DONNERS COMPANY

4000 Warner Blvd., Bldgs. 102 & 103, Suite 4, Burbank CA 91522. (818)954-3611. Fax: (818)954-4908. Production credits include: *Lethal Weapon*, *Maverick*, *Free Willy*.

DOUBLE TREE ENTERTAINMENT

9606 Santa Monica Blvd., 3rd Floor, Beverly Hills CA 90210. (310)859-6644. Fax: (310)859-6650.

DREYFUSS/JAMES PRODUCTIONS

1041 N. Formosa Ave., Pickford Bldg., Room 110, W. Hollywood CA 90046. (323)850-3140. Fax: (323)850-3141. Production credits include: *Quiz Show*, *Mr. Holland's Opus*, *Having Our Say*.

DUCK SOUP STUDIOS

2205 Stoner Ave., Los Angeles CA 90064. (310)478-0771. Produces animation.

EAGLE FILMS

P.O. Box 712, Falls Church VA 22040. (703)237-7160. E-mail: philcook@eaglefilms.com. Web site: www.eaglefilms.com/. **Contact:** Producer/director/writer Philip Cook. Credits include *Invader, Outerworld* and *Despiser.*

EAGLE NATION FILMS

5555 Melrose Ave., Dietrich, Los Angeles CA 90038. (323)956-5989.

EDCON PUBLISHING GROUP

30 Montauk Blvd., Oakdale NY 11769-1399. (631)567-7227. Fax: (631)567-8745. E-mail: editor@edconpublishing.com. Web site: www.edconpublishing.com. **Contact:** Janice Cobas, editor. Estab. 1971. Produces supplementary materials for elementary-high school students, either on grade level or in remedial situations. **100% freelance written.** "All scripts/titles are by assignment only. Do not send manuscripts." Employs video, CD, book, and personal computer media. Buys all rights. Writing samples kept on file unless return requested. Include return envelope and postage if return desired. Responds in 1 month to outline, 6 weeks on final scripts. **Pays $300 and up.**

Tips "Writers must be highly creative and disciplined. We are interested in high interest/low readability materials. Send writing samples, published or unpublished."

EDMONDS ENTERTAINMENT GROUP

1635 N. Cahuenga Blvd., Los Angeles CA 90028. (323)860-1550. Fax: (323)860-1554. Credits include BET's "College Hill." Feature films include *Good Luck Chuck* and *Soul Food*. EEG has film, television and music divisions.

BLAKE EDWARDS PRODUCTIONS

10345 W. Olympic Blvd., Los Angeles CA 90064. (310)234-0989. Fax: (310)207-9305.

EGG PICTURES

555 Melrose Ave., JL Building, Los Angeles CA 90038. (323)956-8400. Fax: (323)862-1414. This production company is run by actress Jodie Foster. Its credits include *Nell* and *The Dangerous Lives of Altar Boys.*

EL DORADO PICTURES

725 Arizona Ave., Suite 404, Santa Monica CA 90401. (310)458-4800. Fax: (310)458-4802. Credits include *State and Main* as well as *The Devil and Daniel Webster.*

EL NORTE PRODUCTIONS

Los Angeles CA. (310)360-1194. Fax: (310)360-1199. Credits include *Bordertown* and "Behind the Mask of Zorro."

ENERGY ENTERTAINMENT

999 N. Doheny Dr., #711, Los Angeles CA 90069. (310)274-3440. Web site: www.energyentertainmen t.net. **Contact:** Brooklyn Weaver, owner/manager-producer. Estab. 2001. Submit query via Web site.

ENTERTAINMENT PRODUCTIONS, INC.

2118 Wilshire Blvd., #744, Santa Monica CA 90403. (310)456-3143. Fax: (310)456-8950. **Contact:** Mary Lee, story editor; Edward Coe, producer. Estab. 1971. Produces theatrical and television productions for worldwide distribution. Query with synopsis and a Writer Submission Release in any form. Responds to queries only if SASE is included. **Purchases rights by negotiations.**

Tips "Submit your strongest writing."

EQUUS ENTERTAINMENT

2121 Ave. of the Stars, 29th Floor, Los Angeles CA 90067. (310)551-2262. Fax: (310)556-3760.

ESCAPE ARTISTS

10202 W. Washington Blvd., Lean, No. 333, Culver City CA 90232. (310)244-8833. Fax: (310)244-2151. **Contact:** Lead developers and producers include Steve Tisch, Todd Black and Jason Blumenthal. Credits include *The Weather Man* (2005), *Alex & Emma* (2003) and *A Knight's Tale (2001)*.

Tips Escape Artists distributes its films domestically via Columbia Pictures and internationally via Summit Entertainment.

ESPARZA-KATZ PRODUCTIONS

8899 Beverly Blvd, Ste 506, Los Angeles CA 90048. (310)281-3770. Fax: (310)281-3777. Credits include *Selena*, *Price of Glory* and *Gettysburg*.

THE ROBERT EVANS COMPANY

5555 Melrose Avenue, Lubitsch Building, Los Angeles CA 90038-3197. Credits include *How to Lose It All* and *How to Lose a Guy In 10 Days*.

EVERYMAN PICTURES

1202 W. Washington Blvd., Old Lab, Culver City CA 90232. (310)244-1686. Fax: (310)244-1315. **Contact:** This studio is headed by director Jay Roach, who has directed the Austin Power films. Credits include *Meet the Fockers, Charlie Bartlett* and *Borat*.

EVIL TWIN PRODUCTIONS

5201 Fulton Ave., Sherman Oaks CA 91401. (818)986-8551. E-mail: info@eviltwinproductions.com. Web site: www.eviltwinproductions.com/eviltwin.html.

EVOLUTION ENTERTAINMENT

7720 Sunset Blvd., Los Angeles CA 90046. (323)850-3232. Fax: (323)850-0521. Credits include the *Saw* series and *Dead Silence*.

FAIR DINKUM PRODUCTIONS

2500 Broadway St., Bldg E-5018, Santa Monica CA 90404. (310)586-8471. Fax: (310)586-5469.

FARRELL/MINOFF PRODUCTIONS

14011 Ventura Blvd., Ste 401, Sherman Oaks CA 91423. (818)789-5766. Fax: (818)789-7459. Web site: www.mikefarrell.org/artist/producer.html.

FAST CARRIER PICTURES, INC.

820 Majorca Place, Los Angeles CA 90049. (213)300-1896. E-mail: fastcarriervp@aol.com. Web site: www.fastcarrier.com. **Contact:** Rory Aylward. Estab. 2000. Mass market motion picture/TV audience. **Buys 1-2 script(s)/year. Works with 1-2 writer(s)/year.** No options or cash up front. No previously produced material. Query with synopsis. Responds to queries immediately; 1-2 months to scripts.

- ➤ "Our bread basket is cable, broadcast, and smaller theatrical films in the following genres: women in jeopardy, low-budget family movies tied to a holiday, low-budget westerns, horror, and romantic comedy." No teen sex comedies, large science fiction movies, historical epics, serial killer movies, or gross violence and humor at the expense of women, children, or minorities.

EDWARD S. FELDMAN COMPANY

520 Evelyn Place, Beverly Hills CA 90210. (416)761-0123. Fax: (416)761-0040.

FGM ENTERTAINMENT

8670 Wilshire Blvd., Ste 301, Beverly Hills CA 90211. (310)358-1370. Fax: (310)358-1380. Produced *Stigmata*, *Species*, *Internal Affairs*, and *Ronin*.

ADAM FIELDS PRODUCTIONS

10390 Santa Monica Blvd., Suite 350, Los Angeles CA 90025. (310)552-8244. Fax: (310)552-8247. This company has produced *Donnie Darko*, among other films.

FIFTY CANNON ENTERTAINMENT

10390 Santa Monica, Ste. 350, Los Angeles CA 90025. (310)552-1518. Fax: (310)552-2310.

FILM ROMAN

A Starz Media Company, 2950 North Hollywood Way, Burbank CA 91505. (818)748-4000. Web site: www.filmroman.com/. This is an anamation studio behind comedy hits such as "King of the Hill" and "The Simpsons." For more than 20 years, this company has worked in the animation business.

FILMCOLONY, LTD

465 South Sycamore Ave., Los Angeles CA 90036. (323)933-4670. Fax: (323)933-4674. E-mail: info@filmcolony.com. Web site: www.filmcolony.com/. This company has produced *Reservoir Dogs*, *Pulp Fiction*, *Killshot*, *54*, *The Cider House Rules*, *Jackie Brown*, and *Mr. Magorium's Wonder Emporium*, among others.

FILMFOUR INTERNATIONAL

76-78 Charlotte St., London W1P 1LX, United Kingdom. (44)(207)868-7700. Fax: (44)(207)868-7766. E-mail: filmfourintl@channel4.co.uk. Web site: www.filmfour.com.

FILMWORLD, INC.

304 N. Edinburgh Ave., Los Angeles CA 90048. (323)655-7705. Fax: (3234)655-7706.

FINE LINE FEATURES

116 N. Robertson Blvd., Suite 200, Los Angeles CA 90048. (212)649-4800; (310)854-5811. Fax: (310)659-1453. Web site: finelinefeatures.com/. This company has produced *Before Night Falls, Deconstructing Harry, American Splendor* and *Invincible*, among other films.

WENDY FINERMAN PRODUCTIONS

10201 W. Pico Blvd., Los Angeles CA 90035. (310)369-8800. Fax: (310)369-8808. This company has produced *Stepmom* and *Forrest Gump*, among other films.

FIREWORKS PICTURES

421 S. Beverly Dr., Suite 700, Beverly Hills CA 90212. (310)789-4700. Fax: (310)789-4747.

FIRST KISS PRODUCTIONS

468 N. Camden Dr., Suite 200, Beverly Hills CA 90210. (310)860-5611. This is actress Alicia Silverstone's company. Production credits include *Braceface* and *Excess Baggage*.

FIRST LOOK STUDIOS, INC.

2000 Avenue of the Stars, Suite 410, Century City CA 90067. (424)202-5000. Web site: www.firstlookmedia.com. Production credits include *Meet Bill, August, War, Inc.*

FIRST STREET FILMS, INC.

120 Broadway Ave., 2nd Floor, Santa Monica CA 90401. (310)393-9150. Fax: (310)393-1430. This is producer Bill Borden's company. Credits include: *La Bamba, End of Days, Get on the Bus.*

⊘ FLATIRON FILMS

171 Pier Ave., No. 396, Santa Monica CA 90405. E-mail: flatiron@flatironers.com. Web site: www.flatironers.com.

Tips Send no unsolicited material.

FLORIDA STRAIGHTS PRODUCTIONS

312 Sixth St., Venice CA 90291. (310)399-0114. Fax: (310)496-3181.

FLOWER FILMS, INC.

9220 Sunset Blvd., No. 309, Los Angeles CA 90069. (310)285-0200. Fax: (310)285-0827. This company, purchased by actress Drew Barrymore, has produced films such as *Fever Pitch* and *Donnie Darko*.

FLYING FREEHOLD PRODUCTIONS

5555 Melrose Ave., Dreire Bldg. No. 216, Los Angeles CA 90038. (310)459-8142. Fax: (310)230-3572.

FOCUS FEATURES

100 Universal City Plaza, Los Angeles CA 91608. (818)777-7373. Web site: www.focusfeatures.com/home.php. This is the specialty films unit of Universal Pictures. Recent films include *Burn After Reading* and *Hamlet 2*.

FORTIS FILMS

8581 Santa Monica Blvd., Ste 1, West Hollywood CA 90069. (310)659-4533. Fax: (310)659-4373. This production company is run by Sandra Bullock, actress. Productions include *Two Weeks Notice* and *Practical Magic*.

FORWARD PASS

12233 W. Olympic Blvd., Los Angeles CA 90064. (310)571-3443.

DAVID FOSTER PRODUCTIONS

5555 Melrose Ave., Clara Bow Ldg. Ste 224, Los Angeles CA 90038. (323)956-5226. Fax: (323)862-2589. This studio's credits include *The Core* and *The Mask of Zorro*.

FOUNDATION ENTERTAINMENT

8800 Venice Blvd., Ste 317, Los Angeles CA 90034. (310)204-4686. Fax: (310)204-4603.

FOUNDRY FILM PARTNERS

140 W. 57th St., New York NY 10019. (212)977-9597. Fax: (212)977-9525. This is producer Robert Greenhut's company. Credits include *Company Man*, *Siegfried & Roy: The Magic Box*, *The Wisdom of Crocodiles*.

FOX FAMILY CHANNEL/FOX FAMILY TELEVISION STUDIOS

10960 Wilshire Blvd., Los Angeles CA 90024. (310)235-9700. Fax: (310)235-5102.

FR PRODUCTIONS

2980 Beverly Glen Circle, Ste 200, Los Angeles CA 90077. (310)470-9212. Fax: (310)470-4905. This company's production credits include *The Virgin Suicides* and *Town and Country*.

FRANCHISE PICTURES, LCC

8228 Sunset Blvd., Ste 311, Los Angeles CA 90046. (323)822-0730. Fax: (323)822-2165. This company's credits include *The Art of War* and *The Boondock Saints*. The company was founded by Elie Samaha and Andrew Stevens.

FRIED FILMS

4503 Glencoe Ave., 2nd Floor, Marina del Rey CA 90292. (310)754-2676. Fax: (310)778-9596. This is Robert Fried's production company.

FURTHER FILMS

100 Universal City Plaza, Bldg. 1320, Universal City CA 91608. (818)777-6700. Fax: (818)866-1278. This is the production company of actor Michael Douglas. Its credits include *The In-Laws* and *It Runs in the Family*.

GAYLORD FILMS

4000 Warner Blvd., Bldg 148, Burbank CA 91522. (818)954-3500. This production company's credits include *Divine Secrets of the Ya-Ya Sisterhood*.

GEISLER/ROBERDEAU

511 Ave. of the Americas, Suite 368, New York NY 10011. (212)475-7472. Production credits include: *The Thin Red Line*.

GEORGE STREET PICTURES

3815 Hughes Ave., Suite 3, Culver City CA 90232. (310)841-4361. Fax: (310)204-6310. This is actor Chris O'Donnell's company. Production credits include: *29 Palms*, *The Triangle*, *The Bachelor*.

GERBER PICTURES

9465 Wilshire Blvd., Suite 318, Beverly Hills CA 90212. (310)385-8219. Fax: (310)385-5881. **Contact:** This production company's credits include *James Dean*.

GILLEN & PRICE

7425 Oakwood Ave., Los Angeles CA 90036. (323)655-8047. Fax: (323)655-8047.

GINTY FILMS

16255 Ventura Blvd., Suite 625, Encino CA 91436. (310)277-1408. E-mail: ginty@robertginty.com. Web site: www.robertginty.com. **Contact:** Robert Ginty. Estab. 1989. Commercial audience. **Buys 12-15 script(s)/year. Works with 10-20 writer(s)/year.** Buys first rights, all rights. Accepts previously produced material. Query with synopsis, production history. Responds in 1 month to queries; 1 month to scripts. **Pays in accordance with WGA standards.**

GITLIN PRODUCTIONS

1741 Ivar Ave., Hollywood CA 90028. (323)802-6950. Fax: (323)802-6951.

GITTES, INC.

10202 W. Washington Blvd., Poitier, Suite 1200, Culver City CA 90232-3195. (310)244-4333. Fax: (310)244-1711. **Contact:** Harry Gittes. Production credits include: *Little Nikita*, *Breaking In*, *About Schmidt*.

GIVEN FILMS

28 Warren St., 5th Floor, New York NY 10007. (212)962-9375. Fax: (212)962-9666. Web site: www.givenfilms.com. **Contact:** Gail Niederhoffen.

GLOBAL NETWORK PICTURES

244 5th Ave., 2nd Floor, Suite A215, New York NY 10001. (212)802-9357. E-mail: globalnetpictures@aol.com. **Contact:** Ricordo Cordero, writer/director. Production credits include: *La Famigila nostra*, *My Heaven Brooklyn*.

GOAT CAY PRODUCTIONS

P.O. Box 38, New York NY 10150. (212)421-8293. Fax: (212)421-8294. E-mail: goatcay@earthlink.net. Web site: home.earthlink.net ~ goatcay/. This is actress Sigourney Weaver's production company. Credits include *Alien 3*.

THE GOATSINGERS

179 Franklin St., 6th Floor, New York NY 10013. (212)966-3045. Fax: (212)966-4362. This is actor Harvey Keitel's production company. Credits include: *Three Seasons*, *Blue in the Face*.

GOEPP CIRCLE PRODUCTIONS

Paramount Pictures, 5555 Melrose, Suite 116, Los Angeles CA 90038. (323)956-4620. Fax: (323)862-1119. Actor Jonathan Frakes' production company. Credits include: *Star Trek: Insurrection*, *Thunderbirds*.

GOLDCREST FILMS INTERNATIONAL, LTD.

1240 Olive Dr., Los Angeles CA 90069. (323)650-4551. Fax: (323)650-3581. Production credits include: *Elvis and Anabelle*, *Rock-A-Doodle*, *A Room With a View*.

GOLDEN HARVEST ENTERTAINMENT CO.

9891 Santa Monica Blvd., Suite 209, Beverly Hills CA 90212. Production credits include: *The Accidental Spy*, *The Big Boss*, *Rumble in the Bronx*.

GOLDEN QUILL

8899 Beverly Blvd., Suite 702, Los Angeles CA 90048. (310)274-5016. Fax: (310)274-5028. Production credits include: *The In-Laws*, *Love Story*, *Outrageous Fortune*.

THE GOLDSTEIN COMPANY

1644 Courtney Ave., Los Angeles CA 90046. (310)659-9511. Fax: (310)659-8779. Production credits include: *The Mothman Prophecies*, *Under Siege*, *Pretty Woman*.

SAMUEL GOLDWYN FILMS

9750 W. Pico Blvd., Suite 400, Los Angeles CA 90035. (310)860-3100. Fax: (310)860-3195. Production credits include *Master and Commander: The Far Side of the World*, *MirrorMask*, *Tortilla Soup*.

GONE FISHIN' PRODUCTIONS

3000 W. Olympic Blvd., Bldg. 2, Suite 1509, Santa Monica CA 90404. (310)315-4737. Fax: (310)315-4715.

GOOD MACHINE INTERNATIONAL, INC.

417 Canal St., 4th Floor, New York NY 10013. (212)343-9230. Fax: (212)343-7412. Production credits include: *The Texas Chainsaw Massacre*, *Adaptation*, *The King Is Alive*.

DAN GORDON PRODUCTIONS

2060-D Ave., Los Arboles, Suite 256, Thousand Oaks CA 91362. (805)496-2566. Production credits include: *Passenger 57*, *Wyatt Earp*, *The Assignment*.

GRACIE FILMS

Sony Pictures, 10202 W. Washington Blvd., Poitier Bldg., Los Angeles CA 90232. (310)244-4222. Fax: (310)244-1530. This is the production company of James L. Brooks, producer/director. Credits include: *Riding in Cars With Boys, As Good As It Gets, Broadcast News*.

GRADE A ENTERTAINMENT

368 N. La Cienega Blvd., Los Angeles CA 90048. (310)358-8600. Fax: (310)652-0718. E-mail: development@gradeaeent.com. **Contact:** Andy Cohen, president. Production credits include: *Captain Ron, It Takes Two, A Chance of Snow*.

GRAHAM/ROSENZWEIG FILMS

6399 Wilshire Blvd., Suite 510, Los Angeles CA 90048. (323)782-6888. Fax: (323)682-6967. E-mail: frfilms@gocybernet.com. **Contact:** Tracie Graham, producer. Production credits include: *Windtalkers, Dumb and Dumber, The War at Home*.

GRAINY PICTURES

75 Main St., Cold Spring NY 10516. (845)265-2241. Fax: (845)265-2543. Production credits include: *How's Your News?, Split Screen, Chasing Amy*.

GRAMMNET PRODUCTIONS

5555 Melrose Ave., Lucy Bldg. #206 (TV); Bob Hope Bldg. #202 (film), Los Angeles CA 90038-3197. (323)956-5547/ (323)956-5840. Fax: (323)862-133. This is actor Kelsey Grammer's company; production credits include: *Kelsey Grammer Salutes Jack Benny, Gary the Rat, The Innocent*.

GRANADA FILM

5225 Wilshire Blvd., Suite 603, Los Angeles CA 90036. (323)692-9940. Fax: (323)692-9944. Production credits include: *The Great Gatsby, The John Denver Story, The Warden*.

GREEN COMMUNICATIONS

255 Parkside Dr., San Fernando CA 91340-3033. (818)557-0050. Production credits include: *Ground Control, Living in Peril, The Last Producer*.

GREEN MOON PRODUCTIONS

3110 Main St., Suite 205, Santa Monica CA 90405. (310)450-6111. Fax: (10)450-1333. Production company of Melanie Griffith and Antonio Banderas. Credits include: *Crazy in Alabama, Along for the Ride, The Body*.

GREENSTREET FILMS, INC.

9 Desbrosses St., 2nd Floor, New York NY 10013. (212)343-1049. Fax: (212)343-0774. **Contact:** Production credits include: *I'm Not Rappaport, Illuminata, Just a Kiss*.

THE ALAN GREISMAN COMPANY

3335 N. Maple Dr., Suite 135, Beverly Hills CA 90210. (310)205-2766. Fax: (310)285-2345.

GREY LINE ENTERTAINMENT

115 W. California Blvd., #310, Pasadena CA 91105-3005. (626)943-0950. E-mail: submissions@greyline.net. Web site: www.greyline.net. **Contact:** Sara Miller, submissions coordinator. "Grey Line Entertainment is a full-service motion picture production and literary management company. We offer direct management of all services associated with the exploitation of stories. When our clients' motion picture screenplays are ready for the marketplace, we place them directly with studios or with major co-producers who can assist in packaging cast and/or director before approaching financiers (Warner Bros., New Line, Fox, Disney, etc.), or broadcasters (HBO, Showtime, etc.)." Query via e-mail only. No attachments. Review online submission guidelines before sending. Responds in 2 weeks to queries.

- ⚷ Queries for screenplays and treatments should consist of a compelling and business-like letter giving us a brief overview of your story and a 1-sentence pitch. Be sure to include your return address and a phone number. No multiple submissions. Treatments and screenplays submitted without a completed and signed Grey Line submission form will be discarded. Include SASE for reply. "We recommend you register your screenplays/treatments with the copyright office or WGA before submitting."

Tips "Your work must be finished and properly edited before seeking our representation (meaning proofread, spell-checked, and rewritten until it's perfect)."

MERV GRIFFIN ENTERTAINMENT

9860 Wilshire Blvd., Beverly Hills CA 90210. (310)385-3160. Fax: (310)385-3162. Production credits include: *Inside the Osmonds*, *Gilda Radner: It's Always Something*, *Jeopardy*.

MATT GROENING PRODUCTIONS

10201 W. Pico Blvd., Bldg. 208, Suite 28, Los Angeles CA 90035. (310)369-3872. Production credits include: *The Simpsons*, *Futurama*, *The Tracey Ullman Show*.

BETH GROSSBARD PRODUCTIONS

9696 Culver Blvd., Suite 208, Culver City CA 90232. (310)841-2555. Fax: (310)841-5934 or (818)705-7366. **Contact:** Jessica Roach, development executive; Beth Grossbard, executive producer. Estab. 1994. Buys first rights and true-life story rights. Query with synopsis, treatment/outline. Responds in 1 month to queries.

Tips "Company develops material for television and the feature film markets. Interested in women's stories/issues, compelling true stories, social issues, contemporary legal issues, literary material, including young adult, children's titles, and small press books. We are also interested in plays, short stories, and original ideas."

RANDA HAINES COMPANY

11693 San Vincente Blvd., Suite 389, Los Angeles CA 90049. (310)889-1843. Fax: (310)472-7951. Production credits include: *Children of a Lesser God*, *The Doctor*, *Dance with Me*.

HALLWAY PICTURES

4929 Wilshire Blvd., Suite 830, Los Angeles CA 90010. (323)937-9210. Fax: (323)937-9222.

HALSTED PICTURES

15 Brooks Ave., Unit B, Venice CA 90291. (310)450-7804. Fax: (310)450-8174. Production credits include *The Day Reagan Was Shot*.

HAMZEH MYSTIQUE FILMS

61 Blaney St., Swampscott MA 01907-2546. (781)596-1281. Fax: (781)599-2424. E-mail: ziad@hamzehmystiquefilms.com. Web site: www.hamzehmystiquefilms.com. Production credits include: *Shadow Glories, Woman, The Letter*.

HANDPRINT ENTERTAINMENT

1100 Glendon Ave., Suite 1000, Los Angeles CA 90024. (310)481-4400. Fax: (310)481-4419. Production credits include: *Fresh Prince of Bel Air, Above the Rim, Booty Call*.

HARPO FILMS, INC.

345 N. Maple Dr., Suite 315, Beverly Hills CA 90210. (310)278-5559. Actress/Producer Oprah Winfrey's company. Production credits include: *Beloved, Before Women Had Wings, Tuesdays with Morrie*.

HART-SHARP ENTERTAINMENT

380 Lafayette St., Suite 304, New York NY 10003. (212)475-7555. Fax: (212)475-1717. Production credits include: *Boys Don't Cry, You Can Count on Me, Nicholas Nickleby*.

HARVE BENNETT PRODUCTIONS

11766 Wilshire Blvd., Ste. 1610, Los Angeles CA 90025. (310) 306-7198. Fax: (310) 306-7598. Credits include *Star Trek II-V, Rich Man, Poor Man, Time Trax, Invasion America*.

HARVEY ENTERTAINMENT

11835 W. Olympic Blvd., #550E, Los Angeles CA 90064. (310)444-4100. Fax: (310)444-4101. Production credits include *Richie Rich*.

HBO ORIGINAL MOVIES

2049 Century Park E., Suite 4200, Los Angeles CA 90067. (310)201-9200. Production credits include: *Six Feet Under, Sex and the City, The Sopranos*.

HEEL & TOE FILMS

650 N. Bronson Ave., Bronson Bldg. 200, Hollywood CA 90293. (323)960-4591. Fax: (323)960-4592. This is Producer Paul Attanasio's company. Production credits include: *Quiz Show, Homicide: Life on the Street, Sum of All Fears*.

JIM HENSON COMPANY

Raleigh Studios, 5358 Melrose Ave., Suite 300 W., Hollywood CA 90038. (323)960-4096. Fax: (212)794-2400 (NYC). Web site: www.henson.com. Production credits include: *Sesame Street, Fraggle Rock, The Great Muppet Caper*.

VICKY HERMAN PRODUCTIONS

8001 Highland Trail, Los Angeles CA 90046. (323)656-4207. Production credits include: *Gilmore Girls*, *A Dangerous Affair*, *Dirty Pictures*.

HERO ENTERTAINMENT

P.O. Box 50811, Santa Barbara CA 93150. (805)695-0757. Fax: (805)695-0757. Production credits include *Blank Check* and *Roger Ramjet: Hero of Our Nation*.

DEBRA HILL PRODUCTIONS

1250 6th St., Suite 205, Santa Monica CA 90401. (310)319-0052. Fax: (310)260-8502. Production credits include: *The Fisher King*, *Crazy in Alabama*, *Halloween*.

HIT & RUN PRODUCTIONS

150 W. 56th St., Suite 5606, New York NY 10019. (212)974-8400. Fax: (212)974-8443. Production credits include *Eye of the Beholder* and *Beautopia*.

HOFFLUND/POLONE

9465 Wilshire Blvd., Suite 820, Beverly Hills CA 90212. (310)859-1971. Fax: (310)859-7250. Production credits include *Stir of Echoes* and *When Trumpets Fade*.

HOGAN MOOREHOUSE PICTURES

1250 6th St., Suite 305, Santa Monica CA 90401. (310)319-9299. Production credits include *Muriel's Wedding* and *Peter Pan*.

HORIZON ENTERTAINMENT, INC.

1040 Hamilton St., Suite 205, Vancouver BC V6B 2R9, Canada. (604)632-1707. Fax: (604)632-1607. E-mail: rhs@filmhorizon.com. Web site: www.filmhorizon.com. Production credits include *The Princess Blade* and *Peter Pan*.

HORSESHOE BAY PRODUCTIONS

710 Wilshire Blvd., Santa Monica CA 90404. (310)587-0787. Production credits include: *Succubus*, *Daredevil*, *Elektra*.

HRD PRODUCTIONS

1041 N. Formosa Ave., W. Hollywood CA 90046. (323)850-3595. Fax: (323)850-3596. Production credits include: *The Replacements*, *Odd Couple II*, *Pretty in Pink*.

HUGHES CAPITAL ENTERTAINMENT

Warner Center, 21550 Oxnard St., 3rd Floor, Woodland Hills CA 91367. (818)592-6379. Fax: (818)888-5219. E-mail: info@trihughes.com. Web site: www.hughescapitalentertainment.com. **Contact:** Faye, creative executive; Patrick Huges, producer; Mark Stefanick, associate manager; Karen Rabesa, VP production/development. Estab. 2006. Produces 2 movies/year. Does not return submissions. Send query and synopsis, or submit complete ms. Mostly accepts agented submissions. Responds in 3 weeks to queries.

☞ "We are looking to produce and develop feature-length screenplays, produced stage plays, well-developed pitches, and detailed treatments. Focus is on broad comedies, urban comedies, socially smart comedies, family films (family adventure), ground-breaking abstract projects, and new writers/directors with an extremely unique and unparalleled point of view. Don't focus on budget, cast, or locations. The story is key to getting things done here."

Tips "Don't back your screenplay or book into a budget. Let the creative lead the way. Never talk about a low budget and a star that's attached or that pre-sold in Egypt for $100 million. We don't care. We care about a unique voice—a filmmaker willing to take risks. Scripts that push the limits without trying for shock value. We care about filmmakers and good writers here."

HUNGRY MAN FILMS

428 Broadway, 6th Floor, New York NY 10013. (212)625-5600. Fax: (212)625-5699.

HUNT-TAVEL PRODUCTIONS

10202 W. Washington Blvd., Bldg. #2410, Culver City CA 90232. (310)244-3144. Fax: (310)244-0164. This is actress Helen Hunt's company. Productions credits include *Then She Found Me*.

HYAMS PRODUCTIONS, INC., PETER

1453 3rd St., Suite 315, Santa Monica CA 90401. (310)393-1553. Fax: (310)393-1554. Production credits include: *The Musketeer, Sudden Death, Timecop*.

HYDE PARK ENTERTAINMENT

2500 Broadway St., Santa Monica CA 90404. (310)449-3191. Fax: (310)449-3356. Production credits include: *Bringing Down the House, Bandits, Original Sin*.

ICON PRODUCTIONS, INC.

5555 Melrose Ave., Los Angeles CA 90038. (323)956-2100. Fax: (323)862-2121. Production credits include: *Maverick, Braveheart, We Were Soldiers*.

IFM FILM ASSOCIATES, INC.

1328 E. Palmer Ave., Glendale CA 91205-3738. (818)243-4976. Fax: (818)550-9728. E-mail: ifmfilm@aol.com. **Contact:** Anthony Ginnane, president. Production credits include: *Sally Marshall Is Not an Alien, The Whole of the Moon, The Hit*.

IMAGEMOVERS

100 Universal City Plaza, Bldg. 484, Universal City CA 91608. (818)733-8313. Fax: (818)733-8333. This is director Robert Zemeckis' company. Production credits include: *Romancing the Stone, Forrest Gump, Back to the Future* franchise.

IMAGINE ENTERTAINMENT

9465 Wilshire Blvd., 7th Floor, Beverly Hills CA 90212. (310)858-2000. Fax: (310)858-2020. This is the production company of Director/Producer Ron Howard/Brian Grazer. Credits include: *American Gangster, Cinderella Man, A Beautiful Mind, 8 Mile*.

INCOGNITO ENTERTAINMENT

345 N. Maple Dr., Suite 348, Beverly Hills CA 90210. (310)246-1500. Fax: (310)246-0469. Production credits include: *Three to Tango, Morning, Freeway II*.

INDICAN PRODUCTIONS

2565 Broadway, Suite 138, New York NY 10025. (212)666-1500. Fax: (212)666-9588. This is actress Julia Ormond's production company; credits include *Calling the Ghosts*.

INDUSTRY ENTERTAINMENT

955 S. Carrilo Dr., 3rd Floor, Los Angeles CA 90048. (323)954-9000. Fax: (323)954-0990. Production company of Keith Addis and Nich Wechsler; credits include: *Drugstore Cowboy, Requiem for a Dream, The Education of Max Bickford*.

INITIAL ENTERTAINMENT GROUP, INC.

3000 W. Olympic Blvd., Suite 1550, Santa Monica CA 90404. (310)315-1722. Fax: (310)315-1723. Production credits include: *Gangs of New York, Ali, Traffic*.

INTERLIGHT

8981 Sunset Blvd., Suite 101, W. Hollywood CA 90069. (310)248-4477. Fax: (310)248-4494. E-mail: contact@interlightusa.com.

INTERMEDIA FILM EQUITIES, USA

9242 Beverly Blvd., Suite 201, Beverly Hills CA 90210. Web site: www.intermediafilm.com. Production credits include: *Adaptation, The Life of David Gale, Terminator 3: The Rise of the Machines*.

INTERNATIONAL FILM GROUP, INC.

7910 Ivanhoe Ave., Suite 529, La Jolla CA 92037. (858)551-7310. Fax: (858)551-7611.

INTERNATIONAL HOME ENTERTAINMENT

1440 Veteran Ave., Suite 650, Los Angeles CA 90024. (323)663-6940. **Contact:** Jed Leland, Jr., assistant to the president. Estab. 1976. Buys first rights. Query. Responds in 2 months to queries. **Pays in accordance with WGA standards.**

Looking for material that is international in scope.

Tips "Our response time is faster on average now (3-6 weeks), but we do not reply without a SASE. No unsolicited mss. We do not respond to unsolicited phone calls or e-mail."

IRISH DREAMTIME

2450 Broadway, Suite E-5021, Santa Monica CA 90404. This is actor Pierce Brosnan's company. Production credits include: *Shattered, The Matador, The Thomas Crown Affair*.

IXTLAN PRODUCTIONS

201 Santa Monica Blvd., Suite 610, Santa Monica CA 90401. (310)395-0525. Fax: (310)395-1536. This is writer/director/producer Oliver Stone's company; production credits include: *Born on the Fourth of July, Nixon, Heaven & Earth*.

THE JACOBSON COMPANY

500 S. Buena Vista St., Burbank CA 91521. (818)560-1600. Fax: (818)655-8746. This is producer Tom Jacobson's company. Production credits include: *Playboys*, *Ladykillers*, *Mission to Mars*.

JAFFILMS

152 W. 57th St., 52nd Floor, New York NY 10019. (212)262-4700. Fax: (212)262-4729. Production credits include: *Four Feathers*, *Fatal Attraction*, *Kramer vs. Kramer*.

JARET ENTERTAINMENT

2017 Pacific Ave., Suite 2, Venice CA 90291. (310)883-8807. Fax: (310)822-0916. Production credits include *10 Things I Hate About You*.

JERSEY FILMS

P.O. Box 491246, Los Angeles CA 90049. (310)550-3200. Fax: (310)550-3210. This is actor/director Danny De Vito's company. Production credits include: *Freedom Writers*, *Erin Brockovich*, *Pulp Fiction*.

THE JINKS/COHEN COMPANY

100 Universal City Plaza, Bldg. 5171, Universal City CA 91608. (818)733-9880. Fax: (818)733-9843. Production credits include: *Big Fish*, *American Beauty*, *The Forgotten*.

JONESING PICTURES, INC.

4502 Jouster Ct., Suite 306, Orlando FL 32817. E-mail: office@jonesingpictures.com. Web site: www. jonesingpictures.com. Production credits include *Loren Cass* and *Straight-Jacket*.

JOVY JUNIOR ENTERPRISES LTD

31 Kingly St., London W1R 5LA, UK. Production credits include *Sorted* and *Holiday Romance*.

JUMP ROPE PRODUCTIONS

10932 Morrison St., Suite 108, Studio City CA 91601. (818)752-2229.

JUNCTION ENTERTAINMENT

500 S. Buena Vista St., Animation 1-B, Burbank CA 91521. (818)560-2800. Fax: (818)841-3176. This is director Jon Turtletaub's company. Directing credits include: *National Treasure*, *Instinct*, *While You Were Sleeping*.

KAPLAN/PERRONE ENTERTAINMENT

10202 W. Washington Blvd., Astaire Bldg., Suite 3003, Culver City CA 90232. (310)244-6681. Fax: (310)244-2151. This is the production company of producers Aaron Kaplan and Sean Perrone; credits include *You, Me and Dupre*.

KAREEM PRODUCTIONS

5458 Wilshire Blvd., Los Angeles CA 90036. (310)201-7960. Fax: (310)201-7964. This is actor Kareem Abdul-Jabbar's production company. Credits include *The Vernon Johns Story*.

MARTY KATZ PRODUCTIONS
1250 6th St., Suite 205, Santa Monica CA 90401. (310)260-8501. Fax: (310)260-8502.

KELLER ENTERTAINMENT GROUP
14225 Ventura Blvd., Sherman Oaks CA 91423. (818)981-4950. Fax: (818)501-6224. E-mail: jimperi10 5@aol.com. Production credits include: *Conan, Tarzan, Acapulco H.E.A.T.*

DAVID E. KELLEY PRODUCTIONS
1600 Rosecrans Ave., Bldg. 4B, Manhattan Beach CA 90266. (310)727-2200. Production credits include: *Life on Mars, Boston Legal, Ally McBeal.*

KENNEDY/MARSHALL COMPANY
3000 W. Olympic Blvd., Bldg. 5, Suite 1250, Santa Monica CA 90404. (310)656-8400. Fax: (310)565-8430. Production credits include: *Alive: 20 Years Later, Seabiscuit, Munich.*

KILLER FILMS, INC.
380 Lafayette St., Suite 302, New York NY 10003. (212)473-3950. Fax: (212)473-6152. Credits include *An American Crime, The Notorious Bettie Page, One Hour Photo.*

KINGSGATE FILMS, INC.
18954 W. Pico, 2nd Floor, Los Angeles CA 90035. (310)281-5880. Fax: (310)281-2633. This is actor Nick Nolte's company. Production credits include: *Affliction, Simpatico, Rules of Attraction.*

KLASKY-CSUPO
6353 Sunset Blvd., Hollywood CA 90028. (323)463-0145. Web site: www.cooltoons.com. Production credits include: *Rugrats, The Wild Thornberrys, Aaahh! Real Monsters.*

KLEISER PRODUCTIONS, RANDAL
3050 Runyon Canyon Rd., Los Angeles CA 90046. (323)850-5511. Fax: (323)850-1074. Production credits include *Getting it Right.*

THE KOCH COMPANY
2791 Ellison Dr., Beverly Hills CA 90210. (310)271-0466. Production credits include: *Rooftops, Keeping the Faith, Frequency.*

KONRAD PICTURES
Columbia Pictures, 10202 W. Washington Blvd., TriStar Bldg., Suite 222, Culver City CA 90232. (310)244-3555. Fax: (310)244-0555. Production credits include *Citizen Ruth, Kate & Leopold.*

KOPELSON ENTERTAINMENT
8490 Sunset Blvd., 2nd Floor, Los Angeles CA 90069. (310)360-3200. Fax: (310)360-3201. This is producers Arnold and Anne Kopelson's company. Production credits include: *U.S. Marshals, Eraser, Platoon.*

ROBERT KOSBERG PRODUCTIONS

% Merv Griffin Entertainment, 9860 Wilshire Blvd., Beverly Hills CA 90210. (310)385-3165. Fax: (310)385-3165. Production credits include: *Commando, In the Mood, Twelve Monkeys*.

KOUF-BIGELOW PRODUCTIONS

10061 Riverside Dr., Suite 1024, Toluca Lake CA 91602. (818)508-1010. Production credits include: *Con Air, Silent Fall, Kalifornia*.

THE JONATHAN KRANE GROUP

8033 Sunset Blvd., Suite 6750, Los Angeles CA 90046. (310)278-0142. Fax: (310)278-0925. Production credits include: *Domestic Disturbance, The General's Daughter, Look Who's Talking Now*.

KUSHNER-LOCKE COMPANY

280 S. Beverly Drive, Suite 205, Beverly Hills CA 90212. Fax: (310)275-7518. E-mail: info@kushner-locke.com. Web site: www.kushner-locke.com. Company credits include: *Pinocchio, Andre, Brave Little Toaster*.

LA LUNA FILMS

335 N. Maple Dr., Suite 235, Beverly Hills CA 90210. (310)285-9696. Fax: (310)285-9691. Production credits include: *The Butcher's Wife, Drop Zone, Dream Lover*.

LA-MONT COMMUNICATIONS, INC.

13323 Washington Blvd., Suite 306, Los Angeles CA 90066. (310)577-6725. Fax: (310)577-6727.

THE LADD COMPANY

9465 Wilshire Blvd., Suite 910, Beverly Hills CA 90212. (310)777-2060. Fax: (310)777-2061. This is producer Alan Ladd, Jr.'s company. Production credits include: *Chariots of Fire, The Right Stuff, Braveheart*.

DAVID LADD FILMS

2450 Broadway St., Santa Monica CA 90404. (310)449-3410. Fax: (310)586-8272. Production credits include: *The Mod Squad, Hart's War, A Guy Thing*.

LAIKA/HOUSE

1400 N.W. 22nd Ave., Portland OR 97210. (503)225-1130. E-mail: ask_us@laika.com. Web site: www.laika.com. **Contact:** Exec. Prod.: Lourri Hammad; Co-Exec. Prod.: Jen Johnson. Produces every type of animation in every medium.

LAKESHORE ENTERTAINMENT

9268 West Third Street, Beverly Hills CA 90210. Web site: www.lakeshoreentertainment.com. Production credits include *Million Dollar Baby, Runaway Bride*.

LAKESHORE INTERNATIONAL

5555 Melrose Ave., Gloria Swanson Blvd., 4th Floor, Hollywood CA 90038. (323)956-4222. Fax: (323)862-1456. Production credits include: *Madhouse, Homegrown*.

LARGER THAN LIFE PRODUCTIONS

100 Universal City Plaza, Bldg. 6111, Universal City CA 91608. (818)777-4004. Fax: (818)866-5677. Production credits include *Pleasantville* and *Trial and Error*.

LARGO ENTERTAINMENT

2029 Century Park E, Suite 4125, Los Angeles CA 90067. (310)203-0055. Fax: (310)203-0254. Production credits include: *Point Break*, *G.I. Jane*, *Finding Graceland*.

ARNOLD LEIBOVIT ENTERTAINMENT

P.O. Box 33544, Santa Fe NM 87594-3544. E-mail: director@scifistation.com. Web site: www.scifistation.com. **Contact:** Barbara Schimpf, vice president, production; Arnold Leibovit, director/producer. Estab. 1988. Produces material for motion pictures and television. **Works with 1 writer(s)/year.** Query with log line and synopsis via e-mail. Do not send full script unless requested. A submission release must be included with all scripts. Responds in 2 months to queries. **Pays in accordance with WGA standards.**

Needs Films (35mm), videotapes. Does not want novels, plays, poems, treatments, or submissions on disk.

LEO FILMS

6249 Langdon Ave., Van Nuys CA 91411. (818)782-6541. Fax: (818)782-3320. E-mail: lustgar@pacbell.net. Web site: www.leofilms.com. **Contact:** Steve Lustgarten, president. Estab. 1989. Has released over 75 feature films. **Buys 5 script(s)/year. Works with 8 writer(s)/year.** Buys all rights. Query by e-mail with synopsis. Responds in 1 week to queries; 2 months to scripts. **Payment varies— options and sales.**

Tips "Will also consider novels, short stories, and treatments that have true movie potential."

LEVIN & ASSOCIATES, CYD

Attn: Rob Gallagher, 8919 Harrat St., Suite 305, Los Angeles CA 90069. (310)271-6484. Web site: www.robgallagher.freeservers.com.

LICHT/MUELLER FILM CORPORATION

132 S. Lasky Dr., Suite 200, Beverly Hills CA 90212. (310)205-5500. Fax: (310)205-5590. Production credits include: *Spinning Boris*, *The Cable Guy*, *Waterworld*.

LIGHTHOUSE PRODUCTIONS

120 El Camino Dr., Suite 212, Beverly Hills CA 90212. (310)859-4923. Fax: (310)859-7511. Production credits include: *The Sting*, *Close Encounters of the Third Kind*, *Taxi Driver*.

LIGHTSTORM ENTERTAINMENT

919 Santa Monica Blvd., Santa Monica CA 90401. (310)656-6100. Fax: (310)656-6102. This is writer/director James Cameron's company. Production credits include: *Titanic*, *Aliens*, *True Lies*.

Production Companies

LION ROCK PRODUCTIONS

2500 Broadway St., Suite E590, Santa Monica CA 90404. (310)449-3205. Fax: (310)449-3512. This is the production company of John Woo and Terence Chang; credits include: *Face/Off*, *Broken Arrow*, *Windtalkers*.

LIONS GATE FILMS INTERNATIONAL

4553 Glencoe Ave., Suite 200, Marina del Rey CA 90292. (310)314-2000. Fax: (310)392-0252. Web site: www.lionsgatefilms.com. Production credits include: *Girl With a Pearl Earring*, *Affliction*, *Monster's Ball*.

LITTLE STUDIO FILMS

270 N. Canon Dr., Suite 1861, Beverly Hills CA 90210. (310)652-5385. Production credits include *Central Booking* and *The Drone Virus*.

LIVE PLANET

2950 31st St., 3rd Floor, Santa Monica CA 90405. (310)664-2400. Production credits include: *The Hero*, *Gone Baby Gone*, *Matchstick Men*.

LOBELL PRODUCTIONS

335 N. Maple Dr., Suite 130, Beverly Hills CA 90210. (310)285-2383. Fax: (310)205-2767. Production credits include: *Tears of the Sun*, *Honeymoon in Vegas*, *The Freshman*.

LONGBOW PRODUCTIONS

4181 Sunswept Dr., Suite 100, Studio City CA 91604. (818)762-6600. Production credits include: *Secret Cutting*, *A Crime of Passion*, *A League of Their Own*.

LOVE SPELL ENTERTAINMENT

10202 W. Washington Blvd., Gable 103, Culver City CA 90232. (310)244-6040. Fax: (310)244-0740. This is actress Jennifer Love Hewitt's company. Production credits include: *Bunny*, *My Romance*, *If Only*.

LOWER EAST SIDE FILMS

302A W. 12th St., Suite 218, New York NY 10014. (212)966-0111. This is actor John Leguizamo's production company; credits include: *Undefeated*, *Joe the King*.

LUCID FILM

8490 Sunset Blvd., Suite 700, Los Angeles CA 90069. (310)777-0007. Fax: (310)360-8613. This is actor Ryan Phillippe's production company; credits include *Honey West* and *White Boy Shuffle*.

LUMIERE FILMS INC.

8079 Selma Ave., Los Angeles CA 90046. (323)650-6773. Fax: (323)650-7339. Distribution credits include *The Three Stages of Stan* and *Dalekmania*.

LYLES PRODUCTIONS, INC.

% Paramount Pictures, 5555 Melerose Ave., Los Angeles CA 90038-3197. (323)956-5819. Fax: (323)862-0256. Production credits include: *The Last Day*, *Dear Mr. President*, *Here's Boomer*.

MAD CHANCE

4000 Warner Blvd., #3, Burbank CA 91522. (818)954-3803. Fax: (818)954-3447. Production credits include: *Get Smart*, *Confessions of a Dangerous Mind*, *Panic*.

MAINLINE RELEASING

1801 Ave. of the Stars, Suite 1035, Los Angeles CA 90067. (310)286-1001. Fax: (310)286-0530. Web site: www.mainlinereleasing.com. Distribution credits include: *Co-Ed Confidential*, *Hangman*, *Indiscreet*.

MAINLINE RELEASING

A Film & TV Production and Distribution Co., 301 Arizona Ave., 4th Floor, Santa Monica CA 90401. (301)255-7999. Fax: (310)255-7998. E-mail: hilda@lightning-ent.com. Web site: www.mainlinerelea sing.com. **Contact:** Hilda Somarriba, coordinator, sales, acquisitions and marketing. Estab. 1997. Produces family films, drama, thrillers, and erotic features.

MALPASO PRODUCTIONS

4000 Warner Blvd., Bldg. 81, Burbank CA 91522-0811. (818)954-3367. Fax: (818)954-4803. This is actor/director Clint Eastwood's production company; credits include: *The Bridges of Madison County*, *Unforgiven*, *Space Cowboys*.

MANDALAY PICTURES

5555 Melrose Ave., Lewis Bldg., Hollywood CA 90038. Production credits include: *Sleepy Hollow*, *Enemy at the Gates*, *The Score*.

MANDATE PICTURES

8750 Wilshire Blvd., Suite 300 E., Beverly Hills CA 90211. (310)360-1441. Fax: (310)360-1447. E-mail: info@mandatepictures.com. Web site: www.senatorinternational.com. Production credits include *Juno*, *Mr. Magorium's Wonder Emporium*, *The Grudge*.

MANDOLIN ENTERTAINMENT

1741 Ivar Ave., Hollywood CA 90028. (323)802-6950. Fax: (323)802-6951. Production credits include: *Trapped*, *Thelma and Louise*, *White Squall*.

MANDY FILMS, INC.

9201 Wilshire Blvd., #206, Beverly Hills CA 90210. (310)246-0500. Fax: (310)246-0350. Production credits include: *Jaws*, *Chocolat*, *A Few Good Men*.

MANIFEST FILM COMPANY

1247 Euclid St., Santa Monica CA 90404. (310)899-5554. Fax: (310)899-5553. This is the production company of Lisa Henson and Janet Wang; credits include: *High Crimes*, *The People vs. Larry Flynt*, *The Joy Luck Club*.

LAURENCE MARK PRODUCTIONS

10202 W. Washington Blvd., Poitier Bldg., Suite 3111, Culver City CA 90232. (310)244-5239. Production credits include: *Riding in Cars with Boys*, *As Good As It Gets*, *Jerry Maguire*.

MARMONT PRODUCTIONS, INC.

1022 Palm Ave., Suite 3, Los Angeles CA 90069. (310)659-0768. Production credits include: *Mountains of the Moon*, *Poodle Springs*, *The Postman Always Rings Twice*.

THE MARSHAK/ZACHARY CO.

8840 Wilshire Blvd., 1st Floor, Beverly Hills CA 90211. Fax: (310)358-3192. E-mail: marshakzachary @aol.com; alan@themzco.com. **Contact:** Alan W. Mills, associate. Estab. 1981. Audience is film goers of all ages and television viewers. **Buys 3-5 script(s)/year. Works with 10 writer(s)/year.** Rights purchased vary. Query with synopsis. Responds in 2 weeks to queries; 3 months to scripts. **Payment varies.**

Tips "Submit logline (1-line description), a short synopsis of storyline, and a short biographical profile (focus on professional background). SASE required for all mailed inquiries. If submissions are sent via e-mail, subject must include specific information or else run the risk of being deleted as junk mail. All genres accepted, but ideas must be commercially viable, high concept, original, and marketable."

MARSTAR PRODUCTIONS

8840 Wilshire Blvd., Suite 102, Beverly Hills CA 90211. (310)358-3210. Fax: (310)820-1850. Production credits include: *Mask*, *Sophie's Choice*, *On Golden Pond*.

MARULLUS PRODUCTIONS

P.O. Box 2435, Venice CA 90291. E-mail: info@marullus.com. Web site: www.marullus.com. **Contact:** Gerhard Schwarz: gerhard@marullus.com; Fernando Ramiros: fernando@marullus.com; Development: development@marullus.com; Company Relations: info@marullus.com. "The goal of Marullus Productions Inc. is nothing short of a revolution in independent film, providing both commercially viable and artistically polished films for both the art house and the local cinema around the block. From family films, mainstream feature films to surreal independent dramas and television series."

MARVEL STUDIOS INC.

10474 Santa Monica Blvd., Suite 206, Los Angeles CA 90025. (310)234-8991. Fax: (310)234-8481. Production credits include: *Spider-Man*, *X-Men*, *Iron Man*.

MATERIAL

4000 Warner Blvd., 139/27, Burbank CA 91522. (818)954-1551. Fax: (818)954-5299. This is producer Jorge Saralegui's company. Production credits include: *Queen of the Damned*, *Red Planet*, *Time Machine*.

MAVERICK FILMS

9348 Civic Center Dr., 1st Floor, Beverly Hills CA 90210. (310)276-6177. Fax: (310)276-9477. This is the production company of Madonna/Guy Oseary. Credits include: *The Riches*, *I'm Going to Tell You a Secret*, *Agent Cody Banks*.

MEDIA 8

15260 Ventura Blvd., Suite 710, Sherman Oaks CA 91403. (818)325-8000. Formerly named MDP Worldwide. Production credits include: *Eye of the Beholder*, *Jungle Book*, *The Musketeer*.

MEERSON-KRIKES

427 N. Canon Dr., Suite 216, Beverly Hills CA 90210. (310)858-0552. Fax: (310)858-0554. Production credits include: *Anna and the King*, *Star Trek IV*, *Double Impact*.

MENDEL PRODUCTIONS, BARRY

100 Universal City Plaza, #5163, Universal City CA 91608. (818)733-3076. Fax: (818)733-4070. Production credits include: *The Royal Tenenbaums*, *The Sixth Sense*, *Rushmore*.

MERCHANT-IVORY

250 W. 57th St., Suite 1825, New York NY 10107. (212)582-8049. Fax: (212)459-9201. This is the production company of director/producer Ismail merchant and James Ivory. Credits include: *Howard's End*, *A Room With a View*, *The Remains of the Day*.

MESTRES PRODUCTIONS, RICARDO

500 S. Buena Vista St., Burbank CA 91521. (818)560-1000. Fax: (818)953-4238. Production credits include: *101 Dalmatians*, *Jack*, *Flubber*.

METAFILMICS, INC.

4250 Wilshire Blvd., Los Angeles CA 90010. (818)734-9320. Production credits include: *What Dreams May Come*, *The Linda McCartney Story*, *Homeless to Harvard*.

MIDDLE FORK PRODUCTIONS

10877 Wilshire Blvd., Suite 1810, Los Angeles CA 90024. (310)271-4200. Fax: (310)271-8200. Production credits include: *Reefer Madness: The Movie Musical*, *Good Rockin' Tonight*, *Anaconda*.

MIKE'S MOVIES

627 N. Las Palmas, Los Angeles CA 90004. (323)462-4690. Fax: (323)462-4699. This is producer Michael Peyser's company. Production credits include *Imagining Argentina* and *Haiku Tunnel*.

MILLAR/GOUGH INK

3800 Barham Blvd., Suite 503, Los Angeles CA 90068. (323)882-1307. Fax: (323)851-6045. Production credits include *Smallville* and *Hannah Montana: The Movie* (2009).

MINDFIRE ENTERTAINMENT

3740 Overland Ave., Los Angeles CA 90034. (310)204-4481. Fax: (310)204-5882. Production credits include: *DOA: Dead or Alive*, *The Darkroom*, *The Specials*.

MINERVISION

8000 Sunset Blvd., Suite 301A, Los Angeles CA 90046. (323)848-3080. Fax: (323)848-3085.

MIRACLE PICTURES

1625 Olympic Blvd., Suite 200, Santa Monica CA 90404. (310)392-3011. Fax: (310)392-2021. This is producer A. Hitman Ho's company. Credits include: *Hotel Rwanda*, *Reservation Road*, *The Weight of Water*.

MIRAGE ENTERPRISES

% Sony Pictures Entertainment, 10202 W. Washington Blvd., Culver City CA 90232. (310)244-2044. This is the company of director Sydney Pollack and Anthony Kinchella. Credits include: *The Talented Mr. Ripley*, *Michael Clayton*, *Iris*.

MODERN ENTERTAINMENT

16255 Ventura Blvd., Suite 1100, Encino CA 91436. (818)386-0444. Fax: (818)728-8294. Production credits include *AFI's 100 Year . . . 100 Passions* and *The Dead Zone*.

MOJO FILMS

90221 Melrose Ave., Suite 302, Los Angeles CA 90069. (310)248-6070. This is producer Gary Fleder's company. Credits include: *A dios momo*, *Imposter*, *Mojo*.

MONAREX HOLLYWOOD CORP.

11605 W. Pico Blvd., Suite 200, Los Angeles CA 90064. (310)478-6666. Fax: (310)478-6866. E-mail: monarexcorp@aol.com. **Contact:** Chris D. Nebe, president. Estab. 1978. All audiences. **Buys 3-4 script(s)/year. Works with 5-10 writer(s)/year.** Buys all rights. Query with synopsis. Responds in 1 month to queries. **Pays in accordance with WGA standards.**

THE MONTECITO PICTURE COMPANY

1482 E. Valley Rd., Suite 477, Montecito CA 93108. (805)565-8590. Fax: (805)565-8590. This is director Ivan Rittman's company. Production credits include: *Disturbia*, *The Pink Panther*, *Old School*.

MOONSTONE ENTERTAINMENT

P.O. Box 7400, Studio City CA 91614-7400. (818)985-3003. Fax: (818)985-3009. Web site: www.moonstonefilms.com. Production credits include: *Hotel*, *Dancing at the Blue Iguana*, *Miss Julie*.

MORGAN CREEK PRODUCTIONS

4000 Warner Blvd., Bldg. 76, Burbank CA 91522. (818)954-4800. Fax: (818)954-4811. Production credits include *Ace Ventura*, *Major League*, *Wild America*.

THE RUDDY MORGAN ORGANIZATION, INC.

9300 Wilshire Blvd., Suite 508, Beverly Hills CA 90212. (310)271-7698. Fax: (310)278-9978. Production credits include *Farewell to the King*, *The Godfather*, *Cannonball Run*.

MOSTOW/LIEBERMAN

100 Universal City Plaza, #4111, Universal City CA 91608. (818)777-4444. Fax: (818)866-128. Production credits include *The Jackal*, *The Game*, *Around the World in 80 Days*.

MOTION PICTURE CORPORATION OF AMERICA

10635 Santa Monica Blvd., Suite 180, Santa Monica CA 90025. (310)319-9500. Fax: (310)319-9501. E-mail: info@mpcafilm.com. Web site: www.mpcafilm.com. Production credits include *Boat Trip*, *Beverly Hills Ninja*, *Kingpin*.

MR. MUDD

5225 Wilshire Blvd., Suite 604, Los Angeles CA 90036. (310)319-9500. Fax: (310)932-5666. This is actor John Malkovich's company. Production credits include *Juno*, *The Libertine*, *Ripley's Game*.

MUTANT ENEMY, INC.

P.O. Box 900, Beverly Hills CA 90213-0900. (310)579-5180. Fax: (310)579-5380. This is producer Joss Whedon's company. Production credits include *Buffy the Vampire Slayer*, *Firefly*, *Serenity*.

MUTUAL FILM COMPANY

650 N. Bronson Ave., Clinton Bldg., Hollywood CA 90004. (323)871-5690. Fax: (323)871-5689. Production credits include *Paulie*, *Lara Croft: Tomb Raider*, *The Patriot*.

MYRIAD PICTURES

3015 Main Street, Suite 400, Santa Monica CA 90405, USA. Web site: www.myriadpictures.com. Production credits include *Dark Matter*, *Van Wilder*, *Being Julia*.

NEUFELD-REHME PRODUCTIONS

10202 W. Washington Blvd., Culver City CA 90232. (310)244-2555. Fax: (310)244-0255. This is the production company of Mace Neufeld/Robert Rehme. Production credits include *Clear and Present Danger*, *The Sum of All Fears*, *Hunt for Red October*.

NEW AMSTERDAM ENTERTAINMENT, INC.

675 third Ave., Suite 2521, New York NY 10017. (212)922-1930. Fax: (212)922-0674. Production credits include *Pet Sematary*, *The Vernon Johns Story*, *Frank Herbert's Dune*.

NEW CRIME PRODUCTIONS

555 Rose Ave., Venice CA 90291. (310)396-2199. Fax: (310)396-4249. This is actor John Cusack's production company. Credits include *Grosse Pointe Blank*, *High Fidelity*, *Grace is Gone*.

NEW REGENCY PRODUCTIONS

10201 W. Pico Blvd., Bldg. 12, Los Angeles CA 90035. (310)369-8300. Fax: (310)369-0470. This is producer Arnon Milchan's company. Credits include *L.A. Confidential*, *The Negotiator*, *City of Angels*.

NHO ENTERTAINMENT

8931 Beverly Blvd., #249, Los Angeles CA 90048. E-mail: mark.costa@nhoentertainment.com; for d.oelman@nhoentertainment.com. Web site: www.nhoentertainment.com. **Contact:** Mark Costa, partner. Estab. 1999. All audiences. **Buys 5 script(s)/year. Works with 10 writer(s)/year.** Buys all rights. Accepts previously produced material. Catalog for #10 SASE. Query with synopsis, résumé, writing samples, production history. Via e-mail. Responds in 1 month to queries. **Pays in accordance with WGA standards.**

Needs Films, videotapes, multimedia kits, tapes and cassettes.

NICKELODEON ANIMATION STUDIOS

231 W. Olive Ave., Burbank CA 91502. (818)736-3000. Web site: www.nick.com. Production credits include *Jimmy Neutron: Boy Genius*, *Harriet the Spy*, *Rugrats: The Movie*.

NITE OWL PRODUCTIONS

126 Hall Rd., Aliquippa PA 15001. (724)775-1993. Fax: (801)881-3017. E-mail: niteowlprods@aol. com; mark@niteowlproductionsltd.com. Web site: www.niteowlproductionsltd.com. **Contact:** Bridget Petrella. Estab. 2001. Production credits include *Shopping Cart Commandos* and *American Playhouse: Three Sovereigns for Sarah*. Send a 1-page, single-spaced query letter via e-mail or mail.

> ⊶ "We will be producing at least 5-10 feature films in the next 2-5 years. We are searching for polished, well-structured, well-written, and professional-looking screenplays that are ready for production. If your screenplay does not meet these standards, do not send us a query. All screenplays must be in English and be in standard industry format. Provide a working title for your screenplay.

Tips "All submissions must include a dated and signed Submission Release Form or they will be discarded immediately. All full-length feature film screenplays must be 80-130 pages in length. One-hour TV spec scripts must be 55-65 pages in length. Do not send us computer disks. One hardcopy of your screenplay will suffice. Do not cheat on your margins—we will notice. Proofread your screenplay thoroughly before submitting to avoid typos and punctuation and grammar mistakes. Copyright your script with the US Copyright Office and register it with the WGA. All screenplays must be firmly bound and include a cover page with the title of the work and your name, address, and contact information. Your materials will not be returned."

NO HANDS PRODUCTIONS

375 Greenwich St., 7th Floor, New York NY 10013. (212)941-4081. Fax: (212)941-4082. Production credits include *Blue's Clues* and *Keith*.

NUANCE PRODUCTIONS

345 N. Maple Dr., Suite 208, Beverly Hills CA 90210. (310)247-1870. Fax: (310)247-8150. This is actor Paul Reiser's production company. Credits include *Mad About You*, *The Thing About My Folks*, *Lovebites*.

NUMENOREAN FILMS

P.O. Box 11409, Beverly Hills CA 90210. E-mail: info@numenoreanfilms.com. Web site: www.nu menoreanfilms.com. Production credits include *Dead Again*, *Inferno*, *The Insatiable*.

LYNDA OBST PRODUCTIONS

5555 Melrose Ave., Millard Bldg. 210, Hollywood CA 90038. (323)956-8744. Fax: (323)862-2287. Web site: www.lyndaobst.com. Production credits include *Sleepless in Seattle*, *The Fisher King*, *One Fine Day*.

OCEAN PICTURES

10201 W. Pico Blvd., Bldg. 12, Los Angeles CA 90035. (310)369-0093. Fax: (310)369-7742. This is actor Harold Ramis's company. Production credits include *Analyze This*, *Bedazzled*, *Groundhog Day*.

OFFROAD ENTERTAINMENT

5555 Melrose Ave., Bldg. 209, Hollywood CA 90038. (323)956-4425. Fax: (323)862-1120. Production credits include *Jury Duty* and *200 Cigarettes*.

OLMOS PRODUCTIONS, INC.

500 S. Buena Vista St., Old Animation Bldg. 3A6, Code 1803, Burbank CA 91521. (818)560-8651. Fax: (818)560-8655. This is actor Edward James Olmos's production company. Credits include *Roosters*, *American Me*, *Lives in Hazard*.

OMEGA ENTERTAINMENT, LTD.

8760 Shoreham Dr., Los Angeles CA 90069. (310)855-0516. Fax: (310)652-2044. Web site: www.omeg apic.com/home.htm. Production credits include *If I Had Known I Was A Genius*, *In the Cold of the Night*, *Blind Date*.

OPEN CITY FILMS

122 Hudson St., 5th Floor, New York NY 10013. (212)255-0500. Fax: (212)244-0455. E-mail: oc@open cityfilms.com. Web site: www.opencityfilms.com. Production credits include *Awake*, *The Best of R.E.M.: In View 1988-2003 The Guys*.

ORIGINAL FILM

4223 Glencoe Ave., Suite B119, Marina Del Ray CA 90292. (310)445-9000. Fax: (310)591-5646. Web site: www.originalfilm.com. This is producer Neal Moritz's company. Credits include *I Know What You Did Last Summer*, *Saving Silverman*, *Urban Legend*.

ORIGINAL VOICES, INC.

2617 3rd St., Santa Monica CA 90405-4108. (310)392-3479. Fax: (310)392-3480. Production credits include *Bruno*, *The Whole Shebang*, *Every Seven Minutes*.

OUT OF THE BLUE ENTERTAINMENT

10202 W. Washington Blvd., Astaire Blvd. #1200, Culver City CA 90232. (310)244-7811. Fax: (310)244-1539. Production credits include *Akeelah and the Bee*, *Mr. Deeds*, *Deuce Bigalow: Male Gigolo*.

OUTASITE NEW MEDIA STUDIOS

1099 Gainard St., Crescent City CA 95531. (707)465-1556/(888)975-8889. Fax: (707)465-1556.

OUTERBANKS ENTERTAINMENT

8000 Sunset Blvd., 3rd Floor, Los Angeles CA 90046. (323)654-3700. Fax: (323)654-3797. This is producer Kevin williamson's company. Production credits include *Dawson's Creek*, *Scream*, *Glory Days*.

THE OUTFIT MANAGEMENT/NOCI PICTURES

No public address available. E-mail: moviegossfilms@aol.com. Web site: www.nocipictures.com.

OUTLAW PRODUCTIONS

9155 Sunset Blvd., W. Hollywood CA 90069. (310)777-2000. Fax: (310)777-2010. Production credits include *Leatherheads*, *National Security*, *Don Juan DeMarco*.

OVERBROOK ENTERTAINMENT

450 N. Roxbury Dr., 4th Floor, Beverly Hills CA 90210. (310)432-2400. This is actor Will Smith's company. Production credits include *Wild Wild West*, *Hancock*, *The Pursuit of Happyness*.

OXYGEN MEDIA, LLC

75 9th Ave., New York NY 10011. (212)651-2000. Fax: (212)651-2099. Web site: www.oxygen.com. Production credits include *Pure Oxygen*, *Oprah: After the Show*, *Girls Behaving Badly*.

PACIFICA ENTERTAINMENT, INC.

335 N. Maple Dr., Suite 235, Beverly Hills CA 90210. (310)285-9696. Fax: (310)285-9691. Production credits include *Nurse Betty*, *Clay Pigeons*, *Where the Money Is*.

PANDORA FILMS

400 Warner Blvd., Bldg. 148, Burbank CA 91522. (818)954-3600. Production credits include *Donnie Darko*, *Kolya*, *Shine*.

PANOPTIC PICTURES

68888 Alta Loma Terrace, Los Angeles CA 90068. (323)874-3060. Fax: (323)876-3290. Production credits include *Takoma Park* and *Just One Night*.

PARKWAY PRODUCTIONS

10202 W. Washington Blvd., Astaire Bldg. 2210, Culver City CA 90232. (310)244-4040. Fax: (310)244-0240. This is director Penny Marshall's company. Production credits include *The Preacher's Wife*, *Awakenings*, *Big*.

ZAK PENN'S COMPANY

10201 W. Pico, Bldg. 31, Room 303, Los Angeles CA 90035. (310)369-7360. Fax: (310)969-0249. Production credits include *Inspector Gadget*, *Last Action Hero*, *Antz*.

PERMUT PRESENTATIONS

9150 Wilshire Blvd., Suite 247, Beverly Hills CA 90212. (310)248-2792. Fax: (310)248-2797. This is actor David Permut's company. Production credits include *Charlie Bartlett*, *Dragnet*, *Richard Pryor Live in Concert*.

PFEFFER FILM

500 S. Buena Vista Blvd., Animation Bldg. 2F-8, Burbank CA 91521. (818)560-3177. Fax: (818)843-7485. Production credits include *Malice*, *A Civil Action*, *A Few Good Men*.

PHASE 1 PRODUCTIONS

3210 Club Dr., Los Angeles CA 90064. (310)842-8401. Fax: (310)280-0415. This is producer Joe Wizan's company. Production credits include *Along Came a Spider* and *Reel Love: The Making of 'Trust the Man'*.

PHOENIX PICTURES

10125 W. Washington Blvd., Frankovich Bldg., Culver City CA 90232. (310)244-6100. Fax: (310)839-8915. Production credits include *Werewolf*, *Zodiac*, *All the King's Men*.

MARC PLATT PRODUCTIONS

100 Universal City Plaza, #5184, Universal City CA 91608. (818)777-1122. Fax: (818)866-6353. Production credits include *Legally Blonde*, *The Path to 9/11*, *Wanted*.

PLAYHOUSE PICTURES

1401 N. La Brea Ave., Hollywood CA 90028. (323)851-2112. This is a visual effects company. Production credits include *The Night Before Christmas* and *Last Action Hero*.

POP/ART FILM FACTORY

23679 Calabasas Rd., Suite 686, Calabasas CA 91302. E-mail: dzpff@earthlink.net. Web site: popartfil mfactory.com. **Contact:** Daniel Zirilli, CEO/director. Estab. 1990. Produces material for all audiences/ feature films. Query with synopsis. **Pays on per project basis.**
- ⛏ "We also have domestic and international distribution, and are always looking for finished films. We're producing 3 feature films/year and 15-20 music-oriented projects. Also exercise and other special-interest videos."

Needs Films (any format), multimedia kits, documentaries.

Tips "Send a query/pitch letter and let me know if you are willing to write on spec (for the first job only; you will be paid if the project is produced). Be original. Do not play it safe. If you don't receive a response from anyone you have ever sent your ideas to, or you continually get rejected, don't give up if you believe in yourself. Good luck and keep writing!"

EDWARD R. PRESSMAN FILM CORPORATION

130 El Camino Dr., Beverly Hills CA 90212. (310)271-8383. Fax: (310)271-9497. Production credits include *City Hall*, *Conan*, *Wall Street*.

PRODUCTION LOGISTICS, INC.

No public address available. E-mail: productionlogistics@msn.com. **Contact:** L.G. Friedman, producer. Buys first rights. No previously produced material. Query with synopsis by e-mail only. **Payment is negotiated on a per picture/per development basis.**

Needs Films (35mm).

Tips "Keep inquiries short, succinct, and impactful."

PROMARK ENTERTAINMENT GROUP

3599 Cahuenga Blvd., Suite 300, Los Angeles CA 90068. (323)878-0404. Fax: (323)878-0486. E-mail: sales@promarkgroup.com. Distribution credits include *Pilgrim*, *After Alice*, *The Stick-Up*.

PROPAGANDA FILMS

1741 N. Ivar Ave., Los Angeles CA 90028. (323)462-6400. Fax: (323)802-7001.

PUNCH PRODUCTIONS

1926 Broadway, #305, New York NY 10023. (212)595-8800/(310)442-4888. Fax: (310)442-4884. This is actor Dustin Hoffman's company. Production credits include *Tootsie*, *Wag the Dog*, *Death of a Salesman*.

THE PUPPETOON STUDIOS

P.O. Box 33544, Santa Fe NM 87594-3544. E-mail: director@scifistation.com. Web site: www.scifistation.com. **Contact:** Arnold Leibovit, director/producer. Estab. 1987. Wants plays geared toward a broad audience. **Works with 1 writer(s)/year.** Query with logline and synopsis via e-mail. Do not send script unless requested. Submission release required with all scripts. Responds in 2 month to queries. **Pays in accordance with WGA standards.**

Needs Films (35mm). No novels, plays, poems, treatments, or submissions on disk.

RADAR PICTURES, INC.

10900 wilshire Blvd., Suite 1400, Los Angeles CA 90024. (310)208-8525. Fax: (310)208-1764. Production credits include *Runaway Bride*, *Jumanji*, *Mr. Holland's Opus*.

RADIANT PICTURES

914 Montana Ave., 2nd Floor, Santa Monica CA 90403. (310)656-1400. Fax: (310)656-1408. Production credits include *Troy*, *The Perfect Storm*, *Air Force One*.

RADICAL MEDIA

435 Hudson St., New York NY 10014. (212)462-1500. Fax: (212)462-1600. Web site: www.radicalmedia.com. Production credits include *Iconoclasts*, *Jay-Z Fade to Black*, *Conservation Int'l*.

RAFFAELLA PRODUCTIONS, INC.

100 Universal City Plaza, #5162, Universal City CA 91608-1085. (818)777-2655. Production credits include *Uprising*, *Dragon: Bruce Lee Story*, *Prancer*.

RAINMAKER PRODUCTIONS, INC.

7255 Santa Monica Blvd., Hollywood CA 90046. (323)874-6770. Fax: (800)858-0520.

RANDWELL PRODUCTIONS, INC.

185 Pier Ave., Suite 103, Santa Monica CA 90405. E-mail: randwellprods@yahoo.com. Web site: www.randwell.com. **Contact:** Christina Wanke, development. Estab. 1997. TV and features audience. **Buys 3-4 script(s)/year. Works with 2-3 writer(s)/year.** Buys all rights. Query with synopsis. Responds in 2 weeks to queries; 3 months to scripts. **Pays in accordance with WGA standards.**

Needs Films (35mm). No sci-fi, no westerns.

Tips "Please keep synopsis to no more than one page. We hardly if ever request a copy of unsolicited material so don't be surprised if we pass."

RANSOHOFF PRODUCTIONS, INC., MARTIN

400 S. Beverly Dr., Suite 308, Beverly Hills CA 90212. (310)551-2680. Fax: (310)551-2094. Production credits include *Guilty as Sin*, *Jagged Edge*, *Switching Channels*.

RASTAR PRODUCTIONS

10202 W. Washington Bldg., Lean Bldg., Room 430, Culver City CA 90232. (310)244-7874. Fax: (310)244-2331. Production credits include *Steel Magnolias*, *Harriet the Spy*, *Brighton Beach Memoirs*.

RAT ENTERTAINMENT

9255 Sunset Blvd., Suite 310, Los Angeles CA 90069. (310)228-5000. Fax: (310)860-9251. This is director Brett Ratner's company. Production credits include *Red Dragon*, *Rush Hour*, *Prison Break*.

RECORDED PICTURE COMPANY

7001 Melrose Ave., Los Angeles CA 90038. (323)937-0733. Fax: (323)936-4913. Production credits include *Sexy Beast*, *The Last Emperor*, *Stealing Beauty*.

RED BIRD PRODUCTIONS

3623 Hayden Ave., Culver City CA 90203. (310)202-1711. Production credits include *Amistad*, *Out of Sync*, *Cool Women*.

RED HOUR FILMS

193 N. Robertson Blvd., Beverly Hills CA 90211. (310)289-2565. Fax: (310)289-5988. This is actor Ben Stiller's company. Production credits include *Blades of Glory*, *Starsky & Hutch*, *Zoolander*.

RED MULLET, INC.

1532 N. Hayworth Ave., #9, Los Angeles CA 90046. (323)874-3372. Fax: (323)874-3372. This is director Mike Figgis's company. Production credits include *Cold Creek Manor* and *One Night Stand*.

RED STROKES ENTERTAINMENT

9465 Wilshire Blvd., Suite 319, Beverly Hills CA 90212. (310)786-7887. Fax: (310)786-7827. This is Garth Brooks's company. Production credits include *Call me Claus*.

RED WAGON PRODUCTIONS

10202 W. Washington Blvd., Hepburn W., Culver City CA 90232. (310)244-4466. Fax: (310)244-1480. This is the company of producer Doug Wick. Credits include *Working Girl*, *Memoirs of a Geisha*, *Gladiator*.

REDEEMABLE FEATURES

381 Park Ave., S., New York NY 10016. (212)685-8585. Fax: (212)685-1455. Production credits include *Interstate 60* and *Ball in the House*.

RENAISSANCE FILMS, LTD.

34-35 Berwick St., London England W1V 8RP, UK. Credits include *Henry V*, *Twelfth Night*, *Much Ado About Nothing*.

RENAISSANCE PICTURES

100 Universal City Plaza, Bldg. 5166, 3rd Floor, Universal City CA 91608. (818)777-0088. Fax: (818)866-0223. This is director Sam Raimi's company. Production credits include *American Gothic*, *Xena: Warrior Princess*, *Hercules and the Amazon Women*.

RENEGADE ANIMATION

116 N. Maryland Ave., Lower Level, Glendale CA 91206. (818)551-2351. Fax: (818)551-2350. Web site: www.renegadeanimation.com. This is an animation studio. Production credits include *Captain Sturdy* and *Christmas is Here Again*.

RENFIELD PRODUCTIONS

1041 N. Formosa Ave., Writers Bldg. 321, W. Hollywood CA 90046. (323)850-3905. Fax: (323)850-3907. This is director Joe Dante's company. Production credits include *Gremlins*, *Innerspace*, *Small Soldiers*.

REPERAGE

8530 Wilshire Blvd., Suite 400, Beverly Hills CA 90211. (310)360-8499. Fax: (310)360-9865. Production credits include *Enemy at the Gates* and *Seven Years in Tibet*.

REVEAL ENTERTAINMENT

Dreamworks, SKG, 100 Universal Plaza, Bldg. 5171, Universal City CA 91608. (818)733-9818. Fax: (818)733-9808. Production credits include *Moonlight Mile*, *City of Angels*, *Casper*.

REVELATIONS ENTERTAINMENT

301 Arizona Ave., Suite 303, Santa Monica CA 90401. (310)394-3131. Fax: (310)394-3133. This is actor Morgan Freeman's company. Production credits include *Along Came a Spider*, *Bopha!*, *Under Suspicion*.

REVOLUTION STUDIOS

2900 W. Olympic Blvd., Santa Monica CA 90404. (310)255-7000. Fax: (310)255-70001. E-mail: info@revolutionstudios.com. Web site: www.revolutionstudios.com. This is producer Joe Roth's company. Credits include *Across the Universe*, *Mona Lisa Smile*, *Anger Management*.

RKO PICTURES, INC.

1875 Century Park E., Suite 2140, Los Angeles CA 90067. (310)277-0707. Fax: (310)226-2490. Production credits include *Laura Smiles*, *Mighty Joe Young*, *The Day the Universe Changed*.

ROADSIDE ATTRACTIONS LLC

7920 Sunset Blvd., Suite 402, Los Angeles CA 90042. (323)882-8490. Fax: (323)882-8493. E-mail: mail@roadsideattractions.com. Web site: www.roadsideattractions.com. Production credits include *Lovely & Amazing*, *Before the Rains* and *The Fall*.

ROCKFISH FILMS

5514 Wilshire Blvd., 6th Floor, Los Angeles CA 90036. (323)937-9060. Fax: (323)937-9361.

ROGUE PICTURES

10202 W. Washington Blvd., Culver City CA 90232. (310)449-4066. Fax: (310)264-4158. Production credits include *Seed of Chucky, Carlito's Way: Rise to Power, Doomsday*.

ROSCOE ENTERPRISES, INC.

3000 W. Olympic Blvd., Suite 2276, Santa Monica CA 90404. (310)449-4066. Fax: (310)264-4158. Production credits include *The Usual Suspects, Hard Eight, Serpent's Kiss*.

ALEX ROSE PRODUCTIONS, INC.

8291 Presson Pl., Los Angeles CA 90069. (323)654-8662. Fax: (323)654-0196. Production credits include *Frankie & Johnny* and *Quigley Down Under*.

HOWARD ROSENMAN PRODUCTIONS

635A Westbourne Dr., Los Angeles CA 90069. (310)659-2100. Production credits include *The Family Man, Eagle's Wings, Foul Play*.

HERBERT ROSS

% F. Altman & Co., 9255 Sunset Blvd., Suite 901, Los Angeles CA 90069. (310)278-4201. Fax: (310)278-5330. Production credits include *The Secret of My Success* and *True Colors*.

ROUNDTABLE INK

6161 Santa Monica Blvd., Suite 202, Hollywood CA 90038. (323)466-4646. Fax: (323)466-4640. Production credits include *What Women Want, Urban Legend, The Wishing Tree*.

RUBY-SPEARS PRODUCTIONS

213 W.Alameda Ave., Suite 102, Burbank CA 91502. (818)840-1234. E-mail: info@rubyspears.com. Web site: www.rubyspears.com. This is an animation company. Production credits include *It's Punky Brewster, The Centurion, Alvin & the Chipmunks*.

SCOTT RUDIN PRODUCTIONS

5555 Melrose Ave., DeMille Bldg., Suite 200, Los Angeles CA 90038. (323)956-4600. Fax: (323)862-0262. Production credits include *No Country for Old Men, The Queen, The School of Rock*.

RYSHER ENTERTAINMENT

2401 Colorado Ave., Suite 200, Santa Monica CA 90404. (310)309-5200. Fax: (310)309-5215. Production credits include *Kiss the Girls, Oz, The Saint*.

SABAN ENTERTAINMENT

10960 Wilshire Blvd., Los Angeles CA 90024. (310)235-5100. Fax: (310)235-5102. Production credits include *Casper Meets Wendy, Au Pair, Rusty: A Dog's Tale*.

THE SAMPLE

110 Hollywood Blvd., Suite 300, Hollywood CA 90210. (330)987-0987. Fax: (330)098-0987. Web site: www.sampleproco.com.

SAMUELSON PRODUCTIONS

10401 Wyton Dr., Los Angeles CA 90024-2527. (310)208-1000. Fax: (310)208-2809. Production credits include *Revenge of the Nerds, Tom & Viv, Arlington Road.*

ARTHUR SARKISSIAN PRODUCTIONS

5455 Wilshire Blvd., Suite 1515, Los Angeles CA 90036. (310)385-1486. Fax: (310)936-2800. Production credits include *Rush Hour, While You Were Sleeping, Wanted: Dead or Alive.*

SATURN FILMS

9000 Sunset Blvd., #911, W. Hollywood CA 90069. (310)887-0900. Fax: (310)248-2965. This is actor Nicholas Cage's company. Production credits include *National Treasure, The Life of David Gale, Sonny.*

PAUL SCHIFF PRODUCTIONS

1741 Ivar Ave., Hollywood CA 90028. (323)462-6400. Fax: (323)852-1640. Production credits include *Maid in Manhattan, My Cousin Vinny, Young Guns.*

SCHINDLER WEISSMAN COMPANY

1710 N. Vermont Ave., Los Angeles CA 90027. (323)666-5566. Fax: (323)666-5565.

ADAM SCHROEDER PRODUCTIONS

4000 Warner Blvd., Burbank CA 91522. (818)954-6000. Production credits include *The Truman Show, Sleepy Hollow, South Park: Bigger, Longer & Uncut.*

JOEL SCHUMACHER PRODUCTIONS

10201 W. Pico Blvd., Bldg. 50, Los Angeles CA 90035. (310)369-2300. Fax: (310)969-1102. Production credits include *The Phantom of the Opera, Batman & Robin, A Time to Kill.*

SCOTT FREE PRODUCTIONS

634 N. La Peer Dr., W. Hollywood CA 90069. (310)360-2250. Fax: (310)360-2251. This is the production company of directors Ridley and Tony Scott. Credits include *Black Hawk Down, Crimson Tide, Thelma & Louise.*

SCREEN GEMS

10202 W. Washington Blvd., Culver City CA 90232. (310)244-4000. Production credits include *Arlington Road, The Mothman Prophesies, Resident Evil.*

SCREEN MEDIA VENTURES, LLC

757 Third Ave., 2nd Floor, New York NY 10017. (212)308-1790. Fax: (212)308-1791.

SECTION EIGHT

4000 Warner Bros., Bldg. 81 #117, Burbank CA 91522. (818)954-4860. This is the production company of George Clooney and Steven Soderbergh. Credits include *Ocean's 11, Syriana, Michael Clayton.*

SERAPHIM FILMS

9326 Readcrest Dr., Beverly Hills CA 90210. (310)246-0050. Fax: (310)246-0051. This is writer Clive Barker's company. Production credits include *Hellraiser* series, *Salome*, *The Forbidden*.

SEVEN ARTS PICTURES

9051 Oriole Way, Los Angeles CA 90069. (310)887-3830. Fax: (310)887-3840. Production credits include *An American Rhapsody*, *The Believer*, *Johnny Mnemonic*.

SHADY ACRES ENTERTAINMENT

100 Universal City Plaza, Bldg. 5225, 2nd Floor, Universal City CA 91608. (818)777-4446. Fax: (818)866-6612. Production credits include *I Now Pronounce You Chuck & Larry*, *Evan Almighty*, *Liar Liar*.

SHOELACE PRODUCTIONS, INC.

16 W. 19th St., 12th Floor, New York NY 10011. (212)243-2900. Fax: (212)243-2973. This is actress Julia Roberts's company. Production credits include *Maid in Manhattan*, *Stepmom*, *America's Sweethearts*.

SHOOTING GALLERY, INC.

3000 Olympic Blvd., Bldg. 3, Suite 1464, Santa Monica CA 90404. (310)315-4880. Production credits include *Sling Blade*, *Niagara, Niagara*, *You Can Count on Me*.

SHORELINE ENTERTAINMENT, INC.

1875 Century Park E., Suite 600, Los Angeles CA 90067. (310)551-2060. Fax: (310)201-0729. E-mail: info@shorelineentertainment.com. Web site: www.shorelineentertainment.com. **Contact:** Production credits include *Glengarry Glen Ross*, *The Visit*, *The Man From Elysian Fields*. Estab. 1993. Mass audience. **Buys 8 script(s)/year. Works with 8 writer(s)/year.** Buys all rights. Query. Responds in 1 week to queries.

Needs Films (35, 70mm).

Tips "Looking for character driven films that are commercial as well as independent. Completed screenplays only. Especially looking for big-budget action, thrillers. We accept submissions by mail, e-mail or fax. No unsolicited screenplays, please."

SHOWCASE ENTERTAINMENT, INC.

21800 Oxnard St., Suite 150, Woodland Hills CA 91367. (818)715-7005. Fax: (818)715-7009. Web site: www.showcaseentertainment.com. Production credits include *Desperate Measures*, *National Lampoon's Cattle Call*, *Anything But Love*.

CHARLES SHYER, INC.

12210 Nebraska, Suite 8, Los Angeles CA 90025. (310)826-0314. Fax: (310)826-2752. Production credits include *Alfie*, *The Parent Trap*, *Private Benjamin*.

SIGNATURE FILMS/MILLENNIUM DANCE COMPLEX

5113 Lankershim Blvd., N. Hollywood CA 91601. (818)752-2991. Fax: (818)752-8386. Web site: www.millenniumdancecomplex.com. Production credits include *Your Chance to Dance* and *Dance Life*.

SILENT SOUND FILMS, LTD.

United Kingdom. E-mail: thj@silentsoundfilms.co.uk. Web site: www.silentsoundfilms.co.uk. **Contact:** Timothy Foster, MD. Estab. 1997. Stage and fiction movies only. TV: arts/travel documentary. No previously produced material. Query with synopsis. Responds in 2 weeks to queries. **Writers paid in accordance with WGA standards or the UK 'pact' agreement, if British production.**

> ☛ "We are interested in excellent writing (specifically musicals, art house, stage plays) with well-developed plot themes and original characters. So if you have a story that is nonparochial, we would be interested to see an e-mailed package that comprises: a 1-page synopsis, no more than 8 pages of scenario, and brief biography. Do not send images, complete screenplays, or large attachments. If it's something that grabs our attention, you will certainly hear from us."

Needs Films (35mm). Does not want "U.S.-based movies, nor storylines with principally American characters set anywhere else. Nothing personal, it's just that we are involved in what is unreliably called art house films and the best American art house films are made by Americans. So why compete?"

Tips "We seek the filmic equivalent of literature as opposed to bestseller."

SILVER PICTURES

4000 Warner Blvd., Bldg. 90, Burbank CA 91522-0001. (818)954-4490. Fax: (818)954-3237. Production credits include *Predator*, *Lethal Weapon*, *The Matrix*.

THE GENE SIMMONS COMPANY

P.O. Box 16075, Beverly Hills CA 90210. (310)859-1694. Fax: (310)859-2631. Production credits include *Detroit Rock City* and *Gene Simmons: Family Jewels*.

RANDY SIMON PRODUCTIONS

1113 N. Hillcrest Rd., Beverly Hills CA 90210. (310)274-7440. Fax: (310)274-9809. Production credits include *Pi*, *Requiem for a Dream*, *Lover's Knot*.

THE ROBERT SIMONDS COMPANY

500 S. Buena Vista St., Animation Bldg. #2G, Burbank CA 91521-1775. (818)560-8900. Fax: (818)842-2078. Production credits include *The Wedding Singer*, *License to Wed*, *Cheaper by the Dozen*.

SINGLE CELL PICTURES

1016 N. Palm Ave., W. Hollywood CA 90069. (310)360-7600. Fax: (310)360-7011. This is producer Michael Stipe's company. Credits include *Being John Malkovich*, *Saved!*, *13 Conversations About One Thing*.

SIRK PRODUCTIONS, LLC

12 West 31st Street, 5th Floor, New York NY 10001, USA. Web site: www.sirkproductions.com. Production credits include *Anytown, USA* and *Inside Reel*.

SKYLARK ENTERTAINMENT/R&R FILMS

12405 Venice Blvd., Suite 237, Los Angeles CA 90066. (310)390-2659. Fax: (310)390-2759. Production credits include *Ace Ventura: When Nature Calls*, *Anacondas: The Hunt for Blood Orchid*, *Facade*.

SKYLARK FILMS

1123 Pacific St., Suite G, Santa Monica CA 90405-1525. (310)396-5753. Fax: (310)396-5753. Production credits include *Terminal Justice*, *Chasing Justice*, *Coal of the Heart*.

SLADEK ENTERTAINMENT CORPORATION, DANIEL

8306 Wilshire Blvd., #510, Beverly Hills CA 90211. (323)934-9268. Fax: (323)934-7362. E-mail: dansladek@aol.com. Web site: www.danielsladek.com.

SNL STUDIOS (L.A.)

5555 Melrose Ave., Room 105, Los Angeles CA 90038-3197. (323)956-5729. Fax: (323)862-8605. Production credits include "Saturday Night Live", *The Ladies Man*, *A Night at the Roxbury*.

SOLARIS ENTERTAINMENT

12 Washington Blvd., 2nd Floor, Venice CA 90292. (310)591-8845. Fax: (310)591-8847. Web site: www.solarisentertainment.com. Production credits include *Tumbleweeds*, *My Generation*, *The Speed of Life*.

SONNENFELD/JOSEPHSON WORLDWIDE ENTERTAINMENT

10202 W. Washington Blvd., Stewart Bldg. #205, Culver City CA 90232. (310)244-8777. Fax: (310)244-1977. Production credits include *Wild, Wild West*, *The Crew*, *Big Trouble*.

SOUTH FORK PICTURES

1101 Montana Ave., Suite B, Santa Monica CA 90403. (310)395-7779. Fax: (310)395-2575. This is actor/director Robert Redford's company. Production credits include *The Horse Whisperer*, *Quiz Show*, *A River Runs Through It*.

SPELLING FILMS

5700 Wilshire Blvd., Suite 375, Los Angeles CA 90036. (323)965-5700. Production credits include *In & Out*, "Charmed," "7th Heaven."

SPENCER PRODUCTIONS, INC.

P.O. Box 2247, Westport CT 06880. E-mail: spencerprods@yahoo.com. **Contact:** Bruce Spencer, general manager; Alan Abel, creative director. Produces material for high school students, college students and adults. Occasionally uses freelance writers with considerable talent. Query. Responds in 1 month to queries. **Payment negotiable.**

Needs Tapes and Cassettes.

Tips "For a comprehensive view of our humor requirements, we suggest viewing our feature film production, *Is There Sex After Death* (Rated R), starring Buck Henry. It is available at video stores. Or read *Don't Get Mad . . . Get Even* and *How to Thrive on Rejection* by Alan Abel (published by W.W. Norton), both available from Barnes & Noble or Amazon." Also Books-on-Tape. "Send brief synopsis (one page) and outline (2-4 pages)."

SPYGLASS ENTERTAINMENT GROUP

500 S. Buena Vista St., Burbank CA 91521-1855. (818)560-3458. Fax: (818)563-1967. This is producer Roger Birnbaum's company. Credits include *Shanghai Noon*, *The Sixth Sense*, *Memoirs of a Geisha*.

STAMPEDE ENTERTAINMENT

3000 W. Olympic Blvd., Bldg. 4, Suite 1308, Santa Monica CA 90404. (310)264-4229. Fax: (310)264-4227. This is producer Ron Underwood's company. Production credits include *City Slickers*, "Tremor" series, *Heart and Souls*.

STARWAY INTERNATIONAL

12021 Wilshire Blvd., Suite 661, Los Angeles CA 90025. (310)458-6202. Fax: (310)458-6102. Production credits include the *Phantasm* series and *Survival Quest*.

STONE VILLAGE PICTURES

9200 W. Sunset Blvd., Suite 250, W. Hollywood CA 90069. (310)402-5171. Web site: www.stonevillagepictures.com. This is producer Scott Steindorff's company. Credits include "Empire Falls," *The Human Stain*, "Las Vegas."

STONE VS. STONE

189 Franklin St., 3rd Floor, New York NY 10013. (212)941-1200. This is executive producer Webster Stone's company. Credits include *Citizen X*, *The Negotiator*, *Gone in 60 Seconds*.

STORM ENTERTAINMENT

127 Broadway, Suite 200, Santa Monica CA 90401. (310)656-2500. Fax: (310)656-2510. Production credits include *Modern Vampires*, *Hurlyburly*, *The Criminal*.

STORYLINE ENTERTAINMENT

10202 W. Washington Blvd., Tristan Bldg. #206, Culver City CA 90232. (310)244-3222. Fax: (310)244-0322. Production credits include *Lucy*, *The Bucket List*, *The Reagans*.

STUDIOCANAL FRANCE

301 N. Canon Dr., Suite 207, Beverly Hills CA 90210. (310)247-0994. Fax: (310)247-0998. Production credits include *The Interpreter*, *Bridget Jones's Diary*, *The Pianist*.

STUDIOS USA

8800 Sunset Blvd., W. Hollywood CA 90069. (310)360-2300. Fax: (310)360-2517. Production credits include "Murder, She Wrote: The Celtic Riddle," "Law & Order: Equal Rights," "Homeward Bound."

SUDDEN STORM PRODUCTIONS INC.

1 Deer Park Crescent, Suite 703, Toronto Ontario M4V 3C4, Canada. Web site: www.suddenstorm.ca. Production credits include "Mod," "The Crypt Club," "The Store."

SUMMIT ENTERTAINMENT

1630 Stewart St., Suite 120, Santa Monica CA 90404. (310)309-8400. Fax: (310)828-4132. Production credits include *Evita*, *American Pie*, *Mr. & Mrs. Smith*.

SUNDANCE INSTITUTE

8530 Wilshire Blvd., 3rd Floor, Beverly Hills CA 90211. (310)360-1981. Fax: (310)360-1969.

TALCO PRODUCTIONS

279 E. 44th St., New York NY 10017-4354. (212)697-4015. Fax: (212)697-4827. **Contact:** Alan Lawrence, president; Marty Holberton, vice president. Estab. 1968. Produces variety of material for TV, radio, business, trade associations, nonprofit organizations, public relations (chiefly political and current events), etc. Audiences range from young children to senior citizens. **20-40% freelance written. Buys scripts from published/produced writers only.** Buys all rights. No previously produced material. Submit résumé, production history. Responds in 3 weeks to queries. **Makes outright purchase. Pays in accordance with WGA standards. Sometimes pays the expenses of writers on assignment.**

Needs Films, videotapes, CDs, DVDs.

Tips "We maintain a file of writers and call on those with experience in the same general category as the project in production. *We do not accept unsolicited manuscripts.* We prefer to receive a writer's résumé listing credits. If his/her background merits, we will be in touch when a project seems right. We are doing more public relations-oriented work (print and DVD) and are concentrating on TV productions. Production budgets are tighter."

TALL TREES PRODUCTIONS

7758 Sunset Blvd., Los Angeles CA 90046. (323)378-1111. Production credits include *Dr. Dolittle, 28 Days, I Spy.*

TANGLEWOOD FILMS

No public address available. E-mail: david@tanglewoodfilms.com. Web site: www.tanglewoodfilms. com/startpage.html.

TAPESTRY FILMS, INC.

9328 Civic Center Dr., Beverly Hills CA 90210. (310)275-1191. Fax: (310)275-1266. Production credits include *Wedding Crashers*, *Point Break*, *Pay It Forward.*

TAURUS ENTERTAINMENT COMPANY

5831 Sunset Blvd., Hollywood CA 90028. (323)860-0807. Fax: (323)860-0834. E-mail: taurusec@aol. com. Production credits include *Morella, Creepshow, The Day of the Dead.*

TAYLOR MADE FILMS

225 Santa Monica Blvd., Suite 610, Santa Monica CA 90401. (310)899-6739. Fax: (310)899-5715. This is producer Geoffrey Taylor's company. Credits include *Down & Out in Beverly Hills, The Tempest, Taking Care of Business.*

TEAM TODD

9021 Melrose Ave., Suite 301, Los Angeles CA 90069. (310)248-6001. Fax: (310)385-8072. Production credits include *Austin Power* series, *Must Love Dogs, Prime.*

TENTH PLANET PRODUCTIONS

833 N. La Cienega, Suite 200, Los Angeles CA 90069. (310)659-8001. Fax: (310)659-8029. E-mail: tenthplanet@aol.com. Web site: www.tenthplanet.net. This is Chris Carter's production company. Credits include "Randy Jackson Presents: America's Best Dance Crew."

THREE STRANGE ANGELS, INC.

2450 Broadway St., Santa Monica CA 90404. (310)449-3425. Fax: (310)449-8858. Production credits include *Stranger Than Fiction* and *Nanny McPhee*.

THRESHOLD ENTERTAINMENT

1649 11th Street, Santa Monica CA 90404, USA. Web site: www.thethreshold.com. This is an animation studio. Production credits include *Mortal Kombat* and *Foodfight!*.

TIG PRODUCTIONS, INC.

100 Universal City Plaza, Universal City CA 91608. (818)777-2737. Fax: (818)733-5616. This is actor/director Kevin Costner's production company. Credits include *Thirteen Days*, *Dances With Wolves*, *Message in a Bottle*.

THE STEVE TISCH COMPANY

3815 Hughes Ave., Culver City CA 90232-2715. (310)838-2500. Fax: (310)204-2713. Production credits include *Wild America*, *Long Kiss Goodnight*, *Forrest Gump*.

TOMORROW FILM CORP

16250 Ventura Blvd., Suite 400, Encino CA 91436, USA. Web site: www.tomorrowfilms.com. Production credits include *Gone in 60 Seconds*, *Focus*, *Just the Ticket*.

TOO NUTS PRODUCTIONS, L.P.

4200 Park Blvd., Suite 241, Oakland CA 94602. (310)967-4532. E-mail: toonutsproductions@yahoo.com. **Contact:** Ralph Scott and Daniel Leo Simpson, co-executive producers. Estab. 1994. Produces illustrated kids books, CDs, DVDs, animation shorts for internet, and half-hour tv/video with a twist. Among our storylines in development: "Our Teacher is a Creature," "Toad Pizza," "The Salivating Salamander," "The Suburban Cowboys," "The Contest-Ants," "The De-Stinktive Skunk," and "Sneeks Peaks." Audience is children, typically ages 3-6 and 7-9. Always looking for talented, new kidlit illustrators as well. **Buys 4-10 script(s)/year. Works with 4-6 writer(s)/year.** Buys both first rights and all rights. Query with synopsis, résumé, writing samples, production history. Creative but brief cover letter/e-mail; Works with 10% first time writers. Illustrators query with creative but brief cover letter, samples of work by e-mail or hyperlink to your online portfolio. Responds in less than 3 months to queries; 6 months to scripts. **Pays royalty and makes outright purchase.**

    ☞ Really good original—clean—content.

Needs Videotapes, multimedia kits, tapes and cassettes, synopses, audio CDs, CD-ROMs. "Please do not submit anything with violence, chainsaws, axes, ice picks, and general blood and guts. We're producing for children, not monsters, or those who aspire to become them."

Tips "Suggestion: Use the words 'Too Nuts' at least twice in your query. (Do the math.) If you don't know how to giggle all the way to the bank, you may want to try someone else. If you've already exorcised your inner child, lizard, monkey, etc., that's a 'no no.' "

TOTEM PRODUCTIONS

8009 Santa Monica Blvd., Los Angeles CA 90046. (323)650-4994. Fax: (323)650-1961. This is director Tony Scott's company. Production credits include *Spy Game*, *Days of Thunder*, *Top Gun*.

⊘ TREASURE ENTERTAINMENT

468 N. Camden Dr., Suite 200, Beverly Hills CA 90210. (310)860-7490. Fax: (310)943-1488. E-mail: acquisitions@treasureentertainment.net. Web site: www.treasureentertainment.net. **Contact:** Mark Heidelberger, Treasure Entertainment co-chairman/chief executive officer. Estab. 2000. Management consideration given to writers with produced credits only. Intended audience is theatrical, festival, television, home video/DVD, Internet. **Buys 1-2 script(s)/year. Works with 8-10 writer(s)/year.** Accepts previously produced material. Does not return submissions unless SASE is included. No Catalog. Query. Responds in up to 6 months to queries; up to 6 months to scripts. **Pays 1-10% royalty, makes outright purchase $1-100,000.**

Needs Films (35 mm and 16mm), videotapes, multimedia kits.

Tips "We reserve the right to reject or return any unsolicited material. We also reserve the right not to purchase any material if we don't feel that any submissions are of sufficient merit. Our needs tend to change with the market and will vary from year to year. We are agreeing to look at writer's queries only. Queries should be sent by mail or e-mail only."

TRIBECA PRODUCTIONS

375 Greenwich St., 8th Floor, New York NY 10013. (212)941-4000. Fax: (212)941-4044. Web site: www.tribecafilm.com. This is actor Robert De Niro's company. Production credits include *A Bronx Tale*, *Analyze This*, *Meet the Fockers*.

TRILOGY ENTERTAINMENT GROUP

2450 Broadway St., Penthouse Suite 675, Santa Monica CA 90404-3061. (310)449-3095. Fax: (310)449-3195. Production credits include *Moll Flanders*, *Backdraft*, *Blown Away*.

TROMA ENTERTAINMENT, INC.

The Troma Bldg., 733 9th Ave., New York NY 10019. (212)757-4555. Fax: (212)399-9885. Web site: www.troma.com. Production credits include *Toxic Avenger* and *Cannibal! The Musical*.

TRUE BLUE PRODUCTIONS

P.O. Box 27127, Los Angeles CA 90027. (323)661-9191. Fax: (323)661-9190. This is actress Kirstie Alley's production company. Credits include *Profoundly Normal*, *Suddenly*, *Bye Bye Blues*.

THE TURMAN-MORRISSEY COMPANY

12220 Dunoon Ln., Los Angeles CA 90049. (213)740-3307. Fax: (213)745-6652. Production credits include *American History X*, *Booty Call*, *The Badge*.

UFLAND PRODUCTIONS

534 21st St., Santa Monica CA 90402. (310)656-3031. Fax: (310)656-3073. Production credits include *Night and the City*, *Not Without My Daughter*, *One True Thing*.

UNIVERSAL ANIMATION STUDIOS

100 Universal City Plaza, Suite 1320-03-M, Universal City CA 91608. (818)777-1213. Web site: www.unistudios.com. Production credits include sequels to *Balto*, *An American Tail*, and *The Land Before Time*.

UPFRONT PRODUCTIONS

12841 S. Hawthorne Blvd., #297, Hawthorne CA 90250. (310)516-0232. Production credits include *Straight From the Streets*, *LA Lakers Victory Parade*, Network Specials.

USA FILMS

65 Bleeckerk St., 2nd Floor, New York NY 10012. (212)539-4000. Fax: (212)539-4099. Production credits include *Traffic*, *The Man Who Wasn't There*, *Monsoon Wedding*.

VALEO FILMS

P.O. Box 1500, Lindale TX 75771. (903)592-2495. E-mail: screenplays@valeofilms.com. Web site: www.valeofilms.com. Query by e-mail or mail.

o➔ Currently considering projects that contain 1 or more of the following: character or story driven, identifies moral values, romance/love story, educational/documentary, presents the human condition, strong visual imagery, coming of age/learning, or intellectual drama/mystery.

Tips ''We require that you provide your name, phone number, address, title of your work, and WGA registration or copyright number. We will send an Unsolicited Project Release letter for you to sign and return with a sing copy of your screenplay/treatment. We don't want projects that contain the following characteristics: 1 character saves the world, SFX based, highly action based, extreme/grotesque violence, high sexual content, or strong explicit language. Although we do have a vast array of production resources available to us, we are a relatively small production copmany who prefers to limit the number of projects we have in production. Consequently, we tend to be very selective when it comes to choosing new material.''

VALHALLA MOTION PICTURES

8530 Wilshire Blvd., Suite 400, Beverly Hills CA 90211. (310)360-8530. Fax: (310)360-8531. This is producer Gale Anne Hurd's company. Production credits include *Terminator*, *Aliens*, *Armageddon*.

VANGUARD FILMS

1230 La Collina Dr., Beverly Hills CA 90210. (310)888-8020. Fax: (310)888-8012. Production credits include *7 Years in Tibet*, *Sarafina*, *Thin Blue Line*, *Shrek*.

VANGUARD PRODUCTIONS

12111 Beatrice St., Culver City CA 90230. **Contact:** Terence M. O'Keefe, president. Estab. 1985. **Buys 1 script(s)/year.** Buys all rights. Accepts previously produced material. Query with synopsis, résumé. Responds in 3 months to queries; 6 months to scripts. **Pays in accordance with WGA standards. Negotiated option.**

Needs Films (35mm), videotapes.

THE VAULT INC.

1831 Centinela Ave., 2nd Floor, Santa Monica CA 90404. (310)315-0012. Fax: (310)315-9322. Production credits include *The Last Supper*, *Campfire Tales*, *Panic*.

VERTIGO ENTERTAINMENT
9348 Civic Center Dr., Mezzanine Level, Beverly Hills CA 90210. (310)288-5170. Fax: (310)278-5295. Production credits include *The Ring, The Departed, Eight Below*.

VIEW ASKEW PRODUCTIONS, INC.
3 Harding Rd., Red Bank NJ 07701. (732)842-6933. Fax: (732)842-3772. E-mail: viewaskew@vie waskew.com. Web site: www.viewaskew.com. Production credits include *Dogma, Mallrats, Chasing Amy*.

VILLAGE ROADSHOW PICTURES INTERNATIONAL
3400 Riverside Dr., Suite 900, Burbank CA 91505. (818)260-6000. Fax: (818)260-6001. Web site: www.villageroadshowpictures.com. Production credits include *Get Smart, Zoolander, The Matrix*.

THE ROBERT D. WACHS COMPANY
345 N. Maple Dr., Suite 179, Beverly Hills CA 90210. (310)276-1123. Fax: (310)276-5572. Production credits include *Another 48 Hours, Beverly Hills Cop II, Raw, Coming to America*.

VINCENT WARD FILMS
1134 N. Gardner St., W. Hollywood CA 90046. (323)850-5703. Fax: (323)850-5743. Production credits include *Map of the Human Heart* and *Rain of the Children*.

WARNER BROS. ANIMATION
15303 Ventura Blvd., Suite 1200, Sherman Oaks CA 91403. (818)977-8700. Animation production credits include *Batman: Gotham Knight* (V), *The Batman/Superman Movie*, "That's Warner Bros.!"

WARNER ROADSHOW STUDIOS
Entertainment Road, Oxenford QLD 4210, Australia. Web site: www.movieworldstudios.com.au.

WEED ROAD PICTURES
4000 Warner Blvd., Bldg. 81, Suite 115, Burbank CA 91522. (818)954-3371. Fax: (818)954-3061. This is writer/director Akiva Goldsman's company. Production credits include *Starsky & Hutch, Constantine, Hancock*.

JERRY WEINTRAUB PRODUCTIONS
4000 Warner Blvd., #1, Burbank CA 91522-0001. (818)954-2500. Fax: (818)954-1399. Production credits include *Ocean's 11, Vegas Vacation, The Specialist*.

WEITZ BROTHERS
300 TV Plaza, Bldg, 136, Suite 234, Burbank CA 91505. (818)954-6485. This is writer/director Chris Weitz's company. Production credits include *American Dreamz, In Good Company, About a Boy*.

WHEELHOUSE ENTERTAINMENT
15464 Ventura Blvd., Sherman Oaks CA 91403-3002. (818)461-3599. Fax: (818)907-0819. Web site: www.wheelhouseentertainment.com. This is writer/director Randall Wallace's production company. Credits include *Braveheart, Pearl Harbor, We Were Soldiers*, "Fight or Die."

WHITE WOLF PRODUCTIONS

2932 wilshire Blvd., Suite 201, Santa Monica CA 90403. (310)829-7500. Fax: (310)586-0717. This is screenwriter David S. Ward's company. Production credits include *Sleepless in Seattle*, *Major League*, *Flyboys*.

WINKLER FILMS

211 S. Beverly Dr., Suite 200, Beverly Hills CA 90212. (310)858-5780. Fax: (310)858-5799. **Contact:** Producer/Director: Irwin Winkler. Production credits include *Rocky*, *Raging Bull*, *Home of the Brave*, *The Shipping News*.

RALPH WINTER PRODUCTIONS

1201 W. 5th St., Maryland Bldg., Rm. M230, Los Angeles CA 90017. (213)534-3654. Fax: (213)534-3078. Production credits include *X-Men* series, *Fantastic Four* series, *Inspector Gadget*.

WITT-THOMAS FILMS

4000 Warner Blvd., Producers 3, Room 20, Burbank CA 91522. (818)954-2545. Fax: (818)954-2660. Production credits include *Insomnia*, *Three Kings*, *Dead Poets Society*.

THE WOLPER ORGANIZATION, INC.

% Warner Bros., 4000 Warner Blvd., Bldg. 14, Burbank CA 91522. (818)954-1421. Fax: (818)954-1593. Production credits include *L.A. Confidential*, *Murder in the First*, *Surviving Picasso*.

WORKING TITLE FILMS

9720 Wilshire Blvd., 4th Fl., Beverly Hills CA 90212. (310)777-3100. Fax: (310)777-5243. Production credits include *Fargo, Oh Brother, Where Art Thou?*, *Elizabeth*, *Pride & Prejudice*, *United 93*.

WORLD INTERNATIONAL NETWORK, LLC

301 N. Canon Dr., Suite 300, Beverly Hills CA 90210. (310)859-2500. Fax: (310)859-7500. Production credits include *The Perfect Wife*, *Facing the Enemy*, *Borderline Normal*.

WORLDWIDE ENTERTAINMENT

280 S. Beverly Dr., Suite 208, Beverly Hills CA 90212. (310)205-9324. Fax: (310)205-9325. Broadway production credits include "Little Women-The Musical" and "Forever Tango."

WYCHWOOD PRODUCTIONS

% Propaganda Films, 1741 Ivar Ave., Hollywood CA 90038. (323)802-7000. Fax: (323)802-7131. This is producer Simon West's company. Credits include *Con-Air*, *Tomb Raider*, *The General's Daughter*.

THE WYLE/KATZ COMPANY

% Warner Bros., 4000 Warner Blvd., Bldg. 138, Burbank CA 91522. (818)954-7440. Fax: (818)954-1846. This is the production company of actor Noah Wyle.

YAK YAK PICTURES

% Warner Bros., 4000 Warner Blvd., Bldg. 138, Burbank CA 91522. (818)954-3861/(818)954-6264. Fax: (818)954-1614. Production credits include *The Peacemaker*, *Deep Impact*, *Pay It Forward*.

BUD YORKIN PRODUCTIONS

345 N. Maple Dr., Suite 206, Beverly Hills CA 90210. (310)274-8111. Fax: (310)274-8112. Production credits include *Intersection*, *Twice in a Lifetime*, "All in the Family."

YORKTOWN PRODUCTIONS, INC.

3000 W. Olympic Blvd., Bldg. 2, Suite 2465, Santa Monica CA 90404. (310)264-4155. Fax: (310)264-4167. This is Norman Jewison's production company. Credits include *Moonstruck*, *The Hurricane*, *A Soldier's Story*.

THE SAUL ZAENTZ COMPANY

2600 10th St., Berkeley CA 94710. (510)549-1528. Web site: www.zaentz.com. Production credits include *One Flew Over the Cuckoo's Nest*, *Amadeus*, *The English Patient*.

THE ZANUCK COMPANY

9465 Wilshire Blvd., Suite 930, Beverly Hills CA 90212. (310)274-0261. Fax: (310)273-9217. Production credits include *The Verdict*, *Driving Miss Daisy*, *Jaws*.

ZIDE/PERRY ENTERTAINMENT

9100 Wilshire Blvd., Suite 615 E., Beverly Hills CA 90212. (310)887-2999. Fax: (310)887-2995. This is the production company of Warren Zide and Chris Perry. Credits include *Final Destination* series, *Cats and Dogs*, *American Pie*.

LAURA ZISKIN PRODUCTIONS

10202 W. Washington Blvd., Culver City CA 90232. (310)244-7373. Fax: (310)244-0073. Production credits include *Pretty Woman*, *To Die For*, *As Good As It Gets*, *Spider-Man*.

ZOLLO PRODUCTIONS, INC.

257 W. 52nd St., 2nd Fl., New York NY 10019. (212)957-1300. Fax: (212)957-1315. Production credits include *Quiz Show*, *In the Gloaming*, *Mississippi Burning*.

ZUCKER PRODUCTIONS

1351 4th St., 3rd Fl., Santa Monica CA 90401. (310)656-9202. Fax: (310)656-9220. Production credits include *Rat Race*, *Ghost*, *First Knight*.

ZUCKER/NETTER PRODUCTIONS

1411 5th St., Suite 402, Santa Monica CA 90401. (310)394-1644. Fax: (310)899-6722. Production credits include *Dude, Where's My Car?* and *Phone Booth*.

Production Companies

Conferences

Writing is a solitary task. It means a lot of time sitting at the computer, researching facts online, checking your e-mail, and staring at a chapter you've rewritten 18 times that still doesn't seem to work. If you want to be a writer, you're going to spend plenty of time alone, but at the same time, you need to understand the importance of networking and making friends who are fellow scribes. That's where writers' conferences come in.

Conferences are rare and invaluable opportunities to simply get out there—to mingle, network, have fun, and meet new contacts that can help further your career. They are events where writers gather to meet one another and celebrate the craft and business of writing. Attendees listen to authors and professionals who present sessions on various topics of interest. Each day is filled with presentations regarding all aspects of writing, and attendees will likely have a choice of which sessions to attend.

Perhaps the most valuable aspect of a conference for writers is the opportunity to meet power players and decision makers in both the entertainment and publishing worlds. In addition, writers can make contacts and form partnerships with fellow scribes. Agents, managers and production executives attend conferences for a specific reason: to find good writers. They are bombarded with pitches and request writing samples from those attendees who dazzle them with a good idea or pitch. Short of an excellent referral, conferences are the best way to snag a rep, so take advantage of meeting one.

Usually it works like this: You schedule a short amount of time to pitch your idea to a rep or executive. Your "elevator pitch" should be relatively short and then there's some time for the professional to ask you questions about the script. If they're interested in seeing some of your work, they will pass you a business card and request part or all of your script. If the agent is not interested, she will say so. When an agent requests pages, you can send it in and put "Requested Material" on the envelope (or in the e-mail) so it gets past the slush pile.

Conferences usually have either a general focus on all subjects of writing, or a more narrow purpose. With some looking, you can find conferences devoted to screenwriting, playwriting, romance, mysteries, fantasy, science fiction, medical thrillers, and more.

SUBHEADS

Each listing is divided into subheads to make locating specific information easier. In the first section, you'll find contact information for conference contacts. You'll also learn conference dates, specific focus, and the average number of attendees. Finally, names of agents who will be speaking or have spoken in the past are listed along with details about their availability during the conference. Calling or e-mailing a conference director to verify the names of speakers and agents in attendance is always a good idea.

Costs: Looking at the price of events, plus room and board, may help writers on a tight budget narrow their choices.

Accommodations: Here conferences list overnight accommodations and travel information. Often conferences held in hotels will reserve rooms at a discount rate and may provide a shuttle bus to and from the local airport.

Additional Information: This section includes information on conference-sponsored contests, individual meetings, the availability of brochures, and more.

AGENTS AND EDITORS CONFERENCE

Writers' League of Texas, 1501 W. Fifth St., Suite E-2, Austin TX 78703. (512)499-8914. Fax: (512)499-0441. E-mail: wlt@writersleague.org. Web site: www.writersleague.org. **Contact:** Kristy Bordine, membership director. Estab. 1982. Annual conference held in the summer. Conference duration: 3 days. Average attendance: 300. Provides writers with the opportunity to meet top literary agents and editors from New York and the West Coast. Topics include: finding and working with agents and publishers, writing and marketing fiction and nonfiction, dialogue, characterization, voice, research, basic and advanced fiction writing, the business of writing, and workshops for genres. Speakers have included Malaika Adero, Stacey Barney, Sha-Shana Crichton, Jessica Faust, Dena Fischer, Mickey Freiberg, Jill Grosjean, Anne Hawkins, Jim Hornfischer, Jennifer Joel, David Hale Smith and Elisabeth Weed.

Costs $295-$345.

Additional Information Contests and awards programs are offered separately. Brochures are available upon request.

ALGONKIAN WRITER WORKSHOPS

2020 Pennsylvania Ave. NW, Suite 43, Washington DC 20006. (800)250-8290. E-mail: algonkian@webdelsol.com. Web site: http://www.algonkianconferences.com/. **Contact:** Michael Neff, director. Estab. 2001. Conference duration: 5 days. Average attendance: 15/craft workshops; 60/pitch sessions. Workshops on fiction, short fiction, and poetry are held 12 times/year in various locations. Speakers have included Paige Wheeler, Elise Capron, Deborah Grosvenor and Kathleen Anderson. Agents will be speaking and available for meetings with attendees.

Costs Housing costs vary depending on the workshop's location.

Additional Information "These workshops are challenging and are not for those looking for praise. Guidelines are available online or via e-mail."

ASJA WRITERS CONFERENCE

American Society of Journalists and Authors, 1501 Broadway, Suite 302, New York NY 10036. (212)997-0947. Fax: (212)768-7414. E-mail: staff@asja.org; director@asja.org. Web site: www.asjaconference.org. **Contact:** Executive director. Estab. 1971. Annual conference held in April. Conference duration: 2 days. Average attendance: 600. Covers nonfiction and screenwriting. Held at the Grand Hyatt in New York. Speakers have included Dominick Dunne, James Brady, and Dana Sobel. Agents will be speaking at the event.

Costs $200+, depending on when you sign up (includes lunch).

Accommodations "The hotel holding our conference always blocks out discounted rooms for attendees."

Additional Information Brochures available in February. Registration form is on the Web site. Inquire by e-mail or fax.

ASPEN SUMMER WORDS LITERARY FESTIVAL & WRITING RETREAT

Aspen Writers' Foundation, 110 E. Hallam St., #116, Aspen CO 81611. (970)925-3122. Fax: (970)925-5700. E-mail: info@aspenwriters.org. Web site: www.aspenwriters.org. **Contact:** Natalie Lacy, programs manager. Estab. 1976. Annual conference held the fourth week of June. Conference duration:

5 days. Average attendance: 150 at writing retreat; 300 + at literary festival. Retreat for fiction, creative nonfiction, poetry, magazine writing, food writing, and literature. Festival includes author readings, craft talks, panel discussions with publishing industry insiders, professional consultations with editors and agents, and social gatherings. Retreat faculty members in 2007: Andrea Barzi, Katherine Fausset, Anjali Singh, Lisa Grubka, Amber Qureshi, Joshua Kendall, Keith Flynn, Robert Bausch, Amy Bloom, Percival Everett, Danzy Senna, Bharti Kirchner, Gary Ferguson, Dorianne Laux. Festival presenters include (in 2007): Ngugi Wa Thiong'o, Wole Soyinka, Chimamanda Ngozi Adichie, Alaa Al Aswany, Henry Louis Gates, Jr., Leila Aboulela, and many more!.

Costs (In 2007:) $475/retreat; $175-250/seminar; Tuition includes daily continental breakfast and lunch, plus one evening reception; a limited number of half-tuition scholarships are available; $200/festival; $35/professional consultation.

Accommodations Discount lodging at the conference site will be available. $170/one-bedroom condo; $255/two-bedroom condo; $127.50/shared two-bedroom condo.

Additional Information Workshops admission deadline is April 1 for the 2008 conference, or until all workshops are filled. Juried admissions for some workshops; writing sample required with application to juried workshops. Mss will be discussed during workshop. Literary festival and some retreat programs are open to the public on first-come, first-served basis; no mss required. Brochure, application and complete admissions information available on Web site, or request by phone, fax or e-mail. Include mailing address with all e-mail requests.

AUSTRALIAN PUBLISHERS AND AUTHORS BOOKSHOW

NSW Writers' Centre, P.O. Box 1056, Rozelle Hospital Grounds, Balmain Road, Rozelle NSW 2039, Australia. (61)(2)9555-9757. Fax: (61)(2)9818-1327. E-mail: nswwc@nswwriterscentre.org.au. Web site: www.nswwriterscentre.org.au. **Contact:** Irina Dunn, executive director. Annual event held the third week in November. Books and magazines from independent, Australian-owned publishing companies, distributors, small presses, niche publishers, self-publishers, and print-on-demand publishers will be showcased. Writers, librarians, booksellers, and members of the public and literary organizations are invited to attend to see what local publishers are doing. Books will also be available for purchase.

Additional Information See the Web site for a complete list concerning program of festivals. There are multiple events with this organization each year. Topics covered during the year include writing novels, short stories, poetry, plays.

BACKSPACE WRITERS CONFERENCE

P.O. Box 454, Washington MI 48094-0454. Phone/Fax: (586)532-9652. E-mail: chrisg@bksp.org. Web site: www.backspacewritersconference.com. **Contact:** Karen Dionne, Christopher Graham. Estab. 2005. The 2008 conference will be held in New York City on Aug. 7-8. Conference duration: 2 days. Average attendance: 150. Conference focuses on all genres of fiction and nonfiction. Offers query letter workshop, writing workshop, and panels with agents, editors, marketing experts, and authors. Speakers have included Pulitzer-Prize-winning playwright Douglas Wright, Michael Cader, David Morrell, Lee Child, Gayle Lynds, Ron McLarty, C. Michael Curtis, Jeff Kleinman, Richard Curtis, Noah Lukeman, Jenny Bent, Dan Lazar and Kristin Nelson.

Costs $355 for Backspace members, $395 for non-members (includes 2-day, 2-track program and refreshments on both days, as well as a cocktail reception).

Additional Information This is a high-quality conference, with much of the program geared toward agented and published authors. Afternoon mixers each day afford plenty of networking opportunities. Go online for brochure, or request information via fax or e-mail.

BALTIMORE WRITERS' CONFERENCE

Citylit Project, 120 S. Curley St., Baltimore MD 21224. E-mail: info@citylitproject.org. Web site: www.tow son.edu/writersconference. **Contact:** Greg Wilhelm, coordinator. Estab. 1994. Annual conference held in November. Conference duration: 1 day. Average attendance: 150-200. Covers all areas of writing and getting published. Held at Towson University. Topics have included: mystery, science fiction, poetry, children's writing, legal issues, grant funding, working with an agent, and book and magazine panels. Speakers have included Dana Gioia, Alice McDermott and Nina Graybill. Agents will be speaking at the event.

Costs $80-100 (includes all-day conference, lunch and reception).

Accommodations Hotels are close by, if required.

Additional Information Writers may register through the BWA Web site. Send inquiries via e-mail.

BIG SUR WRITING WORKSHOPS

Henry Miller Library, Highway One, Big Sur CA 93920. Phone/Fax: (831)667-2574. E-mail: magnus@ henrymiller.org. Web site: www.henrymiller.org/CWW. **Contact:** Magnus Toren, executive director. Annual workshops held in December for children's/young adult writing and in March for adult fiction and nonfiction.

Accommodations Big Sur Lodge in Pfeiffer State Park.

BLOODY WORDS

64 Shaver Ave., Toronto ON M9B 3T5, Canada. E-mail: chair2008@bloodywords.com; info@bloo dywords.com; registrar@bloodywords.com. Web site: www.bloodywords.com. **Contact:** Caro Soles. Estab. 1999. Annual conference held in June. 2008 dates: June 6-8. Conference duration: 3 days. Average attendance: 250. Focuses on mystery fiction and aims to provide a showcase for Canadian mystery writers and readers, as well as provide writing information to aspiring writers. ''We will present 3 tracks of programming: Just the Facts, where everyone from coroners to toxicologists to tactical police units present how things are done in the real works; and What's the Story—where panelists discuss subjects of interest to readers; and the Mystery Cafe, where 12 authors read and discuss their work.''

Costs $175+ (Canadian).

Accommodations A special rate will be available at The Downtown Marriott Hotel in Toronto, Ontario.

Additional Information Registration is available online. Send inquiries via e-mail.

◎ BLUE RIDGE MOUNTAIN CHRISTIAN WRITERS CONFERENCE

No public address available,. E-mail: ylehman@bellsouth.net. Web site: www.lifeway.com/christian writers. **Contact:** Yvonne Lehman. Annual conference held in May. Conference duration: Sunday through lunch on Thursday. Average attendance: 400. A training and networking event for both seasoned and aspiring writers that allows attendees to interact with editors, agents, professional writers, and readers. Workshops and continuing classes in a variety of creative categories are also offered.

Costs $375 (includes sessions and banquet).

Accommodations $49-84, depending on room size, at the LifeWay Ridgecrest Conference Center near Asheville, North Carolina.

Additional Information The event also features a contest for unpublished writers and ms critiques prior to the conference.

BREAD LOAF WRITERS' CONFERENCE

Middlebury College, Middlebury VT 05753. (802)443-5286. Fax: (802)443-2087. E-mail: ncargill@ middlebury.edu. Web site: www.middlebury.edu/blwc. **Contact:** Noreen Cargill, administrative manager. Estab. 1926. Annual conference held in late August. Conference duration: 11 days. Average attendance: 230. Offers workshops for fiction, nonfiction, and poetry. Agents, editors, publicists, and grant specialists will be in attendance.

Costs $2,345 (includes tuition, housing).

Accommodations Bread Loaf Campus in Ripton, Vermont.

BYRON BAY WRITERS FESTIVAL

Northern Rivers Writers' Centre, P.O. Box 1846, 69 Johnson St., Byron Bay NSW 2481, Australia. 040755-2441. E-mail: jeni@nrwc.org.au. Web site: www.byronbaywritersfestival.com. **Contact:** Director. Estab. 1996. Annual festival held the first weekend in August at Becton's Byron Bay Beach Resort. Conference duration: 3 days. Celebrate and reflect with over 100 of the finest writers from Australia and overseas. Workshops, panel discussions, and poetry readings will also be offered.

Costs Early bird: $145/nonmembers; $125/NRWC members and students.

◎ BYU WRITING AND ILLUSTRATING FOR YOUNG READERS WORKSHOP

348 HCEB, Brigham Young University, Provo UT 84602. (801)422-2568. E-mail: cw348@byu.edu. Web site: wfyr.byu.edu. Estab. 2000. Annual workshop held in June. 2008 dates: June 16-20. Conference duration: 5 days. Average attendance: 100. Learn how to write/illustrate and publish in the children's and young adult fiction and nonfiction markets. Beginning and advanced writers/illustrators are tutored in a small-group setting by published authors/artists and receive instruction from editors, a major publishing house representative and a literary agent. Held at Brigham Young University's Harmon Conference Center. Speakers have included Edward Necarsulmer, Tracy Gates, and Jill Davis.

Costs Costs available online.

Accommodations A block of rooms is reserved at the Super 8 Motel for around $49/night. Airport shuttles are available.

Additional Information Guidelines and registration are on the Web site.

CHATTANOOGA FESTIVAL OF WRITERS

Arts & Education Council, 3069 S. Broad St., Suite 2, Chattanooga TN 37408. (423)267-1218. Fax: (423)267-1018. E-mail: info@artsedcouncil.org. Web site: www.artsedcouncil.org/page/chatta nooga-festival-of-writers. **Contact:** Susan Frady Robinson, executive director. Estab. 2006. Biennial conference held in late March. Conference duration: 2 days. Average attendance: 250. This conference covers fiction, nonfiction, drama and poetry through workshops and keynote. Held in downtown

Chattanooga. Speakers have included Suzette Francis, Richard Bausch, David Magee, Philip Gerard, Elizabeth Kostova and Robert Morgan.

Costs $65-175 (depending on attendees participation in workshops, luncheon and dinner).

Additional Information Visit www.chattanoogafun.com for assistance with accomodations and airfare.

CHRISTOPHER NEWPORT UNIVERSITY WRITER CONFERENCE

1 University Place, Center for Community Learning, Newport News VA 23606-2988. (757)594-7938. Fax: (757)594-8736. E-mail: challiday@cnu.edu. Web site: writers.cnu.edu/. **Contact:** Director. Estab. 1981. Annual. Conference held in March. Conference duration: Friday evening and Saturday day. "This is a working conference." Presentations made by editors, agents, fiction writers, poets and more. Site: Christopher Newport University, Newport News, VA. Friday evening and Saturday morning consist of breakout sessions in fiction, nonfiction, poetry, juvenile fiction and publishing. Previous panels included Publishing, Proposal Writing, Internet Research and various breakout sessions. There is one keynote Saturday morning.

Accommodations Provides list of area hotels.

Additional Information Sponsors contest. Full contest info is available online.

CLARION WEST WRITERS' WORKSHOP

340 15th Ave. E, Suite 350, Seattle WA 98112-5156. (206)322-9083. E-mail: info@clarionwest.org. Web site: www.clarionwest.org. **Contact:** Leslie Howle, executive director. Annual workshop that usually goes from late June through early July. Conference duration: 6 weeks. Average attendance: 18. Conference prepares students for professional careers in science fiction and fantasy writing. Held near the University of Washington. Deadline for applications is March 1. Agents are invited to speak to attendees.

Costs $3,200 (for tuition, housing, most meals). $100 discount if application received prior to March 1. Limited scholarships are available based on financial need.

Additional Information This is a critique-based workshop. Students are encouraged to write a story every week; the critique of student material produced at the workshop forms the principal activity of the workshop. Students and instructors critique mss as a group. Students must submit 20-30 pages of ms to qualify for admission. Conference guidelines are available for a SASE. Visit the Web site for updates and complete details.

CLARKSVILLE WRITERS CONFERENCE

1123 Madison St., Clarksville TN 37040. (931)645-2317. E-mail: corneliuswinn@bellsouth.net. Web site: www.artsandheritage.us/writers/. **Contact:** Patricia Winn. Annual. Annual conference held in the summer. Conference duration: 2 days. The conference features a variety of presentations on fiction, nonfiction and more. Previous speakers have included Robert Hicks, Jeanne Ray, David Magee, Alanna Nash, William Gay, River Jordan, Malcolm Glass, David Till.

Costs Costs available online; prices vary depending on how long attendees stay and if they attend the banquet dinner.

Accommodations Hotel specials provided every year.

COLUMBUS WRITERS CONFERENCE

P.O. Box 20548, Columbus OH 43220. (614)451-3075. Fax: (614)451-0174. E-mail: angelapl28@aol.com. Web site: www.creativevista.com. **Contact:** Angela Palazzolo, director. Estab. 1993. Annual conference held in August. Average attendance: 250 +. In addition to literary agent and editor consultations, the conference offers a wide variety of fiction and nonfiction topics presented by writers, editors, and literary agents. Writing topics have included novel, short story, children's, young adult, science fiction, fantasy, humor, mystery, playwriting, finding and working with a literary agent, book proposals, query writing, screenwriting, magazine writing, travel, humor, cookbook, technical queries and freelance writing. The conference has included many writers, editors and literary agents, including Lee K. Abbott, Chuck Adams, Tracy Bernstein, Sheree Bykofsky, Oscar Collier, Lisa Cron, Jennifer DeChiara, Tracey E. Dils, Hallie Ephron, Karen Harper, Scott Hoffman, Jeff Kleinman, Simon Lipskar, Noah Lukeman, Donald Maass, Lee Martin, Erin McGraw, Kim Meisner, Doris S. Michaels, Rita Rosenkrantz, Ben Salmon and Nancy Zafris.

Additional Information For registration fees or to receive a brochure (available in the summer), visit the Web site or contact the conference by e-mail, phone, fax, or postal mail.

DESERT DREAMS

Phoenix Desert Rose Chapter No. 60, P.O. Box 27407, Tempe AZ 85285. (866)267-2249. E-mail: info@desertroserwa.org; desertdreams@desertroserwa.org. Web site: desertroserwa.org. **Contact:** Susan Lanier-Graham, conference coordinator. Estab. 1986. Conference held every other April. Conference duration: 3 days. Average attendance: 250. Covers marketing, fiction, screenwriting, and research. Upcoming speakers and agents will include Jessica Faust (BookEnds), Deirdre Knight (The Knight Agency), other agents, editors, Vicki Lewis Thompson, Lori Wilde, Mary Jo Putney, Sherrilyn Kenyon and more. Agents and editors will be speaking and available for meetings with attendees.

Costs $218 + (includes meals, seminars, appointments with agents/editors).

Accommodations Discounted rates for attendees is negotiated at the Crowne Plaza San Marcos Resort in Chandler, Ariz.

Additional Information Send inquiries via e-mail. Visit Web site for updates and complete details.

EAST OF EDEN WRITERS CONFERENCE

P.O. Box 3254, Santa Clara CA 95055. E-mail: vp@southbaywriters.com; pres@southbaywriters.com. Web site: www.southbaywriters.com. **Contact:** Vice President/Programs Chair of South Bay Writers. Estab. 2000. Biannual conference held in September. 2008 dates: Sept. 5-7. Average attendance: 300. Writers of all levels are welcome. Pitch sessions to agents and publishers are available, as are meetings with authors and editors. Workshops address the craft and the business of writing. Location: Salinas, Calif.—Steinbeck Country.

Costs Costs vary. The full conference (Friday and Saturday) is approximately $250; Saturday only is approximately $175. The fee includes meals, workshops and pitch/meeting sessions. Optional events extra.

Accommodations Negotiated rates at local hotels—$85 per night, give or take.

Additional Information The East of Eden conference is run by writers/volunteers from the California Writers Club, South Bay Branch. For details about our next conference(s), please visit our Web site or send an SASE.

FALL WRITERS' SEMINAR

Council for the Written Word, P.O. Box 298, Franklin TN 37065. (615)790-5918. E-mail: kathyrhodes @pinkbutterbeans.com. Web site: www.asouthernjournal.com/cww. **Contact:** Kathy Rhodes. Annual conference held in September. The Sept. 18 session addresses the five R's of creative nonfiction with Lee Gutkind. An all-day event with local and area authors, agents, editors, publishers, and/or publicists teaching the art and business of writing.

FESTIVAL OF WORDS

217 Main St. N., Moose Jaw SK S6J 0W1, Canada. (306)691-0557. Fax: (306)693-2994. E-mail: word.f estival@sasktel.net. Web site: www.festivalofwords.com. **Contact:** Donna Lee Howes. Estab. 1997. Annual festival held in July. 2008 dates: July 17-20. Conference duration: 4 days. Average attendance: 1,500.

Accommodations A list of motels, hotels, campgrounds, and bed and breakfasts is provided upon request.

Additional Information "Our festival is an ideal place for people who love words to mingle, promote their books, and meet their fans." Brochures are available; send inquiries via e-mail or fax.

FLATHEAD RIVER WRITERS CONFERENCE

P.O. Box 7711, Kalispeil MT 59904-7711. E-mail: answers@authorsoftheflathead.org. Web site: ww w.authorsoftheflathead.org. **Contact:** Val Smith. Estab. 1990. Annual conference held in early mid-October. Conference duration: 3 days. Average attendance: 100. "We provide several small, intense 3-day workshops before the general weekend conference." Workshops, panel discussions, and speakers focus on novels, nonfiction, screenwriting, short stories, magazine articles, and the writing industry. Held at the Grouse Mountain Lodge in Whitefish, Montana. Past speakers have included Sam Pinkus, Randy Wayne White, Donald Maass, Ann Rule, Cricket Pechstein, Marcela Landres, Amy Rennert, Ben Mikaelsen, Esmond Harmsworth, Linda McFall, and Ron Carlson. Agents will be speaking and available for meetings with attendees.

Costs $150 (includes breakfast and lunch, but not lodging).

Accommodations Rooms are available at a discounted rate of $100/night. Whitefish is a resort town, so less expensive lodging can be arranged.

Additional Information "By limiting attendance to 100 people, we assure a quality experience and informal, easy access to the presenters and other attendees." Brochures are available in June; send inquiries via e-mail.

FLORIDA CHRISTIAN WRITERS CONFERENCE

2344 Armour Ct., Titusville FL 32780. (321)269-5831. Fax: (321)264-0037. E-mail: billiewilson@cfl.rr. com. Web site: www.flwriters.org. **Contact:** Billie Wilson. Estab. 1988. Annual conference held in March. Conference duration: 4 days. Average attendance: 200. Covers fiction, nonfiction, magazine writing, marketing, Internet writing, greeting cards, and more. Conference is held at the Christian Retreat Center in Brandenton, Florida.

Costs $485 (includes tuition, meals).

Accommodations "We provide a shuttle from the Sarasota airport." $625/double occupancy; $865/single occupancy.

Additional Information "Each writer may submit 2 works for critique. We have specialists in every area of writing." Brochures/guidelines are available online or for a SASE.

FLORIDA FIRST COAST WRITERS' FESTIVAL

4501 Capper Road, C105, FCCJ, Jacksonville FL 32218. (904)766-6731. Fax: (904)713-4858. E-mail: dathomas@fccj.org. Web site: www.fccj.org/wf. **Contact:** Dana Thomas. Estab. 1985. Annual conference held in the spring. Average attendance: 300. Covers fiction, nonfiction, scriptwriting, poetry, freelancing, etc. Offers seminars on narrative structure and plotting character development. Speakers have included Andrei Codrescu, Gerald Hausman, Connie May Fowler, Leslie Schwartz, Larry Smith, Stella Suberman, Sophia Wadsworth, Amy Gash, David Hale Smith, Katharine Sands, Rita Rosenkranz, Jim McCarthy, David Poyer, Lenore Hart, Steve Berry and S.V. Date. "We offer one-on-one sessions at no additional cost for attendees to speak to selected writers, editors, and agents on a first-come, first-served basis."

Costs Visit the Web site for updated registration fees, including early bird specials.

Additional Information Sponsors a contest for short fiction, poetry, novels and plays. Novel judges are David Poyer and Lenore Hart. Entry fees: $39/novels; $15/short fiction; $7/poetry. Deadline: varies. Visit the Web site often for festival updates and details.

GENEVA WRITERS CONFERENCE

Geneva Writers Group, Switzerland. E-mail: info@GenevaWritersGroup.org. Web site: www.geneva writersgroup.org/conference.html. Estab. 2002. Annual. Conference held in Geneva, Switzerland. The 2008 conference was held at Webster University. Conference duration: 2 days. Past speakers and presenters have included Thomas E. Kennedy, Nahid Rachlin, Jeremy Sheldon, Kwame Kwei Armah, Philip Graham, Mimi Schwartz, Susan Tiberghien, Jo Shapcott, Wallis Wilde Menozzi, David Applefield, Laura Longrigg, Bill Newlin, Zeki Ergas, D-L Nelson, Sylvia Petter, Alistair Scott.

THE GLEN WORKSHOP

Image, 3307 Third Avenue W., Seattle WA 98119. (206)281-2988. Fax: (206)281-2335. E-mail: glenw orkshop@imagejournal.org; jmullins@imagejournal.org. Web site: www.imagejournal.org/glen. Estab. 1991. Annual workshop held in August. Conference duration: 1 week. Workshop focuses on fiction, poetry, spiritual writing, playwriting, screenwriting, songwriting, and mixed media. Writing classes combine general instruction and discussion with the workshop experience, in which each individual's works are read and discussed critically. Held at St. John's College in Santa Fe, New Mexico. Faculty has included Scott Cairns, Jeanine Hathaway, Bret Lott, Paula Huston, Arlene Hutton, David Denny, Barry Moser, Barry Krammes, Ginger Geyer, and Pierce Pettis.

Costs 2007 costs: $500-960 (includes tuition, lodging, meals); $395-475/commuters (includes tuition, lunch). A limited number of partial scholarships are available.

Accommodations Offers dorm rooms, dorm suites, and apartments.

Additional Information "Like *Image*, the Glen is grounded in a Christian perspective, but its tone is informal and hospitable to all spiritual wayfarers." Depending on the teacher, participants may need to submit workshop material prior to arrival (usually 10-25 pages).

◎ GLORIETA CHRISTIAN WRITERS CONFERENCE

CLASServices, Inc., 3311 Candelaria NE, Suite 1, Albuquerque NM 87107-1952. (800)433-6633. Fax: (505)899-9282. E-mail: info@classervices.com. Web site: www.glorietacwc.com. **Contact:** Linda Jewell, seminar manager. Estab. 1997. Annual. Annual conference held in October. Conference duration: Wednesday afternoon through Sunday lunch. Average attendance: 350. Includes programs for all types of writing. Agents, editors, and professional writers will be speaking and available for meetings with attendees.

Costs 2007 costs: $450/early registration (1 month in advance); $495/program only. Critiques are available for an additional charge.

Accommodations Hotel rooms are available at the LifeWay Glorieta Conference Center. Santa Fe Shuttle offers service from the Albuquerque or Santa Fe airports to the conference center. Hotel rates vary. "We suggest you make airline and rental car reservations early due to other events in the area."

Additional Information Brochures are available April 1. Inquire via e-mail, phone, or fax, or visit the Web site.

GOTHAM WRITERS' WORKSHOP

WritingClasses.com, 555 Eighth Ave., Suite 1402, New York NY 10018. (212)974-8377. Fax: (212)307-6325. E-mail: dana@write.org. Web site: www.writingclasses.com. **Contact:** Dana Miller, director of student affairs. Estab. 1993. Classes are held throughout the year. There are four terms, beginning in January, April, June/July, and September/October. Offers craft-oriented creative writing courses in general creative writing, fiction writing, screenwriting, nonfiction writing, article writing, stand-up comedy writing, humor writing, memoir writing, novel writing, children's book writing, playwriting, poetry, songwriting, mystery writing, science fiction writing, romance writing, television writing, article writing, travel writing, business writing and classes on freelancing, selling your screneplay and getting published. Also, Gotham Writers' Workshop offers a teen program, private instruction, and classes on selling your work. Classes are held at various schools in New York City as well as online at www.writingclasses.com. Agents and editors participate in some workshops.

Costs $395/10-week workshops; $125 for the four-week online selling seminars and 1-day intensive courses; $295 for 6-week creative writing and business writing classes.

GREEN LAKE WRITERS CONFERENCE

W2511 State Road 23, Green Lake Conference Center, Green Lake WI 54941-9599. (920)294-3323. E-mail: janwhite@glcc.org. Web site: www.glcc.org. **Contact:** Program coordinator. Estab. 1948. The 60th annual conference will be Aug. 17-22, 2008. Conference duration: 1 week. Attendees may be well-published or beginners, may write for secular and/or Christian markets. Leaders are experienced writing teachers. Attendees can spend 11.5 contact hours in the workshop of their choice: fiction, nonfiction, poetry, inspirational/devotional. Seminars include specific skills: marketing, humor, song-writing, writing for children, self-publishing, writing for churches, interviewing, memoir writing, the magazine market. Evening: panels of experts will answer questions. Social and leisure activities included. GLCC is in south central WI, has 1,000 acres, 2.5 miles of shoreline on Wisconsin's deepest lake, and offers a resort setting.

Additional Information Brochure and scholarship info from Web site or contact Jan White (920-294-7327). To register, call 920-294-3323.

GREEN MOUNTAIN WRITERS CONFERENCE

47 Hazel St., Rutland VT 05701. (802)236-6133. E-mail: ydaley@sbcglobal.net. Web site: www.vermontwriters.com. **Contact:** Yvonne Daley, director. Estab. 1999. Annual conference held in the summer; 2008 dates are July 28—Aug. 1. Covers fiction, creative nonfiction, poetry, journalism, nature writing, essay, memoir, personal narrative, and biography. Held at an old dance pavillion on on a

remote pond in Tinmouth, Vermont. Speakers have included Joan Connor, Yvonne Daley, David Huddle, David Budbill, Jeffrey Lent, Verandah Porche, Tom Smith, and Chuck Clarino.

Costs $500 before June 15; $525 after June 15. Partial scholarships are available.

Accommodations ''We have made arrangements with a major hotel in nearby Rutland and 2 area bed and breakfast inns for special accommodations and rates for conference participants. You must make your own reservations.''

GULF COAST WRITERS CONFERENCE

P.O. Box 35038, Panama City FL 32412. (850)639-4848. E-mail: MichaelLister@mchsi.com. Web site: www.gulfcoastwritersconference.com/. **Contact:** Michael Lister. Estab. 1999. Annual conference held in September in Panama City, Fla. 2008 dates: Sept. 18-20. Conference duration: 2 days. Average attendance: 100+. This conference is deliberately small and writer-centric with an affordable attedance price. Speakers include writers, editors and agents. Cricket Pechstein Freeman of the August Agency is often in attendance. The 2009 keynote speaker is mystery writer Michael Connelly.

HARRIETTE AUSTIN WRITERS CONFERENCE

Georgia Center for Continuing Education, The University of Georgia, Athens GA 30602-3603. E-mail: adminhawc2008@gmail.com. Web site: harrietteaustin.org/default.aspx. **Contact:** Diane Trap. Annual conference held in July. Sessions cover fiction, poetry, freelance writing, computers, how to get an agent, working with editors, and more. Editors and agents will be speaking. Ms critiques and one-on-one meetings with an evaluator are available for $50.

Costs Cost information available online.

Accommodations Accomodations at the Georgia Center Hotel (georgiacenter.uga.edu).

HEARTLAND WRITERS CONFERENCE

P.O. Box 652, Kennett MO 63857. (573)297-3325. Fax: (573)297-3352. E-mail: hwg@heartlandwriters.org. Web site: www.heartlandwriters.org/conference.html. **Contact:** Harry Spiller, conference coordinator. Estab. 1990. Biennial (even years) conference held in June. 2008 date: June 7. Conference duration: 3 days. Average attendance: 160. Covers popular fiction (all genres), nonfiction, children's writing, screenwritin, and poetry. Held at the Best Western Coach House Inn in Sikeston, Missouri. Speakers have included Alice Orr, Jennifer Jackson, Ricia Mainhardt, Christy Fletcher, Sue Yuen, and Evan Marshall. Agents will be speaking and available for meetings with attendees.

Costs $215 for advance registrants; $250 for general registration (includes lunch on Friday and Saturday, awards banquet on Sunday, hospitality room, and get-acquainted mixer Thursday night).

Accommodations Blocks of rooms are available at a special rate ($55-85/night) at the conference venue and 2 nearby motels.

Additional Information Brochures are available in late January. Inquire via e-mail or fax.

HIGHLAND SUMMER CONFERENCE

Box 7014, Radford University, Radford VA 24142-7014. (540)831-5366. Fax: (540)831-5951. E-mail: dcochran7@radford.edu; jasbury@radford.edu. Web site: www.radford.edu/~arsc. **Contact:** JoAnn Asbury, assistant to the director. Estab. 1978. Annual conference held in June. 2008 dates: June 2-13. Conference duration: 2 weeks. Average attendance: 25. Covers fiction, nonfiction, poetry, and screenwriting. Speakers have included Bill Brown, Robert Morgan, Sharyn McCrumb, Nikki Giovanni,

Wilma Dykeman, Jim Wayne Miller, David Huddle, and Diane Fisher. 2008 speakers include: Affrilachian Poet, Frank X. Walker and Poet and Novelist Darnell Arnoult.

Costs The cost is based on current Radford tuition for 3 credit hours, plus an additional conference fee. On-campus meals and housing are available at additional cost. In 2007, conference tuition was $717/in-state undergraduates, $1,686/for out-of-state undergraduates, $780/in-state graduates, and $1,434/out-of-state graduates.

Accommodations "We do not have special rate arrangements with local hotels. We do offer accommodations on the Radford University campus in a recently refurbished residence hall. The 2005 cost was $26-36/night."

Additional Information Conference leaders typically critique work done during the 2-week conference, but do not ask to have any writing submitted prior to the conference." Conference brochures/guidelines are available in March for a SASE. Inquire via e-mail or fax.

HIGHLIGHTS FOUNDATION WRITERS WORKSHOP AT CHAUTAUQUA

814 Court St., Honesdale PA 18431. (570)253-1192. Fax: (570)253-0179. E-mail: contact@highlights foundation.org. Web site: www.highlightsfoundation.org. **Contact:** Kent Brown, executive director. Estab. 1985. Annual conference held July 12-18, 2008, and July 11-18, 2009. Average attendance: 100. Workshops are geared toward those who write for children at the beginner, intermediate, and advanced levels. Offers seminars, small group workshops, and one-on-one sessions with authors, editors, illustrators, critics, and publishers. Workshop site is the picturesque community of Chautauqua, New York. Speakers have included Bruce Coville, Candace Fleming, Linda Sue Park, Jane Yolen, Patricia Gauch, Jerry Spinelli, Eileen Spinelli, Joy Cowley and Pam Munoz Ryan.

Costs $2,400 (includes all meals, conference supplies, gate pass to Chautauqua Institution).

Accommodations "We coordinate ground transportation to and from airports, trains, and bus stations in the Erie, Pennsylvania and Jamestown/Buffalo, New York area. We also coordinate accommodations for conference attendees."

Additional Information "We offer the opportunity for attendees to submit a manuscript for review at the conference." Workshop brochures/guidelines are available upon request.

HOLLYWOOD PITCH FESTIVAL

Fade In Magazine, 287 S. Robertson Blvd., #467, Beverly Hills CA 90211. (800)646-3896. E-mail: inquiries@fadeinonline.com. Web site: hollywoodpitchfestival.com/. Estab. 1996. Annual. Conference duration: Two days. "The Hollywood Pitch Festival is a pitch event that provides non-stop pitch meetings over a two-day period—with 200 of Hollywood's top buyers/representatives under one roof. HPF only has one class—a pitch class taught by a professional A-list filmmaker on Saturday morning, and it is optional. The Hollywood Pitch Festival will e-mail each attendee approximately 7-10 days prior to the event, a list of the companies/industry representatives attending, what each company is currently looking to produce (i.e., genre, budget), along with each company's credits. We also post a genre list at each event for cross-reference."

Costs Our ticket prices are flat fees that cover each attendee's entire weekend (including food and drink). There are no other extra, added costs (i.e., no per pitch meeting fees) involved (unless you're adding hotel rooms).

IDAHO WRITERS LEAGUE WRITERS' CONFERENCE

P.O. Box 492, Kootenai, ID 83840. (208)290-8749. E-mail: president@idahowritersleague.com. Web site: www.idahowritersleague.com/Conference.html. **Contact:** Sherry Ramsey. Estab. 1940. Annual floating conference. Next conference: Sept. 25-27, 2008. Average attendance: 80+. We have such writers as magazine freelance and children's book author, Kelly Milner Halls; and author of the 2006 Christian Women's Fiction Book of the Year, Nikki Arana.

Costs Cost: $125.

Additional Information Check out our Web site at www.idahowritersleague.com. Conference will be held at the Coeur d'Alene Inn in Coeur d'Alene, Idaho.

IMAGINATION WRITERS WORKSHOP AND CONFERENCE

Cleveland State University, English Department, 2121 Euclid Ave., Cleveland OH 44115. (216)687-4522. Fax: (216)687-6943. E-mail: imagination@csuohio.edu. Web site: www.csuohio.edu/imagination/. **Contact:** Neal Chandler, director. Estab. 1990. Annual conference is held in late June/early July. Conference duration: 6 days. Average attendance: 60. Program includes intensive workshops, panels, lectures on poetry, fiction, creative nonfiction, playwriting, and the business of writing by noted authors, editors and agents. Held at Trinity Commons, an award-winning urban renovation and ideal conference center adjacent to the CSU campus. Available both not-for-credit and for university credit.

INDIANA UNIVERSITY WRITERS' CONFERENCE

464 Ballantine Hall, Bloomington IN 47405. (812)855-1877. E-mail: writecon@indiana.edu. Web site: www.indiana.edu/~writecon. Estab. 1940. Annual conference held in June. Participants in the week-long conference join faculty-led workshops (fiction, poetry, and creative nonfiction), take classes, engage in one-on-one consultation with authors, and attend a variety of readings and social events. Previous speakers have included Raymond Carver, Mark Doty, Robert Olen Butler, Aimee Bender, Li-Young Lee, and Brenda Hillman.

Costs Costs available online.

Additional Information ''In order to be accepted in a workshop, the writer must submit the work they would like critiqued. Work is evaluated before the applicant is accepted. Go online or send a SASE for guidelines.

IOWA SUMMER WRITING FESTIVAL

C215 Seashore Hall, University of Iowa, Iowa City IA 52242. (319)335-4160. Fax: (319)335-4039. E-mail: iswfestival@uiowa.edu. Web site: www.uiowa.edu/~iswfest. **Contact:** Amy Margolis, director. Estab. 1987. Annual festival held in June and July. Conference duration: Workshops are 1 week or a weekend. Average attendance: Limited to 12 people/class, with over 1,500 participants throughout the summer. ''We offer courses across the genres: novel, short story, poetry, essay, memoir, humor, travel, playwriting, screenwriting, writing for children, and women's writing.'' Held at the University of Iowa campus. Speakers have included Marvin Bell, Lan Samantha Chang, John Dalton, Hope Edelman, Katie Ford, Patricia Foster, Bret Anthony Johnston, Barbara Robinette Moss, among others.

Costs $500-525/week; $250/weekend workshop. Housing and meals are separate.

Accommodations Iowa House: $75/night; Sheraton: $88/night (rates subject to change).

Additional Information Brochures are available in February. Inquire via e-mail or fax.

JACKSON HOLE WRITERS CONFERENCE

P.O. Box 1974, Jackson WY 83001. (307)413-3332. E-mail: tim@jacksonholewritersconference.com. Web site: jacksonholewritersconference.com/. Estab. 1991. Annual conference held in June. 2008 dates: June 26-29. Conference duration: 4 days. Average attendance: 70. Covers fiction and creative nonfiction and offers ms critiques from authors, agents, and editors. Agents in attendance will take pitches from writers. Paid manuscript critique programs are available.
Costs $360-390.

KARITOS CHRISTIAN ARTS CONFERENCE

24-B N. Belmont Ave., Arlington IL 60004. (847)749-1284. E-mail: bob@karitos.com. Web site: www.karitos.com. **Contact:** RuthAnne Boone, literary department head (ladyruth@ix.netcom.com). Estab. 1996. Annual conference held each summer. 2008 dates: July 31—Aug. 2. Conference duration: Thursday-Saturday night. Average attendance: 300-400. Karitos is a celebration and teaching weekend for Christian artists and writers. Writing Division will focus on teaching the craft of writing, beginning and advanced, fiction and nonfiction. Site for this year's conference is Living Waters Community Church in the Chicago suburb of Bolingbrook, Faculty has included Lori Davis, John DeJarlais, Eva Marie Everson, Lin Johnson, Patricia Hickman, Elma Photikarm, Rajendra Pillai, Jane Rubietta, Travis Thrasher and Chris Wave.
Costs Early registration: $80 (through April 20); $120 thereafter.

KENYON REVIEW WRITERS WORKSHOP

The Kenyon Review, Kenyon College, Gambier OH 43022. (740)427-5207. Fax: (740)427-5417. E-mail: reacha@kenyon.edu. Web site: www.kenyonreview.org. **Contact:** Anna Duke Reach, Director of Summer Programs. Estab. 1990. Annual 8-day workshop held in June. Participants apply in poetry, fiction, or creative nonfiction, and then participate in intensive daily workshops which focus on the generation and revision of significant new work. Held on the campus of Kenyon College in the rural village of Gambier, Ohio. Workshop leaders have included David Baker, Ron Carlson, Rebecca McClanahan, Rosanna Warren and Nancy Zafris.
Costs $1,995 (includes tuition, housing, meals).
Accommodations Participants stay in Kenyon College student housing.

KILLER NASHVILLE

P.O. Box 680686, Franklin TN 37068-0686. (615)599-4032. E-mail: contact@killernashville.com. Web site: www.killernashville.com. **Contact:** Clay Stafford. Estab. 2006. Annual conference held in August. Next conference: Aug. 15-17, 2008. Conference duration: 4 days. Average attendance: 180+. Conference designed for writers and fans of mysteries and thrillers, including fiction and nonfiction authors, playwrights, and screenwriters. There are many opportunities for authors to sign books. Authors/panelists have included Michael Connelly, Carol Higgins Clark, Hallie Ephron, Chris Grabenstein, Rhonda Pollero, P.J. Parrish, Reed Farrel Coleman, Gwen Hunter, Kathryn Wall, Mary Saums, Don Bruns, Bill Moody, Richard Helms, Brad Strickland and Steven Womack. Literary agents and acquisitions editors attend and take pitches from writers. The conference is sponsored by Middle Tennessee State University, Mystery Writers of America, Sisters in Crime and the Nashville Scene, among others. Representatives from the FBI, ATF, police department and sheriff's department present on law enforcement procedures.

LA JOLLA WRITERS CONFERENCE

P.O. Box 178122, San Diego CA 92177. (858)467-1978. Fax: (858)467-1971. E-mail: jkuritz@san.rr. com. Web site: www.lajollawritersconference.com. **Contact:** Jared Kuritz, co-director. Estab. 2001. Annual conference held in October. Conference duration: 3 days. Average attendance: 200. "In addition to covering nearly every genre, we also take particular pride in educating our attendees on the business aspect of the book industry by having agents, editors, publishers, publicists, and distributors teach classes. Our conference offers 2 types of classes: lecture sessions that run for 50 minutes, and workshops that run for 110 minutes. Each block period is dedicated to either workshop or lecture-style classes. During each block period, there will be 6-8 classes on various topics from which you can choose to attend. For most workshop classes, you are encouraged to bring written work for review." Literary agents from The Andrea Brown Literary Agency, The Dijkstra Agency, The McBride Agency and Full Circle Literary Group have participated in the past.

Costs Costs are available online.

Accommodations "We arrange a discounted rate with the hotel that hosts the conference. Please refer to the Web site."

Additional Information "Our conference is completely non-commercial. Our goal is to foster a true learning environment. As such, our faculty is chosen based on their expertise and willingness to make themselves completely available to the attendees." Brochures are online; send inquiries via e-mail or fax.

LAMB'S SPRINGFED WRITING RETREAT

S. Arts, P.O. Box 304, Royal Oak MI 48068-0304. (248)589-3913. Fax: (248)589-9981. E-mail: john dlamb@ameritech.net. Web site: www.springfed.org. **Contact:** John D. Lamb, director. Estab. 1999. Annual conference held in late September. Average attendance: 75. New and established writers and poets attend workshops, readings, and provocative panel discussions. Held at The Birchwood Inn, Harbor Springs, Mich. Speakers have included Thomas Lux, Michael Moore, Dorianne Laux, Billy Collins, Denise Duhamel, Jane Hamilton, Jacquelyn Mitchard, Mary Jo Salter, Brad Leithauser, Doug Stanton, Craig Holden, Chuck Pfarrer, Ivan Raimi, Jonathan Rand and M.L. Liebler.

Costs $535-600/single occupancy; $460-500/double occupancy; $360/no lodging (includes workshops, meals).

Accommodations Attendees stay in comfortable rooms with 1 king bed or two queens. Arranges shuttle ride from Pellston Airport in Pellston, Mich.

Additional Information Attendees may submit their work for craft discussion and/or conference tutorials; send 3 copies of 3 poems or 5 pages of prose.

LAS VEGAS WRITERS CONFERENCE

Henderson Writers Group, 614 Mosswood Drive, Henderson NV 89015. (702)564-2488. E-mail: infoas vegaswritersconference.com. Web site: www.lasvegaswritersconference.com/. **Contact:** Jo Wilkens, president. Annual. Annual conference just outside of Las Vegas. 2008 dates: April 17-19. Conference duration: 3 days. Average attendance: 140. "Join writing professionals, agents, industry experts and your colleagues for four days in Las Vegas, NV, as they share their knowledge on all aspects of the writer's craft. One of the great charms of the Las Vegas Writer's Conference is its intimacy. Registration is limited to 140 attendees so there's always plenty of one-on-one time with the faculty. While there are formal pitch sessions, panels, workshops, and seminars, the faculty is also available throughout the conference for informal discussions and advice. Plus, you're bound to meet a few new friends, too. Workshops, seminars and expert panels will take you through writing in many genres including fiction, creative nonfiction, screenwriting, poetry, journalism and business and technical writing. There will be many Q&A panels for you to ask the experts all your questions."

Accommodations Sam's Town Hotel and Gambling Hall.

THE MACDOWELL COLONY

100 High St., Peterborough NH 03458. (603)924-3886. Fax: (603)924-9142. E-mail: admissions@mac dowellcolony.org. Web site: www.macdowellcolony.org. **Contact:** Admissions Director. Estab. 1907. Open to writers, playwrights, composers, visual artists, film/video artists, interdisciplinary artists and architects. Applicants send information and work samples for review by a panel of experts in each discipline. See application guidelines for details.

Costs There are no residency fees.

◉ MAGNA CUM MURDER

The Mid America Crime Writing Festival, The E.B. and Bertha C. Ball Center, Ball State University, Muncie IN 47306. (765)285-8975. Fax: (765)747-9566. E-mail: magnacummurder@yahoo.com; kenni sonk@aol.com. Web site: www.magnacummurder.com. **Contact:** Kathryn Kennison. Estab. 1994. Annual conference held in October. 2008 dates: Oct. 24-26 in Muncie, IN. Average attendance: 350. Festival for readers and writers of crime writing. Held in the Horizon Convention Center and Historic Hotel Roberts. Dozens of mystery writers are in attendance and there are presentations from agents, editors and professional writers. The Web site has the full list of attending speakers.

Costs $195+ (includes breakfast, boxed lunches, opening reception, Saturday evening banquet).

MALICE DOMESTIC

P.O. Box 8007, Gaithersburg MD 20898-8007. Fax: (301)432-7391. E-mail: malicechair@malicedomesti c.org. Web site: www.malicedomestic.org/. Estab. 1989. The 2008 conference was in April, in Arlington, VA. Future dates: May 1-3, 2009 and April 30—May 2, 2010. The conference is for mystery writers of all kinds and always held in the Washington, DC regional area. The conference includes authors and literary agents.

Costs $225 basic registration. This will convention activities, including Opening Reception, New Authors Breakfast and Closing Festivities. Comprehensive registration also includes your right to vote for the Agatha Awards, a souvenir Program Book, and a subscription to the Usual Suspects.

MAUI WRITERS CONFERENCE

P.O. Box 1118, Kihei HI 96753. (808)879-0061. Fax: (808)879-6233. E-mail: writers@mauiwriters. com. Web site: www.mauiwriters.com. **Contact:** Shannon Tullius. Estab. 1993. Annual. Annual conference held at the end of August (Labor Day weekend). 2008 dates: Aug. 29—Sept. 1. Conference duration: 4 days. Average attendance: 600. Covers fiction, nonfiction, poetry, screenwriting, children's/young adult writing, horror, mystery, romance, science fiction, and journalism. Though previously held in Maui, the conference moved to Honolulu in 2008. Speakers have included Kimberley Cameron (Reece Halsey North), Susan Crawford (Crawford Literary Agency), Jillian Manus (Manus & Associates), Jenny Bent (Trident Media Group), Catherine Fowler (Redwood Agency), James D. Hornfischer (Hornfischer Literary Management), and Debra Goldstein (The Creative Culture).

Costs $600-1,000. See the Web site for full information.

Additional Information "We offer a comprehensive view of the business of publishing, with more than 1,500 consultation slots with industry agents, editors, and screenwriting professionals, as well as workshops and sessions covering writing instruction. Consider attending the MWC Writers Retreat immediately preceding the conference. Write, call, or visit our Web site for current updates and full details on all of our upcoming programs."

MENDOCINO COAST WRITERS CONFERENCE

1211 Del Mar Dr., Fort Bragg CA 95437. (707)962-2600, ext. 2167. E-mail: info@mcwc.org. Web site: www.mcwc.org. **Contact:** Barbara Lee, registrar. Estab. 1988. Annual conference held in August. 2008 dates: July 31—Aug. 3. Conference duration: 3 days. Average attendance: 90. Provides workshops for fiction, nonfiction, scriptwriting, children's, mystery, and writing for social change. Held at a small community college campus on the northern Pacific Coast. Speakers have included Jandy Nelson, Paul Levine, Sally Werner, John Lescroart, and Maxine Schur. Agents will be speaking and available for meetings with attendees.

Costs $400+ (includes panels, meals, 2 socials with guest readers, 1 public event, 1 day intensive in 1 subject and 2 days of several short sessions).

Accommodations Information on overnight accommodations and shared rides from the San Francisco Airport is made available.

Additional Information Emphasis is on writers who are also good teachers. Brochures are online or available with a SASE after January. Send inquiries via e-mail.

MIDWEST LITERARY FESTIVAL

Mayors Office of Special Events, 44 East Downer Place, Aurora IL 60507. (630)844-4731. E-mail: info@midwestliteraryfestival.com; mayorsoffice@aurora-il.org. Web site: www.midwestliteraryfestival.com/press001.htm. Estab. 2002. Annual. Annual conference held in the fall. Conference duration: 3 days. Average attendance: 250+. Annual conference in downtown Aurora, IL, featuring dozens of screenwriters, fiction writers and nonfiction writers—both local and national—who present workshops, meet with writers, and more. Agents in attendance will take pitches from writers and workshop critiques are available. Previous keynote speakers have included Helen Thomas, Joyce Carol Oates, Harry Shearer. Other speakers have included David Morrell, Les Edgerton, Elizabeth Kostova. The conference is paired with a large book festival and book sale.

Costs Costs available online.

Accommodations Hotels are available near the hotel.

MIDWEST WRITERS WORKSHOP

Department of Journalism, Ball State University, 2800 Bethel Ave., Muncie IN 47306. (765)282-1055. Fax: (765)285-5997. E-mail: info@midwestwriters.org. Web site: www.midwestwriters.org. **Contact:** Jama Bigger, registrar. Estab. 1974. Annual workshop held in July. 2008 dates: July 24-26. Conference duration: 3 days. Covers fiction, nonfiction, poetry, writing for children, how to find an agent, memoirs, Internet marketing and more. Speakers have included Steve Brewer, Crescent Dragonwagon, Dennis Hensley, Nickole Brown, Nelson Price, Hanoch McCarty, Jane Friedman (Writer's Digest Books) and more.

Costs $90-275; $25/ms evaluation.

MONTROSE CHRISTIAN WRITERS' CONFERENCE

5 Locust St., Montrose PA 18801. (570)278-1001 or (800)598-5030. Fax: (570)278-3061. E-mail: mbc @montrosebible.org. Web site: www.montrosebible.org. **Contact:** MBC Secretary/Registrar. Estab. 1990. Annual conference held in July. Offers workshops, editorial appointments, and professional critiques. "We try to meet a cross-section of writing needs, for beginners and advanced, covering fiction, poetry, and writing for children. It is small enough to allow personal interaction between attendees and faculty." Speakers have included William Petersen, Mona Hodgson, Jim Fletcher, and Terri Gibbs.

Costs $150/tuition (in 2007); $35/critique.

Accommodations Housing and meals are available on site.

MOUNT HERMON CHRISTIAN WRITERS CONFERENCE

37 Conference Drive, Mount Hermon CA 95041. E-mail: info@mounthermon.org. Web site: www. mounthermon.org/writers. **Contact:** Conference director. Estab. 1970. Annual conference held in the spring. 2008 dates were March 14-16. Average attendance: 450. "We are a broad-ranging conference for all areas of Christian writing, including fiction, children's, poetry, nonfiction, magazines, books, inspirational and devotional writing, educational curriculum and radio and TV scriptwriting. This is a working, how-to conference, with many workshops within the conference involving on-site writing assignments. The conference is sponsored by and held at the 440-acre Mount Hermon Christian Conference Center near San Jose, California, in the heart of the coastal redwoods. The faculty-to-student ratio is about 1 to 6. The bulk of our more than 60 faculty members are editors and publisher representatives from major Christian publishing houses nationwide." Speakers have included Janet Kobobel Grant, Chip MacGregor, Karen Solem, T. Davis Bunn, Sally Suart, Debbie Macomber, Jerry Jenkins and others.

Accommodations Registrants stay in hotel-style accommodations. Meals are taken family style, with faculty joining registrants.

Additional Information "The residential nature of our conference makes this a unique setting for one-on-one interaction with faculty/staff. There is also a decided inspirational flavor to the conference, and general sessions with well-known speakers are a highlight." Registrants may submit 2 works for critique in advance of the conference, then have personal interviews with critiquers during the conference. Brochures/guidelines are available December 1. All conference information is now online only. Send inquiries via e-mail or fax. Tapes of past conferences are also available.

MUSE AND THE MARKETPLACE

160 Boylston St., 4th Floor, Boston MA 02116. (617)695.0075. E-mail: info@grubstreet.org. Web site: www.grubstreet.org. Annual. The conferences are held in the late spring, such as early May. Conference duration: 2 days. Average attendance: 400. Dozens of agents are in attendance to meet writers and take pitches. Previous keynote speakers include Jonathan Franzen. The conferences has workshops on all aspects of writing.

Costs $265 for Members, $305 for Non-Members (includes 6 workshop sessions and 2 "Hour of Power" sessions with options for the Manuscript Mart and a "Five-Star" lunch with authors, editors and agents). Other passes are available for "Saturday only" and "Sunday only" guests. .

NATCHEZ LITERARY AND CINEMA CELEBRATION

P.O. Box 1307, Natchez MS 39121-1307. (601)446-1208. Fax: (601)446-1214. E-mail: carolyn.smith@ colin.edu. Web site: www.colin.edu/NLCC. **Contact:** Carolyn Vance Smith, co-chairman. Estab. 1990. Annual conference held in February. Conference duration: 5 days. Conference focuses on all literature, including film scripts. Each year's conference deals with some general aspect of Southern history. Speakers have included Eudora Welty, Margaret Walker Alexander, William Styron, Willie Morris, Ellen Douglas, Ernest Gaines, Elizabeth Spencer, Nikki Giovanni, Myrlie Evers-Williams, and Maya Angelou.

NATJA ANNUAL CONFERENCE & MARKETPLACE

North American Travel Journalists Association, 531 Main St., #902, El Segundo CA 90245. (310)836-8712. Fax: (310)836-8769. E-mail: chelsea@natja.org ; elizabeth@natja.org. Web site: www.natja.org/conference. **Contact:** Elizabeth H. Beshear, executive director. Estab. 2003. Annual. Annual conference held in May or June. 2008 dates: June 24-27 in Oklahoma City. Conference duration: 3 days. Average attendance: 250. Provides professional development for travel journalists and gives them the chance to market themselves to destinations and cultivate relationships to further their careers. Previous speakers have included Lisa Lenoir (*Chicago Sun-Times*), Steve Millburg (*Coastal Living*) and Peter Yesawich. The dates and location of this event changes each year, so checking the Web site is the best way to go.

Costs $350 + for media attendees (includes hotel accommodations, meals, in-conference transportation); $100 extra for round-trip airline tickets.

Accommodations Different destinations host the conference each year, all at hotels with conference centers.

Additional Information E-mail, call, or go online for more information.

NEBRASKA SUMMER WRITERS' CONFERENCE

Department of English, University of Nebraska, Lincoln NE 68588-0333. (402)472-1834. E-mail: nswc@unl.edu. Web site: www.nswc.org. **Contact:** Jonis Agee, director. Annual conference held in June. Conference duration: 1 week. Faculty include Sara Gruen, Ron Hansen, Li-Young Lee, Sean Doolittle, Lee Martin, Dorianne Laux, Jim Shepard, Judith Kitchen, Joe Mackall, Hilda Raz, William Kloefkorn, agent Sonia Pabley, Timothy Schaffert, Brent Spencer, Stan Sanvel Rubin, agent Emma Sweeney, Jane Von Mehren (vice president, Random House).

Costs Costs available online.

NECON

Northeastern Writers Conference, 330 Olney St., Seekonk MA 02771. (508)557-1218. E-mail: daniel.booth77@gmail.com. Web site: www.campnecon.com. **Contact:** Dan Booth, chairman. Estab. 1980. Annual. July 17-20, 2008. Conference duration: Four days. Average attendance: 200. The conference is dedicated to those who write fiction. Site: Held at Roger Williams University in Bristol, RI. Themes vary from year to year. Agents attend the workshop each year.

Costs $350. This includes meals and lodging.

Accommodations Attendees stay on campus in the dorm rooms. This housing cost is in the registration fee.

Additional Information Shuttle service provided to the convention site as well as the airport and train station. "We are a very laid back, relaxed convention. However, work is accomplished each year and it's a good opportunity to network."

NETWO WRITERS ROUNDUP

Northeast Texas Writers Organization, P.O. Box 411, Winfield TX 75493. (903)856-6724. E-mail: netwomail@netwo.org. Web site: www.netwo.org. **Contact:** Galand Nuchols, president. Estab. 1987. Annual conference held in April. 2008 dates: April 25-26. Conference duration: 2 days. Presenters include agents, writers, editors, and publishers. Agents in attendance will take pitches from writers. The conference features a writing contest, pitch sessions, critiques from professionals, as well as dozens of workshops and presentations.

Costs $60+ (discount offered for early registration).

Additional Information Conference is co-sponsored by the Texas Commission on the Arts. See Web site for current updates.

NEW JERSEY ROMANCE WRITERS PUT YOUR HEART IN A BOOK CONFERENCE

P.O. Box 644, South Plainfield NJ 07080-0644. E-mail: njrwconfchair@yahoo.com; njrw@njromance writers.org. Web site: www.njromancewriters.org. **Contact:** Michele Richter. Estab. 1984. Annual. Annual conference held in October. 2008 dates: Oct. 24-25. Average attendance: 500. Workshops are offered on various topics for all writers of romance, from beginner to multi-published. Speakers have included Nora Roberts, Kathleen Woodiwiss, Patricia Gaffney, Jill Barnett and Kay Hooper. Appointments are offered with editors/agents.

Accommodations Special rate available for conference attendees at the Sheraton at Woodbridge Place Hotel in Iselin, New Jersey.

Additional Information Conference brochures, guidelines, and membership information are available for SASE. Massive bookfair is open to the public with authors signing copies of their books.

THE NEW LETTERS WEEKEND WRITERS CONFERENCE

University of Missouri-Kansas City, 5101 Rockhill Rd., Kansas City MO 64110-2499. (816)235-1168. Fax: (816)235-2611. E-mail: newletters@umkc.edu. Web site: www.newletters.org. **Contact:** Betsy Beasley or Sharon Seaton. Estab. 1970s (as The Longboat Key Writers Conference). Annual conference held in late June. Conference duration: 3 days. Average attendance: 60. The conference brings together talented writers in many genres for seminars, readings, workshops, and individual conferences. The emphasis is on craft and the creative process in poetry, fiction, screenwriting, playwriting, and journalism, but the program also deals with matters of psychology, publications, and marketing. The conference is appropriate for both advanced and beginning writers. The conference meets at the university's beautiful Diastole Conference Center. Two- and 3-credit hour options are available by special permission from the Director Robert Stewart.

Costs Participants may choose to attend as a noncredit student or they may attend for 1 hour of college credit from the University of Missouri-Kansas City. Conference registration includes Friday evening reception and keynote speaker, Saturday and Sunday continental breakfast and lunch.

Accommodations Registrants are responsible for their own transportation, but information on area accomodations is available.

Additional Information Those registering for college credit are required to submit a ms in advance. Ms reading and critique are included in the credit fee. Those attending the conference for noncredit also have the option of having their ms critiqued for an additional fee. Brochures are available for a SASE after March. Accepts inquiries by e-mail and fax.

NIMROD/HARDMAN AWARDS CELEBRATION & WRITING WORKSHOP

University of Tulsa, 800 S. Tucker Drive., Tulsa OK 74104-3189. (918)631-3080. Fax: (918)631-3033. E-mail: nimrod@utulsa.edu. Web site: www.utulsa.edu/nimrod. **Contact:** Francine Ringold, editor-in-chief. Managing Editor: Eilis O'Neal. Estab. 1978. Annual conference held in October. Conference duration: 1 day. Offers one-on-one editing sessions, readings, panel discussions, and master classes in fiction, poetry, nonfiction, memoir, and fantasy writing. Speakers have included Myla Goldberg, B.H. Fairchild, Colleen McElroy, Gina Ochsner, Kelly Link, Rilla Askew, Matthew Galkin, and A.D. Coleman.
Additional Information Full conference details are online in August.

NO CRIME UNPUBLISHED MYSTERY WRITERS' CONFERENCE

No public address available,. E-mail: sistersincrimela@yahoo.com. Web site: www.sistersincrimela. com. Estab. 1995. Annual conference held in June. Next conference June 2009. Conference duration: 1 day. Average attendance: 150. Conference on mystery and crime writing. Offers craft and forensic sessions, a keynote speaker, a luncheon speaker, author and agent panels, and book signings.
Additional Information Conference information is available on the Web site.

NORTH CAROLINA WRITERS' NETWORK FALL CONFERENCE

P.O. Box 954, Carrboro NC 27510-0954. (919)967-9540. Fax: (919)929-0535. E-mail: mail@ncwriter s.org. Web site: www.ncwriters.org. **Contact:** Cynthia Barnett, executive director. Estab. 1985. Annual conference held in November in Research Traingle Park (Durham, North Carolina). Average attendance: 450. This organization hosts two conferences: one in the spring and one in the fall. Each conference is a weekend full of workshops, panels, book signings, and readings (including open mic). There will be a keynote speaker, along with sessions on a variety of genres, including fiction, poetry, creative nonfiction, journalism, children's book writing, screenwriting, and playwriting. "We also offer craft, editing, and marketing classes. We hold the event at a conference center with hotel rooms available." Speakers have included Donald Maass, Noah Lukeman, Joe Regal, Jeff Kleinman, and Evan Marshall. Some agents will teach classes and some are available for meetings with attendees.
Costs Approximately $250 (includes 2 meals).
Accommodations Special rates are available at the Sheraton Hotel, but conferees must make their own reservations.
Additional Information Brochures/guidelines are available online or by sending your street address to mail@ncwriters.org. You can also register online.

NORTHERN COLORADO WRITERS CONFERENCE

2107 Thunderstone Court, Fort Collins CO 80525. (970)282-7754. E-mail: kerrie@ncwc.biz. Web site: www.ncwc.biz/. **Contact:** Kerrie Flanagan. Estab. 2006. Annual. Annual conference held in the spring in Colorado. Conference duration: 3 days. The conference features a variety of speakers, agents and editors. There are workshops and presentations on fiction, nonfiction, screenwriting, staying inspired, and more. Previous agents who have attended and taken pitches from wirters include Jessica Regel,

Kristen Nelson and Rachelle Gardner. Each conference features more than 30 workshops from which to choose from.

Costs $200-300, depending on what package the attendee selects.

Accommodations The conference is hosted at the Fort Collins Hilton, where rooms are available at a special rate.

◎ ODYSSEY FANTASY WRITING WORKSHOP

P.O. Box 75, Mont Vernon NH 03057. E-mail: jcavelos@sff.net. Web site: www.odysseyworkshop.org. **Contact:** Jeanne Cavelos, director. Estab. 1996. Annual workshop held in June (through July). Conference duration: 6 weeks. Average attendance: 16. A workshop for fantasy, science fiction, and horror writers that combines an intensive learning and writing experience with in-depth feedback on students' mss. Held on the campus of Saint Anselm College in Manchester, New Hampshire. Speakers have included George R. Martin, Elizabeth Hand, Jane Yolen, Harlan Ellison, Melissa Scott and Dan Simmons.

Costs $1,800/tuition; $700-1,400/on-campus apartment; approximately $550/on-campus meals. Scholarships are available.

Additional Information Prospective students must include a 15-page writing sample with their application. Accepts inquiries by SASE, e-mail, fax and phone. Application deadline April 10.

OZARK CREATIVE WRITERS CONFERENCE

ETSU-Box 23115, Johnson City TN 37614. (423)439-6024. E-mail: ozarkcreativewriters@earthlink. net. Web site: www.ozarkcreativewriters.org. **Contact:** Chrissy Willis, president. Estab. 1975. Annual conference held the second weekend in October, in Eureka Springs, AR. Includes programs for all types of writing. Speakers have included Dan Slater (Penguin Putnam), Stephan Harrigan (novelist/screenwriter), and Christopher Vogler.

Costs Approximately $100.

Accommodations Special rates are available at the Inn of the Ozarks in Eureka Springs, Arkansas.

Additional Information The conference has a friendly atmosphere and conference speakers are available. Many speakers return to the conference for the companionship of writers and speakers. Brochures are available for a SASE.

PHILADELPHIA WRITERS' CONFERENCE

121 Almatt Terrace, Philadelphia PA 19115-2745. E-mail: info@pwcwriters.org. Web site: www.pwc writers.org. **Contact:** Rhonda O. Hoffman, registrar. Estab. 1949. Annual conference held in June. 2008 dates: June 6-8. Conference duration: 3 days. Average attendance: 150+. Workshops cover short stories, poetry, travel, humor, magazine writing, science fiction, playwriting, memoir, juvenile, nonfiction, and fiction. Speakers have included Ginger Clark (Curtis Brown), Sara Crowe (Harvey Klinger), Samantha Mandor (Berkley), Nancy Springer, Susan Guill, Karen Rile, Gregory Frost, and John Volkmer. Editor/agent critiques are available.

Costs Costs available online.

PIKES PEAK WRITERS CONFERENCE

4164 Austin Bluffs Pkwy., #246, Colorado Springs CO 80918. (719)531-5723. E-mail: info@pikespeak writers.com. Web site: www.pikespeakwriters.com. Estab. 1993. Annual conference held in April.

Conference duration: 3 days. Average attendance: 400. Workshops, presentations, and panels focus on writing and publishing mainstream and genre fiction (romance, science fiction/fantasy, suspense/ thrillers, action/adventure, mysteries, children's, young adult). Agents and editors are available for meetings with attendees on Saturday.

Costs 2007 costs: $295/PPW members; $350/nonmembers (includes all meals).

Accommodations Marriott Colorado Springs holds a block of rooms at a special rate for attendees until late March.

Additional Information Readings with critiques are available on Friday afternoon. Also offers a contest for unpublished writers; entrants need not attend the conference. Deadline: November 1. Registration and contest entry forms are online; brochures are available in January. Send inquiries via e-mail.

PNWA SUMMER WRITERS CONFERENCE

PMB 2717, 1420 NW Gilman Blvd., Issaquah WA 98027. (425)673-2665. E-mail: pnwa@pnwa.org. Web site: www.pnwa.org. Estab. 1955. Annual. All conferences are held in July. Conference duration: 4 days. Average attendance: 400. Attendees have the chance to meet agents and editors, learn craft from authors and uncover marketing secrets. Speakers have included J.A. Jance, Sheree Bykofsky, Kimberley Cameron, Jennie Dunham, Donald Maass, and Jandy Nelson.

Costs For cost and additional information, please see the Web site.

Accommodations The conference is held at the Hilton Seattle Airport & Conference Center.

Additional Information PNWA also holds an annual literary contest every February with more than $12,000 in prize money. Finalists' manuscripts are then available to agents and editors at our summer conference. Visit the Web site for further details.

PORT TOWNSEND WRITERS' CONFERENCE

Box 1158, Port Townsend WA 98368. (360)385-3102. Fax: (360)385-2470. E-mail: info@centrum.org. Web site: http://www.centrum.org/writing/. **Contact:** Carla Vander Ven. Estab. 1974. Annual conference held in mid-July. Average attendance: 180. Conference promotes poetry, fiction, and creative nonfiction and features many of the nation's leading writers. All conference housing and activities are located at beautiful Fort Worden State Park, a historic fort overlooking the Strait of Juan de Fuca, with expansive views of the Olympic and Cascade mountain ranges.

Costs $575/critiqued workshops; $495/open enrollment workshops.

Accommodations $190-380. Participants stay in dorms; meals are taken together in the For Worden Commons. Visitors may also choose to stay in one of Port Townsend's rentals, bed and breakfasts, or hotels.

Additional Information The conference focus is on the craft of writing and the writing life, not on marketing. Guidelines/registration are available online or for SASE.

ROBERT QUACKENBUSH'S CHILDREN'S BOOK WRITING & ILLUSTRATING WORKSHOP

460 E. 79th St., New York NY 10021-1443. (212)744-3822. Fax: (212)861-2761. E-mail: rqstudios@aol .com. Web site: www.rquackenbush.com. **Contact:** Robert Quackenbush, director. Estab. 1982. Annual workshop held during the second week in July. Conference duration: 4 days. Average attendance: Enrollment limited to 10. Workshops promote writing and illustrating books for children and are geared toward beginners and professionals. Generally focuses on picture books, easy-to-read books,

and early chapter books. Held at the Manhattan studio of Robert Quackenbush, author and illustrator of more than 200 books for children. All classes led by Robert Quackenbush.

Costs $750 tuition covers all the costs of the workshop, but does not include housing and meals. A $100 nonrefundable deposit is required with the $650 balance due two weeks prior to attendance.

Accommodations A list of recommended hotels and restaurants is sent upon receipt of deposit.

ROCKY MOUNTAIN FICTION WRITERS COLORADO GOLD

Rocky Mountain Fiction Writers, P.O. Box 545, Englewood CO 80151. E-mail: conference@rmfw.org. Web site: www.rmfw.org/default.aspx. **Contact:** Conference Director. Estab. 1983. Annual conference held in September/October. Conference duration: 3 days. Average attendance: 250. Themes include general novel-length fiction, genre fiction, contemporary romance, mystery, science fiction/fantasy, mainstream, and history. Speakers have included Terry Brooks, Dorothy Cannell, Patricia Gardner Evans, Diane Mott Davidson, Constance O'Day, Connie Willis, Clarissa Pinkola Estes, Michael Palmer, Jennifer Unter, Margaret Marr, Ashley Krass, and Andren Barzvi. Approximately 4 editors and 5 agents attend annually.

Costs Costs available online.

Accommodations Special rates will be available at a nearby hotel.

Additional Information Editor-conducted workshops are limited to 10 participants for critique, with auditing available.

SAN DIEGO STATE UNIVERSITY WRITERS' CONFERENCE

SDSU College of Extended Studies, 5250 Campanile Dr., San Diego State University, San Diego CA 92182-1920. (619)594-2517. Fax: (619)594-8566. E-mail: jgreene@mail.sdsu.edu; rbrown2@mail.sd su.edu. Web site: www.ces.sdsu.edu/writers. **Contact:** Jim Greene, program coordinator. Estab. 1984. Annual conference held in January/February. 2009 dates: Feb. 6-8. Conference duration: 2 days. Average attendance: 375. Covers fiction, nonfiction, scriptwriting and e-books. Held at the Doubletree Hotel in Mission Valley. Each year the conference offers a variety of workshops for the beginner and advanced writers. This conference allows the individual writer to choose which workshop best suits his/her needs. In addition to the workshops, editor reading appointments and agent/editor consultation appointments are provided so attendees may meet with editors and agents one-on-one to discuss specific questions. A reception is offered Saturday immediately following the workshops, offering attendees the opportunity to socialize with the faculty in a relaxed atmosphere. Last year, approximately 60 faculty members attended.

Costs Approximately $365-485 (2009 costs will be published with a fall update of the Web site).

Accommodations Doubletree Hotel (800)222-TREE. Attendees must make their own travel arrangements.

SAN FRANCISCO WRITERS CONFERENCE

1029 Jones St., San Francisco CA 94109. (415)673-0939. Fax: (415)673-0367. E-mail: sfwritersco n@aol.com. Web site: www.sfwriters.org. **Contact:** Michael Larsen, director. Estab. 2003. Annual conference held President's Day weekend in February. Average attendance: 400 +. Top authors, respected literary agents, and major publishing houses are at the event so attendees can make face-to-face contact with all the right people. Writers of nonfiction, fiction, poetry, and specialty writing (children's books, cookbooks, travel, etc.) will all benefit from the event. There are important sessions on marketing, self-publishing, and trends in the publishing industry. Plus, there's an optional 3-hour session called Speed Dating for Agents where attendees can meet with 20+ agents. Speakers have included Gayle Lynds, Jennifer Crusie, ALan Jones, Lalita Tademy, Jamie Raab, Mary Roach, Bob Mayer, Firoozeh Dumas, Zilpha Keatley Snyder. More than 20 agents and editors participate each year, many of whom will be available for meetings with attendees.

Costs $600+ with price breaks for early registration (includes all sessions/workshops/keynotes, Speed Dating with Editors, opening gala at the Top of the Mark, 2 continental breakfasts, 2 lunches). Optional Speed Dating for Agents is $45.

Accommodations The Intercontinental Mark Hopkins Hotel is a historic landmark at the top of Nob Hill in San Francisco. Elegant rooms and first-class service are offered to attendees at the rate of $152/night. The hotel is located so that everyone arriving at the Oakland or San Francisco airport can take BART to either the Embarcadero or Powell Street exits, then walk or take a cable car or taxi directly to the hotel.

Additional Information Present yourself in a professional manner and the contact you will make will be invaluable to your writing career. Brochures and registration are online.

SANDHILLS WRITERS CONFERENCE

No public address available,. E-mail: akellman@aug.edu. Web site: www.sandhills.aug.edu. **Contact:** Anthony Kellman, director. Annual conference held the fourth weekend in March. Covers fiction, poetry, children's literature, nonfiction, plays, and songwriting. Located on the campus of Augusta State University in Georgia. Agents and editors will be speaking at the event.

Accommodations Several hotels are located near the university.

◎ SANDY COVE CHRISTIAN WRITERS CONFERENCE

Sandy Cove Ministries, 60 Sandy Cove Rd., North East MD 21901. (410)287-5433. Fax: (410)287-3196. E-mail: info@sandycove.org. Web site: www.sandycove.org. Estab. 1991. Annual conference held the first week in October. Conference duration: 4 days. Average attendance: 200. There are major workshops in fiction, article writing, and nonfiction books for beginner and advanced writers. The conference has plans to add tracks in screenwriting and musical lyrics. Workshops offer a wide variety of hands-on writing instruction in many genres. While Sandy Cove has a strong emphasis on available markets in Christian publishing, all writers are more than welcome. Speakers have included Francine Rivers, Lisa Bergen, Ken Petersen (Tyndale House), Linda Tomblin (*Guideposts*), and Karen Ball (Zondervan).

Costs Call for rates.

Accommodations Sandy Cove is a full-service conference center located on the Chesepeake Bay. All the facilities are first class, with suites, single rooms, and double rooms available.

Additional Information Conference brochures/guidelines are available. Visit the Web site for exact conference dates.

SANTA BARBARA WRITERS CONFERENCE

P.O. Box 6627, Santa Barbara CA 93160. (805)964-0367. E-mail: info@sbwritersconference.com. Web site: www.sbwritersconference.com. **Contact:** Marcia Meier, conference director. Estab. 1973. Annual conference held in June. Average attendance: 450. Covers poetry, fiction, nonfiction, journalism, playwriting, screenwriting, travel writing, young adult, children's literature, chick lit, humor, and marketing. Speakers have included Kenneth Atchity, Michael Larsen, Elizabeth Pomada, Bonnie Nadell, Stuart Miller, Angela Rinaldi, Katherine Sands, Don Congdon, Mike Hamilburg, Sandra Dijkstra, Paul Fedorko, Andrea Brown and Deborah Grosvenor. Agents appear on a panel, plus there will be an agents and editors day when writers can pitch their projects in one-on-one meetings.

Accommodations Fess Parker's Doubletree Resort.

Additional Information Individual critiques are also available. Submit 1 ms of no more than 3,000 words in advance (include SASE). Competitions with awards are sponsored as part of the conference. E-mail or call for brochure and registration forms.

SANTA FE WRITERS CONFERENCE

Southwest Literary Center, 826 Camino de Monte Rey, A3, Santa Fe NM 87505. (505)577-1125. Fax: (505)982-7125. E-mail: litcenter@recursos.org. Web site: www.santafewritersconference.com. **Contact:** Jenice Gharib, director. Estab. 1985. Annual conference held in June. Conference duration: 5 days. Average attendance: 50. Conference offering intimate workshops in fiction, poetry, and creative nonfiction. Speakers have included Lee K. Abbott, Alice Adams, Lucille Adler, Francisco Alarcon, Agha Shahid Ali, Rudolfo Anaya, Max Apple, Jimmy Santiago Baca, Madison Smartt Bell, Marvin Bell, Molly Bendall, Elizabeth Benedict, Roo Borson, Robert Boswell, Kate Braverman, Mei-Mei Berssenbrugge, Ron Carlson, Denise Chavez, Lisa D. Chavez, Alan Cheuse, Ted Conover, Robert Creeley, C. Michael Curtis, Jon Davis, Percival Everett, Jennifer Foerster, Richard Ford, Judith Freeman, Samantha Gillison, Natalie Goldberg, Jorie Graham, Lee Gutkind, Elizabeth Hardwick, Robert Hass, Ehud Havazelet, Elizabeth Hightower, Tony Hillerman, Brenda Hillman, Tony Hoagland, Garrett Hongo, Lewis Hyde, Mark Irwin, Charles Johnson, Diane Johnson, Teresa Jordan, Donald Justice, Laura Kasischke, Pagan Kennedy, Brian Kiteley, William Kittredge, Carolyn Kizer, Verlyn Klinkenborg, Karla Kuban, Mark Levine, Alison Lurie, Tony Mares, Kevin McIlvoy, Christopher Merrill, Jane Miller, Mary Jane Moffat, Carol Moldow, N. Scott Momaday, David Morrell, Antonya Nelson, Susan Neville, John Nichols, Sharon Niederman, Naomi Shahib Nye, Grace Paley, Ann Patchett, Margaret Sayers Peden, Michael Pettit, Robert Pinsky, Melissa Pritchard, Annie Proulx, Ron Querry, Judy Reeves, Katrina Roberts, Janet Rodney, Pattiann Rogers, Suzanna Ruta, David St. John, Scott Sanders, Bob Shacochis, Julie Shigekuni, John Skoyles, Carol Houck Smith, Gibbs M. Smith, Roberta Smoodin, Marcia Southwick, Kathleen Spivack, Gerald Stern, Robert Stone, Arthur Sze, Elizabeth Tallent, Nathaniel Tarn, James Thomas, Frederick Turner, Leslie Ullman, David Wagoner, Larry Watson, Rob Wilder, Eleanor Wilner, Diane Williams, Kimberly Witherspoon, Charles Wright, Dean Young, Norman Zollinger.

Costs $575 + .

Accommodations A special rate is offered at a nearby hotel.

Additional Information Brochure are available online or by e-mail, fax, or phone.

SCENE OF THE CRIME CONFERENCE

Kansas Writers Association, P.O. Box 2236, Wichita KS 67201. (316) 618-0449; (316)208-6961. E-mail: info@kwawriters.org. Web site: www.kwawriters.org/sceneofthecrime.htm. **Contact:** Gordon Kessler. Annual. Annual conference held in April. Features agent/editor consultations, mixer, banquet and two days of speaker sessions with detectives, government agents, CSI professionals, editors, agents and authors. A full list of each year's speakers is available to see in full on the Web site.

Accommodations Wichita Airport Hilton.

SEWANEE WRITERS' CONFERENCE

735 University Ave., 119 Gailor Hall, Stemlor Center, Sewanee TN 37383-1000. (931)598-1141. E-mail: cpeters@sewanee.edu. Web site: www.sewaneewriters.org. **Contact:** Cheri B. Peters, creative writing programs manager. Estab. 1990. Annual conference held in July. Conference duration: 12 days. Average attendance: 120. "We offer genre-based workshops in fiction, poetry, and playwriting." The conference uses the facilities of Sewanee: The University of the South. The university is a collection of ivy-covered Gothic-style buildings located on the Cumberland Plateau in mid-Tennessee. Editors, publishers, and agents structure their own presentations, but there is always opportunity for questions from the audience." Previous faculty members have included fiction writers Richard Bausch, John Casey, Tony Earley, Diane Johnson, Randall Kenan, Alison Lurie, Jill, McCorkle, and Claire Messud; poets Brad Leithauser, Charles Martin, Mary Jo Salter, Alan Shapiro, Mark Strand, and Greg Williamson; and playwrights Lee Blessing and Melanie Marnich. Visiting agents include Gail Hochman and Georges Borchardt.

Costs $1,600 (includes tuition, board, basic room).

Accommodations Participants are housed in university dormitory rooms. Motel or bed & breakfast housing is available, but not abundantly so. Dormitory housing (shared occupancy) costs are included in the full conference fee. Single rooms are also available for a modest fee.

Additional Information Complimentary chartered bus service is available from the Nashville Airport to Sewanee and back on the first and last days of the conference. "We offer each participant (excepting auditors) the opportunity for a private manuscript conference with a member of the faculty. These manuscripts are due 1 month before the conference begins." Brochures/guidelines are free. The conference provides a limited number of fellowships and scholarships; these are awarded on a competitive basis.

SLEUTHFEST

MWA Florida Chapter,. E-mail: SleuthfestRandy@yahoo.com. Web site: www.mwa-florida.org/sleuthfest.htm. Annual conference held in March. Conference duration: 4 days. Hands-on workshops, 4 tracks of writing and business panels, and 2 keynote speakers for writers of mystery and crime fiction. Also offers agent and editor appointments and paid ms critiques. Honored 2008 speakers included Lee Child and DP Lyle. A full list of attending speakers as well as agents and editors is online. This event is put on by the local chapter of the Mystery Writers of America.

Accommodations The Deerfield Beach Hilton.

☉ SOCIETY OF CHILDREN'S BOOK WRITERS & ILLUSTRATORS ANNUAL SUMMER CONFERENCE ON WRITING AND ILLUSTRATING FOR CHILDREN

8271 Beverly Blvd., Los Angeles CA 90048-4515. (323)782-1010. Fax: (323)782-1892. E-mail: scbwi@scbwi.org. Web site: www.scbwi.org. **Contact:** Stephen Mooser, president. Estab. 1972. Annual conference held in early August. Conference duration: 4 days. Average attendance: 1,000. Held at the Century Plaza Hotel in Los Angeles. Speakers have included Andrea Brown, Steven Malk , Scott Treimel, Ashley Bryan, Bruce Coville, Karen Hesse, Harry Mazer, Lucia Monfried, and Russell Freedman. Agents will be speaking and sometimes participate in ms critiques.

Costs Approximately $400 (does not include hotel room).

Accommodations Information on overnight accommodations is made available.

Additional Information Ms and illustration critiques are available. Brochure/guidelines are available in June online or for SASE.

SOUTH CAROLINA WRITERS WORKSHOP

P.O. Box 7104, Columbia SC 29202. (803)413-5810. E-mail: conference@myscww.org. Web site: www.myscww.org/. Estab. 1991. Annual conference in October. Next conference: Oct. 24-26, 2008 at the Hilton Myrtle Beach Resort in Myrtle Beach, SC. Conference duration: 3 days. The conference features critique sessions, open mic readings, presentations from agents and editors and more. The conference features more than 50 different workshops for writers to choose from, dealing with all subjects of writing craft, writing business, getting an agent and more. Agents will be in attendance. **Costs** $289-389, depending on the package. Cheaper options available for part of the weekend. See the Web site for full registration details.

SOUTHEASTERN WRITERS WORKSHOP

P.O. Box 82115, Athens GA 30608. E-mail: info@southeasternwriters.com. Web site: www.southeasternwriters.com. **Contact:** Tim Hudson. Estab. 1975. Held annually the third week in June at Epworth-by-the-Sea, St. Simons Island, Georgia. Conference duration: 4 days. Average attendance: Limited to 100 students. Classes are offered in all areas of writing, including fiction, poetry, nonfiction, inspirational, juvenile, specialty writing, and others. The faculty is comprised of some of the most successful authors from throughout the southeast and the country. Agent-in-Residence is available to meet with participants. Up to 3 free ms evaluations and critique sessions are also available to participants if mss are submitted by the deadline. **Costs** 2007 tuition was $395.

Additional Information Multiple contests with cash prizes are open to participants. Registration brochure is available in March—e-mail or send a SASE. Full information, including registration material, is on the Web site.

SOUTHWEST WRITERS CONFERENCE MINI-CONFERENCE SERIES

3721 Morris St. NE, Suite A, Albuquerque NM 87111. (505)265-9485. E-mail: swwriters@juno.com. Web site: www.southwestwriters.org. Estab. 1983. Annual mini-conferences held throughout the year. Average attendance: 50. Speakers include writers, editors, agents, publicists, and producers. All areas of writing, including screenwriting and poetry, are represented. **Costs** Fee includes conference sessions and lunch. **Accommodations** Usually have official airline and hotel discount rates.

Additional Information Sponsors a contest judged by authors, editors from major publishers, and agents from New York, Los Angeles, etc. There are 19 categories. Deadline: May 1. Entry fee is $29/members; $44/nonmembers. There are monthly contests with various themes—$5/member, $10/non-member. See Web site for details. Brochures/guidelines are available online or for a SASE. Inquire via e-mail or phone. A one-on-one appointment may be set up at the conference with the editor or agent of your choice on a first-registered, first-served basis.

SPACE COAST WRITERS GUILD ANNUAL CONFERENCE

No public address available,. (321)956-7193. E-mail: scwg-jm@cfl.rr.com. Web site: www.scwg.org/conference.asp. **Contact:** Judy Mammay. Annual. Annual conference held in January along the east coast of central Florida. Conference duration: 2 days. Average attendance: 150 + . This conference is hosted each winter in Florida and features a variety of presenters on all topics writing. Critiques are available for a price, and agents in attendance will take pitches from writers. Previous presenters have included Davis Bunn (writer), Ellen Pepus (agent), Miriam Hees (editor), Lauren Mosko (editor), Lucienne Diver (agent) and many many more.

Accommodations The conference is hosted on a beachside hotel, where rooms are available.

SPRING WRITERS' WORKSHOP

Council for the Written Word, P.O. Box 298, Franklin TN 37065. (615)591-7516. E-mail: kathy@a southernjournal.com. Web site: www.cww-writers.org. **Contact:** Kathy Rhodes, facilitator. Annual workshop held in March. An intensive, half-day event with instruction and hands-on experience in a specific genre.

SQUAW VALLEY COMMUNITY OF WRITERS WORKSHOP

P.O. Box 1416, Nevada City CA 95959-1416. (530)470-8440. E-mail: info@squawvalleywriters.org. Web site: www.squawvalleywriters.org/writers_ws.htm. **Contact:** Ms. Brett Hall Jones, executive director. Estab. 1969. Annual conference held the first full week in August. Conference duration: 1 week. Average attendance: 124. Covers fiction, nonfiction, and memoir. Held in Squaw Valley, California—the site of the 1960 Winter Olympics. The workshops are held in a ski lodge at the foot of this spectacular ski area. Literary agent speakers have recently included Betsy Amster, Julie Barer, Michael Carlisle, Elyse Cheney, Mary Evans, Christy Fletcher, Theresa Park, B.J. Robbins and Peter Steinberg. Agents will be speaking and available for meetings with attendees.

Costs $750 (includes tuition, dinners). Housing is extra.

Accommodations Single room: $550/week; double room: $350/week per person; multiple room: $210/week per person. The airport shuttle is available for an additional cost.

Additional Information Brochures are available online or for a SASE in March. Send inquiries via e-mail.

STEAMBOAT SPRINGS WRITERS CONFERENCE

Steamboat Springs Arts Council, P.O. Box 774284, Steamboat Springs CO 80477. (970)879-8079. E-mail: sswriters@cs.com. Web site: www.steamboatwriters.com. **Contact:** Harriet Freiberger, director. Estab. 1982. Annual conference held in mid-July. Conference duration: 1 day. Average attendance: approximately 35. Attendance is limited. Featured areas of instruction change each year. Held at the restored train depot. Speakers have included Carl Brandt, Jim Fergus, Avi, Robert Greer, Renate Wood, Connie Willis, Margaret Coel and Kent Nelson.

Costs $45 prior to June 1; $55 after June 1 (includes seminars, catered lunch). A post-conference dinner is also available.

Additional Information Brochures are available in April for a SASE. Send inquiries via e-mail.

STONECOAST WRITERS' CONFERENCE

University of Southern Maine, 37 College Avenue, Gorham ME 04038. (207)780-4141. Web site: www.usm.maine.edu/summer/stonecoastwc/. **Contact:** Conference Director. Estab. 1979. Annual conference held in mid-July. Conference duration: 10 days. Average attendance: 90-100. Concentrates on fiction, poetry, popular fiction, and creative nonfiction. Held at Wolfe's Neck on Casco Bay in

Freeport, Maine. Speakers have included Christian Barter, Brian Turner, Chun Yu, Margo Jefferson, Mike Kimball, and Jack Neary.

Costs 2007 costs: $813/tuition; $560/housing and meals at Bowdoin College; $136/commuters. Scholarships are available for various groups.

SURREY INERNATIONAL WRITERS' CONFERENCE

10707 146th St., Surrey BC V3R 1T5, Canada. (640)589-2221. Fax: (604)589-9286. Web site: www.siwc.ca. **Contact:** Lisa Mason. Estab. 1992. Annual conference held in October. 2008 dates: Oct. 24-26. Conference duration: 3 days. Average attendance: 600. Conference for fiction, nonfiction, scriptwriting, and poetry. Held at the Sheraton Guildford Hotel. Speakers have included Donald Maass, Meredith Bernstein, Charlotte Gusay, Denise Marcil, Anne Sheldon, and Michael Vidor. Agents will be speaking and available for one-on-one meetings with attendees.

Costs Approximately $450. See Web site for full cost information and list of upcoming speakers for the next year.

Accommodations Attendees must make their own hotel and transportation arrangements.

TAOS SUMMER WRITERS' CONFERENCE

Department of English Language and Literature, MSC 03 2170, University of New Mexico, Albuquerque NM 87131-0001. (505)277-5572. Fax: (505)277-2950. E-mail: taosconf@unm.edu. Web site: www.unm.edu/~taosconf. **Contact:** Sharon Oard Warner, Barbara van Buskirk. Estab. 1999. Annual conference held in July. Conference duration: 9 days. Offers workshops in novel writing, short story writing, screenwriting, poetry, creative nonfiction, travel writing, historical fiction, memoir, and revision. Participants may also schedule a consultation with a visiting agent/editor.

Costs $300/weekend; $600/week; discounted tuition rate of $250/weekend workshop with weeklong workshop or master class registration.

Accommodations $60-100/night at the Sagebrush Inn; $89/night at Comfort Suites.

TENNESSEE WRITERS ALLIANCE WRITERS CONFERENCE

Tennessee Writers Alliance, Inc., P.O. Box 120396, Nashville TN 37212. E-mail: inquiries@tn-writers.org. Web site: www.tn-writers.org/Workshops.asp. **Contact:** Nancy Fletcher-Blume, president. Annual conference held in June in Franklin, TN, just outside of Nashville. Conference duration: 2 days. Average attendance: 200. The conference is held at Battle Ground Academy, not far from Nashville. Previous speakers have included Robert Hicks, Tama Kieves, Richard Goodman, Ted Swindley and Carl Harris. The conference features a variety of sessions on fiction, nonfiction, playwriting, creative nonfiction, inspiring writers and more.

Costs Costs available online.

Accommodations Hotel accommodations available not far from the conference center in Franklin hotels.

THRILLERFEST

P.O. Box 311, Eureka CA 95502. E-mail: infocentral@thrillerwriters.org. Web site: www.thrillerwriters.org/thrillerfest/. **Contact:** Shirley Kennett. Estab. 2006. Annual. 2008 conference: July 9-12 in Manhattan. Average attendance: 700. Conference dedicated to writing the thriller. Speakers have included Sandra Brown, Eric Van Lustbader, David Baldacci, RL Stine, Steve Martini, Andrew Gross, Donald

Maass, Dr. Kathy Reichs, Brad Thor and James Patterson. Two days of the conference is CraftFest, where the focus is on writing craft, and two days is ThrillerFest, where the focus is on both writers and their readers. There is also AgentFest, where authors can pitch their work to agents in attendance. **Costs** Price will vary from $200 to $1,000 dollars depending on all the events attendees sign up for, including agent pitch slams, award banquets and more. Various event packages are available for attendees.
Accommodations Grand Hyatt in New York City.

TONY HILLERMAN WRITERS CONFERENCE

304 Calle Oso, Santa Fe NM 87501. (505)471-1565. E-mail: wordharvest@wordharvest.com. Web site: www.wordharvest.com/index.php/hillermanconference. Estab. 2001. Annual conference held in November. 2008 dates: Oct. 30—Nov. 2. Conference duration: 4 days. Average attendance: 150-200. Workshops on writing good dialogue, building your platform, writing series that sell, and adding humor to your writing are geared toward mystery writers. Held at the Hyatt Regency in Albuquerque, New Mexico. Speakers have included Tony Hillerman, Michael McGarrity, J.A. Jance, Margaret Coel, Sean Murphy, Virginia Swift, James D. Doss, Gail Larsen, Luther Wilson, and Craig Johnson. 2008 guests include: James Rollins, Michael McGarrity, Craig Johnson, Pari Noskin Taichert and Sandi Ault. The conference has both a short story writing contest and a mystery writing contest.
Costs $250-450, depending on if attendees want an entire weekend pass or just one day. Full cost information available online.
Accommodations Approximately $99/night at the Hyatt Regency.

UNIVERSITY OF NORTH DAKOTA WRITERS CONFERENCE

Department of English, 110 Merrifield Hall, 276 Centennial Drive, Stop 7209, Grand Forks ND 58202. (701)777-3321. E-mail: english@und.edu. Web site: www.undwritersconference.org. **Contact:** Liz Harris-Behling or Heidi Czerwiec, co-directors. Estab. 1970. Annual conference held in March. Offers panels, readings, and films focused around a specific theme. Almost all events take place in the UND Memorial Union, which has a variety of small rooms and a 1,000-seat main hall. Future speakers include Stuart Dybek, Mary Gaitskill, Li-Young Lee, Timothy Liu, Leslie Adrienne Miller, Michelle Richmond, Miller Williams and Anne Harris.
Costs All events are free and open to the public. Donations accepted.

VERMONT COLLEGE POSTGRADUATE WRITERS' CONFERENCE

36 College St., Montpelier VT 05651. (802)223-2133 or (802)828-8764. E-mail: roger.weingarten@tui.edu. Web site: www.tui.edu/pgwc/. **Contact:** Roger Weingarten. Estab. 1996. Annual conference held in August. Conference duration: 6 days. Average attendance: 5-7/workshop. Conference will focus on novel writing, short story writing, short short story writing, creative nonfiction, poetry manuscript, and poetry. Held on the historic Vermont College campus, overlooking Montpelier. Faculty has included Rikki Ducornet, Bret Lott, Mary Ruefle, Sue William Silverman, Robin Hemley, Charles Harper Webb, Richard Jackson and Bruce Weigl.
Costs $800/tuition; $330/private room; $180/shared room; $140/meals. Limited scholarships are available.
Accommodations Single or double rooms are available in the Vermont College campus dormitories.

WASHINGTON INDEPENDENT WRITERS (WIW) SPRING WRITERS CONFERENCE

1001 Connecticut Ave. NW, Suite 701, Washington DC 20036. (202)775-5150. Fax: (202)775-5810. E-mail: info@washwriter.org. Web site: www.washwriter.org. **Contact:** Taryn Carrino. Estab. 1975. Annual conference held in June. Average attendance: 350. Focuses on fiction, nonfiction, screenwriting, poetry, children's writing, and technical writing. Gives participants the chance to hear from and talk with dozens of experts on book and magazine publishing, as well as on the craft, tools, and business of writing. Speakers have included Erica Jong, John Barth, Kitty Kelley, Vanessa Leggett, Diana McLellan, Brian Lamb, and Stephen Hunter. New York and local agents attend the conference. **Additional Information** See the Web site or send a SASE in mid-February for brochures/guidelines and fees information.

WESLEYAN WRITERS CONFERENCE

Wesleyan University, 294 High St., Room 207, Middletown CT 06459. (860)685-3604. Fax: (860)685-2441. E-mail: agreene@wesleyan.edu. Web site: www.wesleyan.edu/writers. **Contact:** Anne Greene, director. Estab. 1956. Annual conference held the third week of June. Average attendance: 100. Focuses on the novel, fiction techniques, short stories, poetry, screenwriting, nonfiction, literary journalism, memoir, mixed media work and publishing. The conference is held on the campus of Wesleyan University, in the hills overlooking the Connecticut River. Features a faculty of award-winning writers, seminars and readings of new fiction, poetry, nonfiction and mixed media forms— as well as guest lectures on a range of topics including publishing. Both new and experienced writers are welcome. Participants may attend seminars in all genres. Speakers have included Esmond Harmsworth (Zachary Schuster Agency), Daniel Mandel (Sanford J. Greenburger Associaties), Dorian Karchmar, Amy Williams (ICM and Collins McCormick), Mary Sue Rucci (Simon & Schuster), Denise Roy (Simon & Schuster), John Kulka (Harvard University Press), Julie Barer (Barer Literary) and many others. Agents will be speaking and available for meetings with attendees. Participants are often successful in finding agents and publishers for their mss. Wesleyan participants are also frequently featured in the anthology *Best New American Voices*.

Costs 2007 Day rate was $1,050 (includes meals for 5 days). Student rate with boarding: $1,250 (includes meals and room for 5 nights); boarding student rate: $1,190 (includes meal and room for 5 nights).

Accommodations Meals are provided on campus. Lodging is available on campus or in town.

Additional Information Ms critiques are available, but not required. Scholarships and teaching fellowships are available, including the Joan Jakobson Awards for fiction writers and poets; and the Jon Davidoff Scholarships for nonfiction writers and journalists. Inquire via e-mail, fax, or phone.

WHIDBEY ISLAND WRITERS' CONFERENCE

Whidbey Island Writers' Association, P.O. Box 1289, Langley WA 98260. (360)331-6714. E-mail: wiwa@whidbey.com. Web site: www.writeonwhidbey.org. **Contact:** Pam Owen, Director. Annual conference held in March. 2008 dates were Feb. 28 through March 2. Conference duration: 3 days. Average attendance: 250. The 11th annual conference, located near Seattle, combines pre-conference workshops, signature fireside chats, professional instruction and island hospitality to encourage and inspire writers. Check out this year's upcoming talent on our Web site. Covers fiction, nonfiction, screenwriting, writing for children, poetry, travel, and nature writing. Class sessions include ''Dialogue That Delivers'' and ''Putting the Character Back in Character.'' Held at a conference hall, with break-out fireside chats held in local homes near the sea. 2008 speakers include Elizabeth George, Maureen Murdock, Steve Berry, M.J. Rose, Katharine Sands, Doris Booth, Eva Shaw, Stephanie Elizondo Griest.

Costs $350 + . Volunteer discounts are available; early registration is encouraged.

Additional Information Brochures are available online or for a SASE. Send inquiries via e-mail.

WILLAMETTE WRITERS CONFERENCE

9045 SW Barbur, Suite 5-A, Portland OR 97219. (503)452-1592. Fax: (503)452-0372. E-mail: wilwrite@willamettewriters.com. Web site: www.willamettewriters.com. **Contact:** Conference director. Estab. 1968. Annual conference held in August. 2008 dates: Aug. 1-3. Average attendance: 600. ''Willamette Writers is open to all writers, and we plan our conference accordingly. We offer workshops on all aspects of fiction, nonfiction, marketing, the creative process, etc. Also, we invite top-notch inspirational speakers for keynote addresses. We always include at least 1 agent or editor panel and offer a variety of topics of interest to screenwriters and fiction and nonfiction writers. Speakers have included Laura Rennert, Kim Cameron, Paul Levine, Angela Rinaldi, Robert Tabian, Joshua Bilmes and Elise Capron. Agents will be speaking and available for meetings with attendees.

Costs Costs available online.

Accommodations If necessary, arrangements can be made on an individual basis. Special rates may be available.

Additional Information Brochure/guidelines are available for a catalog-sized SASE.

WINTER POETRY & PROSE GETAWAY IN CAPE MAY

No public address available,. (609)823-5076. E-mail: info@wintergetaway.com. Web site: www.wintergetaway.com. **Contact:** Peter Murphy, founder/director. Estab. 1994. Annual workshop held in January. Conference duration: 4 days. Offers workshops on short stories, memoirs, creative nonfiction, children's writing, novel, drama, poetry and photography. Classes are small, so each person receives individual attention for the new writing or work-in-progress that they are focusing on. Held at the Grand Hotel on the oceanfront in historic Cape May, New Jersey. Speakers have included Stephen Dunn (recipient of the 2001 Pulitzer Prize for poetry), Christian Bauman, Kurt Brown, Catherine Doty, Douglas Goetsch, James Richardson, Robbie Clipper Sethi and many more.

WISCONSIN BOOK FESTIVAL

222 S. Bedford St., Suite F, Madison WI 53703. (608)262-0706. Fax: (608)263-7970. E-mail: alison@wisconsinbookfestival.org. Web site: www.wisconsinbookfestival.org. **Contact:** Alison Jones Chaim, director. Estab. 2002. Annual festival held in October. Conference duration: 5 days. The festival features readings, lectures, book discussions, writing workshops, live interviews, children's events, and more. Speakers have included Michael Cunningham, Grace Paley, TC Boyle, Marjane Satrapi, Phillip Gourevitch, Myla Goldberg, Audrey Niffenegger, Harvey Pekar, Billy Collins, Tim O'Brien and Isabel Allende.

Costs All festival events are free.

WISCONSIN REGIONAL WRITERS' ASSOCIATION CONFERENCES

No public address available,. E-mail: vpresident@wrwa.net. Web site: www.wrwa.net. **Contact:** Nate Scholze, fall conference chair; Roxanne Aehl, spring conference chair. Estab. 1948. Annual conferences are held in May and September. Conference duration: 1-2 days. Provides presentations for all genres, including fiction, nonfiction, scriptwriting, and poetry. Presenters include authors, agents, editors, and publishers. Speakers have included Jack Byrne, Michelle Grajkowski, Benjamin Leroy, Richard Lederer, and Philip Martin.

Additional Information Go online for brochure or make inquiries via e-mail or with SASE.

WORDS & MUSIC

624 Pirates Alley, New Orleans LA 70116. (504)586-1609. Fax: (504)522-9725. E-mail: faulkhouse@ aol.com. Web site: www.wordsandmusic.org. **Contact:** Rosemary James DeSalvo. Estab. 1997. Annual conference held the first week in November. Conference duration: 5 days. Average attendance: 300. Presenters include authors, agents, editors and publishers. 2006 speakers included agents Deborah Grosvenor, Judith Weber, Stuart Bernstein, Nat Sobel, Jeff Kleinman, Emma Sweeney, Liza Dawson and Michael Murphy; and editors Lauren Marino, Webster Younce, Ann Patty, Will Murphy, Jofie Ferrari-Adler, Elizabeth Stein; critics Marie Arana, Jonathan Yardley, and Michael Dirda; fiction writers Oscar Hijuelos, Robert Olen Butler, Shirley Ann Grau, Mayra Montero, Ana Castillo, H.G. Carrillo. Agents and editors critique manuscripts in advance; meet with them one-on-one during the conference.

Costs $300 fee includes critiques and agent/editor meetings, all discussions. Food, wine, music events, lunches are extra. Hotel and transportation costs not included.

Accommodations Hotel Monteleone in New Orleans.

WRANGLING WITH WRITING

Society of Southwestern Authors, P.O. Box 30355, Tucson AZ 85751-0355. (520)546-9382. Fax: (520)751-7877. E-mail: Penny Porter (wporter202@aol.com); Carol Costa (Ccstarlit@aol.com). Web site: www.ssa-az.org/conference.htm. **Contact:** Penny Porter, Carol Costa. Estab. 1972. Annual. Sept. 27-28, 2008. Conference duration: 2 days. Average attendance: 350. Conference offers 36 workshops covering all genres of writing, plus pre-scheduled one-on-one interviews with 30 agents, editors, and publishers representing major book houses and magazines. Speakers have included Ray Bradbury, Clive Cussler, Elmore Leonard, Ben Bova, Sam Swope, Richard Paul Evans, Bruce Holland Rogers and Billy Collins.

Costs 2007 costs were $275/members; $350/nonmembers. Five meals included.

Additional Information Brochures/guidelines are available as of July 15 by e-mail address above.

WRITE ON THE SOUND WRITERS' CONFERENCE

Edmonds Arts Commission, 700 Main St., Edmonds WA 98020. (425)771-0228. Fax: (425)771-0253. E-mail: wots@ci.edmonds.wa.us. Web site: www.ci.edmonds.wa.us/ArtsCommission/wots.stm. **Contact:** Conference Coordinator. Estab. 1985. Annual conference held in October. Conference duration: 2.5 days. Average attendance: 200. Features over 30 presenters, a literary contest, ms critiques, a reception and book signing, onsite bookstore, and a variety of evening activities. Held at the Frances Anderson Center in Edmonds, just north of Seattle on the Puget Sound. Speakers have included Elizabeth George, Dan Hurley, Marcia Woodard, Holly Hughes, Greg Bear, Timothy Egan, Joe McHugh, Frances Wood, Garth Stein and Max Grover.

Costs $108 before September 19; $130 after September 19; $68/day; $25/ms critiques.

Additional Information Brochures are available Aug. 1. Accepts inquiries via phone, e-mail and fax.

WRITE-TO-PUBLISH CONFERENCE

WordPro Communications Services, 9118 W Elmwood Dr., #1G, Niles IL 60714-5820. (847)296-3964. Fax: (847)296-0754. E-mail: lin@writetopublish.com. Web site: www.writetopublish.com. **Contact:** Lin Johnson, director. Estab. 1971. Annual conference held June 3-6, 2009. Conference duration: 4 days. Average attendance: 250. Conference on writing fiction, nonfiction, devotions, and magazine articles for the Christian market. Held at Wheaton College in Wheaton, Illinois. Speakers have included Dr. Dennis E. Hensley, agent Chip MacGregor, Ken Peterson (Tyndale House), Craig Bubeck (Cook), Joan Alexander, Allan Fisher (Crossway Books & Bibles), Joyce Hart (Hartline Literary Agency), Betsy Newenhuyse (Moody Publishers), and Ginger Kolbaba (Marriage Partnership).

Costs $450 (includes all sessions, Saturday night banquet, 1 ms evaluation); $95/meals.

Accommodations Campus residence halls: $220/double; $300/single. A list of area hotels is also on the Web site.

WRITERS AT THE BEACH: SEAGLASS WRITERS CONFERENCE

Writers at the Beach, P.O. Box 1326, Rehoboth Beach DE 19971. (302)226-8210. E-mail: contactus@ rehobothbeachwritersguild.com. Web site: www.writersatthebeach.com/. **Contact:** Maribeth Fischer, mbfischer1@verizon.net. Annual conference held in the spring. Conference duration: 3 days. "Annual conference on the Delaware coast featuring a variety of editors, agents and writers who present workshops on fiction writing, nonfiction writing and more. Manuscript readings are available, and a 'Meet the Authors' sessions takes place. The beachcoast conference is a great opportunity to learn and charge your batteries. Some proceeds from the conference go to charity."

Accommodations The special room rate for participants is approximately $60.

Additional Information Rehoboth Beach, a popular resort town nicknamed "The Nation's Summer Capital." is a coastal resort town in southern Delaware, 2.5 hours from both Baltimore Maryland and Washington, DC; 2 hours from Philadelphia, and just over 3 hours from New York City. During the conference, you glance outside from any number of the rooms at the Atlantic Sands to the ever-mercurial Atlantic ocean, walk the mile-long boardwalk, or sit on one of the numerous benches where you can watch the sunrise and enjoy our many migrating dolphins. This small town also offers, within a block of the hotel, an eclectic array of boutiques, cafés, souvenir shops and restaurants. And nearby Cape Henlopen State Park is home to the highest sand dune—rising over 80 feet above the shoreline—between Cape Hatteras and Cape Cod.

WRITERS' CONFERENCE AT OCEAN PARK

P.O. Box 7146, Ocean Park ME 04063-7146. (401)598-1424. E-mail: jbrosnan@jwu.edu. Web site: www.oceanpark.org/programs/events/writers/writers.html. **Contact:** Jim Brosnan, Donna Brosnan. Estab. 1941. Annual conference held in mid-August. Conference duration: 4 days. Average attendance: 50. "We try to present a balanced and eclectic conference. In addition to time and attention given to poetry, we also have children's literature, mystery writing, travel, fiction, nonfiction, journalism, and other issues of interest to writers. Our speakers are editors, writers, and other professionals. Our concentration is, by intention, a general view of writing to publish with supportive encouragement. We are located in Ocean Park, a small seashore village 14 miles south of Portland. Ours is a summer assembly center with many buildings from the Victorian age. The conference meets in Porter Hall, one of the assembly buildings which is listed in the National Register of Historic Places." Speakers have included Michael C. White (novelist/short story writer), Betsy Shool (poet), Suzanne Strempek

Shea (novelist), John Perrault (poet), Josh Williamson (newspaper editor), Dawn Potter (poet), Bruce Pratt (fiction writer), Amy McDonald (children's author), Anne Wescott Dodd (nonfiction writer), Kate Chadbourne (singer/songwriter), Wesley McNair (poet/Maine faculty member), and others. "We usually have about 8 guest presenters each year." Publishes writers/editors will be speaking, leading workshops, and available for meetings with attendees.

Costs $175+ (includes conference, reception, Tuesday evening meal). The fee does not include housing or meals, which must be arranged separately by conferees.

Accommodations An accommodations list is available. "We are in a summer resort area where motels, guest houses, and restaurants abound."

Additional Information "We have 7 contests for various genres. An announcement is available in the spring. The prizes (all modest) are awarded at the end of the conference and only to those who are registered." Send SASE in June for the conference program.

WRITING FOR THE SOUL

Jerry B. Jenkins Christian Writers Guild, 5525 N. Union Blvd., Suite 200, Colorado Springs CO 80918. (866)495-5177. Fax: (719)495-5181. E-mail: paul@christianwritersguild.com. Web site: www.christianwritersguild.com/conferences. **Contact:** Paul Finch, admissions manager. Annual conference held in late January and/or early February. Workshops and continuing classes cover fiction, nonfiction, magazine writing, children's books, and teen writing. Appointments with more than 30 agents, publishers, and editors are also available. The keynote speakers are Lee Strobel, Dallas Jenkins, and Richard Lederer. The conference is hosted and emcee'd by Jerry B. Jenkins.

Costs $635/guild members; $795/nonmembers.

Accommodations $150/night at the Broadmoor Hotel in Colorado Springs.

WRITING THE REGION

Gainesville Association for the Creative Arts, P.O. Box 12246, Gainesville FL 32604. (888)917-7001. Fax: (352)373-8854. E-mail: info@artsgaca.org; SarahBewley@sarahbewley.com. Web site: www.writingtheregion.com. **Contact:** Norma Homan, director. Estab. 1997. Annual conference held in July. 2008 dates: July 23-27. Conference duration: 5 days. Average attendance: 100. Conference concentrates on fiction, writing for children, poetry, nonfiction, drama, screenwriting, writing with humor, setting, character, and more. Workshop honors Pulitzer Prize-winning author Marjorie Kinnan Rawlings. Held at the Thomas Center in Gainesville, Floriday. Speakers have included Anne Hawking, Doris Booth, Sarah Bewley, Bill Maxwell, and Robert Fulton. Agent/editor appointments are available.

Costs Costs available online. Lower costs for half-day and one-day registration.

Accommodations Special rates are available at the Holiday Inn, University Center and the Residence Inn, Marriott.

◎ WRITING TODAY

Birmingham-Southern College, Box 549066, Birmingham AL 35254. (205)226-4922. Fax: (205)226-4931. E-mail: agreen@bsc.edu. Web site: www.writingtoday.org. **Contact:** Annie Green. Estab. 1978. Annual conference held during the second weekend in March. The 2009 dates are set for March 13-14. Conference duration: 2 days. Average attendance: 300-350. Conference hosts approximately 18 workshops, lectures, and readings. "We try to offer sessions in short fiction, novels, poetry, children's literature, magazine writing, songwriting, and general information of concern to aspiring writers, such as publishing, agents, markets, and research." The event is held on the Birmingham-Southern College campus in classrooms and lecture halls. Speakers have included Eudora Welty, Pat Conroy, Ernest Gaines, Ray Bradbury, Erskine Caldwell, John Barth, Galway Kinnell, Edward Albee, Horton Foote, and William Styron and other renowned writers.

Costs $150 for both days (includes lunches, reception, morning coffee/rolls).

Accommodations Attendees must arrange own transportation and accommodations.

Additional Information For an additional charge, poetry and short story critiques are offered for interested writers who request and send mss by the deadline. The conference also sponsors the Hackney Literary Competition Awards for poetry, short stories, and novels.

Glossary

#10 Envelope. Standard business-size envelope used for $8^1/_2 \times 11$ sheets of paper.

A-List. The most famous and bankable talent of the current times—usually in reference to actors.

Above the Line. Costs of a film prior to the actual shoot.

Acting Credits. An actor's previous professional work.

Adaptation. The process of rewriting a composition (e.g., novel, article) into a form suitable for some other medium, such as TV or the stage.

Advance. A sum of money paid to a writer prior to publication or production. An advance is made based on anticipated profits not yet realized.

Adventure. A genre of fiction in which action and location are the key elements.

ADR (Automatic Dialogue Replacement). Dialogue that is added or rerecorded in post-production.

AFI. The American Film Institute.

Agent. A writer's business representative who secures work and negotiates contracts in exchange for a portion of the money the writer makes.

All Rights. Complete rights to a work, meaning that the writer now owns nothing—including the characters, concept and dialogue.

Angel. A wealthy individual or private investor who can bankroll a project and provide production capital.

Antagonist. The primary character (or force) in a story with whom the protagonist is in conflict.

Arbitration. A form of legal dispute resolution which forgoes court judgment to determine an award or disputed screenplay credit.

At Rise. The description of setting at the beginning of a stage play.

Auction. A bidding war for the acquisition, purchase or option of a script.

Beat. (1) A one-count pause in the action or in a character's speech. (2) The smallest unit of a story; a moment in which something dramatic occurs.

Beat Sheet. The breakdown of key scenes contained in a screenplay.

Before Rise. What's happening onstage before the curtain opens and a play begins.

Below the Line. Actual production costs of a film.

Bible. A master reference for a television series containing character information and projected storylines.

Bidding War. An instance where two or more studios are trying to outbid one another in terms of money to secure a certain property.

Bio. Short for biography. This term usually identifies a relatively concise paragraph detailing who the writer/producer is.

Blurb. A brief statement, such as one from a reviewer, which accompanies a movie for market and advertising appeal.

Boffo. A box office success.

Boilerplate. A standardized contract in which there is no variance from general terms and conditions offered between one project and another.

Bomb. A box office failure.

Budget. A detailed listing of expenses, potential and actual, for the making of a movie. The budget is used to determine the estimated total cost of the project from screenplay to post-production and distribution.

Character Arc. The emotional journey of a character that details how they change from a story's beginning to end.

Climax. The pinnacle of action and conflict in a story, usually just before the end.

Concept. The general idea regarding a story—i.e., what the story is about on a basic level.

Copyediting. The process of fixing faulty grammar, formatting, spelling and punctuation.

Copyright. A means to protect an author's work.

Cover Page. A one-page sheet before the first page of your script. The cover page lists the title of the work, the author's name, and all pertinent contact information—whether that's for the writer or a representative.

Coverage. A reader's written thoughts and critique of a script created so producers can digest the material quickly. Coverage includes a logline, a synopsis, and the reader's compliments/criticism of the work.

Critiquing Service. Serving the same purpose as a script doctor, this is a service where a professional will help edit a writer's manuscript for a fee.

Curtain. (1) A fabric or screen separating the audience from the setting. (2) A term used to indicate the opening or closing of a scene.

Deal Memo. A rough draft of a contract that comes before the real contract.

Deus ex Machina. Latin for "God from the machine." This term is used to describe a story ending where an impossible scenario is miraculously fixed thanks to a illogical happening or intervention.

Development. The process of bringing a story to the screen. If a script has been commissioned, or is in rewrites, that project is in development.

Development Hell. When the development phase of creating a movie is delayed by endless script changes, delays, and other problems.

Developmental Workshop. When a play is given several rehearsals and performed by actors.

Direct to Video. A movie released to the public for home viewing, bypassing theaters.

Docudrama. A combination of the genres of documentary and drama. The docudrama uses a script, actors, and a set in order to portray real events, either current or historical.

Electronic Rights. Rights pertaining to the Internet and other electronic media.

Elements. (1) The format of a movie script such as headers, character names, dialogue, and narrative. (2) The talent involved in creating a movie or play, such as screenwriters, director, actors, and props.

El-Hi (Elementary-High School). A term used to refer to the publications of books and plays as school texts for adolescents from kindergarten through 12th grade.

Episodic Television. Series television.

Ethnic. A story in which the central characters are typically caught between two conflicting ways of life: mainstream American culture and his or her own ethnic heritage.

Evaluation Fees. Fees charged by agents and companies to consider a manuscript. No WGA-endorsed reps will ask for them.

Resources

Exclusive. Rights or privileges granted to one body that are not awarded to others, usually lasting a specified period of time.

Executive Producer. Someone who provides financing or represents the financial backing for a film. The executive producer is charged with keeping production within the targeted budget.

Experimental. A method of presenting a story in a new way, such as through style or exploring new themes and concepts.

Exposition. Communicating information by explaining something to the audience. In movies and plays, exposition is usually explained through dialogue, and kept to a minimum to keep the story moving.

Family Saga. A story that unfolds over generations through interwoven tales of several members of a genealogical line.

Fantasy. A genre containing magical and supernatural elements such as mythical creatures and legendary characters.

Feature. A full-length film, usually running 90-150 minutes.

Film Noir. A genre of film featuring gritty, dark stories set in urban areas. Other aspects include police detectives, corruption, plot twists and turns, and a femme fatale.

Film Rights. For a book, film rights concern the right to turn the story into a screenplay and produce it.

First-Look Deal. Also known as "first right of refusal" in which a deal is struck providing one person or entity the first chance to develop a screenplay or film. If that entity chooses to pass on the opportunity, the offer can then be opened to others.

Foreign Rights. Rights of selling a writer's work in other countries.

Free Option. When a studio options a script from a writer at no cost.

Genre. A method of categorization based on elements contained within the story, its subject, or the style that is used. Traditional genres in playwriting are tragedy, comedy, romance, and irony; modern genres continue to expand those, including historical, adventure, science fiction, fantasy, western, family, musical, horror, mystery, and so forth. Sub-genres often combine elements of two or more of the genres, such as romantic comedy (rom-com), or action-adventure.

Ghostwriting. The process of writing/rewriting a story for a set fee but receiving little to no credit. Books by celebrities and politicians are usually ghostwritten.

Gofer/Gopher. An employee who handles menial and typically inglorious tasks, such as delivering scripts and fetching coffee.

Graphic Novel. A publication similar in format to comic books, but usually containing a longer, more complex storyline or series of stories. Usually sold in bookstores and bound using the same methods as traditional books.

Green Light. The phrase used to approve a project and let pre-production commence.

Handshake Deal. A deal with no contracts—relying on the "older" practice of two parties and their word.

Hard Sell. A movie without an easy explanation or high concept that will be more difficult to sell.

High Concept. Used to describe a movie with a remarkable idea that is easily summarized.

Hi-Lo. High concept, low budget films.

Historical. A film or story in which the setting and events occur sometime in the past. Historical films are often referred to as "period films" when the events occur during a time frame with specific, recognizable cultural traits.

Hook. Element of the story that grabs attention and compels the viewer's interest in following the story to its resolution.

Horror. Genre of story containing dark themes and in which the intention is to inspire fear or dread.

Hot. Anything that's getting attention or buzz at the moment, such as a script that's deemed a "hot read."

Inciting Incident. An incident or event or happening (usually early in the script) that sets the story in motion.

Independent Producers. A person involved with the production of film or television but is not affiliated with a major company or studio.

Indie. Short for independent. A film created by an individual or smaller company; commonly refers to films that are more experimental or targeted to a specific audience.

Ink Session. A meeting where contracts are signed.

Intermission. A distinct break during a play—usually at the half-way point, lasting approximately 15 minutes.

IRC. International reply coupon, which is used instead of stamps when a writer needs materials sent back from a foreign country.

Joint Contract. A legal agreement in which two or more parties agree to complete a project or perform a service, or may benefit from the completion of a project or performance of service.

Libel. Written words that defame or cause damage through misrepresentation to someone living.

Logline. A concise, one-sentence description of a story that is used to pique interest.

Manager. In screenwriting terms, a representative who will not only rep your work, but also help edit and guide writers on a career path. A manager lacks the legal license to sell a work, and collects a small percentage of any money the writer makes.

Memoir. A story about a person's life written by that person.

Miniseries. A story that borrows the sequential nature of television shows but retains the pacing, resolution, and ending of a movie, usually unfolding in two to four parts.

Montage. A series of shots or short vignettes spliced together in rapid succession to convey the passage of time or to encompass a theme too unwieldy to film in completion.

MOW. Movie of the week.

Multiple Contract. A contract by which the theater/studio agrees to publish, and the author agrees to have produced, two or more consecutive works by the writer.

Musical. A stage production in which songs are used to reinforce the major points of the story being acted out.

Mystery. A story in which one or more elements remain unknown or unexplained until the end of the story.

Narration. The method used to tell a story. In screenplays, this is usually through first-person ("I") or voice-over.

Net Receipts. The amount of money received on the sale of a project after discounts, special sales, etc.

Novelization. The act of creating a novel from a popular movie.

Offscreen. A term used to indicate a sound or voice heard, but not seen, by the audience. It is represented in a script by the letters "O.S."

On Book. A phrase used to describe a play performance where actors still have scripts in hand.

One-Act Play. A form of stage play with a length between 20 and 60 minutes.

Option. A fee paid to a writer for exclusive rights to a script for a certain period of time.

Option Clause. Also called "the right of first refusal," this clause in a contract allows the purchaser to have the first opportunity to review the writer's next similar work.

Orphaned. Used to describe a script/project that was under consideration but is now of little interest to a studio.

Package. A deal that brings together various elements in order to sell a script or product. An agency specializing in package deals will usually attempt to utilize as much of their talent roster as possible.

Pass. The act of officially saying no to a project.

Pitch. Concisely explaining what the story is about in the hopes to pique interest and have the full manuscript requested/read.

Platform. A writer's visibility, and the avenues he or she has to sell their work to the audience(s) who will buy it.

Play. (1) A live performance of a script using actors and setting. (2) A script or book formatted to be performed live containing characters, setting, and dialogue, divided up into acts and scenes.

Plot. The sequence in which an author arranges a series of carefully devised and interrelated incidents so as to form a logical pattern and achieve an intended effect. A plot can also be called the structure, backbone or framework of fiction.

Producer. Person responsible for bringing together all the elements of a film from inception to completion. The producer is responsible for the entire movie, from hiring scriptwriters, directors, and actors to the completion of the project.

Proofreading. The process of reading a work and identifying errors in copy.

Property. Term used to describe a script or other written material.

Proscenium. The walls and arch found in some theaters that contains the curtain and divides the stage area from the audience.

Protagonist. The central character of a story.

Public Domain. Material not protected by copyright, patent or trademark, and therefore available to the general public for use without fee.

Query. A one-page letter designed to interest the reader (agent, editor, etc.) in a story idea.

Reader. (1) The consumer of a written work at whom the story is aimed. (2) The person whose job is to read and evaluate scripts.

Regional Premiere. (1) A formal viewing of a movie in a specific locale, often with a significance to the movie-making process, such as setting or film location. (2) A play or musical's first full production in an area of the country.

Release. (1) To distribute a television show or movie into public either for a limited or general viewing, such as "release date." (2) To give written permission to use a likeness, either pictorial or descriptive, to a script or film without incurring liability.

Residuals. Payments awarded by a union to creative talent in addition to that covered by their contracts.

Resolution. The point at which a solution to the central conflict or driving plot is applied and the story reaches a conclusion.

Romance. A genre in which the plot is centered around two persons having to overcome some obstacle(s) to fall in love.

Royalties. Money received from the individual performance, sale, or use of a published work; for example, the sale of movies for home viewing. Royalties are a percentage of the actualized profits.

SASE. Self-addressed stamped envelope. This is an envelope addressed to oneself and stamped for the return of materials sent with a submission.

Science Fiction. A genre containing impossible or supernatural elements, often set in futuristic or off-world settings. This genre is distinguished from fantasy in that it is technology that makes events occur.

Script. The written version of a film, TV episode or stage play.

Script Doctor. A freelance editor paid to consult on a script.

Script Polish. A final edit or rewrite of a script, usually by a professional who is not the original writer.

Shooting Script. The final version of a script used on set by actors and crew.

Showrunner. The individual(s) responsible for overseeing day-to-day operations on a show—in other words, he or she who "runs the show." The term is sometimes interchanged with "executive producer."

Simultaneous Submission. The act of submitting a query or work to more than one market/agent at the same time.

Sitcom. Short for situation comedy.

Slasher Film. A horror flick with lots of deaths, blood and gore.

Slice of Life. A type of story designed to show a particular way of life in a certain area or time period.

Slug Line. A line in a script designed to show where a scene is taking place. The slug line always begins with EXT. or INT., immediately telling readers whether the scene is set outside or inside.

Slush Pile. A term used to refer to the pile of unsolicited manuscripts received by publishers and/or producers that have not been read or rejected.

Spec Script. A script written "on speculation," meaning that it has not been contracted or commissioned, and no money is assured when writing it.

Staged Reading. A gathering of actors to read a script, so that the writer can hear the dialogue spoken aloud by professionals.

Subplot. A plot line that runs along a story but is smaller in scope and importance than the true plot.

Subsidiary Rights. Also called subrights, these rights refer to a variety of things, such as merchandising, film rights, foreign rights and more.

Subtext. In dialogue, what is meant but never explicitly said aloud.

Synopsis. A summary of a script's plot. It can be as brief as a few lines or several paragraphs long and include explanations of characters, subplots, conflict and resolution.

Tagline. A clever line on a movie poster designed to pique interest.

Theme. The implicit meaning, message, concept, or idea contained within the story; often contains some universal lesson about life, death, love, or human nature.

Thriller. A genre of story dealing with suspense, cat-and-mouse chases, killers, close calls and high-adrenaline storytelling.

Treatment. A loose and somewhat incomplete version of a script that is completed from beginning to end, but lacks details and dialogue in scenes.

Unsolicited Manuscript. A completed work that has not been requested by a studio, person or theater.

Vehicle. A project developed for a specific movie star.

Voice-over. Vocal narration that is spoken by an offscreen character.

Westerns/Frontier. A genre set in western or frontier regions, usually set in the past and dealing with things such as cowboys, train robberies, Native Americans and the natural beauty of open spaces.

White Space. Plenty of empty space on a script page. Preferable to "too much black."

Work-for-Hire. When a writer is contracted and paid to do a specific work or rewrite. This is in contrast to writing a work on speculation.

World Premiere. A play term referring to the first full production of a work.

Agents & Managers Specialties Index

The subject index is divided into script subject categories and formats. To find an agent interested in the type of scripts you've written, see the appropriate sections under the subject headings that best describe your work.

Biography/Autobiography

Cartoon/Animation

Comedy

Contemporary Issues

Detective/Police/Crime

Documentary

Episodic Drama

Erotica

Specialties Index

Specialties Index

Suite A Management Talent & Literary
Agency 159
Swetky Agency, The 159
Talent Source 160

Ethnic

Abrams Artists Agency 109
Acme Talent & Literary 110
Alpern Group, The 112
Anderson Literary, TV & Film Agency,
Darley 114
Bohrman Agency, The 117
Bulger and Associates, Kelvin C. 118
Characters Talent Agency, The 121
Core Group Talent Agency, Inc., The
123
E S Agency, The 126
Evatopia, Inc. 127
French, Inc., Samuel 130
Levine Literary Agency, Paul S. 139
Monteiro Rose Dravis Agency, Inc. 144
Niad Management 145
Sayle Screen, Ltd 154
Sherman & Associates, Ken 156
Steinberg Associates, Micheline 158
Suite A Management Talent & Literary
Agency 159
Swetky Agency, The 159

Experimental

Abrams Artists Agency 109
Acme Talent & Literary 110
Author Literary Agents 115
Bohrman Agency, The 117
Core Group Talent Agency, Inc., The
123
E S Agency, The 126
Levine Literary Agency, Paul S. 139
Omniquest Entertainment 146
Sayle Screen, Ltd 154
Sherman & Associates, Ken 156
Steinberg Associates, Micheline 158

Suite A Management Talent & Literary
Agency 159
Swetky Agency, The 159

Family Saga

Abrams Artists Agency 109
Acme Talent & Literary 110
Anderson Literary, TV & Film Agency,
Darley 114
Author Literary Agents 115
Baskow Agency 116
Bohrman Agency, The 117
Bulger and Associates, Kelvin C. 118
Cedar Grove Agency Entertainment
120
Characters Talent Agency, The 121
Core Group Talent Agency, Inc., The
123
E S Agency, The 126
Evatopia, Inc. 127
Hudson Agency 134
Kay Agency, Charlene 136
Levine Literary Agency, Paul S. 139
Miller Co., The Stuart M. 143
Monteiro Rose Dravis Agency, Inc. 144
Niad Management 145
Omniquest Entertainment 146
Palmer Talent Agency, Inc., Dorothy
147
Sherman & Associates, Ken 156
Steinberg Associates, Micheline 158
Suite A Management Talent & Literary
Agency 159
Swetky Agency, The 159
Talent Source 160
Ware Literary Agents, Cecily 162

Fantasy

Abrams Artists Agency 109
Acme Talent & Literary 110
AEI: Atchity Editorial International,
Inc. Motion Picture Production
& Literary Management 110
Alpern Group, The 112

Specialties Index

Horror

Juvenile

Mainstream

Multimedia

Mystery/Suspense

Psychic/Supernatural

Regional

Religious/Inspirational

Romantic Comedy

Specialties Index

Variety Show

Western/Frontier

Agents Index

To find the individual pages of these agents and agencies, you can cross-reference the agency names in the General Index (page 395) or you can find the agencies in alphabetical order in the Agents & Managers market section of this book (page 107).

A

Abrams, Sheryl (PTI Talent Agency)
Aghassi, Jeff (The Alpern Group)
Ali, Sharif (Aimee Entertainment Agency)
Alpern, Jeff (The Alpern Group)
Amsterdam, Marcia (Marcia Amsterdam Agency)
Anderson, Darley (Darley Anderson Literary, TV & Film Agency)
Apponyi, Rosie (Capel & Land Ltd)
Armitage, Alex (Noel Gay)
Arnaud, Ruth (Casarotto Ramsay & Associates Limited)
Arnold, Frances (Rochelle Stevens & Co.)
Arnold, Michelle (The Dench Arnold Agency)
Assenheim, Lisa-Marie (AIM)
Atchity, Ken (AEI: Atchity Editorial International, Inc.)

B

Baker, Donald (Don Baker Associates)
Balogh, Virág Katalin (HoFra Theatrical and Literary Agency)
Banks, Gaia (Sheil Land Associates, Ltd)

Bartlett, Bruce (Above the Line Agency)
Baskow, Jaki (Baskow Agency)
Bates, Matthew (Sayle Screen, Ltd)
Baxter, Veronique (David Higham Associates Ltd)
Bayer, Jordan (Original Artists)
Beckford, Netta (Canton Smith Agency)
Bell, Jeremy (Foursight Entertainment)
Belushi, Traci (Omniquest Entertainment)
Benedict, Larry (Ann Waugh Talent Agency)
Benson, Ian (The Agency Ltd.)
Betts, Tina (Andrew Mann Ltd)
Bickelmann, Lin (Encore Artists Management)
Blair, Anthony (Cameron Creswell)
Bohrman, Caren (The Bohrman Agency)
Braun, Alan (Kaplan Stahler Gumer Braun Agency)
Brayfield, Chloe (Amanda Howard Associates Ltd.)
Brewster, Phillipa (Capel & Land Ltd)

General Index

L

General Index

General Index

NOTES

NOTES

NOTES

NOTES

NOTES

NOTES

NOTES

NOTES

NOTES

NOTES

NOTES